Facts and Figures on Government Finance

Facts & Figures on Government Finance

1990 Edition

on

Government

Finance

TAX FOUNDATION

The Johns Hopkins University Press
Baltimore and London

Printed in the United States of America

25th edition

The Johns Hopkins University Press
701 West 40th Street
Baltimore, Maryland 21211
The Johns Hopkins Press Ltd., London

ISBN 0-8018-4022-8
ISBN 0-8018-4023-6 pbk.

ISSN 0071-3678
LC 44-7109

Table of Contents

Section B: Selected Economic Series   39

Section C: The Federal Government   87

Fiscal Operations in Summary

Outlays

Lending, Enterprise, and Trust Operations

Section D: State and Local Governments   161

Section F: Local Governments   287

Glossary   325

Index   335

Foreword

With this 25th edition of *Facts and Figures on Government Finance,* a new Tax Foundation renews its tradition of service to the fiscal policy arena. It does so under the auspices of the Citizens for a Sound Economy Foundation, which has reorganized and continued the programs of the Tax Foundation. The resources of this new parent organization will greatly enhance the Tax Foundation's ability to collect and analyze the ever-increasing volume of public finance data coming from governmental and private sources. This explosion of data from hundreds of sources makes *Facts and Figures* all the more valuable and reinforces the importance of the volume's original, unique mission: to document in an independent and unbiased way the taxing and spending practices of government at all levels, and to package this information in a single, convenient volume, readily accessible to business executives, policy analysts, public officials, academicians, the media, and the general public.

This is the second edition of the work to be published under the imprint of the Johns Hopkins University Press and will hereafter be an annual feature of their spring catalog. Although *Facts and Figures* has been published for decades as a biannual, the Foundation sees an increased reliance on public finance data throughout the economy and has decided that annual updating is vital to maintain *Facts and Figures'* preeminence as a public finance reference book.

Finally, the present edition marks *Facts and Figures'* entry into the information age with the introduction of an electronic version of the book on personal computer diskettes. With each table presented in the format of the most popular spreadsheets, users can easily manipulate the data if they have Apple, IBM, or IBM-compatible personal computers. For example, it is possible to access two tables at once, and divide income data from one table by population totals in another to derive per capita figures. With historic economic and tax data, economists can easily perform time series and trend analyses and just as quickly produce computer graphics to represent the data. The fiscal and economic detail provided on the federal, state and local levels makes *Facts and Figures* on diskette a superior data base for economic research.

The 25th edition of any work is a testament to its exceptional value and continued excellence. In the case of *Facts and Figures,* the 25th is a landmark edition not only because of the new electronic version, but because it is the first during the Tax Foundation's new arrangement with Citizens for a Sound Economy Foundation. We are proud to begin the 1990s by presenting this edition and pledge to continue meeting the challenges of public finance research as the nation approaches the twenty-first century.

James C. Miller III   James Q. Riordan
Co-Chairman   Co-Chairman

Introductory Notes to Tables

Data on governmental revenues and expenditures are compiled by many agencies for different purposes. It is not surprising, therefore, that differences among various series on governmental finances may be confusing to the layman and, indeed, to students of public finance. Some introductory explanations, therefore, can be of assistance to the user.

Sources of Federal Data

The chief sources of data on Federal government finances are the Office of Management and Budget and the Treasury Department. The budget division publishes annually *The Budget of the United States Government,* which contains final data for previous fiscal years and the Administration's proposals and estimates for the current and forthcoming fiscal years.

The *Budget* for 1969 was the first to adopt the unified concept recommended by the President's Commission on Budget Concepts. This budget format includes the receipts and outlays of the trust funds, which were excluded from the old "administrative budget." The unified concept also distinguishes "expenditures" from "net lending," primarily for the purpose of evaluating the economic impact of the budget. As in previous budgets, both receipts and outlays are on a cash, rather than an accrual, basis.

In the intervening years since the unified budget concept was adopted, a number of Federal entities – generally those that carry out direct loan programs – have been removed from the budget by law, and two new off-budget entities have been established. To facilitate comparison of overall totals, most Federal budget tables in this volume include both on-budget and off-budget transactions.

The Treasury provides useful historical data in the *Treasury Bulletin* and other publications. These are also the primary sources of detailed data on the Federal debt.

Another official source is Federal receipts and expenditures as they appear in the national income accounts published by the Bureau of Economic Analysis of the Department of Commerce. Since much economic analysis is now based on the national income accounts, there is value in having details of the government sector comparable to the data for the private sector. This "Federal sector of the national income accounts" presentation differs from the unified budget basis chiefly in two respects. First, capital transactions that do not represent current flows of income and production are excluded – these are purely financial transactions or transactions in existing physical assets. Second, business taxes (and certain other items) are on an accrual basis; corporate profits taxes, for example, are shown for the year in which tax liability is incurred rather than in the year actually paid. The same remarks apply to state and local government finances as shown in the national income accounts.

The basic source of data on the operations of state and local governments and all governments combined is the Governments Division, Bureau of the Census, Department of Commerce. It has largely accomplished the tremendous task of establishing and maintaining comparable data on the finances of all three levels of government. For this purpose the Census has adapted data from the Treasury Department and the Office of Management and Budget to concepts appropriate for all governments. For this reason there are differences between the series published by these agencies. For similar reasons Census data on state government finances differ from those published in the budgets of the various states.

There are two important differences between the Census basis for Federal finances and budgetary sources: (1) The classification of functions differs substantially. Thus the Census classification does not include a functional grouping of veterans' benefits; instead, expenditures under this head in the Federal *Budget* are distributed among other functions including education, hospitals, welfare, etc. (2) Various enterprise operations are reported on a gross basis by the Census and on a net basis in the Federal *Budget*. In the Census publications, "general expenditures" include total expenditures of the postal service, not merely the excess of expenditures over receipts as in the *Budget*.

"Total expenditures" include expenditures for utilities, liquor stores, and insurance benefits as well as those for the more typical governmental functions. "General expenditures" include only those for the usual governmental functions, such as education, highways, public welfare, and payment of interest. "Direct expenditures for own purposes" exclude payments to another level of government.

Similar distinctions are made on the revenue side. "Total revenue" includes payments from other governments, and revenue from own sources. "Revenue from own sources" includes utilities, liquor stores, and insurance trust revenue, as well as taxes, charges, and other general revenues. "General revenue from own sources" excludes revenue from utilities, liquor stores, and insurance trusts and payments from another level of government.

Notes on Rounding, Symbols, Fiscal Periods, Per Capita Figures

Because of rounding, the detail shown in the tables may not always add to totals. The abbreviation "n.a." is used for data not available. A dash indicates that a particular series is zero for the year or category concerned. In the case of Alaska and Hawaii, a dash may also indicate that the data is unavailable.

Unless otherwise noted, national totals include Alaska beginning in 1959 and Hawaii beginning in 1960.

Fiscal year figures for the Federal government prior to 1977 relate to the 12-month period beginning July 1 and ending June 30. As of 1977, the fiscal year is October 1 to September 30. For most state governments and school districts, the fiscal year is the 12 months ending June 30. Among other units of local government, where there is more variation in fiscal years; a considerable proportion use a period ending December 31. Beginning in 1963, financial data for local governments, as reported by the Bureau of the Census, are grouped in terms of fiscal years which closed within the 12 months ended June 30. Previously, local government amounts were grouped in terms of fiscal years ended within the particular calendar year.

Per capita figures for fiscal year data are based generally on population as of the middle of the fiscal year. Unless otherwise noted, the population series used exclude armed forces overseas. For this reason per capita figures are slightly higher in wartime periods than they otherwise would be.

Sources and Acknowledgments

The sources cited are the government departments or private organizations which publish the primary data. Detailed sources giving the publications from which the data were obtained are available on request.

The cooperation of the following agencies is particularly appreciated: Department of Agriculture – Commodity Credit Corporation and Economics and Statistics Service; Department of Commerce – Bureau of the Census, Bureau of Economic Analysis, and International Trade Administration; Department of Education – National Center for Education Statistics; Department of Health and Human Services – Health Care Financing Administration and Social Security Administration; Department of Labor – Bureau of Labor Statistics and Employment and Training Administration; Office of Management and Budget; Office of Personnel Management; Treasury Department; Board of Governors of the Federal Reserve System; Federal Trade Commission; Organization for Economic Cooperation and Development; Commerce Clearing House; National Bureau of Economic Research; National Association of State Racing Commissioners; The Bond Buyer; and Sales and Marketing Management, Inc.

The 25th edition of *Facts and Figures on Government Finance* was compiled by the Tax Foundation's research department, under the general supervision of Paul G. Merski, Director of Special Studies. Other staff members who made significant contributions to this publication were: Marion B. Marshall, Information Specialist; Stephanie Gould and Cynthia Reppert, Research Assistants; and William Ahern, Publications Director.

Facts and Figures on Government Finance

Section A
Federal, State, and Local Governments

- Government and the Economy in Summary
- Fiscal Operations of All Governments
- Government in Relation to the Size of the Economy

A1. Government and the Changing Economy

Annual Change in Selected Economic, Business, and Governmental Indicators

Selected Periods 1939-40 to 1987-88[a]

	Percentage Change-Average Per Year				
Section and Item	1939-40 to 1949-50	1949-50 to 1959-60	1959-60 to 1969-70	1969-70 to 1979-80	1979-80 to 1987-88
I. Government - Federal, state, and local					
Expenditures	13.2%	8.0%	8.2%	11.2%	9.2%
Tax receipts	14.4	8.7	8.1	10.2	7.8
Federal, state, and local debt	16.1	2.4	3.7	9.3	13.4
II. Selected economic series					
Gross national product	11.1	5.9	7.0	10.2	7.5
Government purchases of goods and services	10.5	10.0	8.2	9.3	7.8
Private purchases of goods and services	11.2	5.1	6.6	10.5	8.1
Population (July 1)	1.8	1.4	1.3	1.1	1.0
Civilian employment	2.2	1.1	1.8	2.4	1.6
Per capita disposable income in constant dollars	2.6	1.2	3.1	2.0	1.9
Consumer price index	5.6	2.1	2.8	7.8	4.6
III. The Federal government					
Budget receipts	20.0	8.9	7.6	10.4	7.4
Budget outlays	16.2	8.0	7.8	11.7	7.7
Public debt	19.6	1.2	2.8	9.1	14.3
Outlays for national defense and international affairs and finance	27.6	10.7	5.3	5.5	9.5
Domestic-civilian expenditures	11.3	7.1	10.1	14.7	7.1
Federal tax receipts (including social insurance taxes)	21.1	8.9	7.7	10.3	7.5
Federal civilian employment, Executive Branch	6.6	2.1	2.0	.6	.1
IV. State and local governments					
Total revenue	8.1	8.9	9.6	11.6	9.3
Aid received from Federal government	10.2	10.9	12.1	14.3	5.3
Total expenditures	9.5	8.1	9.3	11.4	8.7
Total debt	1.7	11.2	7.5	8.9	11.5
Employment	2.5	4.1	4.7	2.8	1.1
V. State governments					
Total revenue	9.3	9.0	10.5	12.0	9.3
General tax revenue	9.1	8.6	10.3	11.1	8.8
Aid received from Federal government	13.1	10.9	11.7	12.4	6.5
Total expenditures	11.2	7.7	10.4	11.7	8.5
Direct general expenditures	11.4	8.3	10.6	11.4	9.0
State payments to local governments	9.8	8.4	11.8	11.1	7.7
Total debt	3.9	13.4	8.5	11.2	11.8
VI. Local governments					
Total revenue	7.6	8.7	9.1	11.2	8.9
General tax revenue	5.9	8.5	7.9	8.3	9.0
Total expenditures	8.3	8.6	9.0	10.9	8.6
Direct general expenditures	8.5	8.7	9.3	10.5	8.3
Education	9.9	10.2	9.8	9.7	7.7
Other	7.7	7.7	8.8	11.2	8.8
Total debt	1.2	10.6	7.0	7.7	11.4

[a] Economic series in Section II generally relate to calendar years. Governmental series in Sections I, III, IV, V, and VI relate to fiscal years. State and local data are through fiscal year 1987.

Source: Computed by Tax Foundation.

A2. Number of Governmental Units in the United States

Total by Level of Government by State, 1987

Selected Years, 1942-1987

Year and State	All Govern- mental Units[a]	Counties[b]	Municipalities	Townships and Towns	School Districts[c]	Special Districts
A. Total Units						
1942	155,116	3,050	16,220	18,919	108,579	8,299
1952	116,807	3,052	16,807	17,202	67,355	12,340
1962	91,237	3,043	18,000	17,142	34,678	18,323[d]
1972	78,269	3,044	18,517	16,991	15,781	23,885
1982	81,831	3,041	19,076	16,734	14,851	28,078
1987	83,217	3,042	19,205	16,691	14,741	29,487
B. 1987 Detail by State						
Total	83,237	3,042	19,200	16,691	14,721	29,532
Alabama	1,054	67	436	-	129	421
Alaska	173	9	149	-	-	14
Arizona	577	15	81	-	227	253
Arkansas	1,397	75	483	-	333	505
California	4,332	57	442	-	1,098	2,734
Colorado	1,594	62	266	-	180	1,085
Connecticut	478	-	31	149	16	281
Delaware	282	3	57	-	19	202
Florida	966	66	390	-	95	414
Georgia	1,287	158	532	-	186	410
Hawaii	19	3	1	-	-	14
Idaho	1,066	44	198	-	118	705
Illinois	6,628	102	1,279	1,434	1,029	2,783
Indiana	2,807	91	567	1,008	304	836
Iowa	1,878	99	955	-	451	372
Kansas	3,804	105	627	1,360	324	1,387
Kentucky	1,304	119	437	-	178	569
Louisiana	453	61	301	-	66	24
Maine	801	16	22	471	88	203
Maryland	402	23	155	-	-	223
Massachusetts	837	12	39	312	82	391
Michigan	2,700	83	534	1,242	590	250
Minnesota	3,556	87	855	1,798	441	374
Mississippi	854	82	293	-	171	307
Missouri	3,148	114	930	325	561	1,217
Montana	1,244	54	128	-	547	514
Nebraska	3,153	93	534	454	952	1,119
Nevada	198	16	18	-	17	146
New Hampshire	525	10	13	221	160	120
New Jersey	1,626	21	320	247	551	486
New Mexico	332	33	98	-	88	112
New York	3,303	57	618	929	720	978
North Carolina	917	100	495	-	-	321
North Dakota	2,788	53	366	1,355	310	703
Ohio	3,378	88	940	1,318	621	410
Oklahoma	1,803	77	591	-	636	498
Oregon	1,503	36	240	-	350	876
Pennsylvania	4,957	66	1,022	1,548	515	1,805
Rhode Island	126	-	8	31	3	83
South Carolina	708	46	269	-	92	300
South Dakota	1,763	64	309	984	193	212
Tennessee	905	94	334	-	14	462
Texas	4,416	254	1,156	-	1,113	1,892
Utah	531	29	225	-	40	236
Vermont	674	14	55	237	272	95
Virginia	431	95	229	-	-	106
Washington	1,780	39	266	-	297	1,177
West Virginia	631	55	230	-	55	290
Wisconsin	2,720	72	580	1,268	433	366
Wyoming	425	23	95	-	56	250
District of Columbia	2	-	1	-	-	1

[a] Includes the Federal government, the District of Columbia, and the state governments. Alaska and Hawaii are included beginning 1952.
[b] Includes areas corresponding to counties but having no organized county government.
[c] Includes local school systems operated as part of state, county, municipal, or township governments.
[d] Beginning 1962, data are not strictly comparable to prior years because of a change in classification.
Source: Department of Commerce, Bureau of the Census.

A3. Summary of Total Government Revenue, Expenditures, and Debt

Selected Fiscal Years 1927-1987[a]

($Billions)

Item	1927	1940	1950	1960	1970	1980	1987
All governments[b]							
Revenue	$ 12.2	$ 17.8	$ 66.7	$ 153.1	$ 333.8	$ 932.2	$ 1,677.7
General	11.6	14.9	58.5	130.6	272.5	716.6	1,235.7
Utility and liquor stores	0.4	1.0	2.7	4.9	8.6	25.6	49.8
Insurance trust	0.2	1.9	5.5	17.6	52.7	190.0	392.2
Expenditures	11.2	20.4	70.3	151.3	333.0	958.7	1,810.0
General	10.6	18.1	60.7	128.6	275.0	723.1	1,374.3
Utility and liquor stores	0.5	1.3	2.7	5.1	9.4	36.2	68.4
Insurance trust	0.1	1.0	6.9	17.6	48.5	199.4	367.3
Debt outstanding	33.4	63.3	281.5	364.0	514.5	1249.9	3,072.7
Federal							
Revenue	4.5	7.0	43.5	99.8	205.6	565.5	952.6
General	4.4	6.2	40.1	87.1	163.6	419.1	667.0
Intergovernmental	-	-	-	-	-	1.8	2.5
Insurance trust	0.1	0.8	3.5	12.7	42.0	146.4	285.6
Expenditures	3.5	10.1	44.8	97.3	208.2	617.2	1,148.6
Intergovernmental	0.1	0.9	2.4	7.0	23.3	90.8	111.4
Direct	3.4	9.2	42.4	90.3	184.9	526.3	1,037.1
General	3.4	8.9	37.9	76.7	143.7	355.8	832.1
Insurance trust	c	0.3	4.5	13.6	41.2	170.6	316.5
Debt outstanding	18.5	43.0	257.4	286.3	370.9	914.3	2,354.1
State and local							
Revenue	7.8	11.7	25.6	60.3	150.1	451.5	842.6
Intergovernmental	0.1	0.9	2.5	7.0	21.9	83	115.0
Own sources	7.7	10.8	23.2	53.3	128.2	368.5	727.6
General	7.2	8.7	18.4	43.5	108.9	299.3	571.2
Utility and liquor stores	0.4	1.0	2.7	4.9	8.6	25.6	49.8
Insurance trust	0.2	1.1	2.0	4.9	10.7	43.7	106.6
Expenditures	7.8	11.2	27.9	61.0	148.1	434.1	775.3
General	7.2	9.2	22.8	51.9	131.3	369.1	656.1
Utility and liquor stores	0.5	1.3	2.7	5.1	9.4	36.2	68.4
Insurance trust	0.1	0.7	2.4	4.0	7.3	28.8	50.8
Debt outstanding	14.9	20.3	24.1	70.0	143.6	335.6	718.7

[a] Debt as of the end of the fiscal year. Beginning in 1963, data for local governments are reported on a somewhat different chronological basis (see Introductory Notes to Tables).

[b] To avoid duplication, intergovernmental transactions between levels of government are eliminated in the combined totals.

[c] Less than $50 million.

Source: Department of Commerce, Bureau of the Census.

A4. Government Receipts and Expenditures in the National Income Accounts[a]

Selected Calendar Years 1929-1989

($Billions)

Item	1929	1949	1959	1969	1979	1988	1989[e]
Total receipts, national income basis	$ 11.3	$ 56.6	$ 130.3	$ 300.1	$ 779.8	$ 1,566.7	$ 1,657.6
Personal tax and nontax receipts	2.6	18.5	46.1	116.3	304.7	590.3	635.1
Corporate profits tax accruals	1.4	10.2	23.6	39.7	88.0	142.7	147.6
Indirect business tax and nontax accruals	7.1	21.3	41.7	86.3	189.4	389.0	404.0
Contributions for social insurance	.3	6.6	18.8	57.9	197.8	444.7	470.9
Total expenditures, national income basis	10.3	60.0	131.9	290.2	768.3	1,653.8	1,741.9
Purchases of goods and services	8.9	39.0	97.9	207.3	467.8	964.9	1,011.3
Transfer payments	1.0	16.9	27.6	69.7	268.0	568.3	594.4
To persons	.9	11.7	25.7	67.5	262.8	555.4	584.5
To foreigners	b	5.1	1.9	2.2	5.2	12.9	9.9
Net interest paid[c]	.7	4.3	6.3	11.5	30.8	113.1	125.9
Less: Dividends received[d]	-	-	-	.2	2.0	8.2	9.0
Subsidies less current surplus of government enterprises	-.2	-.3	.1	1.9	3.5	15.9	19.3
Less: Wage accruals less disbursements	b	b	b	b	-.2	b	b
Surplus or deficit (-) on national income and product accounts	1.0	-3.4	-1.6	9.9	11.5	-87.1	-84.3
Social insurance funds	.2	2.7	2.2	13.6	27.2	121.7	133.7
Other	.8	-6.0	-3.8	-3.7	-15.7	-208.8	-217.9

[a] See Introductory Notes for a description of the Federal sector in the national income accounts.
[b] Less than $50 million.
[c] Interest paid less interest received by government.
[d] Prior to 1968, dividends received are included in net interest paid.
[e] Seasonally adjusted annual rate QI 1989.
Source: Department of Commerce, Bureau of Economic Analysis.

A5. Federal and State-Local Government Surpluses or Deficits in the National Income Accounts

Selected Calendar Years 1940-1989

($Billions)

Year	All Levels of Government			Federal			State and Local		
	Total	Social Insurance Funds	Other Funds	Total	Social Insurance Funds	Other Funds	Total	Social Insurance Funds	Other Funds
1940	$-.7	$1.3	$-2.0	$-1.3	$1.2	$-2.5	$.6	$.2	$.5
1945	-39.5	4.9	-44.4	-42.1	4.7	-46.8	2.6	.2	2.3
1950	8.0	1.1	6.9	9.2	.4	8.9	-1.2	.7	-1.9
1955	3.1	3.4	-.2	4.4	2.0	2.4	-1.3	1.3	-2.6
1960	3.1	3.8	-.8	3.0	1.6	1.5	.1	2.3	-2.2
1961	-4.3	1.4	-5.6	-3.9	-1.1	-2.8	-.4	2.4	-2.8
1962	-3.8	3.3	-7.1	-4.2	.7	-5.0	.5	2.6	-2.1
1963	.7	5.0	-4.3	.3	2.2	-2.0	.5	2.8	-2.4
1964	-2.3	6.0	-8.2	-3.3	2.8	-6.0	1.0	3.2	-2.2
1965	.5	5.5	-4.9	.5	2.0	-1.5	a	3.4	-3.4
1966	-1.3	11.5	-12.7	-1.8	7.5	-9.3	.5	4.0	-3.5
1967	-14.2	10.9	-25.2	-13.2	6.1	-19.3	-1.1	4.8	-5.9
1968	-6.0	10.5	-16.5	-6.0	5.2	-11.3	.1	5.3	-5.2
1969	9.9	13.6	-3.7	8.4	7.8	.6	1.5	5.8	-4.3
1970	-10.6	10.7	-21.3	-12.4	3.8	-16.2	1.8	6.9	-5.1
1971	-19.5	7.7	-27.1	-22.0	.1	-22.1	2.6	7.6	-5.1
1972	-3.4	11.2	-14.5	-16.8	2.5	-19.3	13.5	8.7	4.8
1973	7.9	18.7	-10.8	-5.6	9.0	-14.6	13.5	9.6	3.9
1974	-4.3	16.9	-21.2	-11.6	5.9	-17.5	7.2	11.0	-3.8
1975	-64.9	-.7	-64.2	-69.4	-13.8	-55.6	4.5	13.1	-8.6
1976	-38.4	2.7	-41.0	-53.5	-12.9	-40.6	15.2	15.6	-.4
1977	-19.1	6.8	-25.9	-46.0	-11.2	-34.9	26.9	18.0	8.9
1978	-.4	18.7	-19.1	-29.3	-1.6	-27.8	28.9	20.3	8.7
1979	11.5	27.2	-15.7	-16.1	3.4	-19.5	27.6	23.8	3.8
1980	-34.5	14.2	-48.7	-61.3	-12.9	-48.4	26.8	27.1	-.3
1981	-29.7	18.3	-48.0	-63.8	-11.7	-52.1	34.1	30.0	4.1
1982	-110.8	6.0	-116.8	-145.9	-30.8	-115.0	35.1	36.9	-1.7
1983	-128.6	10.7	-139.2	-176.0	-32.4	-143.6	47.5	43.1	4.4
1984	-105.0	46.2	-151.2	-169.6	1.4	-171.0	64.6	44.8	19.8
1985	-131.8	62.3	-194.1	-196.9	11.0	-207.9	65.1	51.3	13.8
1986	-144.4	73.6	-218.0	-205.6	17.4	-223.1	61.2	56.2	5.0
1987	-104.9	89.6	-194.5	-157.8	27.5	-185.3	52.9	62.1	-9.2
1988	-87.1	121.7	-208.8	-142.3	53.2	-195.5	55.2	68.5	-13.3
1989b	-84.3	133.7	-217.9	-139.5	61.2	-200.7	55.2	72.5	-17.2

a Less than $50 million.
b Seasonally adjusted annual rate QI 1989.
Source: Department of Commerce, Bureau of Economic Analysis.

A6. Expenditures of All Governments by Function and Level of Government
Fiscal Year 1987
($Millions)

Function	Total	Federal	State	Local
Total expenditures	$ 1,810,006	$ 1,148,584	$ 455,696	$ 463,826
Less: Intergovernmental expenditures	a	111,441	141,426	5,234
To Federal government	a	-	2,455	-
To state governments	a	92,463	-	5,234
To local governments	a	18,978	138,970	-
Equals: Direct expenditures	1,810,006	1,037,143	314,270	458,592
General	1,374,297	720,689	262,513	391,095
National defense and international relations	319,084	319,084	-	-
Education	240,686	14,028	61,647	165,010
Highways	52,822	623	31,488	20,711
Public welfare	106,277	26,187	61,123	18,967
Hospitals	47,894	7,786	17,995	22,113
Health	24,595	7,731	9,207	7,656
Police	28,720	4,036	3,636	21,049
Natural resources	92,801	83,063	7,354	2,384
Housing and urban renewal	21,304	9,538	1,308	10,458
Air transportation	8,699	3,823	476	4,400
Water transport and terminals	3,715	1,971	535	1,209
Social insurance administration	6,775	4,023	2,741	11
Financial administration[b]	39,273	9,230	12,233	17,810
Interest on general debt[c]	187,971	146,155	18,583	23,233
Other[d]	193,681	83,411	34,187	76,084
Utility and liquor stores	68,440	-	8,441	59,998
Insurance trust	367,269	316,454	43,316	7,499
Employee retirement	55,605	25,991	22,189	7,425
Unemployment compensation[e]	15,412	164	15,174	74
Old-age, survivors, disability and health insurance	286,500	282,212	4,288	-
Railroad retirement	6,148	6,148	-	-
Other	3,604	1,939	1,665	-

[a] To avoid duplication, intergovernmental transactions between levels of government are eliminated in the combined total.
[b] Includes general control.
[c] Excluding, as intergovernmental transactions, interest on Federal securities held by Federal agencies and funds.
[d] Includes postal service, space research and technology, correction, sewers, libraries, sanitation, fire, parking facilities, local parks, general (state-local) public buildings, and unallocable services.
[e] Relates to cooperative state-Federal programs administered by state employment security agencies, including regular and extended or supplemental programs.
Source: Department of Commerce, Bureau of the Census.

A7. Expenditures of All Governments by Function

Selected Fiscal Years 1960–1987

($Millions)

Function	1960	1970	1980	1987
Total expenditures	$151,288	$332,985	$958,657	$1,810,006
General expenditures, total[a]	128,600	275,017	723,094	1,374,297
Selected Federal programs:				
National defense and international relations	48,922	84,253	149,459	319,084
Postal service	3,730	7,722	18,177	32,243
Space research and technology	395	3,691	4,892	7,450
Education	19,404	55,771	143,830	240,686
Social services and income maintenance:				
Public welfare	4,462	17,517	64,764	106,277
Hospitals	4,213	9,693	29,208	47,894
Health	1,031	3,895	14,102	24,595
Veterans' services[b]	3,801	5,388	12,504	17,217
Social insurance administration	539	1,790	4,537	6,775
Transportation:				
Highways	9,565	16,746	33,745	52,822
Air transportation	842	2,065	5,071	8,699
Water transport and terminals	1,142	1,905	3,278	3,715
Parking facilities	c	158	343	757
Public safety:				
Police protection	2,030	4,903	15,233	28,720
Fire protection	995	2,024	5,718	10,910
Correction	722	1,709	6,835	17,561
Protective inspection and regulation	c	c	2,318	4,420
Environment and housing:				
Natural resources[d]	7,087	11,469	35,243	92,801
Housing and urban renewal	1,142	3,189	12,142	21,304
Parks and recreation[e]	770	1,888	6,520	12,481
Sanitation and sewerage	1,727	3,413	13,214	21,324
Governmental administration:				
General control	c	3,086	10,518	20,606
Financial administration	2,750	3,284	10,228	18,667
General public buildings[e]	533	1,287	3,018	4,853
Interest on general debt	9,332	18,411	76,033	187,971
Utility expenditures	4,066[f]	7,820[f]	33,599	65,509
Liquor stores expenditures	1,022	1,627	2,591	2,931
Insurance trust expenditures, total[a]	17,596	48,521	199,373	367,269
Old-age, survivors, disability, and health	10,798	35,828	149,451	286,500
Railroad retirement	916	1,586	4,671	6,148
Employee retirement	2,161	6,399	28,870	55,605
Unemployment compensation	2,639	2,816	12,282	15,412
Veterans' life insurance	679	971	1,380	1,939

[a] Total includes items not shown separately.
[b] Not elsewhere classified; other veterans' expenditures are included under education, health and hospitals, welfare, and life insurance benefits.
[c] Included in total general.
[d] Includes Federal stabilization of farm prices and income.
[e] State-local only.
[f] Local only; state utility expenditures included under general prior to 1977.
Source: Department of Commerce, Bureau of the Census.

A8. Percentage Distribution of Government Expenditures by Function

Selected Fiscal Years 1960-1987

Function	1960	1970	1980	1987
Total expenditures	100.0%	100.0%	100.0%	100.0%
General expenditures, total[a]	85.0	82.6	75.4	75.9
Selected Federal programs:				
National defense and international relations	32.3	25.3	15.6	17.6
Postal service	2.5	2.3	1.9	1.8
Space research and technology	.3	1.1	.5	.4
Education	12.8	16.7	15.0	13.3
Social services and income maintenance:				
Public welfare	2.9	5.3	6.8	5.9
Hospitals	2.8	2.9	3.0	2.6
Health	.7	1.2	1.5	1.4
Veterans' services[b]	2.5	1.6	1.3	1.0
Social insurance administration	.4	.5	.5	.4
Transportation:				
Highways	6.3	5.0	3.5	2.9
Air transportation	.6	.6	.5	.5
Water transport and terminals	.8	.6	.3	.2
Parking facilities	c	c	c	c
Public safety:				
Police protection	1.3	1.5	1.6	1.6
Fire protection	.7	.6	.6	.6
Correction	.5	.5	.7	1.0
Protective inspection and regulation	c	c	.2	.2
Environment and housing:				
Natural resources[d]	4.7	3.4	3.7	5.1
Housing and urban renewal	.8	1.0	1.3	1.2
Parks and recreation[e]	.5	.6	.7	.7
Sanitation and sewerage	1.1	1.0	1.4	1.2
Governmental administration:				
General control	c	.9	1.1	1.1
Financial administration	1.8	1.0	1.1	1.0
General public buildings[e]	.4	.4	.3	.3
Interest on general debt	6.2	5.5	7.9	10.4
Utility expenditures	2.7[f]	2.3	3.5	3.6
Liquor stores expenditures	.7	.5	.3	.2
Insurance trust expenditures, total[a]	11.6	14.6	20.8	20.3
Old-age, survivors, disability, and health	7.1	10.8	15.6	15.8
Railroad retirement	.6	.5	.5	.3
Employee retirement	1.4	1.9	3.0	3.1
Unemployment compensation	1.7	.8	1.3	.9
Veterans' life insurance	.4	.3	.1	.1

[a] Total includes items not shown separately.
[b] Not elsewhere classified; other veterans' expenditures are included under education, health and hospitals, welfare, and life insurance benefits.
[c] Less than .05 percent.
[d] Includes Federal stabilization of farm prices and income.
[e] State-local only.
[f] Local only; state utility expenditures included under general prior to 1977.
Source: Computed by Tax Foundation from data in Table A7.

A9. Federal, State, and Local Expenditures[a]
Selected Fiscal Years 1902-1988[b]
($Millions)

Year	Total	Federal	State	Local
1902	$ 1,660	$ 572	$ 179	$ 909
1913	3,215	970	372	1,873
1922	9,297	3,763	1,261	4,273
1927	11,220	3,533	1,882	5,805
1932	12,437	4,266	2,562	5,609
1934	12,807	5,941	2,532	4,334
1936	16,758	9,165	3,144	4,449
1938	17,675	8,449	3,955	5,271
1940	20,417	10,061	4,545	5,811
1942	45,576	35,549	4,456	5,571
1944	109,947	100,520	4,062	5,365
1946	79,707	66,534	6,162	7,011
1948	55,081	35,592	9,531	9,959
1950	70,334	44,800	12,774	12,761
1952	99,847	71,568	13,330	14,948
1953	110,054	79,990	14,086	15,978
1954	111,332	77,692	15,802	17,837
1955	110,717	73,441	17,400	19,875
1956	115,796	75,991	18,379	21,426
1957	125,463	81,783	20,405	23,274
1958	134,931	86,054	23,337	25,539
1959	145,748	93,531	25,106	27,111
1960	151,288	97,284	25,035	28,970
1961	164,875	104,863	28,231	31,782
1962	176,240	113,428	29,210	33,601
1963	184,996	118,805	31,770	34,421
1964	196,431	125,949	33,438	37,045
1965	205,682	130,059	35,726	39,897
1966	224,813	143,022	39,114	42,677
1967	257,800	166,849	45,096	45,855
1968	282,645	184,464	50,046	48,135
1969	308,344	196,165	56,625	55,554
1970	332,985	208,190	64,665	60,130
1971	369,423	226,157	75,882	67,384
1972	399,098	242,186	81,208	75,705
1973	436,907	272,709	87,646	76,552
1974	478,325	295,147	100,513	82,665
1975	560,129	340,542	122,153	97,434
1976	625,076	389,905	127,678	107,493
1977	680,329	430,594	137,683	112,052
1978	745,438	477,825	149,476	118,137
1979	832,385	535,702	168,608	128,075
1980	958,657	615,420	191,806	151,432
1981	1,109,815	717,376	220,511	171,927
1982	1,233,492	794,671	242,075	196,746
1983	1,350,950	872,499	263,630	214,821
1984	1,428,027	926,466	273,518	228,042
1985	1,581,077	1,030,168	305,786	245,123
1986	1,696,980	1,094,295	326,998	275,687
1987	1,810,006	1,146,129	360,576	303,244
1988	1,935,835	1,204,677	397,602	333,556

[a] Grants-in-aid and other intergovernmental payments are counted as expenditures of the first disbursing unit. Total expenditures are shown as defined by the Bureau of the Census including insurance trust expenditures. (See Introductory Notes to Tables.)
[b] Data for 1988 estimated by Tax Foundation. Beginning in 1963, data for local governments are reported on a somewhat different basis.
Source: Department of Commerce, Bureau of the Census.

A10. Federal, State, and Local Expenditures: Per Capita and Percentage Distribution

Selected Fiscal Years 1902-1988[a]

Year	Per Capita				Percentage Distribution			
	Total	Federal	State	Local	Total	Federal	State	Local
1902	$ 21	$ 7	$ 2	$ 12	100.0%	34.5%	10.8%	54.8%
1913	33	10	4	19	100.0	30.2	11.6	58.3
1922	85	34	12	39	100.0	40.5	13.6	46.0
1927	95	30	16	49	100.0	31.5	16.8	51.7
1932	100	34	21	45	100.0	34.3	20.6	45.1
1934	102	47	20	34	100.0	46.4	19.8	33.8
1936	131	72	25	35	100.0	54.7	18.8	26.5
1938	137	65	31	41	100.0	47.8	22.4	29.8
1940	155	77	35	44	100.0	49.3	22.3	28.5
1942	341	626	33	42	100.0	78.0	9.8	12.2
1944	821	751	30	40	100.0	91.4	3.7	4.9
1946	581	485	45	51	100.0	83.5	7.7	8.8
1948	380	246	66	69	100.0	64.6	17.3	18.1
1950	468	298	85	85	100.0	63.7	18.2	18.1
1952	646	463	86	97	100.0	71.7	13.4	15.0
1953	700	509	90	102	100.0	72.7	12.8	14.5
1954	696	486	99	112	100.0	69.8	14.2	16.0
1955	679	451	107	122	100.0	66.3	15.7	18.0
1956	697	458	111	129	100.0	65.6	15.9	18.5
1957	742	484	121	138	100.0	65.2	16.3	18.6
1958	784	500	136	148	100.0	63.8	17.3	18.9
1959	833	534	143	155	100.0	64.2	17.2	18.6
1960	846	544	140	152	100.0	64.3	16.5	19.1
1961	908	577	155	175	100.0	63.6	17.1	19.3
1962	955	615	158	182	100.0	64.4	16.6	19.1
1963	988	634	170	184	100.0	64.2	17.2	18.6
1964	1,034	663	176	195	100.0	64.1	17.0	18.9
1965	1,069	676	186	207	100.0	63.3	17.4	19.4
1966	1,155	735	201	219	100.0	63.6	17.4	19.0
1967	1,311	849	229	233	100.0	64.7	17.5	17.8
1968	1,423	929	252	242	100.0	65.3	17.7	17.0
1969	1,538	978	282	277	100.0	63.6	18.3	18.0
1970	1,643	1,027	319	297	100.0	62.5	19.4	18.1
1971	1,797	1,100	369	328	100.0	61.2	20.5	18.2
1972	1,917	1,163	390	364	100.0	60.7	20.3	19.0
1973	2,076	1,296	417	364	100.0	62.4	20.1	17.5
1974	2,252	1,389	473	389	100.0	61.7	21.0	17.3
1975	2,612	1,588	570	454	100.0	60.8	21.8	17.4
1976	2,886	1,800	589	496	100.0	62.4	20.4	17.2
1977	3,111	1,969	630	512	100.0	63.3	20.3	16.5
1978	3,373	2,162	676	535	100.0	64.1	20.0	15.9
1979	3,726	2,398	755	573	100.0	64.3	20.3	15.4
1980	4,243	2,724	849	670	100.0	64.2	20.0	15.8
1981	4,857	3,140	965	752	100.0	64.8	19.9	15.5
1982	5,345	3,444	1,049	853	100.0	64.4	19.6	16.0
1983	5,798	3,744	1,131	922	100.0	64.6	19.5	15.9
1984	6,065	3,935	1,162	969	100.0	64.9	19.2	15.9
1985	6,652	4,334	1,287	1,031	100.0	65.2	19.3	15.5
1986	7,012	4,522	1,351	1,139	100.0	64.5	19.3	16.2
1987	7,418	4,697	1,478	1,243	100.0	63.3	19.9	16.8
1988	7,837	4,877	1,610	1,350	100.0	62.2	20.5	17.3

[a] Data for 1988 estimated by Tax Foundation.
Source: Computed by Tax Foundation from data in Table A9 and population, excluding armed forces overseas, as of January 1.

A11. Revenue of All Governments by Source and Level of Government

Overlapping in the Sources of Intergovernmental Revenue

Fiscal Year 1987

($Millions)

Source	Total	Federal	State	Local
Total revenue	$ 1,677,737	$ 952,631	$ 516,941	$ 469,317
Intergovernmental	a	2,487	102,381	156,285
From Federal government	a	-	95,463	19,533
From state government	a	2,487	-	136,752
From local government	a	-	6,918	b
Revenue from own sources	1,677,737	950,144	414,560	313,032
General	1,235,685	664,517	317,106	254,062
Taxes	944,549	539,400	246,933	158,216
Property	121,227	-	4,609	116,618
Individual income	476,238	392,557	75,965	7,716
Corporation income	106,598	83,926	20,724	1,947
Sales and gross receipts and customs	192,716	33,285	119,838	24,455
Customs duties	15,138	15,138	-	-
General sales and gross receipts	96,773	-	79,638	17,135
Motor fuel	28,106	11,952	15,705	448
Alcoholic beverages	9,495	6,135	3,091	269
Tobacco products	9,742	4,937	4,605	200
Public utilities	15,557	5,435	5,987	4,135
Other	17,905	4,826[c]	10,811	2,268
Motor vehicle and operators' licenses	9,655	-	9,037	618
Death and gift	10,557	7,493	3,035	29
All other	27,558	7,001	13,725	6,833
Charges and miscellaneous	291,136	125,117	70,173	95,846
Utility and liquor stores	49,810	-	5,776	44,034
Insurance trust	392,242	285,627	91,678	14,936
Employee retirement	83,741	4,486	64,405	14,851
Unemployment compensation[d]	19,129	204	18,839	86[e]
Old-age, survivors, disability and health insurance	275,874	275,874	-	-
Railroad retirement	4,337	4,337	-	-
Other	9,161	726	8,434	-

[a] To avoid duplication, transactions between levels of government are eliminated in the combined total.
[b] Transactions among local units of government are excluded.
[c] Includes windfall profit tax.
[d] Relates to cooperative state-Federal programs administered by state employment security agencies, including regular and extended or supplemental programs.
[e] Washington, DC only.
Source: Department of Commerce, Bureau of the Census.

A12. Tax and Nontax Revenue of All Governments by Source
Selected Fiscal Years 1960-1987
($Millions)

Source	1960	1970	1980	1987
Total revenue	$ 153,102	$ 333,810	$ 932,199	$ 1,677,737
Tax revenue, total	126,678	274,996	729,040	1,243,889
General taxes	113,120	232,877	574,244	944,549
Property	16,405	34,054	68,499	121,227
Individual income	43,178	101,224	286,149	476,238
Corporate income	22,674	36,567	77,921	106,598
Sales and gross receipts and customs	24,452	48,619	111,961	192,716
Customs duties	1,105	2,430	7,436	15,138
General sales and gross receipts	5,177	16,128	51,328	96,773
Motor fuel	5,352	10,100	14,709	28,106
Alcoholic beverages	3,779	6,208	8,327	9,495
Tobacco products	2,915	4,531	6,320	9,742
Public utilities	1,627	3,268	8,755	15,557
Other	4,498	5,954	15,087	17,905
Motor vehicle and operators' licenses	1,700	2,904	5,713	9,655
Death and gift	2,026	4,640	8,424	10,557
All other general	2,685	4,868	15,577	27,558
Insurance trust taxes	13,558	42,119	154,796	299,340
Unemployment compensation	2,295	2,654	12,892	19,129
Old-age, survivors, disability, and health	10,656	38,485	139,370	275,874
Railroad retirement	607	980	2,534	4,337
Nontax revenues, total	26,424	58,814	203,159	433,848
Current charges[a] (general)	12,451	26,274	80,132	163,074
Miscellaneous general revenue[b]	5,048	13,329	62,253	128,062
Utility revenue	3,613[c]	6,608[c]	22,359	46,477
Liquor stores revenue	1,264	2,006	3,201	3,333
Insurance trust, nontax receipts	4,048	10,597	35,214	92,902
Employee retirement	2,868	8,206	29,060	83,741
Veterans' life insurance	527	679	670	726
Other	653	1,712	5,483	8,435

[a] Amounts received from the public for performance of specific services benefitting the person charged; includes fees, toll charges, tuition, other reimbursements for current services, gross income of commercial-type activities, etc.
[b] Includes special assessments, sale of property, interest earnings, etc.
[c] Local only; state utility revenue included under general prior to 1977.
Source: Department of Commerce, Bureau of the Census.

A13. Percentage Distribution of Government Revenue by Source

Selected Fiscal Years 1960-1987

Source	1960	1970	1980	1987
Total revenue	100.0%	100.0%	100.0%	100.0%
Tax revenue, total	82.7	82.4	78.2	74.1
General taxes	73.9	69.8	61.6	56.3
Property	10.7	10.2	7.3	7.2
Individual income	28.2	30.3	30.7	28.4
Corporate income	14.8	11.0	8.4	6.4
Sales and gross receipts	16.0	14.6	12.0	11.5
Customs duties	.7	.7	.8	.9
General sales and gross receipts	3.5	4.8	5.5	5.8
Motor fuel	3.5	3.0	1.6	1.7
Alcoholic beverages	2.5	1.9	.9	.6
Tobacco products	1.9	1.4	.7	.6
Public utilities	1.1	1.0	.9	.9
Other	2.9	1.8	1.6	1.1
Motor vehicle and operators' licenses	1.1	.9	.6	.6
Death and gift	1.3	1.4	.9	.6
All other general	1.8	1.5	1.7	1.6
Insurance trust taxes	8.9	12.6	16.6	17.8
Unemployment compensation	1.5	.8	1.4	1.1
Old-age, survivors, disability, and health	7.0	11.5	15.0	16.4
Railroad retirement	.4	.3	.3	.3
Nontax revenues, total	17.3	17.6	21.8	25.9
Current charges[a] (general)	8.1	7.9	8.6	9.7
Miscellaneous general revenue[b]	3.3	4.0	6.7	7.6
Utility revenue	2.4[c]	2.0[c]	2.4	2.8
Liquor stores revenue	.8	.6	.3	.2
Insurance trust, nontax receipts	2.6	3.2	3.8	5.5
Employee retirement	1.9	2.5	3.1	5.0
Veterans' life insurance	.3	.2	.1	.1
Other	.4	.5	.6	.5

[a] Amounts received from the public for performance of specific services benefitting the person charged; includes fees, toll charges, tuition, other reimbursements for current services, gross income of commercial-type activities, etc.
[b] Includes special assessments, sale of property, interest earnings, etc.
[c] Local only; state utility revenue included under general prior to 1977.
Source: Computed by Tax Foundation from data in Table A12.

A14. Federal, State, and Local Tax Receipts[a]

Selected Fiscal Years 1902-1987

($Millions)

Year	Total	Federal	State	Local
1902	$ 1,373	$ 513	$ 156	$ 704
1913	2,271	662	301	1,308
1922	7,387	3,371	947	3,069
1927	9,451	3,364	1,608	4,479
1932	7,977	1,813	1,890	4,274
1934	8,854	2,942	1,979	3,933
1936	10,606	3,882	2,641	4,083
1938	14,189	5,877	3,834	4,478
1940	14,243	5,583	4,157	4,503
1942	22,962	13,351	4,979	4,632
1944	52,050	41,953	5,390	4,707
1946	48,988	37,887	5,971	5,130
1948	54,584	40,180	7,802	6,602
1950	54,799	37,853	8,958	7,988
1952	84,800	64,036	11,295	9,469
1953	89,779	67,496	11,922	10,361
1954	90,917	67,584	12,352	10,981
1955	87,916	63,291	12,735	11,890
1956	100,025	72,340	14,690	12,995
1957	107,693	77,362	16,041	14,290
1958	108,593	76,716	16,412	15,465
1959	110,209	76,178	17,495	16,536
1960	126,678	88,419	20,172	18,087
1961	131,506	90,322	21,374	19,810
1962	139,471	95,262	23,210	20,999
1963	148,715	101,701	25,109	21,905
1964	158,469	107,630	27,289	23,550
1965	165,475	111,231	29,120	25,124
1966	184,730	124,940	32,420	27,370
1967	207,636	143,716	34,836	29,084
1968	217,697	147,572	38,947	31,178
1969	259,979	180,710	44,481	34,788
1970	274,996	185,670	50,486	38,840
1971	277,822	180,349	54,031	43,442
1972	315,014	202,268	62,998	49,748
1973	348,073	222,463	72,564	53,046
1974	387,611	251,790	79,337	56,484
1975	416,362	267,321	87,691	61,350
1976	446,887	283,794	95,421	67,672
1977	523,237	338,754	109,607	74,876
1978	584,810	381,200	123,155	80,455
1979	659,407	442,057	136,699	80,681
1980	727,984	492,846	148,691	86,447
1981	834,552	572,421	167,227	94,904
1982	872,156	590,089	178,358	103,709
1983	877,253	572,087	192,067	113,099
1984	968,816	632,594	212,735	123,487
1985	1,061,432	695,153	231,763	134,516
1986	1,123,349	733,576	244,686	145,087
1987	1,242,154	819,815	264,044	158,295

[a] Includes social insurance taxes and Federal supplementary medical insurance; excludes contributions to workers' compensation systems.

Source: Department of Commerce, Bureau of the Census.

A15. Federal, State, and Local Tax Receipts: Per Capita and Percentage Distribution

Selected Fiscal Years 1902-1987

Year	Per Capita				Percentage Distribution			
	Total	Federal	State	Local	Total	Federal	State	Local
1902	$ 18	$ 7	$ 2	$ 9	100.0%	37.4%	11.4%	51.3%
1913	24	7	3	14	100.0	29.2	13.3	57.6
1922	68	31	9	28	100.0	45.6	12.8	41.5
1927	80	28	14	38	100.0	35.6	17.0	47.4
1932	64	15	15	34	100.0	22.7	23.7	53.6
1934	70	23	16	31	100.0	33.2	22.4	44.4
1936	83	30	21	32	100.0	36.6	24.9	38.5
1938	110	45	30	35	100.0	41.4	27.0	31.6
1940	108	42	32	34	100.0	39.2	29.2	31.6
1942	172	100	37	35	100.0	58.1	21.7	20.2
1944	389	313	40	35	100.0	80.6	10.4	9.0
1946	357	276	44	38	100.0	77.3	12.2	10.5
1948	377	277	54	46	100.0	73.6	14.3	12.1
1950	365	252	60	53	100.0	69.1	16.3	14.6
1952	548	414	73	61	100.0	75.5	13.3	11.2
1953	571	429	76	66	100.0	75.2	13.3	11.5
1954	569	423	77	69	100.0	74.3	13.6	12.1
1955	539	388	78	73	100.0	72.0	14.5	13.5
1956	602	436	88	78	100.0	72.3	14.7	13.0
1957	637	457	95	85	100.0	71.8	14.9	13.3
1958	631	446	95	90	100.0	70.6	15.1	14.2
1959	630	435	100	94	100.0	69.1	15.9	15.0
1960	709	495	113	101	100.0	69.8	15.9	14.3
1961	724	497	118	109	100.0	68.7	16.3	15.1
1962	756	516	126	114	100.0	68.3	16.6	15.1
1963	794	543	134	117	100.0	68.4	16.9	14.7
1964	834	567	144	124	100.0	67.9	17.2	14.9
1965	859	578	151	130	100.0	67.2	17.6	15.2
1966	949	642	167	141	100.0	67.6	17.5	14.8
1967	1,056	731	177	148	100.0	69.2	16.8	14.0
1968	1,096	743	196	157	100.0	67.8	17.9	14.3
1969	1,297	901	222	174	100.0	69.5	17.1	13.4
1970	1,357	916	249	192	100.0	67.5	18.4	14.1
1971	1,352	877	263	211	100.0	64.9	19.4	15.6
1972	1,513	971	303	239	100.0	64.2	20.0	15.8
1973	1,654	1,057	345	252	100.0	63.9	20.8	15.2
1974	1,825	1,185	373	266	100.0	65.0	20.5	14.6
1975	1,942	1,247	409	286	100.0	64.2	21.1	14.7
1976	2,063	1,310	441	312	100.0	63.5	21.4	15.1
1977	2,392	1,549	501	342	100.0	64.7	20.0	14.3
1978	2,646	1,725	557	364	100.0	65.2	21.1	13.8
1979	2,952	1,979	612	361	100.0	67.0	20.7	12.2
1980	3,222	2,181	658	383	100.0	67.6	20.5	11.9
1981	3,653	2,505	732	415	100.0	68.6	20.0	11.4
1982	3,779	2,557	773	449	100.0	67.7	20.4	11.9
1983	3,765	2,455	824	485	100.0	65.2	21.9	12.9
1984	4,114	2,687	904	524	100.0	65.3	22.0	12.7
1985	4,466	2,925	975	566	100.0	65.5	21.8	12.7
1986	4,681	3,057	1,020	605	100.0	65.3	21.8	12.9
1987	5,126	3,383	1,090	653	100.0	66.0	21.3	12.7

Source: Computed by Tax Foundation from data in Table A14 and population, excluding armed forces overseas, as of January 1.

A16. Tax Index and Tax Receipts by Type of Tax[a]

All Governments

Calendar Years 1965-1988

Year	All Taxes	Personal Income Taxes	Corporate Profits Taxes	Indirect Business Taxes[b]	Social Insurance Contributions	All Other Taxes[c]
\multicolumn{7}{c}{Tax Index, 1967 = 100}
1965	82.8	78.7	94.8	89.3	69.8	89.2
1966	93.1	90.8	103.1	93.0	89.4	95.4
1967	100.0	100.0	100.0	100.0	100.0	100.0
1968	115.3	119.6	120.9	112.6	110.4	104.6
1969	130.2	143.7	121.8	123.6	127.0	118.5
1970	132.5	141.4	105.2	134.7	136.0	124.6
1971	140.9	139.1	116.0	148.0	150.9	143.1
1972	160.9	170.1	128.5	159.0	173.2	161.5
1973	180.8	182.1	151.2	172.7	215.1	163.1
1974	199.9	208.2	158.9	184.0	243.2	161.5
1975	205.4	203.3	156.1	199.4	260.8	167.7
1976	235.5	238.0	196.9	216.0	296.8	186.2
1977	264.6	273.6	223.9	235.6	330.9	220.0
1978	297.6	318.4	256.1	251.9	379.5	195.4
1979	333.3	373.6	269.9	265.5	437.6	206.2
1980	363.8	416.6	260.1	295.4	479.3	233.8
1981	414.7	481.7	248.8	347.4	556.8	247.7
1982	421.4	494.2	193.3	355.1	596.6	267.7
1983	445.6	491.3	236.8	386.7	644.4	250.8
1984	491.9	526.7	288.0	427.0	718.7	261.5
1985	532.7	583.7	296.0	453.0	783.3	281.5
1986	564.2	610.5	327.0	476.0	836.9	304.6
1987	617.4	685.0	410.1	500.1	883.1	326.2
1988	665.7	704.5	437.4	550.8	992.8	349.2
\multicolumn{7}{c}{Tax Receipts ($Billions)}
1965	$ 183.5	$ 55.5	$ 30.9	$ 60.3	$ 31.0	$ 5.8
1966	206.3	64.0	33.6	62.8	39.7	6.2
1967	221.5	70.5	32.6	67.5	44.4	6.5
1968	255.5	84.3	39.4	76.0	49.0	6.8
1969	288.5	101.3	39.7	83.4	56.4	7.7
1970	293.4	99.7	34.3	90.9	60.4	8.1
1971	312.1	98.1	37.8	99.9	67.0	9.3
1972	356.5	119.9	41.9	107.3	76.9	10.5
1973	400.4	128.4	49.3	116.6	95.5	10.6
1974	441.3	146.8	51.8	124.2	108.0	10.5
1975	455.0	143.3	50.9	134.6	115.8	10.9
1976	521.7	167.8	64.2	145.8	131.8	12.1
1977	586.1	192.9	73.0	159.0	146.9	14.3
1978	659.2	224.5	83.5	170.0	168.5	12.7
1979	738.3	263.4	88.0	179.2	194.3	13.4
1980	805.9	293.7	84.8	199.4	212.8	15.2
1981	918.5	339.6	81.1	234.5	247.2	16.1
1982	933.4	348.4	63.0	239.7	264.9	17.4
1983	987.0	346.4	77.2	261.0	286.1	16.3
1984	1,089.5	371.3	93.9	288.2	319.1	17.0
1985	1,179.9	411.5	96.5	305.8	347.8	18.3
1986	1,249.7	430.4	106.6	321.3	371.6	19.8
1987	1,367.5	482.9	133.7	337.6	392.1	21.2
1988	1,474.6	496.7	142.6	371.8	440.8	22.7

[a] Tax receipts, net of refunds, as shown in the national income accounts, generally on an accrual basis. For separate data on Federal and state and local taxes, see Tables C33 and D16.
[b] Sales, excise, and customs levies and real property taxes.
[c] Estate and gift and personal property taxes.
Source: Department of Commerce, Bureau of Economic Analysis; and Tax Foundation computations.

A17. "Tax Freedom Day" and "Tax Bite in the Eight-Hour Day"
Calendar Years 1929-1989

Year	Tax Freedom Day[a]	Tax Bite in the Eight-Hour Day[b] (Hours:Minutes)		
		Total	Federal	State and Local
1929	February 9	:52	:19	:33
1931	February 15	1:00	:13	:47
1933	March 5	1:24	:25	:59
1935	March 1	1:17	:28	:49
1937	March 6	1:24	:40	:44
1939	March 6	1:24	:38	:46
1940	March 8	1:29	:45	:44
1941	March 17	1:40	1:04	:36
1942	March 19	1:43	1:24	:29
1943	April 6	2:06	1:42	:24
1944	March 30	1:58	1:36	:22
1945	April 1	1:59	1:36	:23
1946	March 31	1:57	1:30	:27
1947	April 3	2:01	1:33	:28
1948	March 28	1:55	1:26	:29
1949	March 24	1:48	1:16	:32
1950	April 3	2:02	1:30	:32
1951	April 10	2:11	1:40	:31
1952	April 10	2:12	1:40	:32
1953	April 10	2:12	1:40	:32
1954	April 6	2:05	1:30	:35
1955	April 9	2:09	1:34	:35
1956	April 11	2:13	1:37	:36
1957	April 13	2:14	1:37	:37
1958	April 10	2:12	1:32	:40
1959	April 14	2:16	1:36	:40
1960	April 17	2:22	1:40	:42
1961	April 18	2:22	1:38	:44
1962	April 18	2:21	1:38	:43
1963	April 19	2:23	1:39	:44
1964	April 15	2:18	1:33	:45
1965	April 15	2:17	1:33	:44
1966	April 18	2:21	1:36	:45
1967	April 20	2:24	1:37	:47
1968	April 25	2:32	1:39	:53
1969	May 1	2:38	1:48	:50
1970	April 28	2:34	1:40	:54
1971	April 25	2:31	1:36	:55
1972	April 29	2:36	1:39	:57
1973	April 29	2:36	1:41	:55
1974	May 3	2:41	1:45	:56
1975	April 28	2:35	1:38	:57
1976	May 1	2:40	1:42	:58
1977	May 3	2:41	1:43	:58
1978	May 3	2:41	1:45	:56
1979	May 3	2:41	1:48	:53
1980	May 1	2:39	1:48	:51
1981	May 4	2:43	1:52	:51
1982	May 3	2:41	1:48	:53
1983	April 30	2:38	1:43	:55
1984	April 28	2:36	1:42	:54
1985	May 1	2:38	1:44	:54
1986	May 1	2:38	1:43	:55
1987	May 4	2:42	1:47	:55
1988	May 3	2:42	1:46	:56
1989	May 4	2:43	1:47	:56

[a] "Tax Freedom Day" represents the date on which the average person would finish paying Federal, state, and local taxes if all earnings since January 1 were turned over to governments to fulfill annual tax obligations.

[b] The "Tax Bite in the Eight-Hour Day" reflects the amount of time out of each workday that the average person spends earning enough money to pay tax obligations.

Source: Tax Foundation computations based on data in Table A32.

A18. Gross Debt of Federal, State, and Local Governments[a]
End of Selected Fiscal Years 1902-1988[b]
($Millions)

Year	Total	Federal	State	Local
1902	$ 3,285	$ 1,178	$ 230	$ 1,877
1913	5,607	1,193	379	4,035
1922	33,072	22,963	1,131	8,978
1927	33,393	18,512	1,971	12,910
1932	38,692	19,487	2,832	16,373
1934	45,982	27,053	3,248	15,681
1936	53,253	33,779	3,413	16,061
1938	56,601	37,165	3,343	16,093
1940	63,251	42,968	3,590	16,693
1942	91,759	72,422	3,257	16,080
1944	218,482	201,003	2,776	14,703
1946	285,339	269,422	2,353	13,564
1948	270,948	252,292	3,676	14,980
1950	281,445	257,357	5,258	18,830
1952	289,205	259,105	6,874	23,226
1953	299,852	266,071	7,824	25,957
1954	310,190	271,260	9,600	29,331
1955	318,641	274,374	11,198	33,069
1956	321,619	272,751	12,890	35,978
1957	323,566	270,527	13,738	39,301
1958	334,530	276,343	15,394	42,793
1959	348,816	284,706	16,930	47,180
1960	356,286	286,331	18,543	51,412
1961	363,994	288,971	19,993	55,030
1962	379,479	298,201	22,023	59,255
1963	390,916	305,860	23,176	61,881
1964	403,935	311,713	25,041	67,181
1965	416,786	317,274	27,034	72,478
1966	426,958	319,907	29,564	77,487
1967	439,880	326,221	32,472	81,185
1968	468,736	347,578	35,666	85,492
1969	487,268	353,720	39,555	93,995
1970	514,489	370,919	42,008	101,563
1971	556,957	398,130	47,793	111,034
1972	602,418	427,260	54,453	120,705
1973	656,903	468,418	59,375	129,110
1974	692,851	486,235	65,296	141,320
1975	764,055	544,129	72,127	147,798
1976	871,815	631,283	84,825	155,707
1977	966,668	709,136	90,200	167,332
1978	1,060,856	780,423	102,569	177,864
1979	1,137,853	833,750	111,740	192,363
1980	1,249,919	914,316	121,958	213,645
1981	1,367,831	1,003,939	134,847	229,045
1982	1,551,565	1,146,986	147,470	257,109
1983	1,836,387	1,381,886	167,290	287,211
1984	2,081,778	1,576,748	186,377	318,653
1985	2,395,913	1,827,470	211,904	356,539
1986	2,788,397	2,129,522	247,715	411,160
1987	3,072,943	2,354,286	265,677	452,980
1988	3,419,198	2,614,581	297,053	507,564

[a] Short- and long-term debt outstanding.
[b] State and local debt for 1988 estimated by Tax Foundation.
Source: Department of Commerce, Bureau of the Census; and Treasury Department.

A19. Gross Debt of Federal, State, and Local Governments Per Capita and Percentage Distribution

End of Selected Fiscal Years 1902-1988

Federal, State and Local Governments

Year	Per Capita				Percentage Distribution			
	Total	Federal	State	Local	Total	Federal	State	Local
1902	$41	$15	$3	$24	100.0%	35.9%	7.0%	57.1%
1922	301	209	10	82	100.0	69.4	3.4	27.1
1927	281	156	17	108	100.0	55.4	5.9	38.7
1932	310	156	23	131	100.0	50.4	7.3	42.3
1934	364	214	26	124	100.0	58.8	7.1	34.1
1936	416	264	27	125	100.0	63.4	6.4	30.2
1938	436	286	26	124	100.0	65.7	5.9	28.4
1940	479	326	27	127	100.0	67.9	5.7	26.4
1942	685	541	24	120	100.0	78.9	3.5	17.5
1944	1,644	1,513	21	111	100.0	92.0	1.3	6.7
1946	2,037	1,924	17	97	100.0	94.4	.8	4.8
1948	1,855	1,727	25	103	100.0	93.1	1.4	5.5
1950	1,853	1,695	35	124	100.0	91.4	1.9	6.7
1952	1,849	1,657	44	149	100.0	89.6	2.4	8.0
1954	1,916	1,676	59	181	100.0	87.4	3.1	9.5
1956	1,913	1,623	77	214	100.0	84.8	4.0	11.2
1958	1,921	1,587	88	246	100.0	82.6	4.6	12.8
1960	1,980	1,591	103	286	100.0	80.4	5.2	14.4
1962	2,042	1,605	119	319	100.0	78.5	5.8	15.6
1964	2,113	1,631	131	351	100.0	77.2	6.2	16.6
1966	2,183	1,636	151	396	100.0	74.9	6.9	18.1
1968	2,351	1,743	179	429	100.0	74.2	7.6	18.2
1970	2,522	1,818	206	498	100.0	72.1	8.1	19.7
1971	2,693	1,925	231	537	100.0	71.5	8.6	19.9
1972	2,878	2,042	260	577	100.0	70.9	9.0	20.0
1973	3,108	2,216	281	611	100.0	71.3	9.0	20.0
1974	3,248	2,279	306	662	100.0	70.2	9.4	20.4
1975	3,546	2,525	335	686	100.0	71.2	9.4	19.3
1976	4,007	2,902	390	716	100.0	72.4	9.7	17.9
1977	4,399	3,227	410	761	100.0	73.4	9.3	17.3
1978	4,777	3,514	462	801	100.0	73.6	9.7	16.8
1979	5,067	3,713	498	857	100.0	73.3	9.8	16.9
1980	5,501	4,024	537	940	100.0	73.2	9.8	17.1
1981	5,959	4,374	587	998	100.0	73.4	9.9	16.7
1982	6,688	4,944	636	1,108	100.0	73.9	9.5	16.6
1983	7,838	5,898	714	1,226	100.0	75.2	9.1	15.7
1984	8,803	6,668	788	1,348	100.0	75.7	9.0	15.3
1985	10,036	7,655	888	1,493	100.0	76.3	8.8	14.9
1986	11,565	8,832	1,027	1,705	100.0	76.4	8.9	14.7
1987	12,624	9,672	1,091	1,861	100.0	76.6	8.7	14.7
1988	13,910	10,637	1,208	2,065	100.0	76.5	8.7	14.8

Source: Computed by Tax Foundation from data in Table A18, and population as of July 1.

A20. Government Employees by Level of Government and Major Category

Selected Calendar Years 1929-1987
Number of Full-Time Equivalent Employees (Thousands)

Year	All Governments		Federal		State and Local		Exhibit: All Private Industries
	Total[a]	Total Less Military	Total[a]	Total Less Military	Total[a]	Total Less Education	
1929	3,204	2,923	847	566	2,357	1,275	32,134
1933	3,893	3,623	1,237	967	2,656	1,572	23,321
1939[b]	6,172	5,791	3,312	2,931	2,860	1,636	29,742
1946	8,759	5,322	5,770	2,333	2,989	1,713	38,356
1947	6,762	5,130	3,528	1,896	3,234	1,870	40,364
1948	6,812	5,268	3,460	1,916	3,352	1,934	41,278
1949	7,278	5,561	3,684	1,967	3,594	2,103	39,577
1950	7,505	5,692	3,783	1,970	3,722	2,186	41,099
1951	9,342	6,138	5,535	2,331	3,807	2,226	43,325
1952	10,122	6,410	6,175	2,463	3,947	2,292	43,698
1953	10,095	6,465	5,989	2,359	4,106	2,374	44,677
1954	9,941	6,514	5,669	2,242	4,272	2,460	43,054
1955	9,836	6,691	5,393	2,248	4,443	2,528	44,381
1956	9,936	6,947	5,270	2,281	4,666	2,645	45,605
1957	10,136	7,169	5,263	2,296	4,873	2,745	45,822
1958	10,184	7,387	5,062	2,265	5,122	2,884	43,970
1959	10,306	7,595	5,010	2,299	5,296	2,949	45,365
1960	10,581	7,891	5,055	2,365	5,526	3,036	46,103
1961	10,942	8,168	5,157	2,383	5,785	3,176	45,621
1962	11,348	8,391	5,409	2,452	5,939	3,239	46,734
1963	11,553	8,675	5,351	2,473	6,202	3,318	47,380
1964	11,890	8,994	5,360	2,464	6,530	3,454	48,332
1965	12,264	9,376	5,389	2,501	6,875	3,588	50,338
1966	13,237	9,920	5,988	2,671	7,249	3,732	52,793
1967	13,948	10,341	6,450	2,843	7,498	3,827	54,001
1968	14,395	10,734	6,531	2,870	7,864	3,997	55,419
1969	14,652	11,031	6,484	2,863	8,168	4,120	57,024
1970	14,624	11,351	6,094	2,821	8,530	4,307	56,554
1971	14,589	11,687	5,715	2,813	8,874	4,467	56,206
1972	14,604	12,051	5,344	2,791	9,260	4,680	58,018
1973	14,811	12,372	5,194	2,755	9,617	4,860	61,172
1974	15,080	12,735	5,161	2,816	9,919	5,016	62,005
1975	15,384	13,089	5,116	2,821	10,268	5,248	59,937
1976	15,461	13,208	5,067	2,814	10,394	5,312	62,195
1977	15,588	13,349	5,047	2,808	10,541	5,379	64,770
1978	15,948	13,728	5,065	2,845	10,883	5,597	68,473
1979	16,106	13,917	5,049	2,860	11,057	5,703	71,003
1980	16,350	14,141	5,114	2,905	11,236	5,796	70,726
1981	16,320	14,061	5,137	2,878	11,183	5,703	71,509
1982	16,221	13,928	5,143	2,850	11,078	5,660	69,846
1983	16,274	13,965	5,174	2,865	11,100	5,681	70,465
1984	16,508	14,179	5,249	2,920	11,259	5,773	74,687
1985	16,853	14,507	5,298	2,952	11,555	5,916	76,851
1986	17,148	14,788	5,288	2,928	11,860	6,077	78,292
1987	17,485	15,114	5,353	2,982	12,132	6,228	80,682

[a] Includes government enterprises.
[b] Government figures include work relief.
Source: Department of Commerce, Bureau of Economic Analysis; and Tax Foundation.

A21. Wages and Salaries of Government Employees by Level of Government and Major Category

Selected Calendar Years 1929-1987

($Millions)

Year	All Governments		Federal		State and Local		Exhibit: All Private Industries
	Total[a]	Total Less Military	Total[a]	Total Less Military	Total[a]	Total Less Education	
1929	$ 4,961	$ 4,629	$ 1,417	$ 1,085	$ 3,544	$ 1,981	$ 45,498
1933	5,163	4,874	1,610	1,321	3,553	2,144	23,863
1939[b]	8,241	7,809	4,021	3,589	4,220	2,503	37,742
1946	20,700	12,867	14,371	6,538	6,329	3,745	91,345
1947	17,513	13,342	9,988	5,817	7,525	4,441	105,515
1948	19,007	14,876	10,230	6,099	8,777	5,178	116,444
1949	20,813	16,351	11,110	6,648	9,703	5,720	113,848
1950	22,618	17,365	12,250	6,997	10,368	6,076	124,542
1951	29,213	20,281	17,864	8,932	11,349	6,609	142,364
1952	33,361	22,631	20,823	10,093	12,538	7,294	152,256
1953	34,319	23,695	20,698	10,074	13,621	7,882	164,658
1954	34,884	24,612	20,020	9,748	14,864	8,503	162,415
1955	36,574	26,393	20,582	10,401	15,992	9,083	175,625
1956	38,778	28,608	21,162	10,992	17,616	9,882	190,306
1957	40,988	30,785	21,594	11,391	19,394	10,702	199,016
1958	44,095	33,755	22,732	12,392	21,363	11,644	197,267
1959	46,026	35,660	23,099	12,733	22,927	12,310	213,869
1960	49,150	38,735	24,043	13,628	25,107	13,250	223,828
1961	52,435	41,859	25,067	14,491	27,368	14,346	228,192
1962	56,308	45,052	26,627	15,371	29,681	15,394	243,106
1963	59,984	48,480	27,927	16,423	32,057	16,350	254,888
1964	64,879	52,472	29,897	17,490	34,982	17,592	272,917
1965	69,860	56,930	31,496	18,566	38,364	19,143	293,842
1966	78,333	62,909	35,835	20,411	42,498	20,895	321,908
1967	86,420	69,352	39,104	22,036	47,316	23,068	342,496
1968	96,621	77,776	43,137	24,292	53,484	25,915	375,271
1969	105,526	85,517	46,032	26,023	59,494	28,637	412,711
1970	117,144	96,462	49,640	28,958	67,504	32,456	434,305
1971	126,681	105,963	51,504	30,786	75,177	36,336	457,748
1972	137,773	115,810	55,031	33,068	82,742	40,220	500,899
1973	148,676	126,555	57,154	35,033	91,522	45,026	559,976
1974	160,380	137,882	60,466	37,968	99,914	49,661	611,792
1975	176,092	152,996	64,393	41,297	111,699	55,564	638,641
1976	188,741	165,264	67,770	44,293	120,971	59,794	710,876
1977	202,416	178,113	71,744	47,441	130,672	64,916	791,632
1978	219,699	194,013	77,508	51,822	142,191	71,406	899,968
1979	235,939	208,979	81,989	55,029	153,950	77,355	1,016,053
1980	260,138	230,321	90,149	60,332	169,989	86,005	1,111,918
1981	284,420	249,322	100,705	65,607	183,715	92,714	1,225,978
1982	305,893	266,032	108,416	68,555	197,477	99,621	1,280,331
1983	323,869	281,568	114,411	72,110	209,458	105,904	1,352,382
1984	346,339	301,331	121,986	76,978	224,353	114,094	1,492,460
1985	371,814	323,883	129,098	81,167	242,716	124,038	1,603,357
1986	393,693	343,612	131,936	81,855	261,757	134,570	1,700,205
1987	420,066	367,814	138,377	86,125	281,689	145,699	1,828,202

[a] Includes government enterprises.
[b] Government figures include work relief.
Source: Department of Commerce, Bureau of Economic Analysis; and Tax Foundation.

A22. Average Annual Earnings of Government Employees by Level of Government and Major Category

Selected Calendar Years 1929-1987
(Per Full-Time Equivalent)

Year	All Governments Total[a]	All Governments Total Less Military	Federal Total[a]	Federal Total Less Military	State and Local Total[a]	State and Local Total Less Education	Exhibit: All Private Industries
1929	$1,548	$1,584	$1,673	$1,917	$1,504	$1,554	$1,416
1933	1,326	1,345	1,302	1,366	1,388	1,364	1,023
1939[b]	1,335	1,348	1,214	1,224	1,476	1,530	1,269
1946	2,363	2,418	2,491	2,802	2,117	2,186	2,382
1947	2,590	2,601	2,831	3,068	2,327	2,375	2,614
1948	2,790	2,824	2,957	3,183	2,618	2,677	2,821
1949	2,860	2,940	3,016	3,380	2,700	2,720	2,877
1950	3,014	3,051	3,238	3,552	2,786	2,780	3,030
1951	3,127	3,304	3,227	3,832	2,981	2,969	3,286
1952	3,296	3,531	3,372	4,098	3,177	3,182	3,484
1953	3,400	3,665	3,456	4,270	3,317	3,320	3,686
1954	3,509	3,778	3,531	4,348	3,479	3,457	3,772
1955	3,718	3,945	3,816	4,627	3,599	3,593	3,957
1956	3,903	4,118	4,016	4,819	3,775	3,736	4,173
1957	4,044	4,294	4,103	4,961	3,980	3,899	4,343
1958	4,330	4,570	4,491	5,471	4,171	4,037	4,486
1959	4,466	4,695	4,611	5,538	4,329	4,174	4,714
1960	4,645	4,909	4,756	5,762	4,543	4,364	4,855
1961	4,792	5,125	4,681	6,081	4,731	4,517	5,002
1962	4,962	5,369	4,923	6,269	4,998	4,753	5,202
1963	5,192	5,588	5,219	6,641	5,169	4,928	5,380
1964	5,457	5,834	5,578	7,098	5,357	5,093	5,647
1965	5,696	6,072	5,844	7,423	5,580	5,335	5,837
1966	5,918	6,342	5,984	7,642	5,863	5,599	6,098
1967	6,196	6,707	6,063	7,751	6,310	6,028	6,342
1968	6,712	7,246	6,605	8,464	6,801	6,484	6,772
1969	7,202	7,752	7,099	9,089	7,284	6,951	7,237
1970	8,010	8,498	8,146	10,265	7,914	7,536	7,679
1971	8,683	9,067	9,012	10,944	8,472	8,134	8,144
1972	9,434	9,610	10,298	11,848	8,935	8,594	8,634
1973	10,038	10,229	11,004	12,716	9,517	9,265	9,154
1974	10,635	10,827	11,716	13,483	10,073	9,901	9,867
1975	11,446	11,689	12,587	14,639	10,878	10,588	10,655
1976	12,208	12,512	13,375	15,740	11,639	11,256	11,430
1977	12,985	13,343	14,215	16,895	12,397	12,068	12,222
1978	13,776	14,133	15,303	18,215	13,065	12,758	13,143
1979	14,649	15,016	16,239	19,241	13,923	13,564	14,310
1980	15,911	16,287	17,628	20,768	15,129	14,839	15,721
1981	17,428	17,731	19,604	22,796	16,428	16,257	17,144
1982	18,858	19,101	21,080	24,054	17,826	17,601	18,331
1983	19,901	20,162	22,113	25,169	18,870	18,642	19,190
1984	20,980	21,252	23,240	26,362	19,927	19,763	19,983
1985	22,062	22,326	24,367	27,496	21,005	20,967	20,863
1986	22,959	23,236	24,950	27,956	22,071	22,144	21,716
1987	24,024	24,336	25,850	28,882	23,219	23,394	22,659

[a] Includes government enterprises.
[b] Government figures include work relief.
Source: Department of Commerce, Bureau of Economic Analysis; and Tax Foundation.

A23. Civilian Employment and Payrolls of Governments
October, Selected Years 1940-1987[a]

Government Unit	1940	1949	1959	1969	1979	1987
A. Number of Employees (Thousands)						
All employees[b]	4,474	6,203	8,487	12,691	15,971	17,281
Federal[c]	1,128	2,047	2,399	2,975	2,869	3,091
State and local	3,346	4,156	6,088	9,716	13,102	14,190
Education	1,320	1,658	2,745	5,061	6,732	7,389
Other	2,026	2,497	3,343	4,655	6,370	6,801
State	n.a.	1,037	1,454	2,614	3,699	4,115
Education	n.a.	306	443	1,112	1,577	1,804
Other	551	731	1,011	1,501	2,122	2,311
Local	n.a.	3,119	4,634	7,102	9,403	10,076
Education	n.a.	1,352	2,302	3,949	5,250	5,584
Other	1,475	1,767	2,332	3,154	4,153	4,492
Local by type of government:						
Municipal	n.a.	1,281	1,636	2,165	2,553	2,541
County	n.a.	476	767	1,163	1,804	1,963
Other[d]	n.a.	1,363	2,231	3,775	5,046	578
Full-time equivalent employees:						
Federal	n.a.	n.a.	n.a.	2,893	2,708	n.a.
State and local	n.a.	n.a.	5,342	8,160	10,944	12,086
B. Monthly Payroll ($Millions)						
All employees[b]	$ 565.8	$ 1,406.0	$ 3,114.4	$ 7,593.8	$ 18,077.0	$ 32,382.1
Federal[c]	177.0	539.2	1,072.7	2,341.5	4,727.7	7,924.2
State and local	388.8	866.7	2,041.7	5,252.3	13,349.3	24,457.9
Education	175.3	384.8	999.3	2,830.6	6,757.0	12,315.2
Other	213.5	481.9	1,042.4	2,421.7	6,592.3	12,142.7
State	n.a.	209.8	485.4	1,430.5	3,869.3	7,297.8
Education	n.a.	58.5	139.2	554.4	1,451.4	2,758.3
Other	58.8	151.3	346.2	876.0	2,417.9	4,539.5
Local	n.a.	656.9	1,556.3	3,821.8	9,480.0	17,160.2
Education	n.a.	326.3	860.0	2,276.2	5,305.6	9,556.9
Other	154.7	330.6	696.3	1,545.6	4,174.4	7,603.3
Local by type of government:						
Municipal	n.a.	277.2	547.9	1,195.6	2,728.5	4,687.3
County	n.a.	86.4	229.1	571.6	1,726.0	3,258.0
Other[d]	n.a.	293.5	779.3	2,054.5	5,025.5	1,429.3

[a] Beginning in 1959 data include Alaska and Hawaii.
[b] Full- and part-time employees.
[c] Includes employees outside continental United States; also civilian employees of the National Guard paid directly from the Federal Treasury.
[d] Principally school district personnel.
Source: Department of Commerce, Bureau of the Census.

A24. Civilian Employment of Governments by State
October 1987
(Thousands)

State	Total[a]	Federal	State and Local Governments Total	State and Local Governments State	State and Local Governments Local
Total	17,052	2,862	14,190	4,115	10,076
Alabama	291	59	231	82	150
Alaska	61	14	47	23	25
Arizona	230	36	194	52	142
Arkansas	148	19	130	45	85
California	1,851	314	1,537	348	1,188
Colorado	262	52	210	63	147
Connecticut	196	23	173	64	108
Delaware	45	5	40	22	18
Florida	699	101	598	142	455
Georgia	465	86	380	106	273
Hawaii	90	27	63	50	13
Idaho	72	10	62	20	42
Illinois	742	104	638	159	479
Indiana	360	41	319	96	223
Iowa	205	18	187	59	128
Kansas	197	24	172	54	118
Kentucky	224	33	191	73	118
Louisiana	295	33	262	98	164
Maine	89	17	73	25	47
Maryland	388	129	259	92	167
Massachusetts	386	59	327	105	222
Michigan	617	57	560	159	401
Minnesota	286	31	255	78	177
Mississippi	187	24	163	51	112
Missouri	334	67	267	78	190
Montana	68	11	57	20	37
Nebraska	136	15	121	35	86
Nevada	65	10	55	17	38
New Hampshire	66	7	59	19	39
New Jersey	509	74	435	113	322
New Mexico	129	26	103	45	58
New York	1,408	156	1,252	298	954
North Carolina	424	45	379	113	266
North Dakota	63	8	56	20	35
Ohio	690	90	600	159	441
Oklahoma	246	48	198	75	123
Oregon	204	27	176	59	118
Pennsylvania	673	131	541	142	399
Rhode Island	62	10	52	25	27
South Carolina	279	32	247	79	168
South Dakota	61	9	52	17	35
Tennessee	321	58	263	82	181
Texas	1,106	172	934	232	701
Utah	137	36	101	37	63
Vermont	37	5	33	13	20
Virginia	505	156	349	126	223
Washington	338	63	275	105	170
West Virginia	122	15	107	39	67
Wisconsin	338	27	311	88	223
Wyoming	49	6	43	12	31
District of Columbia	263	206	57	-	57

[a] Full- and part-time employees in the United States; Federal data are for December 1986 and differ from those in Table A23 which pertain to October 1987 and include employees working outside the United States. See Table D47 for monthly payroll of state and local employees by state.

Source: Department of Commerce, Bureau of the Census.

A25. Payments under Social Insurance and Related Programs by Risk and Program

Selected Calendar Years 1949-1986[a]

($Millions)

Risk and Program	1949	1959	1969	1980	1984	1985	1986
Total[b]	$6,555.4	$20,953.3	$46,227.1	$207,796.8	$283,242.1	$302,887.6	$317,701.6
Old-age retirement	1,226.6	9,925.4	24,709.6	113,252.0	175,503.5	186,759.6	200,182.2
Old-age, survivors, disability and health insurance[c]	437.4	7,607.0	17,698.1	77,905.0	123,804.2	132,298.0	140,418.2
Railroad retirement	168.9	523.1	965.5	2,930.6	3,761.6	3,862.1	3,942.8
Federal civil service	123.7	502.5	1,526.8	10,227.5	15,244.8	16,110.8	16,792.3
State and local government retirement	203.0	780.0	2,250.0	10,792.3	17,377.0	20,411.0	22,677.0
Veterans program	61.7	49.7	8.8	e	e	e	e
Other[d]	231.8	463.1	2,260.5	11,396.6	15,315.9	16,077.7	16,352.5
Survivorship (monthly benefits)	794.6	3,315.2	8,774.1	34,986.0	44,846.3	46,296.2	45,751.0
Old-age, survivors, disability and health insurance	196.6	2,063.3	6,219.3	26,654.0	33,916.6	34,806.9	33,785.4
Railroad retirement	39.3	180.9	367.0	1,371.6	1,678.6	1,702.3	1,722.0
Federal civil service	4.3	92.8	354.4	1,930.2	3,006.0	3,176.8	3,311.1
State and local government retirement	25.0	65.0	195.0	63.9	872.0	975.0	1,084.0
Veterans program	477.4	819.0	1,439.2	2,754.9	3,230.1	3,309.5	3,374.8
Workers' compensation	52.0	90.0	185.0	675.0	880.0	980.0	1,032.0
Black lung benefit program	-	-	-	635.0	710.0	730.0	768.0
Other[d]	-	4.3	14.2	301.3	553.0	615.7	673.7
Lump-sum payments	83.3	299.0	545.2	963.6	735.4	955.8	1,311.8
Old-age, survivors, disability and health insurance	33.2	171.3	291.2	395.0	167.9	142.9	136.2
Railroad retirement	11.5	17.8	26.2	13.6	10.5	9.3	9.6
Federal civil service	7.9	11.1	22.3	22.9	37.0	33.9	46.7
State and local government retirement	18.0	60.0	135.0	351.6	391.0	640.0	992.0
Veterans program	12.4	37.7	68.9	177.7	122.9	124.1	119.7
Other[d]	.4	1.2	1.6	2.8	6.1	5.6	7.6
Disability	2,179.9	4,553.8	9,775.2	39,659.4	48,513.4	52,115.1	54,399.7
Old-age, survivors, disability and health insurance	-	456.7	2,542.2	15,437.0	17,732.3	18,645.7	19,524.5
Railroad retirement	72.0	134.2	193.0	564.4	681.1	696.3	705.8
Federal civil service	35.3	134.2	442.5	2,884.7	3,220.7	3,403.7	3,547.7
State and local government retirement	22.0	85.0	255.0	1,210.7	1,565.0	1,834.0	2,038.0
Veterans program	1,630.5	2,424.7	3,706.2	8,602.2	10,577.7	10,748.0	10,886.1
Workers' compensation	331.0	725.0	1,519.0	7,245.0	10,852.0	12,646.4	13,333.0
State temporary disability insurance	59.1	287.9	597.5	1,299.8	1,584.1	1,843.5	1,977.2
Railroad temporary disability insurance	30.1	66.2	57.4	63.2	42.0	42.7	52.2
Black lung benefit program	-	-	-	1,077.0	823.0	796.0	838.0
Other[d]	-	239.9	462.4	1,275.4	1,435.5	1,458.8	1,497.2
Unemployment	2,271.1	2,859.8	2,423.0	18,935.9	13,643.5	14,760.9	16,116.3
State unemployment insurance[f]	1,737.3	2,617.9	2,261.6	18,756.5	13,495.5	14,629.2	15,988.0
Railroad unemployment insurance	103.6	224.5	37.0	179.4	148.0	131.7	128.3
Veterans unemployment allowances	430.2	17.4	-	-	-	-	-
Training and related allowances	-	-	124.4	-	-	-	-

[a] Data for 1986 are preliminary.
[b] Partly estimated; excludes refunds of employee contributions for state and local government, Federal civil service, and other contributory retirement plans.
[c] Includes benefits paid to aged wives, dependent husbands, and children of retired and disabled-worker beneficiaries.
[d] Federal contributory and noncontributory programs.
[e] Negligible amount, included under veterans programs survivorship payments.
[f] Includes payments to unemployed Federal employees made by states as agents of the Federal government, payments under the temporary extended unemployment insurance programs, and under the Ex-Servicemen's Unemployment Act of 1958.
Source: Department of Health and Human Services, Social Security Administration.

A26. Payments under Selected Social Insurance and Related Programs by State

Calendar Year 1986
($Millions)

State	Retirement, Disability, and Survivor Benefits				Unemployment Insurance Benefits			Railroad Temporary Disability Benefits
	Old-Age, Survivors and Disability Insurance	Federal Civil Service	Veterans Programs	Railroad Retirement	Regular State Programs	Federal-State Extended Benefit Program	Other[a]	
Total[b]	$196,692	$23,939	$14,292	$6,380	$15,897	$133.2	$407.0	$52.2
Alabama	3,128	497	313	97	187	c	7.0	.7
Alaska	139	71	15	1	140	21.0	4.5	c
Arizona	2,679	426	165	92	109	-	6.9	.3
Arkansas	2,056	213	257	85	128	-	4.0	.8
California	18,411	2,544	1,130	422	2,093	.3	33.9	3.7
Colorado	1,900	402	162	83	218	-	8.0	.5
Connecticut	2,967	142	125	38	181	-	2.2	.4
Delaware	530	47	30	20	44	-	.5	.3
Florida	12,425	1,805	924	308	298	-	7.2	1.1
Georgia	3,873	591	433	138	227	-	8.4	1.7
Hawaii	667	260	46	2	53	-	2.8	c
Idaho	744	95	56	46	79	c	3.7	.4
Illinois	9,625	639	401	422	907	c	20.3	4.0
Indiana	4,806	307	246	173	190	-	7.3	1.9
Iowa	2,726	189	137	102	168	-	5.7	.8
Kansas	2,107	213	125	146	168	-	7.0	.9
Kentucky	2,895	260	271	145	184	c	10.2	1.6
Louisiana	2,853	237	269	87	570	87.4	6.8	.8
Maine	1,013	118	104	35	59	-	2.2	.4
Maryland	3,078	1,520	238	126	215	c	8.1	1.2
Massachusetts	5,171	544	457	73	458	-	7.3	.4
Michigan	8,039	355	422	142	755	-	16.6	1.6
Minnesota	3,311	260	226	181	346	-	8.1	1.0
Mississippi	1,876	213	243	58	112	-	4.4	.5
Missouri	4,535	473	314	215	224	-	8.5	1.7
Montana	660	95	51	61	53	-	3.6	.6

Continued

A26. Payments under Selected Social Insurance and Related Programs by State (continued)

Calendar Year 1986
($Millions)

State	Retirement, Disability, and Survivor Benefits				Unemployment Insurance Benefits			Railroad Temporary Disability Benefits
	Old-Age, Survivors and Disability Insurance	Federal Civil Service	Veterans Programs	Railroad Retirement	Regular State Programs	Federal-State Extended Benefit Program	Other[a]	
Nebraska	1,362	142	84	98	62	-	4.2	1.3
Nevada	676	118	49	26	74	-	1.5	.1
New Hampshire	814	118	75	12	16	-	.4	.1
New Jersey	6,998	639	359	143	657	-	7.7	1.2
New Mexico	914	237	98	47	86	-	5.6	.3
New York	16,185	1,140	946	328	1,210	-	20.1	3.2
North Carolina	4,662	426	461	94	242	-	7.9	.7
North Dakota	529	47	32	32	51	-	1.7	.2
Ohio	9,365	733	574	364	740	c	22.0	3.0
Oklahoma	2,500	449	309	55	233	-	6.0	.3
Oregon	2,457	307	177	94	250	-	7.6	.7
Pennsylvania	12,024	1,092	709	558	1,106	c	27.7	3.7
Rhode Island	959	118	79	9	73	-	1.1	.1
South Carolina	2,341	307	210	54	111	-	3.1	.4
South Dakota	596	71	51	14	12	-	.9	.1
Tennessee	3,680	331	355	126	177	-	9.1	1.0
Texas	9,787	1,330	952	334	1,232	-	23.6	3.1
Utah	884	284	60	66	99	-	4.0	.5
Vermont	433	47	41	13	29	-	.5	c
Virginia	3,802	1,615	421	191	136	-	7.8	1.6
Washington	3,569	615	268	113	378	c	13.3	.9
West Virginia	1,827	118	167	113	149	c	5.4	1.3
Wisconsin	4,378	213	258	115	371	c	7.8	.8
Wyoming	291	47	24	32	63	-	2.0	.3
District of Columbia	381	591	38	13	66	-	7.4	.1

[a] Includes unemployment compensation for Federal employees, veterans, and railroad employees.
[b] Includes outlying areas and abroad.
[c] Less than $50,000.

Source: Department of Health and Human Services, Social Security Administration.

A27. Employer and Employee Contributions for Social Insurance by Program

Selected Calendar Years 1929-1987[a]

($Billions)

Program	1929	1949	1959	1969	1979	1987
Total Contributions	$.3	$6.6	$18.8	$57.9	$197.8	$399.1
Employer contributions	.1	4.3	10.9	31.6	116.8	227.1
Old-age, survivors, disability and hospital insurance	-	.8	4.6	17.9	60.9	131.8
Old-age, survivors, and disability insurance	-	.8	4.6	15.6	50.3	104.1
Hospital insurance	-	-	-	2.3	10.5	27.6
Unemployment insurance	-	1.6	2.6	3.4	15.8	23.8
State tax	-	1.0	2.0	2.5	12.2	17.6
Federal tax	-	.2	.3	.7	3.0	5.7
Railroad employees	-	-	.2	.1	.2	.2
Federal employees	-	.4	.2	.1	.4	.3
Federal employee retirement	.1	.6	1.4	4.4	17.4	31.0
Civilian	-	.3	.8	1.7	6.8	12.6
Military	-	.3	.7	2.7	10.6	18.4
Railroad retirement	-	.3	.3	.5	1.7	2.4
Veterans' life insurance	-	.5	-	-	-	-
Workers' compensation	-	-	.1	.1	.7	1.2
Military medical insurance	-	-	-	.2	.3	1.1
State and local employee retirement	.1	.4	1.6	4.5	16.8	31.2
Temporary disability insurance	-	-	-	-	.1	.1
Workers' compensation	-	.1	.3	.7	3.0	4.5
Personal contributions	.1	2.2	7.9	26.2	81.0	172.0
Old-age, survivors, disability and hospital insurance	-	.8	5.1	19.7	65.9	146.1
Employees	-	.8	4.6	17.9	61.0	132.1
Old-age, survivors, and disability insurance	-	.8	4.6	15.6	50.4	104.3
Hospital insurance	-	-	-	2.3	10.6	27.7
Self-employed	-	-	.6	1.8	5.0	14.1
Supplemental medical insurance	-	-	-	.9	2.7	6.7
State unemployment insurance	-	-	-	-	.1	.3
Federal civilian employee retirement	-	.4	.8	1.5	3.5	4.7
Railroad retirement	-	.3	.3	.4	.6	1.1
Veterans' life insurance	.1	.4	.5	.6	.7	.8
State and local social insurance fund	-	.4	1.2	3.1	7.5	12.3

[a] Beginning in 1949, totals include employer contributions to workers' compensation systems, previously not classified as social insurance funds.

Source: Department of Commerce, Bureau of Economic Analysis.

A28. Government Transfer Payments to Persons by Level of Government and Major Program

Selected Calendar Years 1929-1987

($Billions)

Program and Level of Government	1929	1939	1949	1959	1969	1979	1987
Total government transfer payments to persons	$.9	$2.5	$11.7	$25.7	$67.5	$262.8	$520.6
Federal government, total	.7	1.3	8.7	20.1	50.8	205.6	402.0
From social insurance funds, total	.1	.8	4.2	16.1	43.0	171.6	353.0
Old-age, survivors, and disability insurance	-	a	.7	10.2	26.4	102.6	201.1
Hospital and supplemental medical insurance	-	-	-	-	6.5	29.2	81.9
Unemployment insurance	-	.4	2.2	2.9	2.3	9.7	14.8
Railroad retirement	-	.1	.3	.8	1.5	4.3	6.5
Federal employee retirement pensions	.1	.1	.5	1.5	5.2	23.6	44.8
Civilian	a	.1	.2	.9	2.6	13.0	26.4
Military	a	.1	.3	.7	2.7	10.6	18.4
Veterans' life insurance	a	.1	.4	.7	.7	1.1	1.7
Workers' compensation	-	a	a	.1	.1	.7	1.2
Military medical insurance	-	-	-	-	.2	.3	1.1
Veterans' benefits	.5	.4	4.2	3.8	5.8	13.0	14.8
Food stamp benefits	-	-	-	-	.3	6.3	10.6
Black lung benefits	-	-	-	-	-	1.7	1.5
Other	.1	a	.3	.2	1.7	12.9	22.0
State and local governments, total	.2	1.3	3.0	5.6	16.7	57.2	118.7
From social insurance funds, total	.1	.2	.5	1.6	4.4	15.8	36.1
State-local employee retirement pensions	.1	.2	.3	1.2	3.5	13.3	30.9
Temporary disability insurance	-	-	a	.1	.4	.7	1.2
Workers' compensation	-	-	.1	.3	.5	1.8	4.0
Direct relief	.1	1.0	2.2	3.7	11.3	36.6	75.5
Medical care	-	-	.5	.5	4.5	21.5	49.7
Aid to families with dependent children	-	.6	.5	.9	3.5	11.0	16.7
Other categorical and general public assistance	-	.4	1.7	2.3	3.3	4.1	12.7
Other	.1	.1	.3	.3	1.0	4.8	3.6

a Less than $50 million.
Source: Department of Commerce, Bureau of Economic Analysis.

A29. Social Welfare Expenditures under Public Programs by Source of Funds and Type

Selected Fiscal Years 1960-1986

Item[a]	1960	1970	1980	1985	1986[b]
	A. Amount ($Millions)				
Total expenditures	$52,293	$145,856	$492,528	$730,399	$770,522
Social insurance	19,307	54,691	229,754	372,529	390,404
OASDHI	11,032	36,835	152,110	260,469	271,980
Public employee retirement	2,570	8,659	39,490	63,044	66,910
Unemployment insurance	2,830	3,820	18,326	18,344	18,550
Workmen's compensation	1,308	2,950	13,457	22,264	24,382
Public aid	4,101	16,488	71,799	96,777	103,079
Public assistance	4,042	14,434	44,888	66,080	71,371
Health and medical programs	4,464	9,907	27,650	41,060	44,334
Veterans' programs	5,479	9,078	21,466	27,042	27,445
Education	17,626	50,846	121,050	166,418	178,518
Elementary and secondary	15,109	38,632	87,150	120,752	142,291
Higher	2,191	9,907	26,175	35,445	34,747
Vocational and adult	298	2,144	7,375	9,891	1,208
Housing	177	701	7,210	12,627	12,037
Other social welfare[c]	1,139	4,145	13,599	13,947	14,705
From Federal funds, total	24,957	77,337	302,631	452,860	472,364
Social insurance	14,307	45,246	191,162	313,108	326,588
Public aid	2,117	9,649	48,667	61,985	65,615
Health and medical programs	1,737	4,775	12,703	18,630	19,926
Veterans' programs	5,367	8,952	21,254	26,704	27,072
Education	868	5,876	13,452	13,796	15,022
Housing	144	582	6,608	11,088	10,164
Other social welfare[c]	417	2,259	8,786	7,548	7,977
From state and local funds, total[a]	27,337	68,519	189,897	277,540	298,158
Social insurance	4,999	9,446	38,592	59,421	63,816
Public aid	1,984	6,839	23,133	34,792	37,465
Health and medical programs	2,727	5,132	14,948	22,430	24,408
Veterans' programs	112	127	212	338	373
Education	16,758	44,970	107,597	152,622	163,495
Housing	33	120	601	1,540	1,872
Other social welfare[c]	733	1,886	4,813	6,398	6,729
	B. Percentage Distribution				
Total social welfare expenditures	100.0	100.0	100.0	100.0	100.0
Federal	47.7	53.0	61.4	62.1	61.3
State-local	52.3	47.0	38.6	38.0	38.7
Exhibit: Total as a percent of GNP	10.3	14.7	18.0	18.2	18.2

[a] Subtotals include items not shown separately. Total financed from state and local funds includes minor amounts for veterans and housing programs.
[b] Preliminary.
[c] Includes institutional care, child nutrition and welfare, vocational rehabilitation, and other social welfare programs not elsewhere classified.
Source: Social Security Administration, Office of Research and Statistics.

A30. National Health Expenditures by Source of Funds and Type
Selected Calendar Years 1965-1986

Item	1965	1970	1975	1980	1985	1986
	A. Amount ($Millions)					
Total expenditures	$ 41,749	$ 74,995	$ 132,680	$ 248,110	$ 422,592	$ 458,214
Private expenditures, total	30,950	47,222	76,356	142,938	246,612	268,517
Health services and supplies	29,482	44,662	73,020	138,666	240,658	262,485
Direct payments	18,522	26,498	38,081	63,039	105,306	116,128
Insurance premiums[a]	9,993	16,871	33,178	72,595	130,139	140,726
Other	966	1,293	1,761	3,032	5,214	5,631
Medical research	176	215	264	305	377	387
Medical facilities construction	1,292	2,345	3,072	3,967	5,577	5,645
Public expenditures, total	10,799	27,773	56,324	105,172	175,980	189,697
Health services and supplies	8,754	24,933	51,259	97,506	166,501	179,473
OASDHI (Medicare)	-	7,496	16,317	36,814	72,294	77,721
Temporary disability insurance[b]	52	66	73	52	56	56
Workers' compensation[b]	798	1,409	2,432	5,151	8,169	8,234
Public assistance medical payments[c]	2,112	6,321	15,098	28,127	42,191	45,782
Department of Defense medical care	853	1,782	2,830	4,207	8,395	8,462
Maternal and child health programs	255	429	589	892	1,191	1,200
Public health activities	814	1,431	3,165	7,294	11,894	11,988
Veterans medical care	1,145	1,764	3,495	5,939	8,733	8,802
Medical vocational rehabilitation	40	149	177	216	264	266
State and local hospitals	2,373	3,320	5,230	5,803	7,340	7,398
Other[d]	313	767	1,851	3,012	5,974	9,564
Medical research	1,340	1,754	3,071	5,134	6,410	6,996
Medical facilities construction	705	1,086	1,995	2,532	2,660	2,571
	B. Percentage Distribution					
Total expenditures	100.0	100.0	100.0	100.0	100.0	100.0
Private	74.1	63	57.5	57.6	58.4	58.6
Public	25.9	37	42.5	42.4	41.6	41.4
Federal	13.3	23.6	27.9	28.6	29.4	29.2
State-local	12.6	13.4	14.6	13.8	12.2	12.2
Exhibit: Total as percent of GNP	6.1	7.4	8.3	9.1	10.5	10.8

[a] Covers insurance benefits and amount retained by insurance companies for expenses, additions to reserves, and profits.
[b] Includes medical benefits paid under public law by private insurance carriers and self-insurers.
[c] After 1965, primarily Medicaid.
[d] Expenditures for Alcohol, Drug Abuse, and Mental Health Administration; Indian Health Service; school health and other programs.
Source: Department of Health and Human Services, Health Care Financing Administration.

A31.   Government Expenditures and Gross National Product

Selected Calendar Years 1929–1989

(Dollar Amounts in Billions)

Year	Gross National Product	Government Expenditures[a]					
		Amount[b]			As a Percentage of GNP		
		Total	Federal	State and Local	Total	Federal	State and Local
1929	$ 103.9	$ 10.3	$ 2.7	$ 7.6	9.9%	2.6%	7.3%
1930	91.1	11.1	2.8	8.3	12.2	3.1	9.1
1935	72.8	13.4	6.6	6.8	18.4	9.1	9.3
1939	91.3	17.6	9.0	8.6	19.3	9.9	9.4
1940	100.4	18.5	10.0	8.5	18.4	10.0	8.5
1941	125.5	28.8	20.5	8.3	22.9	16.3	6.6
1942	159.0	64.1	56.1	8.0	40.3	35.3	5.0
1943	192.7	93.4	85.9	7.5	48.5	44.6	3.9
1944	211.4	103.1	95.6	7.5	48.8	45.2	3.5
1945	213.4	92.9	84.7	8.2	43.5	39.7	3.8
1946	212.4	47.2	37.2	10.0	22.2	17.5	4.7
1947	235.2	43.4	30.8	12.6	18.5	13.1	5.4
1948	261.6	51.1	35.5	15.6	19.5	13.6	6.0
1949	260.4	60.0	42.0	18.0	23.0	16.1	6.9
1950	288.3	61.4	41.2	20.2	21.3	14.3	7.0
1951	333.4	79.5	58.1	21.4	23.8	17.4	6.4
1952	351.6	94.3	71.4	22.9	26.8	20.3	6.5
1953	371.6	102.0	77.6	24.4	27.4	20.9	6.6
1954	372.5	97.5	70.3	27.2	26.2	18.9	7.3
1955	405.9	98.5	68.6	29.9	24.3	16.9	7.4
1956	428.2	105.0	72.5	32.5	24.5	16.9	7.6
1957	451.0	115.8	80.2	35.6	25.7	17.8	7.9
1958	456.8	128.3	89.6	38.7	28.1	19.6	8.5
1959	495.8	131.9	91.7	40.2	26.6	18.5	8.1
1960	515.3	137.3	93.9	43.4	26.6	18.2	8.4
1961	533.8	150.1	102.9	47.2	28.1	19.3	8.8
1962	574.6	161.6	111.4	50.2	28.1	19.4	8.7
1963	606.9	169.1	115.3	53.8	27.9	19.0	8.9
1964	649.8	177.8	119.5	58.3	27.4	18.4	9.0
1965	705.1	189.6	125.3	64.3	26.9	17.8	9.1
1966	772.0	215.6	145.3	70.3	27.9	18.8	9.1
1967	816.4	245.0	165.8	79.2	30.0	20.3	9.7
1968	892.7	272.2	182.9	89.3	30.5	20.5	10.0
1969	963.9	290.2	191.3	98.9	30.1	19.8	10.3
1970	1,015.5	317.4	207.8	109.6	31.3	20.5	10.8
1971	1,102.7	346.8	224.8	122.0	31.5	20.4	11.1
1972	1,212.8	377.3	249.0	128.3	31.1	20.5	10.6
1973	1,359.3	411.7	269.3	142.4	30.3	19.8	10.5
1974	1,472.8	467.4	305.5	161.9	31.7	20.7	11.0
1975	1,598.4	544.9	364.2	180.7	34.1	22.8	11.3
1976	1,782.8	587.5	393.7	193.8	33.0	22.1	10.9
1977	1,990.5	635.7	430.1	205.6	31.9	21.6	10.3
1978	2,249.7	694.8	470.7	224.1	30.9	20.9	10.0
1979	2,508.2	768.3	521.1	247.2	30.6	20.8	9.9
1980	2,732.0	889.6	615.1	274.5	32.6	22.5	10.0
1981	3,052.6	1,006.9	703.3	303.6	33.0	23.0	9.9
1982	3,166.0	1,111.6	781.2	330.4	35.1	24.7	10.4
1983	3,405.7	1,189.9	835.9	354.0	34.9	24.5	10.4
1984	3,772.2	1,277.9	895.6	382.3	33.9	23.7	10.1
1985	4,014.9	1,402.6	985.6	417.0	34.9	24.5	10.4
1986	4,240.3	1,489.0	1,033.9	455.1	35.0	24.4	10.7
1987	4,526.7	1,574.4	1,074.2	500.1	34.8	23.7	11.0
1988	4,864.3	1,654.0	1,117.6	536.4	34.0	23.0	11.0
1989[c]	5,099.0	1,742.0	1,180.6	561.4	34.2	23.2	11.0

[a] Expenditures on income and product account. They are on an accrual basis, include trust account transactions with the public, and exclude capital transactions that do not represent current production, etc. (See Introductory Notes.)

[b] Federal data include expenditures for grants-in-aid to state and local governments. These amounts have been excluded from state and local expenditures to avoid duplication.

[c] Seasonally adjusted annual rate QI 1989.

Source: Department of Commerce, Bureau of Economic Analysis.

A32. Net National Product and Tax Receipts[a]

Selected Calendar Years 1929–1986
(Dollar Amounts in Billions)

Year	Net National Product[b]	Tax Receipts Amount			Tax Receipts As a Percentage of NNP		
		Total	Federal	State and Local	Total	Federal	State and Local
1929	$ 94.0	$ 10.2	$ 3.6	$ 6.6	10.9%	3.8%	7.0%
1930	81.4	9.7	2.9	6.8	11.9	3.6	8.4
1935	64.9	10.6	3.9	6.7	16.3	6.0	10.3
1939	82.3	14.6	6.7	7.9	17.7	8.1	9.6
1940	91.1	16.9	8.6	8.3	18.6	9.4	9.1
1941	115.3	24.1	15.3	8.8	20.9	13.3	7.6
1942	147.7	31.6	22.7	8.9	21.4	15.4	6.0
1943	181.1	47.7	38.5	9.2	26.3	21.3	5.1
1944	199.4	48.9	39.6	9.3	24.5	19.9	4.7
1945	201.0	49.9	40.1	9.8	24.8	20.0	4.9
1946	198.2	49.6	38.5	11.1	25.0	19.4	5.6
1947	217.6	55.6	42.9	12.7	25.6	19.7	5.8
1948	241.2	57.9	43.3	14.6	24.0	18.0	6.1
1949	238.4	54.3	38.3	16.0	22.8	16.1	6.7
1950	264.6	67.3	49.7	17.6	25.4	18.8	6.7
1951	306.2	83.2	63.8	19.4	27.2	20.8	6.3
1952	322.5	88.1	66.9	21.2	27.3	20.7	6.6
1953	340.7	92.5	69.6	22.9	27.1	20.4	6.7
1954	340.0	87.3	63.3	24.0	25.7	18.6	7.1
1955	371.5	98.6	72.2	26.4	26.5	19.4	7.1
1956	390.1	107.0	77.7	29.3	27.4	19.9	7.5
1957	409.9	113.4	81.8	31.6	27.7	20.0	7.7
1958	414.0	111.9	78.6	33.3	27.0	19.0	8.0
1959	451.2	127.0	89.9	37.1	28.1	19.9	8.2
1960	468.9	136.6	96.1	40.5	29.1	20.5	8.6
1961	486.1	141.5	98.0	43.5	29.1	20.2	8.9
1962	525.2	152.9	106.1	46.8	29.1	20.2	8.9
1963	555.5	164.6	114.4	50.2	29.6	20.6	9.0
1964	595.9	169.7	115.0	54.7	28.5	19.3	9.2
1965	647.7	183.4	124.2	59.2	28.3	19.2	9.1
1966	709.9	206.4	141.6	64.8	29.1	19.9	9.1
1967	749.0	221.4	150.3	71.1	29.6	20.1	9.5
1968	818.7	255.5	174.5	81.0	31.2	21.3	9.9
1969	882.5	288.4	197.1	91.3	32.7	22.3	10.3
1970	926.6	293.5	192.5	101.0	31.7	20.8	10.9
1971	1,005.1	312.0	199.5	112.5	31.0	19.8	11.2
1972	1,104.8	356.6	228.7	127.9	32.3	20.7	11.6
1973	1,241.2	400.2	260.3	139.9	32.2	21.0	11.3
1974	1,335.4	441.2	289.9	151.3	33.0	21.7	11.3
1975	1,436.6	455.5	290.6	164.9	31.7	20.2	11.5
1976	1,603.6	521.7	335.6	186.1	32.5	20.9	11.6
1977	1,789.0	586.1	379.0	207.1	32.8	21.2	11.6
1978	2,019.8	659.2	435.5	223.7	32.6	21.6	11.1
1979	2,242.4	738.4	498.1	240.3	32.9	22.2	10.7
1980	2,428.1	805.8	545.1	260.7	33.2	22.5	10.7
1981	2,704.8	918.3	629.2	289.1	34.0	23.3	10.7
1982	2,782.8	933.5	623.6	309.9	33.5	22.4	11.1
1983	3,009.1	987.0	647.8	339.2	32.8	21.5	11.3
1984	3,356.8	1,089.6	712.1	377.5	32.5	21.2	11.2
1985	3,577.6	1,179.9	773.3	406.6	33.0	21.6	11.4
1986	3,784.4	1,248.5	814.7	433.8	33.0	21.5	11.5
1987	4,046.7	1,369.3	900.8	468.5	33.8	22.3	11.6
1988	4,357.9	1,459.3	958.9	500.4	33.5	22.0	11.5
1989[c]	4,574.5	1,545.2	1,024.9	520.3	33.8	22.4	11.4

[a] As shown in the national income accounts, generally on an accrual basis. Tax receipts are net of refunds and include contributions for social insurance.
[b] Gross national product less capital consumption allowances.
[c] Seasonally adjusted annual rate QI 1989.
Source: Department of Commerce, Bureau of Economic Analysis.

A33. Tax Revenues in Relation to Gross Domestic Product in Selected Countries[a]

Selected Years 1960–1986[b]

Country	Taxes As a Percent of Gross Domestic Product									Per Capita Taxes
	1960	1970	1980	1981	1982	1983	1984	1985	1986	1986[c]
Australia	23.5%	24.2%	29.0%	30.0%	30.2%	29.5%	30.9%	30.8%	31.4%	3,419
Austria	30.5	35.7	41.2	42.5	41.2	41.1	42.3	42.9	42.6	5,281
Belgium	26.5	35.2	43.5	44.0	45.4	45.4	46.4	46.6	45.4	5,302
Canada	24.2	31.3	31.6	33.7	33.5	33.0	32.9	32.9	33.2	4,820
Denmark	25.4	40.4	45.5	45.3	44.5	46.5	47.6	48.7	50.6	8,151
Finland	27.7	31.4	33.0	34.6	34.0	34.0	35.5	36.8	38.4	5,499
France	n.a.	35.1	41.7	41.9	42.7	43.6	44.6	44.5	44.2	5,802
Germany	31.3	32.9	38.0	37.6	37.4	37.3	37.5	37.9	37.5	5,484
Greece	n.a.	24.3	28.6	29.1	31.8	33.3	34.9	35.2	36.7	1,461
Ireland	22.0	31.2	34.0	35.2	36.8	38.6	39.4	39.0	40.2	2,781
Italy	34.0	24.2	30.0	31.1	33.7	35.9	35.1	34.7	36.2	3,798
Japan	18.2	19.7	25.5	26.2	26.7	27.2	27.4	28.0	28.8	4,698
Luxembourg	n.a.	30.2	40.9	40.7	40.9	44.8	42.6	42.9	42.4	6,540
Netherlands	30.1	37.6	45.8	45.2	45.4	46.7	45.0	45.1	45.5	5,483
New Zealand	27.3	27.4	33.0	34.0	34.9	32.8	33.1	33.8	32.9	2,775
Norway	31.2	39.3	47.1	48.7	47.9	46.6	45.8	47.4	49.8	8,346
Portugal	16.3	23.1	28.7	30.4	31.0	32.8	32.2	31.5	32.4	968
Spain	n.a.	17.2	24.1	25.5	25.8	27.9	29.2	28.8	30.4	1,798
Sweden	27.2	40.2	49.4	51.1	49.9	50.6	50.3	50.6	53.5	8,385
Switzerland	21.3	23.8	30.8	30.6	31.0	31.6	32.3	32.0	32.6	6,707
Turkey	n.a.	17.7	21.7	23.4	22.4	20.7	17.3	19.7	22.7	259
United Kingdom	28.5	37.1	35.3	36.7	39.3	37.9	38.3	38.1	39.0	3,762
United States	26.6	29.2	29.5	30.0	29.9	28.4	28.4	29.2	28.9	4,944

[a] Tax revenues collected by all levels of government, recorded on a cash basis.
[b] Primarily calendar years; however, data from some countries recorded on a fiscal year basis.
[c] In U.S. dollars.

Source: Organization for Economic Cooperation and Development.

A34. Percentage Distribution of Tax Revenues in Selected Countries by Source

Fiscal Year 1986

Country	All Taxes	Taxes on Income and Profits[a]		Social Security Taxes			Taxes on Goods and Services			Property Taxes[d]	Other and Unallocable[e]
		Individual Income	Corporate Profits	Total[b]	Employers' Share	Employees' Share	Total[c]	General	Specific		
Australia	100.0%	46.6%	9.0%	-	-	-	30.5%	7.8%	18.5%	8.0%	5.5%
Austria	100.0	23.4	3.4	31.9%	15.8%	13.3%	32.1	20.7	10.2	2.4	6.8
Belgium	100.0	33.7	6.6	33.6	17.3	13.7	24.0	15.5	6.8	1.9	0.2
Canada	100.0	37.0	8.1	13.7	8.7	4.8	29.7	14.6	11.4	9.4	2.1
Denmark	100.0	47.8	6.2	3.1	1.2	1.8	35.4	19.5	14.7	4.7	2.8
Finland	100.0	48.1	3.7	9.0	9.0	-	35.8	21.5	13.9	3.1	0.3
France	100.0	13.0	5.1	42.7	27.4	11.9	29.4	19.5	8.9	4.8	5.0
Germany	100.0	28.6	6.0	37.2	19.1	16.1	25.2	15.3	8.6	3.1	-
Greece	100.0	13.1	4.0	32.6	14.3	13.7	45.4	17	24.4	2.7	2.2
Ireland	100.0	32.6	3.5	14.2	9.1	5.0	44.1	20.8	21.4	3.9	1.7
Italy	100.0	28.0	9.9	34.3	24.6	6.5	24.6	14.6	8.6	2.7	0.5
Japan	100.0	25.1	20.7	29.8	15.4	10.9	13.4	-	11.4	10.9	0.1
Luxembourg	100.0	26.5	16.7	25.6	13.8	10.3	24.5	13.3	10.5	6.2	0.5
Netherlands	100.0	20.3	7.3	42.5	17.3	18.1	26.0	16.5	7.3	3.6	0.3
New Zealand	100.0	62.6	7.0	-	-	-	26.9	12.9	13.2	1.7	1.3
Norway	100.0	22.8	13.3	22.2	14.9	6.5	38.8	19.7	17.8	2.1	0.8
Portugal	100.0	[f]	[f]	28.1	18.5	8.5	48.0	21.0	25.7	1.9	22.0
Spain	100.0	17.7	5.9	39.1	29.4	6.9	32.0	18.0	13.4	3.2	2.1
Sweden	100.0	38.0	4.7	25.0	24.1	-	24.8	13.4	10.2	2.8	4.7
Switzerland	100.0	34.9	6.2	31.6	9.9	10.0	18.8	9.3	8.1	8.4	0.1
Turkey	100.0	26.9	12.1	12.8	7.5	4.3	31.5	23.0	8.0	3.3	13.4
United Kingdom	100.0	27.9	10.3	17.9	9.1	8.2	30.9	15.5	13.7	12.9	0.1
United States	100.0	35.4	7.0	29.8	17.3	11.5	17.5	7.6	7.5	10.3	-

a Includes taxes on capital gains.
b Includes taxes on self-employed.
c Includes import duties, profits on public fiscal monopolies, licenses, and other business taxes.
d Includes taxes on movable and immovable property, net wealth taxes, and estate and gift taxes.
e Includes general and selective taxes on payrolls which are not earmarked for social security purposes, and other taxes not elsewhere classified.
f Income and profit taxes are 21.2% of total taxes and are included under "other and unallocable", as they are not segregable between individuals and corporations.
Source: Organization for Economic Cooperation and Development.

Section B
Selected Economic Series

- Population and Employment
- National Output, Income, and Prices
- Selected Financial Data

B1. Total and Resident Population of the United States[a]

July 1, Selected Years 1901-1989

(Thousands)

Year	Total Population[b]	Population Residing in United States	Year	Total Population[b]	Population Residing in United States
1901	77,585	77,585	1965	194,303	193,526
1921	108,541	108,541	1966	196,560	195,576
1933	125,690	125,579	1967	198,712	197,457
1935	127,362	127,250	1968	200,706	199,399
1937	128,961	128,825	1969	202,677	201,385
1939	131,028	130,880	1970	205,052	203,984
1941	133,402	133,121	1971	207,661	206,827
1943	136,739	134,245	1972	209,896	209,284
1945	139,928	132,481	1973	211,909	211,357
1947	144,126	143,446	1974	213,854	213,342
1949	149,188	148,665	1975	215,973	215,465
1950	151,684	151,235	1976	218,035	217,563
1951	154,287	153,310	1977	220,239	219,760
1952	156,954	155,687	1978	222,585	222,095
1953	159,565	158,242	1979	225,055	224,567
1954	162,391	161,164	1980	227,757	227,255
1955	165,275	164,308	1981	230,138	229,637
1956	168,221	167,306	1982	232,520	231,996
1957	171,274	170,371	1983	234,799	234,284
1958	174,141	173,320	1984	237,001	236,477
1959	177,073	176,289	1985	239,279	238,736
1960	180,671	179,979	1986	241,625	241,107
1961	183,691	182,992	1987	243,934	243,419
1962	186,538	185,771	1988	246,329	245,807
1963	189,242	188,483	1989[c]	247,968	247,448
1964	191,889	191,141			

[a] Includes Alaska and Hawaii beginning 1960.
[b] Includes armed forces overseas beginning 1931.
[c] March 1, 1989.
Source: Department of Commerce, Bureau of the Census.

B2. Number of Households and Average Population Per Household[a]

March, Selected Years 1900-1988[b]

(Thousands)

Year	Number of Households	Population Per Household	Year	Number of Households	Population Per Household
1900[b]	15,964	4.76	1975	71,120	2.94
1910[b]	20,256	4.54	1976	72,867	2.89
1920[b]	24,352	4.34	1977	74,142	2.86
1930[b]	29,905	4.11	1978	76,030	2.81
1940[b]	34,949	3.67	1979	77,330	2.78
1950	43,554	3.37	1980	80,776	2.76
1955[b]	47,874	3.33	1981	82,368	2.73
1960	52,799	3.33	1982	83,527	2.72
1965	57,436	3.29	1983	83,918	2.73
1970	63,401	3.14	1984	85,290	2.71
1971	64,778	3.11	1985	86,789	2.69
1972	66,676	3.06	1986	88,458	2.67
1973	68,251	3.01	1987	89,479	2.66
1974	69,859	2.97	1988	91,066	2.64

[a] A "household" comprises all persons who occupy a housing unit; that is, an apartment or other group of rooms, or a room that constitutes separate living quarters. Data are not strictly comparable over time because of changes in the definition of household.
[b] Data for 1900 as of June; for 1920 as of January; for 1910, 1930, 1940, and 1955 as of April. Data for 1971 through 1979 not adjusted for consistency with 1980 census.
Source: Department of Commerce, Bureau of the Census.

B3. Resident Population and Number of Households by State
Selected Years 1960-1987

State	Resident Population (Thousands)			Number of Households (Thousands)		
	April 1, 1960	April 1, 1970	July 1, 1987[a]	April 1, 1960	April 1, 1970	July 1, 1987[a]
Total	179,323	203,302	243,400	53,021	63,450	90,031
Alabama	3,267	3,444	4,083	884	1,034	1,483
Alaska	226	303	525	57	79	175
Arizona	1,302	1,775	3,386	367	539	1,240
Arkansas	1,786	1,923	2,388	524	615	895
California	15,717	19,971	27,663	4,981	6,574	10,076
Colorado	1,754	2,210	3,296	529	691	1,255
Connecticut	2,535	3,032	3,211	753	933	1,189
Delaware	446	548	644	129	165	238
Florida	4,952	6,791	12,023	1,550	2,285	4,787
Georgia	3,943	4,588	6,222	1,070	1,369	2,258
Hawaii	633	770	1,083	153	203	345
Idaho	667	713	998	194	219	357
Illinois	10,081	11,110	11,582	3,085	3,502	4,271
Indiana	4,662	5,195	5,531	1,388	1,609	2,049
Iowa	2,758	2,825	2,834	841	896	1,072
Kansas	2,179	2,249	2,476	673	727	943
Kentucky	3,038	3,221	3,727	852	984	1,366
Louisiana	3,257	3,645	4,461	892	1,052	1,566
Maine	969	994	1,187	280	303	447
Maryland	3,101	3,924	4,535	863	1,175	1,656
Massachusetts	5,149	5,689	5,855	1,535	1,760	2,190
Michigan	7,823	8,882	9,200	2,239	2,653	3,355
Minnesota	3,414	3,806	4,246	992	1,154	1,585
Mississippi	2,178	2,217	2,625	568	637	909
Missouri	4,320	4,678	5,103	1,360	1,521	1,940
Montana	675	694	809	202	217	303
Nebraska	1,411	1,485	1,594	433	474	608
Nevada	285	489	1,007	92	160	397
New Hampshire	607	738	1,057	180	225	391
New Jersey	6,067	7,171	7,672	1,806	2,218	2,807
New Mexico	951	1,017	1,500	251	289	533
New York	16,782	18,241	17,825	5,248	5,914	6,722
North Carolina	4,556	5,084	6,413	1,205	1,510	2,390
North Dakota	632	618	672	173	182	247
Ohio	9,706	10,657	10,784	2,852	3,289	4,035
Oklahoma	2,328	2,559	3,272	735	851	1,244
Oregon	1,769	2,092	2,724	558	692	1,074
Pennsylvania	11,319	11,801	11,936	3,351	3,705	4,447
Rhode Island	859	950	986	257	292	369
South Carolina	2,383	2,591	3,425	604	734	1,199
South Dakota	681	666	709	195	201	264
Tennessee	3,567	3,926	4,855	1,003	1,213	1,820
Texas	9,580	11,199	16,789	2,778	3,434	5,960
Utah	891	1,059	1,680	242	298	518
Vermont	390	445	548	111	132	204
Virginia	3,967	4,651	5,904	1,074	1,391	2,171
Washington	2,853	3,413	4,538	894	1,106	1,761
West Virginia	1,860	1,744	1,897	521	547	707
Wisconsin	3,952	4,418	4,807	1,146	1,329	1,785
Wyoming	330	332	490	99	105	177
District of Columbia	764	757	622	252	263	248

[a] Resident population figures are provisional. Household figures are estimates.
Source: Department of Commerce, Bureau of the Census.

B4. Estimates and Projections of the Population by Age Groups[a]
July 1, Selected Years 1960-2080
(Millions)

Age Group	1960	1970	1980	1987	1990	2000	2030	2050	2080
Total	180.7	205.1	227.7	243.9	249.7	268.0	304.8	309.5	310.8
Under 5 years	20.3	17.2	16.4	18.3	19.2	17.6	17.7	17.7	17.2
5 to 13 years	33.0	36.7	31.1	30.8	32.2	34.4	33.0	32.6	31.7
14 to 17 years	11.2	15.9	16.1	14.4	13.0	15.4	15.2	14.6	14.3
18 to 24 years	16.1	24.7	30.3	27.4	25.8	24.6	26.2	25.7	25.3
25 to 34 years	22.9	25.3	37.6	43.5	43.5	36.4	37.2	38.4	37.2
35 to 44 years	24.2	23.2	25.9	34.4	37.8	43.7	40.2	38.8	38.2
45 to 54 years	20.6	23.3	22.7	23.3	25.4	37.1	36.8	37.0	37.4
55 to 64 years	15.6	18.7	21.8	22.0	21.1	23.8	34.0	37.3	36.3
65 and over	16.7	20.1	25.7	29.8	31.8	34.9	64.6	67.4	73.1

[a] Total population includes armed forces abroad.
Source: Department of Commerce, Bureau of the Census.

43

B5. Labor Force by Employment Status

Annual Averages for Selected Calendar Years 1929-1989[a]

(Numbers in Thousands)

Year	Total	Resident Armed Forces	Civilian Labor Force Total	Employed Total	Agricultural	Nonagricultural	Unemployed	Unemployment as a Percent of Civilian Labor Force
(Thousands of Persons 14 Years of Age and Over)								
1929	n.a.	n.a.	49,180	47,630	10,450	37,180	1,550	3.2%
1933	n.a.	n.a.	51,590	38,760	10,090	28,670	12,830	24.9
1939	n.a.	n.a.	55,230	45,750	9,610	36,140	9,480	17.2
1946	n.a.	n.a.	57,520	55,250	8,320	46,930	2,270	3.9
(Thousands of Persons 16 Years of Age and Over)								
1947	n.a.	n.a.	59,350	57,038	7,890	49,148	2,311	3.9
1948	n.a.	n.a.	60,621	58,343	7,629	50,714	2,276	3.8
1949	n.a.	n.a.	61,286	57,651	7,658	49,993	3,637	5.9
1950	63,377	1,169	62,208	58,918	7,160	51,758	3,288	5.3
1951	64,160	2,143	62,017	59,961	6,726	53,235	2,055	3.3
1952	64,524	2,386	62,138	60,250	6,500	53,749	1,883	3.0
1953[b]	65,246	2,231	63,015	61,179	6,260	54,919	1,834	2.9
1954	65,785	2,142	63,643	60,109	6,205	53,904	3,532	5.5
1955	67,087	2,064	65,023	62,170	6,450	55,722	2,852	4.4
1956	68,517	1,965	66,552	63,799	6,283	57,514	2,750	4.1
1957	68,877	1,948	66,929	64,071	5,947	58,123	2,859	4.3
1958	69,486	1,847	67,639	63,036	5,586	57,450	4,602	6.8
1959	70,157	1,788	68,369	64,630	5,565	59,065	3,740	5.5
1960[b]	71,489	1,861	69,628	65,778	5,458	60,318	3,852	5.5
1961	72,359	1,900	70,459	65,746	5,200	60,546	4,714	6.7
1962[b]	72,675	2,061	70,614	66,702	4,944	61,759	3,911	5.5
1963	73,839	2,006	71,833	67,762	4,687	63,076	4,070	5.7
1964	75,109	2,018	73,091	69,305	4,523	64,782	3,786	5.2
1965	76,401	1,946	74,455	71,088	4,361	66,726	3,366	4.5
1966	77,892	2,122	75,770	72,895	3,979	68,915	2,875	3.8
1967	79,565	2,218	77,347	74,372	3,844	70,527	2,975	3.8
1968	80,990	2,253	78,737	75,920	3,817	72,103	2,817	3.6
1969	82,972	2,238	80,734	77,902	3,606	74,296	2,832	3.5
1970	84,889	2,118	82,771	78,678	3,463	75,215	4,093	4.9
1971	86,355	1,973	84,382	79,367	3,394	75,972	5,016	5.9
1972[b]	88,847	1,813	87,034	82,153	3,484	78,669	4,882	5.6
1973[b]	91,203	1,774	89,429	85,064	3,470	81,594	4,365	4.9
1974	93,670	1,721	91,949	86,794	3,515	83,279	5,156	5.6
1975	95,453	1,678	93,775	85,846	3,408	82,438	7,929	8.5
1976	97,826	1,668	96,158	88,752	3,331	85,421	7,406	7.7
1977	100,665	1,656	99,009	92,017	3,283	88,734	6,991	7.1
1978[b]	103,882	1,631	102,251	96,048	3,387	92,661	6,202	6.1
1979	106,559	1,597	104,962	98,824	3,347	95,477	6,137	5.8
1980	108,544	1,604	106,940	99,303	3,364	95,938	7,637	7.1
1981	110,315	1,645	108,670	100,397	3,368	97,030	8,273	7.6
1982	111,872	1,668	110,204	99,526	3,401	96,125	10,678	9.7
1983	113,226	1,676	111,550	100,834	3,383	97,450	10,717	9.6
1984	115,241	1,697	113,544	105,005	3,321	101,685	8,539	7.5
1985	117,167	1,706	115,461	107,150	3,179	103,971	8,312	7.2
1986[b]	119,540	1,706	117,834	109,597	3,163	106,434	8,237	7.0
1987	121,602	1,737	119,865	112,440	3,208	109,232	7,425	6.2
1988	123,378	1,709	121,669	114,968	3,169	111,800	6,701	5.5
1989[c]	124,995	1,690	123,304	116,782	3,262	113,521	6,522	5.3

[a] Beginning in 1960, data include Alaska and Hawaii.
[b] Not strictly comparable with previous data due to population adjustments.
[c] Estimate.
Source: Department of Labor, Bureau of Labor Statistics.

B6. Estimates and Projections of the Civilian Labor Force by Sex and Age

Annual Averages in Selected Calendar Years 1980-2000[a]

(Thousands)

Sex and Age Cohort	Actual		Projected					
			High Growth		Intermediate Growth		Low Growth	
	1980	1989	1995	2000	1995	2000	1995	2000
Total								
Total, 16 and over	106,940	121,906	132,893	141,107	131,598	138,775	128,515	134,517
16 to 24	25,302	28,374	21,612	23,176	21,258	22,631	20,924	22,159
16 to 19	9,380	7,199	7,913	9,034	7,826	8,880	7,622	8,586
20 to 24	15,922	13,975	13,699	14,142	13,432	13,751	13,302	13,573
25 to 54	66,600	85,618	97,151	102,496	96,247	100,780	93,538	97,050
25 to 34	29,228	35,667	35,028	32,706	34,407	31,657	33,390	30,427
35 to 44	20,463	30,291	36,748	39,079	36,543	38,571	35,474	37,111
45 to 54	16,909	19,660	25,375	30,711	25,297	30,552	24,674	29,512
55 and over	15,039	15,113	14,130	15,435	14,093	15,364	14,053	15,308
55 to 64	11,984	11,755	11,384	13,032	11,353	12,970	11,357	12,977
65 and over	3,054	3,358	2,746	2,403	2,740	2,394	2,696	2,331
Male								
Total, 16 and over	61,453	66,752	71,139	74,464	70,392	73,136	69,521	71,729
16 to 24	13,606	14,812	11,081	11,811	10,881	11,506	10,729	11,261
16 to 19	4,999	3,721	4,023	4,584	3,977	4,501	3,910	4,389
20 to 24	8,607	7,370	7,058	7,227	6,904	7,005	6,819	6,872
25 to 54	38,712	46,905	52,014	54,009	51,488	53,024	50,875	52,043
25 to 34	16,971	19,726	18,752	17,170	18,386	16,559	18,158	16,246
35 to 44	11,836	16,424	19,512	20,420	19,394	20,133	19,160	19,757
45 to 54	9,905	10,755	13,750	16,419	13,708	16,332	13,557	16,040
55 and over	9,135	8,757	8,044	8,644	8,023	8,606	7,917	8,425
55 to 64	7,242	6,751	6,455	7,271	6,438	7,238	6,359	7,099
65 and over	1,893	2,006	1,589	1,373	1,585	1,368	1,558	1,326
Female								
Total, 16 and over	45,487	55,154	61,754	66,643	61,206	65,639	58,994	62,788
16 to 24	11,696	13,561	10,531	11,365	10,377	11,125	10,195	10,898
16 to 19	4,381	3,478	3,890	4,450	3,849	4,379	3,712	4,197
20 to 24	7,315	6,605	6,641	6,915	6,528	6,746	6,483	6,701
25 to 54	27,888	38,712	45,137	48,487	44,759	47,756	42,663	45,007
25 to 34	12,257	15,941	16,276	15,536	16,021	15,098	15,232	14,181
35 to 44	8,627	13,867	17,236	18,659	17,149	18,438	16,314	17,354
45 to 54	7,004	8,905	11,625	14,292	11,589	14,220	11,117	13,472
55 and over	5,904	6,358	6,086	6,791	6,070	6,758	6,136	6,883
55 to 64	4,742	5,005	4,929	5,761	4,915	5,732	4,998	5,878
65 and over	1,161	1,353	1,157	1,030	1,155	1,026	1,138	1,005

[a] Data for 1989 are as of February.

Source: Department of Labor, Bureau of Labor Statistics.

B7. Gross National Product by Purchaser and Type of Product

Selected Calendar Years 1929-1989

($Billions)

Item	1929	1939	1949	1959	1969	1979	1988	1989[a]
Gross national product	$ 103.9	$ 91.3	$ 260.4	$ 495.8	$ 963.9	$ 2,508.2	$ 4,864.3	$ 5,099.0
Personal consumption expenditures	77.3	67.0	178.3	316.3	597.9	1,566.8	3,227.5	3,378.1
Durable goods	9.2	6.7	25.0	42.8	86.2	219.0	451.1	459.9
Nondurable goods	37.7	35.1	94.9	148.5	252.2	613.2	1,046.9	1,092.7
Services	30.4	25.2	58.4	125.0	259.4	734.6	1,729.6	1,825.5
Gross private domestic investment	16.7	9.5	36.5	80.2	153.2	454.8	766.5	788.9
Fixed investment	14.9	9.1	39.5	74.4	143.4	441.9	718.1	748.5
Nonresidential	11.0	6.1	24.9	46.3	102.3	302.8	488.4	511.3
Residential structures	4.0	3.0	14.6	28.1	41.2	139.1	229.7	237.2
Change in business inventories	1.7	0.4	-3.1	5.8	9.8	13.0	48.4	40.4
Net exports of goods and services	1.1	1.2	6.5	1.5	5.6	18.8	-94.6	-79.3
Government purchases of goods and services	8.9	13.6	39.0	97.9	207.3	467.8	964.9	1,011.3
Federal	1.5	5.2	21.1	54.6	100.0	178.0	381.0	397.6
National defense	-	1.3	13.9	46.4	78.9	121.9	298.4	299.5
Other	-	3.9	7.2	8.2	21.1	56.1	82.6	98.1
State and local	7.4	8.3	18.0	43.3	107.2	289.9	583.9	613.7

[a] Seasonally adjusted annual rate QI 1989.
Source: Department of Commerce, Bureau of Economic Analysis.

B8. Rates of Change in Selected Economic Measures

Calendar Years 1950-1989[a]

(Percent Change From Preceding Year)

Year	Gross National Product			Civilian Labor Force	Civilian Employ- ment	Productivity[b]	Consumer Price Index
	Current Dollars	Constant 1982 Dollars	Implicit Price Deflator				
1950	10.0	8.5	2.0	1.5	2.2	8.3	1.0
1951	15.7	10.3	4.8	-.3	1.8	4.0	7.9
1952	5.5	3.9	1.5	.2	.5	3.1	2.2
1953	5.7	4.0	1.6	1.4[c]	1.5[c]	3.6	.8
1954	.2	-1.3	1.6	1.0	-1.7	1.6	.5
1955	9.0	5.6	3.2	2.2	3.4	3.0	-.4
1956	5.5	2.1	3.4	2.4	2.6	1.3	1.5
1957	5.3	1.7	3.6	.6	-.4	2.6	3.6
1958	1.3	-.8	2.1	1.1	-1.6	3.0	2.7
1959	8.5	5.8	2.4	1.1	2.5	3.3	.8
1960	3.9	2.2	1.6	1.8[c]	1.8[c]	1.7	1.6
1961	3.6	2.6	1.0	1.2	.0	3.5	1.0
1962	7.6	5.3	2.2	.2[c]	1.5[c]	3.6	1.1
1963	5.6	4.1	1.6	1.7	1.6	4.0	1.2
1964	7.1	5.3	1.5	1.8	2.3	4.3	1.3
1965	8.5	5.8	2.7	1.9	2.6	3.0	1.7
1966	9.5	5.8	3.6	1.8	2.5	2.8	2.9
1967	5.8	2.9	2.6	2.1	2.0	2.7	2.9
1968	9.3	4.1	5.0	1.8	2.1	2.7	4.2
1969	8.0	2.4	5.6	2.5	2.6	.1	5.4
1970	5.4	-.3	5.5	2.5	1.0	.7	5.9
1971	8.6	2.8	5.7	1.9	.9	3.2	4.3
1972	10.0	5.0	4.7	3.1[c]	3.5[c]	3.0	3.3
1973	12.1	5.2	6.5	2.8[c]	3.5	2.0	6.2
1974	8.3	-.5	9.1	2.8	2.0	-2.1	11.0
1975	8.5	-1.3	9.8	2.0	-1.1	2.0	9.1
1976	11.5	4.9	6.4	2.5	3.4	2.8	5.8
1977	11.7	4.7	6.7	3.0	3.7	1.7	6.5
1978	13.0	5.3	7.3	3.3[c]	4.4[c]	.8	7.7
1979	11.5	2.5	8.9	2.7	2.9	-1.2	11.3
1980	8.9	-.2	9.0	1.9	.5	-.3	13.5
1981	11.7	1.9	9.7	1.6	1.1	1.4	10.4
1982	3.7	-2.5	6.4	1.4	-.9	-.4	6.1
1983	7.6	3.6	3.9	1.2	1.3	2.7	3.2
1984	10.8	6.8	3.7	1.8	4.1	2.5	4.3
1985	6.4	3.4	3.0	1.7	2.0	2.1	3.6
1986	5.6	2.8	2.7	2.1	2.3	2.2	1.9
1987	6.8	3.4	3.3	1.7	2.6	.8	3.6
1988	7.5	3.9	3.4	1.5	2.2	1.1	4.1
1989[d]	8.7	4.3	3.9	1.6	1.9	3.5	4.8

[a] Computed from total or average level for year.
[b] Output per hour of all persons in private business sector.
[c] Not entirely comparable with earlier data because of adjustments in population data.
[d] Seasonally adjusted annual rate QI 1989. Change from same quater of previous year.
Source: Department of Commerce, Bureau of Economic Analysis; Department of Labor, Bureau of Labor Statistics; and Tax Foundation computations.

B9. Alternative Measures of Aggregate Income and Product in Current and in Constant (1982) Dollars

Selected Calendar Years 1929-1989

($Billions)

Year	Current Dollars				Constant 1982 Dollars[a]		
	Gross National Product	Net National Product	National Income	Personal Income	Gross National Product	Net National Product	National Income
1929	$103.9	$94.0	$84.7	$84.3	$709.6	$622.8	$574.0
1930	91.1	81.4	73.5	75.5	642.8	554.1	517.7
1939	91.3	82.3	71.2	72.1	716.6	632.2	575.1
1940	100.4	91.1	79.6	77.6	772.9	687.9	630.7
1941	125.5	115.3	102.8	95.2	909.4	823.1	766.5
1942	159.0	147.7	136.2	122.4	1,080.3	993.4	952.8
1943	192.7	181.1	169.7	150.7	1,276.2	1,190.5	1,162.3
1944	211.4	199.4	182.6	164.5	1,380.6	1,295.7	1,242.9
1945	213.4	201.0	181.6	170.0	1,354.8	1,269.4	1,204.9
1946	212.4	198.2	180.7	177.6	1,096.9	1,008.9	947.4
1947	235.2	217.6	196.6	190.2	1,066.7	975.0	904.7
1948	261.6	241.2	221.6	209.2	1,108.7	1,011.9	950.0
1949	260.4	238.4	215.2	206.4	1,109.0	1,007.3	933.2
1950	288.3	264.6	239.8	228.1	1,203.7	1,097.1	1,015.0
1951	333.4	306.2	277.3	256.5	1,328.2	1,216.4	1,123.4
1952	351.6	322.5	291.6	273.8	1,380.0	1,263.0	1,169.0
1953	371.6	340.7	306.6	290.5	1,435.3	1,313.2	1,211.2
1954	372.5	340.0	306.3	293.0	1,416.2	1,288.8	1,183.0
1955	405.9	371.5	336.3	314.2	1,494.9	1,362.3	1,251.5
1956	428.2	390.1	356.3	337.2	1,525.6	1,387.3	1,284.6
1957	451.0	409.9	372.8	356.3	1,551.1	1,407.7	1,298.7
1958	456.8	414.0	375.0	367.1	1,539.2	1,391.5	1,276.2
1959	495.8	451.2	409.2	390.7	1,629.1	1,477.2	1,358.8
1960	515.3	468.9	424.9	409.4	1,665.3	1,508.9	1,390.5
1961	533.8	486.1	439.0	426.0	1,708.7	1,548.1	1,421.8
1962	574.6	525.2	473.3	453.2	1,799.4	1,634.3	1,497.3
1963	606.9	555.5	500.3	476.3	1,873.3	1,703.0	1,561.9
1964	649.8	595.9	537.6	510.2	1,973.3	1,797.0	1,650.2
1965	705.1	647.7	585.2	552.0	2,087.6	1,903.9	1,746.9
1966	772.0	709.9	642.0	600.8	2,208.3	2,016.1	1,840.6
1967	816.4	749.0	677.7	644.5	2,271.4	2,070.3	1,896.2
1968	892.7	818.7	739.1	707.2	2,365.6	2,155.8	1,972.9
1969	963.9	882.5	798.1	772.9	2,423.3	2,203.4	2,019.1
1970	1,015.5	926.6	832.6	831.8	2,416.2	2,186.4	1,989.0
1971	1,102.7	1,005.1	898.1	894.0	2,484.8	2,245.3	2,032.5
1972	1,212.8	1,104.8	994.1	981.6	2,608.5	2,355.2	2,137.3
1973	1,359.3	1,241.2	1,122.7	1,101.7	2,744.1	2,480.5	2,255.0
1974	1,472.8	1,335.4	1,203.5	1,210.1	2,729.3	2,453.2	2,227.6
1975	1,598.4	1,436.6	1,289.1	1,313.4	2,695.0	2,408.0	2,172.0
1976	1,782.8	1,603.6	1,441.4	1,451.4	2,826.7	2,529.4	2,278.9
1977	1,990.5	1,789.0	1,617.8	1,607.5	2,958.6	2,649.0	2,393.3
1978	2,249.7	2,019.8	1,838.2	1,812.4	3,115.2	2,791.5	2,526.7
1979	2,508.2	2,242.4	2,047.3	2,034.0	3,192.4	2,851.1	2,582.3
1980	2,732.0	2,428.1	2,203.5	2,258.5	3,187.1	2,831.0	2,562.6
1981	3,052.6	2,704.8	2,443.5	2,520.9	3,248.8	2,879.1	2,610.4
1982	3,166.0	2,782.8	2,518.4	2,670.8	3,166.0	2,782.8	2,518.5
1983	3,405.7	3,009.1	2,719.5	2,838.6	3,279.1	2,884.7	2,603.7
1984	3,772.0	3,356.8	3,028.6	3,108.7	3,501.4	3,094.2	2,799.9
1985	4,014.9	3,577.6	3,234.0	3,325.3	3,618.7	3,192.0	2,896.9
1986	4,240.3	3,784.4	3,437.1	3,531.1	3,721.7	3,278.5	2,978.5
1987	4,526.7	4,046.7	3,678.7	3,780.0	3,847.0	3,386.2	3,074.0
1988	4,864.3	4,357.9	3,968.4	4,062.1	3,996.1	3,516.4	3,200.9
1989[b]	5,099.0	4,574.5	4,188.9	4,315.7	4,077.5	3,586.3	3,280.7

[a] No appropriate deflator for personal income. See Table B14 for disposable personal income in 1982 dollars.
[b] Seasonally adjusted annual rate QI 1989.
Source: Department of Commerce, Bureau of Economic Analysis.

B10. International Transactions of the United States

Calendar Years 1984-1988

($Millions)

Item	1984	1985	1986	1987	1988[a]
Merchandise trade balance	$-112,522	$-122,148	$-144,547	$-160,280	$-126,525
Balance on goods and services	-94,975	-100,093	-123,520	-140,519	-121,748
Current account transactions balance	-107,077	-115,103	-138,828	-153,964	-135,332
Exports of goods and services[b]	360,619	360,528	374,952	424,765	n.a.
Merchandise, excluding military	219,900	215,935	223,969	249,570	319,570
Transfers under military sales contracts	9,817	8,738	8,583	11,529	n.a.
Transportation and travel	28,308	29,519	32,095	37,161	n.a.
Income on U.S. investments abroad[c]	85,908	88,837	90,110	103,756	108,190
Miscellaneous services[d]	16,839	17,547	20,296	22,807	n.a.
Imports of goods and services	-455,746	-460,667	-498,573	-565,342	-629,569
Merchandise, excluding military	-332,422	-338,083	-365,516	-409,850	-446,430
Military expenditures, direct	-11,916	-12,169	-12,955	-13,897	n.a.
Transportation and travel	-36,903	-39,568	-41,439	-47,415	n.a.
Income on foreign investments in the U.S.[e]	-67,419	-62,901	-66,968	-83,381	-105,589
Miscellaneous services	-7,079	-7,947	-8,696	-10,772	n.a.
Unilateral transfers, net[f]	-12,102	-15,010	-15,308	-13,445	-13,584
Capital account transactions					
U.S. Government capital flows[g]	18,251	18,372	3,863	-9,258	22,249
U.S. direct investment abroad	-2,821	-18,068	-27,811	-44,455	-20,435
Foreign direct investment in the U.S.	25,359	19,022	34,091	41,977	42,224
Foreign purchases of U.S. securities other other than Treasury issues	12,568	50,962	70,969	42,213	26,961
Short-term private capital flows and other long-term capital transactions, net[h]	27,689	32,798	8,385	48,086	n.a.
Allocation of special drawing rights (SDRs)	-	-	-	-	-
Errors and omissions	26,760	17,839	15,566	18,461	16,548
Official reserve transactions balance	-730	-5,821	33,765	56,941	36,724
Financed by changes in:					
Increase (-) in U.S. official reserve assets	-3,131	-3,858	312	9,149	-3,566
Increase (+) in foreign official assets in the U.S.	2,401	-1,963	33,453	47,792	40,290

[a] Preliminary.
[b] Excludes transfers under military grants of $153 million in 1984, $46 million in 1985, and $101 million in 1986, and $58 million in 1987.
[c] Includes direct investments, other private assets, and U.S. Government assets.
[d] Includes fees and royalties from direct investments and unaffiliated foreigners, and other private and public services.
[e] Includes private and public payments.
[f] Includes private remittances, U.S. Government grants (excluding military), U.S. Government pensions and other transfers.
[g] Includes net U.S. Government assets, foreign-held U.S. Treasury securities, and other U.S. Government liabilities arranged with or through foreign official agencies.
[h] Includes U.S. purchases of foreign securities, and changes in claims and liabilities reported by banking and nonbanking concerns.
Source: Deparment of Commerce, Bureau of Economic Analysis.

B11. National Income by Distributive Shares

Selected Calendar Years 1929-1989

($Billions)

Item	1929	1939	1949	1959	1969	1979	1988	1989[b]
National income	$84.7	$71.2	$215.2	$409.2	$798.1	$2,047.3	$3,968.4	$4,188.9
Compensation of employees	51.1	48.2	142.0	281.2	578.4	1,491.4	2,904.7	3,060.9
Wages and salaries	50.5	46.0	134.7	259.8	518.3	1,251.9	2,436.9	2,574.7
Government and government enterprises	5.0	8.2	20.8	46.0	105.5	235.9	446.1	465.9
Other	45.5	37.7	113.9	213.8	412.7	1,016.0	1,990.7	2,108.8
Supplements to wages and salaries	0.7	2.2	7.3	21.4	60.1	239.5	467.8	486.2
Employer contributions for social insurance	0.1	1.6	4.3	10.9	31.6	116.8	249.6	260.8
Other labor income	0.5	0.6	2.9	10.6	28.5	122.7	218.3	225.4
Proprietors' income with inventory valuation and capital consumption adjustments	14.4	11.4	35.9	51.7	79.3	191.9	324.5	358.1
Business and professional	8.3	7.1	23.1	40.9	64.7	160.1	288.2	300.9
Proprietors' income	8.8	7.6	22.2	40.1	65.1	164.0	254.0	270.4
Inventory valuation adjustment	0.1	-0.2	0.5	a	-0.5	-2.9	-1.3	-2.3
Capital consumption adjustment	-0.6	-0.4	0.5	0.9	0.1	-1.0	35.6	32.8
Farm	6.1	4.4	12.8	10.8	14.6	31.7	36.3	57.1
Proprietors' income with inventory valuation adjustment	6.3	4.5	13.5	11.7	15.8	38.0	43.4	63.9
Capital consumption adjustment	-0.2	-0.1	-0.7	-0.9	-1.1	-6.3	-7.2	-6.8
Rental income of persons	4.9	2.6	6.7	14.6	18.4	5.6	19.3	14.4
Corporate profits with inventory valuation and capital consumption adjustments	9.6	5.5	28.0	51.4	87.4	200.1	328.4	319.4
Corporate profits before tax	10.0	7.2	29.2	52.6	87.2	257.2	306.6	320.2
Corporate profits tax liability	1.4	1.4	10.2	23.6	39.7	88.0	142.7	147.6
Corporate profits after tax	8.6	5.7	19.0	28.9	47.5	169.2	163.9	172.6
Dividends	5.8	3.8	7.2	12.2	22.5	50.1	104.5	111.1
Undistributed profits	2.8	2.0	11.8	16.7	25.0	119.1	59.4	61.5
Inventory valuation adjustment	0.5	-0.7	1.9	-0.3	-5.9	-43.2	-23.8	-34.1
Capital consumption adjustment	-0.9	-1.0	-3.0	-0.8	6.1	-14.0	45.6	33.3
Net interest	4.7	3.6	2.6	10.2	34.6	158.3	391.5	436.2

a Less than $50 million.
b Seasonally adjusted annual rate QI 1989.
Source: Department of Commerce, Bureau of Economic Analysis.

B12. Sources of Government Receipts in Relation to National Income and Product

Selected Calendar Years 1929-1989

($Billions)

Item	1929	1949	1959	1969	1979	1988	1989[d]
Total government receipts[a]	$11.3	$56.6	$130.3	$300.1	$779.8	$1,752.4	$1,829.4
Less: Nontax receipts[b]	1.1	2.4	3.4	11.8	41.4	293.1	284.2
Equals: Tax receipts[c]	10.2	54.3	127.0	288.4	738.4	1,459.3	1,545.2
Gross national product	103.9	260.4	495.8	963.9	2,508.2	4,864.3	5,099.0
Less: Capital consumption allowances	9.9	22.0	44.6	81.4	265.8	506.3	524.5
Equals: Net national product	94.0	238.4	451.2	882.5	2,242.4	4,357.9	4,575.5
Less: Indirect business tax and nontax liability	7.1	21.3	41.7	86.3	189.4	389.0	403.9
Business transfer payments	.6	.8	1.8	3.9	10.3	30.7	32.6
Statistical discrepancy	1.5	.8	-1.5	-3.9	-1.0	-14.3	-31.5
Plus: Subsidies less current surplus of government enterprises	-.2	-.3	.1	1.9	3.5	15.9	19.4
Equals: National income	84.7	215.2	409.2	798.1	2,047.3	3,968.4	4,188.9
Less: Corporate profits tax liability	1.4	10.2	23.6	39.7	88.0	328.4	319.4
Contributions for social insurance	.3	6.6	18.8	57.9	197.8	444.7	471.0
Undistributed corporate profits	2.8	11.8	16.7	25.0	119.1	59.4	61.5
Dividends	5.8	7.2	12.2	22.5	50.1	104.5	111.1
Net interest	4.7	2.6	10.2	34.6	158.3	391.5	436.2
Corporate inventory valuation adjustment	.5	1.9	-.3	-5.9	-43.2	-23.8	-34.1
Capital consumption adjustment	-.9	-3.0	-.8	6.1	-14.0	45.6	33.3
Wage accruals less disbursements	e	e	e	e	-.2	e	e
Plus: Government transfers to persons	.9	11.7	25.7	67.5	262.8	555.3	584.5
Personal interest income	6.9	8.7	22.3	60.9	221.5	575.9	634.2
Personal dividend income	5.8	7.2	12.2	22.4	48.1	96.3	102.1
Business transfer payments	.6	.8	1.8	3.9	10.3	30.7	32.6
Equals: Personal income	84.3	206.4	390.7	772.9	2,034.0	4,062.1	4,315.7
Less: Personal tax and nontax payments	2.6	18.5	46.1	116.3	304.7	590.3	635.1
Equals: Disposable personal income	81.7	187.9	344.6	656.7	1,729.3	3,471.8	3,680.6
Less: Personal outlays	79.2	180.6	322.8	614.5	1,611.3	3,327.5	3,482.7
Equals: Personal savings	2.6	7.4	21.8	42.2	118.1	144.3	197.9

[a] Sum of indirect business tax and nontax liability, corporate profits tax liability, contributions for social insurance, and personal tax and nontax payments.
[b] Consists mainly of charges for products and services not accounted for under government enterprises, fines and penalties, rents and royalties, licenses, donations, and special assessments for operators.
[c] See Table A32.
[d] Seasonally adjusted annual rate QI 1989.
[e] Less than $50 million.
Source: Department of Commerce, Bureau of Economic Analysis; and Tax Foundation computations.

B13. Total and Per Capita Personal Income by State[a]
Selected Calendar Years 1971-1988

Total Personal Income ($Millions)

State	1971	1981	1985	1986	1987	1988
Total	$888,536	$2,514,231	$3,317,239	$3,522,203	$3,768,696	$4,042,110
Alabama	11,084	33,243	43,038	45,776	48,781	52,019
Alaska	1,679	6,456	9,777	9,805	9,624	10,014
Arizona	7,720	28,333	40,954	44,834	48,425	51,592
Arkansas	6,025	19,169	24,825	26,194	27,555	29,478
California	100,865	308,730	422,142	454,086	493,547	531,100
Colorado	10,054	35,403	47,461	49,411	51,397	54,004
Connecticut	16,021	42,016	57,847	62,372	68,070	73,772
Delaware	2,743	6,631	9,082	9,765	10,632	11,682
Florida	30,232	110,295	158,315	171,067	187,377	204,792
Georgia	17,058	51,830	75,376	82,135	89,097	95,887
Hawaii	4,060	11,052	14,576	15,639	16,970	18,466
Idaho	2,723	8,942	10,863	11,217	11,856	12,644
Illinois	54,376	137,093	169,921	179,015	190,203	203,305
Indiana	21,300	55,461	68,378	72,434	77,078	82,076
Iowa	11,268	31,503	36,208	38,017	40,329	41,844
Kansas	9,186	26,774	33,855	35,697	37,501	39,561
Kentucky	11,011	32,572	40,168	41,857	44,711	47,603
Louisiana	12,175	42,234	50,638	50,568	51,219	53,891
Maine	3,635	10,230	13,834	15,089	16,584	18,065
Maryland	19,134	50,954	70,175	75,558	82,415	89,692
Massachusetts	27,368	67,818	94,944	102,603	111,565	121,538
Michigan	39,985	100,094	127,264	135,372	141,933	152,400
Minnesota	16,206	45,308	59,289	63,140	67,533	72,285
Mississippi	6,366	19,514	24,143	25,422	27,038	28,875
Missouri	19,238	50,886	66,729	70,548	74,825	79,605

Per Capita Personal Income

State	1971	1981	1985	1986	1987	1988
Total	$4,296	$10,949	$13,895	$14,608	$15,482	$16,444
Alabama	3,169	8,463	10,705	11,300	11,944	12,604
Alaska	5,305	15,543	18,726	18,479	18,353	19,514
Arizona	4,071	10,063	12,955	13,670	14,241	14,887
Arkansas	3,055	8,333	10,523	11,046	11,537	12,172
California	4,958	12,723	16,016	16,818	17,846	18,855
Colorado	4,364	11,865	14,678	15,132	15,605	16,417
Connecticut	5,233	13,453	18,217	19,528	21,192	22,761
Delaware	4,852	11,116	14,590	15,332	16,407	17,699
Florida	4,221	10,820	13,921	14,634	15,584	16,546
Georgia	3,621	9,305	12,618	13,461	14,306	14,980
Hawaii	5,129	11,276	13,867	14,702	15,683	16,898
Idaho	3,685	9,272	10,823	11,184	11,859	12,657
Illinois	4,853	11,948	14,728	15,393	16,417	17,611
Indiana	4,057	10,103	12,433	13,161	13,937	14,721
Iowa	3,951	10,795	12,570	13,384	14,284	14,764
Kansas	4,090	11,207	13,826	14,513	15,152	15,905
Kentucky	3,621	8,862	10,775	11,243	12,008	12,795
Louisiana	3,281	9,822	11,291	11,243	11,515	12,193
Maine	3,579	9,016	11,876	12,880	13,984	14,976
Maryland	4,757	11,972	15,980	16,934	18,167	19,314
Massachusetts	4,769	11,787	16,305	17,583	19,050	20,701
Michigan	4,457	10,867	14,008	14,805	15,418	16,387
Minnesota	4,207	11,017	14,149	14,985	15,910	16,787
Mississippi	2,810	7,668	9,239	9,687	10,303	10,992
Missouri	4,074	10,303	13,256	13,923	14,648	15,492

Continued

B13. Total and Per Capita Personal Income by State[a] (continued)

Selected Calendar Years 1971-1988

State	Total Personal Income ($Millions)						Per Capita Personal Income					
	1971	1981	1985	1986	1987	1988	1971	1981	1985	1986	1987	1988
Montana	2,614	7,861	9,095	9,565	9,946	10,186	3,676	9,877	11,021	11,702	12,291	12,670
Nebraska	6,127	16,843	20,829	21,637	22,796	24,305	4,073	10,641	12,982	13,538	14,300	15,184
Nevada	2,661	10,464	13,791	14,959	16,515	18,479	5,117	12,372	14,671	15,481	16,412	17,440
New Hampshire	3,111	10,165	15,349	17,047	18,916	20,860	4,082	10,847	15,373	16,601	17,906	19,016
New Jersey	37,161	95,189	133,403	143,517	155,909	168,923	5,103	12,853	17,626	18,819	20,313	21,882
New Mexico	3,554	12,061	16,248	16,927	17,797	18,842	3,374	9,032	11,203	11,459	11,898	12,481
New York	94,627	209,179	280,397	298,959	321,169	345,425	5,153	11,914	15,786	16,789	18,005	19,299
North Carolina	17,898	52,907	73,029	78,717	85,415	92,199	3,441	8,879	11,665	12,441	13,325	14,128
North Dakota	2,235	6,692	8,163	8,427	8,709	8,430	3,567	10,122	11,921	12,420	12,971	12,720
Ohio	45,618	114,008	142,033	148,764	157,497	168,344	4,250	10,555	13,219	13,837	14,598	15,485
Oklahoma	9,549	33,184	40,209	40,482	41,092	43,292	3,647	10,676	12,124	12,264	12,607	13,269
Oregon	8,920	27,884	33,955	35,748	38,182	41,068	4,149	10,446	12,628	13,226	14,019	14,982
Pennsylvania	50,540	129,100	161,029	169,617	181,533	194,459	4,253	10,869	13,573	14,257	15,200	16,168
Rhode Island	4,079	9,990	13,305	14,271	15,421	16,709	4,232	10,490	13,763	14,641	15,633	16,793
South Carolina	8,528	26,685	35,783	38,255	41,204	44,586	3,204	8,377	10,734	11,313	12,027	12,764
South Dakota	2,336	6,402	7,801	8,348	8,900	8,917	3,480	9,255	11,017	11,798	12,545	12,475
Tennessee	13,618	40,837	53,681	57,550	62,522	67,183	3,396	8,804	11,263	11,988	12,876	13,659
Texas	44,033	164,197	220,694	225,526	233,107	245,663	3,826	11,120	13,466	13,518	13,889	14,640
Utah	3,904	13,105	17,496	18,285	19,129	20,315	3,547	8,647	10,642	10,988	11,389	12,013
Vermont	1,739	4,948	6,626	7,189	7,839	8,546	3,827	9,592	12,383	13,315	14,325	15,382
Virginia	19,095	59,214	82,511	89,427	97,506	105,774	4,018	10,878	14,472	15,422	16,486	17,640
Washington	14,961	49,269	61,953	66,470	70,993	76,538	4,340	11,629	14,060	14,899	15,630	16,569
West Virginia	5,900	16,711	19,553	20,229	20,860	21,960	3,333	8,522	10,099	10,551	10,992	11,658
Wisconsin	18,445	50,070	62,906	66,537	70,767	75,028	4,136	10,573	13,174	13,907	14,720	15,444
Wyoming	1,408	6,095	6,536	6,451	6,230	6,455	4,140	12,342	12,827	12,720	12,719	13,718
District of Columbia	4,367	8,627	11,065	11,675	12,475	13,431	5,817	13,632	17,756	18,674	20,084	21,667

[a] Personal income by state is the current income received by residents of the states from all sources, inclusive of transfers from government and business but exclusive of transfers among persons. Total personal income for all states differs from total personal income of the United States in that the latter includes income disbursed by the Federal government to its civilian and military personnel outside the United States.

Source: Department of Commerce, Bureau of Economic Analysis.

B14. Disposable Personal Income in Current and Constant (1982) Dollars and Personal Savings Rate

Selected Calendar Years 1929-1989

Year	Disposable Personal Income[a]				Personal Savings Rate[b]
	Amount ($Billions)		Per Capita		
	In Current Dollars	In 1982 Dollars	In Current Dollars	In 1982 Dollars	
1929	$ 81.7	$ 498.6	$ 671	$ 4,091	3.2%
1933	44.9	370.8	357	2,950	-3.6
1940	75.0	530.7	568	4,017	4.0
1941	91.9	604.1	689	4,528	10.9
1943	132.9	721.4	972	5,276	24.6
1945	149.2	739.5	1,066	5,285	19.2
1947	168.8	694.8	1,171	4,820	3.1
1949	187.9	733.2	1,260	4,915	3.9
1950	207.5	791.8	1,368	5,220	6.1
1951	227.6	819.0	1,475	5,308	7.3
1952	239.8	844.3	1,528	5,379	7.3
1953	255.1	880.0	1,599	5,515	7.2
1954	260.5	894.0	1,604	5,505	6.3
1955	278.8	944.5	1,687	5,714	5.8
1956	297.5	989.4	1,769	5,881	7.2
1957	313.9	1,012.1	1,833	5,909	7.2
1958	324.9	1,028.8	1,865	5,908	7.5
1959	344.6	1,067.2	1,946	6,027	6.3
1960	358.9	1,091.1	1,986	6,036	5.8
1961	373.8	1,123.2	2,034	6,113	6.6
1962	396.2	1,170.2	2,123	6,271	6.5
1963	415.8	1,207.3	2,197	6,378	5.9
1964	451.4	1,291.0	2,352	6,727	7.0
1965	486.8	1,365.7	2,505	7,027	7.0
1966	525.9	1,431.3	2,675	7,280	6.8
1967	562.1	1,493.2	2,828	7,513	8.0
1968	609.6	1,551.3	3,037	7,728	7.0
1969	656.7	1,599.8	3,239	7,891	6.4
1970	715.6	1,668.1	3,489	8,134	8.1
1971	776.8	1,728.4	3,740	8,322	8.5
1972	839.6	1,797.4	4,000	8,562	7.3
1973	949.8	1,916.3	4,481	9,042	9.4
1974	1,038.4	1,896.6	4,855	8,867	9.3
1975	1,142.8	1,931.7	5,291	8,944	9.2
1976	1,252.6	2,001.0	5,744	9,175	7.6
1977	1,379.3	2,066.6	6,262	9,381	6.6
1978	1,551.2	2,167.4	6,968	9,735	7.1
1979	1,729.3	2,212.6	7,682	9,829	6.8
1980	1,918.0	2,214.3	8,421	9,722	7.1
1981	2,127.6	2,248.6	9,243	9,769	7.5
1982	2,261.4	2,261.5	9,724	9,725	6.8
1983	2,428.1	2,331.9	10,340	9,930	5.4
1984	2,668.6	2,469.8	11,257	10,419	6.1
1985	2,838.7	2,542.8	11,861	10,625	4.4
1986	3,019.6	2,640.9	12,496	10,929	4.0
1987	3,209.7	2,686.3	13,157	11,012	3.2
1988	3,471.8	2,788.3	14,103	11,326	4.2
1989[c]	3,696.4	2,881.1	14,925	11,633	5.7

[a] Consists of total personal income less personal tax and nontax payments to governments.
[b] Personal saving as a percent of disposable personal income.
[c] Preliminary.
Source: Department of Commerce, Bureau of Economic Analysis.

B15. Number of Families and Unrelated Individuals and Median Income
Selected Calendar Years 1947-1987[a]

Year	Number (Thousands)			Median Money Income	
	Total	Families[b]	Unrelated Individuals[c]	Families	Unrelated Individuals
1947	45,402	37,237	8,165	$ 3,031	$ 980
1950	49,295	39,929	9,366	3,319	1,045
1951	49,720	40,578	9,142	3,709	1,195
1952	50,537	40,832	9,705	3,890	1,409
1953	50,716	41,202	9,514	4,242	1,396
1954	51,675	41,951	9,724	4,167	1,222
1955	52,778	42,889	9,889	4,418	1,317
1956	53,276	43,497	9,779	4,780	1,426
1957	54,131	43,696	10,435	4,966	1,493
1958	55,116	44,232	10,884	5,087	1,486
1959	55,990	45,111	10,879	5,417	1,557
1960	56,606	45,539	11,067	5,620	1,720
1961	57,624	46,418	11,206	5,735	1,754
1962	58,094	47,059	11,035	5,956	1,753
1963	58,776	47,540	11,236	6,249	1,800
1964	60,080	47,956	12,124	6,569	1,983
1965	60,727	48,509	12,218	6,957	2,153
1966	61,681	49,214	12,467	7,532	2,290
1967	63,317	50,111	13,206	7,933	2,379
1968	64,722	50,823	13,899	8,632	2,786
1969	66,212	51,586	14,626	9,433	2,931
1970	67,714	52,227	15,487	9,867	3,137
1971	69,607	53,296	16,311	10,285	3,316
1972	71,184	54,373	16,811	11,116	3,521
1973	73,313	55,053	18,260	12,051	4,134
1974	74,624	55,698	18,926	12,902	4,603
1975	76,479	56,245	20,234	13,719	4,882
1976	78,169	56,710	21,459	14,958	5,375
1977	80,325	57,215	23,110	16,009	5,907
1978	82,389	57,804	24,585	17,640	6,705
1979	85,720	59,550	26,170	19,587	7,537
1980	87,442	60,309	27,133	21,023	8,296
1981	88,733	61,019	27,714	22,388	9,138
1982	89,301	61,393	27,908	23,433	9,976
1983	91,173	62,015	29,158	24,674	10,682
1984	92,974	62,706	30,268	26,433	11,204
1985	94,909	63,558	31,351	27,735	11,808
1986	96,170	64,491	31,679	29,458	12,116
1987	97,993	65,133	32,860	30,853	12,559

[a] The number of families and unrelated individuals applies to March of the following year.
[b] A "family" is defined as a group of two or more persons related by blood, marriage, or adoption, residing together.
[c] Persons, other than institutional inmates and military personnel on post, who are not with any relatives.
Source: Department of Commerce, Bureau of the Census.

B16. Distribution of Families by Total Money Income in Constant (1987) Dollars

Selected Calendar Years 1950-1987[a]

Total Money Income[b] (1987 dollars)	1950	1960	1970	1980	1986	1987
Number of Families (Thousands)[c]						
Total	39,929	45,539	52,227	60,309	64,491	65,133
Under $2,500	2,516	1,594	731	905	1,161	1,172
$2,500 to $4,999	2,476	1,822	1,097	1,327	1,741	1,693
$5,000 to $7,499	2,835	2,414	1,828	2,231	2,322	2,345
$7,500 to $9,999	3,035	2,596	2,141	2,714	2,515	2,410
$10,000 to $12,499		3,188	2,298	2,835	2,967	2,996
$12,500 to $14,999		2,368	2,455	3,076	2,967	2,931
$15,000 to $19,999		8,743	5,170	6,152	6,191	6,188
$20,000 to $24,999	29,068[d]	5,055	5,902	6,152	6,127	5,992
$25,000 to $34,999			11,490	12,062	11,415	11,398
$35,000 to $49,999		17,760[e]	11,072	12,303	12,769	13,157
$50,000 and over			8,043	10,554	14,317	14,850
Median money income	$15,670	$21,568	$28,880	$28,996	$30,534	$30,853
Percentage Distribution						
Total	100.0	100.0	100.0	100.0	100.0	100.0
Under $2,500	6.3	3.5	1.4	1.5	1.8	1.8
$2,500 to $4,999	6.2	4.0	2.1	2.2	2.7	2.6
$5,000 to $7,499	7.1	5.3	3.5	3.7	3.6	3.6
$7,500 to $9,999	7.6	5.7	4.1	4.5	3.9	3.7
$10,000 to $12,499		7.0	4.4	4.7	4.6	4.6
$12,500 to $14,999		5.2	4.7	5.1	4.6	4.5
$15,000 to $19,999		19.2	9.9	10.2	9.6	9.5
$20,000 to $24,999	72.8[d]	11.1	11.3	10.2	9.5	9.2
$25,000 to $34,999			22.0	20.0	17.7	17.5
$35,000 to $49,999		39.0[e]	21.2	20.4	19.8	20.2
$50,000 and over			15.4	17.5	22.2	22.8

[a] Number of families applies to March of the following year.
[b] Before taxes.
[c] A "family" is defined as a group of two or more persons related by blood, marriage, or adoption, residing together.
[d] Includes income brackets $10,000 through $50,000 and over.
[e] Includes income brackets $25,000 through $50,000 and over.
Source: Department of Commerce, Bureau of the Census; and Tax Foundation computations.

B17. Persons Below the Poverty Level, by Family Status and Age Group

Selected Calendar Years 1959-1987[a]

Year	All Persons[b]	Persons in Families				Persons 65 Years and Older
		Total	Householders	Related Children under 18 Years	Other Family Members	
		Number Below the Poverty Level (Thousands)				
1959	39,490	34,562	8,320	17,208	9,034	5,481
1960	39,851	34,925	8,243	17,288	9,394	n.a.
1961	39,628	34,509	8,391	16,577	9,541	n.a.
1963	36,436	31,498	7,554	15,691	8,253	n.a.
1965	33,185	28,358	6,721	14,388	7,249	n.a.
1967	27,769	22,771	5,667	11,427	5,677	5,388
1969	24,147	19,175	5,008	9,501	4,667	4,787
1970	25,420	20,330	5,260	10,235	4,835	4,793
1971	25,559	20,405	5,303	10,344	4,757	4,273
1972	24,460	19,577	5,075	10,082	4,420	3,738
1973	22,973	18,299	4,828	9,453	4,018	3,354
1974	23,370	18,817	4,922	9,967	3,928	3,085
1975	25,877	20,789	5,450	10,882	4,457	3,317
1976	24,975	19,632	5,311	10,081	4,240	3,313
1977	24,720	19,505	5,311	10,028	4,165	3,177
1978	24,497	19,062	5,280	9,722	4,059	3,233
1979	26,072	19,964	5,461	9,993	4,509	3,682
1980	29,272	22,601	6,217	11,114	5,270	3,871
1981	31,822	24,850	6,851	12,068	5,931	3,853
1982	34,398	27,349	7,512	13,139	6,698	3,751
1983	35,303	27,933	7,647	13,427	6,859	3,625
1984	33,700	26,458	7,277	12,929	6,251	3,330
1985	33,064	25,729	7,223	12,483	6,032	3,456
1986	32,370	24,754	7,023	12,257	5,475	3,477
1987	32,546	24,479	7,059	12,435	4,985	3,491
		Percent Below the Poverty Level				
1959	22.4	20.8	18.5	26.9	15.9	35.2
1960	22.2	20.7	18.1	26.5	16.2	n.a.
1961	21.9	20.3	18.1	25.2	16.5	n.a.
1963	19.5	17.9	15.9	22.8	13.8	n.a.
1965	17.3	15.8	13.9	20.7	11.8	n.a.
1967	14.2	12.5	11.4	16.3	9.1	29.5
1969	12.1	10.4	9.7	13.8	7.2	25.3
1970	12.6	10.9	10.1	14.9	7.4	24.6
1971	12.5	10.8	10.0	15.1	7.2	21.6
1972	11.9	10.3	9.3	14.9	6.6	18.6
1973	11.1	9.7	8.8	14.2	5.9	16.3
1974	11.2	9.9	8.8	15.1	5.7	14.6
1975	12.3	10.9	9.7	16.8	6.4	15.3
1976	11.8	10.3	9.4	15.8	6.0	15.0
1977	11.6	10.2	9.3	16.0	5.9	14.1
1978	11.4	10.0	9.1	15.7	5.7	14.0
1979	11.7	10.2	9.2	16.0	6.1	15.2
1980	13.0	11.5	10.3	17.9	7.1	15.7
1981	14.0	12.5	11.2	19.5	7.8	15.3
1982	15.0	13.6	12.2	21.3	8.7	14.6
1983	15.2	13.9	12.3	21.8	8.8	13.8
1984	14.4	13.1	11.6	21.0	8.0	12.4
1985	14.0	12.6	11.4	20.1	7.7	12.6
1986	13.6	12.0	10.9	19.8	6.9	12.4
1987	13.5	11.8	10.8	20.0	6.3	12.2

[a] Beginning in 1969 and 1974, data are based on revised methodologies for processing income data. Beginning in 1969, data are based on 1970 Census population controls. Family status is reported as of March of following year. Beginning in 1979, includes members of unrelated subfamilies not shown separately, that were previously included in "families."

[b] Includes unrelated individuals not shown separately.

Source: Department of Commerce, Bureau of the Census.

B18. Personal Consumption Expenditures by Type of Product or Service

Selected Calendar Years 1929-1989

A. Amount ($Billions)

Product or Service	1929	1939	1949	1959	1969	1979	1989[b]
Food and tobacco[a]	$ 21.2	$ 20.9	$ 56.6	$ 87.2	$ 140.3	$ 336.6	$ 619.1
Clothing, accessories, and jewelry	11.2	8.4	23.3	32.0	56.2	125.0	241.9
Personal care	1.1	1.0	2.3	5.2	11.1	25.3	50.0
Housing	11.7	9.4	19.6	45.0	86.8	231.1	522.0
Household operations	10.7	9.5	25.6	45.0	81.1	211.2	394.1
Medical care expenses	3.0	2.9	8.5	19.6	49.5	162.9	489.2
Personal business	4.0	3.2	5.9	13.3	29.3	85.3	242.1
Transportation	7.7	6.5	21.8	40.7	79.8	222.0	410.9
Recreation	4.3	3.5	10.0	17.5	39.6	106.2	254.9
Private education and research	.7	.6	1.7	3.6	9.2	24.0	61.2
Religious and welfare activities	1.2	1.0	2.3	5.0	10.9	32.4	78.7
Foreign travel and remittances (net)	.5	.2	.6	2.0	4.0	4.6	14.0
Total personal consumption expendituries	77.3	67.0	178.3	316.3	597.9	1,566.8	3,378.2
Commodities	46.8	41.8	119.9	191.3	338.4	832.2	1,552.7
Durable	9.1	6.6	25.0	42.8	86.2	219.0	460.0
Nondurable	37.7	35.2	94.9	148.5	252.2	613.2	1,092.7
Services	30.5	25.2	58.4	125.0	259.4	734.6	1,825.5

B. As a Percentage of Personal Consumption Expenditures

Product or Service	1929	1939	1949	1959	1969	1979	1989[b]
Food and tobacco[a]	27.4	31.2	31.7	27.6	23.5	21.5	18.3
Clothing, accessories, and jewelry	14.5	12.5	13.1	10.1	9.4	8.0	7.2
Personal care	1.4	1.5	1.3	1.6	1.9	1.6	1.5
Housing	15.1	14.0	11.0	14.2	14.5	14.7	15.5
Household operations	13.8	14.2	14.4	14.2	13.6	13.5	11.7
Medical care expenses	3.9	4.3	4.8	6.2	8.3	10.4	14.5
Personal business	5.2	4.8	3.3	4.2	4.9	5.4	7.2
Transportation	10.0	9.7	12.2	12.9	13.3	14.2	12.2
Recreation	5.6	5.2	5.6	5.5	6.6	6.8	7.5
Private education and research	.9	.9	1.0	1.1	1.5	1.6	1.8
Religious and welfare activities	1.6	1.5	1.3	1.6	1.8	2.1	2.3
Foreign travel and remittances (net)	.6	.3	.3	.6	.7	.3	.4
Total personal consumption expenditures	100.0	100.0	100.0	100.0	100.0	100.0	100.0
Commodities	60.5	62.4	67.2	60.5	56.6	53.1	46.0
Durable	11.8	9.9	14.0	13.5	14.4	14.0	13.6
Nondurable	48.8	52.5	53.2	46.9	42.2	39.1	32.3
Services	39.5	37.6	32.8	39.5	43.4	46.9	54.0

[a] Includes expenditures for alcoholic beverages for all years except 1929.
[b] Seasonally adjusted annual rate QI 1989.
Source: Department of Commerce, Bureau of Economic Analysis. Percentage computations by Tax Foundation.

B19. Business Expenditures for New Plant and Equipment by Industry[a]
Calendar Years 1947-1989[b]
($Billions)

Year	Total	Manu-facturing	Mining	Railroad Trans-portation	Other Trans-portation[c]	Public Utilities	Commercial and other[d]
1947	$ 20.11	$ 8.73	$ .69	$ 1.39	$ 1.30	$ 1.64	$ 6.38
1948	22.78	9.25	.93	1.89	1.28	2.67	6.77
1949	20.28	7.32	.88	1.92	.88	3.28	6.01
1950	21.56	7.73	.84	1.67	1.19	3.42	6.70
1951	26.81	11.07	1.11	2.13	1.47	3.75	7.29
1952	28.16	12.12	1.21	2.09	1.47	3.96	7.31
1953	29.96	12.43	1.25	2.06	1.52	4.61	8.09
1954	28.86	12.00	1.29	1.45	1.46	4.23	8.42
1955	30.94	12.50	1.31	1.55	1.55	4.26	9.77
1956	37.90	16.33	1.64	1.90	1.66	4.78	11.59
1957	40.54	17.50	1.69	2.13	1.71	5.95	11.56
1958	33.84	12.98	1.43	1.28	1.44	5.74	10.97
1959	35.88	13.76	1.35	1.46	2.01	5.46	11.84
1960	39.44	16.36	1.29	1.59	1.95	5.40	12.86
1961	38.34	15.53	1.26	1.19	1.95	5.20	13.21
1962	40.86	16.03	1.41	1.43	2.16	5.12	14.71
1963	43.67	17.27	1.26	1.72	1.92	5.33	16.17
1964	51.26	21.23	1.33	2.20	2.51	5.80	18.20
1965	59.52	25.41	1.36	2.60	3.06	6.49	20.60
1966	70.40	31.37	1.42	3.09	3.59	7.82	23.11
1967	72.75	32.25	1.38	2.50	4.07	9.33	23.22
1968	76.42	32.34	1.44	2.15	4.76	10.52	25.22
1969	85.74	36.27	1.77	2.61	4.62	11.70	28.77
1970	91.91	36.99	2.02	2.48	4.69	13.03	32.71
1971	92.91	33.60	2.67	2.39	4.03	14.70	35.52
1972	103.40	35.42	2.88	2.35	4.79	16.26	41.69
1973	120.03	42.35	3.30	2.91	5.09	17.99	48.39
1974	139.67	52.48	4.58	3.63	5.53	19.96	53.49
1975	142.42	53.66	6.12	3.88	6.07	20.23	52.47
1976	158.44	58.53	7.63	4.25	6.85	22.90	58.29
1977	184.82	67.48	9.81	4.67	7.53	27.83	67.51
1978	217.76	78.58	11.22	5.19	8.17	31.50	83.09
1979	254.96	95.92	12.81	6.61	9.44	35.63	94.56
1980	282.80	112.33	15.99	7.09	9.51	37.74	100.14
1981	315.22	126.54	21.39	6.28	9.56	41.21	110.24
1982	310.58	120.68	20.05	5.33	9.46	45.43	109.63
1983	304.78	116.20	15.19	4.88	9.09	44.96	114.45
1984	354.44	138.82	16.86	6.79	9.73	47.48	134.75
1985	387.13	153.48	15.88	7.08	10.94	48.81	150.94
1986	379.47	142.69	11.22	6.66	12.15	46.38	160.38
1987	389.67	145.90	11.39	5.92	12.93	44.88	168.65
1988	429.67	165.70	12.67	7.06	14.29	46.51	183.44
1989	468.78	178.66	11.79	8.04	17.14	49.56	203.60

[a] Excludes agricultural business, real estate operators, medical, legal, educational, and cultural service.
[b] Data for 1989 are preliminary estimates based on planned capital expenditures reported by business January through March 1989.
[c] Includes air transportation.
[d] Includes trade, service, construction, communication, finance, and insurance.
Source: Department of Commerce, Bureau of the Census.

B20. Corporate Profits and Related Data by Industry

Selected Calendar Years 1929-1987

($Millions)

Industry and Item	1929	1939	1949	1959	1969	1979	1987
All industries:[a]							
Corporate profits before tax[b]	$9,990	$7,181	$29,206	$52,552	$87,222	$257,230	$276,699
Federal, state, and local corporate profits taxes[c]	1,369	1,441	10,203	23,646	39,674	87,996	133,759
Corporate profits after tax	8,621	5,740	19,003	28,906	47,548	169,234	142,940
Net corporate dividend payments	5,801	3,766	7,210	12,171	22,529	50,099	95,522
Undistributed corporate profits	2,820	1,974	11,793	16,735	25,019	119,135	47,418
Corporate depreciation charges	4,204	3,736	7,972	23,619	53,380	144,341	349,198
Agriculture, forestry and fisheries:							
Corporate profits before tax[b]	6	3	121	34	208	1,182	-81
Federal, state, and local corporate profits taxes[c]	6	7	58	46	116	412	488
Corporate profits after tax	0	-4	63	-12	92	770	-569
Net corporate dividend payments	8	14	45	10	60	303	513
Undistributed corporate profits	-8	-18	18	-22	32	467	-1,082
Corporate depreciation charges	34	28	46	138	437	2,039	3,416
Mining:							
Corporate profits before tax[b]	460	338	1,038	733	766	4,016	-1,734
Federal, state, and local corporate profits taxes[c]	47	43	221	186	229	1,373	540
Corporate profits after tax	413	295	817	547	537	2,643	-2,274
Net corporate dividend payments	309	159	196	384	666	-2,647	156
Undistributed corporate profits	104	136	621	163	-129	5,290	-2,430
Corporate depreciation charges	290	240	412	948	1,011	3,794	8,279
Contract construction:							
Corporate profits before tax[b]	134	43	631	849	2,171	6,197	7,858
Federal, state, and local corporate profits taxes[c]	19	14	232	411	826	2,075	2,964
Corporate profits after tax	115	29	399	438	1,345	4,122	4,894
Net corporate dividend payments	60	21	68	97	277	440	653
Undistributed corporate profits	55	8	331	341	1,068	3,682	4,241
Corporate depreciation charges	71	42	181	656	1,638	4,782	9,513
Manufacturing:							
Corporate profits before tax[b]	4,898	3,797	15,055	26,584	40,439	107,014	102,919
Federal, state, and local corporate profits taxes[c]	618	741	5,631	12,579	19,696	42,157	46,734
Corporate profits after tax	4,280	3,056	9,424	14,005	20,743	64,857	56,185
Net corporate dividend payments	2,548	1,701	3,462	5,300	10,308	17,605	28,614
Undistributed corporate profits	1,732	1,355	5,962	8,705	10,435	47,252	27,571
Corporate depreciation charges	1,884	1,570	3,619	10,943	24,470	59,897	130,061

Continued

B20. Corporate Profits and Related Data by Industry (continued)

Selected Calendar Years 1929-1987

($Millions)

Industry and Item	1929	1939	1949	1959	1969	1979	1987
Wholesale and retail trade:							
Corporate profits before tax[b]	$856	$929	$3,973	$5,870	$12,058	$43,992	$50,782
Federal, state, and local corporate profits taxes[c]	124	195	1,527	2,747	5,050	12,748	22,940
Corporate profits after tax	732	734	2,446	3,123	7,008	31,244	27,842
Net corporate dividend payments	531	424	827	831	1,819	7,616	15,476
Undistributed corporate profits	201	310	1,619	2,292	5,189	23,628	12,366
Corporate depreciation charges	327	305	900	2,155	4,810	17,018	44,903
Finance, insurance, and real estate:							
Corporate profits before tax[b]	1,420	671	3,803	7,835	12,547	31,656	29,775
Federal, state, and local corporate profits taxes[c]	282	149	1,158	3,451	7,248	20,549	39,267
Corporate profits after tax	1,138	522	2,645	4,384	5,299	11,107	-9,492
Net corporate dividend payments	832	295	539	794	257	-3,070	3,663
Undistributed corporate profits	306	227	2,106	3,590	5,042	14,177	-13,155
Corporate depreciation charges	396	427	633	1,898	4,497	10,829	38,843
Transportation:							
Corporate profits before tax[b]	1,004	157	1,132	1,160	586	4,477	5,774
Federal, state, and local corporate profits taxes[c]	135	89	461	710	597	1,632	2,826
Corporate profits after tax	869	68	671	450	-11	2,845	2,948
Net corporate dividend payments	565	227	256	449	727	1,382	2,395
Undistributed corporate profits	304	-159	415	1	-738	1,463	553
Corporate depreciation charges	484	312	897	2,267	5,308	10,581	16,771
Communications and public utilities:							
Corporate profits before tax[b]	810	839	1,764	5,918	9,998	15,343	30,302
Federal, state, and local corporate profits taxes[c]	110	172	696	3,030	4,881	4,108	13,051
Corporate profits after tax	700	667	1,068	2,888	5,117	11,235	17,251
Net corporate dividend payments	628	681	848	2,366	4,201	11,832	29,105
Undistributed corporate profits	72	-14	220	522	916	-597	-11,854
Corporate depreciation charges	575	671	909	3,259	7,402	23,955	64,106
Services:							
Corporate profits before tax[b]	170	80	564	904	1,946	9,655	14,695
Federal, state, and local corporate profits taxes[c]	28	31	219	486	1,031	2,942	4,949
Corporate profits after tax	142	49	345	418	915	6,713	9,746
Net corporate dividend payments	88	60	137	131	470	1,528	2,842
Undistributed corporate profits	54	-11	208	287	445	5,185	6,904
Corporate depreciation charges	143	141	375	1,355	3,807	11,446	33,306

[a] Includes estimates for the rest of the world, not shown separately.
[b] Depletion charges are not deducted in arriving at corporate profits for national income purposes.
[c] All taxes shown on a liability basis.
Source: Department of Commerce, Bureau of Economic Analysis.

B21. Sales, Profits, and Stockholders' Equity In Manufacturing Corporations
Calendar Years 1958-1988[a]
(Dollar Figures in Billions)

Year	Sales (Net)	Profits Before Income Taxes[b]	Profits After Income Taxes	Stockholders' Equity[c]	After-Tax Profits As a Percentage of Sales	After-Tax Profits As a Percentage of Equity
1958	$305.3	$22.7	$12.7	$147.4	4.2%	8.6%
1959	338.0	29.7	16.3	157.1	4.8	10.4
1960	345.7	27.5	15.2	165.4	4.4	9.2
1961	356.4	27.5	15.3	172.6	4.3	8.9
1962	389.4	31.9	17.7	181.4	4.5	9.8
1963	412.7	34.9	19.5	189.7	4.7	10.3
1964	443.1	39.6	23.2	199.8	5.2	11.6
1965	492.2	46.5	27.5	211.7	5.6	13.0
1966	554.2	51.8	30.9	230.3	5.6	13.4
1967	575.4	47.8	29.0	247.6	5.0	11.7
1968	631.9	55.4	32.1	265.9	5.1	12.1
1969	694.6	58.1	33.2	289.9	4.8	11.5
1970	708.8	48.1	28.6	306.8	4.0	9.3
1971	751.1	52.9	31.0	320.8	4.1	9.7
1972	849.5	63.2	36.5	343.4	4.3	10.6
1973	1,017.2	81.4	48.1	374.1	4.7	12.8
1974	1,060.6	92.1	58.7	395.0	5.5	14.9
1975	1,065.2	79.9	49.1	423.4	4.6	11.6
1976	1,203.2	104.9	64.5	462.7	5.4	13.9
1977	1,328.1	115.1	70.4	496.7	5.3	14.2
1978	1,496.4	132.5	81.1	540.5	5.4	15.0
1979	1,741.8	154.2	98.7	600.5	5.7	16.4
1980	1,912.8	145.8	92.6	668.1	4.8	13.9
1981	2,144.7	158.6	101.3	743.4	4.7	13.6
1982	2,039.4	108.2	70.9	770.2	3.5	9.2
1983	2,114.3	133.1	85.8	812.8	4.1	10.6
1984	2,335.0	165.6	107.6	864.2	4.6	12.5
1985	2,331.4	137.0	87.6	866.2	3.8	10.1
1986	2,220.9	129.3	83.1	874.7	3.7	9.5
1987	2,378.2	173.0	115.6	900.9	4.9	12.8
1988	2,587.4	213.5	152.3	954.2	5.9	16.0

[a] Because of changes in accounting and other procedures, data are not strictly comparable from one period to another.
[b] Through 1973, "income taxes" refers to Federal income taxes only, as state and local income taxes had already been deducted; after 1973, no income taxes have been deducted.
[c] Annual average based on four end-of-quarter equity figures.
Source: Department of Commerce, Bureau of the Census.

B22. Profits of Nonfinancial Corporations and Related Data

Calendar Years 1946-1989

(Dollar Figures in Billions)

Year	Profits Before Tax[a]	Capital Consumption Adjustment[b]	Inventory Valuation Adjustment	Adjusted Profits Before Tax	Federal and State Income Taxes	Effective Tax Rate (percent)
1946	$22.0	$-3.0	$-5.3	$13.8	$8.6	62.3%
1947	29.1	-3.5	-5.9	19.7	10.8	54.8
1948	31.8	-4.0	-2.2	25.6	11.8	46.1
1949	24.9	-3.9	1.9	22.9	9.3	40.6
1950	38.5	-3.9	-5.0	29.6	16.9	57.1
1951	39.1	-4.6	-1.2	33.4	21.2	63.5
1952	33.8	-4.5	1.0	30.2	17.8	58.9
1953	34.9	-3.9	-1.0	30.0	18.5	61.7
1954	32.1	-3.2	-0.3	28.6	15.6	54.5
1955	42.0	-2.0	-1.7	38.3	20.2	52.7
1956	41.8	-3.2	-2.7	35.9	20.1	56.0
1957	39.8	-3.4	-1.5	34.9	19.1	54.7
1958	33.7	-3.2	-0.3	30.2	16.2	53.6
1959	43.1	-2.7	-0.3	40.1	20.7	51.6
1960	39.7	-2.1	-0.2	37.4	19.2	51.3
1961	39.5	-1.5	0.3	38.3	19.5	50.9
1962	44.2	1.4	c	45.6	20.6	45.2
1963	48.9	2.3	0.1	51.2	22.8	44.5
1964	55.4	2.9	-0.5	57.7	24.0	41.6
1965	65.2	3.7	-1.2	67.7	27.2	40.2
1966	70.3	3.9	-2.1	72.2	29.5	40.9
1967	66.5	5.5	-1.6	70.4	27.8	39.5
1968	73.1	5.3	-3.7	74.7	33.6	45.0
1969	69.6	5.9	-5.9	69.6	33.3	47.8
1970	57.0	5.0	-6.6	55.4	27.2	49.1
1971	65.6	4.2	-4.6	65.2	29.9	45.9
1972	76.8	5.5	-6.6	75.7	33.8	44.6
1973	96.9	5.6	-20.0	82.5	40.2	48.7
1974	107.2	1.7	-39.5	69.4	42.2	60.8
1975	109.2	-6.6	-11.0	91.6	41.5	45.3
1976	138.3	-10.2	-14.9	113.2	53.0	46.8
1977	160.5	-9.0	-16.6	134.9	59.9	44.4
1978	182.1	-10.9	-25.3	145.9	67.1	46.0
1979	195.8	-13.5	-43.2	139.1	69.6	50.0
1980	181.8	-15.5	-43.1	123.2	67.0	54.4
1981	181.5	-13.1	-24.2	144.2	63.9	44.3
1982	129.7	-7.5	-10.4	111.8	46.3	41.4
1983	159.3	17.1	-10.9	165.6	59.4	35.9
1984	196.0	32.1	-5.8	222.4	73.5	33.0
1985	170.2	56.7	-1.7	225.3	69.9	31.0
1986	172.6	49.6	8.3	230.6	76.8	33.3
1987	210.2	45.3	-18.0	237.5	99.0	41.7
1988	239.0	37.5	-23.8	252.7	108.6	43.0
1989[d]	246.3	25.7	-34.1	237.9	112.7	47.4

[a] Book profits, measured after deduction of tax-return based capital consumption allowance; inventory profits are included.
[b] Based on straight-line depreciation, 85% of Bulletin F lives.
[c] Less than $50 million.
[d] Seasonally adjusted annual rate QI 1989.
Source: Department of Commerce, Bureau of Economic Analysis. Computations by Tax Foundation.

B23. Number, Receipts, and Net Profits of Business Firms By Form of Organization[a]

Selected Fiscal Years 1939-1985

(Number of Firms in Thousands; Dollar Figures in Billions)

Item	1939	1945	1960	1970	1980	1984	1985
Number of firms, total	1,793	6,737	11,172	12,001	16,793	16,077	16,920
Proprietorships[b]	1,052	5,689	9,090	9,400	12,702	11,262	11,929
Partnerships	271	627	941	936	1,380	1,644	1,714
Corporations	470	421	1,141	1,665	2,711	3,171	3,277
Business receipts, total	$171	$382	$1,095	$2,082	$7,159	$8,752	$9,306
Proprietorships[b]	24	79	171	238	506	516	540
Partnerships	15	47	74	93	292	375	368
Corporations	133	255	849	1,751	6,361	7,861	8,398
Net profits, total[c]	$11	$40	$73	$109	$302	$301	$310
Proprietorships[b]	2	12	21	33	55	71	79
Partnerships	2	7	8	10	8	-3	-9
Corporations[d]	7	21	44	66	239	233	240

[a] The concept of business firm as used here relates primarily to the legal entity used for Federal income tax purposes. While a few corporations file consolidated tax returns (i.e., one return for the parent firm and all its subsidiaries), most corporate tax returns represent individual corporations.
[b] Through 1980 includes individually owned businesses and farms; thereafter nonfarm business.
[c] Before tax.
[d] For 1970 and after, includes constructive taxable income from related foreign corporations.
Source: Treasury Department, Internal Revenue Service.

B24. Number and Receipts of Business Firms by Size of Receipts and Form of Organization

Income Year 1985

Size of Receipts (Dollars)	Number of Firms (Thousands)				Receipts ($Billions)			
	Total	Proprietor-ships	Partner-ships[a]	Corpora-tions[a]	Total	Proprietor-ships	Partner-ships[a]	Corpora-tions[a]
Total	16,920	11,929	1,714	3,277	$8,213	$540	$303	$7,370
Under 25,000[b]	9,801	8,250	840	711	60	54	2	4
25,000-49,999	1,826	1,394	195	237	61	50	3	8
50,000-99,999	1,624	1,094	200	330	107	77	8	22
100,000-499,999	2,526	1,060	356	1,110	532	213	49	270
500,000-999,999	508	89	67	352	334	61	29	244
1,000,000 or more	635	41	56	538	7,120	85	212	6,823

[a] Active firms only.
[b] Includes firms with no receipts.
Source: Treasury Department.

B25. Productivity and Related Data, Private Business Sector

Calendar Years 1958-1988

Index Numbers 1977=100

Year	Output[a]	Hours of All Persons[b]	Output Per Hour of All Persons	Compen-sation Per Hour[c]	Unit Labor Cost	Implicit Price Deflator[d]
1958	50.7	78.8	64.4	30.9	48.0	46.9
1959	54.4	81.8	66.5	32.2	48.5	47.8
1960	55.4	81.9	67.6	33.6	49.7	48.5
1961	56.5	80.7	70.0	34.9	49.9	48.8
1962	59.4	81.9	72.5	36.6	50.4	49.7
1963	62.1	82.4	75.4	37.9	50.3	50.2
1964	65.9	83.7	78.7	39.9	50.7	50.7
1965	70.0	86.4	81.0	41.5	51.2	51.9
1966	73.6	88.5	83.2	44.3	53.3	53.6
1967	75.6	88.5	85.5	46.7	54.7	54.9
1968	78.9	89.9	87.8	50.4	57.4	57.5
1969	81.1	92.3	87.8	53.9	61.4	60.4
1970	80.3	90.8	88.4	57.8	65.4	63.2
1971	82.5	90.4	91.3	61.6	67.4	66.4
1972	87.7	93.2	94.1	65.5	69.6	69.0
1973	92.9	96.9	95.9	70.9	73.9	73.4
1974	91.3	97.3	93.9	77.6	82.7	80.5
1975	89.4	93.4	95.7	85.2	89.0	88.7
1976	94.5	96.1	98.3	92.8	94.3	94.0
1977	100.0	100.0	100.0	100.0	100.0	100.0
1978	105.8	104.9	100.8	108.5	107.6	107.3
1979	107.9	108.3	99.6	119.1	119.5	117.0
1980	106.7	107.5	99.3	131.5	132.5	127.6
1981	108.9	108.2	100.7	143.7	142.7	139.8
1982	105.5	105.2	100.3	154.9	154.5	148.1
1983	109.9	106.8	103.0	161.4	156.7	153.0
1984	119.2	112.9	105.5	167.9	159.1	158.2
1985	124.2	115.8	107.7	175.5	162.9	162.2
1986	128.6	116.8	110.1	183.1	166.3	165.8
1987	133.3	120.1	111.0	190.4	171.5	170.5
1988	138.8	123.6	112.3	198.3	176.6	174.6

[a] Output refers to gross domestic product originating in the sector in 1982 dollars.
[b] Hours of all persons in private industry engaged in the sector, including hours of proprietors and unpaid family workers. Estimates based primarily on establishment data.
[c] Wages and salaries of employees plus employers' contributions for social insurance and private benefit plans. Also includes an estimate of wages, salaries, and supplemental payments for the self-employed.
[d] Current dollar gross domestic product divided by constant dollar gross domestic product.
Source: Department of Labor, Bureau of Labor Statistics.

B26. Unit Labor Costs and Productivity in Manufacturing In Selected Countries

Selected Calendar Years 1950-1988

Year	United States	Canada	Japan	France	Italy	F.R. Germany	Nether- lands	United Kingdom
			Unit Labor Costs in U.S. Dollars (1977=100)					
1950	41.8	41.8	28.8	34.5	22.3	32.4	19.2	28.0
1955	48.9	53.6	30.4	48.6	23.0	33.1	22.3	36.9
1960	58.7	59.4	28.5	40.3	25.9	35.1	25.1	43.7
1965	55.8	50.4	35.4	46.8	32.6	44.5	35.2	50.5
1970	71.0	64.5	39.1	45.2	42.9	54.7	41.2	53.7
1975	91.7	93.1	86.7	98.5	88.7	106.8	92.8	102.5
1980	130.6	121.5	116.8	156.4	147.9	138.4	134.1	220.6
1985	142.7	128.9	105.6	109.5	101.2	103.8	80.0	143.5
1986	143.3	132.1	154.4	146.6	143.0	137.4	112.2	168.6
1987	141.7	142.3	170.5	174.2	177.0	164.0	138.6	188.3
1988	142.1	157.8	188.4	172.9	180.3	168.8	139.9	210.5
			Output Per Hour (1977=100)					
1950	51.1	34.9	9.4	23.1	19.3	21.3	20.4	45.6
1955	58.7	42.8	15.9	28.8	27.8	29.7	25.5	49.3
1960	62.2	50.7	23.2	37.4	40.3	37.2	32.4	55.9
1965	76.6	65.0	35.0	50.5	54.0	51.4	42.1	66.2
1970	80.8	75.6	64.8	71.4	71.2	69.8	64.3	80.3
1975	92.9	88.6	87.7	88.7	90.1	86.2	86.2	94.9
1980	101.4	98.2	122.7	110.6	108.6	122.1	113.6	101.9
1985	123.6	117.3	161.1	132.7	128.4	156.8	145.1	134.1
1986	127.7	117.7	163.7	135.2	128.3	158.3	144.8	138.6
1987	132.0	120.5	176.5	136.8	129.9	162.3	145.9	147.6
1988	136.2	124.3	190.0	144.1	135.9	167.1	153.2	154.9

Source: Department of Labor, Bureau of Labor Statistics.

B27. Industrial Production and Manufacturing Capacity Utilization

Calendar Years 1958-1988

Year	Total Industrial Production	Indexes of Industrial Production, 1977=100					Capacity Utilization Rate in Manu-facturing
		Manufacturing			Mining	Utilities	
		Total	Durable	Nondurable			
1958	42.6	41.7	41.5	42.1	67.1	34.9	75.0%
1959	47.7	47.0	47.7	46.3	70.2	38.4	81.6
1960	48.8	48.0	48.5	47.4	71.6	41.1	80.1
1961	49.1	48.1	47.6	48.8	72.1	43.4	77.3
1962	53.2	52.4	52.8	51.8	74.1	46.6	81.4
1963	56.3	55.5	56.3	54.6	77.1	49.8	83.5
1964	60.1	59.3	60.3	58.2	80.2	54.1	85.6
1965	66.1	65.7	68.6	62.1	83.1	57.4	89.5
1966	72.0	71.7	76.2	66.0	87.6	61.8	91.1
1967	73.5	73.1	77.0	68.1	89.3	64.9	86.7
1968	77.6	77.2	80.8	72.5	92.7	70.2	87.0
1969	81.2	80.6	84.0	76.3	96.4	76.4	86.7
1970	78.5	77.0	77.6	76.3	98.9	81.1	79.2
1971	79.6	78.2	77.3	79.4	96.4	85.0	77.4
1972	87.3	86.4	86.3	86.5	98.4	90.4	82.8
1973	94.4	94.0	96.3	90.8	99.3	94.0	87.0
1974	93.0	92.6	94.3	90.2	98.8	92.8	82.6
1975	84.8	83.4	82.6	84.5	96.6	93.7	72.3
1976	92.6	91.9	91.1	93.1	97.4	97.4	77.4
1977	100.0	100.0	100.0	100.0	100.0	100.0	81.4
1978	106.5	107.1	108.2	105.5	103.6	103.1	84.2
1979	110.7	111.5	113.9	108.2	106.4	105.9	84.6
1980	108.6	108.2	109.1	107.0	112.4	107.3	79.3
1981	111.0	110.5	111.1	109.7	117.5	107.1	78.2
1982	103.1	102.2	99.9	105.5	109.3	104.8	70.3
1983	109.2	110.2	107.7	113.7	102.9	105.2	73.9
1984	121.4	123.4	124.2	122.3	111.1	110.7	80.5
1985	123.7	126.4	127.6	124.6	108.9	111.1	80.1
1986	125.1	129.1	128.4	130.1	100.4	108.5	79.7
1987	129.8	134.7	133.1	136.8	100.7	110.3	81.1
1988	136.6	141.8	141.6	143.6	103.2	113.9	83.5

Source: Board of Governors of the Federal Reserve System.

B28. Capital Investment Per Production Worker in Manufacturing[a]

Selected Calendar Years 1949-1985

Industry	1949	1959	1963	1975	1985
All manufacturing[b]	$ 8,089	$ 17,528	$ 20,426	$ 60,054	$ 155,165
Food, beverages, and tobacco	10,790	19,770	22,315	62,398	152,049
Food and beverages	9,837	18,485	20,680	56,384	134,216
Tobacco manufactures	23,446	38,468	47,239	170,378	567,401
Textiles and their products	4,483	6,789	7,283	16,630	32,809
Textile-mill products	5,850	9,566	11,122	23,499	41,391
Apparel and fabric products	3,050	4,607	4,607	11,785	27,296
Leather and leather products	3,624	5,049	7,128	17,959	52,430
Rubber products	7,438	15,330	16,645	33,221	56,178
Lumber and furniture products	4,565	9,512	9,358	31,847	62,759
Lumber and wood products	4,666	10,528	10,103	42,514	80,442
Furniture and fixtures	4,310	7,640	8,148	15,500	36,549
Paper and allied products	9,533	18,173	20,575	50,174	113,886
Printing and publishing	8,279	12,945	15,192	37,496	96,850
Chemicals and allied products	20,737	36,291	44,732	119,472	338,195
Stone, clay, and glass products	6,594	16,174	18,634	40,346	96,274
Metal products and processes	8,898	16,843	19,756	60,723	111,487
Primary metal industries	10,345	23,766	26,449	79,638	155,445
Fabricated metal products[c]	7,221	11,695	14,240	31,638	86,670
Electrical machinery	7,190	12,537	15,655	58,520	168,725
Machinery, except electrical	10,432	18,034	19,181	57,665	135,493
Motor vehicles and transportation equipment	8,428	17,914	22,788	83,264	243,737
Instruments and related products	7,116	17,655	22,572	46,988	117,856
Miscellaneous manufacturing[c]	8,205	13,681	14,536	38,612	127,947

[a] Capital investment is total assets less investments in government obligations and securities of corporations. It is measured in book values. Data for 1959 and later years are not strictly comparable with earlier years.

[b] Includes some categories not shown separately (principally highly capitalized petroleum and coal products manufacturing.)

[c] Prior to 1963, ordnance and accessories are included in fabricated metal products; in 1963, 1975, and 1985 included in miscellaneous manufacturing.

Source: Department of the Treasury, Internal Revenue Service; Bureau of Labor Statistics; and Tax Foundation computations.

B29. Gross Fixed Capital Formation as a Percentage of Gross Domestic Product in Selected Countries

Selected Years 1960-1986

(Percent)

Country	1960	1968	1974	1979	1984	1985	1986
Australia	25.0	26.2	23.2	23.3	22.3	23.4	23.3
Austria	25.0	25.7	28.4	25.1	22.0	22.3	22.4
Belgium	19.3	21.5	22.7	20.7	16.1	15.7	16.1
Canada	22.6	22.0	23.7	23.1	19.2	19.9	20.2
Denmark	21.6	23.4	24.0	20.9	17.1	18.4	20.3
Finland	28.3	23.1	29.8	23.5	23.7	23.8	23.1
France	20.6	24.0	25.0	22.4	19.3	19.0	18.8
Germany	24.3	22.4	21.6	21.8	20.2	19.7	19.5
Greece	19.0	23.2	22.2	25.8	18.5	19.1	18.5
Ireland	14.4	20.9	24.6	30.5	21.7	20.4	18.7
Italy	27.7	24.9	27.5	23.1	21.2	21.2	20.1
Japan	29.5	33.2	34.8	31.7	27.9	27.8	27.7
Luxembourg	20.9	22.1	24.6	24.4	19.6	18.1	20.7
Netherlands	24.1	26.9	21.9	21.0	18.6	19.0	19.6
New Zealand	21.3	19.6	27.5	20.6	24.8	25.4	22.3
Norway	29.0	26.9	30.5	27.7	26.0	21.7	27.5
Portugal	23.2	22.2	26.0	26.6	23.9	21.7	21.6
Spain	20.1	25.7	28.0	21.6	18.8	18.9	18.7
Sweden	22.7	23.9	21.5	19.8	18.6	19.1	18.2
Switzerland	24.8	25.6	27.6	21.8	23.4	23.8	24.3
Turkey	16.0	17.3	19.0	20.8	18.4	20.2	23.6
United Kingdom	16.4	19.4	20.9	18.8	17.3	17.2	17.2
United States	18.0	18.1	18.6	20.4	18.0	18.1	17.8

Source: Organization for Economic Cooperation and Development.

B30. New Public and Private Construction Activity

Selected Calendar Years 1929-1988[a]

(Dollar Figures in Millions)

Year	Total	Private Construction				Public Construction[b]			Public as Percent of Total New Construction
		Total	Residential Buildings	Nonresidential Buildings[c]	Other[d]	Total	Federally Owned	State and Locally Owned	
1929	$10,793	$8,307	$3,772	$2,694	$1,841	$2,486	$155	$2,331	23.0%
1939	8,198	4,389	2,786	786	817	3,809	759	3,050	46.5
1944	5,259	2,186	923	351	912	3,073	2,505	568	58.4
1946	14,308	12,077	6,656	3,362	2,059	2,231	865	1,366	15.6
1949	26,722	20,453	13,111	3,383	3,959	6,269	1,488	4,781	23.5
1959	55,392	39,322	24,251	8,859	6,212	16,070	3,724	12,346	29.0
1960	54,738	38,875	22,975	10,149	5,751	15,863	3,622	12,241	29.0
1961	56,445	39,297	23,107	10,734	5,456	17,148	3,879	13,269	30.4
1962	60,205	42,336	25,150	11,617	5,569	17,869	3,913	13,956	29.7
1963	64,812	45,455	27,874	11,646	5,935	19,357	4,001	15,356	29.9
1964	67,675	47,292	28,010	12,955	6,327	20,383	3,898	16,485	30.1
1965	73,747	51,685	27,934	16,509	7,242	22,062	4,014	18,048	29.9
1966	76,414	52,407	25,715	18,279	8,413	24,007	3,964	20,043	31.4
1967	78,082	52,546	25,568	17,589	9,389	25,536	3,475	22,061	32.7
1968	87,093	59,488	30,565	18,164	10,759	27,605	3,367	24,238	31.7
1969	93,917	65,953	33,200	21,155	11,598	27,964	3,313	24,651	29.8
1970	94,855	66,759	31,864	21,417	13,478	28,096	3,290	24,806	29.6
1971	109,950	80,079	43,267	22,479	14,333	29,871	3,983	25,888	27.2
1972	124,085	93,901	54,288	24,038	15,575	30,184	4,392	25,792	24.3
1973	137,917	105,412	59,727	27,584	18,101	32,505	4,851	27,654	23.6
1974	138,501	100,166	50,376	29,637	20,153	38,334	5,293	33,042	27.7
1975	134,535	93,651	46,472	26,407	20,772	40,884	6,318	34,566	30.4
1976	151,054	111,931	60,520	26,091	25,320	39,123	7,017	32,106	25.9
1977	173,975	135,801	80,956	28,695	26,150	38,174	7,320	30,855	21.9
1978	205,561	159,665	93,424	36,293	29,947	45,896	8,398	37,497	22.3
1979	230,413	181,621	99,030	47,298	35,293	48,792	8,564	40,227	21.2
1980	230,712	175,699	87,261	52,434	36,004	55,013	9,641	45,372	23.8
1981	239,111	185,762	86,566	60,818	38,378	53,349	10,413	42,935	22.3
1982	244,412	193,570	85,390	69,355	38,825	50,842	10,008	40,834	20.8
1983	281,266	227,494	125,521	65,675	36,298	53,772	10,558	43,214	19.1
1984	328,641	270,977	153,849	81,147	35,981	57,664	11,240	46,422	17.5
1985	355,735	291,665	158,474	95,317	37,874	64,070	12,004	52,066	18.0
1986	386,093	314,652	187,148	91,171	36,333	71,441	12,412	59,030	18.5
1987	398,850	323,820	194,772	91,994	37,054	75,030	14,076	60,956	18.8
1988	403,122	325,111	195,281	93,186	36,644	78,012	12,882	65,130	19.4

[a] Years prior to 1946 not strictly comparable to other years. Data for Alaska and Hawaii included beginning 1959. For public construction, data beginning 1975 not directly comparable to prior data.
[b] For public construction by type, see Table B31.
[c] Excludes farm.
[d] Public utilities, nonresidential farm, and all other private.
Source: Department of Commerce, Bureau of the Census.

B31. Value of New Public Construction by Type[a]

Selected Calendar Years 1929-1988[b]

($Millions)

Year	Total	Housing and Redevelopment Buildings	Nonresidential Buildings Total	Nonresidential Buildings Educational	Sewer and Water Systems	Highways and Streets	Conservation and Development	Military Facilities[c]	All Other[d]
1929	$2,486	.	$659	$389	$253	$1,266	$115	$19	$174
1939	3,809	$65	970	468	371	1,381	570	125	327
1944	3,073	211	1,361	41	79	362	163	837	60
1946	2,231	374	354	101	194	764	260	188	97
1949	6,269	359	2,049	934	619	2,015	852	137	238
1959	16,070	962	4,514	2,656	1,467	5,761	1,121	1,465	780
1960	15,863	716	4,759	2,818	1,487	5,437	1,175	1,366	887
1961	17,148	842	5,169	3,052	1,581	5,854	1,384	1,371	947
1962	17,869	938	5,154	2,984	1,754	6,365	1,523	1,266	869
1963	19,357	531	6,003	3,477	1,829	7,084	1,694	1,179	1,037
1964	20,383	567	6,610	3,790	2,281	7,133	1,750	910	1,132
1965	22,062	603	7,290	4,284	2,461	7,550	2,019	830	1,309
1966	24,007	655	8,265	5,333	2,366	8,405	2,194	727	1,395
1967	25,536	709	9,273	5,988	2,328	8,591	2,124	695	1,816
1968	27,605	746	9,693	6,061	3,065	9,321	1,973	808	1,999
1969	27,964	1,047	10,183	5,868	2,680	9,250	1,783	879	2,142
1970	28,096	1,107	9,550	5,619	2,638	9,981	1,908	718	2,194
1971	29,871	1,136	10,261	5,564	2,825	10,658	2,095	901	1,995
1972	30,184	875	10,625	5,720	2,778	10,429	2,172	1,087	2,218
1973	32,505	941	12,054	6,647	3,022	10,505	2,313	1,166	2,504
1974	38,334	1,006	13,984	7,310	4,062	12,065	2,714	1,185	3,290
1975	40,884	754	14,720	7,760	6,566	10,854	3,257	1,389	3,345
1976	39,123	720	13,039	6,342	6,972	9,743	3,742	1,630	3,276
1977	38,174	908	11,891	5,459	7,184	9,380	3,862	1,429	3,520
1978	45,896	1,053	14,188	6,264	9,426	10,706	4,457	1,502	4,563
1979	48,792	1,212	14,346	6,903	9,788	11,996	4,588	1,647	5,215
1980	55,013	1,648	16,869	8,050	10,437	13,770	5,091	1,880	5,318
1981	53,349	1,722	16,070	6,737	8,939	13,599	5,300	1,964	5,755
1982	50,842	1,658	15,339	5,927	8,431	13,292	5,027	2,205	4,890
1983	53,772	1,700	15,576	5,374	7,343	17,199	4,820	2,544	4,590
1984	57,664	1,636	16,247	5,557	8,860	18,771	4,654	2,839	4,655
1985	64,070	1,511	18,603	6,708	9,860	21,540	4,779	3,235	4,542
1986	71,441	1,456	22,000	8,440	11,475	22,682	4,647	3,867	5,314
1987	75,030	1,519	23,639	8,838	13,272	22,757	5,161	4,324	4,358
1988	78,012	1,522	25,584	10,736	12,999	25,720	4,535	3,951	3,701

[a] "Public" construction relates to government ownership, not source of funds.
[b] Beginning in 1959, data include Alaska and Hawaii. Years prior to 1946 not strictly comparable to other years. Data beginning 1975 not directly comparable to prior data.
[c] Beginning in 1963, military hospitals are included in the nonresidential buildings category.
[d] Includes publicly owned parks and playgrounds, memorials, public service enterprises, etc., and in 1942-1944, petroleum pipelines.

Source: Department of Commerce, Bureau of the Census.

B32. Number of New Housing Starts

Calendar Years 1960-1988
(Thousands of Units)

Year	Total	Publicly Owned	Privately Owned			Percent Change from Previous Year		
			Total	Single Family	Multi-family	Total	Publicly Owned	Privately Owned
1960	1,296.1	43.9	1,252.2	994.7	257.5	-16.6	19.6	-17.5
1961	1,365.0	52.0	1,313.0	974.3	338.7	5.3	18.5	4.9
1962	1,492.5	29.6	1,462.9	991.4	471.5	9.3	-43.1	11.4
1963	1,634.9	31.7	1,603.2	1,012.4	590.8	10.1	7.1	9.6
1964	1,561.0	32.2	1,528.8	970.5	558.3	-4.5	1.6	-4.6
1965	1,509.7	36.9	1,472.8	963.7	509.1	-3.3	14.6	-3.7
1966	1,195.8	30.9	1,164.9	778.6	386.3	-20.8	-16.3	-20.9
1967	1,321.9	30.3	1,291.6	843.9	447.7	10.5	-1.9	10.9
1968	1,545.4	37.8	1,507.6	899.4	608.2	16.9	24.7	16.7
1969	1,499.5	32.7	1,466.8	810.6	656.2	-3.0	-13.5	-2.7
1970	1,469.0	35.4	1,433.6	812.9	620.7	-2.0	8.3	-2.3
1971	2,084.5	32.3	2,052.2	1,151.0	901.2	41.9	-8.8	43.2
1972	2,378.5	21.9	2,356.6	1,309.2	1,047.4	27.1	-32.2	14.8
1973	2,057.5	12.2	2,045.3	1,132.0	913.3	-13.5	-44.3	-13.2
1974	1,352.5	14.8	1,337.7	888.1	449.6	-34.3	21.3	-34.6
1975	1,171.4	10.9	1,160.4	892.2	268.2	-13.4	-26.4	-13.3
1976	1,547.6	10.1	1,537.5	1,162.4	375.1	32.1	-7.3	32.5
1977	2,001.7	14.6	1,987.1	1,450.9	536.2	29.3	44.6	29.2
1978	2,036.1	15.8	2,020.3	1,433.3	587.0	1.7	8.2	1.7
1979	1,760.0	14.8	1,745.1	1,194.1	551.0	-13.6	-6.3	-13.6
1980	1,312.6	20.4	1,292.2	852.2	440.0	-25.4	37.8	-26.0
1981	1,100.3	16.1	1,084.2	705.4	378.8	-16.2	-21.1	-16.1
1982	1,072.0	9.8	1,062.2	662.6	399.6	-2.6	-39.1	-2.0
1983	1,712.5	9.4	1,703.0	1,067.6	635.4	59.7	-4.1	60.3
1984	1,755.8	6.3	1,749.5	1,084.2	665.3	2.5	-33.0	2.7
1985	1,745.0	3.1	1,741.8	1,072.4	669.4	-.6	-50.8	-.4
1986	1,807.1	1.7	1,805.4	1,179.4	626.0	3.6	-45.2	3.7
1987	1,622.7	2.2	1,620.5	1,146.4	474.1	-10.2	29.4	-10.2
1988	1,488.1	n.a.	1,488.1	1,081.3	406.8	-8.3	n.a.	-8.2

Source: Department of Commerce, Bureau of the Census; and Tax Foundation computations.

B33. Income of Farm Operators in Current and in Constant (1982) Dollars

Selected Calendar Years 1910-1987

| | Current Income ($Millions) | | | | | | Income of Farm Operator Families in 1982 Dollars | | | | |
| | | | Gross Farm Income | | | | Net Income From Farming | | Personal Income of Farm Population[c] | | |
Year	Net Farm Income[a]	Production Expenses	Total	Nonmoney and Other Farm Income[b]	Cash Receipts From Marketings	Government Payments	Total ($Billions)	Per Farm	Total ($Millions)	Per Capita	Number of Farms (Thousands)
1910-14[d]	$3,984	$3,790	$7,774	$1,845	$5,929	-	$20.1	$3,134	n.a.	n.a.	6,429
1915-19[d]	7,029	6,187	13,216	2,640	10,576	-	25.5	3,930	n.a.	n.a.	6,479
1920-24[d]	5,086	7,318	12,404	2,604	9,801	-	13.9	2,131	n.a.	n.a.	6,500
1925-29[d]	6,101	7,520	13,621	2,698	10,923	-	17.2	2,652	n.a.	n.a.	6,475
1930-34[d]	3,023	5,207	8,230	1,740	6,374	$116	10.1	1,524	n.a.	$585	6,672
1935-39[d]	4,873	5,824	10,698	2,224	7,994	479	17.0	2,565	$14,962	593	6,611
1940	4,482	6,858	11,340	2,235	8,382	723	34.5	2,461	18,088	1,225	6,350
1950	13,648	19,455	33,103	4,359	28,461	283	57.1	1,011	28,218	1,324	5,648
1960	11,212	27,376	38,588	3,873	34,012	703	36.3	916	20,701	1,522	3,963
1962	12,063	30,279	42,342	4,128	36,468	1,746	37.8	1,024	21,785	1,558	3,692
1964	10,489	31,812	42,301	2,797	37,325	2,179	31.9	923	21,265	2,113	3,457
1966	13,962	36,507	50,469	3,756	43,436	3,277	39.9	1,225	24,499	2,212	3,257
1968	12,323	39,524	51,847	4,201	44,183	3,463	32.7	1,065	23,128	2,432	3,071
1970	14,366	44,452	58,818	4,592	50,509	3,717	34.2	1,160	23,616	2,885	2,949
1972	19,457	51,689	71,146	6,078	61,106	3,962	41.8	1,462	27,724	3,299	2,860
1974	27,266	70,981	98,247	5,326	92,391	530	50.5	1,807	30,567	3,110	2,795
1975	25,547	75,043	100,590	10,881	88,902	807	43.1	1,710	25,118	2,846	2,521
1976	20,176	82,741	102,719	6,630	95,355	734	32.0	1,282	21,421	3,358	2,497
1977	19,882	88,884	108,766	10,713	96,235	1,818	29.5	1,201	20,799	3,742	2,456
1978	25,197	103,250	128,447	13,057	112,360	3,030	34.9	1,433	24,327	3,912	2,436
1979	27,416	123,304	150,720	17,815	131,529	1,376	34.9	1,435	24,418	3,107	2,432
1980	16,134	133,139	149,273	8,251	139,737	1,285	18.8	773	18,799	3,499	2,433
1981	26,879	139,444	166,323	22,774	141,616	1,933	28.6	1,175	20,260	3,029	2,434
1982	23,525	139,980	163,505	17,418	142,595	3,492	23.5	979	17,021	2,717	2,401
1983	12,676	140,377	153,053	7,190	136,567	9,296	12.2	514	15,727	n.a.	2,370
1984	32,218	142,669	174,887	24,031	142,435	8,431	29.9	1,284	n.a.	n.a.	2,328
1985	32,292	133,957	166,249	14,529	144,015	7,705	29.1	1,279	n.a.	n.a.	2,275
1986	37,498	122,335	159,833	12,917	135,102	11,814	32.9	1,487	n.a.	n.a.	2,212
1987	46,263	123,502	169,765	14,924	138,094	16,747	39.3	1,806	n.a.	n.a.	2,176

a Net farm income is the difference between total gross farm income and production expenses.
b Nonmoney income includes value of farm products consumed directly in farm households and gross rental value of farm dwellings. Other farm income includes recreation, machine hire and customwork receipts.
c Income from all sources, including off-farm.
d Annual average for period.
Source: Department of Agriculture, Economics and Statistics Service.

B34. Indexes of Farm Output, Prices Received and Paid by Farmers

Calendar Years 1948-1988[a]

(1977=100)

Year	Farm Output	Prices Received by Farmers	Prices Paid by Farmers[b]
1948	63	63	38
1949	62	55	36
1950	61	56	37
1951	63	66	41
1952	66	63	42
1953	66	56	40
1954	66	54	40
1955	69	51	40
1956	69	50	40
1957	67	51	42
1958	73	55	43
1959	74	53	43
1960	76	52	44
1961	76	53	44
1962	77	53	45
1963	80	53	45
1964	79	52	45
1965	82	54	47
1966	79	58	49
1967	83	55	49
1968	85	56	51
1969	85	59	53
1970	84	60	55
1971	92	62	58
1972	91	69	62
1973	93	98	71
1974	88	105	81
1975	95	101	89
1976	97	102	97
1977	100	100	100
1978	104	115	108
1979	111	132	123
1980	104	134	138
1981	118	139	150
1982	116	133	159
1983	96	135	161
1984	112	142	165
1985	118	128	163
1986	111	123	159
1987	110	127	162
1988	97	138	170

[a] Annual averages.
[b] Includes interest, taxes, and wage rates.
Source: Department of Agriculture.

B35. Indexes of Producer Prices and Consumer Prices

Calendar Years 1959-1988

Year	Producer Prices		Consumer Prices	
	1967 = 100	1982 = 100	1967 = 100	1982-84 = 100
1959	93.0	33.1	87.1	29.1
1960	93.8	33.4	88.6	29.6
1961	93.8	33.4	89.5	29.9
1962	94.1	33.5	90.4	30.2
1963	93.8	33.4	91.6	30.6
1964	94.1	33.5	92.8	31.0
1965	95.8	34.1	94.3	31.5
1966	98.9	35.2	97.0	32.4
1967	100.0	35.6	100.0	33.4
1968	102.8	36.6	104.2	34.8
1969	106.7	38.0	109.9	36.7
1970	110.4	39.3	116.2	38.8
1971	113.8	40.5	121.3	40.5
1972	117.4	41.8	125.1	41.8
1973	128.1	45.6	132.9	44.4
1974	147.8	52.6	147.6	49.3
1975	163.5	58.2	161.1	53.8
1976	170.8	60.8	170.4	56.9
1977	181.7	64.7	181.4	60.6
1978	196.1	69.8	195.2	65.2
1979	218.0	77.6	217.4	72.6
1980	247.2	88.0	246.7	82.4
1981	269.9	96.1	272.2	90.9
1982	280.9	100.0	288.9	96.5
1983	285.4	101.6	298.2	99.6
1984	291.3	103.7	311.1	103.9
1985	294.1	104.7	322.2	107.6
1986	289.9	103.2	328.1	109.6
1987	296.1	105.4	340.1	113.6
1988	303.4	108.0	354.2	118.3

Source: Department of Labor, Bureau of Labor Statistics; and Tax Foundation computations.

B36. Purchasing Power of the Dollar

Calendar Years 1959-1988

Year	Purchasing Power As Measured By			
	Producer Prices		Consumer Prices	
	1967 = $100	1982 = $100	1967 = $100	1982-84 = $100
1959	$ 1.08	$ 3.02	$ 1.15	$ 3.44
1960	1.07	2.99	1.13	3.38
1961	1.07	2.99	1.12	3.34
1962	1.06	2.99	1.11	3.31
1963	1.07	2.99	1.09	3.27
1964	1.06	2.99	1.08	3.23
1965	1.04	2.93	1.06	3.17
1966	1.01	2.84	1.03	3.09
1967	1.00	2.81	1.00	2.99
1968	.97	2.73	.96	2.87
1969	.94	2.63	.91	2.72
1970	.91	2.54	.86	2.58
1971	.88	2.47	.82	2.47
1972	.85	2.39	.80	2.39
1973	.78	2.19	.75	2.25
1974	.68	1.90	.68	2.03
1975	.61	1.72	.62	1.86
1976	.59	1.64	.59	1.76
1977	.55	1.55	.55	1.65
1978	.51	1.43	.51	1.53
1979	.46	1.29	.46	1.38
1980	.40	1.14	.41	1.21
1981	.37	1.04	.37	1.10
1982	.36	1.00	.35	1.04
1983	.35	.98	.34	1.00
1984	.34	.96	.32	.96
1985	.34	.96	.31	.93
1986	.34	.97	.30	.91
1987	.34	.95	.29	.88
1988	.33	.93	.28	.85

Source: Computed from data in Table B35.

B37. Implicit Price Deflators for Gross Domestic Product and Selected Components

Selected Calendar Years 1929-1989

(Index Numbers 1982=100)

Year	Gross National Product	Personal Consumption Expenditures	Gross Private Domestic Investment		Government Purchases of Goods and Services
			Nonresidential Structures and Producers' Goods	Residential Structures	
1929	14.6	16.4	11.8	11.2	9.4
1930	14.2	15.9	11.2	10.9	9.2
1935	12.5	13.5	10.7	8.8	9.1
1939	12.7	13.9	11.5	10.5	9.4
1940	13.0	14.1	11.9	10.9	9.5
1941	13.8	15.2	12.7	11.9	10.6
1942	14.7	16.8	13.3	12.8	12.4
1943	15.1	18.4	13.8	13.8	12.5
1944	15.3	19.4	14.0	14.9	12.3
1945	15.7	20.2	14.3	15.8	11.8
1946	19.4	22.0	16.4	17.5	12.3
1947	22.1	24.3	19.3	21.1	14.7
1948	23.6	25.7	21.0	22.8	16.3
1949	23.5	25.6	21.7	23.0	17.3
1950	23.9	26.2	22.4	23.7	16.8
1951	25.1	27.8	24.2	25.4	18.3
1952	25.5	28.4	24.4	26.1	19.4
1953	25.9	29.0	25.1	26.3	19.8
1954	26.3	29.1	25.2	26.4	20.1
1955	27.2	29.5	25.8	27.0	20.8
1956	28.1	30.1	27.7	27.9	21.9
1957	29.1	31.0	29.5	28.0	22.9
1958	29.7	31.6	29.5	28.0	24.1
1959	30.4	32.3	30.2	28.0	24.6
1960	30.9	32.9	30.6	28.2	24.9
1961	31.2	33.3	30.5	28.2	25.4
1962	31.9	33.9	30.9	28.3	26.3
1963	32.4	34.4	31.3	28.2	26.9
1964	32.9	35.0	31.5	28.5	27.6
1965	33.8	35.6	32.1	29.0	28.5
1966	35.0	36.7	33.3	29.9	29.8
1967	35.9	37.6	34.4	30.9	31.2
1968	37.7	39.3	35.9	32.5	33.1
1969	39.8	41.0	37.9	35.6	35.1
1970	42.0	42.9	39.9	37.0	38.1
1971	44.4	44.9	42.4	39.0	41.0
1972	46.5	46.7	44.4	41.2	43.8
1973	49.5	49.6	46.0	44.8	47.1
1974	54.0	54.8	50.5	49.8	52.2
1975	59.3	59.2	57.9	54.2	57.7
1976	63.1	62.6	61.9	58.0	61.5
1977	67.3	66.7	66.1	64.6	65.8
1978	72.2	71.6	71.5	72.6	70.4
1979	78.6	78.2	77.8	81.4	76.8
1980	85.7	86.6	85.1	89.4	85.5
1981	94.0	94.6	93.4	96.6	93.4
1982	100.0	100.0	100.0	100.0	100.0
1983	103.9	104.1	98.8	102.2	104.0
1984	107.7	108.1	97.9	106.0	108.6
1985	110.9	111.6	97.7	108.3	112.3
1986	113.9	114.3	100.2	111.1	114.6
1987	117.7	119.5	100.4	116.2	118.5
1988	121.7	124.5	100.2	119.8	123.3
1989[a]	125.1	128.2	102.2	122.1	126.7

[a] Seasonally adjusted annual rate QI 1989.
Source: Department of Commerce, Bureau of Economic Analysis.

B38. Selected Bond Yields and Interest Rates

Average for Calendar Years 1950-1989

(Percent Per Year)

Year	U.S. Treasury 3-Month Bills (New Issues)[a]	High-grade Municipal Bonds (Standard & Poor's)	Corporate Bonds-Aaa (Moody's)	New Home Mortgage Yields[b] (FHLBB)	Bank Prime Rate	Federal Reserve Discount Rate[c]
1950	1.218%	1.98%	2.62%	-	2.07%	1.59%
1951	1.552	2.00	2.86	-	2.56	1.75
1952	1.766	2.19	2.96	-	3.00	1.75
1953	1.931	2.72	3.20	-	3.17	1.99
1954	.953	2.37	2.90	-	3.05	1.60
1955	1.753	2.53	3.06	-	3.16	1.89
1956	2.658	2.93	3.36	-	3.77	2.77
1957	3.267	3.60	3.89	-	4.20	3.12
1958	1.839	3.56	3.79	-	3.83	2.15
1959	3.405	3.95	4.38	-	4.48	3.36
1960	2.928	3.73	4.41	-	4.82	3.53
1961	2.378	3.46	4.35	-	4.50	3.00
1962	2.778	3.18	4.33	-	4.50	3.00
1963	3.157	3.23	4.26	5.89%	4.50	3.23
1964	3.549	3.22	4.40	5.82	4.50	3.55
1965	3.954	3.27	4.49	5.81	4.54	4.04
1966	4.881	3.82	5.13	6.25	5.63	4.50
1967	4.321	3.98	5.51	6.46	5.61	4.19
1968	5.339	4.51	6.18	6.97	6.30	5.16
1969	6.677	5.81	7.03	7.80	7.96	5.87
1970	6.458	6.51	8.04	8.45	7.91	5.95
1971	4.348	5.70	7.39	7.74	5.72	4.88
1972	4.071	5.27	7.21	7.60	5.25	4.50
1973	7.041	5.18	7.44	7.96	8.03	6.44
1974	7.886	6.09	8.57	8.92	10.81	7.83
1975	5.838	6.89	8.83	9.00	7.86	6.25
1976	4.989	6.49	8.43	9.00	6.84	5.50
1977	5.265	5.56	8.02	9.02	6.83	5.46
1978	7.221	5.90	8.73	9.56	9.06	7.46
1979	10.041	6.39	9.63	10.78	12.67	10.28
1980	11.506	8.51	11.94	12.66	15.27	11.77
1981	14.029	11.23	14.17	14.70	18.87	13.42
1982	10.686	11.57	13.79	15.14	14.86	11.02
1983	8.630	9.48	12.04	12.57	10.79	8.50
1984	9.580	10.15	12.71	12.38	12.04	8.80
1985	7.480	9.18	11.37	11.55	9.93	7.69
1986	5.980	7.38	9.02	10.17	8.33	6.33
1987	5.820	7.73	9.38	9.31	8.22	5.66
1988	6.690	7.76	9.71	9.19	9.32	6.20
1989[d]	9.100	7.64	9.85	9.81	11.50	7.00

[a] Rate on new issues within period; bank-discount basis.
[b] Effective rate (in the primary market) on conventional mortgages, reflecting fees and charges as well as contract rate and assuming on the average repayment in 10 years. Beginning 1973, data not strictly comparable with prior rates.
[c] Applies to Federal Reserve Bank of New York.
[d] 1989 as of April.
Source: Compiled by Council of Economic Advisers; basic data from Treasury Department, Board of Governors of the Federal Reserve System, Federal Home Loan Bank Board (FHLBB), Moody's Investors Service, and Standard & Poor's Corporation.

B39. Business Cycle Expansions and Contractions
Period 1854-1988

Business Cycle Reference Dates		Duration in Months			
		Contraction (Trough from Previous Peak)	Expansion (Trough to Peak)	Cycle	
				Trough from Previous Trough	Peak from Previous Peak
Trough	Peak				
December 1854	June 1857	-	30	-	-
December 1858	October 1860	18	22	48	40
June 1861	April 1865	8	46[a]	30	54[a]
December 1867	June 1869	32[a]	18	78[a]	50
December 1870	October 1873	18	34	36	52
March 1879	March 1882	65	36	99	101
May 1885	March 1887	38	22	74	60
April 1888	July 1890	13	27	35	40
May 1891	January 1893	10	20	37	30
June 1894	December 1895	17	18	37	35
June 1897	June 1899	18	24	36	42
December 1900	September 1902	18	21	42	39
August 1904	May 1907	23	33	44	56
June 1908	January 1910	13	19	46	32
January 1912	January 1913	24	12	43	36
December 1914	August 1918	23	44[a]	35	67[a]
March 1919	January 1920	7[a]	10	51[a]	17
July 1921	May 1923	18	22	28	40
July 1924	October 1926	14	27	36	41
November 1927	August 1929	13	21	40	34
March 1933	May 1937	43	50	64	93
June 1938	February 1945	13	80[a]	63	93[a]
October 1945	November 1948	8[a]	37	88[a]	45
October 1949	July 1953	11	45[a]	48	56[a]
May 1954	August 1957	10[a]	39	55[a]	49
April 1958	April 1960	8	24	47	32
February 1961	December 1969	10	106[a]	34	116[a]
November 1970	November 1973	11[a]	36	117[a]	47
March 1975	January 1980	16	58	52	74
July 1980	July 1981	6	12	64	18
November 1982		16	-	28	-
Average, all cycles:					
1854-1982 (30 cycles)		18	33	51	51[b]
1854-1919 (16 cycles)		22	27	48	49[c]
1919-1945 (6 cycles)		18	35	53	53
1945-1982 (8 cycles)		11	45	56	55
Average, peacetime cycles:					
1854-1982 (25 cycles)		19	27	46	46[d]
1854-1919 (14 cycles)		22	24	46	47[e]
1919-1945 (5 cycles)		20	26	46	45
1945-1982 (6 cycles)		11	34	46	44

[a] Indicates wartime expansions (Civil War, World Wars I and II, Korean War, and Vietnam War), postwar contractions, and full cycles including wartime expansions.
[b] 29 cycles.
[c] 15 cycles.
[d] 24 cycles.
[e] 13 cycles.
Source: National Bureau of Economic Research, Inc.

B40. Net Stock of Fixed Reproducible Tangible Wealth in Current and Constant (1982) Dollars

End of Selected Calendar Years 1929-1987

($Billions)

Type of Wealth	1929	1935	1945	1950	1955	1960	1965	1970	1975	1980	1985	1987
Current Dollars												
Net stock, total	$279	$222	$479	$758	$1,068	$1,347	$1,701	$2,637	$4,600	$8,312	$10,912	$12,198
Private business	203	152	250	476	662	846	1,062	1,637	2,934	5,484	7,255	8,091
Nonresidential equipment	32	23	38	95	141	192	244	395	719	1,337	1,797	1,964
Nonresidential structures	73	55	76	132	179	228	292	470	852	1,471	1,975	2,137
Residential	97	74	136	249	342	426	526	722	1,364	2,676	3,483	3,991
Government	37	44	182	174	248	307	403	627	1,070	1,808	2,259	2,423
Nonresidential equipment:												
Military	1	1	77	29	50	54	64	77	101	180	318	357
Other	1	2	12	9	17	21	25	40	60	93	127	149
Nonresidential structures	35	41	90	131	174	222	301	493	876	1,478	1,742	1,838
Residential	a	a	3	5	7	10	12	18	33	57	72	80
Households (consumer durables)	39	26	46	108	157	194	236	372	596	1,020	1,398	1,684
Constant (1982) Dollars												
Net stock, total	$2,392	$2,260	$2,961	$3,073	$3,806	$4,487	$5,397	$6,566	$7,743	$8,972	$10,079	$10,765
Private business	1,908	1,719	1,629	2,042	2,501	2,979	3,567	4,313	5,130	6,005	6,741	7,132
Nonresidential equipment	258	196	242	395	505	579	695	940	1,193	1,506	1,738	1,879
Nonresidential structures	765	685	569	629	738	879	1,046	1,272	1,462	1,632	1,839	1,881
Residential	986	839	817	1,108	1,257	1,521	1,825	2,100	2,476	2,867	3,164	3,372
Government	329	409	1,196	789	968	1,119	1,351	1,594	1,753	1,878	2,012	2,106
Nonresidential equipment:												
Military	11	8	572	133	173	164	181	178	176	208	299	337
Other	8	15	77	36	57	62	71	91	97	103	118	133
Nonresidential structures	309	386	587	600	713	860	1,056	1,275	1,420	1,506	1,540	1,568
Residential	a	a	19	19	25	34	43	51	60	61	65	67
Households (consumer durables)	155	131	136	243	337	389	480	659	860	1,090	1,327	1,528

a Represents or rounds to zero.
Source: Department of Commerce, Bureau of Economic Analysis.

B41. Measures and Components of the Money Supply

December Averages 1983-1989[a]

($Billions)

Item	1983	1984	1985	1986	1987	1988	1989
Measures[b]							
M-1	$ 522.1	$ 551.9	$ 620.5	$ 725.9	$ 752.3	$ 790.3	$ 786.6
M-2	2,186.0	2,367.2	2,567.4	2,811.2	2,909.9	3,069.3	3,071.6
M-3	2,694.3	2,982.3	3,201.7	3,494.9	3,677.6	3,919.0	3,937.9
L	3,155.5	3,523.4	3,830.6	4,137.1	4,340.5	4,685.2	4,695.3
Components[c]							
Currency	146.3	156.1	167.8	180.5	196.4	211.8	214.4
Demand deposits	238.7	244.2	267.3	303.2	288.3	288.6	284.3
Savings deposits	305.6	285.4	301.6	371.0	416.4	431.3	424.5
Small-denomination time deposits[d]	784.0	886.3	882.6	853.9	914.1	1,025.3	1,085.3
Large-denomination time deposits[e]	327.4	417.2	436.6	439.0	487.4	537.7	551.4

[a] Averages of daily figures seasonally adjusted. 1989 is first quarter preliminary.

[b] Measures consist of components as follows: M1 = currency outside the Treasury, Federal Reserve Banks, and the vaults of commercial banks; traveler's checks of non-bank issuers; demand deposits at all commercial banks other than those due to domestic banks, the U.S. government, and foreign banks and official institutions less cash items in the process of collection and Federal Reserve float; and negotiable order of withdrawal (NOW) and automatic transfer service (ATS) accounts at banks and thrift institutions, credit union share draft (CUSD) accounts, and demand deposits at mutual savings banks; M2 = M1 plus savings and small-denomination time deposits at all depository institutions, overnight repurchase agreements at commercial banks, overnight Eurodollars held by U.S. residents other than banks at Caribbean branches of member banks, and balances of money market mutual funds (general purpose and broker/dealer); M3 = M2 plus large-denomination time deposits at all depository institutions and term RPs at commercial banks and savings and loan associations and balances of institution-only money market mutual funds; L = M3 plus other liquid assets such as term Eurodollars held by U.S. residents other than banks, bankers acceptances, commercial paper, Treasury bills and other liquid Treasury securities, and U.S. savings bonds.

[c] Selected.

[d] Issued in amounts of less than $100,000.

[e] Issued in amounts of $100,000 or more. Net of the holdings of domestic banks, thrift institutions, the U.S. Government, money market mutual funds, and foreign banks and official institutions.

Source: Board of Governors of the Federal Reserve System.

B42. Net Financial Investment of Households[a]

Selected Calendar Years 1960-1988

($Billions)

Category	1960	1970	1980	1987	1988
Net financial investment	$12.2	$51.5	$131.7	$109.0	$141.5
Net acquisition of financial assets	30.1	74.6	260.1	358.2	400.6
Deposits, plus credit market instruments[b]	21.0	56.3	190.8	260.1	309.7
Deposits	13.7	52.4	158.5	128.3	170.1
Checkable deposits and currency	1.7	8.8	10.2	12.4	24.6
Small time and savings deposits	11.7	30.1	83.4	72.4	97.1
Large time deposits	.4	13.4	40.4	14.6	24.6
Money market fund shares	-	-	24.5	28.9	23.9
Credit market instruments	7.3	3.9	32.3	131.8	139.7
U.S. Government securities	-.5	-4.6	23.5	87.8	138.1
Tax-exempt obligations	2.6	-.9	7.0	43.0	20.5
Corporate and foreign bonds	.7	10.7	-13.2	5.3	-18.7
Mortgages	2.8	2.4	17.5	-10.4	-11.0
Open-market paper	1.7	-3.7	-2.4	6.1	10.7
Mutual fund shares	1.4	2.6	1.1	79.8	-7.9
Other corporate equities	-2.0	-4.3	-12.0	-99.3	-105.5
Life insurance reserves	3.2	5.3	9.7	26.0	12.9
Pension funds	8.3	18.6	108.8	170.4	231.8
Net investment in noncorporate business	-2.5	-5.6	-49.1	-88.9	-72.4
Security credit	.1	-.9	5.2	-6.8	3.9
Miscellaneous assets	.5	2.6	5.6	17.0	28.2
Net increase in liabilities	17.9	23.1	128.5	249.2	259.1
Credit market instruments	17.7	23.9	118.4	260.3	248.9
Home mortgages	11.7	13.4	96.4	219.7	195.7
Other mortgages	.8	1.2	1.9	2.3	2.3
Installment consumer credit	3.9	4.4	.1	42.3	55.7
Other consumer credit	.4	1.1	2.8	-1.6	-6.4
Tax-exempt debt	-	-	3.1	-1.0	.9
Bank loans, n.e.c.	c	1.3	5.3	-4.3	-4.2
Other loans	.8	2.6	8.8	2.9	4.9
Security	-.1	-1.8	6.5	-15.3	3.6
Trade debt	.1	.6	2.3	2.9	3.3
Miscellaneous	.2	.4	1.2	1.2	3.4

[a] Includes personal trusts and nonprofit corporations.
[b] Excludes corporate equities.
[c] Less than $50 million.
Source: Board of Governors of the Federal Reserve System.

B43. Financial Assets and Liabilities of Households[a]

End of Selected Calendar Years 1970-1987

($Billions)

Category	1970	1980	1986	1987
Total financial assets	$2,480.7	$6,548.4	$10,715.3	$11,277.1
Deposits and credit market instruments[b]	790.9	2,130.4	3,740.2	4,028.9
Deposits	543.9	1,577.7	2,732.7	2,860.1
Demand deposits and currency	118.2	260.7	471.5	481.5
Small time and savings deposits	410.7	1,140.7	1,946.2	2,017.9
Large time deposits	15.0	111.5	66.2	83.1
Money market fund shares	-	64.9	248.7	277.6
Credit market instruments	247.0	552.6	1,007.5	1,168.9
U.S. Government securities	102.1	259.1	532.4	586.7
Treasury issues	84.2	218.9	463.7	507.6
Savings bonds	52.1	72.5	93.3	101.1
Other Treasury	32.1	146.4	370.4	406.5
Agency issues	17.9	40.2	68.6	79.1
Tax-exempt obligations	46.0	86.9	217.8	281.9
Corporate and foreign bonds	35.6	59.3	82.4	92.2
Mortgages	51.5	107.0	127.8	134.2
Open-market paper	11.8	40.3	47.1	73.8
Corporate equities	727.2	1,163.4	2,207.5	2,106.8
Mutual fund shares	44.5	52.1	356.8	409.1
Other corporate equities	682.7	1,111.3	1,850.6	1,697.8
Life insurance reserves	130.7	216.4	274.2	300.3
Pension fund reserves	240.8	916.1	2,057.7	2,261.8
Equity in noncorporate business	560.4	2,033.5	2,238.1	2,371.5
Security credit	4.4	16.2	44.0	37.2
Miscellaneous assets	26.3	72.4	153.6	170.6
Total liabilities	492.6	1,488.7	2,703.6	2,934.7
Credit market instruments	471.8	1,430.2	2,594.2	2,836.5
Home mortgages	290.0	942.4	1,669.9	1,878.1
Other mortgages	19.0	31.5	46.1	48.4
Installment consumer credit	105.5	302.1	581.3	623.6
Other consumer credit	28.5	53.3	74.9	73.3
Tax-exempt debt	-	16.7	79.1	78.2
Bank loans n.e.c.	7.7	29.5	54.4	47.4
Other loans	20.9	54.7	88.4	87.4
Security credit	10.4	28.5	65.0	49.7
Trade credit	5.3	17.2	30.5	33.4
Deferred and unpaid life insurance premiums	5.1	12.9	13.9	15.1

[a] Includes holdings by personal trusts and nonprofit organizations.
[b] Excludes corporate equities.
Source: Board of Governors of the Federal Reserve System.

B44. Savings and Investment of Corporate Business[a]

Selected Calendar Years 1960-1988

($Billions)

Item	1960	1970	1980	1986	1987	1988
Gross investment	$ 28.8	$ 58.5	$ 206.3	$ 294.5	$ 306.9	$ 333.2
Capital expenditures	37.8	79.3	243.7	333.9	361.7	395.8
Fixed investment	35.4	76.2	238.0	319.8	323.9	359.8
Plant and equipment	34.1	74.5	238.2	316.0	321.6	358.0
Home construction	-.3	.2	-1.4	2.5	1.2	.5
Multi-family residential	.6	1.5	1.1	1.3	1.0	1.4
Change in inventories[b]	2.5	2.8	.7	7.0	34.8	31.9
Mineral rights from U.S. Government	-	.3	5.0	7.2	2.9	4.1
Net financial investment	-9.0	-20.7	-37.4	-39.5	-54.8	-62.6
Net acquisition of financial assets[c]	3.9	18.7	108.4	122.8	75.6	40.9
Liquid assets	-4.8	.5	27.7	87.7	13.2	3.4
Demand deposits and currency	-.9	.9	4.8	19.0	-1.0	-1.6
Time deposits	1.5	1.7	6.5	12.2	4.1	4.5
Security repurchase agreements	-	-3.1	6.6	12.2	5.8	8.2
Foreign deposits	d	-.4	2.8	5.9	-2.8	-4.3
U.S. Government securities	-6.0	.2	5.6	19.5	3.6	-5.9
Tax-exempt obligations	.6	-.6	-.2	3.1	2.6	-1.0
Commercial paper	d	1.8	-2.3	8.6	1.7	2.4
Consumer credit	d	.6	.2	.1	2.6	2.7
Trade credit	4.5	8.5	48.2	3.2	49.2	16.5
Miscellaneous assets[e]	4.2	9.2	32.0	30.3	15.6	14.5
Net increase in liabilities	13.0	39.5	145.8	162.3	130.4	103.5
Net funds raised in markets	11.8	34.2	92.7	121.3	68.9	62.4
Net new equity issues	1.4	5.7	12.9	-80.8	-76.5	-130.5
Debt instruments	10.4	28.5	79.8	202.1	145.4	192.9
Tax-exempt debt[f]	-	-	10.9	-9.9	-.9	.1
Corporate bonds[g]	3.4	19.8	27.7	121.3	99.9	97.4
Mortgages	2.6	.9	1.7	28.4	16.0	13.2
Home mortgages	-.2	.1	-1.1	2.0	1.0	.4
Multi-family	.8	1.2	3.0	.5	.7	1.0
Commercial	2.1	-.5	-.2	26.0	14.3	11.8
Bank loans, n.e.c.	2.1	4.7	27.4	47.9	4.6	36.9
Foreign loans	-	-	-	11.1	1.2	18.2
Commercial paper	.5	1.8	4.0	-9.3	2.3	11.6
Acceptances	.1	.4	1.6	-.2	5.1	.1
Finance company loans	1.6	.6	3.8	11.3	17.0	16.0
U.S. Government loans	.1	.3	1.5	1.5	.1	-.5
Profit taxes payable	-2.2	-3.7	-1.7	2.5	1.4	-.7
Trade debt	3.1	7.5	39.6	3.1	18.0	-.3
Foreign direct investment in U.S.	.3	1.5	15.3	35.4	42.2	42.1

[a] Nonfarm and nonfinancial corporate business only.
[b] Includes inventory valuation adjustment.
[c] Total includes money market and mutual fund shares.
[d] Less than $50 million.
[e] Primarily foreign direct investment net of bond issues abroad.
[f] Industrial revenue bonds, issued by state and local governments to finance private investment.
[g] Excludes bond issues abroad.
Source: Board of Governors of the Federal Reserve System.

B45. Sources of Gross Savings

Calendar Years 1929-1989

($Billions)

Year	Total[a]	Private			Government Surplus or Deficit (-)			Gross Savings Rate[b]
		Total	Personal	Business	Total	Federal	State and Local	
1929	$ 15.9	$ 14.9	$ 2.6	$ 12.3	$ 1.0	$ 1.2	$ -.2	15.3
1930	11.3	11.6	1.9	9.7	-.3	.3	-.6	12.4
1931	4.7	7.6	1.4	6.2	-2.9	-2.1	-.8	6.2
1933	.6	1.9	-1.6	3.5	-1.4	-1.3	-.1	1.1
1935	6.3	8.3	1.5	6.8	-2.0	-2.6	.6	8.7
1937	11.8	11.5	2.9	8.6	.3	-.4	.7	12.9
1939	8.9	11.1	1.8	9.3	-2.2	-2.2	c	9.7
1940	13.6	14.3	3.0	11.3	-.7	-1.3	.6	13.5
1941	18.8	22.6	10.0	12.6	-3.8	-5.1	1.3	15.0
1942	10.9	42.3	27.0	15.3	-31.4	-33.1	1.8	6.9
1943	5.8	50.0	32.7	17.3	-44.2	-46.6	2.4	3.0
1944	3.0	54.9	36.5	18.4	-51.8	-54.5	2.7	1.4
1945	5.9	45.4	28.7	16.7	-39.5	-42.1	2.6	2.8
1946	35.7	30.3	13.6	16.7	5.4	3.5	1.9	16.8
1947	42.5	28.1	5.2	22.9	14.4	13.4	1.0	18.1
1948	50.8	42.4	11.1	31.3	8.4	8.3	.1	19.4
1949	36.5	39.9	7.4	32.5	-3.4	-2.6	-.7	14.0
1950	52.5	44.5	12.6	31.9	8.0	9.2	-1.2	18.2
1951	58.7	52.6	16.6	36.0	6.1	6.5	-.4	17.6
1952	52.3	56.1	17.4	38.7	-3.8	-3.7	c	14.9
1953	51.0	58.0	18.4	39.6	-7.0	-7.1	.1	13.7
1954	51.6	58.8	16.4	42.4	-7.1	-6.0	-1.1	13.9
1955	68.4	65.2	16.0	49.2	3.1	4.4	-1.3	16.9
1956	77.3	72.1	21.3	50.8	5.2	6.1	-.9	18.1
1957	77.1	76.1	22.7	53.4	.9	2.3	-1.4	17.1
1958	64.5	77.1	24.3	52.8	-12.6	-10.3	-2.4	14.1
1959	80.5	82.1	21.8	60.3	-1.6	-1.1	-.4	16.2
1960	84.2	81.1	20.8	60.3	3.1	3.0	.1	16.3
1961	82.6	86.8	24.9	61.9	-4.3	-3.9	-.4	15.5
1962	91.4	95.2	25.9	69.3	-3.8	-4.2	.5	15.9
1963	98.7	97.9	24.6	73.3	.7	.3	.5	16.3
1964	108.5	110.8	31.5	79.3	-2.3	-3.3	1.0	16.7
1965	123.5	123.0	34.3	88.7	.5	.5	c	17.5
1966	130.3	131.6	36.0	95.6	-1.3	-1.8	.5	16.9
1967	129.5	143.8	45.1	98.7	-14.2	-13.2	-1.1	15.9
1968	139.7	145.7	42.5	103.2	-6.0	-6.0	.1	15.6
1969	158.8	148.9	42.2	106.7	9.9	8.4	1.5	16.5
1970	154.7	164.5	57.7	106.8	-10.6	-12.4	1.8	15.2
1971	171.9	190.6	66.3	124.3	-19.5	-22.0	2.6	15.6
1972	200.7	203.4	61.4	142.0	-3.4	-16.8	13.5	16.5
1973	251.9	244.0	89.0	155.0	7.9	-5.6	13.5	18.5
1974	247.9	254.3	96.7	157.6	-4.3	-11.6	7.2	16.8
1975	238.7	303.6	104.6	199.0	-64.9	-69.4	4.5	14.9
1976	283.0	321.4	95.8	225.6	-38.4	-53.5	15.2	15.9
1977	335.4	354.5	90.7	263.8	-19.1	-46.0	26.9	16.9
1978	408.6	409.0	110.2	298.8	-.4	-29.3	28.9	18.2
1979	458.4	445.8	118.1	327.7	11.5	-16.1	27.6	18.3
1980	445.0	478.4	136.9	341.5	-34.5	-61.3	26.8	16.3
1981	522.0	550.5	159.4	391.1	-29.7	-63.8	34.1	17.1
1982	446.4	557.1	153.9	403.2	-110.8	-145.9	35.1	14.1
1983	463.6	592.2	130.6	461.6	-128.6	-176.0	47.5	13.6
1984	568.5	673.5	164.1	509.4	-105.0	-169.6	64.6	15.1
1985	533.5	665.3	125.4	539.9	-131.8	-196.9	65.1	13.3
1986	537.2	681.6	121.7	559.9	-144.4	-205.6	61.2	12.7
1987	560.4	665.3	104.2	561.1	-104.9	-157.8	52.9	12.4
1988	644.6	731.8	144.3	587.5	-87.2	-142.3	55.2	13.3
1989[d]	698.8	783.1	197.9	585.2	-84.3	-139.5	55.2	13.7

[a] Includes net capital grants received by the United States.
[b] Gross savings as a percent of gross national product.
[c] Less than $50 million.
[d] Seasonally adjusted annual rate QI 1989.
Source: Department of Commerce, Bureau of Economic Analysis; computations by Tax Foundation.

Section C
The Federal Government

- ■ Fiscal Operations in Summary
- ■ Outlays
- ■ Lending, Enterprise, and Trust Operations
- ■ Debt
- ■ Federal Civilian Employment

C1. Summary of Federal Fiscal Operations[a]

Fiscal Years 1940-1990[b]

($Millions)

Fiscal Year	Receipts	Outlays	Surplus or Deficit (-)	Gross Federal Debt Outstanding End of Year
1940	$ 6,548	$ 9,468	$ -2,920	$ 50,696
1941	8,712	13,653	-4,941	57,531
1942	14,634	35,137	-20,503	79,200
1943	24,001	78,555	-54,554	142,648
1944	43,747	91,304	-47,557	204,079
1945	45,159	92,712	-47,553	260,123
1946	39,296	55,232	-15,936	270,991
1947	38,514	34,496	4,018	257,149
1948	41,560	29,764	11,796	252,031
1949	39,415	38,835	580	252,610
1950	39,443	42,562	-3,119	256,853
1951	51,616	45,514	6,102	255,288
1952	66,167	67,686	-1,519	259,097
1953	69,608	76,101	-6,493	265,963
1954	69,701	70,855	-1,154	270,812
1955	65,451	68,444	-2,993	274,366
1956	74,587	70,640	3,947	272,763
1957	79,990	76,578	3,412	272,353
1958	79,636	82,405	-2,769	279,693
1959	79,249	92,098	-12,849	287,767
1960	92,492	92,191	301	290,862
1961	94,388	97,723	-3,335	292,895
1962	99,676	106,821	-7,146	303,291
1963	106,560	111,316	-4,756	310,807
1964	112,613	118,528	-5,915	316,763
1965	116,817	118,228	-1,411	323,154
1966	130,835	134,532	-3,698	329,474
1967	148,822	157,464	-8,643	341,348
1968	152,973	178,134	-25,161	369,769
1969	186,882	183,640	3,242	367,144
1970	192,812	195,649	-2,837	382,603
1971	187,139	210,172	-23,033	409,467
1972	207,309	230,681	-23,373	437,329
1973	230,799	245,707	-14,908	468,426
1974	263,224	269,359	-6,135	486,247
1975	279,090	332,332	-53,242	544,131
1976	298,060	371,779	-73,719	631,866
1977	355,559	409,203	-53,644	709,138
1978	399,740	458,729	-58,989	780,425
1979	463,302	503,464	-40,161	833,751
1980	517,112	590,920	-73,808	914,317
1981	599,272	678,209	-78,936	1,003,941
1982	617,766	745,706	-127,940	1,146,987
1983	600,562	808,327	-207,764	1,381,886
1984	666,457	851,781	-185,324	1,576,748
1985	734,057	946,316	-212,259	1,827,234
1986	769,091	989,815	-220,724	2,132,913
1987	854,143	1,004,586	-150,444	2,345,578
1988	908,954	1,064,044	-155,090	2,600,753
1989	975,534	1,137,030	-161,496	2,868,792
1990	1,059,339	1,151,848	-92,509	3,107,207

[a] Data include on-budget and off-budget transactions. For consistency, figures for all years are adjusted to include transactions that were legally off-budget in fiscal years 1971-1985, as well as transactions of the Federal Old-Age, Survivors, and Disability Insurance trust funds which were removed from the budget totals by legislation in 1985.

[b] Data for 1989 and 1990 are estimates.

Source: Office of Management and Budget and Treasury Department.

C2. Federal Receipts and Outlays by Fund Group[a]
Fiscal Years 1960-1990[b]
($Billions)

Fiscal Year	Federal Funds		Trust Funds		Interfund Transac-tions	Surplus or Deficit (-)	
	Receipts	Outlays	Receipts	Outlays		Federal Funds	Trust Funds
1960	$ 75.6	$ 74.9	$ 19.3	$ 19.7	$ -2.4	$ .8	$ -.5
1961	75.2	79.4	22.3	21.5	-3.1	-4.2	.9
1962	79.7	86.5	23.0	23.3	-3.0	-6.8	-.3
1963	84.0	90.6	25.8	23.9	-3.2	-6.6	1.9
1964	87.5	96.1	28.5	25.8	-3.4	-8.6	2.7
1965	90.9	94.9	29.2	26.7	-3.3	-3.9	2.5
1966	101.4	106.6	33.0	31.5	-3.6	-5.2	1.5
1967	111.8	127.5	42.2	35.1	-5.2	-15.7	7.1
1968	114.7	143.1	44.0	40.8	-5.8	-28.4	3.2
1969	143.3	148.2	51.1	43.0	-7.5	-4.9	8.1
1970	143.2	156.3	58.4	48.1	-8.8	-13.2	10.3
1971	133.8	163.7	64.9	58.1	-11.6	-29.9	6.9
1972	148.8	178.1	71.6	65.7	-13.2	-29.3	5.9
1973	161.4	187.0	90.8	80.0	-21.3	-25.7	10.8
1974	181.2	201.4	103.8	89.8	-21.8	-20.1	14.0
1975	187.5	248.2	117.6	110.2	-26.1	-60.7	7.4
1976	201.1	277.2	132.5	130.1	-35.5	-76.1	2.4
1977	241.3	304.5	151.5	142.0	-37.3	-63.1	9.5
1978	270.5	342.4	166.5	153.8	-37.4	-71.9	12.7
1979	316.4	374.9	188.1	169.7	-41.1	-58.5	18.3
1980	350.9	433.5	212.1	203.3	-45.9	-82.6	8.8
1981	410.4	496.2	240.6	233.8	-51.8	-85.8	6.8
1982	409.3	543.4	270.1	263.9	-61.6	-134.2	6.2
1983	382.3	613.2	318.6	296.7	-100.0	-230.8	21.9
1984	419.6	637.8	338.6	305.7	-91.3	-218.2	32.9
1985	459.5	725.9	397.9	343.7	-122.9	-266.4	54.2
1986	473.5	756.5	423.5	361.6	-127.7	-283.0	61.9
1987	537.8	760.2	444.2	371.7	-128.0	-222.4	72.5
1988	560.2	813.1	491.3	393.5	-142.5	252.9	97.8
1989	560.2	877.2	539.5	417.6	-157.7	-283.4	121.9
1990	593.8	884.6	586.0	437.5	-170.4	-241.0	148.5

[a] Data include on-budget and off-budget transactions. See footnote *a* to Table C1.
[b] Data for 1989 and 1990 are estimates from the *Budget* presented in January 1989.
Source: Office of Management and Budget, and Tax Foundation.

C3. Federal Receipts by Source, Outlays by Function, and Total Public Debt

Fiscal Years 1987-1990[a]

($Billions)

Source or Function	1987	1988	1989	1990
Receipts	$ 854.1	$ 909.0	$ 975.5	$ 1,059.3
Individual income taxes	392.6	401.2	425.2	466.7
Corporation income taxes	83.9	94.5	107.0	117.4
Employment taxes	303.3	334.3	363.9	391.5
Excise taxes	32.5	35.2	34.0	35.3
Estate and gift taxes	7.5	7.6	7.8	8.1
Customs	15.1	16.2	16.3	18.0
All other	19.3	19.9	21.4	22.4
Outlays	1,004.6	1,064.0	1,137.0	1,151.8
National defense[b]	282.0	290.4	298.3	303.0
International affairs	11.6	10.5	10.7	17.3
General science, space, and technology	9.2	10.8	12.6	14.9
Agriculture	27.4	17.2	20.9	15.9
Natural resources and environment	13.4	14.6	16.5	14.4
Energy	4.1	2.3	4.1	2.3
Commerce and housing credit	6.2	18.8	20.0	8.3
Transportation	26.2	27.3	28.0	28.3
Community and regional development	5.1	5.3	6.3	6.4
Education, training, employment and social services	29.7	31.9	36.4	39.5
Health	40.0	44.5	49.8	52.2
Medicare	75.1	78.9	86.7	94.9
Social security	207.4	219.3	232.3	246.7
Income security	123.2	129.3	136.9	136.8
Veterans' benefits	26.8	29.4	29.2	29.9
Net interest	138.6	151.7	165.7	170.1
General government	7.6	9.5	10.0	10.0
Administration of justice	7.5	9.2	9.4	10.6
Allowances[c]	-	-	-	-.3
Undistributed offsetting receipts	-36.5	-37.0	-36.9	-49.2
Budget surplus(+) or deficit (-)	-170.0	-193.9	-217.5	-161.3
Deficit (-) of off-budget entities[d]	19.6	38.8	56.0	68.8
Total surplus (+) or deficit (-)	-150.4	-155.1	-161.5	-92.5
Means of financing:				
Borrowing from the public	151.7	162.1	143.6	91.2
Reduction of cash and money assets, etc.	-1.3	-7.0	17.9	1.3
Gross debt outstanding at end of year[e]	2,355.3	2,600.8	2,868.8	3,107.2
Debt held by public[f]	1,897.8	2,050.2	2,193.8	2,285.0

[a] Data for 1989 and 1990 are estimates from the *Budget* presented in January 1989.
[b] Includes allowances for Department of Defense.
[c] Includes allowances for civilian agency pay raises and contingencies.
[d] Refers to the social security trust fund, which was moved off-budget.
[e] Includes public debt securities and agency securities.
[f] Change in debt held by public equals borrowing from the public.
Source: Treasury Department and Office of Management and Budget.

C4. Federal Receipts and Expenditures in the National Income Accounts[a]

Selected Calendar Years 1929-1988

($Billions)

Source and Function	1929	1949	1959	1969	1979	1988
Total receipts, national-income basis	$ 3.8	$ 39.4	$ 90.6	$ 199.7	$ 505.0	$ 975.2
Personal tax and nontax receipts	1.3	16.1	39.9	95.1	231.0	413.4
Corporate profits tax accruals	1.2	9.6	22.5	36.1	74.4	92.9
Indirect business tax and nontax accruals	1.2	8.0	12.5	18.9	29.3	56.7
Contributions for social insurance	.2	5.6	15.7	49.6	170.3	393.7
Total expenditures, national-income basis	2.7	42.0	91.7	191.3	521.1	1,117.6
Purchase of goods and services	1.5	21.1	54.6	100.0	178.0	381.0
Transfer payments	.7	13.9	22.0	53.0	210.9	440.1
To persons	.7	8.7	20.1	50.8	205.6	427.2
Foreign (net)	b	5.1	1.9	2.2	5.2	12.9
Grants-in-aid to state and local governments	.1	2.2	6.8	20.3	80.5	111.5
Net interest paid[c]	.3	4.3	6.2	12.7	42.5	153.9
Subsidies less current surplus of government enterprises	.1	.6	2.1	5.2	9.2	31.1
Surplus or deficit (-) on national income and products account	1.2	-2.6	-1.1	8.4	-16.1	-142.3
Social insurance funds	.1	2.1	.2	7.8	3.4	53.2
Other funds	1.1	-4.7	-1.3	.6	-19.5	-195.5

[a] See Introductory Notes for a description of the Federal sector in the national income accounts.
[b] Less than $50 million.
[c] Interest paid less interest received.
Source: Department of Commerce, Bureau of Economic Analysis.

C5. Federal Finances and Gross National Product

Fiscal Years 1970–1990[a]

Fiscal Year	Gross National Product ($Billions)	Percentage of GNP					
		Budget Receipts[b]	Total Receipts[c]	Budget Outlays[b]	Total Outlays[c]	Surplus or Deficit (-)[c]	Federal Debt[d]
1970	$ 990.2	16.1%	19.5%	17.0%	19.8%	-.3%	38.5%
1971	1,055.9	14.3	17.7	16.8	19.9	-2.2	38.7
1972	1,153.1	14.5	18.0	16.8	20.0	-2.0	37.8
1973	1,281.4	14.4	18.0	15.6	19.2	-1.2	36.4
1974	1,416.5	14.8	18.6	15.3	19.0	-.4	34.2
1975	1,522.5	14.2	18.3	17.9	21.8	-3.5	35.6
1976	1,698.2	13.6	17.6	17.8	21.9	-4.3	37.0
1977	1,933.0	14.4	18.4	17.0	21.2	-2.8	36.5
1978	2,171.8	14.5	18.4	17.0	21.1	-2.7	35.8
1979	2,447.8	14.9	18.9	16.5	20.6	-1.6	33.9
1980	2,670.6	15.1	19.4	17.8	22.1	-2.8	34.0
1981	2,986.4	15.7	20.1	18.2	22.7	-2.6	33.3
1982	3,139.1	15.1	19.7	18.9	23.8	-4.1	36.2
1983	3,321.9	13.6	18.1	19.9	24.3	-6.3	41.3
1984	3,687.7	13.6	18.1	18.6	23.1	-5.0	42.4
1985	3,952.4	13.9	18.6	19.5	23.9	-5.4	46.0
1986	4,186.8	13.6	18.4	19.3	23.7	-5.3	50.6
1987	4,433.8	14.5	19.3	18.3	22.6	-3.4	52.9
1988	4,780.0	14.0	19.0	18.0	22.3	-3.2	54.4
1989	5,119.7	13.8	19.1	18.1	22.2	-3.2	56.0
1990	5,475.7	14.1	19.3	17.0	21.0	-1.7	56.7

[a] Data for 1989 and 1990 are estimates from the *Budget* presented in January 1989.
[b] Budget receipts and outlays include formerly off-budget transactions, but exclude social security trust funds removed from the budget in 1985.
[c] Includes off-budget social security trust funds.
[d] End of year.
Source: Office of Management and Budget.

C6. The Federal Credit Budget

Fiscal Years 1986-1990[a]

($Millions)

Item	1986	1987	1988	1989	1990
New obligations and commitments, total	$ 591,595	$ 599,399	$ 505,952	$ 520,817	$ 546,076
New direct loan obligations	41,329	29,817	27,222	16,933	12,255
New guaranteed loan commitments	159,243	142,064	100,668	112,819	111,689
GSE lending obligations[b]	391,023	427,518	378,062	391,065	422,132
Net change in outstanding loans and loan guarantees, total	45,719	41,373	26,899	24,023	22,635
Net direct loans	11,155	-18,984	-13,359	-12,648	-9,866
Net loan guarantees	34,564	60,357	40,258	36,671	32,501

[a] Data for fiscal year 1989 and 1990 are estimates from the *Budget* presented in January 1989.
[b] Government Sponsored Enterprise (GSE).
Source: Office of Management and Budget.

C7. Federal Participation in Domestic Credit Markets

Fiscal Years 1980-1990[a]

(\$Billions)

Item	1980	1981	1982	1983	1984	1985	1986	1987	1988	1989	1990
Total funds loaned in U.S. credit markets[b]	$351.4	$405.4	$394.0	$509.8	$697.4	$748.8	$904.3	$727.9	$745.5	c	c
Federal and Federally assisted lending	79.9	86.5	87.6	86.5	79.5	110.3	129.1	149.2	109.4	$77.4	$87.4
Direct loans	24.2	26.1	23.4	15.3	6.3	28.0	11.2	-19.0	-13.4	-12.6	-9.9
Guaranteed loans	31.6	28.0	20.9	34.1	20.1	21.6	34.6	60.4	40.3	36.7	32.5
Government-sponsored enterprise loans	24.1	32.4	43.3	37.1	53.1	60.7	83.3	107.8	82.5	53.3	64.8
Federal lending participation rate (percent)	22.7	21.3	22.2	17.0	11.4	14.7	14.3	20.5	14.7	c	c
Total funds borrowed in U.S. credit markets[b]	351.4	405.4	394.0	509.8	697.4	748.8	904.3	727.9	745.5	c	c
Federal and Federally assisted borrowing	122.5	138.3	198.9	280.0	244.5	278.9	374.6	327.9	295.9	251.1	194.6
Federal borrowing from public	69.5	75.5	134.4	211.8	168.9	199.4	236.8	152.0	162.1	143.6	91.2
Borrowing for guaranteed loans	31.6	28.0	20.9	34.1	20.1	21.6	34.6	60.4	40.3	36.7	32.5
Government-sponsored enterprise borrowing	21.4	34.8	43.6	34.1	55.5	57.9	103.2	115.5	93.5	70.8	70.9
Federal borrowing participation rate (percent)	34.9	34.1	50.5	54.9	35.1	37.2	41.4	45.0	39.7	c	c

[a] Data for 1989 and 1990 are estimates from the *Budget* presented in January 1989.
[b] Nonfinancial sectors, excluding equities.
[c] Not estimated.
Source: Office of Management and Budget.

C8. Relation of Federal Receipts and Expenditures in the Unified Budget and National Income Accounts[a]

Selected Fiscal Years 1980–1988[b]

($Billions)

Item	1980	1985	1986	1987	1988
Receipts					
Federal receipts - unified budget	$ 520.1	$ 734.1	$ 769.1	$ 854.1	$ 909.0
Less: Adjustments for agency coverage and financial transactions	1.1	1.2	1.5	1.7	1.7
Plus: Netting differences[c]	25.2	46.9	46.3	49.3	59.2
Timing differences[d]	-5.7	-3.0	1.1	-.1	-6.1
Miscellaneous	.1	-	-	-	-
Equals: Federal receipts - national income accounts	538.6	776.8	815.0	901.7	909.0
Expenditures					
Federal outlays - unified budget	579.0	936.8	989.8	1,002.3	1,064.0
Less: Coverage differences[f]	-9.7	-3.4	3.8	4.1	5.1
Financial transactions[g]	22.6	24.0	9.5	1.0	-7.7
Plus: Netting differences[c]	25.2	46.9	46.3	49.3	59.2
Timing differences[h]	-2.4	-.9	5.1	12.5	2.6
Miscellaneous	.2	.1	-.2	-	e
Equals: Federal expenditures - national income accounts	589.0	962.3	1,027.8	1,058.9	1,128.3

[a] See Introductory Notes for definitions.
[b] Data for 1988 are estimates based on the *Budget* presented in January 1989.
[c] Largely for contributions to government employee retirement funds.
[d] Relates primarily to the corporate income tax, withheld personal income tax, Federal and state unemployment insurance taxes, social security contributions, and excise taxes.
[e] Less than $50 million.
[f] Relates primarily to Federal home loans and Federal land banks.
[g] Includes net lending and net purchases of foreign currency and net purchases of land.
[h] Relates to the increase in payables (net of advances) on purchases of goods and services, accrued interest less interest paid, transfer payments, and subsidies less current surplus of government enterprises.
Source: Department of Commerce, Bureau of Economic Analysis.

C9. Federal Outlays by Selected Function

Selected Fiscal Years 1789-1990[a]

($Millions)

Year	Total Outlays	National Defense	International Affairs and Finance	Veterans' Benefits and Services	Net Interest[b]	All Other[c]
1789-91	$ 4	$ 1	d	d	$ 2	$ 1
1800	11	6	d	d	3	1
1810	8	4	d	d	3	1
1820	18	7	d	d	5	6
1830	15	8	d	d	2	5
1840	24	13	d	d	e	11
1850	40	17	d	d	4	18
1860	63	28	d	d	3	32
1870	310	79	d	d	129	101
1880	268	52	d	d	96	120
1890	318	67	d	d	36	215
1900	521	191	d	$ 141	40	149
1910	694	284	d	161	21	228
1920	6,357	3,997	$ 435	332	1,024	569
1930	3,320	734	14	821	697	1,054
New Series[f]						
1940	9,468	1,660	51	570	899	6,288
1950	42,562	13,724	4,673	8,834	4,812	10,519
1951	45,514	23,566	3,647	5,526	4,665	8,110
1952	67,686	46,089	2,691	5,341	4,701	8,864
1953	76,101	52,802	2,119	4,519	5,156	11,505
1954	70,855	49,266	1,596	4,613	4,811	10,569
1955	68,444	42,729	2,223	4,675	4,850	13,967
1956	70,640	42,523	2,414	4,891	5,079	15,733
1957	76,578	45,430	3,147	5,005	5,354	17,642
1958	82,405	46,815	3,364	5,350	5,604	21,272
1959	92,098	49,015	3,144	5,443	5,762	28,734
1960	92,191	48,130	2,988	5,441	6,947	28,685
1961	97,723	49,601	3,184	5,705	6,716	32,517
1962	106,821	52,345	5,639	5,628	6,889	36,320
1963	111,316	53,400	5,308	5,521	7,740	39,347
1964	118,528	54,757	4,945	5,682	8,199	44,945
1965	118,228	50,620	5,273	5,723	8,591	48,021
1966	134,532	58,111	5,580	5,923	9,386	55,532
1967	157,464	71,417	5,566	6,901	10,268	63,312
1968	178,134	81,926	5,301	6,884	11,090	72,933
1969	183,640	82,497	4,600	7,642	12,669	76,202
1970	195,649	81,692	4,330	8,679	14,380	86,562
1971	210,172	78,872	4,159	9,778	14,841	102,522
1972	230,681	79,174	4,781	10,732	15,478	120,516
1973	245,707	76,681	4,149	12,015	17,349	135,513
1974	269,359	79,347	5,710	13,388	21,449	149,465
1975	332,332	86,509	7,097	16,599	23,244	198,883
1976	371,779	89,619	6,433	18,433	26,714	230,580
1977	409,203	97,241	6,353	18,038	29,886	257,635
1978	458,729	104,495	7,482	18,978	35,441	292,333
1979	503,464	116,342	7,459	19,931	42,615	317,117
1980	590,920	133,995	12,714	21,185	52,512	370,514
1981	678,209	157,513	13,104	22,991	68,734	415,867
1982	745,706	185,309	12,300	23,958	84,995	439,144
1983	808,327	209,903	11,848	24,846	89,774	471,956
1984	851,781	227,413	15,876	25,614	111,058	471,820
1985	946,316	252,748	16,176	26,291	129,430	521,671
1986	990,258	273,375	14,152	26,356	135,969	540,406
1987	1,003,830	281,999	11,649	26,782	138,570	544,830
1988	1,064,044	290,361	10,471	29,428	151,748	582,036
1989	1,137,030	298,255	10,748	29,218	165,704	633,105
1990	1,151,848	302,991	17,322	29,872	170,109	631,554

[a] Data for 1989 and 1990 are estimates from the *Budget* presented January 1989.
[b] Prior to new series, interest is on a gross basis, before deducting interest received by trust funds.
[c] After deduction of undistributed intragovernmental transactions in new series.
[d] Included in "All other."
[e] Less than $500,000.
[f] New series includes net lending and is based on new budget concepts adopted in 1969.
Source: Office of Management and Budget and Treasury Department.

C10. Federal Outlays by Type in Current and in Constant (1982) Dollars[a]

Fiscal Years 1969-1989[b]
(Dollar Figures in Billions)

Year	Total Outlays	National Defense	Total Non-Defense	Non-Defense Payments for Individuals	Net Interest	All Other	Percent Change in Total Outlays from Previous Year
1969	$183.6	$82.5	$101.1	$57.1	$12.7	$31.3	3.1%
1970	195.6	81.7	114.0	64.7	14.4	34.9	6.5
1971	210.2	78.9	131.3	80.4	14.8	36.1	7.5
1972	230.7	79.2	151.5	92.9	15.5	43.1	9.8
1973	245.7	76.7	169.0	104.5	17.3	47.2	6.5
1974	269.4	79.3	190.0	120.1	21.4	48.5	9.6
1975	332.3	86.5	245.8	153.5	23.2	69.1	23.3
1976	371.8	89.6	282.2	180.1	26.7	75.4	11.9
1977	409.2	97.2	312.0	196.3	29.9	85.8	10.1
1978	458.7	104.5	354.2	211.0	35.4	107.8	12.1
1979	503.5	116.3	387.1	232.9	42.6	111.6	9.8
1980	590.9	134.0	456.9	277.5	52.5	126.9	17.4
1981	678.2	157.5	520.7	323.4	68.7	128.6	14.8
1982	745.7	185.3	560.4	356.7	85.0	118.7	10.0
1983	808.3	209.9	598.4	395.3	89.8	113.3	8.4
1984	851.8	227.4	624.4	399.8	111.1	113.5	5.4
1985	946.3	252.7	693.6	425.6	129.4	138.6	11.1
1986	990.3	273.4	716.9	449.4	136.0	131.5	4.7
1987	1,003.8	282.0	721.8	469.4	138.6	113.8	1.4
1988	1,064.0	290.4	773.7	498.8	151.7	123.2	6.0
1989	1,137.0	298.3	838.8	534.5	165.7	138.6	6.9

Constant (Fiscal 1982) Dollars

Year	Total Outlays	National Defense	Total Non-Defense	Payments for Individuals	Net Interest	All Other	Percent Change
1969	510.4	243.4	267.0	140.6	32.4	94.0	c
1970	509.4	225.6	283.8	152.2	34.7	96.9	c
1971	509.4	202.7	306.7	181.0	34.0	91.7	c
1972	527.6	190.9	336.7	200.1	33.6	103.0	3.6
1973	527.5	175.1	352.4	215.7	35.9	100.8	c
1974	528.7	163.3	365.3	228.3	41.1	95.9	.2
1975	586.0	159.8	426.2	265.8	40.4	120.0	10.8
1976	609.8	153.6	456.2	291.7	43.0	121.5	4.1
1977	622.6	154.3	468.3	295.5	44.6	128.2	2.1
1978	652.2	155.0	497.1	296.8	49.4	150.9	4.8
1979	660.2	159.1	501.0	301.6	54.7	144.7	1.2
1980	699.1	164.0	535.1	324.7	62.0	148.4	5.9
1981	726.5	171.4	555.2	344.3	73.7	137.2	3.9
1982	745.7	185.3	560.4	356.7	85.0	118.7	2.6
1983	775.0	201.3	573.7	378.6	86.1	109.0	3.9
1984	788.1	211.3	576.8	368.7	102.6	105.5	1.7
1985	849.6	230.0	619.7	380.0	116.0	123.7	7.8
1986	867.5	243.7	623.8	390.6	118.7	114.5	2.1
1987	857.8	250.3	607.4	393.1	117.2	97.1	-1.1
1988	879.2	252.9	626.3	400.1	124.4	101.8	2.5
1989	902.4	250.0	652.4	412.3	130.7	109.4	2.6

[a] Data include on-budget and off-budget outlays.
[b] Data for 1989 are estimates from the *Budget* presented in January 1989.
[c] Less than .05 percent change.
Source: Office of Management and Budget, and Tax Foundation computations.

C11. Federal Outlays by Function[a]

Selected Fiscal Years 1960-1990[b]

($Billions)

Function	1960	1970	1980	1988	1989	1990
Total outlays	$ 92.2	$ 195.6	$ 590.9	$ 1,064.0	$ 1,137.0	$ 1,151.8
National defense	48.1	81.7	134.0	290.4	298.3	303.0
International affairs	3.0	4.3	12.7	10.5	10.7	17.3
General science, space, and technology	.6	4.5	5.8	10.8	12.6	14.9
Agriculture	2.6	5.2	8.8	17.2	20.9	15.9
Natural resources and environment	1.6	3.1	13.9	14.6	16.5	14.4
Energy	.5	1.0	10.2	2.3	4.1	2.3
Commerce and housing credit	1.6	2.1	9.4	18.8	20.0	8.3
Transportation	4.1	7.0	21.3	27.3	28.0	28.3
Community and regional development	.2	2.4	11.3	5.3	6.3	6.4
Education, training, employment, and social services	1.0	8.6	31.8	31.9	36.4	39.5
Health	.8	5.9	23.2	44.5	49.8	52.2
Social security	11.6	30.3	118.5	219.3	232.3	246.7
Medicare	-	6.2	32.1	78.9	86.7	94.9
Income security	7.4	15.6	86.5	129.3	136.9	136.8
Veterans' benefits and services	5.4	8.7	21.2	29.4	29.2	29.9
Net interest	6.9	14.4	52.5	151.7	165.7	170.1
Administration of justice	.4	1.0	4.6	9.2	9.4	10.6
General government	1.0	1.8	4.4	7.7	8.0	8.2
General purpose fiscal assistance	.2	.5	8.6	1.8	1.9	1.8
Special allowances[c]	-	-	-	-	-	-.4
Undistributed offsetting receipts	-4.8	-8.6	-19.9	-37.0	-36.9	-49.2

[a] Data include on-budget and off-budget outlays.
[b] Data for 1989 and 1990 are estimates from the *Budget* presented in January 1989.
[c] Pay increases and contingencies.
Source: Office of Management and Budget.

C12. Federal Outlays by Agency[a]

Selected Fiscal Years 1962-1990[b]

($Billions)

Department or Other Unit	1962	1970	1980	1986	1987	1988	1989	1990
Total outlays	$ 106.8	$ 195.6	$ 590.9	$ 989.8	$ 1,004.6	$ 1,064.0	$ 1,094.2	$ 1,148.3
Legislative branch	.2	.4	1.2	1.7	1.8	1.9	2.1	2.2
Judiciary	.1	.1	.6	1.1	1.2	1.3	1.7	1.7
Executive Office of the President	c	c	.1	.1	.1	.1	.1	.1
Funds appropriated to the President	3.2	2.8	9.1	11.4	10.4	7.3	8.7	7.9
Agriculture	6.4	8.4	34.8	58.7	50.4	44.0	48.3	48.2
Commerce	.2	.8	3.1	2.1	2.1	2.3	2.6	3.5
Defense								
Military	50.1	80.2	131.0	265.6	274.0	281.9	285.5	297.3
Civil	1.9	4.1	15.2	20.3	20.7	22.0	23.7	25.0
Education	.8	4.7	14.8	17.7	16.8	18.2	22.7	23.9
Health and Human Services	3.5	17.9	76.4	143.3	148.9	159.1	168.6	181.3
Social Security	14.4	29.8	117.9	190.7	202.4	214.5	228.2	243.1
Housing and Urban Development	.8	2.4	12.7	14.1	15.5	18.9	21.6	22.6
Interior	.6	1.1	4.5	4.8	5.1	5.1	5.0	2.8
Justice	.3	.6	2.6	3.8	4.3	5.4	5.8	6.2
Labor	4.1	5.1	29.7	24.1	23.5	21.9	23.1	23.7
State	.3	.4	1.9	2.9	2.8	3.4	3.4	3.5
Transportation	4.1	6.7	19.8	27.4	25.4	26.4	26.4	26.5
Treasury								
Interest and other	8.6	19.3	76.5	179.2	180.3	202.4	205.7	216.7
Energy	2.8	2.4	6.5	11.0	10.7	11.2	11.8	12.8
Environmental Protection Agency	.1	.4	5.6	4.9	4.9	4.9	5.1	5.4
General Service Administration	.4	.4	.2	.2	.5	-.3	-.5	.2
National Aeronautics and Space Administration	1.3	3.8	5.0	7.4	7.6	9.1	11.0	12.7
Office of Personnel Management	1.0	2.7	15.1	24.0	27.0	29.2	30.5	33.9
Small Busines Administration	.2	.3	2.0	.6	-.7	-.1	-.4	-.2
Veterans Administration	5.6	8.7	21.1	26.5	27.0	29.3	29.5	30.6
Other independent agencies	2.8	5.1	15.5	11.4	14.3	23.4	13.3	13.6
Undistributed allowances	-	-	-	-	-	-	-.5	.9
Undistributed intragovernmental transactions	-6.7	-12.6	-32.0	-65.0	-72.3	78.9	-89.7	-97.8

[a] Total outlays include on-budget and off-budget outlays.
[b] Data for 1989 and 1990 are estimates from the Mid-Session Review of the 1988 Budget, August 1987.
[c] Less than $50 million.
Source: Office of Management and Budget.

C13. Federal Outlays for National Defense, International, and Domestic Programs[a]

Selected Fiscal Years 1962-1990[b]

($Millions)

Program	1962	1970	1980	1988	1989	1990
Total outlays	$ 106,821	$ 195,649	$ 590,920	$ 1,064,044	$ 1,137,030	$ 1,151,848
National defense	52,345	81,692	133,995	290,361	298,255	302,991
Defense-military	50,124	80,221	130,976	281,935	289,800	293,820
Atomic energy defense activities	2,074	1,415	2,878	7,913	7,945	8,647
Defense-related activities	146	55	142	512	510	524
International affairs	5,639	4,330	12,714	10,471	10,748	17,322
Conduct of foreign affairs	249	398	1,366	2,729	2,822	3,117
Foreign economic and financial assistance	2,883	2,341	3,626	4,703	4,907	4,805
Foreign information and exchange activities	197	235	534	1,051	1,154	1,263
International financial programs	353	261	2,425	-2,513	-957	-291
International security assistance	1,958	1,094	4,763	4,500	2,823	8,428
Domestic-civilian	54,111	118,259	464,153	800,179	864,958	881,093
Direct outlays	46,185	94,194	372,702	684,885	741,395	757,111
Aid to state and local governments	7,926	24,065	91,451	115,294	123,563	123,622
Special allowances[c]	-	-	-	-	-	-360
Undistributed offsetting receipts	-5,274	-8,632	-19,942	-36,967	-36,931	-49,198

[a] Data include on-budget and off-budget outlays.
[b] Data for 1989 and 1990 are estimates from the *Budget* presented in January 1989.
[c] Includes allowances for civilian agency pay raises and contingencies.

Source: Office of Management and Budget.

C14. Federal Domestic-Civilian Outlays, Direct and Intergovernmental, by Function

Fiscal Years 1988-1990[a]

($Millions)

Function	1988 Direct Expenditures	1988 Aid to State and Local Governments[b]	1989 Direct Expenditures	1989 Aid to State and Local Governments[b]	1990 Direct Expenditures	1990 Aid to State and Local Governments[b]
Total domestic-civilian outlays[c]	**$ 663,208**	**$ 116,972**	**$ 734,101**	**$ 121,855**	**$ 762,246**	**$ 118,842**
General science, space and technology	10,841	-	12,593	-	14,863	-
Agriculture	15,049	2,161	19,190	1,713	14,521	1,371
Natural resources and environment	10,965	3,641	13,042	3,445	12,030	2,404
Energy	2,152	145	3,937	200	2,277	-
Commerce and housing credit	18,808	-	20,040	-	8,262	-
Transportation	8,380	18,892	8,902	19,125	11,121	17,166
Community and regional development	1,431	3,863	3,018	3,285	3,207	3,158
Education, training, employment, and social services	9,919	22,019	12,937	23,414	17,261	22,270
Health	11,448	33,042	12,778	36,983	13,668	38,509
Medicare	78,878	-	86,734	-	94,918	-
Social security	219,341	-	232,334	-	246,724	-
Income security	98,673	30,659	105,920	31,027	104,983	31,805
Veterans' benefits and services	29,309	119	29,081	137	29,726	146
Interest	151,748	-	165,704	-	170,109	-
General government	7,364	2,110	7,871	2,119	8,155	1,838
Administration of justice	8,902	321	9,020	408	10,421	177

[a] Data for 1989 and 1990 are estimates from the *Budget* presented in January 1989.
[b] Excludes aid to state and local governments classified under national defense of $204 million in 1988, $237 million in 1989, and $198 million in 1990.
[c] Before adjustment for undistributed offsetting receipts.
Source: Office of Management and Budget, and Tax Foundation computations.

C15. Federal Expenditures by State[a]

Fiscal Year 1988

State	Amount ($Millions)					Per Capita	
	Total[b]	Grants to State & Local Governments	Salaries and Wages	Direct Payments to Individuals	Procurement[c]	Amount	State Ranking
Total	$ 884,131	$ 114,610	$ 134,285	$ 409,229	$ 188,670	$ 3,545	-
Alabama	14,354	1,721	2,665	7,182	2,428	3,478	20
Alaska	2,664	593	1,031	450	561	5,193	3
Arizona	12,248	1,177	1,763	6,019	3,034	3,534	19
Arkansas	7,485	1,011	822	4,406	835	3,090	37
California	102,366	11,676	16,380	41,941	29,457	3,634	16
Colorado	12,973	1,241	2,522	4,681	3,831	3,943	11
Connecticut	13,770	1,542	1,142	5,215	5,250	4,249	8
Delaware	2,088	319	336	1,066	318	3,163	33
Florida	42,997	3,419	5,662	26,800	6,590	3,474	21
Georgia	18,451	2,964	4,175	8,866	1,944	2,882	42
Hawaii	4,957	477	2,078	1,715	591	4,535	5
Idaho	3,407	477	440	1,495	669	3,410	24
Illinois	31,962	4,670	4,271	18,181	2,606	2,769	46
Indiana	14,807	1,960	1,606	8,583	1,681	2,656	49
Iowa	9,697	1,199	666	4,827	699	3,422	23
Kansas	8,995	880	1,553	4,251	1,111	3,617	17
Kentucky	10,686	1,766	1,861	6,142	629	2,872	43
Louisiana	12,682	2,135	1,585	6,479	2,036	2,869	44
Maine	4,025	665	496	2,114	690	3,338	27
Maryland	23,745	2,004	5,403	8,265	6,309	5,113	4
Massachusetts	25,079	3,328	2,383	10,456	7,862	4,272	7
Michigan	23,651	4,243	2,167	14,835	1,598	2,543	50
Minnesota	13,840	2,120	1,163	6,168	2,306	3,214	31
Mississippi	9,895	1,324	1,208	4,465	2,586	3,767	12
Missouri	21,559	1,942	2,622	9,015	6,553	4,195	9
Montana	2,929	546	445	1,368	149	3,643	15
Nebraska	5,935	712	832	2,679	392	3,707	14
Nevada	3,429	336	517	1,658	880	3,235	30
New Hampshire	3,198	398	612	1,601	516	2,916	41
New Jersey	23,984	3,328	3,148	13,174	3,972	3,107	36
New Mexico	8,685	831	1,202	2,369	4,124	5,752	2
New York	60,677	12,494	5,952	31,110	9,243	3,390	26
North Carolina	17,743	2,299	3,691	9,504	1,690	2,719	47
North Dakota	2,881	462	464	1,071	166	4,345	6
Ohio	33,521	4,693	3,484	17,968	6,442	3,083	38
Oklahoma	10,762	1,406	2,232	5,640	870	3,298	28
Oregon	8,237	1,322	1,001	4,878	749	3,005	39
Pennsylvania	39,569	5,793	4,752	23,469	4,526	3,290	29
Rhode Island	3,567	644	503	1,848	489	3,585	18
South Carolina	10,934	1,354	2,322	5,139	1,932	3,130	34
South Dakota	2,691	443	428	1,195	128	3,764	13
Tennessee	15,705	2,225	2,356	7,855	2,927	3,193	32
Texas	49,485	5,168	8,600	23,118	10,564	2,949	40
Utah	5,750	725	1,267	2,063	1,546	3,400	25
Vermont	1,550	324	181	843	154	2,788	45
Virginia	35,698	1,961	9,841	10,597	12,288	5,954	1
Washington	18,306	2,170	3,427	7,669	4,204	3,963	10
West Virginia	5,861	1,056	530	3,838	372	3,111	35
Wisconsin	13,127	2,228	1,049	7,794	1,192	2,702	48
Wyoming	1,626	448	281	640	199	3,453	22
District of Columbia	15,257	1,615	8,223	1,693	2,759	24,608	-
Territories[d]	7,278	2,717	909	3,074	513	-	-
Undistributed	27,361	2,058	35	1,759	23,509	-	-

[a] Because of accounting and timing differences, amounts in this table cannot be directly compared to outlays in the Federal Budget. Also, not included are amounts that could not be geographically allocated, such as net interest on the Federal debt, international aid, and others, as well as some amounts for which data were not available.

[b] Totals include expenditures on other programs not shown separately. For the entire United States and territories, this amounted to $37,336 million.

[c] Represents contract awards, not expenditures.

[d] Includes distributions to American Samoa, Guam, Northern Marianas, Puerto Rico, and the Virgin Islands.

Source: Department of Commerce, Bureau of the Census.

C16. Federal Aid to State and Local Governments by Form of Aid and Function

Fiscal Years 1988-1990[a]

($Millions)

Form of Aid and Function	1988	1989	1990
Total aid to state and local governments[b]	$ 112,661	$ 122,669	$ 123,478
Grants-in-aid, Federal funds accounts	97,113	105,168	104,977
Veterans' benefits and services	106	128	145
Health	32,586	36,615	38,369
Education, employment, training, and social services	18,932	21,400	21,291
Agriculture	2,069	1,715	1,467
Natural resources and environment	3,540	3,409	3,164
Commerce and housing credit	1	-	-
Transportation	2,669	2,733	2,319
Community and regional development	4,267	4,316	4,271
Income security	30,010	31,734	31,044
General government	1,950	2,090	1,883
Administration of justice	338	359	433
National defense	188	232	195
Energy	457	437	396
Grants-in-aid, trust funds	18,181	18,395	18,645
Airport and airways trust fund	825	1,123	1,256
Highway trust funds	14,558	14,302	14,294
Unemployment trust fund[c]	2,559	2,613	2,690
Hazardous substance response fund	85	166	240
Other trust fund aid[d]	154	191	165
Loans and repayable advances (net of collections)[e]	-2,633	-894	-144
Natural resources, environment, and energy	-447	67	43
Agriculture, commerce and housing credit	12	12	10
Transportation	-22	-19	-
Community and regional development	-1,519	-578	279
Education, training, employment, and social services	-371	-42	-118
Health	-1	-	-
Income security[f]	-255	-300	-325
General purpose fiscal assistance[g]	-30	-34	-33

[a] Data for 1989 and 1990 are estimates from the *Budget* presented in January 1989.
[b] Includes net direct Federal loans (either expenditure account or loan account) to state and local governments for purposes similar to those for which grants are made.
[c] Includes administrative expenses.
[d] Includes funds for sport fish restoration and boat safety.
[e] Not included in grants-in-aid and shared revenue categories.
[f] Represents net loans for low-rent public housing under the Department of Housing and Urban Development.
[g] Refers to repayable advances made to the District of Columbia.
Source: Office of Management and Budget, and Tax Foundation computations.

C17. Federal Aid to State and Local Governments by State[a]

Selected Fiscal Years 1949-1988

($Millions)

State	1949	1959	1970	1980	1988	1988 Total Less Federal Aid for Highways
Total	$ 1,848.5	$ 6,343.0	$ 24,194.1	$ 91,365.2	$ 114,610.3	$ 100,791.5
Alabama	35.5	131.5	523.5	1,583.5	1,721.4	1,427.2
Alaska	-	36.5	115.9	451.2	592.8	479.0
Arizona	15.4	70.1	237.2	837.9	1,176.7	964.8
Arkansas	27.6	90.7	274.8	940.4	1,011.0	910.1
California	145.5	552.7	2,998.3	8,804.4	11,676.2	10,772.2
Colorado	33.4	99.4	282.3	995.2	1,240.9	1,015.5
Connecticut	15.3	63.8	295.5	1,156.8	1,542.1	1,283.9
Delaware	3.7	14.4	51.1	275.4	318.5	257.6
Florida	41.8	142.9	509.4	2,854.4	3,418.5	2,942.8
Georgia	45.9	154.3	553.8	2,373.4	2,964.1	2,519.5
Hawaii	-	-	123.6	463.3	477.2	415.6
Idaho	10.7	43.6	95.3	393.1	477.0	372.0
Illinois	92.6	272.3	950.8	4,477.0	4,670.3	4,152.8
Indiana	34.1	97.2	352.2	1,608.5	1,960.0	1,717.4
Iowa	33.9	110.1	244.3	994.7	1,199.5	1,000.0
Kansas	29.1	100.3	231.7	818.5	880.5	713.3
Kentucky	31.3	124.3	456.6	1,471.2	1,766.3	1,578.1
Louisiana	60.9	198.0	527.0	1,567.6	2,135.2	1,866.0
Maine	11.2	41.2	112.5	522.5	664.8	598.9
Maryland	17.8	85.1	395.0	1,843.2	2,004.2	1,666.4
Massachusetts	57.2	157.0	715.8	2,886.7	3,327.7	3,065.2
Michigan	74.9	201.4	768.8	3,928.5	4,242.9	3,917.7
Minnesota	41.6	127.7	407.4	1,667.3	2,119.6	1,866.4
Mississippi	29.7	108.6	413.0	1,191.0	1,324.4	1,192.8
Missouri	66.5	205.5	502.0	1,702.9	1,941.5	1,702.5
Montana	14.9	49.0	135.5	486.4	546.3	445.0
Nebraska	18.8	49.5	129.8	546.5	712.1	600.8
Nevada	7.5	26.7	76.8	335.5	336.0	282.1
New Hampshire	6.9	24.9	72.2	345.9	398.0	337.3
New Jersey	33.2	100.0	619.7	2,833.1	3,327.5	3,098.5
New Mexico	15.0	78.5	218.8	668.5	830.9	734.6
New York	116.2	451.2	2,365.6	9,569.6	12,494.2	11,820.7
North Carolina	38.7	140.5	507.1	1,929.2	2,298.9	2,075.0
North Dakota	12.6	43.0	87.7	347.2	462.0	377.2
Ohio	75.5	318.2	888.5	3,433.7	4,693.5	4,310.6
Oklahoma	60.0	177.0	403.8	1,061.5	1,405.8	1,207.8
Oregon	25.9	93.7	298.0	1,237.3	1,322.4	1,174.4
Pennsylvania	94.3	319.6	1,343.2	4,515.6	5,792.9	5,107.4
Rhode Island	9.0	30.9	132.7	477.4	643.5	544.5
South Carolina	25.9	79.3	278.1	1,067.7	1,353.9	1,173.8
South Dakota	13.7	35.6	103.7	443.3	443.2	365.2
Tennessee	44.6	137.8	487.0	1,695.7	2,225.4	1,955.3
Texas	117.2	353.7	1,153.4	3,964.4	5,167.8	4,492.3
Utah	12.9	50.2	173.8	571.7	725.2	607.5
Vermont	6.1	18.3	77.1	355.6	323.8	278.4
Virginia	21.3	108.9	465.7	1,775.5	1,960.9	1,633.7
Washington	44.1	138.9	400.5	1,674.1	2,170.4	1,798.3
West Virginia	19.1	77.7	303.7	950.4	1,056.2	871.9
Wisconsin	39.2	104.8	368.7	2,024.5	2,227.8	2,064.1
Wyoming	12.2	49.2	83.5	294.4	447.6	386.5
District of Columbia	7.9	56.6	405.1	1,336.4	1,615.1	1,547.4
Puerto Rico	8.1	59.2	325.4	1,430.5	2,389.8	2,346.3
Virgin Islands	1.2	4.9	27.1	295.8	120.8	116.3
Other territories	-13.0	7.1	66.5	215.2	206.6	203.8
Adjustments	-	23.1	57.5	-324.9	2,058.3	436.8

[a] Includes Federal grants-in-aid and shared revenues. Direct loans included in 1970.
Source: Treasury Department and Department of Commerce, Bureau of the Census.

C18. Controllability of Federal Outlays
Selected Fiscal Years 1987-1990[a]
($Billions)

Item	1987	1988	1989	1990
Total outlays[b]	$ 1,003.8	$ 1,064.0	$ 1,137.0	$ 1,151.8
Relatively uncontrollable under present law, total	769.3	807.4	865.1	902.9
Open-ended programs and fixed costs, total	584.0	620.6	668.2	690.9
Payments for individuals	421.7	448.0	481.5	516.5
Social security and railroad retirement	208.6	220.3	233.7	248.1
Federal employees' retirement and insurance	55.2	59.3	60.9	65.7
Unemployment assistance	15.7	13.8	14.3	14.8
Medical assistance	105.9	114.7	128.7	145.1
Assistance to students	3.7	3.9	4.2	4.0
Food and nutrition assistance	4.1	4.3	4.7	5.0
Public assistance and related programs	25.7	28.8	31.2	30.8
Other	2.9	2.9	3.7	3.0
Net interest	138.6	151.7	165.7	169.9
General revenue-sharing	.1	c	c	-
Farm price supports (CCC)	22.4	12.2	13.9	11.8
Other	1.3	8.7	7.1	-7.3
Outlays from prior-year contracts and obligations, total	185.3	186.8	196.9	212.0
National defense	112.7	115.3	116.3	113.2
Civilian programs	72.5	71.5	80.5	98.8
Relatively controllable outlays, total	265.1	290.1	306.3	282.3
National defense	169.1	174.8	181.9	189.7
Civilian programs	96.0	115.3	124.4	92.6
Undistributed employer share, employee retirement	-30.1	-33.3	-34.3	-33.4

Memorandum: Percent of Total Outlays

	1987	1988	1989	1990
Total budget outlays	100.0%	100.0%	100.0%	100.0%
Relatively uncontrollable under present law	76.6	75.9	76.1	78.4
Open-ended programs and fixed costs	58.2	58.3	58.8	60.0
Payments for individuals	42.0	42.1	42.3	44.8
Other	16.2	16.2	16.4	15.1
Outlays from prior-year contracts and obligations	18.5	17.6	17.3	18.4
Relatively controllable outlays	26.4	27.3	26.9	24.5
Undistributed employer share, employee retirement	-3.0	-3.1	-3.0	-2.9

[a] Data for 1989 and 1990 are estimates from the *Budget* presented in January 1989.
[b] Data include on-budget and off-budget outlays.
[c] $50 million or less.
Source: Office of Management and Budget.

C19. Outlays for the Legislative Branch of the Federal Government by Unit

Selected Fiscal Years 1970-1989[a]

(\$Thousands)

Unit	1970	1980	1988	1989
Total	\$ 343,147	\$ 1,217,985	\$ 1,851,958	\$ 2,233,439
Congress, total	179,159	581,543	993,367	1,049,816
Senate	57,585	183,890	335,235	356,570
House of Representatives	108,279	324,569	566,542	565,423
Joint activities	13,295	73,084	91,590	127,823
Legislative agencies, total	163,988	636,442	858,591	1,183,623
Architect of the Capitol	18,797	89,496	118,821	167,361
Botanic Garden	620	1,583	2,091	2,613
Congressional Budget Office	-	12,101	17,199	18,382
General Accounting Office	69,857	201,192	326,316	338,477
Government Printing Office	34,141	115,747	78,207	121,613
Library of Congress	49,804	192,740	283,235	492,235
Office of Technology Assessment	-	11,131	16,905	17,638
U.S. Tax Court	2,972	9,703	24,342	29,356
Other	-	13,675	1,973	7,040
Deductions for offsetting receipts	-12,203	-10,926	-10,498	-11,092

[a] Data for 1989 are estimates from the *FY 1990 Budget* presented in January 1989.
Source: Office of Management and Budget.

C20. Federal Direct Expenditures by Character and Payments to Other Governments

Selected Fiscal Years 1902-1987

($Millions)

Year	Total	Direct						Payments to Other Governments
		Total Direct[a]	Current Operation	Capital Outlay	Assistance and Subsidies	Interest	Insurance Trust[b]	
1902	$572	$565	$498	$38	-	$29	-	$7
1913	970	958	816	119	-	23	-	12
1922	3,763	3,645	2,487	161	-	988	$9	118
1927	3,533	3,410	2,442	174	-	764	30	123
1932	4,266	4,034	3,083	318	-	582	51	232
1936	9,165	8,257	6,312	1,162	-	717	66	908
1940	10,061	9,177	6,686	1,311	-	899	281	884
1942	35,549	34,662	26,276	6,991	-	1,026	369	887
1944	100,520	99,448	92,254	4,555	-	2,151	488	1,072
1946	66,534	65,640	59,123	1,566	-	3,865	1,086	894
1948	35,592	33,821	26,790	1,291	-	4,323	1,417	1,771
1950	44,800	42,429	31,839	1,671	-	4,404	4,515	2,371
1952	71,568	68,984	37,579[c]	17,437[c]	$5,916	4,262	3,790	2,585
1954	77,692	74,725	40,986	18,244	5,637	4,796	5,061	2,967
1956	75,991	72,644	38,582	14,956	6,595	5,311	7,200	3,347
1958	86,054	81,219	40,775	16,852	7,119	6,116	10,356	4,835
1960	97,284	90,289	45,336	16,842	6,884	7,662	13,565	6,994
1962	113,428	105,693	55,410	18,429	7,952	7,162	16,740	7,735
1964	125,949	115,852	61,809	17,818	8,865	8,293	19,067	10,097
1966	143,022	129,907	70,276	17,652	9,048	9,589	23,342	13,115
1968	184,464	166,411	90,204	21,326	10,801	11,607	32,474	18,053
1970	208,190	184,933	99,105	17,869	12,674	14,037	41,248	23,257
1972	242,186	208,602	100,130	20,816	16,456	17,114	54,086	33,584
1974	295,488	252,634	115,019	19,166	21,924	22,450	74,075	42,854
1976	391,085	322,028	130,944	25,100	35,245	29,306	101,433	69,057
1978	479,297	400,125	152,946	36,289	40,263	39,330	131,297	79,172
1980	617,166	526,330	209,199	36,492	48,776	61,286	170,576	90,836
1981	719,249	624,640	241,196	48,903	51,692	80,510	202,339	94,609
1982	796,483	710,469	265,891	62,835	51,817	101,816	228,110	86,014
1983	874,264	781,578	286,634	80,744	55,371	108,735	250,094	92,686
1984	928,188	829,173	324,919	72,456	58,447	109,209	264,142	99,015
1985	1,032,131	924,889	360,281	77,014	62,680	140,281	284,633	107,242
1986	1,096,401	980,769	386,388	85,647	64,375	144,167	300,192	115,632
1987	1,148,584	1,037,141	412,126	96,871	65,537	146,155	316,454	111,441

a Amounts for capital outlay other than construction (equipment and land and existing structures) and for assistance and subsidies included in current operation for fiscal years 1902 through 1950. Capital outlay expenditures for these years include construction only.

b Includes withdrawals of retirement contributions and employee retirement benefits; Old-Age, Survivors, Disability and Health Insurance; Veterans' Life Insurance; and Railroad Retirement benefits.

c Capital outlay expenditures for land and existing structures included in current operation for fiscal year 1952.

Source: Department of Commerce, Bureau of the Census.

C21. Postal Receipts and Expenditures

Selected Fiscal Years 1939-1989[a]

($Millions)

Fiscal Year	Postal Revenues[b]	Postal Expenditures[c]	Surplus or Deficit (-)
1939	$ 746	$ 785	$ -39
1940	767	808	-41
1950	1,677	2,223	-545
1951	1,777	2,341	-565
1952	1,947	2,667	-720
1953	2,092	2,742	-650
1954	2,263	2,575	-312
1955	2,337	2,693	-356
1956	2,419	2,882	-463
1957	2,548	3,065	-518
1958	2,583	3,257	-674
1959	3,061	3,835	-774
1960	3,334	3,822	-488
1961	3,483	4,348	-865
1962	3,609	4,343	-734
1963	3,870	4,640	-770
1964	4,394	4,971	-578
1965	4,663	5,467	-805
1966	5,039	5,927	-888
1967	5,326	6,468	-1,141
1968	5,714	6,794	-1,080
1969	6,353	7,273	-920
1970	6,570	8,080	-1,510
1971	6,907	9,090	-2,183
1972	9,489	9,843	-355
1973	9,934	10,091	-157
1974	12,071	12,344	-273
1975	12,551	13,664	-1,112
1976	12,937	14,113	-1,176
1977	14,842	15,530	-688
1978	16,388	15,923	465
1979	18,341	17,465	876
1980	19,612	19,182	430
1981	21,223	21,468	-246
1982	23,856	23,127	729
1983	24,790	24,173	617
1984	26,557	26,440	117
1985	29,016	29,267	-251
1986	31,135	30,830	305
1987	32,505	32,729	-224
1988	35,938	36,536	-598
1989	39,176	38,614	562

[a] Data for 1989 are estimates from the 1990 *Budget* of the U.S. Government.
[b] Excludes advances from Treasury to cover postal deficiencies.
[c] Beginning 1954, excludes extraordinary expenditures (e.g., estimated amounts of postage that would have been collected on certain free or reduced-rate mailings).
Source: Treasury Department and Office of Management and Budget.

C22. Commodity Credit Corporation Net Realized Losses or Costs of Price-Support and Related Programs[a]

October 17, 1933 — September 30, 1987

($Millions)

	Realized Losses and Costs[b]	
Commodity or Item	October 17, 1933 - September 30, 1987	Fiscal Year 1987
Total	$ 166,010.5	$ 26,133.8
Commodity operations	139,468.7	22,146.7
Feed grains	59,591.4	11,471.8
Corn (and products)	48,689.6	10,053.0
Grain sorghum	7,798.9	925.2
Barley	2,592.7	484.4
Oats and rye (and products)	510.2	9.2
Wheat (and products)	29,994.4	4,206.6
Rice (and products)	5,099.9	1,277.9
Tobacco	662.5	251.6
Cotton	20,057.5	1,836.0
Dairy	19,999.2	2,648.9
Butter	5,533.9	405.6
Cheese	6,767.9	946.7
Milk and whey	855.9	847.8
Dairy product stabilization, milk marketing fees collected, and other	168.3	448.8
Oil and oilseeds[c]	2,040.0	161.6
Beans, dry edible	132.9	.1
Other commodities	1,891.0	292.3
Other costs and losses		
Storage facilities	15.1	.1
Research expenses[d]	43.6	-
Emergency feed program	693.1	85.8
Crop insurance indemnity payments	250.0	-
Accounts and notes receivable	78.7	15.4
Other assets charged off	498.8	450.0
Offshore procurement premiums	79.0	-
Strategic and other materials	9.2	-
Ocean transportation on commodities donated through voluntary agencies	88.6	38.9
Eradication of animal and plant diseases	103.2	-
Export market promotion program	94.1	68.0
Guarantee fees collected	(133.8)	(20.9)
Agricultural Trade and Export Policy Commission	1.3	.3
Export enhancement program	652.7	643.0
Ethanol plant assistance program	54.3	29.1
Conservation reserve program	1,473.5	1,362.8
Other[e]	156.5	156.5
Interest, net	15,647.4	562.2
Operating expenses, net	4,642.0	595.5
Net income (expense), general	20,289.4	1,157.7
Wartime consumer subsidy program	2,102.3	-

[a] After deduction of realized gains. Includes price-support and commodity export programs, supply and foreign purchase, emergency feed program, and special milk program for children. Excludes cost of programs operated under specific statutory authority for separate reimbursement.

[b] Totals are net, including gains (negative figures) in some commodities or items.

[c] Chiefly peanuts, soybeans and products.

[d] Includes $28.8 million for cotton research and promotion.

[e] 1986 Disaster Program payments.

Source: Department of Agriculture, Commodity Credit Corporation.

C23. Major U.S. Government Foreign Assistance by Program
Selected Periods 1946-1987[a]
($Millions)

Program	Total 1946-1985	1984	1985	1986	1987
Total, net	$ 275,780	$ 13,986	$ 14,321	$ 14,983	$ 9,184
Investment in international financial institutions[b]	14,441	1,427	1,302	1,481	1,212
Assistance programs, net	261,338	12,558	13,019	13,502	7,972
New grants, net[c]	191,203	8,839	11,387	11,982	10,327
Gross new grants	193,580	8,845	11,390	12,037	10,332
Military aid[d]	87,912	2,467	3,286	4,346	3,310
Economic and technical aid[e]	105,668	6,378	8,104	7,691	7,022
Less: Reverse grants and returns	2,378	6	3	55	5
New credits, net[c]	68,370	3,713	1,623	1,516	-2,339
Gross new credits	137,006	7,777	5,913	7,165	4,832
Export-Import Bank[f]	47,099	2,493	1,794	1,253	990
Foreign Assistance Act	55,492	3,945	2,759	2,932	2,516
Country program loans	26,582	753	671	595	334
Financing military sales	27,633	3,185	2,090	2,307	2,169
Social progress trust fund	855	-4	-16	-5	-9
Other	425	11	13	35	22
Agricultural Trade Development and Assistance Act[g]	19,190	909	1,055	991	825
Commodity Credit Corporation Charter Act[h]	7,992	428	300	1,989	500
Other	7,232	2	6	-	-
Less: Principal collections	68,636	4,064	4,290	5,649	7,171
Other assistance programs[i]	1,766	7	9	4	-15

[a] Data for 1987 are preliminary.
[b] The Inter-American Development Bank, Asian Development Bank, International Bank for Reconstruction and Development, International Development Association, International Finance Corporation, African DevelopmenFund, and African Development Bank.
[c] New grants are largely outright gifts. New credits are loans or other agreements which give rise to specific obligations to repay, over a period of years, usually with interest.
[d] Includes military supplies and services, multilateral construction program contributions, lend-lease, Chinese and Japanese military aid under the Foreign Assistance Act; and other military aid.
[e] Includes surplus agricultural commodities, civilian supplies, Inter-American and other special country programs, the Peace Corps, and other technical and economic aid.
[f] Direct loans less reimbursements by private participants.
[g] Public Law 83-480.
[h] Public Law 80-806.
[i] Through net accumulation of foreign currency claims and including aid under the Mutual Security Acts, Commodity Credit Corporation Charter Act, Agricultural Trade Development and Assistance Act, and triangular trade operations.
Source: Department of Commerce, Bureau of Economic Analysis.

C24. Net U.S. Foreign Grants and Credits by Region and Country[a]

Selected Periods 1946 - 1987[b]

($Millions)

Region and Country	Total 1946 - 1985	Calendar Years			
		1984	1985	1986	1987
Total (net)	$ 275,780	$ 13,986	$ 14,321	$ 14,983	$ 9,184
Under assistance programs[c]	261,338	12,558	13,019	13,502	7,972
Western Europe	42,449	253	-202	-8	-167
Austria	1,209	3	10	-9	-9
Belgium and Luxembourg	1,846	-17	-15	-9	-9
France	8,175	-17	-47	-26	-13
Germany	3,657	-6	-2	-	-3
Italy	5,504	-12	-84	-107	-21
Netherlands	1,974	-14	-9	-1	-1
Portugal	1,526	129	101	178	9
Spain	3,033	222	-85	66	-11
United Kingdom	6,053	-134	-121	-202	-347
Yugoslavia	2,765	17	18	-21	-41
Other and unspecified	4,265	116	102	200	290
Eastern Europe	2,579	5	15	1,249	-150
Poland	1,846	67	45	1,348	-33
Near East and South Asia	89,755	6,458	7,437	7,924	6,221
Bangladesh	2,371	265	175	178	140
Egypt	14,920	1,926	2,231	2,727	1,608
Greece	4,574	-14	-21	72	304
India	10,086	84	42	36	48
Iran	1,415	-	-	-	-
Israel	30,049	3,094	3,807	4,030	3,111
Pakistan	7,300	415	481	347	226
Turkey	10,778	442	479	298	450
Other and unspecified	1,419	22	-3	27	33
Africa	17,102	1,803	2,004	1,299	1,052
Far East and Pacific	70,290	658	220	-64	-2,666
China (Taiwan)	6,119	-144	-255	-262	-970
Indonesia	3,746	224	37	13	-13
Japan	4,030	-99	-87	-88	-319
Korea, Republic of	15,108	208	58	-146	-1,717
Philippines	3,777	141	334	449	281
Thailand	2,648	110	68	62	-77
Other and unspecified	3,737	31	26	27	18
Western Hemisphere	23,104	2,077	2,142	1,825	2,016
Other international organizations and unspecified areas	16,061	1,304	1,404	1,278	1,665
Investment in international agencies	14,441	1,427	1,302	1,481	1,212
African Development Bank	54	18	18	15	20
African Development Fund	125	57	20	53	45
Asian Development Bank	712	80	135	110	95
Inter-American Development Bank	4,391	353	321	351	189
International Bank for Reconstruction and Development	1,001	27	41	241	232
International Development Association	8,012	892	768	658	546
International Finance Corporation	146	-	-	28	7

[a] Region totals include countries not shown separately.
[b] Data for 1987 are preliminary.
[c] Includes military grants.
Source: Department of Commerce, Bureau of Economic Analysis.

C25. Net Federal Direct Loan Outlays by Agency or Program

Fiscal Years 1988-1990[a]

($Millions)

Agency or Program	Net Outlays[b]		
	1988	1989	1990
Total, direct loan outlays[c]	$ -13,359	$ -12,648	$ -9,866
Funds appropriated to the President:	-2,307	-4,457	1,021
International security assistance	-2,205	-4,296	1,195
International development assistance	-102	-161	-174
Agriculture:	-9,242	-4,847	-9,279
Farmers Home Administration	-2,822	-3,371	-9,097
Agricultural credit	-2,119	-3,081	-3,871
Rural housing	587	335	-5,354
Rural development	-1,290	-625	128
Commodity Credit Corporation	-6,578	-2,180	-603
Public Law 480 long-term export credits	413	582	549
Rural Electrification and telephone	-255	122	-128
Commerce	-218	-51	-104
Defense	-29	-38	-48
Education	103	794	217
Energy	34	d	d
Health programs	87	17	-163
Housing and Urban Development:	241	1,129	196
Low-rent public housing	-37	-42	-44
Government National Mortgage Association	-422	-34	-
Other housing programs	700	1,205	240
Interior	-460	29	17
Transportation:	-506	-162	118
Railroad programs	-175	-318	-16
Other	-331	156	134
Veterans Affairs	43	4	-28
Loans to the District of Columbia	-30	-34	-33
Export-Import Bank	-1,308	-1,376	-658
Federal Deposit Insurance Corporation	559	-3,283	-4
Federal Savings and Loan Insurance Corporation	83	66	26
National Credit Union Administration	7	7	-28
Small Business Administration:	-818	-618	-987
Business and investment loans	-359	-290	-413
Disaster loans	-459	-328	-574
Tennessee Valley Authority	-6	-13	-16
NASA	84	96	-126
Other agencies and programs	326	87	13

[a] Data for 1989 and 1990 are estimates from the *Budget* presented in January 1989.
[b] Net loan outlays equal disbursements less repayments. Foreign currency transactions are excluded from the budget totals.
[c] Direct loan activities of the Federal Financing Bank are not shown separately, but are attributed to the originating agency or program.
[d] $500,000 or less.
Source: Office of Management and Budget.

C26. Outstanding Federal Direct, Guaranteed, and Insured Loans by Agency or Program

End of Fiscal Years 1988-1990[a]

($Millions)

Agency or Program	1988 Guaranteed Loans[b]	1988 Direct Loans[b]	1989 Guaranteed Loans[b]	1989 Direct Loans[b]	1990 Guaranteed Loans[b]	1990 Direct Loans[b]
Total	$ 549,966	$ 221,973	$ 586,637	$ 209,325	$ 619,138	$ 199,460
Funds appropriated to the President:						
International security assistance	2,600	30,365	7,580	26,069	7,357	27,262
International development assistance	1,775	12,920	1,980	12,759	2,202	12,585
Agriculture:						
Farmers Home Administration						
Agricultural credit	3,507	25,481	5,209	22,400	6,772	18,528
Rural housing	50	27,098	46	27,432	41	22,078
Rural development	1,688	5,173	1,596	4,548	1,511	4,669
Commodity Credit Corporation	4,919	11,999	7,937	9,820	10,214	9,216
Public Law 480 long-term export credits	-	11,632	-	12,214	-	12,764
Rural Electrification Administration:						
Rural electrification and telephone revolving fund	2,868	34,354	3,353	34,384	3,338	34,237
Rural Telephone Bank	-	1,413	-	1,505	629	1,525
Commerce:						
Economic development	123	442	125	389	113	290
National Oceanic and Atmospheric Administration	315	94	370	96	345	91
International Trade Administration and other	-	-	-	-	-	-
Defense	-	1,759	-	1,721	-	1,672
Education	47,610	11,955	52,043	12,748	56,192	12,965
Energy	-	54	-	54	-	54
Health and Human Services:						
Health programs	2,504	799	2,589	816	2,542	654
Housing and Urban Development:						
Low-rent public housing	5,998	2,037	5,698	1,995	5,373	1,951
Federal Housing Administration	300,758	5,123	321,804	6,054	344,767	6,619
Government National Mortgage Association	333,445	34	361,037	-	385,718	-
Other housing programs	59	7,879	49	8,155	37	7,828
Interior	170	176	204	204	236	211
Transportation:						
Federal ship financing fund	3,864	1,294	3,516	1,478	3,218	1,612
Railroad programs	-	462	-	144	-	128
Other	1,112	169	1,096	141	1,079	141
Treasury:						
Financial Assistance Corporation	450	-	1,450	-	2,260	-
Biomass energy development	150,207	-	149,021	-	148,522	-
Veterans Affairs	-	1,383	-	1,388	-	1,361
Loans to the District of Columbia	-	685	-	652	-	619
Export-Import Bank	5,703	9,905	6,664	8,530	7,475	7,871
Federal Deposit Insurance Corporation	-	3,649	-	366	-	361
Federal Savings and Loan Insurance Corporation	3,077	1,852	3,005	1,918	2,971	1,944
National Credit Union Administration	2	123	2	130	-	102
Small Business Administration:						
Business and investment loans	9,711	4,149	10,320	3,859	11,160	3,446
Disaster loan fund	1	3,260	1	2,932	1	2,358
Pollution control bond guarantees	262	-	248	-	-	-
Tennessee Valley Authority	1	2,425	-	2,522	-	2,543
Other agencies and programs	666	1,827	730	1,902	783	1,753
Deduction for secondary guaranteed loans	333,445	-	361,037	-	385,718	-
Deduction for guaranteed loans held as direct loans	34	-	-	-	-	-

[a] Data for 1989 and 1990 are estimates from the *Budget* presented in January 1989.
[b] Data include transactions of the Federal Financing Bank. Agency-guaranteed loans that are disbursed as direct loans by the FFB are shown in the table only as direct loans and are attributed to the appropriate agency or program. The guaranteed loan totals are primary guarantees only. To avoid double counting, secondary guarantees and guaranteed loans held as direct loans are deducted.

Source: Office of Management and Budget.

C27. Gross Outlays and Applicable Collections of Public Enterprise Funds by Agency or Program[a]

Fiscal Years 1988-1990[b]

($Millions)

Agency or Program	1988 Gross Outlays	1988 Applicable Receipts	1989 Gross Outlays	1989 Applicable Receipts	1990 Gross Outlays	1990 Applicable Receipts
Total	$ 140,912	$ 112,811	$ 133,588	$ 99,988	$ 124,846	$ 114,142
Funds appropriated to the President:						
Foreign assistance	1,485	921	1,402	939	1,129	578
Agriculture:						
Commodity Credit Corporation	36,183	24,008	26,396	12,502	22,339	11,618
Farmers Home Administration:						
Rural housing insurance fund	6,368	2,757	6,135	2,840	4,729	4,833
Agricultural credit insurance fund	5,653	3,035	6,307	2,872	3,988	2,713
Rural development insurance fund	2,135	1,685	1,711	1,115	1,359	539
Federal Crop Insurance Corporation	544	322	1,456	407	771	400
Rural Electrification Administration	3,538	5,747	3,533	3,742	3,394	3,536
Commerce	65	133	43	69	23	38
Education	10	383	39	87	48	287
Energy	2,650	2,791	2,741	3,028	2,799	3,610
Health and Human Services	67	58	96	57	89	127
Housing and Urban Development:						
Public and Indian Housing Programs	1,302	129	964	42	679	44
Federal Housing Administration Fund	7,551	6,417	8,135	6,688	7,644	5,962
Government National Mortgage Association	1,043	853	639	852	394	688
Other	1,096	1,017	1,119	806	1,120	1,288
Interior	406	459	496	487	657	676
Labor	283	560	851	1,082	867	1,209
Transportation	500	624	356	549	284	285
Treasury[c]	61	1,558	9	108	5,633	12,974
General Services Administration	5	3	4	3	5	3
Veterans Administration	3,970	2,859	4,233	3,143	3,062	2,712
Other independent agencies:						
Export-Import Bank	2,114	3,008	1,906	2,768	1,771	1,982
Federal Emergency Management Agency	261	461	561	622	635	658
Federal Savings and Loan Insurance Corporation	16,415	8,338	15,914	7,182	9,078	7,008
National Credit Union Administration	499	716	492	656	458	669
Small Business Administration	1,066	1,451	1,136	1,332	970	1,357
Postal Service	37,882	36,170	39,563	39,421	42,275	40,077
Tennessee Valley Authority	6,735	5,646	6,297	5,652	6,077	5,721
Other	1,027	705	1,051	938	2,569	2,547

[a] These are funds which finance a cycle of operations, in which the expenditures generate receipts available for continuing use. They include most government-owned corporations and various unincorporated enterprises, as well as agencies financed outside the budget.
[b] Data for 1989 and 1990 are estimates from the *Budget* presented in January 1989.
[c] Includes two new Federal credit revolving funds in 1990.
Source: Office of Management and Budget.

C28. Federal Trust Fund Receipts and Expenditures by Fund[a]

Selected Fiscal Years 1959-1990[b]
($Millions)

Trust Fund	1959	1969	1988	1989	1990
Total[c]					
Receipts	$ 16,769	$ 52,009	$ 473,713	$ 517,034	$ 559,442
Outlays	18,291	43,284	375,916	395,132	410,966
Old-age, survivors, and disability insurance trust funds					
Receipts	9,038	31,053	259,056	289,278	315,492
Outlays	9,741	27,303	220,257	233,268	246,717
Health insurance trust funds					
Receipts	-	7,255	103,001	119,124	138,994
Outlays	-	6,598	87,676	98,408	108,525
Railroad employees retirement funds					
Receipts	758	1,614	10,012	10,017	10,032
Outlays	778	1,498	8,977	9,332	9,630
Unemployment trust fund					
Receipts	1,997	3,852	26,984	26,397	26,294
Outlays	3,054	2,792	18,598	17,800	18,300
Federal employees retirement funds					
Receipts	1,741	3,776	47,016	48,967	51,207
Outlays	792	1,826	28,431	29,944	29,777
Airport and airway trust funds					
Receipts	-	-	4,081	4,690	5,074
Outlays	-	-	2,896	2,790	4,549
Highway trust funds					
Receipts	2,088	4,690	15,307	16,143	16,123
Outlays	2,613	4,151	14,733	14,585	14,613
Foreign military sales trust fund					
Receipts	-	959	8,964	8,594	8,330
Outlays	-	1,062	9,057	8,719	8,450
Veterans' life insurance funds[d]					
Receipts	697	751	1,423	1,436	1,432
Outlays	642	703	1,134	1,198	1,230
Black lung disability trust fund					
Receipts	-	-	640	680	662
Outlays	-	-	639	682	662
Military retirement trust fund[e]					
Receipts	-	-	33,117	34,680	34,892
Outlays	-	-	19,009	20,088	20,611
Other trust funds[f]					
Receipts	585	288	4,035	4,436	4,138
Outlays	806	288	3,439	3,545	3,871
Trust revolving funds[g]					
Outlays	-	-708	993	2,181	-2,741
Intrafund transactions	-135	-523	-20,432	-25,282	-29,663
Proprietary receipts from the public	-	-1,705	-19,491	-22,124	-23,566

[a] Does not include operations of deposit funds and government-sponsored enterprises.
[b] Data for 1989 and 1990 are estimates from the *Budget* presented in January 1989.
[c] Totals are net of intrafund transactions and proprietary receipts from the public.
[d] Includes Government Life Insurance Fund.
[e] This fund was established beginning in 1985.
[f] Includes principally District of Columbia, Indian tribal funds, adjusted certificates fund, National Mortgage Association Trust Fund, increment resulting from reduction in weight of gold dollar, and funds appropriated to the President.
[g] Outlays are stated net of offsetting collections.
Source: Office of Management and Budget and Treasury Department.

C29. Estimated Growth of Old-Age and Survivors and Disability Insurance Trust Funds

Selected Calendar Years 1940-1993[a]

($Millions)

Year	Contributions	Benefit Payments	Administrative Expenses	Transfers to Railroad Retirement Account	Interest on Fund[b]	Balance in Fund at End of Year[c]
		A. Old-Age and Survivors Insurance Trust Fund				
1940	$ 325	$ 35	$ 26	-	$ 43	$ 2,031
1945	1,285	274	30	-	134	7,121
1950	2,667	961	61	-	257	13,721
1955	5,713	4,968	119	$ -7	454	21,663
1960	10,866	10,677	203	318	516	20,324
1965	16,017	16,737	328	436	593	18,235
1970	30,256	28,798	471	579	1,515	32,454
1975	56,816	58,517	896	982	2,364	36,987
1980	103,456	105,083	1,154	1,442	1,845	22,823
1981	122,627	123,803	1,307	1,585	2,060	21,490
1982	123,673	138,806	1,519	1,793	845	22,088
1983	138,337	149,221	1,528	2,251	6,706	19,672
1984	164,122	157,841	1,638	2,404	2,266	27,117
1985	176,958	167,248	1,592	2,310	1,871	35,842
1986	190,741	176,813	1,601	2,585	3,069	39,081
1987	202,735	183,587	1,524	2,557	4,690	62,149
1988	229,775	195,454	1,776	2,790	7,568	102,899
1989	252,809	207,601	1,601	2,828	12,247	159,812
1990	270,362	220,791	1,678	3,001	17,724	227,150
1991	287,001	234,755	1,746	3,135	23,534	302,835
1992	304,053	247,224	1,807	3,324	29,337	389,050
1993	321,762	259,750	1,864	3,438	35,198	486,532
		B. Disability Insurance Trust Fund				
1960	$ 1,010	$ 568	$ 36	$ -5	$ 53	$ 2,289
1965	1,188	1,573	90	24	59	1,606
1970	4,481	3,085	164	10	277	5,614
1975	7,444	8,505	256	29	502	7,354
1980	13,255	15,515	368	-12	485	3,629
1981	16,738	17,192	436	29	172	3,049
1982	21,995	17,376	590	26	546	2,691
1983	17,991	17,524	625	28	1,569	5,195
1984	15,945	17,898	626	22	1,174	3,959
1985	17,191	18,827	608	43	870	6,321
1986	18,399	19,853	600	68	803	7,780
1987	19,691	20,519	849	57	648	6,658
1988	22,039	21,695	737	61	600	6,864
1989	24,230	22,922	717	37	711	8,336
1990	28,804	24,100	762	44	1,002	13,563
1991	30,755	25,437	799	36	1,483	19,804
1992	32,574	26,920	837	39	1,969	26,858
1993	34,472	28,606	878	40	2,450	34,593

[a] Beginning in 1989, data are projections reflecting changes that would occur, under automatic provisions of the law, based on an intermediate level of assumptions as to the future course of real gross national product, average wages, the consumer price index, and unemployment.

[b] Amounts shown include interest on retroactive government contributions on wage credits for military service from 1957 and unnegotiated benefit checks totaling: $6,677 million for OASI and $660 million for DI in 1983; $1,732 million for OASI and $169 million for DI in 1984; and $88 million for OASI and $15 million for DI in 1985.

[c] In addition to the items shown here, transactions affecting fund balances are income from taxation of benefits (beginning in 1984), reimbursements from the general fund of the Treasury, and interfund borrowing transfers.

Source: Board of Trustees, Federal Old-Age and Survivors Insurance and Disability Insurance Trust Funds.

C30. Estimated Progress of the Federal Highway Trust Fund
Actual Fiscal Years 1957-1988 and Estimated Fiscal Years 1989-1993[a]
($Millions)

Fiscal Year	Receipts			Expenditures			Balance in Fund End of Fiscal Year
	Total	Excise Taxes[b] (Net)	Interest on Investments (Net)[c]	Total	Interstate	Non-Interstate	
Actual:							
1957	$ 1,482	$ 1,479	$ 3	$ 966	$ 211	$ 755	$ 516
1958	2,044	2,026	18	1,511	673	838	1,049
1959	2,087	2,074	13	2,613	1,501	1,112	523
1960	2,536	2,539	-3	2,940	1,861	1,079	119
1961	2,799	2,798	1	2,619	1,719	900	299
1962	2,956	2,949	7	2,784	1,914	870	471
1963	3,293	3,279	14	3,017	2,109	908	747
1964	3,539	3,519	20	3,645	2,635	1,010	641
1965	3,670	3,659	11	4,026	3,016	1,010	285
1966	3,924	3,917	7	3,965	2,978	987	244
1967	4,455	4,441	14	3,974	2,976	998	725
1968	4,428	4,394	34	4,171	3,207	964	982
1969	4,690	4,637	53	4,151	3,149	1,002	1,521
1970	5,469	5,354	115	4,378	3,289	1,089	2,612
1971	5,725	5,542	183	4,685	3,456	1,229	3,652
1972	5,528	5,322	206	4,690	3,468	1,222	4,490
1973	5,912	5,665	247	4,811	3,395	1,416	5,591
1974	6,675	6,260	415	4,599	3,017	1,582	7,667
1975	6,774	6,188	586	4,844	2,902	1,942	9,597
1976	6,000	5,413	587	6,520	3,429	3,091	9,077
1977	7,302	6,709	593	6,147	2,979	3,168	10,164
1978	7,567	6,905	662	6,058	2,846	3,212	11,673
1979	8,046	7,189	857	7,155	3,449	3,706	12,564
1980	7,647	6,620	1,027	9,212	n.a.	n.a.	10,999
1981	7,434	6,305	1,129	9,174	n.a.	n.a.	9,259
1982	7,822	6,743	1,079	8,035	n.a.	n.a.	9,046
1983	9,375	8,297	1,078	8,841	n.a.	n.a.	9,581
1984	12,858	11,743	1,116	10,617	n.a.	n.a.	11,822
1985	14,328	13,015	1,313	13,263	n.a.	n.a.	12,886
1986	14,700	13,363	1,337	14,813	n.a.	n.a.	12,773
1987	14,310	13,032	1,278	13,469	n.a.	n.a.	13,613
1988	15,307	14,114	1,193	14,734	n.a.	n.a.	14,187
Estimated:							
1989	16,143	14,919	1,224	14,585	n.a.	n.a.	15,745
1990	16,123	14,804	1,319	14,613	n.a.	n.a.	17,254
1991	16,417	15,037	1,380	14,347	n.a.	n.a.	19,325
1992	16,646	15,245	1,401	14,424	n.a.	n.a.	21,548
1993	16,816	15,442	1,374	14,446	n.a.	n.a.	23,918

[a] Under present law the fund is scheduled to terminate on September 30, 1993. Effective March 31, 1983, a portion of the fund is earmarked for mass transit.
[b] Taxes on motor fuels, trucks, buses, trailers, tires, use of certain vehicles, lubricating oils, parts and accessories, inner tubes, and tread rubber. (For tax rates see Table C50.)
[c] Receipts of interest on investments netted by payment of interest on general fund advances.
Source: Treasury Department.

C31. Total and Per Capita Federal Receipts[a]

Selected Fiscal Years 1789-1988[b]

($Millions, Except Per Capita)

Year	Total Receipts[c]		Income and Profit Taxes	Customs[d]	Employment Taxes[e]	Other[f]
	Amount	Per Capita				
1789-91	$ 4	$ 1.02	-	$ 4	-	-
1800	10	1.89	-	9	-	$ 1
1810	9	1.25	-	9	-	g
1820	15	1.56	-	15	-	g
1830	22	1.71	-	22	-	g
1840	14	.82	-	13	-	g
1850	40	1.72	-	40	-	g
1860	53	1.68	-	53	-	g
1870	380	9.50	$ 38	195	-	147
1880	311	6.19	-	187	-	124
1890	373	5.90	-	230	-	143
1900	528	6.94	-	233	-	295
1910	624	6.75	21	334	-	269
1920	5,728	53.80	3,945	323	-	1,460
1930	3,626	29.46	2,411	587	-	628
1940	5,696	43.34	2,125	349	$ 834	2,388
1950	39,882	264.61	28,263	423	2,645	8,551
1960	97,730	546.81	67,151	1,123	11,337	18,118
1961	100,365	552.58	67,918	1,008	12,775	18,664
1962	105,941	574.18	71,945	1,171	12,977	19,848
1963	113,132	604.07	75,324	1,241	14,886	21,682
1964	119,810	630.67	78,891	1,284	17,125	22,509
1965	122,863	638.15	79,792	1,478	17,550	24,043
1966	138,112	709.54	92,132	1,811	20,890	23,279
1967	159,134	809.45	104,288	1,972	28,105	24,769
1968	165,047	831.14	108,149	2,113	29,487	25,298
1969	200,676	1,000.89	135,778	2,387	34,841	27,669
1970	209,883	1,035.35	138,689	2,494	39,520	29,180
1971	207,348	1,010.68	131,072	2,657	42,217	31,401
1972	227,544	1,097.15	143,805	3,394	46,568	33,777
1973	257,975	1,233.53	164,157	3,308	55,356	35,154
1974	293,014	1,390.72	184,648	3,444	66,428	38,494
1975	321,050	1,512.66	202,146	3,782	75,565	39,557
1976	333,708	1,559.73	205,752	4,209	80,317	43,430
1977	393,195	1,821.07	246,976	5,287	92,610	48,322
1978	440,598	2,024.82	278,438	6,729	104,411	51,020
1979	506,721	2,307.36	322,994	7,640	120,711	55,376
1980	572,641	2,583.28	359,928	7,482	139,273	65,958
1981	663,991	2,901.69	406,583	8,523	163,516	85,369
1982	690,421	2,988.54	418,600	9,278	181,027	81,516
1983	687,581	2,944.71	411,410	9,060	186,197	80,914
1984	750,269	3,183.98	434,905	11,791	212,612	90,961
1985	817,965	3,434.32	477,716	12,498	235,317	92,434
1986	860,764	3,578.99	501,275	13,808	255,806	89,875
1987	948,234	3,904.61	568,312	15,574	273,562	90,786
1988	999,510	4,076.17	583,351	16,690	305,833	93,636

[a] On the basis of warrants issued from 1789 to 1915; on Daily Treasury Statement basis from 1916 to 1952; on Monthly Treasury Statement basis for 1953 and subsequent years. General, special, emergency, and trust accounts combined from 1789 through 1930.
[b] Data for 1954 onward reflect changes in the concept of the Federal budget.
[c] Internal revenue plus customs and Federal unemployment insurance taxes before refunds. Tax receipts by source net of refunds are shown in Table C3.
[d] Includes the tonnage tax through 1931.
[e] Includes old-age, survivors, disability, and hospital insurance; and railroad retirement taxes. Excludes state unemployment insurance tax deposits.
[f] Includes excise, estate and gift, Federal unemployment, railroad unemployment, and state unemployment taxes deposited with the Treasury (1954-1988); other contributions for social insurance; and miscellaneous receipts and taxes.
[g] Less than $500,000.

Source: Treasury Department; per capita computations by Tax Foundation.

C32. Federal Tax Collections by Type of Tax[a]
Selected Fiscal Years 1960-1990[b]

Type of Tax	1960	1970	1975	1980	1988	1989	1990
	Amount ($Millions)						
Total	$ 90,514	$ 187,689	$ 269,996	$ 500,933	$ 884,522	$ 949,689	$ 1,032,562
Individual income tax	40,715	90,412	122,386	244,069	401,181	425,193	466,711
Corporate income tax	21,494	32,829	40,621	64,600	94,508	106,997	117,413
Employment taxes[c]	11,248	39,133	75,199	138,748	305,093	336,037	364,363
Unemployment taxes[d]	2,667	3,470	6,771	15,336	24,584	23,097	22,435
Excise taxes[e]	11,676	15,705	16,551	24,329	35,227	33,977	35,270
Estate and gift taxes	1,606	3,644	4,611	6,389	7,594	7,850	8,084
Customs duties	1,105	2,430	3,676	7,174	16,198	16,281	17,988
Miscellaneous taxes	3	66	181	288	137	257	298
	Percentage Distribution						
All taxes	100.0%	100.0%	100.0%	100.0%	100.0%	100.0%	100.0%
Individual income tax	45.0	48.2	45.3	48.7	45.4	44.8	45.2
Corporate income tax	23.7	17.5	15.0	12.9	10.7	11.3	11.4
Employment taxes	12.4	20.9	27.9	27.7	34.5	35.4	35.3
Unemployment taxes	2.9	1.8	2.5	3.1	2.8	2.4	2.2
Excise taxes	12.9	8.4	6.1	4.9	4.0	3.6	3.4
Estate and gift taxes	1.8	1.9	1.7	1.3	.9	.8	.8
Customs duties	1.2	1.3	1.4	1.4	1.8	1.7	1.7
Miscellaneous taxes	f	f	.1	.1	f	f	f

[a] Net of refunds.
[b] Data for 1989 and 1990 are estimates from the *Budget* presented in January 1989.
[c] Old-age, survivors, disability, and hospital insurance; and railroad retirement.
[d] Includes state taxes deposited in Treasury.
[e] For details by type of tax, see Table C49. Includes collections from windfall profits tax beginning 1980.
[f] Less than .05%.
Source: Office of Management and Budget, and Tax Foundation computations.

C33. Federal Tax Index and Tax Receipts by Type of Tax[a]
Calendar Years 1965-1988

Year	All Taxes	Personal Income Taxes	Corporate Profits Taxes	Indirect Business Taxes[b]	Social Insurance Contributions	Estate and Gift
Tax Index, 1967 = 100						
1965	82.6	79.3	96.3	102.0	69.0	90.3
1966	94.1	91.0	104.7	95.4	90.2	96.8
1967	100.0	100.0	100.0	100.0	100.0	100.0
1968	116.0	118.8	120.3	111.8	110.9	100.0
1969	131.1	142.1	120.3	117.8	127.6	116.1
1970	128.0	137.9	102.0	119.7	135.8	119.4
1971	132.8	133.1	111.7	125.7	150.7	148.4
1972	152.1	159.5	122.0	122.4	173.5	174.2
1973	173.1	170.0	144.3	131.6	218.8	164.5
1974	192.8	196.3	150.3	132.9	247.7	154.8
1975	193.2	187.6	145.3	146.1	262.6	158.1
1976	223.1	219.7	182.0	142.1	297.1	180.6
1977	252.1	252.3	205.3	151.3	331.0	232.3
1978	289.6	294.3	238.0	167.8	381.4	171.0
1979	331.1	349.7	248.0	171.1	442.7	177.4
1980	362.4	389.9	234.3	223.7	485.7	212.9
1981	418.5	453.0	219.0	330.9	569.5	225.8
1982	414.6	460.4	163.3	271.7	607.7	245.2
1983	430.7	447.4	204.3	295.4	656.8	190.3
1984	473.4	471.6	250.7	316.4	739.8	196.8
1985	514.3	527.0	254.3	307.8	808.0	209.7
1986	541.7	549.1	280.0	292.8	863.7	229.0
1987	599.2	616.1	352.7	310.5	912.5	238.7
1988	640.0	627.3	371.0	325.7	1,033.9	254.8
Tax Receipts ($Billions)						
1965	$ 124.3	$ 51.1	$ 28.9	$ 15.5	$ 26.0	$ 2.8
1966	141.5	58.6	31.4	14.5	34.0	3.0
1967	150.4	64.4	30.0	15.2	37.7	3.1
1968	174.5	76.5	36.1	17.0	41.8	3.1
1969	197.2	91.5	36.1	17.9	48.1	3.6
1970	192.5	88.8	30.6	18.2	51.2	3.7
1971	199.7	85.7	33.5	19.1	56.8	4.6
1972	228.7	102.7	36.6	18.6	65.4	5.4
1973	260.4	109.5	43.3	20.0	82.5	5.1
1974	289.9	126.4	45.1	20.2	93.4	4.8
1975	290.5	120.8	43.6	22.2	99.0	4.9
1976	335.6	141.5	54.6	21.6	112.3	5.6
1977	379.1	162.5	61.6	23.0	124.8	7.2
1978	435.5	189.5	71.4	25.5	143.8	5.3
1979	498.0	225.2	74.4	26.0	166.9	5.5
1980	545.1	251.1	70.3	34.0	183.1	6.6
1981	629.4	291.7	65.7	50.3	214.7	7.0
1982	623.5	296.5	49.0	41.3	229.1	7.6
1983	647.8	288.1	61.3	44.9	247.6	5.9
1984	712.0	303.7	75.2	48.1	278.9	6.1
1985	773.5	339.3	76.3	46.8	304.6	6.5
1986	814.7	353.6	83.9	44.5	325.6	7.1
1987	901.2	396.8	105.8	47.2	344.0	7.4
1988	962.5	404.0	111.3	49.5	389.8	7.9

[a] Tax receipts, net of refunds, as shown in the national income accounts, generally on an accrual basis.
[b] Excise taxes and customs duties.
Source: Department of Commerce, Bureau of Economic Analysis; and Tax Foundation computations.

C34. Federal Individual Income Tax: Exemptions and Treatment of Dividends

Income Years 1913-1989

Revenue Act	Income Years	Personal and Dependency Exemptions			Treatment of Dividends
		Married Person[a]	Single Person	Amount for Each Dependent	
1913[b]	1913-1915	$ 4,000	$ 3,000	None	Exempt
1916	1916	4,000	3,000	None	do
1917	1917, 1918	2,000	1,000	$ 200	do
1918	1918-1920	2,000	1,000	200	do
1921	1920-1923	2,500[c]	1,000	400	do
1924	1924	2,500	1,000	400	do
1926, 1928	1925-1931	3,500	1,500	400	do
1932	1932, 1933	2,500	1,000	400	do
1934	1934, 1935	2,500	1,000	400	do
1936, 1938	1936-1939	2,500	1,000	400	Fully taxable
1940[d]	1940	2,000	800	400	do
1941	1941	1,500	750	400	do
1942	1942, 1943	1,200	500	350	do
1944, 1945	1944-1947	1,000[e]	500[e]	500[e]	do
1948, 1950, 1951	1948-1953	1,200	600	600	do
Internal Revenue Code of 1954	1954-1963	1,200	600	600	First $50 exempt
1964	1964-1967	1,200	600	600	First $100 exempt
1968	1968, 1969	1,200	600	600	do
Tax Reform Act of 1969	1970	1,250	625	625	do
1971	1971	1,350[f]	675[f]	675[f]	do
	1972-1974	1,500	750	750	do
Tax Reduction Act of 1975	1975	1,500	750	750	do
Tax Reform Act of 1976	1976	1,500	750	750	do
Tax Reduction and Simplification Act of 1977	1977, 1978	1,500	750	750	do
1978	1979, 1980	2,000	1,000	1,000	do
Crude Oil Windfall Profits Tax of 1980	1981, 1982	2,000	1,000	1,000	g
Economic Recovery Tax Act of 1981	1982-1984	2,000[h]	1,000[h]	1,000[h]	g
Tax Equity and Fiscal Responsibility Act of 1982	1982-1984	2,000	1,000	1,000	First $100 exempt
	1985	2,080[h]	1,040[h]	1,040[h]	Fully taxable
	1986	2,160[h]	1,080[h]	1,080[h]	-
Tax Reform Act of 1986	1987	3,800	1,900	1,900	-
	1988[i]	3,900	1,950	1,950	-
	1989	4,000[h]	2,000[h]	2,000[h]	-

[a] For the years 1916-1943, the personal exemption allowed to married persons was also allowed to heads of families. For 1948 and subsequent years, an additional exemption is granted to persons over 65 and to the blind.
[b] Tariff Act of October 3, 1913. Tax effective on income for last 10 months in 1913.
[c] For net incomes in excess of $5,000, personal exemption was $2,000.
[d] Revenue acts passed after February 10, 1939 (the date of the enactment of the Internal Revenue Code) and prior to 1954 are not complete taxing statutes in themselves, but consist of amendments to the 1939 Code.
[e] Surtax exemptions, 1944 and 1945; in these years the normal tax exemption was $500 per taxpayer.
[f] Increased personal and dependency exemptions to $750 effective for one-half of year 1971.
[g] For 1981-1982 first $200 of combined dividend and interest income ($400 for joint returns) is exempt. For income years 1981-1986, up to $750 ($1,500 for joint returns) of reinvested dividends of public utilities is exempt.
[h] Effective in 1985-1986, and after 1989, personal exemption allowances are adjusted by changes in the Department of Labor's Consumer Price Index.
[i] Beginning in 1988, the personal exemption will be phased out for higher income taxpayers.
Source: Treasury Department and Commerce Clearing House.

C35. Federal Internal Revenue Collections by State[a]
Selected Fiscal Years 1949-1987
($Millions)

State[c]	1949 Total	1949 Income and Employment Taxes	1959 Total	1959 Income and Employment Taxes	1969 Total	1969 Income and Employment Taxes	1979 Total	1979 Income and Employment Taxes	1987[b] Total	1987[b] Income and Employment Taxes
Total[c]	$40,351.4	$31,983.3	$78,652.1	$66,642.2	$187,919.3	$168,846.7	$453,859.1	$432,697.8	$935,106.6	$901,388.2
Alabama	259.5	236.2	534.7	512.6	1,332.6	1,222.5	4,130.5	3,948.6	9,011.4	8,720.8
Alaska	-	-	47.9	46.1	132.1	129.7	796.2	781.3	1,548.7	1,515.1
Arizona	82.1	74.2	266.4	254.2	717.3	688.3	3,262.0	3,186.4	8,039.8	7,778.9
Arkansas	115.9	105.6	197.5	188.6	651.8	609.5	2,018.9	1,939.4	5,040.5	4,764.9
California	2,955.9	2,419.0	6,923.6	6,069.2	16,777.4	15,291.5	49,558.1	46,911.1	108,332.5	104,319.7
Colorado	277.0	222.5	976.0	889.1	2,243.4	2,058.3	6,730.5	6,422.7	12,886.8	12,543.2
Connecticut	642.6	535.5	1,335.8	1,194.5	3,478.0	3,215.4	9,108.1	8,693.0	22,697.0	22,241.1
Delaware	306.2	293.6	686.1	676.2	1,318.6	1,276.4	2,217.5	2,168.4	5,227.7	5,106.0
Florida	342.6	286.6	1,147.3	1,039.3	3,625.6	3,381.7	13,328.6	12,482.9	36,806.0	35,540.9
Georgia	403.5	322.9	888.9	778.7	2,614.8	2,428.8	7,314.7	6,735.2	21,001.1	19,997.6
Hawaii					526.6	493.9	1,455.2	1,421.0	3,310.8	3,224.1
Idaho	76.4	71.0	147.1	142.1	379.6	369.7	1,313.0	1,291.8	2,571.3	2,520.8
Illinois	3,569.8	2,924.1	6,394.9	5,570.5	14,286.1	13,070.4	33,432.9	31,648.3	57,783.7	55,793.0
Indiana	950.5	586.8	1,759.1	1,432.3	3,409.7	2,943.3	9,820.1	9,334.9	18,607.6	18,197.7
Iowa	407.9	330.7	683.7	647.2	1,442.2	1,383.3	4,081.4	3,935.8	6,773.7	6,567.3
Kansas	401.9	301.3	582.7	534.0	1,185.1	1,128.6	3,935.9	3,770.2	7,711.6	7,376.0
Kentucky	812.3	282.1	1,541.0	547.3	2,541.0	1,314.1	5,272.0	3,928.0	8,059.2	7,567.2
Louisiana	357.4	291.8	689.2	610.7	1,639.9	1,542.3	5,486.7	5,334.5	8,362.9	8,154.6
Maine	117.5	107.8	192.9	183.4	470.4	451.2	1,144.3	1,111.0	2,909.1	2,831.0
Maryland[d]	1,068.1	842.1	1,937.5	1,652.3	5,425.3	4,951.9	13,111.1	12,470.9	29,967.4	29,201.5
Massachusetts	1,232.0	1,063.6	2,209.8	2,001.6	5,455.4	5,059.8	11,311.7	10,898.6	29,374.8	28,647.0
Michigan	2,564.5	1,876.0	5,010.8	3,586.9	13,871.7	11,201.4	26,664.1	25,528.0	42,341.3	41,761.0
Minnesota	669.0	573.8	1,291.9	1,174.0	3,195.7	3,021.1	10,353.7	10,035.1	20,953.5	20,352.7
Mississippi	100.7	91.6	193.1	176.7	619.6	574.0	1,755.6	1,702.8	3,932.7	3,767.5
Missouri	1,095.2	892.3	1,945.9	1,672.6	4,782.8	4,342.7	11,581.5	10,973.5	22,495.3	21,640.3
Montana	78.9	72.1	145.0	136.1	273.2	257.6	828.4	792.9	1,582.3	1,524.5
Nebraska	276.2	224.4	484.8	430.2	1,031.8	937.1	2,976.0	2,833.6	5,356.5	5,181.2
Nevada	38.1	33.7	114.9	101.3	351.4	330.6	1,471.3	1,430.8	3,506.4	3,420.7
New Hampshire	71.5	63.8	152.8	146.3	447.7	432.7	1,286.7	1,234.3	3,641.5	3,584.6
New Jersey	1,151.1	937.9	2,442.8	2,114.8	6,670.0	6,081.0	16,775.4	16,061.0	43,647.8	42,042.2
New Mexico	55.4	50.5	177.7	170.0	367.9	351.0	1,240.4	1,206.9	2,660.1	2,552.7
New York	7,427.2	6,260.5	15,433.2	13,634.8	33,245.3	31,149.5	51,800.4	50,004.2	101,392.9	99,549.3

Continued

C35. Federal Internal Revenue Collections by State[a] (continued)

Selected Fiscal Years 1949-1987

($Millions)

State	1949 Total	1949 Income and Employment Taxes	1959 Total	1959 Income and Employment Taxes	1969 Total	1969 Income and Employment Taxes	1979 Total	1979 Income and Employment Taxes	1987[b] Total	1987[b] Income and Employment Taxes
North Carolina	1,166.7	423.7	1,983.7	875.0	4,065.6	2,801.4	8,936.4	7,427.8	18,226.6	17,677.3
North Dakota	61.7	58.0	95.6	92.5	201.8	193.8	761.0	731.8	1,299.0	1,257.7
Ohio	2,626.3	2,148.0	5,047.4	4,405.8	12,407.0	11,317.0	27,411.8	25,920.4	42,534.0	40,893.6
Oklahoma	418.8	337.3	809.8	596.7	1,598.2	1,262.5	5,029.8	4,611.1	8,764.0	7,651.9
Oregon	298.8	275.8	491.9	468.6	1,288.3	1,238.6	4,863.9	4,676.1	7,829.3	7,652.8
Pennsylvania	3,213.4	2,578.4	5,392.8	4,607.5	11,110.9	10,007.3	24,948.8	23,712.1	45,732.1	44,309.5
Rhode Island	214.8	194.4	311.3	282.9	891.3	852.9	1,826.2	1,783.9	3,795.4	3,723.3
South Carolina	205.0	191.5	287.6	272.6	963.1	931.4	3,030.6	2,959.5	7,103.7	6,924.7
South Dakota	64.1	58.2	107.6	103.8	218.8	208.7	671.0	645.2	1,384.1	1,341.3
Tennessee	333.2	295.7	644.7	605.4	1,868.1	1,788.4	5,669.7	5,447.1	13,777.3	13,349.9
Texas	1,381.2	1,218.9	2,682.5	2,413.8	7,615.5	6,624.4	29,862.5	27,766.3	57,579.2	51,136.6
Utah	90.7	76.7	217.1	199.8	434.7	415.0	1,607.7	1,571.7	3,582.0	3,410.1
Vermont	40.7	36.2	78.1	70.6	211.6	202.5	508.6	496.2	1,429.3	1,402.0
Virginia	770.3	393.4	1,231.5	843.3	2,829.1	2,250.5	7,626.9	6,761.7	19,322.6	18,800.9
Washington	488.8	438.4	970.3	891.4	2,472.3	2,296.7	7,629.4	7,302.0	16,209.7	15,890.0
West Virginia	242.7	219.8	308.0	287.4	630.1	595.6	1,770.7	1,708.7	3,077.7	2,933.2
Wisconsin	788.2	629.9	1,409.5	1,241.9	3,353.7	3,070.3	8,777.3	8,366.1	15,222.0	14,888.6
Wyoming	38.8	35.0	77.8	69.1	145.5	129.6	640.6	593.0	993.8	886.5
Alaska (territory)	18.2	16.5			-	-	-	-	-	-
Hawaii (territory)	91.2	81.8	175.2	163.5	-	-	-	-	-	-
Other[e]	2.3	f	970.8	874.3	1,103.7	971.0	3,276.5	3,145.8	9,711.2	9,270.7

[a] Collections in various states do not necessarily indicate the actual Federal tax burden on the residents of each state. For estimated tax burden by state, see Table C55.
[b] Data for 1987 are not strictly comparable to prior years because amounts in 1987 are classified according to state of taxpayer's residence; previously amounts were classified according to state where tax payments were made.
[c] Excludes collections outside of states recognized as of fiscal year.
[d] Includes District of Columbia.
[e] Includes Puerto Rico, Canal Zone, Philippine Islands, other foreign countries, and undistributed.
[f] Less than $50,000.
Source: Treasury Department.

C36. Federal Individual Income Tax: Combined Normal and Surtax Rates

Selected Income Years 1913-1989[a]

Taxable Income[b]	1913-1915	1916	1917	1918	1919-1921	1922, 1923[c]	1925, 1931[d]	1932, 1933	1934, 1935	1936-1939	Taxable Income[b]
Under 2	-	-	-	6%	4%	4%	-	4%	-	4%	Under 2
2-4	1%	2%	2%	6	4	4	1-1/2%	4	4%	4	2-4
4-5	1	2	4	6	4	4	1-1/2	4	8	8	4-5
5-6	1	2	5	7	5	4	1-1/2	4	8	8	5-6
6-7.5	1	2	5	14	10	9	1-1/2	9	9	9	6-7.5
7.5-8	1	2	6	14	10	9	1-1/2	9	9	9	7.5-8
8-10	1	2	6	15	11	9	3	9	10	10	8-10
10-12	1	2	7	16	12	10	4	10	11	11	10-12
12-14	1	2	7,8	17	13	11	6	11	12	12	12-14
14-16	1	2	8,9	18	14	12	7	12	13	13	14-16
16-18	1	2	9	19	15	13	8	13	15	15	16-18
18-20	1	2	9	20	16	14	9	14	17	17	18-20
20-22	2	3	12	21	17	16	10	16	19	19	20-22
22-26	2	3	12	22,23	18,19	17,18	11,12	17,18	21	21	22-26
26-28	2	3	12	24	20	19	12	19	23	23	26-28
28-30	2	3	12	25	21	20	13	20	23	23	28-30
30-32	2	3	12	26	22	21	13	21	23	23	30-32
32-36	2	3	12	27,28	23,24	23	14	23	25	25	32-36
36-40	2	3	12	29,30	25,26	24,25	15	24,25	25,28	25,28	36-40
40-44	2	4	16	31,32	27,28	26,27	16	26,27	28	28	40-44
44-48	2	4	16	33,34	29,30	28,29	17	28,29	31	31	44-48
48-52	2,3	4	16	35,36	31,32	30,31	18	30,31	31,34	31,35	48-52
52-56	3	4	16	37,38	33,34	32,33	19	32,33	34	35	52-56
56-60	3	4	16	39,40	35,36	34,35	20	34,35	37	39	56-60
60-66	3	5	21	41-43	37-39	36-38	21,22	36-38	37,40	39,43	60-66
66-70	3	5	21	44,45	40,41	39,40	22	39,40	40,43	43,47	66-70
70-74	3	5	21	46,47	42,43	41,42	23	41,42	43	47	70-74
74-76	3,4	5	21	48	44	43	23	43	46	51	74-76
76-80	4	5	26	49,50	45,46	44,45	23	44,45	46	51	76-80
80-86	4	6	26	51-53	47-49	46-48	24	46-48	49	55	80-86
86-90	4	6	26	54,55	50,51	49,50	24	49,50	49	55	86-90
90-96	4	6	26	56-58	52-54	51-53	24	51-53	54	59	90-96
96-100	4	6	31	59,60	55,56	54,55	24	54,55	54	59	96-100
100-150	5	7	35	64	60	56	25	56	56	62	100-150
150-200	5	8	41,46	68	64	57	25	57	57	64	150-200
200-300	5,6	9,10	50	72	68	58	25	58	58	66,68	200-300
300-500	6	11	54,59	75	71	58	25	59,60	59,60	70,72	300-500
500-1,000	7	12	65	76	72	58	25	61,62	61,62	74,76	500-1,000
1,000-1,500	7	13	66,67	77	73	58	25	63	63	77	1,000-1,500
Over 1,500	7	14,15		77	73	58	25	63	63	77-79	Over 1,500

Continued

C36. Federal Individual Income Tax: Combined Normal and Surtax Rates (continued)

Selected Income Years 1913-1989[a]

Taxable Income[b]	1944-1945	1952-1953	1954-1963	1965-1976[e]	1977-1978	1979-1981[f]	1982	1983	1984-1986[a]	1987 Taxable Income[b]	1987 Tax Rate[h]	1988-89+ Taxable Income[b]	1988-89+ Tax Rate[h]
Under .5	23%	22.2%	20%	14%	-	-	-	-	-	0-$3	11%	up to $29.75	15%
.5- 1	23	22.2	20	15	-	-	-	-	-	3-28	15	over $29.75	28
1- 1.5	23	22.2	20	16	-	-	-	-	-	28-45	28		
1.5- 2	25	22.2	20	17	-	-	-	-	-	45-90	35		
2- 4	29	24.6	22	19	0, 14%	0, 14%	0, 12%	0, 11%	0, 11%	over 90	38.5		
4- 6	33	29	26	22	14-19	14-18	12-16	11-15	11-14				
6- 8	37	34	30	25	19, 22	18, 21	16, 19	15, 17	14,16				
8- 10	41	38	34	28	22, 25	21	19	17	16				
10- 12	46	42	38	32	25, 28	24	22	19	18				
12- 14	50	48	43	36	28 ,32	24 ,28	22, 25	19, 23	18, 22				
14- 16	53	53	47	39	32, 36	28, 32	25, 29	23, 26	22, 25				
16- 18	56	56	50	42	36, 39	32, 37	29, 33	26, 30	25, 28				
18- 20	59	59	53	45	39, 42	37, 43	33, 39	30, 35	28, 33				
20- 22	62	62	56	48	42, 45	43	39	35	33				
22- 26	65	66	59	50	45, 48	43, 49	39, 44	35, 40	33, 38				
26- 32	68	67	62	53	48, 50	49, 54	44, 49	40, 44	38, 42				
32- 38	72	68	65	55	50, 53	54	49	44	42				
38- 44	75	72	69	58	53, 55	54, 59	49, 50	44, 48	42, 45				
44- 50	78	75	72	60	55, 58	59	50	48	45				
50- 60	81	77	75	62	58, 60	59, 64	50	48, 50	45, 49				
60- 70	84	80	78	64	60, 62	64	50	50	49				
70- 80	87	83	81	66	62, 64	64, 68	50	50	49				
80- 90	90	85	84	68	64, 66	68	50	50	49				
90- 100	92	88	87	69	66, 68	68, 70	50	50	49, 50				
100- 150	93	90	89	70	68, 69	70	50	50	50				
150- 200	94	91	90	70	69, 70	70	50	50	50				
200- 300	94	92	91	70	70	70	50	50	50				
300- 500	94[g]	92	91	70	70	70	50	50	50				
500- 1,000	94[g]	92[g]	91[g]	70	70	70	50	50	50				
over 1,000	94[g]	92[g]	91[g]	70[g]	70	70	50	50	50				

[a] For income years 1941-43, 1946-51 and 1964, see 1981 edition of *Facts and Figures on Government Finance*. Before 1934 all net income was subject to surtax; for 1934 and later years, net income less personal exemptions and credits for dependents was subject to surtax. For this table, in the years before 1934, normal tax rates were added to the surtax by including in "taxable income" for normal tax the exemptions for a married couple with one child. Beginning in 1948, rates shown apply only to married taxpayers filing joint returns who may split their income for tax purposes. In 1954, these income-splitting provisions were extended to a surviving spouse with dependent children. Special rates, not shown in the table, were provided for heads of households beginning in 1952 and for single persons beginning in 1971. For tax years beginning after December 31, 1984 (except 1987 and 1988) tax brackets are adjusted for inflation as measured by the Consumer Price Index.

[b] Thousands of dollars. From 1977-1986 taxable income excludes zero bracket amounts.

[c] The tax for 1923, computed at these rates, was reduced 25% by credit or refund under the Revenue Act of 1924.

[d] Normal tax rates for 1929 were reduced by one percentage point by Joint Resolution of Congress, No. 133, approved by the President on December 16, 1929.

[e] Excludes effect of surtax of 7.5%, 10%, and 2.5% in 1968, 1969, and 1970, respectively.

[f] For 1981, tax liability was reduced for all brackets by 1.25 percent under the Economic Recovery Tax Act of 1981.

[g] The maximum effective rates of the income tax on net income were as follows: 1944 and 1945, 90%; 1946 and 1947, 85.5%; 1948 and 1949, 77%; 1950, 80%; 1951, 87.2%; 1952 and 1953, 88%. Under the Internal Revenue Code of 1954, the maximum was 87% of taxable income. Maximum marginal tax rate on earned income was 60% in 1971 and 50% thereafter, under the Tax Reform Act of 1969.

[h] Maximum marginal tax rate on all taxable income is 50% under the Economic Recovery Tax Act of 1981.

For joint returns, The Tax Reform Act of 1986 consolidated the rate schedule and lowered tax rates. Instead of the 14 rates that ranged from 11 to 50 percent in the 1986 income year, there is a five-bracket rate structure for income year 1987 ranging from 11 to 38.5 percent. Starting in the 1988 income year there are only two rates of 15 and 28 percent. Most families with taxable income over $71,900 ($43,150 for single individuals), will be subject to an additional 5 percent surcharge, making their true marginal rate 33 percent.

Source: Commerce Clearing House, and Treasury Department.

C37. Federal Income Tax Liability[a] for Selected Income Groups

Selected Income Years 1954-1985

Adjusted Gross Income	1954-1963	1965	1970[b]	1975	1977-1978	1979-1980[c]	1982	1983	1984	1985
Single Person, No Dependents										
$5,000	$ 818	$ 671	$ 683	$ 404	$ 279	$ 250	$ 216	$ 199	$ 193	$ 177
10,000	2,096	1,742	1,726	1,476	1,221	1,177	1,043	951	915	888
20,000	5,900	4,918	4,405	4,123	4,007	3,837	3,442	3,089	2,945	2,845
25,000	8,324	6,982	6,091	5,865	5,715	5,484	4,942	4,445	4,205	4,125
35,000	13,778	11,627	10,028	9,698	9,548	9,194	8,292	7,485	7,065	6,916
50,000	22,788	19,230	17,235	16,710	16,560	16,032	14,468	13,073	12,335	12,067
75,000	39,702	33,206	31,560	30,680	30,530	29,487	25,718	23,873	22,595	22,195
Married Couple, 2 Dependents										
$5,000	$ 420	$ 290	$ 290	$ -300[d]	$ -500[d]	$ -500[d]	$ -500[d]	$ -500[d]	$ -500[d]	$ -550[d]
10,000	1,372	1,114	1,112	709	446	374	332	296	291	132[d]
20,000	3,800	3,160	3,213	2,740	2,530	2,265	2,013	1,846	1,741	1,682
25,000	5,318	4,412	4,490	4,092	3,864	3,497	3,137	2,828	2,673	2,566
35,000	9,037	7,529	7,677	7,175	7,115	6,571	5,904	5,334	5,070	4,916
50,000	15,976	13,388	13,674	12,980	12,920	12,118	10,911	9,844	9,310	9,086
75,000	29,635	25,025	25,594	24,575	24,515	23,404	21,086	19,050	18,066	17,649

[a] Computations assume the low income allowance, standard deduction, zero bracket amount, or itemized deductions equal to 10% of adjusted gross income, whichever is greatest.
[b] Includes surtax.
[c] Tax liabilities for 1981 were 98.75% of the 1980 tax liabilities.
[d] Refundable earned income credit.
Source: Treasury Department.

C38. Effective Rates[a] of Federal Income Tax Liability for Selected Income Groups

Selected Income Years 1954-1985

Adjusted Gross Income	1954- 1963	1965	1970[b]	1975	1977- 1978	1979- 1980[c]	1982	1983	1984	1985
Single Person, No Dependents										
$ 5,000	16.4%	13.4%	13.7%	8.1%	5.6%	5.0%	4.3%	4.0%	3.9%	3.5%
10,000	21.0	17.4	17.3	14.8	12.2	11.8	10.4	9.5	9.2	8.9
20,000	29.5	24.6	22.0	20.6	20.0	19.2	17.2	15.4	14.7	14.3
25,000	33.3	27.9	24.4	23.5	22.9	21.9	19.8	17.8	16.8	16.5
35,000	39.4	33.2	28.7	27.7	27.3	26.3	23.7	21.4	20.2	19.8
50,000	45.6	38.5	34.5	33.4	33.1	32.1	28.9	26.1	24.7	24.1
75,000	52.9	44.3	42.1	40.9	40.7	39.3	34.3	31.8	30.1	29.6
Married Couple, 2 Dependents										
$ 5,000	8.4%	5.8%	5.8%	-6.0%[d]	-6.0%[d]	-10.0%[d]	-10.0%[d]	-10.0%[d]	-10.0%[d]	-11.0%[d]
10,000	13.7	11.1	11.2	7.1	4.5	3.7	3.2	3.0	2.9	1.3[d]
20,000	19.0	15.8	16.1	13.7	12.6	11.3	10.1	9.2	8.7	8.4
25,000	21.3	17.6	18.0	16.4	15.5	14.0	12.5	11.3	10.7	10.3
35,000	25.8	21.5	21.9	20.5	20.3	18.8	16.9	15.2	14.5	14.0
50,000	32.0	26.8	27.3	26.0	25.8	24.2	21.8	19.7	18.6	18.2
75,000	39.5	33.4	34.1	32.8	32.7	31.2	28.1	25.4	24.1	23.5

[a] Tax liability as shown in Table C37 divided by stated income.
[b] Includes surtax.
[c] Tax rates for 1981 were 98.75% of the 1980 tax rates.
[d] Refundable earned income credit.
Source: Treasury Department.

C39. Federal Individual Income Tax Data
Selected Calendar Years 1960-1987[a]
(\$Millions)

Item	1960	1965	1970	1975	1980	1985	1987[a]
Number of returns (000)	61,028	67,596	74,280	82,229	93,902	101,660	107,070
Adjusted gross income [b]	\$315,466	\$429,201	\$631,693	\$947,785	\$1,613,731	\$2,305,951	\$2,788,011
Itemized deductions	35,313	50,739	88,178	122,261	218,028	405,024	383,917
Exemptions	105,183	114,445	127,531	159,141	227,569	253,720	217,530
Taxable income	171,628	255,082	401,154	595,493	1,279,985	1,820,741	1,858,714
Total statutory adjustments	n.a.	3,143	7,665	15,102	28,614	95,082	29,565
Income tax liability	39,464	49,530	83,909	124,526	250,341	338,765	371,258
Sources of adjusted gross income:							
Salaries and wages	257,918	347,150	531,884	795,399	1,349,843	1,928,201	2,169,144
Business and profession [c]	21,072[d]	24,588	30,554	39,421	55,129	78,773	103,930
Farm [c]	[e]	3,365	2,789	3,563	-1,792	-12,005	-770
Partnership [c]	8,966[f]	10,606[f]	10,900	10,751	9,429	-2,527[f]	32,075[f]
Small business corporations [c]	[g]	[g]	1,738	2,060	671	[g]	[g]
Sales of capital assets [c]	5,300	10,181	9,007	14,072	30,029	68,278	133,483
Sales of property other than capital assets [c]	-83	-39	-110	136	76	1,527	-
Dividends after exclusion	9,530	12,961	15,807	21,892	38,761	55,046	66,442
Interest received	5,057	11,296	22,021	43,434	102,009	182,109	163,981
Pensions and annuities	1,617	3,568	7,879	20,887	43,340	95,096	125,352
Rents [c]	2,728	2,454	2,426	3,433	200	-19,822	7,144[h]
Royalties [c]	584	621	806	1,769	3,905	6,858	[i]
Estates and trusts [c]	635	-	1,449	2,554	4,560	9,730	-
State income tax refunds	-	[k]	[k]	1,450	3,630	8,553	-
Alimony	2,474[l]	5,592[m]	2,206[m]	725	1,422	2,884	-
Unemployment compensation	-	-	-	-	2,082	6,356	12,324
Other income less loss	[k]	[k]	[k]	1,340	-579	-19,426	-
Tax credits	445	615	370	8,070	7,216	10,248	6,108
Additional tax for tax preferences	-	-	122	144	1,263	3,793	1,234

[a] Data for 1987 are preliminary.
[b] Adjusted gross income less deficit.
[c] Net gain, net income, or net profit minus net loss.
[d] Includes "Farm."
[e] Included in "Business and profession."
[f] Includes "Small business corporations."
[g] Included in "Small business corporations."
[h] Included in "Partnership."
[i] Includes "Royalties."
[k] Included in "Alimony."
[l] Includes "Other income less loss."
[m] Includes "State income tax refunds" and "Other income less loss."
Source: Treasury Department.

C40. Income and Tax Liability on Federal Individual Income Tax Returns by Income Class[a]

Selected Years 1916-1987
($Millions)

Year	Under $10,000[b]			$10,000 under $50,000			$50,000 under $100,000			$100,000 and over		
	Number of Returns	Income	Income Tax Liability	Number of Returns	Income	Income Tax Liability	Number of Returns	Income	Income Tax Liability	Number of Returns	Income	Income Tax Liability
1916	307,702	$1,662	$7	104,614	$2,058	$23	10,452	$723	$16	6,633	$1,856	$127
1918	4,265,508	11,540	238	145,111	2,715	273	9,996	680	147	4,499	990	470
1920	7,033,824	18,343	264	210,378	3,856	327	12,093	810	164	3,649	727	321
1924	7,109,980	18,896	76	238,277	4,455	187	15,816	1,067	137	5,715	1,238	304
1928	3,688,730	12,553	36	338,937	6,364	219	27,207	1,858	194	15,977	4,451	714
1933	3,621,420	8,399	72	94,066	1,742	107	6,021	401	57	2,051	467	138
1939	7,424,307	18,459	174	196,699	3,497	305	9,272	618	147	2,921	618	302
1944	46,286,469	102,539	10,763	595,948	10,719	3,432	28,963	1,926	1,022	8,210	1,531	999
1948	50,533,412	137,390	8,918	1,143,280	20,210	3,768	52,725	3,516	1,247	16,280	3,057	1,509
1952	54,311,136	179,337	17,682	1,712,673	29,085	6,534	65,403	4,341	1,811	17,877	3,324	1,776
1954	54,177,685	188,191	16,716	2,039,909	33,830	6,537	70,400	4,656	1,709	18,710	3,559	1,704
1956	55,686,142	210,254	19,604	3,000,654	47,977	8,957	89,170	5,905	2,129	22,877	4,447	2,042
1958	54,875,502	214,354	20,005	3,711,028	57,479	10,319	91,715	6,050	2,107	22,679	4,283	1,905
1960	55,274,088	226,825	21,636	5,192,825	78,132	13,441	101,272	6,661	2,273	24,523	4,940	2,113
1962	55,210,606	233,407	22,680	6,931,263	102,993	17,244	121,552	7,984	2,685	27,174	5,477	2,294
1964	55,465,669	242,683	20,613	9,281,886	137,629	20,383	159,229	10,463	3,204	36,501	7,437	2,953
1966	56,752,667	250,363	20,667	13,136,210	194,840	26,969	218,382	14,380	4,229	53,166	10,689	4,223
1968	55,277,521	245,422	22,635	18,067,170	273,931	40,762	301,794	19,983	6,205	82,223	16,969	7,036
1970	50,611,101	230,611	20,294	23,240,062	363,603	51,269	350,978	23,107	6,646	77,690	14,372	5,700
1971	48,598,527	221,769	17,030	25,482,168	408,033	54,331	404,692	26,695	7,314	91,020	17,123	6,733
1972	48,139,166	218,131	15,469	28,835,251	474,360	61,389	483,677	31,983	8,528	114,636	21,501	8,190
1973	47,619,350	212,338	15,505	32,340,931	551,350	73,170	595,663	39,382	10,367	135,643	24,077	9,040
1974	47,353,290	210,788	15,965	35,119,936	619,018	84,184	700,528	46,275	12,232	166,436	29,502	11,225
1975	44,854,767	199,922	11,926	36,407,204	663,711	87,002	781,406	51,551	13,362	185,955	32,601	12,236
1976	43,828,707	197,134	10,997	39,666,745	754,441	99,070	948,034	62,416	16,257	226,903	39,905	15,478
1977	42,605,454	192,279	9,117	42,609,849	841,847	112,170	1,140,784	74,932	19,392	278,553	49,434	19,119
1978	41,821,473	191,392	9,504	46,124,857	952,059	130,578	1,471,406	96,283	24,380	353,815	62,713	23,770
1979	40,528,425	188,206	8,952	49,324,396	1,069,617	143,811	1,889,878	123,163	29,811	451,603	84,409	31,921
1980	38,426,526	173,545	8,479	52,346,752	1,169,791	163,232	2,568,427	165,928	39,758	560,764	104,468	38,872
1981	36,274,740	162,194	8,039	54,871,125	1,271,184	181,766	3,472,117	221,152	51,495	666,831	124,829	44,550
1982	35,142,933	170,617	7,309	55,602,781	1,310,571	171,576	3,804,140	241,594	50,655	747,648	148,572	48,933
1983	34,529,701	146,660	6,204	56,506,800	1,348,926	160,654	4,425,812	282,263	53,877	831,321	172,940	55,350
1984	33,692,123	133,073	6,282	59,034,486	1,430,526	163,341	5,707,146	364,336	66,114	1,004,953	211,968	66,184
1985	32,221,027	134,352	5,589	60,407,162	1,484,857	165,430	6,907,057	441,598	78,068	1,221,813	261,082	79,646
1986	32,555,710	120,071	5,404	61,024,903	1,511,801	166,680	7,974,601	513,758	88,740	1,489,956	336,050	106,453
1987	33,653,138	132,737	4,702	61,164,723	1,531,479	147,648	10,187,358	659,485	101,292	2,046,868	464,310	117,587

a Income shown is adjusted gross income for 1944-1987 and net income for 1916-1943. Includes data for fiduciary returns for 1916-1939. Nontaxable returns are included throughout.
b Prior to 1944, the major influence on the number of returns, etc., in this income class is the level of personal exemptions and filing requirements. The history of personal exemptions is shown in Table C34.

Source: Treasury Department.

C41. Relationship of Personal Income and Taxable Income
Selected Calendar Years 1950-1986
($Billions)

Item		1950	1960	1970	1986
Personal income		$ 226.1	$ 399.7	$ 801.3	$ 3,531.1
Deduct:	Portion of personal income not included in adjusted gross income	32.9	72.8	172.8	1,103.2
	Transfer payments	14.6	27.0	73.0	437.5
	Other labor income	3.5	11.0	31.4	192.5
	Income in kind and imputed income	9.4	20.3	38.2	70.0
	Other types of personal income	5.3	14.6	30.2	403.2
Add:	Portion of adjusted gross income not included in personal income	9.0	19.5	49.2	403.0
	Employee and self-employed persons' contributions for social insurance	2.9	9.3	28.0	161.1
	Net gain from sale of assets	2.9	5.3	9.0	137.4
	Other types of income[a]	3.3	4.9	12.2	104.5
Equals:	Adjusted gross income of all individuals, estimated from personal income	202.3	346.4	677.7	2,830.8
Less:	Difference between BEA and IRS estimates of adjusted gross income[b]	23.1	30.9	46.0	308.3
Equals:	Adjusted gross income reported on individual returns[c]	179.1	315.5	631.7	2,522.5
Less:	Adjusted gross income reported on non-taxable returns[c]	20.6	18.3	21.4	40.8
Equals:	Adjusted gross income reported on taxable returns[c]	158.5	297.2	610.3	2,481.7
Less:	Deductions on taxable returns	19.0	44.5	102.6	-
	(a) Standard deductions	10.1	11.7	18.4	-
	(b) Itemized deductions	8.9	32.8	84.1	447.1[d]
Less:	Exemptions on taxable returns	55.2	81.2	107.0	87.6
Plus:	Tax preferences adjustment	-	-	0.1	*e*
Plus:	Unused zero-bracket amount	-	-	-	*e*
Equals:	Taxable income on taxable returns	84.3	171.5	400.9	1,947.0

[a] Largely taxable private pensions.
[b] Department of Commerce, Bureau of Economic Analysis; and Internal Revenue Service estimates.
[c] Net of deficits.
[d] Excess itemized deductions only; i.e., total itemized deductions less the zero-bracket amount.
[e] Included in taxable income.
Source: Department of Commerce, Bureau of Economic Analysis; and Treasury Department, Internal Revenue Service.

C42. Relationship of Federal Individual Income Tax to Alternative Measures of Income

Calendar Years 1948-1987

(Dollar Figures in Billions)

Calendar Year	Personal Income	Adjusted Gross Income	Income Tax Base Amount	Income Tax Base As Percent of Personal Income	Income Tax after Credits Amount	Income Tax after Credits As a Percent of Personal Income	Income Tax after Credits As a Percent of Adjusted Gross Income	Income Tax after Credits As a Percent of Tax Base
1948	$ 209.2	$ 163.6	$ 74.7	35.7%	$ 15.4	7.4%	9.4%	20.6%
1949	206.4	160.6	71.6	34.7	14.5	7.0	9.0	20.3
1950	228.1	179.1	84.3	37.0	18.4	8.1	11.6	21.8
1951	256.5	202.4	97.1	37.9	24.2	9.4	13.2	24.9
1952	273.8	215.3	107.4	39.2	27.8	10.2	14.1	25.9
1953	290.5	228.7	115.5	39.8	29.4	10.1	14.0	25.5
1954	293.0	229.2	115.2	39.3	26.7	9.1	12.7	23.2
1955	314.2	248.5	127.9	40.7	29.6	9.4	12.9	23.1
1956	337.2	267.8	141.4	41.9	32.7	9.7	13.1	23.1
1957	356.3	280.4	149.2	41.9	34.4	9.7	13.1	23.1
1958	367.1	281.2	149.2	40.6	34.3	9.3	13.1	23.0
1959	390.7	305.1	166.4	42.6	38.6	9.9	13.4	23.2
1960	409.4	315.5	171.5	41.9	39.5	9.6	13.3	23.0
1961	426.0	329.9	181.6	42.6	42.2	9.9	13.6	23.2
1962	453.2	348.7	195.0	43.0	44.9	9.9	13.6	23.0
1963	476.3	368.8	208.6	43.8	48.2	10.1	13.8	23.1
1964	510.2	396.7	229.3	44.9	47.2	9.3	12.6	20.6
1965	552.0	429.2	254.3	46.1	49.5	9.0	12.1	19.5
1966	600.8	468.5	285.5	47.5	56.1	9.3	12.5	19.6
1967	644.5	504.8	314.3	48.8	62.9	9.8	12.9	20.0
1968	707.2	554.4	352.0	49.8	76.6	10.8	14.2	21.8
1969	772.9	603.5	388.2	50.2	86.6	11.2	14.7	22.3
1970	831.8	631.7	401.2	48.2	83.8	10.1	13.7	20.9
1971	894.0	673.6	413.4	46.2	85.2	9.5	13.1	20.6
1972	981.6	746.0	444.6	45.3	93.4	9.5	13.0	21.0
1973	1,101.7	827.1	510.6	46.3	107.9	9.8	13.5	21.1
1974	1,210.1	905.5	572.4	47.3	123.5	10.2	14.0	21.6
1975	1,313.4	947.8	595.5	45.3	124.4	9.5	13.8	20.9
1976	1,451.4	1,053.9	669.4	46.1	140.8	9.7	14.0	21.0
1977	1,607.5	1,158.5	905.9	56.4	158.5	9.9	14.4	17.5
1978	1,812.4	1,302.4	1,027.3	56.7	186.7	10.3	15.0	18.2
1979	2,034.0	1,465.4	1,127.5	55.4	213.3	10.5	15.2	18.9
1980	2,258.5	1,613.7	1,280.0	56.7	249.1	11.0	16.0	19.5
1981	2,520.9	1,772.6	1,383.7	54.9	282.3	11.2	16.4	20.4
1982	2,670.8	1,852.1	1,445.7	54.1	276.1	10.3	15.3	19.1
1983	2,838.6	1,942.6	1,516.3	53.4	271.7	9.6	14.3	17.9
1984	3,108.7	2,139.9	1,701.4	54.7	297.4	9.6	14.2	17.5
1985	3,325.3	2,306.0	1,820.7	54.8	321.9	9.7	14.3	17.7
1986	3,531.1	2,481.7	1,947.0	55.1	360.6	10.2	14.3	18.5
1987[a]	3,780.0	2,788.0	1,858.7	49.2	370.0	9.8	14.3	19.9

[a] Income tax data preliminary.
Source: Treasury Department, Department of Commerce, and Tax Foundation computations.

C43. Federal Income Taxes Generated Measured by Adjusted Gross Income Class

Tax Years 1979 and 1987[a]

Adjusted Gross Income Class	Income Level		Percent of Tax Paid		Average Tax	
	1979	1987	1979	1987	1979	1987
Highest 5%	$39,000 or more	$71,125 or more	37.6%	43.0%	$17,407	$29,820
Highest 10%	32,710 or more	54,700 or more	49.5	55.4	11,456	19,214
Highest 25%	21,760 or more	34,260 or more	73.1	76.7	6,769	10,643
Highest 50%	11,870 or more	17,598 or more	93.2	94.1	4,315	6,526
Lowest 50%	11,869 or less	17,597 or less	6.8	5.9	313	410
Lowest 25%	5,565 or less	7,800 or less	0.5	0.7	46	90
Lowest 10%	2,212 or less	2,880 or less	b	b	9	25

1987 Income and Tax Data

Adjusted Gross Income Class	Total Individual Returns (thousands)	Total Adjusted Gross Income ($billions)	Percentage of Adjusted Gross Income	Average Tax Rate
Highest 5%	5,353	$713.4	25.6%	22.4%
Highest 10%	10,705	1,032.5	37.0	19.9
Highest 25%	26,763	1,705.4	61.2	16.7
Highest 50%	53,526	2,383.6	85.5	14.7
Lowest 50%	53,526	404.5	14.5	5.4
Lowest 25%	26,763	73.0	2.6	3.3
Lowest 10%	10,705	-13.1	—	—

[a] Data for 1987 are preliminary.
[b] Less than .07 percent.
Source: Tax Foundation computations based on Statistics of Income, Internal Revenue Service, U.S. Department of the Treasury.

C44. Federal Individual Income Tax Returns and Related Data by State

Income Year 1987

(Dollar Amounts in Thousands)

State	Number of Returns		Adjusted Gross Income	Total Tax Liability		
					Average	
	With Tax Liability	With No Tax Liability		Amount	Per Taxable Return	Per Capita[a]
Total[b]	91,119,609	16,282,452	$ 2,772,619,841	$ 386,357,209	$ 4,240	$ 1,587
Alabama	1,281,165	302,719	35,491,432	4,426,484	3,455	1,084
Alaska	305,104	28,423	6,926,876	1,043,533	3,420	1,988
Arizona	1,222,666	243,087	36,151,357	4,615,277	3,775	1,363
Arkansas	726,249	182,051	18,302,823	2,185,528	3,009	915
California	10,512,603	1,935,926	355,446,757	50,216,312	4,777	1,815
Colorado	1,259,984	205,647	36,992,444	4,885,027	3,877	1,482
Connecticut	1,495,588	155,905	55,089,657	9,183,726	6,141	2,860
Delaware	266,355	39,262	8,240,864	1,124,878	4,223	1,747
Florida	4,633,080	899,456	140,278,994	20,736,508	4,476	1,725
Georgia	2,229,724	431,492	66,241,101	8,759,810	3,929	1,408
Hawaii	439,394	66,908	12,670,065	1,640,755	3,734	1,515
Idaho	313,332	64,646	7,810,313	904,315	2,886	906
Illinois	4,355,429	722,867	139,481,851	20,912,962	4,802	1,806
Indiana	2,004,654	380,592	56,972,232	7,532,781	3,758	1,362
Iowa	1,021,053	178,778	26,435,242	3,359,015	3,290	1,185
Kansas	908,592	154,760	25,880,407	3,535,965	3,892	1,428
Kentucky	1,168,913	259,094	31,244,592	3,924,439	3,357	1,053
Louisiana	1,259,820	345,600	34,439,198	4,456,136	3,537	999
Maine	466,153	75,220	12,362,604	1,555,973	3,338	1,311
Maryland	1,960,048	260,766	65,237,577	9,070,694	4,628	2,000
Massachusetts	2,617,242	284,900	85,613,540	12,911,003	4,933	2,205
Michigan	3,421,729	570,605	106,118,816	14,632,718	4,276	1,591
Minnesota	1,718,690	231,111	49,166,071	6,368,518	3,705	1,500
Mississippi	712,645	229,662	18,120,118	2,094,264	2,939	798
Missouri	1,856,091	333,323	52,928,425	7,217,637	3,889	1,414
Montana	270,459	65,637	6,429,208	778,279	2,878	962
Nebraska	591,741	102,521	15,195,086	1,955,460	3,305	1,227
Nevada	430,511	71,842	13,020,220	1,908,668	4,433	1,895
New Hampshire	478,414	55,272	15,125,319	2,211,103	4,622	2,092
New Jersey	3,528,569	419,585	122,658,740	18,919,420	5,362	2,466
New Mexico	477,467	129,929	12,699,844	1,523,963	3,192	1,016
New York	6,908,152	1,006,829	235,394,545	34,943,260	5,058	1,960
North Carolina	2,374,741	464,765	65,454,953	8,182,060	3,445	1,276
North Dakota	237,805	42,427	5,613,528	706,667	2,972	1,052
Ohio	4,091,529	694,596	117,266,957	15,568,112	3,805	1,444
Oklahoma	1,016,186	226,089	27,519,432	3,515,864	3,460	1,075
Oregon	1,002,296	196,483	27,523,256	3,369,459	3,362	1,237
Pennsylvania	4,547,167	763,750	131,421,755	18,199,689	4,002	1,525
Rhode Island	407,961	54,816	11,856,788	1,624,975	3,983	1,648
South Carolina	1,157,729	253,515	31,120,046	3,677,911	3,177	1,074
South Dakota	242,398	51,733	5,536,434	709,149	2,926	1,000
Tennessee	1,684,986	361,992	46,293,009	6,202,822	3,681	1,278
Texas	5,516,129	1,256,684	164,815,221	23,936,483	4,339	1,426
Utah	517,880	101,518	14,379,025	1,583,725	3,058	943
Vermont	220,774	31,984	5,916,723	762,160	3,452	1,391
Virginia	2,363,623	346,047	74,654,147	10,170,891	4,303	1,723
Washington	1,765,588	285,580	52,165,381	7,214,494	4,086	1,590
West Virginia	549,736	121,622	14,483,000	1,746,777	3,177	921
Wisconsin	1,829,563	291,176	50,642,199	6,362,271	3,477	1,324
Wyoming	164,777	31,698	4,509,276	605,029	3,672	1,235
District of Columbia	276,709	48,103	9,058,484	1,381,825	4,994	2,222

[a] Per capita figures by state based on resident population as of July 1, 1987; for total U.S. based on total U.S. population (including armed forces overseas) as of July 1, 1987.

[b] Total includes returns with addresses outside the United States.

Source: Treasury Department and Department of Commerce, Bureau of the Census.

C45. Median Incomes, Before and After Direct Federal Taxes And Inflation

Calendar Years 1959-1989

Year	Median Family Income[a]	Direct Federal Taxes			After-Tax Income	
		Income Tax[b]	Social Security	Total	Current Dollars	1967 Dollars[c]
1959	$ 5,661	$ 475	$ 120	$ 595	$ 5,066	$ 5,803
1960	5,847	501	144	645	5,202	5,865
1961	6,051	534	144	678	5,373	5,997
1962	6,202	558	150	708	5,494	6,064
1963	6,469	599	174	773	5,696	6,212
1964	6,724	539	174	713	6,011	6,470
1965	6,914	515	174	689	6,225	6,587
1966	7,463	597	277	874	6,589	6,779
1967	7,883	658	290	948	6,935	6,935
1968	8,444	802	343	1,145	7,299	7,005
1969	9,277	958	374	1,332	7,945	7,236
1970	9,750	939	374	1,313	8,437	7,255
1971	10,314	933	406	1,339	8,975	7,399
1972	11,152	982	468	1,450	9,702	7,743
1973	11,895	1,098	632	1,730	10,165	7,637
1974	13,004	1,267	761	2,028	10,976	7,431
1975	14,156	1,172	825	1,997	12,159	7,543
1976	15,016	1,388	878	2,266	12,750	7,478
1977	15,949	1,466	933	2,399	13,550	7,466
1978	17,318	1,717	1,048	2,765	14,553	7,448
1979	19,048	1,881	1,168	3,049	15,999	7,359
1980	20,586	2,143	1,262	3,405	17,181	6,962
1981	21,462	2,267	1,427	3,694	17,768	6,523
1982	23,036	2,342	1,543	3,885	19,151	6,624
1983	23,943	2,277	1,604	3,881	20,062	6,723
1984	25,415	2,395	1,703	4,098	21,317	6,852
1985	25,992	2,466	1,832	4,298	21,694	6,733
	Two-Earner Median Family Income[d]					1989 Dollars[c]
1980	29,627	4,050	1,816	5,866	23,761	35,731
1981	32,224	4,386	2,143	6,529	25,695	35,007
1982	34,515	4,450	2,313	6,763	27,752	35,625
1983	36,106	4,300	2,419	6,719	29,387	36,551
1984	38,713	4,634	2,710	7,344	31,369	37,389
1985	40,593	4,787	2,862	7,649	32,944	37,954
1986	42,492	5,158	3,038	8,196	34,296	38,753
1987	44,536	5,291	3,184	8,475	36,061	39,325
1988[e]	46,870	5,632	3,510	9,142	37,728	39,423
1989[e]	49,326	6,164	3,684	9,848	39,478	39,478

[a] Median income for all families with one earner employed full-time, year-round.
[b] Married couple filing joint return, two children.
[c] Adjusted by Consumer Price Index, (1967 = 100).
[d] Median income for all married-couple families with wife in paid labor force.
[e] Estimate by Tax Foundation.

Source: Department of Commerce, Bureau of the Census; Department of Labor, Bureau of Labor Statistics; and Tax Foundation computations.

C46. Federal Corporation Income Tax Data[a]

Selected Income Years 1939-1985[b]

Item	1939	1949	1959	1969	1979	1981	1985
				Thousands			
Total number of returns	470	615	1,074	1,659	2,557	2,812	3,277
Return with net income	199	385	671	1,046	1,586	1,597	1,820
Returns with no net income	270	230	404	613	970	1,215	1,457
				$Millions			
Total compiled receipts	$ 132,878	$ 393,450	$ 816,800	$1,680,483	$ 5,598,689	$ 7,026,352	$ 8,398,278
Returns with net income	105,658	350,169	719,416	1,461,061	4,890,972	5,461,362	6,420,237
Return with no net income	27,220	43,281	97,384	219,422	707,717	1,564,990	1,978,041
Total net income	6,735	28,195	46,797	80,219	284,616	213,649	240,119
Returns with net income	8,827	30,577	51,651	93,433	321,650	301,441	363,867
Returns with no net income (deficit)	2,092	2,382	4,854	13,214	37,034	87,792	123,748
Total dividends paid[c]	5,747	9,569	16,242	32,951	86,614	120,295	n.a.
Return with net income	5,562	9,409	15,797	31,827	82,396	110,555	n.a.
Return with no net income	184	160	445	1,124	4,218	9,740	n.a.
Total tax liability	1,232	9,817	22,525	33,477	65,888	58,445	63,348[d]

[a] Active corporations only.
[b] For most large corporations, the accounting period coincides with the calendar year. Returns for each year also include those corporations with fiscal years ending within six months before or after the end of the calendar year.
[c] Dividends paid in cash and assets other than own stock.
[d] Amount due after credits, including U.S. possessions tax credits of $2,451 million and foreign tax credits of $24,263 million.
Source: Treasury Department.

C47. Federal Corporation Income Tax Rates

Income Years 1909-1989

Year	Rate Brackets or Exemptions	Rate[a] (Percent)
1909-1913	$5,000 exemption	1
1913-1915	No exemption after March 1, 1913	1
1916	None	2
1917	None	6
1918	$2,000 exemption	12
1919-1921	$2,000 exemption	10
1922-1924	$2,000 exemption	12.5
1925	$2,000 exemption	13
1926-1927	$2,000 exemption	13.5
1928	$3,000 exemption	12
1929	$3,000 exemption	11
1930-1931	$3,000 exemption	12
1932-1935	None	13.75
1936-1937	Graduated normal tax ranging from—	
	First $2,000	8
	Over $40,000	15
	Graduated surtax on undistributed profits ranging from—	7-27
1938-1939	First $25,000	12.5-16
	Over $25,000	19[b]
1940	First $25,000	14.85-18.7
	$25,000 to $31,964.30	38.3
	$31,964.30 to $38,565.89	36.9
	Over $38,565.89	24
1941	First $25,000	21-25
	$25,000 to $38,461.54	44
	Over $38,461.54	31
1942-1945	First $25,000	25-29
	$25,000 to $50,000	53
	Over $50,000	40
1946-1949	First $25,000	21-25
	$25,000 to $50,000	53
	Over $50,000	38
1950	First $25,000	23
	Over $25,000	42
1951	First $25,000	28.75
	Over $25,000	50.75

Continued

C47. Federal Corporation Income Tax Rates (continued)
Income Years 1909-1989

Year	Rate Brackets or Exemptions	Rate[a] (Percent)
1952-1963	First $25,000	30
	Over $25,000	52
1964	First $25,000	22
	Over $25,000	50
1965-1967	First $25,000	22
	Over $25,000	48
1968-1969	First $25,000	24.2[c]
	Over $25,000	52.8[c]
1970	First $25,000	22.55[c]
	Over $25,000	49.2[c]
1971-1974	First $25,000	22
	Over $25,000	48
1975-1978	First $25,000	20
	Next $25,000	22
	Over $50,000	48
1979-1981	First $25,000	17
	$25,000 to $50,000	20
	$50,000 to $75,000	30
	$75,000 to $100,000	40
	Over $100,000	46
1982	First $25,000	16
	$25,000 to $50,000	19
	$50,000 to $75,000	30
	$75,000 to $100,000	40
	Over $100,000	46
1983-1986	First $25,000	15
	$25,000 to $50,000	18
	$50,000 to $75,000	30
	$75,000 to $100,000	40
	Over $100,000	46
1987-1989[d]	First $50,000	15
	$50,000 to $75,000	25
	Over $75,000[e]	34

[a] In addition to the rates shown, certain types of "excess profits" levies were in effect in 1917-1921, 1933-1945, and 1950-1953.
[b] Less adjustments: 14.025% of dividends received and 2.5% of dividends paid.
[c] Includes surcharge of 10% in 1968 and 1969 and 2.5% in 1970.
[d] Rates shown effective for tax years beginning on or after July 1, 1987. Income in taxable years that include July 1, 1987 (other than as the first date of such year) is subject to a blended rate.
[e] An additional 5% tax is imposed on a corporation's taxable income in excess of $100,000 up to a $335,000 maximum, making the marginal rate 39%. Maximum additional tax is $11,750; this provision phases out the benefit of graduated rates for corporations with taxable income between $100,000 and $335,000; corporations with income above $335,000, in effect, pay a flat tax at a 34% rate.
Source: Treasury Department, Office of Tax Analysis.

C48. Income on Federal Corporation Income Tax Returns by Income Class[a]
Selected Income Years 1939-1985[b]

Income Subject to Tax ($Thousands)	1939		1949		1959		1969		1985[c]	
	Number of Returns	Net Income ($Millions)	Number of Returns	Net Income ($Millions)	Number of Returns	Net Income ($Millions)	Number of Returns	Net Income ($Millions)	Number of Returns	Net Income ($Millions)
Total	199,479	$ 8,827	384,772	$ 30,577	670,581	$ 51,651	778,290	$ 83,878	1,015,325	$ 257,512
Under 5	131,275	170	185,907	309	314,233	470	296,318	821	911,004	22,924
5 under 25	43,758	512	123,432	1,543	232,847	2,899	297,287	4,389		
25 under 100	15,705	775	50,014	2,424	90,891	4,036	136,234	6,785	63,201	12,114
100 under 250	4,649	718	14,324	2,218	18,141	2,771	28,621	4,784	21,747	11,784
250 under 500	1,885	662	5,173	1,812	6,576	2,293	9,702	3,685	8,574	9,673
500 under 1,000	1,046	729	2,766	1,933	3,528	2,459	4,901	3,788	4,975	10,384
1,000 under 5,000	943	1,997	2,441	5,054	3,247	6,835	3,914	8,907	5,083	53,384
5,000 under 10,000	125	888	354	2,483	512	3,558	577	4,467		
10,000 and over	93	2,376	361	12,800	606	26,332	734	46,252	743	137,248

[a] Returns with net income.
[b] For most large corporations, the accounting period coincides with the calendar year. Returns for each year also include those corporations with fiscal years ending within six months before or after the end of the calendar year.
[c] Data for 1985 exclude returns and income of corporations filing tax forms 1120S, 1120-DISC, and 1120-FSC.
Source: Treasury Department.

C49. Federal Excise Tax Collections by Type of Tax

Selected Fiscal Years 1959-1988

($Millions)

Type of Tax	1959	1969	1979	1988
Total	$ 10,759.5	$ 15,542.8	$ 19,049.5	$ 36,259.0
Alcohol taxes[a]	3,002.1	4,555.6	5,647.9	5,709.0
Distilled spirits	2,137.1	3,390.8	3,945.0	3,876.0
Wines	92.4	157.4	198.3	280.0
Beer	772.5	1,007.3	1,504.6	1,610.0
Tobacco taxes	1,806.8	2,137.6	2,495.5	4,616.0
Cigars	51.1	54.2	36.2	40.0
Cigarettes	1,738.1	2,082.1	2,454.8	4,550.0
Other[b]	17.7	1.3	4.5	26.0
Manufacturers' excise taxes	3,958.8	6,501.1	7,057.6	10,643.4
Gasoline and gasohol	1,700.3	3,186.2	4,525.1	9,456.6
Lubricating oils[c]	73.7	97.5	108.6	-
Passenger automobiles, bodies, etc.[d]	1,039.3	1,864.0	p	-
Trucks, buses, trailers, etc.[d]	215.3	589.3	965.5	-
Parts and accessories for automobiles, trucks, etc.[e]	166.2	81.4	223.7	-
Tires, tubes, and tread rubber[f]	278.9	631.5	878.3	319.1
Fishing rods, creels, reels, etc.	5.6	11.9	30.4	76.8
Firearms, shells, and cartridges	13.9	33.1	71.4	85.0
Pistols and revolvers	2.0	6.2	17.5	29.1
Black lung (coal excises)	-	-	232.1	601.3
Other[g]	463.6	.1	5.0	75.5
Retailers' excise taxes	408.3	224.7	553.3	4,528.3
Noncommercial aviation gasoline	-	-	10.7	7.7
Noncommercial aviation fuel other than gasoline	-	-	35.9	214.7
Diesel and special motor fuels[c]	52.5	224.7	506.7	3,148.7
Other[h]	355.7	p	-	1,157.2
Stamp taxes[i]	133.8	1.5	-	-
Miscellaneous excise taxes[j]	383.4	1,922.9	3,223.0	8,717.1
Toll telephone, telegraph, radio and cable facilities, telephone service, etc.	690.4	1,316.4	1,362.2	2,555.1
Transportation of persons by air	227.0	223.7	1,272.0	2,875.0
Transportation of property by air	143.3	-	79.0	172.4
Use of international air travel facilities	-	-	74.6	98.1
Coin-operated gaming devices[k]	16.9	12.3	4.9	-
Sugar[l]	86.4	108.2	-	-
Narcotics and marijuana[a, m]	1.0	1.9	-	-
Firearms, transfer, and occupational taxes	p	.1	.7	p
Wagering[a]	6.8	4.7	10.0	11.4
Use tax on highway motor vehicles weighing over 26,000 pounds	32.5	124.3	251.8	570.1
Use tax on civil aircraft[n]	-	-	27.7	-
Interest equalization	-	111.7	-	-
Foreign insurance	-	18.5	69.3	721.2
Exempt organizations	-	-	68.6	244.9
Employee pension plans	-	-	2.1	171.2
Windfall profits tax[o]	-	-	-	372.8
Unclassified excise taxes	66.4	199.5	72.1	2,045.3

[a] Includes occupational taxes.
[b] Includes taxes on cigarette papers and tubes and miscellaneous tobacco collections.
[c] Repealed, effective after January 6, 1983.
[d] Taxes on passenger automobiles and light trucks repealed effective December 11, 1971.
[e] Repealed for parts and accessories for automobiles effective January 1, 1966; tax on truck parts and accessories repealed effective after January 6, 1983.
[f] Taxes on inner tubes and tread rubber repealed effective January 1, 1984.
[g] Includes amounts collected or adjusted for taxes that have been repealed or expired, mainly under Excise Tax Reduction Act of 1965. See footnotes to Table C50. Also includes excise tax collections on bows and arrows, and alcohol sold but not used as fuel. For 1979, also includes excise taxes on sugar and interest equalization, which have expired.
[h] Includes excise taxes on inland waterway fuel, truck and bus chassis, bodies, etc. (imposed at the retailer rather than manufacturer level, effective April 1, 1983), jewelry, furs, toilet preparations, luggage, handbags, etc.
[i] Tax on issues and transfers of stocks and bonds repealed effective January 1, 1966. Tax on silver bullion sales or transfers repealed effective June 3, 1963. Tax on playing cards repealed effective June 22, 1965.
[j] Total includes items not shown separately.
[k] Repealed effective June 30, 1980.
[l] Terminated effective June 30, 1975.
[m] Repealed effective May 1, 1971.
[n] Expired September 30, 1980. Officially repealed.
[o] Tax on windfall profit from domestically-produced oil effective March 1, 1980. Figure for 1988 is incomplete and reflects only the amount from returns processed by the end of the reporting period. Repealed August 1988.
[p] Less than $50 thousand.
Source: Treasury Department; and Office of Management and Budget.

C50. Federal Excise Tax Rates on Selected Items

Selected Dates 1944-1989

Item Taxed	As of December 31			January 1, 1989
	1944	1954	1964	
Liquor taxes				
Distilled spirits (per proof gallon)	$ 9	$ 10.50	$ 10.50	$ 12.50
Still wines (per wine gallon)[a]				
Not over 14% alcohol	15¢	17¢	17¢	17¢
14 to 21% alcohol	60¢	67¢	67¢	67¢
21 to 24% alcohol	$ 2	$ 2.25	$ 2.25	$ 2.25
Beer (per 31-gallon barrel)	$ 8	$ 9	$ 9	$ 9
Tobacco taxes				
Small cigars, not over 3 lbs. per thousand (per thousand)	75¢	75¢	75¢	75¢
Large cigars, over 3 lbs. per thousand (per thousand)	$ 2.50 to $ 20	$ 2.50 to $ 20	$ 2.50 to $ 20	8-1/2% of wholesale price to $ 20
Cigarettes (per thousand, 3 lbs. or less)[b]	$ 3.50	$ 4	$ 4	$ 8
Tobacco and snuff (per pound)	18¢	10¢	10¢	c
Stamp taxes, documentary, etc.				
Documentary stamps on conveyances (per $500 of value and fractional part thereof)	50¢	55¢	55¢	c
Documentary stamps on issuance of bonds and stock (per $100 of value, respectively)	10¢, 10¢	11¢, 11¢	11¢, 10¢	c
Transfers of bonds and stock (per $100 of value, respectively)	4¢	5¢	5¢, 4¢	c
Playing cards (per package of not more than 54)	10¢	13¢	13¢	d
Manufacturers' excise taxes				
Lubricating oils (per gallon)	6¢	6¢	6¢	e
Matches, white phosphorous (per hundred)	2¢	2¢	2¢	d
Matches, in general (per thousand)	2¢	2¢	2¢	d
Gasoline (per gallon)	1.5¢	2¢	2¢	9¢
Highway tires (per pound respectively)	5¢	5¢	10¢	15¢ to 50¢[f]
Inner tubes (per pound)	9¢	9¢	10¢	g
Tread rubber (per pound)	-	-	5¢	g
Automobiles (sale price)	7%	10%	10%	h
Automotive accessories (sale price)	5%	8%	8%	c
Trucks (sale price)	7%	10%	10%	12%
Radios and accessories (sale price)	10%	10%	10%	d
Refrigerators, household-type (sale price)	10%	10%	5%	d
Electric, gas, and oil appliances (sale price)	10%	10%	5%	d
Firearms, shells, cartridges (sale price)	11%	11%	11%	11%
Pistols and revolvers (sale price)	11%	11%	10%	10%
Sporting goods, except fishing equipment (sale price)	10%	10%	10%	d
Musical instruments and phonographs (sale price)	10%	10%	10%	d
Records (sale price)	10%	10%	10%	d
Business and store machines (sale price)	10%	10%	10%	d
Cameras and photographic apparatus (sale price)	25%	10%	10%	d
Photographic film (sale price)	15%	20%	10%	d
Bows and arrows (sale price)	-	-	-	11%
Fishing equipment (sale price)	-	10%	10%	10%
Gas guzzler tax	-	-	-	i
Miscellaneous excise taxes				
General telephone service (amount paid)	15%	10%	10%	3%[j]
Toll telephone service (amount paid)	25%	10%	10%	3%[j]
Cable and radio messages (amount paid)	25%	10%	10%	c

Continued

C50. Federal Excise Tax Rates on Selected Items (continued)
Selected Dates 1944-1989

Item Taxed	As of December 31			January 1, 1989
	1944	1954	1964	
Leased wires, or teletypewriter and wire message service (amount paid)	25%	10%	10%	c
Wire and equipment services (amount paid)	25%	10%	10%	c
Bowling alleys, pool tables (per unit, per year)	$ 20	$ 20	$ 20	k
Transportation of persons by air (amount paid)	15%	10%	5%	8%
International departure ticket	-	-	-	$ 3
Air freight (domestic waybills)	-	-	-	5%
Lease of safe deposit boxes (amount paid)	20%	10%	10%	h
Cabarets, roof gardens, etc. (amount paid)	20%	20%	10%	l
Admissions (for every 5¢ or major fraction, 1944-1953; 10¢ or major fraction, 1954-1964)	1¢	1¢	1¢	l
Leases of boxes or seats (amount for which similar accommodations are sold)	20%	10%	10%	l
Wagers (amount wagered except parimutuel)	10%	10%	10%	2%[m]
Occupation of accepting wagers (per year)	-	$ 50	$ 50	m
Dues and initiation fees (amount paid)	20%	20%	20%	l
Coin-operated amusement and gambling devices (per unit, per year, respectively)	$ 10, $100	$ 10, $250	$ 10, $250	l
Foreign insurance policies (premium paid)				
Life insurance	1%	1%	1%	1%
Other insurance	4%	4%	4%	4%
Coal sales, underground and surface mines (per ton, respectively)	-	-	-	$1.10, 55¢
Windfall profits tax (percent of windfall profit)	-	-	-	n
Use tax on heavy highway vehicles (per year)	-	-	o	p
Environmental ("superfund") excise taxes				
Crude oil (per barrel[i], domestic and imported, respectively)	-	-	-	8.2¢, 11.7¢
Chemicals (per ton)[i]	-	-	-	22¢ to $4.87[q]
Retailers' excise taxes				
Jewelry (sale price)	20%	10%	10%	d
Furs (sale price)	20%	20%	10%	d
Toilet preparations (sale price)	20%	20%	10%	d
Luggage (sale price)	20%	20%	20%	d
Diesel fuel for highway vehicles (per gallon)	-	-	-	15¢
Gasoline substitute fuels for highway vehicles and motor boats	-	-	-	9¢
Gasoline used in noncommercial aviation (per gallon)	-	-	-	12¢
Aviation fuel other than gasoline (per gallon)	-	-	-	14¢
Inland waterways users' fuel (per gallon)	-	-	-	10¢[q]
Gasohol (per gallon)	-	-	-	3¢

a Artificially carbonated wines are taxed at $2.40 per wine gallon; sparkling wines at $3.40 per wine gallon.
b Cigarettes weighing more than 3 lbs. per thousand are currently taxed at $16.80 per thousand.
c Repealed January 1, 1966. Snuff at 24 cents per pound, chewing tobacco at 8 cents per pound as of 7/1/86.
d Repealed June 22, 1965.
e Repealed January 7, 1983.
f On tires weighing 40 lbs. or less, no tax; over 40 lbs. but under 70 lbs. tax is 15¢ per lb. over 40 lbs.; over 70 lbs. but under 90 lbs., $4.50 plus 30¢ per lb. over 70 lbs.; over 90 lbs., $10.50 plus 50¢ per lb. over 90 lbs.
g Repealed January 1, 1984.
h Repealed August 16, 1971.
i Imposed on passenger automobiles weighing 6,000 lbs. or less that fail to meet prescribed fuel efficiency standards. In 1987, for a 1986 or later model car, tax ranges from $500 for cars with fuel economy rating (in miles per gallon) of at least 21.5 but less than 22.5 to $3,850 for cars with rating of less than 12.5 miles per gallon.
j Tax expires December 31, 1990.
k Repealed July 1, 1965.
l Repealed December 31, 1965.
m For wagers authorized under state law, rate is .25%. An occupational tax of $500 per year is imposed on businesses accepting wagers ($50 if authorized under state law).
n Repealed August 1988.
o $3 per 1,000 lbs. of gross weight over 26,000 lbs.
p On vehicles under 55,000 lbs., no tax; 55,000-75,000 lbs. – $100 plus $22 per 1,000 lbs. over 55,000; over 75,000 lbs – $550.
q Scheduled to rise in graduated steps to 20¢ per gallon in 1995 and thereafter.
Source: Commerce Clearing House and Joint Committee on Taxation.

C51. Federal Estate and Gift Tax Rates

September 9, 1916 to October 1, 1989[a]

($Thousands)

A. Federal Estate Tax

Revenue Act or Internal Revenue Code[a]	Effective Date	Specific Exemption	Minimum Rate (Percent)	Minimum On Taxable Estate Under[b]	Maximum Rate (Percent)	Maximum On Taxable Estate Above[b]	Credit for State Death Taxes (Percent of Federal Tax)[c]
1916	9/9/16	$50	1	$50	10	$5,000	-
1917	3/3/17	50	1.5	50	15	5,000	-
	10/4/17	50	2	50	25	10,000	-
1918, 1921	2/24/19	50	1	50	25	10,000	-
1924	6/2/24	50	1	50	25	10,000	25
1926	2/26/26	100	1	50	20	10,000	80
1932	6/6/32	50	1	10	45	10,000	} 80% of basic tax[c]
1934	5/11/34	50	1	10	60	10,000	
1935	8/31/35[d]	40	2	10	70	50,000	
1941	9/21/41	40	3	5	77	10,000	
1942	10/22/42[e]	60	3	5	77	10,000	
1954	8/17/54	60	3	5	77	10,000	f
1976	1/1/77	g	h	h	70	5,000	f
1981	1/1/82	g	h	h	65[i]	4,000[i]	f

B. Federal Gift Tax

Revenue Act or Internal Revenue Code[a]	Effective Date	Specific Exemption[j]	Annual Exclusion Per Donee[k]	Minimum Rate (Percent)	Minimum On Taxable Gifts Under[b]	Maximum Rate (Percent)	Maximum On Taxable Gifts Above[b]
1924	6/2/24	$50	$5	1	$5	25	$10,000
1932	6/7/32	50	5	.75	10	33.5	10,000
1934	1/1/35	50	5	.75	10	45	10,000
1935	1/1/36[d]	40	4[l]	1.5	10	52.5	50,000
1941	1/1/42	40	4	2.25	5	57.75	10,000
1942	1/1/43[e]	30	3	2.25	5	57.75	10,000
1954	8/17/54	30	3	2.25	5	57.75	10,000
1976	1/1/77	g	3	h	h	70	5,000[i]
1981	1/1/82	g	10	h	h	65[i]	4,000[i]

a   The October 1, 1989 date is solely for a cut-off date for the table. Only those acts which made a significant change in the statutory rate structure are listed. (See also footnote e below.)

b   After deduction of the specific exemption, and, in the case of the gift tax, of the annual exclusion for donees.

c   For the period June 6, 1932- August 16, 1954, the credit for state taxes was 80% of the "basic tax," which was the Federal tax under the Revenue Act of 1926.

d   A defense tax of 10% of the gift and net estate was added by the 1940 Act (effective June 26, 1940) and integrated with the ordinary rates by the Revenue Act of 1941.

e   The Revenue Act of 1948 provided a marital deduction by which property passing to a spouse may be tax-exempt up to one-half of the "adjusted gross estate" or of amount of gift to a third person (effective January 1, 1948 for estate tax and April 3, 1948 for gift tax). The Tax Reform Act of 1976 established a limit of $250,000 or one-half of the "adjusted gross estate," whichever is greater, for persons dying after December 31, 1976.

f   The credit is limited to a percentage of the taxable estate through a graduated set of rates, starting at 0.8% of the taxable estate from $40,000 to $90,000 and rising to 16% of taxable estate in excess of $10,400,000. This was merely a change in the method of calculating the credit for state taxes; it did not affect the amount of tax.

g   The Tax Reform Act of 1976 established a unified credit against estate and gift taxes in lieu of specific exemptions. The amount of the credit was phased in over a period of five years; $30,000 in 1977, $34,000 in 1978, $38,000 in 1979, $42,500 in 1980, $47,000 in 1981. The Economic Recovery Tax Act of 1981 raised the credit to $62,800 in 1982, $79,300 in 1983, $96,300 in 1984, $121,800 in 1985, $155,800 in 1986, and $192,800 in 1987 and subsequent years.

h   Although the nominal minimum rate is 18% of combined gifts and estates under $10,000, the effect of the credit was a minimum rate of 30% of taxable estates and gifts over $120,666 in 1977, rising to a minimum rate of 37% of taxable estates and gifts over $600,000 in 1987 and thereafter.

i   A 60% maximum rate applied for 1983 for amounts in excess of $3.5 million; for 1984-1987, 55% for amounts in excess of $3 million; in 1988 and thereafter, a 50% rate is applied for amounts in excess of $2.5 million.

j   Under the Revenue Act of 1924, the specific exemption was allowed for each calendar year. Under later acts, the specific exemption was allowed but once and taken all in one year or over a period of years, at the option of the donor.

k   Not applicable to gifts of future interest for 1932 and later years, nor to gifts in trust 1939-1942.

l   The reduction in the annual exclusion from $5,000 to $4,000 was effective January 1, 1939.

Source: Treasury Department.

C52. Federal Estate and Gift Tax Burden
Calendar Years 1983, 1985, 1988

Taxable Estate Including Cumulative Gifts[a]	1983[b]		1985[b]		1988[b]	
	Amount of Tax[c]	Effective Rate[d]	Amount of Tax[c]	Effective Rate[d]	Amount of Tax[c]	Effective Rate[d]
$ 500,000	$ 66,500	13.3	$ 24,000	4.8	-	-
750,000	148,600	19.8	106,100	14.1	$ 35,100	4.7
1,000,000	233,300	23.3	190,800	19.1	119,800	12.0
2,000,000	601,900	30.1	559,400	28.0	488,400	24.4
5,000,000	2,004,900	40.1	1,877,400	37.5	1,691,400	33.8
7,500,000	3,191,300	42.6	2,938,800	39.2	2,627,800	35.0
10,000,000	4,328,900	43.3	3,951,400	39.5	3,515,400	35.2
15,000,000	6,529,700	43.5	5,902,200	39.3	5,216,200	34.8
25,000,000	10,929,700	43.7	9,802,200	39.2	8,616,200	34.5
50,000,000	21,929,700	43.9	19,552,200	39.1	17,116,200	34.2
100,000,000	43,929,700	43.9	39,052,200	39.1	34,116,200	34.1

[a] Gross estate less any allowable deductions. Deductions are available for funeral expenses, administrative expenses, losses incurred during administration of the estate, debts, charitable contributions, and bequests to spouse.

[b] In 1983, the maximum unified Federal credit was $79,300, and the maximum tax rate was 60% on amounts over $3.5 million. For 1985, the maximum credit is $121,800, with a maximum tax rate of 55% on amounts over $3 million. For 1988 and later years, the maximum credit will be $192,800 and the maximum tax rate 50% on amounts over $2.5 million.

[c] Amounts of tax shown are after allowances for the maximum credit for state death taxes and the unified Federal credit. The former credit is computed in accordance with current Federal law, which no longer provides for personal exemptions in arriving at taxable estate. For many states, therefore, Federal credit may exceed actual state taxes paid. In practice, however, the Federal credit is limited to the amount of state taxes paid.

[d] Tax as a percentage of taxable estate, including cumulative gifts.

Source: Computed by Tax Foundation from Treasury Department data.

C53. Old-Age, Survivors, Disability, and Hospital Insurance: Tax Rates And Maximum Tax[a]

Calendar Years 1937-2000

Year	Maximum Taxable Base	Tax Rate (Percent)			Maximum Tax (Dollars)		
		Combined Employer-Employee	Employer or Employee Alone	Self-Employed	Combined Employer-Employee	Employer or Employee Alone	Self-Employed
1937-1949	$ 3,000	2.0	1.0	b	$ 60	$ 30	b
1950	3,000	3.0	1.5	b	90	45	b
1951-1953	3,600	3.0	1.5	2.25	108	54	$81
1954	3,600	4.0	2.0	3.0	144	72	108
1955-1956	4,200	4.0	2.0	3.0	168	84	126
1957-1958	4,200	4.5	2.25	3.375	189	95	142
1959	4,800	5.0	2.5	3.75	240	120	180
1960-1961	4,800	6.0	3.0	4.5	288	144	216
1962	4,800	6.25	3.125	4.7	300	150	226
1963-1965	4,800	7.25	3.625	5.4	348	174	259
1966	6,600	8.4	4.2	6.15	554	277	406
1967	6,600	8.8	4.4	6.4	580	290	422
1968	7,800	8.8	4.4	6.4	686	343	499
1969-1970	7,800	9.6	4.8	6.9	748	374	538
1971	7,800	10.4	5.2	7.5	811	406	585
1972	9,000	10.4	5.2	7.5	936	468	675
1973	10,800	11.7	5.85	8.0	1,264	632	864
1974	13,200	11.7	5.85	7.9	1,544	772	1,043
1975	14,100	11.7	5.85	7.9	1,650	825	1,114
1976	15,300	11.7	5.85	7.9	1,790	895	1,209
1977	16,500	11.7	5.85	7.9	1,930	965	1,304
1978	17,700	12.1	6.05	8.1	2,142	1,071	1,434
1979	22,900	12.3	6.13	8.1	2,817	1,404	1,855
1980	25,900	12.3	6.13	8.1	3,186	1,588	2,098
1981	29,700	13.3	6.65	9.3	3,950	1,975	2,762
1982	32,400	13.4	6.70	9.35	4,342	2,171	3,029
1983	35,700	13.4	6.70	9.35	4,784	2,392	3,338
1984	37,800	14.0	7.00[d]	14.0[e]	5,292[d]	2,646[d]	5,292[e]
1985	39,600	14.1	7.05	14.1[e]	5,584	2,792	5,584[e]
1986	42,000	14.3	7.15	14.3[e]	6,006	3,003	6,006[e]
1987	43,800	14.3	7.15	14.3[e]	6,263	3,132	6,263[e]
1988	45,000	15.02	7.51	15.02[e]	6,759	3,380	6,759[e]
1989	48,000	15.02	7.51	15.02[e]	7,210	3,605	7,210[e]
1990-1999	c	15.3	7.65	15.3[e]	c	c	c
2000 & later	c	15.3	7.65	15.3[e]	c	c	c

[a] Disability insurance not included until 1956; hospital insurance not until 1966.
[b] Not covered until January 1, 1951.
[c] The base will be increased annually in line with wage levels whenever there has been a cost-of-living benefit adjustment in the preceding year. Maximum tax will vary accordingly.
[d] A credit of .3% of wages was allowed against 1984 employee taxes to reduce the net rate to 6.7%.
[e] For 1984-1989 credits will be allowed at the following rates of self-employment income: 2.7% in 1984; 2.3% in 1985; 2.0% in 1986-1989. Credit is to be replaced by a new arrangement beginning in 1990.
Source: Department of Health and Human Services, Social Security Administration.

C54. Old-Age, Survivors, Disability, and Health Insurance: Selected Benefits

A. Selected Monthly OASDI Benefits for Workers First Eligible in 1987[a]
December 1988

	Worker with Yearly Earnings Equal to:				
Beneficiary Family	Federal Minimum Wage[b]	75% of the Average Wage	Average Wage[c]	150% of the Average Wage	Maximum Wage Creditable[d]
Retired workers families[e]					
Average indexed monthly earnings[f]	$ 759.00	$ 1,084.00	$ 1,446.00	$ 1,964.00	$ 2,311.00
Primary insurance amount[g]	445.00	553.10	673.60	838.50	892.70
Maximum family benefit	693.90	988.20	1,230.10	1,467.80	1,562.70
Monthly benefit amount:					
Retired worker at age 62	356.00	442.00	538.00	670.00	714.00
Retired worker with spouse:					
age 65 or older	578.00	718.00	874.00	1,089.00	1,160.00
age 62	522.00	649.00	790.00	984.00	1,048.00
Survivor families[h]					
Maximum family benefits	661.10	990.70	1,231.80	1,525.50	1,753.40
Disabled worker families[i]					
Maximum family benefits	665.90	830.20	1,010.80	1,279.30	1,391.60

B. Hospital and Medical Benefits, 1989[j]

Beneficiary Cost Sharing	Period	Deductible	Coinsurance Payment
Hospitalization			
All covered services	k	First $ 560	l
Post-hospital extended care[m,n]			
Supplementary medical insurance[o]			

a The year of eligibility is defined as the year in which the worker attained age 62, became disabled, or died.
b Worker earned the federal minimum wage (currently $3.35 per hour) and worked 2,080 hours per year in all years used in the computation of the benefit.
c Worker earned the national average wage in each year used in the computation of the benefit.
d Worker earned the maximum amount of wages that can be credited to a worker's Social Security record in all years used in the computation of the benefit.
e Assumes the worker retired at age 62 in 1988 and had no prior period of disability.
f The indexing method for computing benefits was introduced by the 1977 Amendments and was effective in 1979. Under this method, the worker's earnings are first indexed to reflect average wage levels in the economy during his or her working years before the averaging of earnings takes place.
g The primary insurance amount (PIA) is derived from the following formula: 90% of first $310 of AIME, plus 32% of AIME over $310 through $1,866, plus 15% of AIME over $1,866. The result is rounded down to the lower $0.10.
h Assumes the deceased worker began to work at age 22, was deceased in 1988 at age 40, had no earnings in that year, and had no prior disability.
i Assumes the worker began to work at age 22, became disabled in 1988 at age 50, and had no prior period of disability.
j Available to most individuals age 65 and over and certain disabled workers at any age. Does not cover special cases of limited applicability.
k For 1989 and subsequent years, once the annual deductible has been paid, Medicare pays the balance of covered charges regardless of the number of days of hospitalization.
l For 1989 and subsequent years, the beneficiary pays a coinsurance amount equal to 20% of the national daily cost of SNF care for the first 8 days of care.
m The Medicare Catastrophic Coverage Act of 1988 increased to 150 the number of days in a skilled nursing facility per year.
n Hospice care extended beyond 210 days when enrollee certified as terminally ill.
o Includes the standard monthly SMI premium rate of $27.90 and a $4.00 monthly premium under the Medicare Catastrophic Coverage Act of 1988, which affects most Part B beneficiaries.
Source: Department of Health and Human Services, Social Security Administration.

C55. Allocation of the Federal Tax Burden by State

Fiscal Year 1989

State	Total Federal Tax Burden[a]		
	Percentage Distribution	Amount ($Millions)	Per Capita[b]
Total	100.00	$ 949,627	$ 3,825
Alabama	1.22	11,576	2,799
Alaska	.26	2,430	4,301
Arizona	1.24	11,788	3,278
Arkansas	.66	6,290	2,623
California	12.80	121,620	4,214
Colorado	1.31	12,423	3,637
Connecticut	2.03	19,295	5,959
Delaware	.32	2,996	4,553
Florida	5.17	49,109	3,857
Georgia	2.29	21,791	3,381
Hawaii	.42	4,034	3,612
Idaho	.29	2,707	2,673
Illinois	5.23	49,609	4,270
Indiana	1.99	18,954	3,422
Iowa	.97	9,254	3,292
Kansas	.95	9,055	3,613
Kentucky	1.10	10,471	2,798
Louisiana	1.27	12,057	2,705
Maine	.42	3,975	3,301
Maryland	2.24	21,299	4,606
Massachusetts	3.10	29,422	4,999
Michigan	3.86	36,609	3,989
Minnesota	1.78	16,923	3,943
Mississippi	.63	5,946	2,241
Missouri	1.96	18,631	3,616

State	Total Federal Tax Burden[a]		
	Percentage Distribution	Amount ($Millions)	Per Capita[b]
Montana	.24	2,299	2,821
Nebraska	.56	5,353	3,345
Nevada	.45	4,272	3,985
New Hampshire	.53	5,040	4,594
New Jersey	4.58	43,453	5,603
New Mexico	.44	4,196	2,691
New York	8.80	83,634	4,675
North Carolina	2.19	20,845	3,176
North Dakota	.22	2,051	3,030
Ohio	4.20	39,893	3,703
Oklahoma	1.04	9,901	2,963
Oregon	.98	9,293	3,382
Pennsylvania	4.85	46,010	3,850
Rhode Island	.43	4,094	4,107
South Carolina	1.03	9,818	2,796
South Dakota	.21	1,978	2,771
Tennessee	1.64	15,546	3,155
Texas	6.20	58,871	3,352
Utah	.46	4,400	2,521
Vermont	.20	1,903	3,410
Virginia	2.54	24,111	3,976
Washington	1.86	17,599	3,781
West Virginia	.51	4,850	2,577
Wisconsin	1.80	17,111	3,540
Wyoming	.16	1,523	3,076
Dist. of Columbia	.35	3,323	5,386

[a] The burden by state is estimated on the basis of a special formula designed for this purpose, since data on Federal tax collections by state do not accurately reflect the distribution of the burden.
[b] Based on estimates of resident population as of July 1, 1989.
Source: Office of Management and Budget; and Tax Foundation.

C56. Trends in State Shares of Federal Tax Burden[a]
Selected Fiscal Years 1961-1989
(Percent)

State	1961	1965	1970	1975	1980	1989
Total	100.00	100.00	100.00	100.00	100.00	100.00
Alabama	1.05	1.06	1.11	1.20	1.30	1.22
Alaska	.11	.12	.14	.18	.29	.26
Arizona	.59	.69	.69	.92	.99	1.24
Arkansas	.50	.55	.59	.66	.69	.66
California	11.00	11.49	11.42	10.80	11.61	12.80
Colorado	.95	1.01	.95	1.15	1.27	1.31
Connecticut	2.08	2.14	2.11	1.88	1.75	2.03
Delaware	.52	.48	.36	.34	.30	.32
Florida	2.49	2.65	2.87	3.82	3.83	5.17
Georgia	1.39	1.51	1.69	1.97	1.89	2.29
Hawaii	.31	.34	.38	.43	.44	.42
Idaho	.28	.26	.26	.29	.33	.29
Illinois	7.03	6.80	6.69	6.39	6.16	5.23
Indiana	2.32	2.36	2.45	2.49	2.45	1.99
Iowa	1.23	1.19	1.21	1.34	1.32	.97
Kansas	.99	1.00	1.02	1.08	1.07	.95
Kentucky	1.09	1.10	1.10	1.21	1.28	1.10
Louisiana	1.22	1.18	1.36	1.31	1.54	1.27
Maine	.43	.43	.38	.37	.37	.42
Maryland	1.92	2.05	2.20	2.22	2.13	2.24
Massachusetts	3.40	3.33	3.18	2.99	2.62	3.10
Michigan	4.44	4.48	4.78	4.71	4.67	3.86
Minnesota	1.63	1.64	1.67	1.80	1.86	1.78
Mississippi	.50	.55	.59	.68	.69	.63
Missouri	2.32	2.30	2.19	2.15	2.06	1.96
Montana	.30	.29	.28	.29	.32	.24
Nebraska	.65	.67	.64	.73	.68	.56
Nevada	.21	.28	.27	.32	.39	.45
New Hampshire	.33	.32	.35	.38	.39	.53
New Jersey	4.26	4.26	4.27	4.34	3.94	4.58
New Mexico	.39	.38	.36	.38	.44	.44
New York	13.20	12.73	11.74	9.95	8.40	8.80
North Carolina	1.45	1.62	1.77	2.04	2.01	2.19
North Dakota	.20	.21	.22	.27	.26	.22
Ohio	5.75	5.47	5.49	5.16	5.04	4.20
Oklahoma	.97	.97	.99	1.05	1.17	1.04
Oregon	.97	.94	.95	1.04	1.19	.98
Pennsylvania	6.83	6.28	5.95	5.61	5.27	4.85
Rhode Island	.53	.50	.48	.45	.40	.43
South Carolina	.65	.73	.82	.95	1.00	1.03
South Dakota	.23	.24	.23	.24	.24	.21
Tennessee	1.24	1.36	1.42	1.57	1.62	1.64
Texas	4.43	4.43	4.78	5.10	6.12	6.20
Utah	.38	.42	.38	.42	.48	.46
Vermont	.18	.18	.18	.18	.17	.20
Virginia	1.78	1.92	1.98	2.23	2.31	2.54
Washington	1.64	1.57	1.76	1.65	1.95	1.86
West Virginia	.70	.65	.61	.64	.69	.51
Wisconsin	2.07	2.00	2.04	2.03	1.99	1.80
Wyoming	.17	.18	.14	.16	.23	.16
District of Columbia	.70	.69	.51	.44	.39	.35

[a] See Table C32 for dollar amounts of Federal tax collections in selected years and Table C55 for 1989 state-by-state amounts.

Source: Tax Foundation estimates based on a special formula designed to show the geographic burden of taxes, as distinct from the initial impact of taxes that is shown by tax collections as reported by the Treasury Department.

C57. Federal Tax Burden by Type of Tax and State

Fiscal Year 1989
($Millions)

State	Individual Income Taxes	Corporate Income Taxes	Social Insurance Taxes	Highway Trust Fund Taxes	Alcoholic Beverage Excises	Tobacco Products Excises	Other Excise Taxes	Estate and Gift Taxes
Total	$ 425,193.0	$ 106,997.0	$ 359,077.0	$ 14,916.0	$ 5,503.0	$ 4,468.0	$ 25,623.0	$ 7,850.0
Alabama	4,944.7	1,226.7	4,581.6	274.1	79.9	73.7	329.3	65.9
Alaska	1,093.5	219.6	988.0	36.2	13.4	8.8	66.2	4.2
Arizona	5,187.0	1,428.0	4,371.7	234.1	81.2	61.3	337.1	87.2
Arkansas	2,426.2	756.0	2,594.6	196.2	44.6	43.3	191.3	37.5
California	54,308.7	13,883.6	46,175.4	1,565.3	664.7	505.8	3,354.6	1,161.5
Colorado	5,485.3	1,468.2	4,705.8	195.7	77.9	60.2	347.5	82.2
Connecticut	10,031.9	1,995.1	6,315.2	184.7	83.3	61.0	457.5	166.0
Delaware	1,278.2	303.9	1,238.7	46.1	17.3	12.0	70.1	29.7
Florida	24,013.1	6,521.6	15,562.6	694.4	322.1	231.5	1,282.3	481.7
Georgia	9,754.0	2,281.2	8,267.0	516.1	141.1	111.4	594.0	126.3
Hawaii	1,726.0	452.4	1,624.5	37.2	24.3	19.8	116.7	33.5
Idaho	993.6	334.4	1,176.3	68.9	19.2	17.2	83.2	14.6
Illinois	22,490.3	5,523.1	18,815.2	546.8	268.2	212.3	1,306.9	445.9
Indiana	8,491.1	2,132.5	7,086.2	391.6	114.1	100.9	525.3	112.4
Iowa	3,594.5	1,250.9	3,748.4	176.3	55.7	52.2	277.3	99.1
Kansas	3,827.9	1,107.8	3,524.4	175.3	47.7	45.3	253.0	73.5
Kentucky	4,441.0	1,213.7	4,077.2	220.8	72.4	67.8	309.2	69.3
Louisiana	5,031.5	1,407.8	4,710.3	274.1	92.9	78.1	354.9	107.7
Maine	1,727.1	460.2	1,510.9	90.6	27.9	22.0	114.9	21.1
Maryland	9,932.8	2,251.0	7,949.9	274.7	114.2	84.7	549.6	142.0
Massachusetts	14,165.2	3,177.2	10,533.8	302.4	153.7	112.3	750.1	227.0
Michigan	16,277.1	3,850.7	14,481.8	492.0	208.4	167.4	962.9	168.6
Minnesota	7,075.9	1,910.5	6,960.3	231.9	99.5	77.9	457.0	109.7
Mississippi	2,341.1	678.3	2,414.4	194.7	51.2	45.5	186.4	34.8
Missouri	8,191.5	2,233.4	6,927.5	390.8	110.5	94.3	517.4	165.3
Montana	852.7	308.9	948.4	69.4	17.8	14.5	69.9	17.7
Nebraska	2,153.4	673.9	2,140.0	111.3	33.2	29.1	159.4	52.2
Nevada	2,141.5	460.9	1,380.8	75.6	36.9	18.8	112.1	44.9
New Hampshire	2,528.8	520.1	1,725.5	59.6	37.3	19.7	130.1	18.6
New Jersey	20,961.7	4,518.5	15,892.7	453.9	190.5	145.1	1,062.0	228.1
New Mexico	1,706.5	502.2	1,658.8	123.0	31.3	26.2	121.5	26.4
New York	38,325.4	9,290.5	31,431.0	723.8	419.0	334.5	2,093.3	1,016.5
North Carolina	9,030.4	2,202.9	8,195.5	455.6	135.5	118.9	577.3	128.5
North Dakota	802.8	274.2	809.1	52.2	15.0	12.0	62.0	24.0
Ohio	16,959.0	4,361.3	16,161.4	619.7	218.2	197.4	1,075.7	300.0
Oklahoma	3,934.8	1,171.8	3,847.4	265.2	61.8	59.1	264.4	296.9
Oregon	3,719.6	1,125.3	3,820.0	190.8	59.7	50.6	261.0	65.8
Pennsylvania	19,885.2	5,201.8	18,242.8	657.0	252.1	225.7	1,251.2	294.0
Rhode Island	1,790.3	437.6	1,644.8	48.6	24.6	18.8	106.8	22.9
South Carolina	4,126.5	1,040.1	3,931.7	248.6	77.5	61.7	280.9	50.9
South Dakota	756.7	268.5	793.5	56.1	15.1	12.7	64.7	11.0
Tennessee	6,916.3	1,605.3	5,947.1	365.6	97.7	89.5	435.9	89.0
Texas	26,928.1	6,451.3	21,395.0	1,236.0	339.3	293.3	1,598.4	629.4
Utah	1,774.5	486.1	1,819.7	111.2	25.9	26.1	130.9	25.6
Vermont	833.6	226.6	726.2	34.0	13.7	10.1	49.4	9.1
Virginia	11,266.3	2,678.4	8,730.6	376.7	128.8	110.4	661.1	157.7
Washington	7,871.9	2,005.0	6,660.2	279.3	101.8	83.7	500.7	96.2
West Virginia	1,988.4	566.0	1,941.1	112.2	34.0	35.0	145.7	27.2
Wisconsin	6,881.3	2,031.1	7,102.9	292.1	115.3	87.9	489.6	110.4
Wyoming	655.7	180.4	546.2	65.6	10.7	8.5	41.0	14.5
District of Columbia	1,572.6	339.9	1,242.9	21.6	24.7	12.1	83.2	26.1

Source: Office of Management and Budget; and Tax Foundation computations.

C58. Percentage Distribution of the Federal Tax Burden by Type of Tax and State

Fiscal Year 1989

State	Individual Income Taxes	Corporate Income Taxes	Social Insurance Taxes	Highway Trust Fund Taxes	Alcoholic Beverage Excises	Tobacco Product Excises	Other Excise Taxes	Estate and Gift Taxes
Total	100.00%	100.00%	100.00%	100.00%	100.00%	100.00%	100.00%	100.00%
Alabama	1.16	1.15	1.28	1.84	1.45	1.65	1.29	.84
Alaska	.26	.21	.28	.24	.24	.20	.26	.05
Arizona	1.22	1.33	1.22	1.57	1.48	1.37	1.32	1.11
Arkansas	.57	.71	.72	1.32	.81	.97	.75	.48
California	12.77	12.98	12.86	10.49	12.08	11.32	13.09	14.80
Colorado	1.29	1.37	1.31	1.31	1.42	1.35	1.36	1.05
Connecticut	2.36	1.86	1.76	1.24	1.51	1.36	1.79	2.11
Delaware	.30	.28	.34	.31	.31	.27	.27	.38
Florida	5.65	6.10	4.33	4.66	5.85	5.18	5.00	6.14
Georgia	2.29	2.13	2.30	3.46	2.56	2.49	2.32	1.61
Hawaii	.41	.42	.45	.25	.44	.44	.46	.43
Idaho	.23	.31	.33	.46	.35	.39	.32	.19
Illinois	5.29	5.16	5.24	3.67	4.87	4.75	5.10	5.68
Indiana	2.00	1.99	1.97	2.63	2.07	2.26	2.05	1.43
Iowa	.85	1.17	1.04	1.18	1.01	1.17	1.08	1.26
Kansas	.90	1.04	.98	1.18	.87	1.01	.99	.94
Kentucky	1.04	1.13	1.14	1.48	1.32	1.52	1.21	.88
Louisiana	1.18	1.32	1.31	1.84	1.69	1.75	1.39	1.37
Maine	.41	.43	.42	.61	.51	.49	.45	.27
Maryland	2.34	2.10	2.21	1.84	2.08	1.90	2.14	1.81
Massachusetts	3.33	2.97	2.93	2.03	2.79	2.51	2.93	2.89
Michigan	3.83	3.60	4.03	3.30	3.79	3.75	3.76	2.15
Minnesota	1.66	1.79	1.94	1.55	1.81	1.74	1.78	1.40
Mississippi	.55	.63	.67	1.31	.93	1.02	.73	.44
Missouri	1.93	2.09	1.93	2.62	2.01	2.11	2.02	2.11
Montana	.20	.29	.26	.46	.32	.33	.27	.23
Nebraska	.51	.63	.60	.75	.60	.65	.62	.66
Nevada	.50	.43	.38	.51	.67	.42	.44	.57
New Hampshire	.59	.49	.48	.40	.68	.44	.51	.24
New Jersey	4.93	4.22	4.43	3.04	3.46	3.25	4.14	2.91
New Mexico	.40	.47	.46	.82	.57	.59	.47	.34
New York	9.01	8.68	8.75	4.85	7.61	7.49	8.17	12.95
North Carolina	2.12	2.06	2.28	3.05	2.46	2.66	2.25	1.64
North Dakota	.19	.26	.23	.35	.27	.27	.24	.31
Ohio	3.99	4.08	4.50	4.15	3.97	4.42	4.20	3.82
Oklahoma	.93	1.10	1.07	1.78	1.12	1.32	1.03	3.78
Oregon	.87	1.05	1.06	1.28	1.08	1.13	1.02	.84
Pennsylvania	4.68	4.86	5.08	4.40	4.58	5.05	4.88	3.75
Rhode Island	.42	.41	.46	.33	.45	.42	.42	.29
South Carolina	.97	.97	1.09	1.67	1.41	1.38	1.10	.65
South Dakota	.18	.25	.22	.38	.27	.29	.25	.14
Tennessee	1.63	1.50	1.66	2.45	1.78	2.00	1.70	1.13
Texas	6.33	6.03	5.96	8.29	6.17	6.56	6.24	8.02
Utah	.42	.45	.51	.75	.47	.58	.51	.33
Vermont	.20	.21	.20	.23	.25	.23	.19	.12
Virginia	2.65	2.50	2.43	2.53	2.34	2.47	2.58	2.01
Washington	1.85	1.87	1.85	1.87	1.85	1.87	1.95	1.23
West Virginia	.47	.53	.54	.75	.62	.78	.57	.35
Wisconsin	1.62	1.90	1.98	1.96	2.10	1.97	1.91	1.41
Wyoming	.15	.17	.15	.44	.19	.19	.16	.19
District of Columbia	.37	.32	.35	.14	.45	.27	.32	.33

Source: Table C57.

C59. Federal Grants-in-Aid to State and Local Governments and Estimated Federal Tax Burden for Grants

Fiscal Year 1988

State	$Millions		Tax Burden Per Dollar of Aid	
	Grants[a]	Estimated Tax Burden for Grants[b]	Amount	State Rank
Total	$ 108,724.7	$ 108,724.7	$ 1.00	-
Alabama	1,667.9	1,324.7	.79	33
Alaska	579.8	278.9	.48	50
Arizona	1,160.7	1,347.9	1.16	13
Arkansas	1,004.5	719.4	.72	37
California	11,583.8	13,917.3	1.20	10
Colorado	1,199.6	1,421.7	1.19	12
Connecticut	1,542.1	2,210.4	1.43	5
Delaware	318.5	342.8	1.08	16
Florida	3,415.2	5,616.8	1.64	1
Georgia	2,959.3	2,494.0	.84	30
Hawaii	477.2	461.6	.97	21
Idaho	458.1	310.0	.68	40
Illinois	4,669.4	5,684.5	1.22	8
Indiana	1,959.8	2,168.0	1.11	14
Iowa	1,199.2	1,058.9	.88	26
Kansas	873.3	1,035.7	1.19	11
Kentucky	1,750.7	1,199.3	.69	38
Louisiana	2,131.9	1,381.9	.65	43
Maine	664.7	455.1	.68	39
Maryland	2,004.2	2,435.5	1.22	9
Massachusetts	3,327.6	3,368.8	1.01	18
Michigan	4,240.6	4,198.0	.99	19
Minnesota	2,117.4	1,936.4	.91	24
Mississippi	1,304.6	680.1	.52	46
Missouri	1,938.1	2,130.9	1.10	15
Montana	504.5	262.9	.52	47
Nebraska	711.5	611.3	.86	28
Nevada	322.8	490.2	1.52	2
New Hampshire	397.3	576.8	1.45	4
New Jersey	3,327.5	4,979.9	1.50	3
New Mexico	726.1	479.9	.66	42
New York	12,494.2	9,571.3	.77	34
North Carolina	2,296.2	2,383.8	1.04	17
North Dakota	451.3	235.0	.52	48
Ohio	4,693.1	4,570.2	.97	20
Oklahoma	1,402.2	1,133.3	.81	32
Oregon	1,110.9	1,064.5	.96	22
Pennsylvania	5,790.4	5,273.6	.91	25
Rhode Island	643.5	469.4	.73	36
South Carolina	1,351.3	1,123.8	.83	31
South Dakota	439.5	225.8	.51	49
Tennessee	2,084.4	1,779.6	.85	29
Texas	5,162.2	6,742.9	1.31	7
Utah	683.7	503.4	.74	35
Vermont	323.5	218.2	.67	41
Virginia	1,958.8	2,757.3	1.41	6
Washington	2,131.4	2,020.0	.95	23
West Virginia	1,054.7	556.1	.53	45
Wisconsin	2,226.9	1,961.7	.88	27
Wyoming	273.8	174.5	.64	44
District of Columbia	1,615.1	380.8	.24	51

[a] Excludes shared revenues and payments in lieu of taxes; includes trust fund aid.
[b] The tax burden for grants is assumed to equal grant payments.
Source: Tax Foundation computations based on data from the Treasury Department and U.S. Department of Commerce, Bureau of the Census.

C60. Trends in Federal Tax Burdens per Dollar of Federal Aid by State[a]

Selected Fiscal Years 1961-1988

State	1961	1965	1970	1975	1980	1988[b]
Alabama	$ .51	$ .55	$ .50	$ .74	$ .73	$ .79
Alaska	.17	.15	.33	.42	.52	.48
Arizona	.68	.69	.72	1.00	1.13	1.16
Arkansas	.46	.53	.51	.65	.67	.72
California	1.17	1.11	.89	1.08	1.20	1.20
Colorado	.75	.77	.82	1.01	1.20	1.19
Connecticut	1.51	1.50	1.70	1.36	1.35	1.43
Delaware	2.01	1.54	1.61	1.36	.93	1.08
Florida	1.05	1.23	1.41	1.46	1.23	1.64
Georgia	.64	.73	.75	.81	.72	.84
Hawaii	.69	.70	.76	.88	.84	.97
Idaho	.59	.54	.67	.76	.79	.68
Illinois	1.21	1.32	1.65	1.36	1.18	1.22
Indiana	1.24	1.47	1.64	1.41	1.34	1.11
Iowa	.96	1.06	1.17	1.07	1.13	.88
Kansas	.85	.98	1.03	1.12	1.20	1.19
Kentucky	.61	.62	.58	.69	.78	.69
Louisiana	.47	.45	.59	.75	.91	.65
Maine	.80	.84	.82	.66	.63	.68
Maryland	1.33	1.41	1.32	1.10	.98	1.22
Massachusetts	1.24	1.13	1.04	.98	.80	1.01
Michigan	1.25	1.36	1.45	1.06	1.03	.99
Minnesota	.86	.81	.98	.93	.96	.91
Mississippi	.41	.48	.34	.52	.53	.52
Missouri	.85	.91	1.01	1.08	1.09	1.10
Montana	.52	.45	.48	.65	.60	.52
Nebraska	.75	1.04	1.16	.97	1.10	.86
Nevada	.71	.60	.93	1.15	1.10	1.52
New Hampshire	.77	1.05	1.14	1.04	1.03	1.45
New Jersey	2.07	1.87	1.62	1.36	1.21	1.50
New Mexico	.51	.54	.40	.50	.74	.66
New York	1.63	1.44	1.14	.83	.76	.77
North Carolina	.87	.96	.85	.96	.92	1.04
North Dakota	.45	.49	.57	.71	.67	.52
Ohio	1.27	1.30	1.45	1.40	1.27	.97
Oklahoma	.49	.57	.57	.76	1.05	.81
Oregon	.92	.81	.96	.91	1.02	.96
Pennsylvania	1.42	1.25	1.05	1.00	1.02	.91
Rhode Island	.97	.75	.87	.87	.76	.73
South Carolina	.68	.90	.71	.85	.82	.83
South Dakota	.42	.44	.50	.55	.48	.51
Tennessee	.60	.81	.72	.89	.90	.85
Texas	.98	1.04	.99	1.14	1.40	1.31
Utah	.60	.49	.54	.74	.79	.74
Vermont	.48	.49	.58	.59	.45	.67
Virginia	1.00	.78	1.01	1.08	1.14	1.41
Washington	.97	.85	1.06	1.09	1.10	.95
West Virginia	.56	.47	.47	.56	.63	.53
Wisconsin	1.34	1.46	1.28	1.08	.89	.88
Wyoming	.47	.41	.51	.89	1.11	.64
District of Columbia	.60	.55	.27	.28	.32	.24

[a] Federal aid refers to grants-in-aid to state and local governments; excludes shared revenues and payments in lieu of taxes but includes general revenue sharing and trust fund aids. The total tax burden for grants is assumed to equal grant payments.
[b] See Table C59 for additional details for 1988.
Source: Tax Foundation computations based on tax burdens shown in Table C56 and grants-in-aid published by Treasury Department through 1980 and by Department of Commerce, Bureau of the Census for 1988.

C61. Course of the Federal Debt

As of Selected Dates 1917-1988

($Millions, except Per Capita)

Item	World War I		Post-World War I Low Debt Dec. 31, 1930	World War II		Post-World War II	
	Pre-War Debt Mar. 31, 1917	Highest War Debt Aug. 31, 1919		Debt Preceding Defense Program June 30, 1940	Highest War Debt Feb. 28, 1946	Lowest Post-War Debt Apr. 30, 1949	Debt Sept. 30, 1988
Total debt	$ 1,282	$ 26,597	$ 16,026	$ 48,497	$ 279,764	$ 251,553	$ 2,602,458
Direct (gross)	1,282	26,597	16,026	42,968	279,214	251,530	2,602,338
Guaranteed[a,b]	-	-	-	5,529	551	23	120
Interest-bearing debt, total	1,023	26,349	15,774	47,874	278,451	249,528	2,599,997
Direct	1,023	26,349	15,774	42,376	277,912	249,509	2,599,877
Guaranteed[a]	-	-	-	5,498	539	19	120
Per capita total debt[c]	12	250	130	367	1,990	1,690	10,535
General fund balance	74	1,118	307	1,891	25,961	3,995	7,963[d]
Computed annual interest rate on direct debt (percent)	2.40	4.20	3.75	2.58	1.97	2.24	8.83
Federal interest payments for the fiscal year	25	1,020	612	1,041	4,722	5,339	214,145

[a] Excludes obligations owned by the Treasury.
[b] Includes outstanding matured principal of guaranteed debt of U.S. Government agencies, cash for payment of which is held by Treasury in the general fund balance.
[c] Based on population including armed forces overseas.
[d] Budget estimate full fiscal year.
Source: Treasury Department.

C62. Composition of the Federal Debt by Type of Obligation
End of Selected Fiscal Years 1939-1988
($Millions)

Type of Obligation	1939	1949	1959	1969	1979	1988
Total public debt and debt of U.S. Government agencies	$ 45,890	$ 252,798	$ 284,817	$ 354,317	$ 827,088	$ 2,602,458
Total public debt	40,440	252,770	284,706	353,720	826,519	2,602,338
Interest-bearing debt	39,886	250,762	281,883	351,729	819,007	2,599,877
Public issues, total	36,116	217,986	237,077	284,940	642,647	2,063,419
Marketable, total	33,965	155,147	178,027	226,107	506,693	1,802,905
Treasury bills	1,308	11,536	32,017	68,356	161,378	398,451
Treasury notes and bonds	32,461	114,021	112,117	157,751	345,315	1,389,453
Other[a]	197	29,589	33,893	-	-	15,000
Nonmarketable, total	2,151	62,839	59,050	58,833	135,954	260,514
Foreign series[b]	-	-	-	4,070	28,115	6,320
Treasury bonds[c]	-	5,814	8,365	2,459	2,245	147,602
U.S. savings bonds	1,868	56,260	50,503	51,711	80,440	106,176
Other	283	765	183	592	25,155	416
Special issues, total	3,770	32,776	44,756	66,790	176,360	536,455
OASDHI trust funds	-	9,003	18,760	26,918	41,651	170,299
Unemployment trust fund	1,267	7,340	5,636	9,957	12,048	35,743
Highway trust fund	-	-	429	1,513	12,469	13,445
Railroad retirement account	67	1,720	3,417	3,434	2,794	7,090
Other[d]	2,436	14,713	16,514	24,968	107,398	309,878
Matured debt, no interest payments	142	245	476	461	6,668	1,745
Debt bearing no interest	411	1,764	2,396	1,530	844	715
Guaranteed debt of U.S. Government agencies	5,451	27	111	597	569	120
Debt not subject to statutory limitation (deduct)	5,519	770	418	636	609	598
Participation certificates subject to limitation (add)	-	-	-	3,250	1,135	10
Total debt subject to limitation	40,371	252,028	284,399	356,932	827,614	2,586,869

[a] Principally certificates of indebtedness.
[b] Includes foreign currency series. Consists of Treasury notes, certificates of indebtedness, and bonds.
[c] Other than foreign series. Includes Treasury certificates of indebtedness, and state and local government series.
[d] Principally Federal employees' retirement funds and national service life insurance funds.
Source: Treasury Department.

C63. Estimated Ownership of Federal Securities
End of Selected Fiscal Years 1939-1988[a]
($Billions at Par)

Year	Total Securities Outstanding[b]	Held by Banks			U.S. Government Investment Accounts	Held by Nonbank Investors							
		Total	Commercial Banks[c]	Federal Reserve Banks		Total	Individuals[d]	Insurance Companies	Mutual Savings Banks	Corporations[e]	State and Local Governments	Foreign and International	Miscellaneous Investors[f]
1939[g]	$42.4	$15.2	$12.7	$2.5	$6.5	$20.7	$9.4	$5.7	$2.7	$2.0	$.4	$.2	$.3
1946[g]	262.3	97.8	74.5	23.3	30.9	133.6	64.1	24.9	11.8	15.3	6.3	1.9	9.3
1950	259.4	83.9	65.6	18.3	37.8	137.7	67.4	19.1	11.6	18.4	8.7	2.2	9.6
1952	260.7	84.0	61.1	22.9	44.3	132.4	64.8	15.7	9.6	18.8	10.4	3.4	9.7
1954	272.8	88.6	63.6	25.0	49.3	134.9	64.8	15.4	9.1	16.5	13.9	4.6	10.6
1956	274.1	81.1	57.3	23.8	53.5	139.5	66.6	13.6	8.3	17.3	16.1	6.2	11.4
1958	278.4	90.6	65.2	25.4	55.9	131.9	64.4	12.2	7.4	14.1	16.3	5.9	11.6
1960	286.3	81.8	55.3	26.5	55.3	149.2	69.7	12.0	6.6	19.5	18.8	10.1	12.5
1962	297.6	94.8	65.1	29.7	56.5	146.3	65.5	11.4	6.2	18.2	20.1	11.3	13.6
1964	310.7	95.0	60.2	34.8	61.1	154.6	68.5	11.1	5.8	18.9	22.5	12.0	15.8
1966	318.7	97.0	54.8	42.2	66.7	155.0	72.8	10.0	5.0	14.2	24.5	11.6	16.9
1968	345.1	111.9	59.7	52.2	76.0	157.2	74.2	8.5	4.0	12.0	25.1	10.7	22.7
1970	370.2	110.3	52.6	57.7	95.2	164.7	81.8	7.2	3.2	8.5	29.0	14.0	21.0
1972	426.4	132.3	60.9	71.4	111.5	182.8	73.2	6.7	3.5	9.3	26.9	49.2	14.0
1974	474.2	133.7	53.2	80.5	138.2	202.5	80.7	5.9	2.6	10.8	28.3	56.9	17.3
1976	620.4	186.9	92.5	94.4	149.6	283.9	96.4	10.6	5.4	24.3	39.3	69.8	38.1
1977	698.8	204.5	99.8	104.7	155.5	338.8	103.9	14.3	6.2	23.3	53.0	95.5	42.6
1978	771.5	211.1	96.3	114.8	168.0	392.0	109.4	15.1	5.2	21.3	69.0	121.0	51.1
1979	826.5	205.6	90.1	115.5	187.7	433.3	115.5	14.6	4.8	24.0	67.1	125.2	82.1
1980	907.7	221.6	100.9	120.7	197.7	488.3	123.0	14.4	5.3	25.5	73.4	126.0	120.7
1981	997.9	237.0	112.7	124.3	208.1	552.7	109.7	27.6	11.4	18.0	99.8	130.7	155.5
1982	1,142.0	252.2	117.8	134.4	216.4	673.4	115.6	38.6	38.6	21.6	109.0	140.6	209.4
1983	1,377.2	331.7	176.3	155.4	239.0	806.4	128.9	58.5	22.1	35.9	137.0	160.1	263.8
1984	1,572.3	339.6	184.6	155.0	263.1	969.5	142.4	56.5	13.6	47.7	170.0	175.5	363.8
1985	1,824.4	373.3	203.6	169.7	316.5	1,134.6	151.4	71.4	22.7	59.0	203.0	209.8	417.3
1986	2,127.0	391.7	200.9	190.8	382.9	1,352.4	158.0	96.4	24.9	65.7	251.2	253.4	502.8
1987	2,351.7	416.9	205.0	211.9	457.2	1,477.6	168.9	118.4	15.2	81.8	273.0	267.0	553.3
1988	2,603.3	432.2	203.0	229.2	550.4	1,620.7	184.5	135.0	10.8	86.0	287.0	334.3	583.1

[a] The Export-Import Bank was moved on-budget effective October 1, 1976. Adjustments are made to include totals for the period it was off-budget. Also, adjustments are now made to reflect certain Export-Import Bank borrowing transactions now classified as agency debt.
[b] Securities issued or guaranteed by the United States Government, excluding guaranteed securities held by the Treasury.
[c] Consists of commercial banks, trust companies, and stock savings banks in the United States and in territories and island possessions; excludes securities held in trust departments.
[d] Includes partnerships and personal trust accounts.
[e] Exclusive of banks and insurance companies.
[f] Includes savings and loan associations, nonprofit institutions, corporate pension trust funds, and dealers and brokers. Also included are certain government deposit accounts and government sponsored agencies.
[g] As of end of calendar year.
Source: Treasury Department and Federal Reserve System.

C64. Indebtedness of Foreign Countries to the United States Government by Region and Country[a]

End of Selected Fiscal Years 1954-1988

($Millions)

Region and Country	1954	1965	1975	1981	1988
Total	$ 11,816	$ 18,315	$ 34,549	$ 62,178	$ 69,614
Western Europe	9,127	6,687	6,680	6,623	4,697
France	1,911	607	336	151	44
Germany, F.R.	1,196	225	126	14	2
Italy	300	130	245	422	79
Netherlands	322	66	158	45	-
Norway	106	29	249	82	15
Portugal	46	105	101	559	405
Spain	61	411	788	1,394	1,511
United Kingdom	4,648	3,987	3,520	2,821	1,912
Yugoslavia	55	629	578	611	561
Other	482	497	578	524	168
Eastern Europe	310	293	1,241	2,180	3,173
Poland	70	86	134	975	2,337
Union of Soviet Socialist Republics	222	195	1,015	1,077	778
Other	18	12	92	127	58
East Asia and Pacific	493	1,677	5,162	10,251	7,271
Australia and New Zealand	20	3	373	313	119
Taiwan	156	334	730	1,743	67
Indonesia	127	177	1,250	2,186	2,488
Japan	90	804	594	610	3
Korea, Republic of (Seoul)	21	58	1,248	3,526	2,289
Philippines	79	96	336	714	1,262
Other	-	205	632	1,158	1,043
Western Hemisphere	927	3,135	7,440	10,488	12,872
Brazil	437	1,014	2,134	2,071	2,453
Canada	11	-	254	481	320
Chile	79	517	1,098	552	514
Colombia	33	269	894	848	1,149
Mexico	115	245	524	2,308	1,891
Other	252	1,090	2,535	4,228	6,545
Near East	353	1,988	5,239	20,162	25,834
Egypt	6	521	506	6,578	11,637
Greece	81	174	325	679	1,304
Iran	24	243	1,006	403	64
Israel	123	391	1,698	8,289	7,872
Turkey	95	623	1,527	3,001	3,984
Other	24	36	176	1,212	973
South Asia	397	3,872	6,481	7,486	8,804
Bangladesh	-	-	241	969	1,265
India	361	2,858	3,650	3,305	2,897
Pakistan	15	955	2,368	2,740	3,932
Other	21	59	223	472	710
Africa	142	529	2,252	4,968	6,964
Algeria	-	-	218	874	280
Morocco	10	243	481	629	1,235
Zaire	-	b	275	818	1,305
Sudan	-	10	39	350	657
Other	132	276	1,239	2,298	3,487
Worldwide	67	134	55	20	b
United Nations	62[c]	107	54	19	b
Unspecified	5	27	1	1	b

[a] Outstanding long-term principal indebtedness. Excludes indebtedness arising out of World War I. Includes the debt of private agencies as well as governments to the U.S. Government and its agencies.
[b] Less than $500,000.
[c] International organizations, including United Nations.
Source: Treasury Department.

C65. Federal Civilian Employment by Branch and Type of Agency

Selected Dates 1918-1988

Branch and Agency	End of World War I Nov. 11, 1918	As of Dec. 31, 1932	Prewar Emergency Peak June 30, 1939	World War II Peak June 30, 1945	Postwar Low April 30, 1950	As of June 30, 1988
Total	927,780	576,741	964,342	3,761,635	1,972,700	3,126,171
Legislative Branch	7,980	11,159	15,802	26,959	22,896	39,504
Judicial Branch	2,040	1,777	2,292	2,706	3,772	21,123
Executive Branch	917,760	563,805	946,248	3,731,970	1,946,032[a]	3,065,544
Departments (except military establishment)	n.a.	467,768	579,589	684,719	837,606[a]	2,005,068
Post Office (Postal Service)[c]	n.a.	n.a.	n.a.	378,849	510,727	833,281
Agriculture	n.a.	n.a.	n.a.	84,573	77,559	122,943
Treasury	n.a.	n.a.	n.a.	96,493	90,573	164,870
Health and Human Services	n.a.	n.a.	n.a.	n.a.	n.a.	124,762
Interior	n.a.	n.a.	n.a.	44,354	58,206	78,091
Other	n.a.	n.a.	n.a.	80,450	100,541[a]	257,735
Independent agencies[c]	n.a.	[b]	171,373	250,214	353,720	423,386
Emergency agencies	n.a.	-	-	169,027	-	-
Postwar agencies	n.a.	-	-	-	9,687	-
Military establishment	n.a.	96,037	195,286	2,628,010	745,019	1,060,476

[a] Excludes 147,264 temporary employees engaged in taking the Seventeenth Decennial Census.
[b] Unallocable, included in departments (except military establishment).
[c] The U.S. Postal Service became an independent agency effective July 1, 1971; total for independent agencies in 1988 excludes Postal Service.
Source: Office of Personnel Management.

C66. Federal Civilian Employment in the Executive Branch
Selected Fiscal Years 1881-1901, Fiscal Years 1908-1988[a]

Year	Employees	Year	Employees
1881	94,679	1947	2,082,258
1891	150,844	1948	2,043,981
1901	231,056	1949	2,075,148
1908	348,479	1950	1,934,040
1909	364,078	1951	2,455,901
1910	380,428	1952	2,574,132
1911	387,673	1953	2,532,160
1912	391,918	1954	2,381,659
1913	388,217	1955	2,371,462
1914	393,555	1956	2,372,266
1915	387,294	1957	2,390,561
1916	391,133	1958	2,355,292
1917	429,727	1959	2,355,054
1918	844,480	1960	2,370,826
1919	784,180	1961	2,407,025
1920	645,408	1962	2,484,655
1921	550,020	1963	2,497,699
1922	532,210	1964	2,469,645
1923	525,746	1965	2,496,064
1924	532,048	1966	2,726,144
1925	541,792	1967	2,967,964
1926	537,251	1968	3,019,976
1927	535,599	1969	3,040,129
1928	549,238	1970	2,884,307
1929	567,721	1971	2,822,884
1930	588,951	1972	2,769,848
1931	596,745	1973	2,722,131
1932	592,560	1974	2,847,140
1933	590,984	1975	2,848,014
1934	685,108	1976	2,832,471
1935	765,712	1977	2,840,149
1936	850,395	1978	2,874,547
1937	878,214	1979	2,895,007
1938	864,534	1980	3,065,672
1939	935,797	1981	2,891,844
1940	1,022,853	1982	2,860,754
1941	1,416,444	1983	2,863,071
1942	2,272,082	1984	2,901,137
1943	3,273,887	1985	3,001,540
1944	3,304,379	1986	3,008,938
1945	3,786,645	1987	3,077,290
1946	2,665,520	1988	3,072,602

[a] Data for 1881-1976 as of end of fiscal year, June 30, except 1919 (as of November 11), and 1921 (as of July 31). Data for 1977 through 1988 as of June 30. 1988 is preliminary.
Source: Office of Personnel Management.

C67. Federal Civilian Employment in the Executive Branch by Agency And State

As of December 31, 1988

State	Total[a]	Department of Defense	Postal Service[b]	Veterans Administration	All Other
Total	3,089,681	1,052,616	848,079	249,831	939,155
Alabama	58,443	26,321	8,927	4,933	18,262
Alaska	14,549	4,992	2,260	167	7,130
Arizona	38,451	10,547	10,536	3,418	13,950
Arkansas	19,432	4,941	5,606	3,991	4,894
California	324,702	133,329	101,759	23,594	66,020
Colorado	52,980	13,935	13,336	3,329	22,380
Connecticut	24,242	5,011	13,796	2,446	2,989
Delaware	5,369	1,805	2,162	711	691
Florida	109,157	32,589	43,313	11,661	21,594
Georgia	88,219	38,288	19,211	5,785	24,935
Hawaii	26,973	20,745	2,969	286	2,973
Idaho	9,880	1,342	2,214	713	5,611
Illinois	106,976	21,353	48,757	12,496	24,370
Indiana	41,639	15,038	15,242	4,078	7,281
Iowa	18,515	1,497	9,150	3,101	4,767
Kansas	24,826	6,829	7,934	3,142	6,921
Kentucky	35,423	13,422	8,440	3,669	9,892
Louisiana	33,915	9,069	10,685	4,583	9,578
Maine	17,659	10,591	4,104	1,119	1,845
Maryland	132,277	42,754	18,781	3,112	67,630
Massachusetts	62,175	12,157	28,766	7,789	13,463
Michigan	57,761	12,381	27,416	6,586	11,378
Minnesota	32,323	2,972	15,719	5,342	8,290
Mississippi	24,022	10,429	5,003	3,136	5,454
Missouri	66,553	20,025	19,557	6,136	20,835
Montana	11,370	1,352	2,224	650	7,144
Nebraska	15,688	4,042	5,539	2,127	3,980
Nevada	10,338	2,066	3,181	891	4,200
New Hampshire	8,028	1,629	3,996	744	1,659
New Jersey	76,975	26,189	37,628	4,347	8,811
New Mexico	26,685	10,230	3,486	1,972	10,997
New York	158,969	19,684	83,502	20,577	35,206
North Carolina	46,353	15,265	15,727	5,184	10,177
North Dakota	8,059	2,035	2,085	649	3,290
Ohio	92,993	34,333	35,203	8,601	14,856
Oklahoma	47,395	24,715	8,922	2,727	11,031
Oregon	28,922	3,295	8,516	3,379	13,732
Pennsylvania	135,591	54,031	43,935	11,926	25,699
Rhode Island	10,511	4,317	4,147	1,078	969
South Carolina	33,066	19,894	6,606	2,713	3,853
South Dakota	9,205	1,556	2,032	1,850	3,767
Tennessee	56,773	7,383	13,991	7,256	28,143
Texas	175,607	62,756	49,816	15,984	47,051
Utah	36,965	22,241	3,870	1,853	9,001
Vermont	5,087	639	2,126	880	1,442
Virginia	159,554	107,660	18,815	5,734	27,345
Washington	64,979	28,715	13,933	4,818	17,513
West Virginia	15,521	1,750	4,438	2,956	6,377
Wisconsin	27,808	3,183	13,543	5,185	5,897
Wyoming	6,464	1,173	1,214	852	3,225
District of Columbia	210,494	390	10,166	550	176,614
Outside U.S.	148,598	102,433	3,795	2,609	39,761

[a] Excludes employees in the Central Intelligence Agency and the National Security Agency.
[b] Excludes temporary Christmas assistance in the Postal Service in all areas.
Source: Office of Personnel Management.

C68. Full-Time Federal Civilian Employment (General Schedule), Aggregate Pay, and Average Salary, By Grade[a]

June 30, 1968 and March 31, 1988

Grade	June 30, 1968			March 31, 1988		
	Employees[b]	Aggregate Pay ($Millions)	Average Salary[c]	Employees[b]	Aggregate Pay ($Millions)	Average Salary[c]
Total	1,301,503	$ 11,263.1	$ 8,654	1,480,150	$ 41,613.3	$ 28,114
1	3,514	13.6	3,878	1,544	15.5	10,039
2	47,280	200.7	4,244	11,908	137.8	11,568
3	156,091	759.4	4,865	57,764	759.8	13,153
4	190,894	1,071.9	5,615	153,645	2,323.1	15,120
5	158,729	1,006.7	6,342	200,208	3,439.8	17,181
6	63,373	449.3	7,089	95,678	1,858.6	19,425
7	112,822	856.9	7,596	145,391	3,081.2	21,193
8	20,462	172.9	8,451	30,505	735.7	24,116
9	139,516	1,263.1	9,054	156,344	4,025.4	25,747
10	15,916	160.0	10,053	28,984	851.5	29,378
11	138,285	1,497.9	10,832	185,479	5,824.0	31,400
12	111,796	1,422.0	12,720	189,892	7,215.0	37,995
13	81,234	1,214.1	14,945	125,807	5,734.3	45,580
14	37,548	660.8	17,600	65,352	3,546.6	54,270
15	19,450	401.8	20,656	30,829	2,005.9	65,067
16	3,294	77.7	23,590	652	46.8	71,786
17	920	23.9	25,996	106	7.7	72,500
18	379	10.3	27,055	62	4.5	72,500

[a] The General Schedule Federal career system covers most positions in the Executive Branch, the District of Columbia government, and certain agencies in the Legislative and Judicial Branches; personnel of the Central Intelligence Agency and National Security Agency are excluded.

[b] Salaries for certain employees of the Veterans Administration, the Foreign Service, U.S. Postal Service, blue collar workers, and others are covered under smaller special pay systems.

[c] Arithmetic mean. The rate of basic pay for employees in the General Schedule is limited by statute to the rate for level V of the Executive Schedule (currently $72,500), which in turn is tied to Congressional salary adjustments.

Source: Office of Personnel Management.

C69. Federal Personnel Compensation and Benefits

Fiscal Years 1988-1990[a]

($Millions)

Item	1988	1989	1990
A. Costs of Current Personnel			
Current personnel costs, total[b]	$ 183,571	$ 190,264	$ 195,157
Direct compensation	138,197	142,278	147,568
Personnel benefits	45,374	47,986	47,589
Civilian personnel, total[b]	109,888	114,458	118,562
Executive branch, total	78,862	81,918	84,802
Direct compensation	63,085	65,646	67,792
Personnel benefits[c]	15,777	16,272	17,010
Legislative and judiciary, total[d]	1,498	1,596	1,773
Direct compensation	1,299	1,375	1,494
Personnel benefits	199	221	279
Postal Service, total	29,528	30,944	31,987
Direct compensation	23,571	24,595	25,439
Personnel benefits	5,957	6,349	6,548
Military personnel, total[e]	73,683	75,806	76,595
Direct compensation	50,242	50,662	52,843
Personnel benefits[f]	23,441	25,144	23,752
B. Costs of Retired Pay for Former Personnel			
Retired pay, total	$ 20,422	$ 21,523	$ 22,699
Civilian personnel	962	1,003	1,030
Military personnel	19,460	20,519	21,669

[a] Data for 1989 and 1990 are estimates from the *Budget* submitted in February 1989.
[b] Includes Postal Service, which was converted to independent status by the Postal Service Reorganization Act of 1970.
[c] Includes employing agency's contributions for the costs of life and health insurance, retirement, and transfers from general revenues to amortize the effects of general pay increases on Federal retirement systems for employees (non-postal) in the executive, legislative, and judicial branches. Excludes transfers from general revenues, mandated by law, for interest on unfunded liabilities and annuities attributable to military service totaling (in millions): $10,836 in 1988, $11,307 in 1989; and $11,567 in 1990.
[d] Excludes members and officers of Congress.
[e] Excludes reserve components; includes allowances for military pay raises of $1,839 million in 1990.
[f] Effective October 1, 1984, the *Budget* reflects establishment of a military retirement trust fund. Military personnel benefits include payments by the Defense Department to finance retirement benefits that accrue to current military personnel totaling (in millions): $18,382 in 1988; $18,798 in 1989; and $16,608 in 1990.
Source: Office of Management and Budget.

Section D
State and Local Governments

- Summary Data
- Expenditures
- Revenue and Taxation
- Major State and Local Functions

D1. State and Local Total Expenditures, Revenue, and Debt

Selected Fiscal Years 1902-1987

($Millions)

Year	Expenditures[a] Total	Expenditures State Total[c]	Expenditures State Direct[d]	Expenditures Local Direct	Revenue Total State and Local[e]	Revenue From Own Sources State	Revenue From Own Sources Local	Revenue From Federal Government	Gross Debt[b] Total	Gross Debt[b] State	Gross Debt[b] Local
1902	$1,095	$188	$136	$959	$1,048	$183	$858	$7	$2,107	$230	$1,877
1913	2,257	388	297	1,960	2,030	360	1,658	12	4,414	379	4,035
1922	5,652	1,397	1,085	4,567	5,169	1,234	3,827	108	10,109	1,131	8,978
1927	7,810	2,047	1,451	6,359	7,838	1,994	5,728	116	14,881	1,971	12,910
1932	8,403	2,829	2,028	6,375	7,887	2,274	5,381	232	19,205	2,832	16,373
1940	11,240	5,209	3,555	7,685	11,749	5,012	5,792	945	20,283	3,590	16,693
1942	10,914	5,343	3,563	7,351	13,148	6,012	6,278	858	19,337	3,257	16,080
1946	14,067	7,066	4,974	9,093	15,983	7,712	7,416	855	15,917	2,353	13,564
1950	27,905	15,082	10,864	17,041	25,639	11,480	11,673	2,486	24,115	5,285	18,830
1952	30,863	15,834	10,790	20,073	31,013	14,330	14,117	2,566	30,100	6,874	23,226
1954	36,607	18,686	13,008	23,599	35,386	15,951	16,468	2,966	38,931	9,600	29,331
1956	43,152	21,686	15,148	28,004	41,692	18,903	19,453	3,335	48,868	12,890	35,978
1958	53,712	28,080	19,991	33,721	49,262	21,427	22,970	4,865	58,187	15,394	42,793
1960	60,999	31,596	22,152	38,847	60,277	26,094	27,209	6,974	69,955	18,543	51,412
1962	70,547	36,402	25,495	45,053	69,492	30,115	31,506	7,871	81,278	22,023	59,255
1964	80,579	42,583	29,616	50,964	81,455	35,703	35,749	10,002	92,222	25,041	67,181
1966	94,906	51,123	34,195	60,711	97,619	43,000	41,499	13,214	107,051	29,564	77,487
1968	116,234	66,254	44,304	71,930	117,581	52,525	47,875	17,181	121,158	35,666	85,492
1970	148,052	85,055	56,163	91,889	150,106	68,691	59,557	21,857	143,570	42,008	101,563
1972	190,496	109,255	72,496	118,001	190,798	84,362	75,097	31,342	175,158	54,453	120,705
1973	205,466	118,836	78,014	127,452	217,616	97,108	81,253	39,256	188,485	59,375	129,110
1974	226,032	132,134	86,193	139,498	237,856	107,645	88,391	41,820	206,616	65,296	141,320
1975	269,215	158,882	106,905	161,336	264,013	119,206	97,773	47,034	219,926	72,127	147,798
1976	304,226	180,926	123,069	179,980	303,287	139,104	108,594	55,589	240,532	84,825	155,707
1977	324,554	191,225	128,765	194,403	337,870	155,799	119,626	62,444	259,658	90,200	169,458
1978	346,786	203,832	136,545	208,768	371,607	171,550	130,464	69,592	280,433	102,569	177,864
1979	381,867	224,644	148,690	231,684	404,934	189,917	139,853	75,164	304,103	111,740	192,363
1980	434,073	257,812	173,308	259,010	451,537	212,636	155,873	83,029	335,603	121,958	213,645
1981	487,048	291,527	198,347	286,827	506,728	240,042	176,391	90,294	363,892	134,847	229,045
1982	524,817	310,358	211,615	311,408	547,719	261,733	198,703	87,282	404,579	147,470	257,109
1983	566,990	334,019	233,132	332,093	593,461	284,933	218,522	90,006	454,501	167,290	287,211
1984	600,576	351,445	243,072	355,781	652,114	315,637	239,425	97,052	505,030	186,377	318,653
1985	658,101	390,828	269,257	386,881	719,607	349,077	264,372	106,158	568,442	211,904	356,539
1986	718,316	424,216	292,249	423,961	783,193	382,600	287,495	113,099	658,875	247,715	411,160
1987	775,318	455,696	314,270	458,592	842,589	414,560	313,032	114,996	718,657	265,677	452,980

a Includes expenditures for utility, liquor stores, and insurance trust, as well as general functions; excludes payments for debt retirement.
b Short- and long-term debt outstanding at end of fiscal year.
c Expenditures for state functions and intergovernmental payments to local governments; beginning 1974 also includes state payments to Federal government, largely for the supplemental security income program for the aged, blind, and disabled, initiated in January 1974.
d Direct expenditures are disbursements to final recipients of government payments; i.e., all expenditures other than intergovernmental.
e Excludes duplicating interlevel transfers of funds.

Source: Department of Commerce, Bureau of the Census.

D2. State and Local Revenue, Expenditures, and Surpluses or Deficits; Total and General Accounts

Selected Fiscal Years 1942-1986

($Millions)

Year	Total			General[a]		
	Revenue	Expenditure	Surplus or Deficit (-)	Revenue	Expenditure	Surplus or Deficit (-)
1942	$ 13,148	$ 10,914	$ 2,234	$ 10,418	$ 9,190	$ 1,228
1944	14,133	10,449	3,684	10,908	8,863	2,045
1946	15,983	14,067	1,916	12,356	11,028	1,328
1948	21,613	21,260	353	17,250	17,684	-434
1950	25,639	27,905	-2,266	20,911	22,787	-1,876
1952	31,013	30,863	150	25,181	26,098	-917
1954	35,386	36,607	-1,221	29,012	30,701	-1,689
1956	41,692	43,152	-1,460	34,667	36,711	-2,044
1957	45,929	47,553	-1,624	38,164	40,375	-2,211
1958	49,262	53,712	-4,450	41,219	44,851	-3,632
1959	53,972	58,572	-4,600	45,302	48,887	-3,585
1960	60,277	60,999	-722	50,505	51,876	-1,371
1961	64,531	67,023	-2,492	54,037	56,201	-2,164
1962	69,492	70,547	-1,055	58,252	60,206	-1,954
1963	74,408	74,698	-290	62,269	63,977	-1,708
1964	81,455	80,579	876	68,443	69,302	-859
1965	87,777	86,686	1,091	74,000	74,678	-678
1966	97,619	94,906	2,713	83,036	82,843	193
1967	106,581	105,978	603	91,197	93,350	-2,153
1968	117,581	116,234	1,347	101,264	102,411	-1,147
1969	132,153	131,600	553	114,500	116,728	-2,228
1970	150,106	148,052	2,054	130,756	131,332	-576
1971	166,090	170,766	4,676	144,927	150,674	-5,747
1972	190,798	190,496	302	167,541	168,549	-1,008
1973	217,616	205,466	12,150	190,214	181,357	8,857
1974	237,856	226,032	11,824	207,670	198,959	8,711
1975	264,013	269,215	-5,202	228,171	230,721	-2,550
1976	303,287	304,228	-941	256,176	256,731	-555
1977	337,870	324,554	13,316	285,157	274,215	10,942
1978	371,607	346,786	24,821	315,960	296,983	18,977
1979	404,934	381,867	23,067	343,278	327,517	15,761
1980	451,537	434,073	17,464	382,322	369,086	13,236
1981	506,728	487,048	19,680	423,404	407,449	15,955
1982	547,719	524,817	22,902	457,654	436,896	20,758
1983	593,461	566,990	26,471	486,753	466,844	19,909
1984	651,997	600,222	51,775	542,730	505,008	37,722
1985	720,062	657,888	62,174	598,121	553,899	44,222
1986	783,349	717,430	65,919	641,457	605,594	35,863

[a] Excludes utilities, liquor stores, and insurance trust transactions.

Source: Department of Commerce, Bureau of the Census, and Tax Foundation computations.

D3. State and Local Receipts and Expenditures in the National Income Accounts[a]

Selected Calendar Years 1929-1988

($Billions)

Source and Function	1929	1949	1959	1969	1979	1988
Total receipts, national income basis	$ 7.6	$ 19.5	$ 46.6	$ 120.8	$ 355.3	$ 702.6
Personal tax and nontax receipts	1.3	2.4	6.2	21.1	73.7	176.9
Corporate profits tax accruals	.1	.6	1.2	3.6	13.6	30.8
Indirect business tax and nontax accruals	5.9	13.3	29.3	67.4	160.1	332.4
Contributions for social insurance	.1	.9	3.1	8.3	27.4	51.0
Federal grants-in-aid	.1	2.2	6.8	20.3	80.5	111.5
Total expenditures, national income basis	7.8	20.2	47.0	119.3	327.7	647.7
Purchase of goods and services	7.4	18.0	43.3	107.2	289.9	583.6
Transfer payments to persons	.2	3.0	5.6	16.7	57.2	128.2
Net interest paid[b]	.4	.1	.1	-1.2	-11.8	-40.8
Less: Dividends received by government[c]	-	-	-	.2	2.0	8.2
Subsidies less current surplus of government enterprises	-.2	-.9	-2.0	-3.3	-5.7	-15.1
Surplus or deficit (-) in national income and products accounts	-.2	-.7	-.4	1.5	27.6	54.9
Social insurance funds	.1	.6	2.0	5.8	23.8	68.5
Other	-.3	-1.3	-2.5	-4.3	3.8	-13.5

[a] See Introductory Notes for a description of the Federal sector in the national income and products accounts.
[b] Interest paid less interest received.
[c] Prior to 1968, net interest paid included dividends received.
Source: Department of Commerce, Bureau of Economic Analysis.

D4. State and Local Direct General Expenditures, Revenue, and Debt, by State

Fiscal Year 1987

($Millions)

State	Expenditures			Revenue				Gross Debt[a]	
	Total State and Local	State	Local	Total State and Local	From Own Sources State	From Own Sources Local	From Federal Government	Total State and Local	State
Total	$653,608	$262,513	$391,095	$686,164	$317,106	$254,062	$114,996	$718,657	$265,677
Alabama	8,473	4,140	4,332	8,914	4,439	2,733	1,742	9,384	3,729
Alaska	5,227	3,100	2,127	5,502	3,756	1,186	560	11,175	6,189
Arizona	9,490	3,421	6,069	8,939	4,213	3,549	1,176	14,103	1,937
Arkansas	4,553	2,229	2,324	4,596	2,340	1,240	1,017	4,321	1,441
California	84,581	27,814	56,767	89,010	43,191	31,430	14,390	71,961	22,405
Colorado	9,345	3,186	6,159	9,574	3,680	4,465	1,429	11,200	2,320
Connecticut	9,394	4,763	4,631	10,323	5,659	3,291	1,373	10,753	8,014
Delaware	1,925	1,168	757	2,119	1,420	381	318	3,816	2,787
Florida	28,271	8,680	19,590	28,578	11,534	13,377	3,668	40,627	7,806
Georgia	14,912	5,632	9,281	15,686	6,289	6,641	2,756	14,253	2,601
Hawaii	3,066	2,348	718	3,274	2,209	538	528	3,504	2,868
Idaho	2,078	966	1,112	2,121	1,047	651	423	1,146	614
Illinois	29,170	11,933	17,236	30,273	13,167	11,960	5,147	27,476	12,665
Indiana	11,956	5,095	6,862	12,623	6,281	4,133	2,210	7,689	2,731
Iowa	7,126	3,136	3,990	7,540	3,544	2,770	1,227	4,892	1,776
Kansas	6,169	2,321	3,849	6,772	2,615	3,257	900	6,658	370
Kentucky	7,776	4,279	3,497	7,972	4,435	1,949	1,588	12,419	4,669
Louisiana	11,013	5,394	5,620	11,727	5,243	3,749	2,735	19,790	11,075
Maine	2,938	1,579	1,359	3,166	1,667	816	683	2,606	1,621
Maryland	12,527	5,683	6,845	13,683	6,663	4,811	2,210	13,909	5,336
Massachusetts	20,979	10,124	10,855	18,783	10,505	5,161	3,118	9,236	12,800
Michigan	26,662	11,360	15,302	27,551	12,956	9,874	4,721	18,674	7,700
Minnesota	13,930	4,986	8,944	14,617	6,840	5,502	2,274	17,228	3,587
Mississippi	5,319	2,209	3,110	5,642	2,452	1,876	1,314	5,338	1,322
Missouri	10,553	4,538	6,015	10,667	4,914	3,898	1,854	8,658	4,307
Montana	2,331	1,111	1,219	2,313	933	815	565	2,222	1,146

Continued

D4. State and Local Direct General Expenditures, Revenue, and Debt, by State (continued)

Fiscal Year 1987
($Millions)

State	Expenditures			Revenue				Gross Debt[a]	
	Total State and Local	State	Local	Total State and Local	From Own Sources State	Local	From Federal Government	Total State and Local	State
Nebraska	3,950	1,662	2,288	4,215	1,670	1,838	677	6,321	1,478
Nevada	2,829	979	1,850	2,810	1,354	1,060	396	3,341	1,226
New Hampshire	2,365	1,113	1,252	2,466	1,022	1,055	388	3,063	2,362
New Jersey	23,281	9,627	13,654	24,926	12,931	8,572	3,423	28,951	17,489
New Mexico	4,041	1,908	2,134	4,370	2,667	1,006	697	5,297	1,780
New York	69,520	23,804	40,980	75,614	29,930	33,212	12,472	77,247	40,631
North Carolina	13,325	5,728	7,597	14,308	7,570	4,355	2,382	13,735	2,726
North Dakota	1,946	1,092	854	1,909	970	516	423	1,678	792
Ohio	26,255	10,789	15,466	27,147	12,815	9,792	4,541	9,364	9,440
Oklahoma	8,598	4,149	4,449	7,408	3,650	2,481	1,277	8,544	4,105
Oregon	7,653	3,251	4,403	8,048	3,418	3,148	1,482	10,944	7,143
Pennsylvania	28,050	11,883	16,167	30,928	14,161	11,118	5,648	36,509	8,820
Rhode Island	2,749	1,644	1,104	2,922	1,632	739	551	3,400	2,785
South Carolina	7,264	3,641	3,622	7,587	4,039	2,196	1,352	8,920	3,722
South Dakota	1,804	1,031	772	1,682	695	582	405	1,968	1,544
Tennessee	10,086	4,575	5,511	10,309	4,425	3,752	2,131	11,041	2,261
Texas	39,017	13,049	25,968	39,585	15,083	18,902	5,600	53,274	5,329
Utah	4,276	2,144	2,132	4,366	2,005	1,467	894	9,119	1,418
Vermont	1,507	897	610	1,596	813	421	362	1,316	955
Virginia	14,167	6,279	7,888	14,452	7,139	5,050	2,264	11,081	4,199
Washington	12,602	5,473	7,129	13,132	6,683	4,005	2,444	19,721	3,841
West Virginia	4,313	2,344	1,969	4,327	2,312	1,028	988	5,176	2,241
Wisconsin	13,666	5,260	8,406	13,944	7,006	4,520	2,418	9,747	4,795
Wyoming	2,168	901	1,267	2,452	1,098	895	459	2,151	780
District of Columbia	3,211	-	3,211	3,695	-	2,301	1,393	3,711	-

[a] Includes general and utility debt.
Source: Department of Commerce, Bureau of the Census.

D5. State and Local Total Expenditures by Function

Selected Fiscal Years 1902-1987

($Millions)

Year	Total	General by Function								Insurance Trust[c]	Utility and Liquor Stores[d]
		Total General	Education	Highways	Public Welfare	Health and Hospitals	Police and Fire	Financial Administration[a]	Other General[b]		
1902	$1,095	$1,013	$255	$175	$37	$60	$90	$141	$255	-	$82
1913	2,257	2,064	577	419	52	108	165	211	532	$7	186
1922	5,652	5,218	1,705	1,294	119	258	348	313	1,181	75	359
1927	7,810	7,210	2,235	1,809	151	355	473	412	1,775	109	491
1932	8,403	7,765	2,311	1,741	444	456	528	470	1,815	120	518
1942	10,914	9,190	2,586	1,490	1,225	591	630	578	2,090	617	1,106
1944	10,499	8,863	2,793	1,200	1,133	656	665	599	1,817	354	1,281
1946	14,067	11,028	3,356	1,672	1,409	818	773	703	2,297	1,306	1,733
1948	21,260	17,684	5,379	3,036	2,099	1,229	1,050	880	4,011	1,197	2,379
1950	27,905	22,787	7,177	3,803	2,940	1,748	1,264	1,041	4,814	2,379	2,739
1952	30,863	26,098	8,318	4,650	2,788	2,185	1,525	1,193	5,436	1,698	3,067
1954	36,607	30,701	10,557	5,527	3,060	2,409	1,783	1,375	5,990	2,423	3,482
1956	43,152	36,711	13,220	6,953	3,139	2,772	2,067	1,560	7,000	2,376	4,065
1958	53,712	44,851	15,919	8,567	3,818	3,462	2,483	1,843	8,759	4,168	4,693
1960	60,999	51,876	18,719	9,428	4,404	3,794	2,852	2,113	10,565	4,031	5,088
1962	70,547	60,206	22,216	10,357	5,084	4,342	3,254	2,338	12,615	4,888	5,453
1964	80,579	69,302	26,286	11,664	5,766	4,910	3,588	2,567	14,521	5,094	6,184
1966	94,906	82,843	33,287	12,770	6,757	5,910	4,152	2,974	16,993	4,782	7,282
1968	116,234	102,411	41,158	14,481	9,857	7,546	5,033	3,647	20,688	5,653	8,170
1970	148,052	131,332	52,718	16,427	14,679	9,669	6,518	4,682	26,639	7,263	9,447
1972	190,496	168,549	65,814	19,021	21,117	13,023	8,584	5,920	35,070	10,548	11,398
1974	226,032	198,959	75,833	19,946	25,085	15,945	10,326	7,536	44,289	12,667	14,406
1976	304,228	256,731	97,216	23,907	32,604	20,686	13,429	9,671	59,218	27,954	19,542
1978	346,786	296,983	110,758	24,609	39,140	24,951	16,108	12,293	69,124	23,526	26,277
1980	434,073	369,086	133,211	33,311	47,288	32,174	19,212	15,416	88,474	28,797	36,190
1981	487,048	407,449	145,784	34,603	54,121	36,101	21,283	16,771	98,786	36,583	43,016
1982	524,817	436,896	154,282	34,520	57,996	40,881	23,537	18,841	106,839	39,508	48,413
1983	566,990	466,844	163,876	36,655	60,906	44,118	25,516	20,883	114,890	47,335	52,811
1984	600,576	505,006	176,108	39,516	66,414	46,419	27,464	22,496	126,589	40,508	55,062
1985	658,101	554,111	192,686	45,022	71,532	49,711	29,873	24,786	140,501	44,191	59,800
1986	718,316	606,561	210,819	49,368	76,730	53,613	32,272	27,697	156,062	46,459	65,297
1987	775,318	656,064	226,658	52,199	82,520	56,972	35,594	30,043	172,078	50,815	68,440

[a] Includes general control.

[b] Includes natural resources, sanitation and sewerage, recreation, housing and urban renewal, interest on the general debt, and other and unallocable expenditures.

[c] Cash payments of contributory employee retirement, unemployment compensation, workmen's compensation, sickness, and other cash benefit social insurance programs. Includes withdrawals of retirement contributions for 1975-1987 and includes revenue and benefits of extended and special unemployment compensation programs.

[d] Utility covers water supply, electric power, gas supply, and transit systems owned and operated by local governments.

Source: Department of Commerce, Bureau of the Census.

D6. Per Capita State and Local Direct General Expenditures by Function[a]

Selected Fiscal Years 1902-1987

Year	Total General	Education	Highways	Public Welfare	Health and Hospitals	Police and Fire	Financial Administration[b]	All Other[c]
1902	$ 12.80	$ 3.22	$ 2.21	$ .47	$ .78	$ 1.14	$ 1.78	$ 3.22
1913	21.23	5.93	4.31	.53	1.11	1.70	2.17	5.48
1922	47.41	15.49	11.76	1.08	2.35	3.17	2.84	10.72
1927	60.57	18.78	15.20	1.27	2.98	3.98	3.46	14.90
1932	62.15	18.50	13.93	3.55	3.65	4.23	3.76	14.53
1934	56.77	14.48	11.93	7.03	3.30	3.79	3.42	12.82
1936	59.63	16.98	11.12	6.45	3.64	4.05	3.90	13.49
1938	67.38	19.17	12.70	8.23	4.24	4.54	4.17	14.33
1940	69.85	19.97	11.91	8.75	4.61	4.54	4.25	15.82
1942	68.14	19.18	11.05	9.08	4.38	4.67	4.29	15.49
1944	64.04	20.18	8.67	8.19	4.74	4.80	4.33	13.13
1946	78.00	23.74	11.83	9.97	5.79	5.47	4.97	16.23
1948	120.60	36.68	20.71	14.31	8.38	7.16	6.00	27.36
1950	150.22	47.31	25.07	19.38	11.52	8.34	6.86	31.74
1952	166.29	53.00	29.63	17.76	13.92	9.71	7.60	34.67
1954	189.06	65.01	34.04	18.84	14.83	10.98	8.47	36.89
1956	219.42	79.02	41.56	18.76	16.57	12.35	9.32	41.84
1958	258.76	91.84	49.43	22.03	19.97	14.33	10.63	50.53
1960	288.21	104.00	52.38	24.47	21.08	15.85	11.74	58.69
1962	324.00	119.56	55.74	27.36	23.37	17.51	12.58	67.88
1964	362.20	137.38	60.96	30.13	25.66	18.75	13.40	75.90
1966	422.97	169.95	65.20	34.50	30.17	21.20	15.18	86.75
1968	512.41	205.93	72.46	49.32	37.75	25.18	18.25	103.52
1970	646.20	259.39	80.83	72.23	47.57	32.07	23.04	131.05
1971	730.52	288.05	87.73	88.36	54.32	36.50	25.68	149.88
1972	801.38	316.06	91.35	101.19	62.54	41.23	28.43	160.58
1973	862.93	332.20	88.71	112.37	65.97	45.67	31.70	186.31
1974	939.58	358.74	94.36	117.06	75.43	48.85	35.65	209.49
1975	1,078.01	412.24	105.71	127.58	88.43	56.54	40.54	246.97
1976	1,190.50	452.89	111.37	151.89	96.37	62.56	45.06	270.36
1977	1,260.86	474.99	106.56	159.57	106.48	68.66	49.67	294.93
1978	1,355.15	507.91	112.85	172.79	114.41	73.87	56.38	316.94
1979	1,481.26	542.70	129.22	183.64	128.21	78.84	62.75	355.90
1980	1,621.77	588.11	147.07	201.11	142.05	84.82	68.06	390.55
1981	1,790.25	643.51	152.74	230.63	159.35	93.95	74.02	436.05
1982	1,920.59	681.02	152.37	248.14	180.45	103.89	83.48	471.24
1983	1,987.68	700.38	156.66	252.83	188.56	109.05	89.25	490.95
1984	2,131.13	745.72	167.33	274.01	196.56	116.29	95.26	535.96
1985	2,312.97	807.10	188.58	291.43	208.22	125.13	103.77	588.74
1986	2,507.31	874.49	204.78	309.64	222.39	133.87	116.53	645.61
1987	2,685.33	931.22	214.46	329.05	234.06	146.24	125.16	705.14

a Based on resident population (including armed forces overseas, 1930-1955) at the middle of the calendar year.
b Includes general control.
c Includes natural resources, parks and recreation, sanitation and sewerage, interest on general debt, housing and urban redevelopment, correction, and other unallocable expenditures.
Source: Department of Commerce, Bureau of the Census.

D7. State and Local Direct General Expenditures by Function and State

Fiscal Year 1987
($Millions)

State	Total General	Education	Highways	Public Welfare	Health and Hospitals	Police and Fire	Financial Administration[a]	Other[b]
Total	$ 653,608	$ 226,658	$ 52,199	$ 80,090	$ 56,971	$ 35,595	$ 30,043	$ 172,052
Alabama	8,473	3,191	711	642	1,434	376	389	1,730
Alaska	5,227	1,246	584	291	128	162	319	2,496
Arizona	9,490	3,625	1,231	726	427	582	524	2,375
Arkansas	4,553	1,893	511	543	414	167	187	838
California	84,581	27,014	3,904	11,292	7,441	6,141	4,950	23,839
Colorado	9,345	3,419	820	923	681	531	520	2,451
Connecticut	9,394	2,850	815	1,187	663	538	456	2,885
Delaware	1,925	740	176	139	95	75	108	592
Florida	28,271	9,034	2,104	2,059	2,911	2,035	1,527	8,601
Georgia	14,912	5,226	1,236	1,303	2,689	684	627	3,147
Hawaii	3,066	821	148	309	200	158	186	1,244
Idaho	2,078	815	251	170	195	100	96	451
Illinois	29,170	9,999	2,549	3,905	1,824	1,892	1,304	7,697
Indiana	11,957	5,008	975	1,410	1,176	474	512	2,402
Iowa	7,126	2,809	892	857	709	273	287	1,299
Kansas	6,169	2,375	776	530	493	264	314	1,417
Kentucky	7,776	2,679	927	1,006	484	308	364	2,008
Louisiana	11,013	3,415	1,016	1,053	1,307	554	470	3,198
Maine	2,938	1,046	286	507	139	116	120	724
Maryland	12,527	4,243	1,170	1,405	514	739	542	3,914
Massachusetts	17,525	5,005	973	2,987	1,629	1,070	791	5,070
Michigan	26,662	10,001	1,628	4,247	2,641	1,317	1,134	5,694
Minnesota	13,930	4,802	1,338	2,036	1,098	480	593	3,583
Mississippi	5,319	1,931	552	556	850	199	194	1,037
Missouri	10,553	4,038	965	1,108	1,119	580	432	2,311
Montana	2,331	870	307	247	120	74	118	595
Nebraska	3,950	1,573	453	415	422	151	158	778

Continued

D7. State and Local Direct General Expenditures by Function and State (continued)

Fiscal Year 1987
($Millions)

State	Total General	Education	Highways	Public Welfare	Health and Hospitals	Police and Fire	Financial Administration[a]	Other[b]
Nevada	2,829	806	281	163	194	214	192	979
New Hampshire	2,365	854	276	271	130	127	115	592
New Jersey	23,281	7,647	1,826	2,689	1,339	1,278	1,040	7,462
New Mexico	4,041	1,509	477	329	304	194	218	1,010
New York	69,520	20,262	3,812	11,423	7,038	3,927	2,845	20,213
North Carolina	13,325	5,769	1,036	1,263	1,302	629	556	2,770
North Dakota	1,946	727	226	236	111	53	71	522
Ohio	26,255	9,620	1,900	4,220	2,215	1,412	1,075	5,813
Oklahoma	7,249	2,749	660	847	682	322	320	1,669
Oregon	7,653	2,900	626	579	480	426	431	2,211
Pennsylvania	28,050	9,908	2,581	4,425	1,545	1,151	1,215	7,225
Rhode Island	2,749	877	164	492	194	166	129	727
South Carolina	7,264	3,029	458	621	1,009	288	270	1,589
South Dakota	1,804	590	246	155	86	58	71	598
Tennessee	10,087	3,401	930	1,216	1,289	461	368	2,422
Texas	39,017	15,754	4,040	2,665	3,158	1,993	1,537	9,870
Utah	4,276	1,787	361	393	293	187	196	1,059
Vermont	1,507	607	186	190	76	46	70	332
Virginia	14,167	5,536	1,494	1,111	1,303	763	711	3,249
Washington	12,602	4,580	1,131	1,427	889	621	636	3,318
West Virginia	4,313	1,611	507	511	274	113	190	1,107
Wisconsin	13,666	5,112	1,252	2,341	826	721	531	2,883
Wyoming	2,168	791	322	114	259	82	95	505
District of Columbia	3,211	567	116	558	302	319	174	1,175

a Includes general control.
b Sewerage, other sanitation, local parks and recreation, interest on general debt, and all other general expenditures.
Source: Department of Commerce, Bureau of the Census.

D8. State and Local Direct General Expenditures by Major Function and State[a]
Selected Fiscal Years 1967-1987
($Millions)

State	Total[b] 1967	Total[b] 1977	Total[b] 1987	Education 1967	Education 1977	Education 1987	Highways 1967	Highways 1977	Highways 1987	Public Welfare 1967	Public Welfare 1977	Public Welfare 1987
Total	$93,350.2	$273,001.8	$653,608.2	$37,918.7	$102,805.2	$226,657.9	$13,932.4	$23,104.5	$52,199.3	$8,217.8	$34,664.0	$80,089.7
Alabama	1,337.3	3,696.3	8,472.8	559.9	1,454.9	3,190.7	229.9	435.4	711.1	130.1	375.9	641.8
Alaska	323.9	1,333.1	5,226.7	84.1	436.5	1,245.8	119.8	190.7	583.6	9.6	57.3	291.2
Arizona	868.4	2,853.4	9,490.4	397.4	1,288.4	3,624.7	166.1	285.1	1,230.8	39.6	127.0	726.1
Arkansas	697.3	1,878.6	4,553.0	275.1	758.4	1,892.6	132.6	262.1	510.6	83.2	237.2	543.2
California	12,301.2	32,532.1	84,581.5	4,391.4	12,217.8	27,016.5	1,336.9	1,504.6	3,904.5	1,626.4	5,178.6	11,292.3
Colorado	1,060.2	3,524.6	9,345.3	495.9	1,587.0	3,418.6	145.6	334.1	819.8	107.0	323.8	923.2
Connecticut	1,364.0	3,579.3	9,393.6	509.6	1,296.0	2,849.7	197.3	244.5	814.5	108.3	437.5	1,186.6
Delaware	322.1	848.7	2,116.4	125.7	345.9	740.0	70.3	67.7	175.6	15.4	74.0	139.1
Florida	2,527.5	9,287.5	28,270.5	997.5	3,438.2	9,033.5	371.8	726.0	2,103.8	145.5	488.3	2,058.7
Georgia	1,709.6	5,060.9	14,912.2	709.7	1,860.5	5,226.2	261.8	476.7	1,235.5	138.6	516.6	1,302.9
Hawaii	490.8	1,714.1	3,066.3	178.6	478.2	820.8	55.3	133.4	147.9	23.9	189.5	308.8
Idaho	315.9	977.7	2,078.0	124.3	375.1	815.4	64.3	159.6	250.7	23.7	78.5	169.9
Illinois	4,505.9	14,237.0	19,169.9	1,842.5	5,357.1	9,999.3	587.2	1,403.6	2,548.7	394.4	2,082.2	3,904.5
Indiana	2,052.8	5,080.1	11,956.5	1,047.3	2,286.6	5,007.8	300.8	496.0	975.0	88.0	474.8	1,410.4
Iowa	1,352.6	3,556.3	7,126.2	603.4	1,499.7	2,808.5	302.9	520.5	891.6	91.2	361.5	857.0
Kansas	1,019.7	2,775.5	6,169.5	461.4	1,102.0	2,375.2	186.5	339.9	776.1	71.3	296.5	529.5
Kentucky	1,278.1	3,479.5	7,775.6	504.0	1,359.8	2,679.1	272.3	456.8	926.5	126.9	471.6	1,006.2
Louisiana	1,783.5	4,733.5	11,013.4	681.1	1,570.3	3,415.3	320.9	661.9	1,015.9	215.0	442.2	1,053.4
Maine	389.0	1,214.9	2,937.6	152.8	405.4	1,046.3	85.9	158.8	286.2	34.5	170.2	507.2
Maryland	1,689.9	3,013.0	12,527.4	715.4	2,353.8	4,242.8	207.6	466.2	1,169.6	123.5	586.3	1,405.3
Massachusetts	2,537.5	7,968.4	17,525.5	825.7	2,612.1	5,005.4	272.1	516.2	973.1	299.3	1,371.1	2,986.9
Michigan	4,323.4	12,687.3	26,662.1	2,065.0	5,060.0	10,000.8	515.6	906.8	1,628.2	326.8	1,996.0	4,247.0
Minnesota	1,934.0	5,803.2	13,930.2	852.0	2,167.2	4,802.2	343.4	613.9	1,337.9	168.5	773.0	2,035.7
Mississippi	837.8	2,431.6	5,319.2	331.1	905.2	1,931.1	168.0	375.7	552.0	86.1	234.0	556.3
Missouri	1,830.8	4,523.6	10,552.8	776.7	1,834.6	4,037.9	280.9	508.1	964.7	174.2	449.3	1,108.2
Montana	357.3	1,072.3	2,330.9	144.3	438.0	870.3	95.4	197.7	307.0	19.7	78.7	247.3
Nebraska	648.4	1,799.1	3,949.9	263.6	763.5	1,573.4	140.8	260.2	452.8	38.5	141.6	414.9
Nevada	309.8	930.4	2,829.4	97.7	293.5	906.2	64.8	108.0	280.7	13.2	57.8	163.4

Continued

D8. State and Local Direct General Expenditures by Major Function and State[a] (continued)

Selected Fiscal Years 1967-1987

($Millions)

State	Total[b]			Education			Highways			Public Welfare		
	1967	1977	1987	1967	1977	1987	1967	1977	1987	1967	1977	1987
New Hampshire	289.6	947.9	2,365.1	122.3	377.9	854.4	60.6	148.4	276.0	19.2	113.2	270.5
New Jersey	2,897.3	9,722.8	23,280.6	1,138.2	3,475.8	7,647.3	380.7	562.2	1,826.0	168.2	1,239.3	2,688.6
New Mexico	551.6	1,400.3	4,041.1	275.1	642.9	1,508.6	95.6	149.7	477.5	39.9	109.0	329.0
New York	11,262.7	32,177.9	69,520.5	4,140.0	9,643.5	20,261.9	1,092.5	1,472.4	3,811.6	1,086.1	5,321.1	11,422.5
North Carolina	1,728.1	5,426.0	13,324.9	805.1	2,417.4	5,768.9	277.6	513.3	1,035.6	119.7	432.4	1,263.2
North Dakota	359.9	854.3	1,946.3	140.0	322.7	726.6	79.3	149.5	226.0	23.6	68.0	236.2
Ohio	4,065.1	11,871.5	26,255.4	1,728.5	4,868.6	9,619.8	695.3	933.9	1,900.2	354.5	1,327.3	4,219.6
Oklahoma	1,156.7	2,937.0	7,249.1	461.0	1,172.3	2,749.4	181.3	311.2	659.7	208.3	360.5	847.2
Oregon	1,098.1	3,359.7	7,653.4	506.4	1,386.7	2,900.3	181.4	262.6	625.5	63.3	351.0	579.3
Pennsylvania	4,647.4	13,746.5	28,049.8	1,934.5	4,898.8	9,908.1	724.2	1,161.0	2,580.7	366.3	2,367.2	4,424.7
Rhode Island	440.2	1,199.7	2,749.3	150.4	421.4	876.9	78.2	62.8	163.5	47.4	212.5	491.9
South Carolina	795.6	2,814.3	7,263.6	371.4	1,144.4	3,028.6	126.1	179.5	457.9	39.7	242.2	620.8
South Dakota	336.7	813.3	1,803.5	145.8	311.2	589.7	89.5	135.1	246.1	21.4	70.4	154.6
Tennessee	1,522.0	4,266.1	10,086.8	604.0	1,593.7	3,400.8	283.2	490.4	930.4	105.2	430.9	1,215.6
Texas	4,162.8	12,873.1	39,016.7	1,859.6	5,595.1	15,754.2	787.4	1,136.6	4,039.5	290.6	1,200.2	2,664.8
Utah	534.2	1,523.0	4,276.2	284.3	759.4	1,786.9	89.3	157.2	360.5	31.8	120.6	392.6
Vermont	236.2	618.0	1,506.6	90.6	240.9	605.6	68.1	96.4	185.9	18.0	80.6	189.8
Virginia	1,699.6	5,671.8	14,166.9	728.4	2,182.9	5,536.0	353.7	742.0	1,494.4	70.8	515.0	1,110.9
Washington	1,746.7	4,963.9	12,602.9	747.6	2,024.2	4,579.7	313.0	501.9	1,130.7	134.9	512.2	1,426.6
West Virginia	717.9	2,013.6	4,313.3	289.5	742.9	1,611.2	183.5	361.0	506.8	65.4	187.8	511.1
Wisconsin	2,220.9	6,147.0	13,666.5	968.8	2,496.2	5,111.8	374.1	612.1	1,251.8	170.9	940.5	2,341.5
Wyoming	233.2	638.3	2,167.6	95.0	258.6	791.2	68.9	112.2	322.2	8.3	26.7	133.7
District of Columbia	479.5	1,424.0	3,211.3	119.1	321.8	566.9	51.6	52.8	116.4	39.8	265.1	558.1

[a] Direct general expenditures exclude utility, liquor stores, and insurance trust. See Table D4 for fiscal 1987 total direct general expenditures by level of government.

[b] Totals include other expenditures, including health and hospitals, police and fire, general control, and miscellaneous expenditures not shown separately. Fiscal 1987 expenditures for these functions are shown in Table D7.

Source: Department of Commerce, Bureau of the Census.

D9. Per Capita State and Local Direct General Expenditures by Function and State[a]

Fiscal Year 1987

State	Total	Education	Highways	Public Welfare	Health and Hospitals	Police and Fire	Financial Administra- tion[b]	Other[c]
Total	$ 2,685	$ 931	$ 214	$ 329	$ 234	$ 146	$ 125	$ 706
Alabama	2,074	781	174	157	325	92	96	449
Alaska	9,956	2,373	1,112	555	245	308	606	4,757
Arizona	2,803	1,071	364	214	126	172	124	732
Arkansas	1,907	793	214	227	173	70	97	333
California	3,058	977	141	408	269	222	164	877
Colorado	2,835	1,037	249	280	207	161	165	736
Connecticut	2,925	887	254	370	207	168	153	886
Delaware	2,990	1,149	273	216	147	116	176	913
Florida	2,351	751	175	171	242	169	137	706
Georgia	2,397	840	199	209	432	110	101	506
Hawaii	2,831	758	137	285	185	146	179	1,141
Idaho	2,082	817	251	170	195	101	100	448
Illinois	2,519	863	220	337	157	163	110	669
Indiana	2,162	905	176	255	213	86	86	441
Iowa	2,515	991	315	302	250	96	103	458
Kansas	2,492	959	313	214	199	107	133	567
Kentucky	2,086	719	249	270	130	83	96	539
Louisiana	2,469	766	228	236	293	124	104	718
Maine	2,475	881	241	427	117	98	77	634
Maryland	2,762	936	258	310	113	163	126	856
Massachusetts	2,993	855	166	510	278	183	139	862
Michigan	2,898	1,087	177	462	287	143	122	620
Minnesota	3,281	1,131	315	479	259	113	138	846
Mississippi	2,026	736	210	212	324	76	78	390
Missouri	2,068	791	189	217	219	114	85	453
Montana	2,881	1,076	380	306	148	91	145	735
Nebraska	2,478	987	284	260	265	95	96	491
Nevada	2,810	801	279	162	192	213	195	968
New Hampshire	2,238	808	261	256	123	120	105	565
New Jersey	3,034	997	238	350	175	167	147	960
New Mexico	2,694	1,006	318	219	203	129	143	676
New York	3,900	1,137	214	641	395	220	167	1,126
North Carolina	2,078	900	161	197	203	98	89	430
North Dakota	2,896	1,081	336	351	166	79	149	734
Ohio	2,435	892	176	391	205	131	108	532
Oklahoma	2,215	840	202	259	209	99	96	510
Oregon	2,810	1,065	230	213	176	156	151	819
Pennsylvania	2,350	830	216	371	129	96	102	606
Rhode Island	2,788	889	166	499	197	169	131	737
South Carolina	2,121	884	134	181	295	84	79	464
South Dakota	2,544	832	347	218	121	82	106	838
Tennessee	2,078	700	192	250	266	95	83	492
Texas	2,324	938	241	159	188	119	96	583
Utah	2,545	1,064	215	234	174	111	130	617
Vermont	2,749	1,105	339	346	98	85	139	637
Virginia	2,400	938	253	188	221	129	126	545
Washington	2,777	1,009	249	314	196	137	132	740
West Virginia	2,248	840	264	266	143	59	100	576
Wisconsin	2,843	1,063	260	487	172	150	108	603
Wyoming	4,424	1,615	657	232	528	167	196	1,029
District of Columbia	5,163	911	187	897	485	513	313	1,857

[a] Based on resident population at the end of the fiscal year.
[b] Includes general control.
[c] Sewerage, other sanitation, local parks and recreation, interest on general debt, all other direct general expenditures.
Source: Department of Commerce, Bureau of the Census.

D10. Ranking of States According to Per Capita State and Local Direct General Expenditures by Function

Fiscal Year 1987

State	Total	Education	Highways	Public Welfare	Health and Hospitals	Police and Fire	Financial Administration	Other
Alabama	48	45	45	51	5	41	40	46
Alaska	1	1	1	3	16	2	1	1
Arizona	19	10	4	39	46	7	26	21
Arkansas	51	43	33	34	37	50	39	51
California	6	20	49	10	11	3	9	10
Colorado	15	14	22	23	22	15	8	18
Connecticut	10	30	19	13	23	10	10	9
Delaware	9	3	14	38	42	27	6	8
Florida	36	48	44	47	17	8	19	23
Georgia	35	35	37	43	3	31	36	40
Hawaii	16	47	50	22	33	18	5	3
Idaho	45	40	21	48	30	33	37	47
Illinois	27	33	30	17	40	13	28	25
Indiana	42	26	42	29	20	43	46	48
Iowa	28	18	9	21	15	37	34	44
Kansas	29	21	11	40	27	32	20	34
Kentucky	44	50	23	24	44	46	41	37
Louisiana	32	46	29	31	8	24	33	22
Maine	31	32	25	9	49	35	51	27
Maryland	22	24	18	19	50	14	24	12
Massachusetts	8	34	46	4	10	6	16	11
Michigan	11	7	41	8	9	19	27	28
Minnesota	5	5	10	7	14	29	18	13
Mississippi	50	49	35	42	6	49	50	50
Missouri	49	44	39	37	19	28	47	45
Montana	13	9	3	20	41	42	14	19
Nebraska	30	19	12	26	13	39	42	42
Nevada	17	42	13	49	31	5	4	6
New Hampshire	40	41	16	28	47	25	32	35
New Jersey	7	17	27	15	35	11	13	7
New Mexico	24	16	8	35	25	22	15	24
New York	4	4	34	2	4	4	7	4
North Carolina	46	27	48	44	26	36	45	49
North Dakota	12	8	7	14	39	48	12	20
Ohio	33	28	43	11	24	21	29	38
Oklahoma	41	36	36	27	21	34	43	39
Oregon	18	11	28	41	34	16	11	15
Pennsylvania	37	39	31	12	45	38	35	30
Rhode Island	20	29	47	5	28	9	22	17
South Carolina	43	31	51	46	7	45	49	43
South Dakota	26	38	5	36	48	47	31	14
Tennessee	47	51	38	30	12	40	48	41
Texas	38	22	26	50	32	26	44	32
Utah	25	12	32	32	36	30	23	29
Vermont	23	6	6	16	51	44	17	26
Virginia	34	23	20	45	18	23	25	36
Washington	21	15	24	18	29	20	21	16
West Virginia	39	37	15	25	43	51	38	33
Wisconsin	14	13	17	6	38	17	30	31
Wyoming	3	2	2	33	1	12	3	5
District of Columbia	2	25	40	1	2	1	2	2

Source: Computed by Tax Foundation from data in Table D9.

D11. State and Local Direct General Expenditures Per $1,000 of Personal Income by Function

Selected Fiscal Years 1940-1987

Year	Total General	Education	Highways	Public Welfare	Health and Hospitals	Police and Fire	Financial Administration[a]	All Other[b]
1940	$117.53	$33.60	$20.03	$14.72	$7.76	$7.64	$7.14	$26.64
1942	75.07	21.12	12.17	10.01	4.83	5.15	4.72	17.07
1944	55.35	17.44	7.49	7.08	4.10	4.15	3.74	11.35
1946	62.77	19.10	9.52	8.02	4.66	4.40	4.00	13.07
1948	85.26	25.93	14.64	10.12	5.93	5.06	4.24	19.34
1950	101.06	31.83	16.87	13.04	7.75	5.61	4.62	21.35
1952	97.00	30.92	17.28	10.36	8.12	5.67	4.43	20.20
1953	98.46	33.13	17.59	10.28	8.08	5.77	4.46	19.16
1954	107.82	37.08	19.41	10.75	8.46	6.26	4.83	21.04
1955	109.40	38.63	20.93	10.28	8.19	6.24	4.71	20.43
1956	111.08	40.00	21.04	9.50	8.39	6.25	4.72	21.18
1957	115.78	40.53	22.41	9.99	8.95	6.53	4.95	22.42
1958	125.12	44.41	23.90	10.65	9.66	6.93	5.14	24.43
1959	128.32	45.37	25.18	10.86	9.78	6.89	5.26	25.00
1960	130.10	46.95	23.65	11.05	9.52	7.15	5.30	26.50
1961	135.74	49.69	23.78	11.40	9.87	7.50	5.40	28.10
1962	136.91	50.52	23.55	11.56	9.87	7.41	5.32	28.69
1963	140.73	52.13	24.18	11.90	10.17	7.38	5.30	29.67
1964	150.12	57.47	25.26	12.49	10.63	7.77	5.56	30.94
1965	152.66	59.00	24.89	12.86	10.92	7.85	5.65	31.49
1966	155.67	62.55	23.99	12.69	11.10	7.80	5.59	31.95
1967	160.81	65.32	24.00	14.16	11.44	7.79	5.68	32.42
968	163.84	65.84	23.16	15.77	12.07	8.05	5.83	33.12
1969	170.66	69.03	22.54	17.71	12.46	8.33	6.00	34.59
1970	176.40	70.81	22.06	19.71	12.98	8.76	6.29	35.79
1971	188.59	74.36	22.64	22.81	14.02	9.43	6.63	38.68
1972	196.65	76.79	22.19	24.64	15.19	9.99	6.89	40.96
1973	193.60	74.38	19.90	25.21	14.80	10.14	7.11	42.06
1974	187.76	71.69	18.66	23.39	15.07	9.76	7.12	42.07
1975	199.26	76.29	19.56	23.61	16.36	10.28	7.50	45.65
1976	203.25	77.32	19.01	25.00	16.45	10.68	7.69	47.10
1977	199.65	74.83	16.79	26.14	16.77	10.82	7.82	46.47
1978	194.62	72.94	16.21	24.82	16.43	10.61	8.10	45.51
1979	190.82	69.91	16.65	23.65	16.52	10.16	8.08	45.85
1980	190.26	68.99	17.25	23.59	16.66	9.95	7.98	45.82
1981	187.51	67.40	16.00	24.16	16.69	9.84	7.75	45.67
1982	180.87	64.13	14.35	23.37	16.99	9.78	7.83	44.42
1983	180.85	63.73	14.25	23.00	17.16	9.92	8.12	44.67
1984	184.08	64.41	14.45	23.67	16.98	10.04	8.23	46.30
1985	182.81	63.80	14.91	23.04	16.46	9.89	8.21	46.50
1986	182.58	63.68	14.91	22.55	17.20	9.75	8.48	46.01
1987	185.18	64.22	14.79	22.69	16.14	10.08	8.63	48.63

[a] Includes general control.
[b] Includes natural resources, parks and recreation, sanitation and sewerage, interest on general debt, housing and urban redevelopment, corrections, and all other and unallocable expenditures.

Source: Department of Commerce, Bureau of the Census and Bureau of Economic Analysis; and Tax Foundation computations.

D12. State and Local Direct General Expenditures Per $1,000 of Personal Income by Function and State

Fiscal Year 1987

State	Total	Education	Highways	Public Welfare	Health and Hospitals	Police and Fire	Financial Adminis-tration[a]	Other[b]
Total	185.18	64.22	14.79	22.69	16.14	10.08	8.63	48.63
Alabama	184.44	69.46	15.48	13.97	28.87	8.18	8.50	39.98
Alaska	550.46	131.20	61.46	30.67	13.53	17.03	33.50	263.07
Arizona	212.22	81.06	27.52	16.24	9.54	13.02	11.63	53.21
Arkansas	173.33	72.05	19.44	20.68	15.75	6.36	6.99	32.06
California	185.45	59.23	8.56	24.76	16.32	13.47	9.92	53.19
Colorado	187.77	68.69	16.47	18.55	13.69	10.66	10.91	48.80
Connecticut	150.29	45.59	13.03	18.98	10.61	8.61	7.83	45.64
Delaware	202.71	77.91	18.48	14.64	9.99	7.86	11.94	61.89
Florida	165.34	52.83	12.30	12.04	17.03	11.90	9.62	49.62
Georgia	181.68	63.67	15.05	15.87	32.76	8.33	7.69	38.31
Hawaii	193.90	51.90	9.35	19.52	12.68	9.99	12.24	78.22
Idaho	184.71	72.48	22.29	15.10	17.30	8.91	8.87	39.76
Illinois	162.01	55.54	14.16	21.69	10.12	10.51	7.10	42.89
Indiana	165.39	69.27	13.49	19.51	16.26	6.55	6.57	33.74
Iowa	187.27	73.81	23.43	22.52	18.64	7.17	7.67	34.03
Kansas	171.17	65.90	21.53	14.69	13.69	7.33	9.13	38.90
Kentucky	185.57	63.94	22.11	24.01	11.56	7.34	8.50	48.11
Louisiana	218.60	67.79	20.16	20.91	25.95	11.00	9.19	63.60
Maine	195.75	69.72	19.07	33.79	9.23	7.75	8.09	48.10
Maryland	166.43	56.37	15.54	18.67	6.82	9.82	7.59	51.62
Massachusetts	169.57	48.43	9.41	28.90	15.76	10.36	7.87	48.84
Michigan	197.33	74.02	12.05	31.43	19.55	9.74	8.28	42.26
Minnesota	220.47	76.00	21.18	32.22	17.38	7.59	9.19	56.91
Mississippi	208.56	75.72	21.64	21.81	33.33	7.78	8.02	40.26
Missouri	151.07	57.80	13.81	15.86	16.02	8.31	6.24	33.03
Montana	241.15	90.03	31.77	25.58	12.38	7.65	12.15	61.59
Nebraska	179.89	71.66	20.62	18.89	19.23	6.89	6.98	35.62
Nevada	190.28	54.22	18.88	10.99	13.03	14.41	13.19	65.56
New Hampshire	144.75	52.29	16.89	16.56	7.94	7.79	6.76	36.52
New Jersey	164.04	53.88	12.87	18.94	9.44	9.01	7.92	51.98
New Mexico	239.21	89.30	28.26	19.48	17.98	11.49	12.68	60.02
New York	228.61	66.63	12.53	37.56	23.14	12.91	9.78	66.06
North Carolina	169.18	73.24	13.15	16.04	16.53	7.98	7.24	35.00
North Dakota	229.79	85.79	26.68	27.89	13.14	6.24	8.75	61.30
Ohio	175.26	64.21	12.68	28.17	14.79	9.43	7.76	38.22
Oklahoma	178.57	67.73	16.25	20.87	16.80	7.94	7.80	41.18
Oregon	212.86	80.66	17.40	16.11	13.34	11.85	11.48	62.02
Pennsylvania	165.59	58.49	15.24	26.12	9.12	6.80	7.15	42.67
Rhode Island	193.44	61.70	11.51	34.61	13.64	11.71	9.10	51.17
South Carolina	190.38	79.38	12.00	16.27	26.44	7.54	7.05	41.70
South Dakota	215.63	70.50	29.42	18.48	10.28	6.95	9.02	70.98
Tennessee	174.98	59.00	16.14	21.09	22.36	8.00	7.03	41.36
Texas	173.50	70.06	17.96	11.85	14.04	8.86	7.15	43.58
Utah	233.82	97.71	19.71	21.47	16.02	10.24	11.96	56.71
Vermont	208.67	83.88	25.74	26.29	7.45	6.44	10.53	48.34
Virginia	158.88	62.08	16.76	12.46	14.62	8.56	8.37	36.03
Washington	188.15	68.38	16.88	21.30	13.27	9.28	8.93	50.11
West Virginia	212.59	79.41	24.98	25.20	13.51	5.59	9.42	54.48
Wisconsin	205.36	76.81	18.81	35.18	12.41	10.85	7.80	43.50
Wyoming	334.25	122.01	49.69	17.35	39.88	12.60	14.84	77.88
District of Columbia	264.48	46.69	9.58	45.97	24.86	26.31	16.01	95.06

[a] Includes general control.
[b] Sewerage, other sanitation, local parks and recreation, interest on general debt, and all other direct general expenditures.
Source: Department of Commerce, Bureau of the Census; and Tax Foundation computations.

D13.   Ranking of States According to State and Local Direct General Expenditures Per $1,000 of Personal Income by Function

Fiscal Year 1987

State	Total	Education	Highways	Public Welfare	Health and Hospitals	Police and Fire	Financial Administra- tion	Other
Alabama	31	25	33	47	4	30	26	39
Alaska	1	1	1	8	31	2	1	1
Arizona	14	8	6	39	45	5	10	17
Arkansas	38	20	19	26	24	49	47	51
California	29	38	51	16	19	4	14	18
Colorado	26	27	29	34	28	14	12	25
Connecticut	50	51	40	30	41	26	34	29
Delaware	18	12	23	46	44	34	9	10
Florida	45	46	44	49	16	8	16	23
Georgia	32	35	35	42	3	28	38	42
Hawaii	21	48	50	27	37	18	6	3
Idaho	30	19	11	44	15	24	24	40
Illinois	47	43	36	20	43	15	44	32
Indiana	44	26	38	28	20	47	50	49
Iowa	27	17	10	18	12	43	39	48
Kansas	39	32	14	45	29	42	20	41
Kentucky	28	34	12	17	40	41	27	27
Louisiana	10	29	17	24	6	12	18	8
Maine	20	24	20	5	47	37	30	28
Maryland	42	42	32	33	51	19	40	20
Massachusetts	40	49	49	9	23	16	33	24
Michigan	19	16	45	7	10	20	29	34
Minnesota	9	14	15	6	14	39	19	14
Mississippi	16	15	13	19	2	36	31	38
Missouri	49	41	37	43	21	29	51	50
Montana	4	4	3	14	39	38	7	11
Nebraska	33	21	16	32	11	45	48	46
Nevada	24	44	21	51	36	3	4	7
New Hampshire	51	47	26	37	49	35	49	44
New Jersey	46	45	41	31	46	23	32	19
New Mexico	5	5	5	29	13	11	5	13
New York	8	31	43	2	8	6	15	6
North Carolina	41	18	39	41	18	32	41	47
North Dakota	7	6	7	11	35	50	25	12
Ohio	35	33	42	10	25	21	37	43
Oklahoma	34	30	30	25	17	33	35	37
Oregon	12	9	25	40	33	9	11	9
Pennsylvania	43	40	34	13	48	46	42	33
Rhode island	22	37	47	4	30	10	21	21
South Carolina	23	11	46	38	5	40	45	35
South Dakota	11	22	4	35	42	44	22	5
Tennessee	36	39	31	23	9	31	46	36
Texas	37	23	24	50	27	25	43	30
Utah	6	3	18	21	22	17	8	15
Vermont	15	7	8	12	50	48	13	26
Virginia	48	36	28	48	26	27	28	45
Washington	25	28	27	22	34	22	23	22
West Virginia	13	10	9	15	32	51	17	16
Wisconsin	17	13	22	3	38	13	36	31
Wyoming	2	2	2	36	1	7	3	4
District of Columbia	3	50	48	1	7	1	2	2

Source: Computed by Tax Foundation from data in Table D12.

D14. State and Local Revenue by Source

Selected Fiscal Years 1902-1987

($Millions, Except Per Capita)

Year	Total[a]	Total Own Sources	General Revenue Total General	General Revenue Taxes[f]	General Revenue Charges and Miscellaneous	Liquor Stores[c]	Utility[d]	Insurance Trust[e]	From Federal Government	Per Capita[b] (Dollars) Total	Per Capita[b] (Dollars) Taxes[f]
1902	$1,048	$1,041	$979	$860	$119	$2	$60	-	$7	$13.37	$10.97
1913	2,030	2,018	1,900	1,609	291	-	116	$2	12	21.08	16.71
1922	5,169	5,061	4,673	4,016	657	-	266	122	108	47.29	36.74
1927	7,638	7,722	7,155	6,087	1,068	-	403	164	116	66.30	51.49
1932	7,887	7,655	7,035	6,164	871	-	463	157	232	63.38	49.53
1942	13,148	12,290	9,560	8,528	1,031	390	887	1,454	858	98.30	63.76
1944	14,333	13,379	9,954	8,774	1,180	567	1,066	1,792	954	107.06	65.54
1946	15,983	15,128	11,501	10,094	1,407	864	1,169	1,593	855	116.47	73.56
1948	21,613	19,752	15,389	13,342	2,047	946	1,565	1,851	1,861	149.14	92.07
1950	25,639	23,153	18,425	15,914	2,511	904	1,808	2,016	2,486	170.76	105.99
1952	31,013	28,447	22,615	19,323	3,292	1,037	2,071	2,724	2,566	200.51	124.93
1954	35,386	32,420	26,046	22,067	3,979	1,093	2,403	2,877	2,966	221.35	138.03
1956	41,692	38,357	31,332	26,368	4,964	1,136	2,718	3,171	3,335	251.09	158.80
1958	49,262	44,397	36,354	30,380	5,974	1,170	3,041	3,832	4,865	286.30	176.56
1960	60,277	53,302	43,530	36,117	7,414	1,264	3,613	4,896	6,974	337.25	202.08
1962	69,492	61,621	50,381	41,554	8,827	1,282	4,026	5,932	7,871	376.63	225.22
1964	81,455	71,453	58,440	47,785	10,665	1,359	4,616	7,038	10,002	428.77	251.54
1966	97,619	84,405	69,822	56,647	13,174	1,550	5,069	7,964	13,214	501.51	291.02
1968	117,581	100,400	84,083	67,572	16,511	1,819	5,683	8,815	17,181	592.12	340.28
1970	150,106	128,248	108,898	86,795	22,103	2,006	6,608	10,736	21,857	740.47	428.16
1972	190,798	159,456	136,199	109,609	26,590	2,188	7,641	13,428	31,342	919.97	528.50
1974	237,656	196,036	165,850	130,673	35,177	2,355	9,392	18,439	41,820	1,128.93	620.21
1975	264,013	216,979	181,137	141,465	39,668	2,468	10,867	22,507	47,034	1,243.91	666.52
1976	303,287	247,697	200,586	156,813	43,774	2,553	12,573	31,985	55,589	1,417.49	732.91
1977	337,747	275,172	223,221	175,879	47,343	2,612	14,191	35,148	62,575	1,566.65	815.82
1978	371,607	302,014	246,368	193,642	52,726	2,759	17,252	35,635	69,592	1,704.11	888.03
1979	404,934	329,770	268,115	205,514	62,600	2,898	19,730	39,027	75,164	1,812.77	920.03
1980	451,537	368,509	299,293	223,463	75,830	3,201	22,359	43,656	83,029	1,998.44	989.02
1981	506,728	416,433	333,109	244,514	88,595	3,278	26,617	53,429	90,294	2,217.22	1,069.89
1982	547,719	460,436	370,371	266,390	103,982	3,343	30,697	56,025	87,282	2,372.18	1,153.74
1983	593,461	503,455	396,746	284,436	112,310	3,311	34,033	69,364	90,006	2,544.67	1,219.62
1984	651,997	555,062	445,794	320,194	125,600	3,240	37,374	68,654	96,935	2,769.22	1,359.96
1985	720,062	613,905	491,963	350,367	141,596	3,235	41,537	77,170	106,158	3,029.58	1,474.13
1986	783,349	670,251	528,359	373,051	155,308	3,313	43,850	94,729	113,099	3,263.90	1,554.35
1987	842,589	727,593	571,168	405,149	166,019	3,333	46,477	106,615	114,996	3,477.35	1,672.04

a Excludes duplicating interlevel transfers of funds.
b Based on estimated population, excluding armed forces overseas, at the middle of the fiscal year.
c Principally receipts from sales in states with alcoholic beverage monopoly systems. Excludes alcoholic beverage taxes.
d State utility revenues included under general revenue until 1977.
e Collections from employers and employees for financing unemployment compensation, accident and sickness, workmen's compensation, retirement, and like social insurance programs.
f Excludes unemployment compensation tax collections included in insurance trust revenue.

Source: Department of Commerce, Bureau of the Census. Per capita computations by Tax Foundation.

D15. Percentage Distribution of State and Local General Revenue by Source

Selected Fiscal Years 1940-1985

Fiscal Year	Total General	From Own Sources					From Federal Government
		Total	Taxes			Charges and Miscellaneous	
			Total	Property	Other		
1940	100.0%	90.2%	81.3%	46.1%	35.2%	8.9%	9.8%
1942	100.0	91.8	81.9	43.6	38.3	9.9	8.2
1944	100.0	91.3	80.4	42.2	38.2	10.8	8.7
1946	100.0	93.1	81.7	40.4	41.3	11.4	6.9
1948	100.0	89.2	77.3	35.5	41.8	11.9	10.8
1950	100.0	88.1	76.1	35.1	41.0	12.0	11.9
1952	100.0	89.8	76.7	34.4	42.4	13.1	10.2
1953	100.0	89.5	76.6	34.3	42.2	12.9	10.5
1954	100.0	89.8	76.1	34.4	41.7	13.7	10.2
1955	100.0	89.9	75.6	34.5	41.0	14.4	10.1
1956	100.0	90.4	76.1	33.9	42.2	14.3	9.6
1957	100.0	89.9	75.5	33.7	41.8	14.4	10.1
1958	100.0	88.2	73.7	34.1	39.6	14.5	11.8
1959	100.0	85.9	71.5	33.1	38.4	14.5	14.1
1960	100.0	86.2	71.5	32.5	39.0	14.7	13.8
1961	100.0	86.8	71.9	33.3	38.6	14.9	13.2
1962	100.0	86.5	71.3	32.7	38.6	15.2	13.5
1963	100.0	86.1	70.4	31.9	38.5	15.7	13.9
1964	100.0	85.4	69.8	31.0	38.8	15.6	14.6
1965	100.0	85.2	69.4	30.8	38.5	15.8	14.8
1966	100.0	84.2	68.3	29.7	38.6	15.9	15.8
1967	100.0	83.1	66.9	28.6	38.3	16.3	16.9
1968	100.0	83.0	66.7	27.4	39.3	16.3	17.0
1969	100.0	83.3	67.0	26.8	40.2	16.3	16.7
1970	100.0	83.3	66.4	26.0	40.3	16.9	16.7
1971	100.0	82.0	65.5	26.1	39.4	16.4	18.0
1972	100.0	81.3	65.4	25.6	39.8	15.9	18.7
1973	100.0	79.4	63.7	23.8	39.9	15.7	20.6
1974	100.0	79.9	62.9	23.0	39.9	16.9	20.1
1975	100.0	79.4	62.0	22.6	39.4	17.4	20.6
1976	100.0	78.2	61.2	22.2	39.0	17.1	21.7
1977	100.0	78.1	61.7	21.9	39.8	16.4	21.9
1978	100.0	78.0	61.3	21.0	40.3	16.7	22.0
1979	100.0	78.1	59.9	18.9	41.0	18.2	21.9
1980	100.0	78.3	58.4	17.9	40.5	19.8	21.7
1981	100.0	78.7	57.8	17.7	40.0	20.9	21.3
1982	100.0	80.9	58.2	17.9	40.3	22.7	19.1
1983	100.0	81.5	58.4	18.3	40.1	23.1	18.5
1984	100.0	82.1	59.0	17.8	41.2	23.1	17.9
1985	100.0	82.2	58.5	17.4	41.1	23.7	17.8

Source: Department of Commerce, Bureau of the Census; and Tax Foundation computations.

D16. State and Local Tax Index and Tax Receipts by Type of Tax[a]
Calendar Years 1965-1988

Year	All Taxes	Personal Income Taxes	Corporate Profits Taxes	Indirect Business Taxes[b]	Social Insurance Contributions	All Other Taxes[c]
Tax Index, 1967 = 100						
1965	83.3	72.1	76.9	85.7	74.6	88.2
1966	91.1	88.5	84.6	92.4	85.1	94.1
1967	100.0	100.0	100.0	100.0	100.0	100.0
1968	113.9	127.9	126.9	112.8	107.5	108.8
1969	128.4	160.7	138.5	125.2	123.9	120.6
1970	141.9	178.7	142.3	139.0	137.3	129.4
1971	158.1	203.3	165.4	154.5	152.2	138.2
1972	179.7	282.0	203.8	169.6	171.6	150.0
1973	196.9	309.8	230.8	184.7	194.0	161.8
1974	212.9	334.4	257.7	198.9	217.9	167.6
1975	232.1	368.9	280.8	214.9	250.7	176.5
1976	261.7	431.1	369.2	237.5	291.0	191.2
1977	291.1	498.4	438.5	260.0	329.9	208.8
1978	314.6	573.8	465.4	276.3	368.7	217.6
1979	338.0	626.2	523.1	292.9	409.0	232.4
1980	366.8	698.4	557.7	316.3	443.3	252.9
1981	406.6	785.2	592.3	352.2	485.1	267.6
1982	435.9	850.8	538.5	379.3	534.3	288.2
1983	477.1	955.7	611.5	413.2	574.6	305.9
1984	530.9	1,108.2	719.2	459.1	600.0	320.6
1985	571.6	1,183.6	776.9	495.2	644.8	347.1
1986	611.8	1,259.0	873.1	529.3	686.6	373.5
1987	655.8	1,411.5	1,073.1	555.3	717.9	405.9
1988	720.3	1,519.7	1,203.8	616.3	761.2	435.3
Tax Receipts ($Billions)						
1965	$ 59.2	$ 4.4	$ 2.0	$ 44.8	$ 5.0	$ 3.0
1966	64.8	5.4	2.2	48.3	5.7	3.2
1967	71.1	6.1	2.6	52.3	6.7	3.4
1968	81.0	7.8	3.3	59.0	7.2	3.7
1969	91.3	9.8	3.6	65.5	8.3	4.1
1970	100.9	10.9	3.7	72.7	9.2	4.4
1971	112.4	12.4	4.3	80.8	10.2	4.7
1972	127.8	17.2	5.3	88.7	11.5	5.1
1973	140.0	18.9	6.0	96.6	13.0	5.5
1974	151.4	20.4	6.7	104.0	14.6	5.7
1975	165.0	22.5	7.3	112.4	16.8	6.0
1976	186.1	26.3	9.6	124.2	19.5	6.5
1977	207.0	30.4	11.4	136.0	22.1	7.1
1978	223.7	35.0	12.1	144.5	24.7	7.4
1979	240.3	38.2	13.6	153.2	27.4	7.9
1980	260.8	42.6	14.5	165.4	29.7	8.6
1981	289.1	47.9	15.4	184.2	32.5	9.1
1982	309.9	51.9	14.0	198.4	35.8	9.8
1983	339.2	58.3	15.9	216.1	38.5	10.4
1984	377.5	67.6	18.7	240.1	40.2	10.9
1985	406.4	72.2	20.2	259.0	43.2	11.8
1986	435.0	76.8	22.7	276.8	46.0	12.7
1987	466.3	86.1	27.9	290.4	48.1	13.8
1988	512.1	92.7	31.3	322.3	51.0	14.8

[a] Tax Receipts, net of refunds, as shown in the national income accounts, generally on an accrual basis.
[b] Sales, excise, and customs levies and real property taxes.
[c] Estate and gift and personal property taxes.
Source: Department of Commerce, Bureau of Economic Analysis; and Tax Foundation computations.

D17. State and Local General Revenue by Source and State

Fiscal Year 1987
($Millions)

State	Total General	From Own Sources					From Federal Government
		Total	Taxes			Charges and Miscellaneous	
			Total	Property	Other		
Total	$ 686,164	$ 571,168	$ 405,149	$ 121,227	$ 283,922	$ 166,019	$ 114,996
Alabama	8,914	7,172	4,441	505	3,936	2,731	1,742
Alaska	5,502	4,942	1,660	623	1,037	3,282	560
Arizona	8,939	7,763	5,399	1,584	3,815	2,363	1,176
Arkansas	4,596	3,579	2,475	470	2,005	1,104	1,017
California	89,011	74,620	53,272	13,703	39,569	21,348	14,390
Colorado	9,574	8,145	5,280	1,885	3,395	2,864	1,429
Connecticut	10,323	8,950	7,116	2,705	4,411	1,834	1,373
Delaware	2,119	1,801	1,128	155	973	673	318
Florida	28,578	24,910	16,412	5,445	10,967	8,498	3,668
Georgia	15,686	12,930	8,535	2,161	6,374	4,396	2,756
Hawaii	3,275	2,746	2,117	346	1,771	629	528
Idaho	2,121	1,698	1,176	334	842	522	423
Illinois	30,273	25,126	19,113	6,598	12,515	6,014	5,147
Indiana	12,623	10,413	7,214	2,304	4,910	3,200	2,210
Iowa	7,541	6,313	4,336	1,639	2,697	1,977	1,227
Kansas	6,772	5,872	3,733	1,394	2,339	2,139	900
Kentucky	7,972	6,384	4,511	763	3,748	1,873	1,588
Louisiana	11,727	8,992	5,473	882	4,591	3,518	2,735
Maine	3,166	2,483	1,916	630	1,286	567	683
Maryland	13,683	11,473	8,633	2,103	6,530	2,840	2,210
Massachusetts	18,783	15,666	12,327	3,747	8,580	3,339	3,118
Michigan	27,551	22,830	16,335	6,156	10,179	6,495	4,721
Minnesota	14,617	12,342	8,086	2,431	5,655	4,256	2,274
Mississippi	5,642	4,328	2,599	616	1,983	1,729	1,314
Missouri	10,667	8,813	6,362	1,385	4,977	2,451	1,854
Montana	2,313	1,748	1,105	533	572	643	565

Continued

D17. State and Local General Revenue by Source and State (continued)

Fiscal Year 1987

($Millions)

State	Total General	From Own Sources					From Federal Government
		Total	Taxes			Charges and Miscellaneous	
			Total	Property	Other		
Nebraska	4,215	3,538	2,328	1,014	1,314	1,210	677
Nevada	2,810	2,414	1,633	363	1,270	781	396
New Hampshire	2,466	2,077	1,468	911	557	609	388
New Jersey	24,926	21,503	16,105	6,486	9,619	5,398	3,423
New Mexico	4,370	3,673	1,962	229	1,733	1,711	697
New York	75,614	63,142	49,422	14,249	35,173	13,720	12,472
North Carolina	14,308	11,926	8,740	1,867	6,873	3,186	2,382
North Dakota	1,909	1,486	857	272	585	629	423
Ohio	27,147	22,607	16,278	4,461	11,817	6,329	4,541
Oklahoma	7,408	6,131	3,987	802	3,185	2,145	1,277
Oregon	8,048	6,566	4,392	1,948	2,444	2,174	1,482
Pennsylvania	30,928	25,279	18,547	4,923	13,624	6,732	5,648
Rhode Island	2,922	2,370	1,696	644	1,052	674	551
South Carolina	7,587	6,235	4,223	985	3,238	2,013	1,352
South Dakota	1,682	1,277	846	351	495	430	405
Tennessee	10,309	8,177	5,612	1,207	4,405	2,565	2,131
Texas	39,585	33,985	22,313	9,215	13,098	11,672	5,600
Utah	4,366	3,472	2,284	661	1,623	1,188	894
Vermont	1,596	1,234	894	353	541	340	362
Virginia	14,452	12,189	9,141	2,536	6,605	3,048	2,264
Washington	13,132	10,688	7,702	2,192	5,510	2,986	2,444
West Virginia	4,327	3,340	2,335	409	1,926	1,005	988
Wisconsin	13,944	11,526	8,592	2,965	5,627	2,935	2,418
Wyoming	2,452	1,993	1,124	543	581	869	459
District of Columbia	3,695	2,301	1,915	546	1,369	387	1,393

Source: Department of Commerce, Bureau of the Census.

D18. State and Local General Revenue by Originating Level of Government and by State[a]

Fiscal Year 1987

(Dollar Amounts in Millions)

State	Total General Revenue	Amount			Percent		
		Federal	State	Local	Federal	State	Local
Total	$ 686,164	$ 114,996	$ 317,106	$ 254,062	16.8%	46.2%	37.0%
Alabama	8,914	1,742	4,439	2,733	19.5	49.8	30.7
Alaska	5,502	560	3,756	1,186	10.2	68.3	21.6
Arizona	8,939	1,176	4,213	3,549	13.2	47.1	39.7
Arkansas	4,596	1,017	2,340	1,240	22.1	50.9	27.0
California	89,011	14,390	43,191	31,430	16.2	48.5	35.3
Colorado	9,574	1,429	3,680	4,465	14.9	38.4	46.6
Connecticut	10,323	1,373	5,659	3,291	13.3	54.8	31.9
Delaware	2,119	318	1,420	381	15.0	67.0	18.0
Florida	28,578	3,668	11,534	13,377	12.8	40.4	46.8
Georgia	15,686	2,756	6,289	6,641	17.6	40.1	42.3
Hawaii	3,275	528	2,209	538	16.1	67.4	16.4
Idaho	2,121	423	1,047	651	19.9	49.4	30.7
Illinois	30,273	5,147	13,167	11,960	17.0	43.5	39.5
Indiana	12,623	2,210	6,281	4,133	17.5	49.8	32.7
Iowa	7,540	1,227	3,544	2,770	16.3	47.0	36.7
Kansas	6,772	900	2,615	3,257	13.3	38.6	48.1
Kentucky	7,972	1,588	4,435	1,949	19.9	55.6	24.4
Louisiana	11,727	2,735	5,243	3,749	23.3	44.7	32.0
Maine	3,166	683	1,667	816	21.6	52.6	25.8
Maryland	13,683	2,210	6,663	4,811	16.1	48.7	35.2
Massachusetts	18,783	3,118	10,505	5,161	16.6	55.9	27.5
Michigan	27,551	4,721	12,956	9,874	17.1	47.0	35.8
Minnesota	14,617	2,274	6,840	5,502	15.6	46.8	37.6
Mississippi	5,642	1,314	2,452	1,876	23.3	43.5	33.3
Missouri	10,667	1,854	4,914	3,898	17.4	46.1	36.5
Montana	2,313	565	933	815	24.4	40.4	35.2
Nebraska	4,215	677	1,700	1,838	16.1	40.3	43.6
Nevada	2,810	396	1,354	1,060	14.1	48.2	37.7
New Hampshire	2,466	388	1,022	1,055	15.8	41.4	42.8
New Jersey	24,926	3,423	12,931	8,572	13.7	51.9	34.4
New Mexico	4,370	697	2,667	1,006	15.9	61.0	23.0
New York	75,614	12,471	29,930	33,212	16.5	39.6	43.9
North Carolina	14,308	2,382	7,570	4,355	16.7	52.9	30.4
North Dakota	1,909	423	970	516	22.2	50.8	27.0
Ohio	27,147	4,541	12,815	9,792	16.7	47.2	36.1
Oklahoma	7,408	1,277	3,650	2,481	17.2	49.3	33.5
Oregon	8,048	1,482	3,418	3,148	18.4	42.5	39.1
Pennsylvania	30,928	5,648	14,161	11,118	18.3	45.8	35.9
Rhode Island	2,922	551	1,632	739	18.9	55.8	25.3
South Carolina	7,587	1,352	4,039	2,196	17.8	53.2	28.9
South Dakota	1,682	405	695	582	24.1	41.3	34.6
Tennessee	10,309	2,131	4,425	3,752	20.7	42.9	36.4
Texas	39,585	5,600	15,083	18,902	14.1	38.1	47.8
Utah	4,366	894	2,005	1,467	20.5	45.9	33.6
Vermont	1,596	362	813	421	22.7	51.0	26.4
Virginia	14,452	2,264	7,139	5,050	15.7	49.4	34.9
Washington	13,132	2,444	6,683	4,005	18.6	50.0	30.5
West Virginia	4,327	986	2,312	1,028	22.8	53.4	23.7
Wisconsin	13,944	2,418	7,006	4,520	17.3	50.2	32.4
Wyoming	2,452	459	1,098	895	18.7	44.8	36.5
District of Columbia	3,695	1,393	-	2,301	37.7	-	62.3

[a] Before transfers among governments.
Source: Department of Commerce, Bureau of the Census.

D19. State and Local General Revenue by Final Recipient Level of Government and by State[a]

Fiscal Year 1987

(Dollar Amounts in Millions)

State	Total General Revenue	Amount		Percent	
		State	Local	State	Local
Total	$ 686,164	$ 282,734	$ 403,430	41.2%	58.8%
Alabama	8,914	4,462	4,452	50.1	49.9
Alaska	5,502	3,479	2,023	63.2	36.8
Arizona	8,939	3,089	5,850	34.6	65.4
Arkansas	4,596	2,367	2,229	51.5	48.5
California	89,011	29,657	59,353	33.3	66.7
Colorado	9,574	3,414	6,160	35.7	64.3
Connecticut	10,323	5,746	4,577	55.7	44.3
Delaware	2,119	1,378	741	65.0	35.0
Florida	28,578	8,712	19,867	30.5	69.5
Georgia	15,686	5,504	10,182	35.1	64.9
Hawaii	3,275	2,572	702	78.6	21.4
Idaho	2,121	1,006	1,116	47.4	52.6
Illinois	30,273	12,462	17,811	41.2	58.8
Indiana	12,623	5,362	7,261	42.5	57.5
Iowa	7,541	3,168	4,373	42.0	58.0
Kansas	6,772	2,541	4,231	37.5	62.5
Kentucky	7,972	4,375	3,597	54.9	45.1
Louisiana	11,727	6,005	5,722	51.2	48.8
Maine	3,166	1,858	1,308	58.7	41.3
Maryland	13,683	6,450	7,233	47.1	52.9
Massachusetts	18,783	9,345	9,438	49.8	50.2
Michigan	27,551	12,525	15,026	45.5	54.5
Minnesota	14,617	5,151	9,465	35.2	64.8
Mississippi	5,642	2,331	3,311	41.3	58.7
Missouri	10,667	4,899	5,768	45.9	54.1
Montana	2,313	1,141	1,172	49.3	50.7
Nebraska	4,215	1,819	2,396	43.2	56.8
Nevada	2,810	983	1,827	35.0	65.0
New Hampshire	2,466	1,228	1,238	49.8	50.2
New Jersey	24,926	11,397	13,529	45.7	54.3
New Mexico	4,370	2,177	2,192	49.8	50.2
New York	75,314	27,876	47,738	36.9	63.1
North Carolina	14,308	6,296	8,012	44.0	56.0
North Dakota	1,909	1,020	889	53.4	46.6
Ohio	27,147	11,314	15,833	41.7	58.3
Oklahoma	7,408	3,510	3,898	47.4	52.6
Oregon	8,048	3,528	4,520	43.8	56.2
Pennsylvania	30,928	13,450	17,478	43.5	56.5
Rhode Island	2,922	1,849	1,073	63.3	36.7
South Carolina	7,587	4,009	3,578	52.8	47.2
South Dakota	1,682	865	817	51.4	48.6
Tennessee	10,309	4,717	5,591	45.8	54.2
Texas	39,585	13,111	26,475	33.1	66.9
Utah	4,366	2,047	2,319	46.9	53.1
Vermont	1,596	991	604	62.1	37.9
Virginia	14,452	6,607	7,846	45.7	54.3
Washington	13,132	5,791	7,341	44.1	55.9
West Virginia	4,327	2,354	1,973	54.4	45.6
Wisconsin	13,944	5,722	8,222	41.0	59.0
Wyoming	2,452	1,074	1,378	43.8	56.2
District of Columbia	3,695	-	3,695	-	100.0

[a] After intergovernmental transfers.
Source: Department of Commerce, Bureau of the Census.

D20. Per Capita State and Local General Revenue by Source[a]

Selected Fiscal Years 1902-1987

| Year | Total General | From Own Sources | | | From Federal Government |
		Total	Taxes	Charges and Miscellaneous	
1902	$ 12	$ 12	$ 11	$ 2	-
1913	20	20	17	3	-
1922	43	42	36	6	$ 1
1927	61	60	51	9	1
1932	58	56	49	7	2
1934	61	53	47	6	8
1936	65	58	52	6	7
1938	71	65	59	6	6
1940	73	66	59	6	7
1942	77	71	63	8	6
1944	79	72	63	9	7
1946	87	81	71	10	6
1948	118	105	91	14	13
1950	138	121	105	17	16
1952	160	144	123	21	16
1954	179	160	136	24	18
1956	207	187	158	30	20
1958	238	210	175	34	28
1960	281	242	201	41	39
1961	295	256	212	44	39
1962	313	271	224	48	42
1963	330	284	233	51	46
1964	358	305	250	56	52
1965	382	325	264	61	57
1966	424	356	289	67	67
1967	461	383	308	75	78
1968	507	421	338	83	86
1969	567	472	380	93	95
1970	643	536	427	109	108
1971	703	576	460	115	127
1972	805	654	526	128	151
1973	906	719	577	142	187
1974	983	785	618	166	198
1975	1,071	850	664	186	221
1976	1,193	934	731	204	259
1977	1,318	1,029	813	216	289
1978	1,449	1,130	888	242	319
1979	1,560	1,218	934	284	341
1980	1,688	1,321	987	335	367
1981	1,869	1,470	1,079	391	399
1982	2,020	1,635	1,176	459	385
1983	2,080	1,696	1,216	480	385
1984	2,299	1,888	1,356	532	411
1985	2,503	2,059	1,465	593	445
1986	2,661	2,191	1,547	644	469
1987	2,819	2,347	1,665	682	472

[a] Based on resident population, excluding armed forces overseas, at the end of the fiscal year.
Source: Department of Commerce, Bureau of the Census.

D21. Per Capita State and Local General Revenue by Source and State[a]

Fiscal Year 1987

State	Total General	From Own Sources					From Federal Government
		Total	Taxes			Charges and Miscellaneous	
			Total	Property	Other		
Total	$ 2,819	$ 2,347	$ 1,665	$ 498	$ 1,167	$ 682	$ 472
Alabama	2,183	1,757	1,088	124	964	669	427
Alaska	10,481	9,414	3,162	1,187	1,974	6,252	1,067
Arizona	2,640	2,293	1,595	468	1,127	698	347
Arkansas	1,925	1,499	1,037	197	840	462	426
California	3,218	2,697	1,926	495	1,430	772	520
Colorado	2,905	2,471	1,602	572	1,030	869	434
Connecticut	3,215	2,787	2,216	842	1,374	571	428
Delaware	3,290	2,797	1,752	241	1,511	1,045	493
Florida	2,377	2,072	1,365	453	912	707	305
Georgia	2,521	2,078	1,372	347	1,024	706	443
Hawaii	3,024	2,536	1,955	320	1,635	581	488
Idaho	2,126	1,702	1,178	334	844	523	424
Illinois	2,614	2,169	1,650	570	1,081	519	444
Indiana	2,282	1,883	1,304	417	888	579	400
Iowa	2,661	2,228	1,530	578	952	698	433
Kansas	2,735	2,372	1,508	563	945	864	363
Kentucky	2,139	1,713	1,210	205	1,006	503	426
Louisiana	2,629	2,016	1,227	198	1,029	789	613
Maine	2,667	2,092	1,614	531	1,084	477	576
Maryland	3,017	2,530	1,904	464	1,440	626	487
Massachusetts	3,208	2,676	2,105	640	1,465	570	532
Michigan	2,995	2,482	1,776	669	1,107	706	513
Minnesota	3,442	2,907	1,904	572	1,332	1,002	536
Mississippi	2,149	1,649	990	235	756	659	500
Missouri	2,090	1,727	1,247	271	975	480	363
Montana	2,859	2,161	1,366	659	707	795	698
Nebraska	2,644	2,220	1,460	636	824	759	425
Nevada	2,791	2,397	1,622	360	1,262	775	394
New Hampshire	2,333	1,965	1,389	862	528	576	367
New Jersey	3,249	2,803	2,099	845	1,254	704	446
New Mexico	2,913	2,449	1,308	153	1,155	1,141	464
New York	4,242	3,542	2,773	799	1,973	770	700
North Carolina	2,231	1,860	1,363	291	1,072	497	372
North Dakota	2,841	2,211	1,276	404	871	936	630
Ohio	2,517	2,096	1,509	414	1,096	587	421
Oklahoma	2,264	1,874	1,218	245	973	655	390
Oregon	2,954	2,410	1,612	715	897	798	544
Pennsylvania	2,591	2,118	1,554	412	1,141	564	473
Rhode Island	2,963	2,404	1,720	653	1,067	684	559
South Carolina	2,215	1,820	1,233	288	945	588	395
South Dakota	2,372	1,801	1,194	495	699	607	571
Tennessee	2,123	1,684	1,156	249	907	528	439
Texas	2,358	2,024	1,329	549	780	695	334
Utah	2,599	2,066	1,360	393	966	707	532
Vermont	2,912	2,251	1,631	643	987	620	661
Virginia	2,448	2,064	1,548	430	1,119	516	383
Washington	2,894	2,355	1,697	483	1,214	658	539
West Virginia	2,255	1,740	1,217	213	1,003	524	515
Wisconsin	2,901	2,398	1,787	617	1,171	610	503
Wyoming	5,004	4,067	2,293	1,108	1,185	1,774	937
District of Columbia	5,940	3,700	3,078	878	2,200	622	2,240

[a] Based on resident population at end of fiscal year.
Source: Department of Commerce, Bureau of the Census.

D22. Ranking of States According to Per Capita State and Local General Revenue by Source

Fiscal Year 1987

State	Total General	From Own Sources					From Federal Government
		Total	Taxes			Charges and Miscellaneous	
			Total	Property	Other		
Alabama	45	44	49	51	35	25	34
Alaska	1	1	1	1	2	1	2
Arizona	28	22	23	26	18	21	49
Arkansas	51	51	50	49	45	51	36
California	8	9	9	23	8	13	17
Colorado	18	14	22	18	26	7	31
Connecticut	9	8	5	6	9	39	33
Delaware	6	7	14	44	5	4	22
Florida	36	33	33	28	39	16	51
Georgia	33	32	31	36	28	18	29
Hawaii	11	11	8	38	4	36	23
Idaho	48	48	47	37	44	44	38
Illinois	30	27	17	19	23	45	28
Indiana	40	39	38	30	42	37	40
Iowa	26	24	26	16	36	22	32
Kansas	24	20	28	20	38	8	47
Kentucky	47	47	45	47	29	47	35
Louisiana	29	37	42	48	27	11	8
Maine	25	31	20	22	22	50	9
Maryland	12	12	11	27	7	29	24
Massachusetts	10	10	6	13	6	40	15
Michigan	13	13	13	9	20	19	19
Minnesota	5	5	10	17	10	5	14
Mississippi	46	50	51	45	48	26	21
Missouri	50	46	40	41	32	49	48
Montana	21	28	32	10	49	10	5
Nebraska	27	25	29	14	46	15	37
Nevada	23	19	19	35	11	12	42
New Hampshire	39	38	30	4	51	38	46
New Jersey	7	6	7	5	12	20	27
New Mexico	16	15	37	50	16	3	26
New York	4	4	3	7	3	14	4
North Carolina	43	41	34	39	24	48	45
North Dakota	22	26	39	33	43	6	7
Ohio	34	30	27	31	21	35	39
Oklahoma	41	40	43	43	33	28	43
Oregon	15	16	21	8	41	9	12
Pennsylvania	32	29	24	32	17	41	25
Rhode Island	14	17	15	11	25	24	11
South Carolina	44	42	41	40	37	34	41
South Dakota	37	43	46	24	50	33	10
Tennessee	49	49	48	42	40	42	30
Texas	38	36	36	21	47	23	50
Utah	31	34	35	34	34	17	16
Vermont	17	23	18	12	31	31	6
Virginia	35	35	25	29	19	46	44
Washington	20	21	16	25	13	27	13
West Virginia	42	45	44	46	30	43	18
Wisconsin	19	18	12	15	15	32	20
Wyoming	3	2	4	2	14	2	3
District of Columbia	2	3	2	3	1	30	1

Source: Computed by Tax Foundation from data in Table D21.

D23. State and Local General Revenue per $1,000 of Personal Income by Source

Selected Fiscal Years 1940-1987

Fiscal Year	Total General	From Own Sources					From Federal Government
		Total	Taxes			Charges and Miscellaneous	
			Total	Property	Other		
1940	$ 122.37	$ 110.34	$ 99.46	$ 56.42	$ 43.05	$ 10.88	$ 12.03
1942	85.10	78.10	69.67	37.07	32.60	8.43	7.01
1944	68.12	62.17	54.80	28.75	26.04	7.37	5.96
1946	70.32	65.46	57.45	28.38	29.07	8.01	4.87
1948	83.17	74.19	64.33	29.54	34.79	9.87	8.97
1950	92.74	81.72	70.58	32.59	37.99	11.14	11.03
1952	93.59	84.06	71.82	32.16	39.66	12.24	9.54
1953	96.44	86.31	73.84	33.11	40.73	12.46	10.14
1954	101.89	91.47	77.50	35.00	42.49	13.97	10.42
1955	102.42	92.10	77.40	35.38	42.02	14.70	10.32
1956	104.93	94.84	79.81	35.56	44.25	15.03	10.09
1957	109.44	98.42	82.64	36.89	45.75	15.78	11.02
1958	115.68	102.02	85.26	39.42	45.84	16.76	13.65
1959	118.85	102.12	84.93	39.30	45.63	17.18	16.73
1960	126.26	108.82	90.29	41.01	49.28	18.53	17.44
1961	130.52	113.29	93.86	43.48	50.38	19.43	17.22
1962	132.47	114.57	94.49	43.33	51.16	20.07	17.90
1963	136.55	117.61	96.14	43.62	52.52	21.47	18.94
1964	148.27	126.60	103.52	46.02	57.50	23.08	21.66
1965	151.41	128.94	105.04	46.68	58.36	23.90	22.46
1966	156.04	131.38	106.63	46.36	60.27	24.75	24.65
1967	157.11	130.63	105.09	44.87	60.21	25.54	26.48
1968	161.99	134.51	108.10	44.39	63.71	26.41	27.48
1969	167.54	139.53	112.20	44.86	67.34	27.33	28.01
1970	175.62	146.27	116.58	45.74	70.84	29.68	29.35
1971	181.39	148.67	118.87	47.37	71.50	29.79	32.72
1972	195.47	158.90	127.88	50.02	77.85	31.02	36.57
1973	203.33	161.36	129.47	48.41	81.06	31.89	41.97
1974	196.38	156.83	123.58	45.14	78.44	33.25	39.54
1975	198.15	157.29	122.84	44.71	78.13	34.45	40.86
1976	203.74	159.33	124.72	45.33	79.41	34.81	44.21
1977	207.61	162.15	128.09	45.52	82.57	34.06	45.46
1978	208.09	162.26	127.53	43.74	83.79	34.72	45.83
1979	200.92	156.93	120.29	38.01	82.28	36.64	43.99
1980	198.02	155.01	115.74	35.48	80.26	39.28	43.01
1981	195.75	154.01	113.05	34.66	78.39	40.96	41.74
1982	190.25	153.96	110.74	34.12	76.62	43.22	36.28
1983	189.27	154.28	110.61	34.65	75.96	43.67	34.99
1984	198.55	163.05	117.11	35.28	81.83	45.94	35.50
1985	197.88	162.73	115.82	34.35	81.47	46.91	35.15
1986	193.75	159.58	112.69	33.74	78.95	46.90	34.16
1987	194.41	161.83	114.79	34.35	80.44	47.03	32.58

Source: Department of Commerce, Bureau of the Census and Bureau of Economic Analysis; and Tax Foundation computations.

D24. State and Local General Revenue Per $1,000 of Personal Income by Source and State

Fiscal Year 1987

State	Total General	From Own Sources					From Federal Government
		Total	Taxes			Charges and Miscel- laneous	
			Total	Property	Other		
Total	$ 194.41	$ 161.83	$ 114.79	$ 34.35	$ 80.44	$ 47.03	$ 32.58
Alabama	194.04	156.12	96.67	11.00	85.67	59.44	37.93
Alaska	579.50	520.50	174.82	65.66	109.16	345.67	59.00
Arizona	199.89	173.59	120.74	35.43	85.31	52.85	26.30
Arkansas	174.97	136.26	94.23	17.88	76.35	42.03	38.71
California	195.16	163.61	116.80	30.04	86.76	46.80	31.55
Colorado	192.36	163.64	106.09	37.88	68.21	57.56	28.71
Connecticut	165.16	143.19	113.85	43.27	70.58	29.34	21.97
Delaware	223.09	189.65	118.79	16.34	102.45	70.87	33.44
Florida	167.14	145.69	95.99	31.84	64.15	49.70	21.45
Georgia	191.12	157.54	103.98	26.33	77.65	53.56	33.58
Hawaii	207.07	173.66	133.89	21.89	112.00	39.77	33.42
Idaho	188.57	150.97	104.54	29.67	74.87	46.43	37.60
Illinois	168.14	139.55	106.15	36.64	69.51	33.40	28.59
Indiana	174.61	144.04	99.78	31.87	67.91	44.26	30.57
Iowa	198.16	165.91	113.95	43.07	70.88	51.96	32.25
Kansas	187.89	162.93	103.57	38.69	64.88	59.36	24.96
Kentucky	190.25	152.36	107.66	18.20	89.46	44.70	37.89
Louisiana	232.75	178.47	108.64	17.50	91.14	69.84	54.28
Maine	210.96	165.44	127.68	41.97	85.71	37.75	45.53
Maryland	181.78	152.43	114.69	27.93	86.76	37.73	29.36
Massachusetts	181.74	151.57	119.27	36.25	83.02	32.31	30.17
Michigan	203.91	168.97	120.90	45.57	75.33	48.06	34.94
Minnesota	231.33	195.34	127.98	38.47	89.51	67.36	36.00
Mississippi	221.22	169.71	101.90	24.14	77.76	67.81	51.51
Missouri	152.70	126.15	91.07	19.83	71.24	35.08	26.54
Montana	239.29	180.87	114.36	55.19	59.17	66.50	58.43
Nebraska	191.96	161.13	106.02	46.19	59.83	55.11	30.83
Nevada	188.98	162.32	109.81	24.38	85.43	52.51	26.66
New Hampshire	150.91	127.14	89.86	55.74	34.12	37.28	23.77
New Jersey	175.64	151.52	113.48	45.70	67.78	38.03	24.12
New Mexico	258.65	217.41	116.13	13.56	102.57	101.27	41.24
New York	248.65	207.64	162.52	46.86	115.66	45.12	41.01
North Carolina	181.66	151.41	110.97	23.70	87.27	40.44	30.25
North Dakota	225.37	175.42	101.20	32.08	69.12	74.23	49.94
Ohio	181.22	150.90	108.66	29.78	78.88	42.25	30.31
Oklahoma	182.48	151.03	98.21	19.76	78.45	52.83	31.45
Oregon	223.83	182.60	122.14	54.19	67.95	60.46	41.23
Pennsylvania	182.58	149.23	109.49	29.06	80.43	39.74	33.35
Rhode Island	205.56	166.78	119.33	45.29	74.04	47.44	38.78
South Carolina	198.87	163.42	110.67	25.82	84.85	52.75	35.44
South Dakota	201.06	152.64	101.19	41.97	59.22	51.44	48.43
Tennessee	178.83	141.85	97.35	20.93	76.42	44.51	36.97
Texas	176.03	151.13	99.22	40.98	58.24	51.91	24.90
Utah	238.74	189.83	124.89	36.12	88.77	64.94	48.91
Vermont	220.99	170.85	123.76	48.83	74.93	47.09	50.13
Virginia	162.08	136.69	102.51	28.44	74.07	34.18	25.39
Washington	196.06	159.57	114.99	32.72	82.27	44.58	36.49
West Virginia	213.27	164.60	115.07	20.17	94.90	49.53	48.67
Wisconsin	209.53	173.20	129.10	44.55	84.55	44.10	36.33
Wyoming	378.10	307.32	173.29	83.73	89.56	134.04	70.78
District of Columbia	304.28	189.53	157.69	44.98	112.71	31.85	114.75

Source: Department of Commerce, Bureau of the Census; and Tax Foundation computations.

D25. Ranking of States According to State and Local General Revenue Per $1,000 of Personal Income by Source

Fiscal Year 1987

State	Total General	From Own Sources					From Federal Government
		Total	Taxes			Charges and Miscellaneous	
			Total	Property	Other		
Alabama	27	31	47	51	17	12	18
Alaska	1	1	1	2	4	1	3
Arizona	22	14	13	25	19	17	44
Arkansas	44	49	49	47	30	38	17
California	26	24	17	30	14	29	32
Colorado	28	23	34	21	41	14	40
Connecticut	48	45	24	14	38	51	50
Delaware	12	7	16	49	6	5	28
Florida	47	43	48	29	46	24	51
Georgia	30	30	37	36	28	16	27
Hawaii	18	13	5	41	3	40	29
Idaho	33	40	36	32	33	30	20
Illinois	46	47	33	22	39	48	41
Indiana	45	44	43	28	43	35	35
Iowa	24	20	23	15	37	21	31
Kansas	34	26	38	19	45	13	46
Kentucky	31	34	32	46	11	32	19
Louisiana	8	11	31	48	8	6	5
Maine	16	21	8	16	16	43	12
Maryland	37	33	21	35	15	44	39
Massachusetts	38	35	15	23	22	49	38
Michigan	20	18	12	10	31	26	26
Minnesota	9	5	7	20	10	8	24
Mississippi	13	17	40	39	27	7	6
Missouri	50	51	50	44	36	46	43
Montana	6	10	22	4	49	9	4
Nebraska	29	28	35	8	47	15	34
Nevada	32	27	28	38	18	20	42
New Hampshire	51	50	51	3	51	45	49
New Jersey	43	36	25	9	44	42	48
New Mexico	4	3	18	50	5	3	13
New York	5	4	3	7	1	31	15
North Carolina	39	37	26	40	13	39	37
North Dakota	10	12	41	27	40	4	8
Ohio	40	41	30	31	25	37	36
Oklahoma	36	39	45	45	26	18	33
Oregon	11	9	11	5	42	11	14
Pennsylvania	35	42	29	33	24	41	30
Rhode Island	19	19	14	11	35	27	16
South Carolina	23	25	27	37	20	19	25
South Dakota	21	32	42	17	48	23	11
Tennessee	41	46	46	42	29	34	21
Texas	42	38	44	18	50	22	47
Utah	7	6	9	24	12	10	9
Vermont	14	16	10	6	32	28	7
Virginia	49	48	39	34	34	47	45
Washington	25	29	20	26	23	33	22
West Virginia	15	22	19	43	7	25	10
Wisconsin	17	15	6	13	21	36	23
Wyoming	2	2	2	1	9	2	2
District of Columbia	3	8	4	12	2	50	1

Source: Computed by Tax Foundation from data in Table D24.

D26. State and Local Tax Collections by Level of Government and Source[a]

Selected Fiscal Years 1902-1987

($Millions)

	Level of Government			State and Local by Source				
Year	Total	State	Local	Individual Income	Corpo-ration Income	Sales and Gross Receipts	Property	Other Taxes Including Licenses
1902	$ 860	$ 156	$ 704	-	-	$ 28	$ 706	$ 126
1913	1,609	301	1,308	-	-	58	1,332	219
1922	4,016	947	3,069	$ 43	$ 58	154	3,321	440
1927	6,087	1,608	4,479	70	92	470	4,730	725
1932	6,164	1,890	4,274	74	79	752	4,487	772
1934	5,912	1,979	3,933	80	49	1,008	4,076	699
1936	6,701	2,618	4,083	153	113	1,484	4,093	858
1938	7,605	3,132	4,473	218	165	1,794	4,440	988
1940	7,810	3,313	4,497	224	156	1,982	4,430	1,018
1942	8,528	3,903	4,625	276	272	2,351	4,537	1,092
1944	8,774	4,071	4,703	342	451	2,289	4,604	1,089
1946	10,094	4,937	5,157	422	447	2,986	4,986	1,254
1948	13,342	6,743	6,599	543	592	4,442	6,126	1,638
1950	15,914	7,930	7,984	788	593	5,154	7,349	2,030
1952	19,323	9,857	9,466	998	846	6,357	8,652	2,471
1953	20,908	10,552	10,356	1,065	817	6,927	9,375	2,723
1954	22,067	11,089	10,978	1,127	778	7,276	9,967	2,918
1955	23,483	11,597	11,886	1,237	744	7,643	10,735	3,125
1956	26,368	13,375	12,992	1,538	890	8,691	11,749	3,501
1957	28,817	14,531	14,286	1,754	984	9,467	12,864	3,748
1958	30,380	14,919	15,461	1,759	1,018	9,829	14,047	3,725
1959	32,379	15,848	16,531	1,994	1,001	10,437	14,983	3,966
1960	36,117	18,036	18,081	2,463	1,180	11,849	16,405	4,220
1961	38,861	19,057	19,804	2,613	1,266	12,463	18,002	4,518
1962	41,554	20,561	20,993	3,037	1,308	13,494	19,054	4,662
1963	44,014	22,117	21,897	3,267	1,505	14,446	19,833	4,963
1964	47,785	24,243	23,542	3,791	1,695	15,762	21,241	5,296
1965	51,243	26,126	25,116	4,090	1,929	17,118	22,583	5,521
1966	56,647	29,380	27,267	4,760	2,038	19,085	24,670	6,094
1967	61,000	31,926	29,074	5,825	2,227	20,530	26,047	6,371
1968	67,572	36,400	31,171	7,308	2,518	22,911	27,747	7,087
1969	76,712	41,931	34,781	8,908	3,180	26,519	30,673	7,432
1970	86,795	47,962	38,833	10,812	3,738	30,322	34,054	7,868
1971	94,975	51,541	43,434	11,900	3,424	33,233	37,852	8,567
1972	109,609	59,870	49,739	15,227	4,416	37,518	42,877	9,572
1973	121,102	68,069	53,032	17,994	5,425	42,047	45,283	10,354
1974	130,673	74,207	56,466	19,491	6,015	46,098	47,705	11,364
1975	141,465	80,155	61,310	21,454	6,642	49,815	51,491	12,063
1976	156,813	89,256	67,557	24,575	7,273	54,547	57,001	13,417
1977	175,936	101,085	74,852	29,246	9,174	60,641	62,527	14,348
1978	193,642	113,261	80,381	33,176	10,738	67,956	66,422	15,350
1979	205,514	124,908	80,606	36,932	12,128	74,247	64,944	17,263
1980	223,463	137,075	86,388	42,080	13,321	79,927	68,499	19,636
1981	244,514	149,738	94,776	46,426	14,143	85,971	74,969	23,004
1982	266,390	162,607	103,783	50,738	15,028	93,613	82,067	24,944
1983	284,436	171,440	112,996	55,129	14,258	100,247	89,105	25,697
1984	320,194	196,795	123,399	64,623	17,047	114,097	96,457	27,970
1985	349,793	215,320	134,473	70,097	19,158	126,281	103,757	30,500
1986	373,051	228,054	144,997	74,417	19,951	134,971	111,711	32,001
1987	405,149	246,933	158,216	83,681	22,672	144,293	121,227	33,276

[a] Excludes unemployment compensation taxes included in insurance trust revenue in Table D14.
Source: Department of Commerce, Bureau of the Census.

D27. Percentage Distribution of State and Local Tax Collections by Level of Government and Source[a]

Selected Fiscal Years 1902-1987

Year	By Level of Government		State and Local by Source					
	State	Local	Individual Income	Corporation Income	Sales and Gross Receipts	Property	Other Taxes Including Licenses
			Percent of Total					
1902	18.1%	81.9%	-	-	3.3%	82.1%	14.7%
1913	18.7	81.3	-	-	3.6	82.8	13.6
1922	23.6	76.4	1.1%	1.4%	3.8	82.7	11.0
1927	26.4	73.6	1.1	1.5	7.7	77.7	11.9
1932	30.7	69.3	1.2	1.3	12.2	72.8	12.5
1940	42.4	57.6	2.9	2.0	25.4	56.7	13.0
1942	45.8	54.2	3.2	3.2	27.6	53.2	12.8
1944	46.4	53.6	3.9	5.1	26.1	52.5	12.4
1946	48.9	51.1	4.2	4.4	29.6	49.4	12.4
1948	50.5	49.5	4.1	4.4	33.3	45.9	12.3
1950	49.8	50.2	5.0	3.7	32.4	46.2	12.8
1952	51.0	49.0	5.2	4.4	32.9	44.8	12.8
1954	50.3	49.7	5.1	3.5	33.0	45.2	13.2
1956	50.7	49.3	5.8	3.4	33.0	44.6	13.3
1958	49.1	50.9	5.8	3.4	32.4	46.2	12.3
1960	49.9	50.1	6.8	3.3	32.8	45.4	11.7
1962	49.5	50.5	7.3	3.1	32.5	45.9	11.2
1964	50.7	49.3	7.9	3.5	33.0	44.5	11.1
1966	51.9	48.1	8.4	3.6	33.6	43.5	10.9
1968	53.9	46.1	10.8	3.7	33.9	41.1	10.5
1970	55.3	44.7	12.5	4.3	35.0	39.2	9.0
1972	55.0	45.0	14.0	4.1	34.5	38.7	8.8
1974	56.8	43.2	14.9	4.6	35.3	36.5	8.7
1976	56.9	43.1	15.7	4.6	34.8	36.4	8.6
1978	58.5	41.5	17.1	5.5	34.9	34.3	8.1
1980	61.3	38.7	18.8	6.0	35.8	30.7	8.8
1981	61.2	38.8	19.0	5.8	35.2	30.7	9.4
1982	61.0	39.0	19.0	5.6	35.1	30.8	9.4
1983	60.3	39.7	19.4	5.0	35.2	31.3	9.0
1984	61.5	38.5	20.2	5.3	35.6	30.1	8.7
1985	61.6	38.4	20.0	5.5	36.1	29.7	8.7
1986	61.1	38.9	19.9	5.4	36.2	29.9	8.6
1987	60.9	39.1	20.7	5.6	35.6	29.9	8.2

[a] Total excludes unemployment compensation taxes included in insurance trust revenue in Table D14.
Source: Computed from data in Table D26.

D28. State and Local Total and Per Capita Tax Collections by State

Selected Fiscal Years 1957-1987

State	Amount ($Millions)			Per Capita[a]		
	1957	1967	1987	1957	1967	1987
Total	$ 28,817	$ 61,000	$ 405,149	$ 169.14	$ 308.29	$ 1,664.54
Alabama	320	677	4,441	102.92	191.37	1,087.65
Alaska	-	86	1,660	-	315.60	3,161.73
Arizona	183	524	5,399	162.74	320.57	1,594.65
Arkansas	179	393	2,475	103.05	199.46	1,036.56
California	3,311	7,785	53,272	232.13	406.47	1,925.77
Colorado	314	678	5,280	188.93	343.15	1,602.02
Connecticut	462	983	7,116	195.83	335.92	2,216.05
Delaware	59	178	1,128	137.98	339.52	1,751.91
Florida	667	1,623	16,412	152.51	270.74	1,365.07
Georgia	470	1,025	8,535	124.79	227.33	1,371.71
Hawaii	-	300	2,117	-	406.60	1,955.00
Idaho	100	205	1,176	156.25	293.49	1,178.47
Illinois	1,732	3,250	19,113	179.10	298.32	1,650.21
Indiana	638	1,471	7,214	140.98	294.27	1,304.21
Iowa	490	919	4,336	180.28	333.77	1,530.10
Kansas	369	717	3,733	173.23	315.21	1,507.62
Kentucky	325	674	4,511	110.99	211.40	1,210.38
Louisiana	498	959	5,473	159.95	261.81	1,226.94
Maine	141	253	1,916	149.20	260.20	1,614.18
Maryland	461	1,172	8,633	160.53	318.42	1,903.67
Massachusetts	1,018	2,004	12,327	206.50	369.70	2,105.39
Michigan	1,396	2,715	16,335	184.48	316.31	1,775.60
Minnesota	600	1,256	8,086	183.29	350.74	1,904.46
Mississippi	234	461	2,599	112.23	196.47	990.03
Missouri	554	1,199	6,362	132.14	260.46	1,246.64
Montana	126	213	1,105	188.89	303.59	1,366.36
Nebraska	201	390	2,328	144.38	271.48	1,460.42
Nevada	60	166	1,633	231.78	374.31	1,621.52
New Hampshire	87	177	1,468	152.25	257.86	1,389.11
New Jersey	991	2,240	16,105	172.67	319.84	2,099.24
New Mexico	128	272	1,962	151.25	270.98	1,307.97
New York	3,723	8,424	49,422	227.40	459.40	2,772.60
North Carolina	503	1,129	8,740	115.20	224.56	1,362.85
North Dakota	108	178	857	176.14	279.11	1,275.50
Ohio	1,404	2,612	16,278	149.21	249.77	1,509.44
Oklahoma	346	629	3,987	151.85	252.09	1,218.41
Oregon	350	631	4,392	204.20	315.80	1,612.19
Pennsylvania	1,777	3,242	18,547	162.21	278.77	1,553.89
Rhode Island	130	267	1,696	152.92	296.60	1,720.18
South Carolina	246	511	4,223	108.05	196.52	1,232.87
South Dakota	113	204	846	169.37	303.34	1,193.78
Tennessee	404	821	5,612	117.73	210.86	1,155.89
Texas	1,259	2,471	22,313	138.78	227.36	1,329.00
Utah	137	300	2,284	165.59	292.59	1,359.54
Vermont	65	134	894	172.53	321.05	1,630.60
Virginia	492	1,071	9,141	127.89	236.04	1,548.23
Washington	514	1,209	7,702	188.67	359.11	1,697.18
West Virginia	220	400	2,335	119.48	222.69	1,216.60
Wisconsin	709	1,518	8,592	187.00	362.29	1,787.34
Wyoming	61	110	1,124	193.14	350.20	2,293.41
District of Columbia	143	275	1,915	187.76	339.84	3,078.23

[a] Based on population, excluding armed forces overseas, at end of fiscal year.
Source: Department of Commerce, Bureau of the Census.

D29. State and Local Revenue from Charges and Miscellaneous General Revenue by Source and Level of Government

Selected Fiscal Years 1960-1987

($Millions)

Source	1960	1970	1980	1983	1984	1985	1986	1987
				A. Total by Source				
Total	$ 7,414	$ 22,103	$ 75,830	$ 112,310	$ 125,600	$ 141,732	$ 155,257	$ 166,019
Current charges, total	5,319	14,873	44,373	62,625	69,022	74,504	80,400	86,199
Education	1,796	5,803	13,756	18,829	20,614	21,936	23,745	24,976
School lunch sales	688	1,394	2,013	2,363	2,499	2,616	2,794	3,026
Higher education	} 1,108	3,742	10,409	14,808	16,362	17,512	19,060	20,231
Other education	}	667	1,335	1,658	1,753	1,808	1,891	1,719
Hospitals	883	3,053	12,733	19,244	20,554	21,611	22,830	24,082
Sewerage and sanitation	422	1,172	4,873	7,460	8,583	9,573	10,808	11,998
Parks and recreation	105 [a]	273	1,174	1,711	1,898	2,097	2,203	2,471
Natural resources	179	305	726	901	977	1,040	1,139	1,189
Housing and urban renewal	339	589	1,310	1,643	1,874	2,072	2,202	2,337
Air transportation	147	498	1,826	2,535	2,745	3,118	3,454	3,806
Water transport and terminals	143	273	821	986	1,073	1,142	1,230	1,304
Parking facilities	b	175	335	453	526	663	632	681
Other	1,305	2,732	6,819	8,863	10,180	11,254	12,157	13,355
Miscellaneous general, total	2,094	7,230	31,457	49,685	56,578	67,228	74,857	79,820
Special assessments	369	573	1,288	1,625	1,905	2,111	2,163	2,386
Sale of property	241	335	517	1,033	934	850	1,086	947
Interest earnings	644	2,952	17,025	26,102	27,456	33,259	35,850	36,899
Other	840	3,371	12,628	20,925	26,283	31,009	35,757	39,588
				B. Total by Level of Government				
State, total	2,583	9,545	32,190	46,312	52,495	60,102	66,848	70,173
Current charges	1,783	6,102	16,545	23,182	25,738	27,590	29,987	31,900
Miscellaneous general	800	3,443	15,646	23,130	26,757	32,512	36,861	38,272
Local, total	4,831	12,558	43,640	65,998	73,105	81,630	88,409	95,846
Current charges	3,536	8,770	27,828	39,443	43,284	46,914	50,413	54,299
Miscellaneous general	1,295	3,788	15,812	26,555	29,821	34,716	37,996	41,548

[a] Local only.
b Not segregable, included in "Other."
Source: Department of Commerce, Bureau of the Census.

D30. State and Local Tax Collections by Level of Government, Source, and State[a]

Fiscal Year 1987

	Level of Government			Source			
State	Total	State	Local	Income	Sales and Gross Receipts	Property	Other Taxes Including Licenses
Total	$ 405,149.2	$ 246,933.2	$ 158,216.0	$ 106,352.3	$ 96,772.7	$ 121,226.9	$ 80,797.3
Alabama	4,440.9	3,222.2	1,218.7	1,096.5	1,341.2	505.2	1,498.0
Alaska	1,659.9	1,062.4	597.5	141.5	55.3	623.4	839.7
Arizona	5,399.5	3,469.5	1,930.0	961.1	1,876.6	1,584.3	977.5
Arkansas	2,475.3	1,889.1	586.2	650.9	776.1	469.7	578.6
California	53,272.5	35,790.8	17,481.7	18,633.1	13,706.1	13,702.7	7,230.6
Colorado	5,280.2	2,561.5	2,718.8	1,158.8	1,408.1	1,885.3	828.0
Connecticut	7,115.7	4,359.2	2,756.6	1,146.2	1,823.0	2,704.5	1,442.0
Delaware	1,128.2	941.9	186.3	483.8	-	155.2	489.2
Florida	16,412.2	9,846.2	6,566.0	596.4	5,515.4	5,444.7	4,855.7
Georgia	8,534.8	5,323.7	3,211.1	2,598.3	2,387.3	2,161.2	1,388.0
Hawaii	2,117.3	1,697.4	419.8	619.9	817.5	346.2	333.7
Idaho	1,176.1	829.7	346.4	312.7	297.9	333.8	231.7
Illinois	19,112.7	10,429.5	8,683.1	3,958.0	4,623.2	6,597.8	3,933.7
Indiana	7,213.6	4,774.2	2,439.4	1,820.6	2,252.1	2,304.2	836.7
Iowa	4,336.3	2,662.1	1,674.2	1,104.9	827.7	1,638.8	764.9
Kansas	3,732.9	2,085.5	1,647.4	771.5	917.9	1,394.3	649.2
Kentucky	4,511.1	3,520.4	990.7	1,434.6	892.0	762.8	1,421.7
Louisiana	5,473.4	3,448.6	2,024.7	629.8	2,164.8	881.7	1,797.1
Maine	1,916.0	1,228.5	627.6	491.5	439.4	629.8	355.3
Maryland	8,633.2	5,204.5	3,428.7	3,435.0	1,302.5	2,102.7	1,793.0
Massachusetts	12,327.1	8,463.9	3,863.2	5,183.3	1,866.7	3,746.8	1,530.3
Michigan	16,335.5	9,857.1	6,478.4	5,217.0	2,828.5	6,156.5	2,133.5
Minnesota	8,086.3	5,546.4	2,539.9	2,735.0	1,479.7	2,430.8	1,440.8
Mississippi	2,598.8	1,943.4	655.4	418.3	1,015.7	615.7	549.1
Missouri	6,361.6	3,942.3	2,419.3	1,655.8	2,142.6	1,385.2	1,178.0
Montana	1,105.4	591.0	514.4	229.2	-	533.5	342.7
Nebraska	2,327.9	1,203.3	1,124.6	427.2	458.1	1,014.2	428.4
Nevada	1,632.9	1,131.3	501.6	-	558.8	362.5	711.6
New Hampshire	1,468.1	562.7	905.6	160.5	-	910.7	397.1
New Jersey	16,105.4	9,491.4	6,614.0	3,691.6	2,911.8	6,486.3	3,015.7
New Mexico	1,962.0	1,574.7	387.3	341.8	818.3	229.0	572.9
New York	49,421.5	24,676.3	24,745.2	18,592.2	9,481.9	14,249.3	7,098.1
North Carolina	8,740.0	6,235.2	2,504.8	3,132.4	2,083.7	1,866.6	1,657.3
North Dakota	857.1	573.5	283.7	113.6	200.2	271.7	271.6
Ohio	16,277.8	9,717.1	6,560.6	5,163.9	3,802.5	4,460.5	2,850.9
Oklahoma	3,986.6	2,669.2	1,317.5	762.5	1,050.0	802.2	1,371.9
Oregon	4,391.6	2,235.1	2,156.5	1,598.0	-	1,948.5	845.1
Pennsylvania	18,547.2	11,378.8	7,168.4	5,344.7	3,568.9	4,923.0	4,710.6
Rhode Island	1,696.1	1,050.1	646.0	446.7	350.8	643.7	254.9
South Carolina	4,222.7	3,158.5	1,064.1	1,119.4	1,175.4	984.9	1,943.0
South Dakota	846.4	416.4	430.0	24.2	265.3	351.1	205.8
Tennessee	5,611.9	3,603.3	2,008.5	366.8	2,575.8	1,206.5	1,462.8
Texas	22,312.6	11,227.8	11,084.8	-	5,727.1	9,215.2	7,370.3
Utah	2,284.0	1,438.3	845.7	592.6	682.7	660.6	348.1
Vermont	893.6	537.9	355.7	200.4	109.5	352.6	231.1
Virginia	9,140.7	5,526.6	3,614.2	2,766.4	1,480.5	2,536.1	2,357.7
Washington	7,701.8	5,639.4	2,062.4	-	3,701.2	2,191.8	1,808.8
West Virginia	2,334.6	1,830.2	504.5	572.1	790.4	409.2	562.9
Wisconsin	8,591.8	5,673.6	2,918.2	2,694.7	1,651.9	2,964.7	1,280.5
Wyoming	1,123.8	631.7	492.1	-	191.1	543.0	389.7
District of Columbia	1,914.7	-	1,914.7	676.7	379.3	546.2	312.5

[a] Excludes unemployment compensation taxes in insurance trust revenue in Table D14.
Source: Department of Commerce, Bureau of the Census.

D31. Per Capita State and Local Tax Collections by Level of Government, Source, and State[a]

Fiscal Year 1987

State	Level of Government			Source			
	Total	State	Local	Income	Sales and Gross Receipts	Property	Other Taxes Including Licenses
Total	$ 1,665	$ 1,015	$ 650	$ 437	$ 398	$ 498	$ 332
Alabama	1,088	789	298	269	328	124	367
Alaska	3,162	2,024	1,138	270	105	1,187	1,599 b
Arizona	1,595	1,025	570	284	554	468	289
Arkansas	1,037	791	246	273	325	197	242
California	1,926	1,294	632	674	495	495	261
Colorado	1,602	777	825	352	427	572	251
Connecticut	2,216	1,358	858	357	568	842	449
Delaware	1,752	1,463	289	751	-	241	760
Florida	1,365	819	546	50	459	453	404
Georgia	1,372	856	516	418	384	347	223
Hawaii	1,955	1,568	388	572	755	320	308
Idaho	1,179	831	347	313	299	335	232
Illinois	1,650	900	750	342	399	570	340
Indiana	1,304	863	441	329	407	417	151
Iowa	1,530	939	591	390	292	578	270
Kansas	1,508	842	665	312	371	563	262
Kentucky	1,210	945	266	385	239	205	381
Louisiana	1,227	773	454	141	485	198	403
Maine	1,614	1,035	529	414	370	531	299
Maryland	1,904	1,148	756	757	287	464	395
Massachusetts	2,105	1,446	660	885	319	640	261
Michigan	1,776	1,071	704	567	307	669	232
Minnesota	1,905	1,306	598	644	349	573	339
Mississippi	990	740	250	159	387	235	209
Missouri	1,247	772	474	324	420	271	231
Montana	1,367	731	636	283	-	660	424
Nebraska	1,460	755	705	268	287	636	269
Nevada	1,621	1,123	498	-	555	360	707
New Hampshire	1,389	532	857	152	-	862	376
New Jersey	2,099	1,237	862	481	380	845	393
New Mexico	1,308	1,050	258	228	546	153	382
New York	2,773	1,384	1,388	1,043	532	799	398
North Carolina	1,363	972	391	488	325	291	258
North Dakota	1,276	854	422	169	298	404	404
Ohio	1,509	901	608	479	353	414	264
Oklahoma	1,218	816	403	233	321	245	419
Oregon	1,612	820	792	587	-	715	310
Pennsylvania	1,554	953	601	448	299	412	395
Rhode Island	1,720	1,065	655	453	356	653	259
South Carolina	1,233	922	311	35	343	288	567
South Dakota	1,194	588	607	34	374	495	290
Tennessee	1,156	742	414	76	531	248	301
Texas	1,329	669	660	-	341	549	439
Utah	1,360	856	503	353	406	393	207
Vermont	1,630	981	649	366	200	643	422
Virginia	1,548	936	612	469	251	430	399
Washington	1,697	1,243	454	-	816	483	399
West Virginia	1,216	954	263	298	412	213	293
Wisconsin	1,787	1,180	607	561	344	617	266
Wyoming	2,293	1,289	1,004	-	390	1,108	795
District of Columbia	3,078	-	3,078	1,088	610	878	502

[a] Excludes unemployment compensation taxes included in insurance trust revenue in Table D14.
[b] Primarily severance tax collection.
Source: Department of Commerce, Bureau of the Census; and Tax Foundation computations.

D32. Percentage Distribution of State and Local Tax Collections by Level of Government, Source, and State[a]

Fiscal Year 1987

| State | Level of Government | | | Source | | | |
	Total	State	Local	Income	Sales and Gross Receipts	Property	Other Taxes Including Licenses
Total	100.0%	60.9%	39.1%	26.3%	23.9%	29.9%	19.9%
Alabama	100.0	72.6	27.4	24.7	30.2	11.4	33.7
Alaska	100.0	64.0	36.0	8.5	3.3	37.6	50.6
Arizona	100.0	64.3	35.7	17.8	34.8	29.3	18.1
Arkansas	100.0	76.3	23.7	26.3	31.4	19.0	23.4
California	100.0	67.2	32.8	35.0	25.7	25.7	13.6
Colorado	100.0	48.5	51.5	21.9	26.7	35.7	15.7
Connecticut	100.0	61.3	38.7	16.1	25.6	38.0	20.3
Delaware	100.0	83.5	16.5	42.9	-	13.8	43.4
Florida	100.0	60.0	40.0	3.6	33.6	33.2	29.6
Georgia	100.0	62.4	37.6	30.4	28.0	25.3	16.3
Hawaii	100.0	80.2	19.8	29.3	38.6	16.4	15.8
Idaho	100.0	70.5	29.5	26.6	25.3	28.4	19.7
Illinois	100.0	54.6	45.4	20.7	24.2	34.5	20.6
Indiana	100.0	66.2	33.8	25.2	31.2	31.9	11.6
Iowa	100.0	61.4	38.6	25.5	19.1	37.8	17.6
Kansas	100.0	55.9	44.1	20.7	24.6	37.4	17.4
Kentucky	100.0	78.0	22.0	31.8	19.8	16.9	31.5
Louisiana	100.0	63.0	37.0	11.5	39.6	16.1	32.8
Maine	100.0	64.1	32.8	25.7	22.9	32.9	18.5
Maryland	100.0	60.3	39.7	39.8	15.1	24.4	20.8
Massachusetts	100.0	68.7	31.3	42.0	15.1	30.4	12.4
Michigan	100.0	60.3	39.7	31.9	17.3	37.7	13.1
Minnesota	100.0	68.6	31.4	33.8	18.3	30.1	17.8
Mississippi	100.0	74.8	25.2	16.1	39.1	23.7	21.1
Missouri	100.0	62.0	38.0	26.0	33.7	21.8	18.5
Montana	100.0	53.5	46.5	20.7	-	48.3	31.0
Nebraska	100.0	51.7	48.3	18.4	19.7	43.6	18.4
Nevada	100.0	69.3	30.7	-	34.2	22.2	43.6
New Hampshire	100.0	38.3	61.7	10.9	-	62.0	27.0
New Jersey	100.0	58.9	41.1	22.9	18.1	40.3	18.7
New Mexico	100.0	80.3	19.7	17.4	41.7	11.7	29.2
New York	100.0	49.9	50.1	37.6	19.2	28.8	14.4
North Carolina	100.0	71.3	28.7	35.8	23.8	21.4	19.0
North Dakota	100.0	66.9	33.1	13.3	23.4	31.7	31.7
Ohio	100.0	59.7	40.3	31.7	23.4	27.4	17.5
Oklahoma	100.0	67.0	33.0	19.1	26.3	20.1	34.4
Oregon	100.0	50.9	49.1	36.4	-	44.4	19.2
Pennsylvania	100.0	61.4	38.6	28.8	19.2	26.5	25.4
Rhode Island	100.0	61.9	38.1	26.3	20.7	38.0	15.0
South Carolina	100.0	74.8	25.2	2.8	27.8	23.3	46.0
South Dakota	100.0	49.2	50.8	2.9	31.3	41.5	24.3
Tennessee	100.0	64.2	35.8	6.5	45.9	21.5	26.1
Texas	100.0	50.3	49.7	-	25.7	41.3	33.0
Utah	100.0	63.0	37.0	25.9	29.9	28.9	15.2
Vermont	100.0	60.2	39.8	22.4	12.3	39.5	25.9
Virginia	100.0	60.5	39.5	30.3	16.2	27.7	25.8
Washington	100.0	73.2	26.8	-	48.1	28.5	23.5
West Virginia	100.0	78.4	21.6	24.5	33.9	17.5	24.1
Wisconsin	100.0	66.0	34.0	31.4	19.2	34.5	14.9
Wyoming	100.0	56.2	43.8	-	17.0	48.3	34.7
District of Columbia	100.0	-	100.0	35.3[b]	19.8	28.5	16.3

[a] Excludes unemployment compensation taxes included in insurance trust revenue in Table D14.
[b] Includes corporation net income tax collections.
Source: Department of Commerce, Bureau of the Census; and Tax Foundation computations.

D33. State and Local Debt Outstanding, Issued, and Retired

Fiscal Years 1957-1987

($Millions)

Year	Debt Outstanding[a]			Long-Term Debt Issued	Long-Term Debt Retired
	Total	Long-Term	Short-Term		
1957	$53,039	$50,845	$2,194	$6,776	$2,716
1958	58,187	55,737	2,450	7,865	2,839
1959	64,110	61,127	2,983	8,147	3,222
1960	69,955	66,801	3,154	7,955	3,458
1961	75,023	71,540	3,483	8,081	3,696
1962	81,278	77,543	3,735	9,585	4,227
1963	85,056	81,110	3,946	8,744	4,358
1964	92,222	87,527	4,695	11,243	5,045
1965	99,512	94,204	5,309	11,249	5,040
1966	107,051	101,000	6,051	12,129	5,641
1967	113,659	106,649	7,010	12,110	5,694
1968	121,158	112,731	8,427	13,357	6,002
1969	133,548	123,466	10,083	15,453	6,538
1970	143,570	131,415	12,155	12,848	7,011
1971	158,827	143,617	15,210	19,232	7,670
1972	175,158	159,098	16,061	22,104	8,174
1973	188,485	172,605	15,879	21,804	9,013
1974	206,616	189,953	16,663	12,218	9,955
1975	219,926	200,140	19,786	21,125	10,904
1976	240,532	221,754	18,777	31,671	11,348
1977	257,532	244,147	13,385	32,342	13,219
1978	280,433	269,003	11,430	39,980	16,715
1979	304,103	292,302	11,801	42,085	27,056
1980	335,603	322,456	13,147	42,364	17,404
1981	363,892	348,330	15,562	43,819	18,929
1982	404,579	385,786	18,793	49,182	20,955
1983	454,501	435,946	18,554	72,451	26,894
1984	505,030	485,069	19,960	71,621	33,941
1985	568,442	548,859	19,583	101,164	43,509
1986	658,875	640,550	18,325	162,045	74,360
1987	718,657	702,881	15,775	131,811	82,149

[a] End of fiscal year.
Source: Department of Commerce, Bureau of the Census.

D34. State and Local Debt Outstanding, Issued, and Retired, by State

Fiscal Year 1987

($Millions)

State	Debt Outstanding[a]			Long-Term Debt Issued	Long-Term Debt Retired
	Total	Long-Term	Short-Term		
Total	$ 718,657	$ 702,881	$ 15,775	$ 131,811	$ 82,149
Alabama	9,384	9,283	101	1,296	964
Alaska	11,175	11,142	33	1,049	1,762
Arizona	14,103	13,701	402	1,664	836
Arkansas	4,321	4,296	25	658	452
California	71,961	70,950	1,011	12,886	6,562
Colorado	11,200	11,164	36	3,116	1,652
Connecticut	10,753	10,471	282	1,777	1,292
Delaware	3,816	3,773	43	631	433
Florida	40,627	40,451	176	15,218	6,594
Georgia	14,253	14,009	244	2,835	1,729
Hawaii	3,504	3,421	83	763	651
Idaho	1,146	1,130	16	148	212
Illinois	27,476	26,655	821	4,826	3,505
Indiana	7,689	7,471	218	1,459	992
Iowa	4,892	4,346	546	492	438
Kansas	6,658	6,521	137	1,055	1,030
Kentucky	12,419	12,416	2	1,760	730
Louisiana	19,790	19,743	47	5,468	4,100
Maine	2,606	2,582	24	447	292
Maryland	13,909	13,694	214	1,897	1,936
Massachusetts	19,236	18,293	943	2,918	1,925
Michigan	18,674	18,220	454	2,965	2,202
Minnesota	17,228	16,864	364	2,580	2,012
Mississippi	5,338	5,327	11	949	669
Missouri	8,658	8,569	89	1,339	671
Montana	2,222	2,184	39	258	360
Nebraska	6,321	6,290	31	554	465
Nevada	3,341	3,325	16	715	414
New Hampshire	3,063	3,037	25	444	316
New Jersey	28,951	27,651	1,300	4,560	2,417
New Mexico	5,297	5,277	20	624	513
New York	77,247	73,851	3,396	16,310	9,063
North Carolina	13,735	13,446	289	2,885	1,859
North Dakota	1,678	1,659	20	229	180
Ohio	19,364	17,974	1,390	2,461	1,467
Oklahoma	8,544	8,483	61	1,505	1,230
Oregon	10,944	10,692	253	1,057	976
Pennsylvania	36,509	35,711	797	7,525	3,765
Rhode Island	3,400	3,279	120	393	550
South Carolina	8,920	8,870	50	1,958	1,664
South Dakota	1,968	1,967	1	565	295
Tennessee	11,041	10,796	245	2,367	1,101
Texas	53,274	52,685	589	9,332	6,138
Utah	9,119	9,101	19	1,336	1,104
Vermont	1,316	1,294	22	224	230
Virginia	11,081	10,978	103	1,800	1,010
Washington	19,721	19,461	260	2,165	1,284
West Virginia	5,176	5,171	5	396	287
Wisconsin	9,747	9,352	395	1,239	1,062
Wyoming	2,151	2,149	2	251	383
District of Columbia	3,711	3,706	5	465	378

[a] End of fiscal year.
Source: Department of Commerce, Bureau of the Census.

D35. Cash and Security Holdings of State and Local Governments by Purpose of Holding

End of Selected Fiscal Years 1952-1987

($Millions)

Year	Total	Insurance Trust Systems				Other Than Insurance Trust Systems			
		Total	Unemployment Compensation	Employee Retirement	Other Insurance Trust Systems	Total	Long-term[a] Debt Offsets	Bond Funds[b]	All Other
1952	$33,959	$15,257	$7,838	$6,406	$1,014	$18,702	$3,207	c	$15,495
1957	48,482	22,678	8,480	12,825	1,373	25,804	4,167	$5,374	16,263
1960	56,050	26,737	6,675	18,539	1,523	29,313	5,205	5,892	18,216
1962	63,985	30,599	5,659	23,294	1,646	33,386	5,887	7,283	20,217
1964	76,306	37,034	6,643	28,639	1,752	39,272	7,577	7,773	23,922
1965	85,036	41,215	7,541	31,814	1,860	43,821	8,261	9,764	25,795
1966	95,221	46,183	8,902	35,272	2,010	49,038	9,798	10,988	28,252
1967	102,598	51,522	10,075	39,265	2,183	51,076	8,819	11,314	30,942
1968	111,428	56,984	10,922	43,681	2,382	54,444	8,685	12,511	33,247
1969	123,177	63,340	11,925	48,876	2,539	59,837	9,098	14,278	36,461
1970	133,517	70,000	12,312	54,925	2,762	63,517	9,682	13,251	40,585
1971	142,490	75,057	10,489	61,605	2,964	67,433	10,264	16,008	41,161
1972	158,626	81,036	9,029	68,760	3,247	77,590	11,258	17,671	48,661
1973	185,590	91,761	9,830	78,448	3,482	93,829	13,855	19,450	60,524
1974	212,059	102,215	10,818	87,486	3,912	109,844	15,904	23,134	70,806
1975	222,951	109,068	6,860	98,003	4,206	113,883	18,088	22,842	72,954
1976	243,304	120,216	4,440	111,333	4,443	123,088	26,048	22,131	74,909
1977	270,621	133,818	4,968	123,638	5,213	136,803	31,933	23,492	81,378
1978	318,676	154,772	7,463	140,746	6,563	163,904	43,794	26,918	93,192
1979	362,359	179,597	11,387	159,651	8,559	182,763	43,666	33,231	105,866
1980	407,815	205,697	11,971	183,696	10,030	202,118	59,529	33,206	109,382
1981	454,393	232,169	11,649	209,862	10,658	222,224	74,514	31,649	116,062
1982	506,793	262,813	6,787	243,248	12,318	243,981	83,034	32,344	128,603
1983	585,848	305,728	4,818	287,282	13,628	280,120	101,989	38,570	139,561
1984	669,293	341,717	5,735	323,008	12,974	327,576	125,449	37,516	164,611
1985	786,769	395,228	8,653	370,551	16,024	391,540	151,937	47,584	192,019
1986	926,182	466,467	18,079	431,121	17,266	459,715	181,618	65,589	212,508
1987	1,047,766	547,143	22,510	505,520	19,113	500,623	193,010	72,236	235,377

[a] Comprises cash and investment assets of sinking funds and other reserve funds that are specifically held for redemption of long-term debt.
[b] Holdings in funds or accounts established to maintain the proceeds of bond issues, pending their disbursement.
[c] Unallocable; included in "all other."
Source: Department of Commerce, Bureau of the Census.

D36. Cash and Security Holdings of State and Local Governments by Purpose of Holding and Level of Government by State

End of Fiscal Year 1987
($Millions)

State	Total			Insurance Trust Systems			Other Than Insurance Trust Systems		
	State and Local	State	Local	State and Local	State	Local	State and Local	State	Local
Total	$1,047,765.9	$695,823.8	$351,942.0	$547,142.8	$443,168.0	$103,974.8	$500,623.0	$252,655.8	$247,967.2
Alabama	11,942.5	9,446.7	2,495.8	6,440.8	5,931.0	509.8	5,501.7	3,515.7	1,986.0
Alaska	20,633.8	18,412.8	2,221.0	3,282.1	3,123.0	159.1	17,351.7	15,289.8	2,062.0
Arizona	14,599.9	8,906.6	5,693.3	7,091.1	6,521.5	569.6	7,508.8	2,385.1	5,123.7
Arkansas	6,418.2	4,929.0	1,489.2	3,146.9	3,042.5	104.4	3,271.3	1,886.6	1,384.8
California	162,328.3	91,409.2	70,919.1	92,232.5	67,256.8	24,975.7	70,095.9	24,152.5	45,943.4
Colorado	16,458.8	9,386.6	6,772.2	8,091.2	6,948.2	1,142.9	8,067.6	2,438.4	5,629.2
Connecticut	11,882.7	9,272.9	2,609.8	5,973.2	4,616.1	1,357.0	5,909.6	4,656.8	1,252.8
Delaware	3,320.8	2,546.1	774.6	1,430.6	1,342.2	88.4	1,890.2	1,203.9	686.3
Florida	45,877.2	23,604.3	22,273.0	16,180.7	13,660.5	2,520.2	29,696.6	9,943.8	19,752.8
Georgia	18,841.2	11,807.5	7,033.7	10,015.2	9,032.8	982.4	8,826.0	2,774.7	6,051.3
Hawaii	5,048.9	4,535.9	513.0	2,895.7	2,895.7	-	2,153.2	1,640.2	513.0
Idaho	2,728.3	2,340.8	387.5	1,260.7	1,256.1	4.6	1,467.6	1,084.6	383.0
Illinois	42,610.5	22,719.6	19,890.9	22,771.1	13,937.4	8,833.7	19,839.4	8,782.2	11,057.1
Indiana	10,971.3	8,307.8	2,663.5	4,316.0	4,265.5	50.6	6,655.3	4,042.4	2,612.9
Iowa	7,991.0	5,434.9	2,556.0	4,216.0	3,685.4	530.6	3,774.9	1,749.9	2,025.4
Kansas	7,094.2	3,831.9	3,262.3	3,328.0	3,067.7	260.4	3,766.2	764.2	3,001.9
Kentucky	10,777.1	8,755.2	2,022.0	5,393.5	5,103.5	290.0	5,383.6	3,651.6	1,732.0
Louisiana	17,577.9	12,464.4	5,113.4	7,171.6	6,632.2	539.4	10,406.3	5,832.2	4,574.1
Maine	3,401.9	3,007.3	394.7	1,303.2	1,303.9	-	2,098.8	1,704.1	394.7
Maryland	16,684.1	10,923.1	5,761.0	9,273.7	7,096.7	2,177.0	7,410.5	3,826.4	3,584.1
Massachusetts	20,837.6	14,378.1	6,459.6	8,550.6	5,510.6	3,039.9	12,287.1	8,867.4	3,419.6
Michigan	37,648.6	24,636.5	13,012.1	23,378.1	16,468.3	6,909.7	14,270.5	8,168.2	6,102.3
Minnesota	21,760.0	13,462.5	8,297.4	9,848.6	8,283.3	1,565.3	11,911.3	5,179.3	6,732.1
Mississippi	6,552.8	5,446.7	1,106.2	3,989.6	3,938.2	51.4	2,563.2	1,508.5	1,054.7
Missouri	16,965.4	11,829.1	5,136.3	9,073.3	7,374.8	1,698.5	7,892.1	4,454.3	3,437.8
Montana	3,672.7	3,086.4	586.3	1,258.6	1,257.8	0.9	2,414.1	1,828.7	585.4

Continued

D36. Cash and Security Holdings of State and Local Governments by Purpose of Holding and Level of Government by State (continued)

End of Fiscal Year 1987
($Millions)

State	Total			Insurance Trust Systems			Other Than Insurance Trust Systems		
	State and Local	State	Local	State and Local	State	Local	State and Local	State	Local
Nebraska	5,039.6	2,645.9	2,393.7	1,338.5	756.4	582.1	3,701.1	1,889.5	1,811.7
Nevada	5,072.5	4,135.9	936.6	2,931.7	2,931.7	-	2,140.7	1,204.1	936.6
New Hampshire	2,618.4	2,110.7	507.7	1,047.2	1,043.3	3.9	1,571.2	1,067.3	503.9
New Jersey	35,908.2	29,239.1	6,669.1	17,042.6	16,989.0	53.6	18,865.6	12,250.2	6,615.5
New Mexico	10,704.5	9,009.6	1,695.0	2,847.2	2,847.2	-	7,857.3	6,162.3	1,695.0
New York	124,182.6	78,643.9	45,538.7	84,294.4	53,531.3	30,763.1	39,888.2	25,112.6	14,775.6
North Carolina	20,825.5	15,788.4	5,037.1	12,744.4	12,670.2	74.2	8,081.1	3,118.2	4,962.9
North Dakota	2,574.0	2,010.9	563.0	792.7	746.0	46.7	1,781.3	1,264.9	516.3
Ohio	48,322.8	40,220.5	8,102.2	33,865.5	33,235.3	630.2	14,457.3	6,985.2	7,472.1
Oklahoma	11,707.0	8,135.1	3,571.9	4,282.6	4,099.9	182.7	7,424.3	4,035.1	3,389.2
Oregon	17,526.0	14,828.2	2,697.8	7,319.9	7,313.8	6.0	10,206.2	7,514.4	2,691.8
Pennsylvania	39,157.5	25,383.7	13,773.7	21,429.9	18,607.3	2,822.6	17,727.6	6,776.4	10,951.2
Rhode Island	3,805.3	3,406.2	399.1	1,781.7	1,602.4	179.3	2,023.6	1,803.9	219.8
South Carolina	12,542.4	10,110.5	2,431.8	7,575.6	7,540.8	34.7	4,966.8	2,569.7	2,397.1
South Dakota	3,187.0	2,686.5	500.5	1,033.8	986.6	47.2	2,153.2	1,699.9	453.3
Tennessee	14,430.5	8,773.9	5,656.6	7,632.9	6,048.6	1,584.3	6,797.5	2,725.2	4,072.3
Texas	63,660.9	36,456.8	27,204.1	23,513.5	20,363.8	3,149.7	40,147.3	16,093.0	24,054.4
Utah	7,461.8	4,279.1	3,182.7	2,564.5	2,564.5	-	4,897.3	1,714.6	3,182.7
Vermont	1,597.2	1,446.3	150.9	578.2	551.1	27.1	1,019.1	895.3	123.8
Virginia	18,766.1	12,828.7	5,937.4	8,923.3	6,993.7	1,929.7	9,842.8	5,835.1	4,007.7
Washington	20,780.7	14,808.5	5,972.2	13,371.1	12,787.0	584.1	7,409.6	2,021.4	5,388.1
West Virginia	6,106.7	4,249.1	1,857.6	2,501.5	2,443.4	58.1	3,605.2	1,805.8	1,799.5
Wisconsin	19,996.9	15,180.5	4,816.4	13,524.9	11,824.8	1,700.1	6,472.0	3,355.7	3,116.3
Wyoming	5,252.4	4,563.8	688.6	1,153.4	1,138.6	14.8	4,098.9	3,425.1	673.8
District of Columbia	2,213.8	-	2,213.8	1,139.3	-	1,139.3	1,074.5	-	1,074.5

Source: Department of Commerce, Bureau of the Census.

D37. New State and Local Security Issues by Type and Use of Proceeds
Calendar Years 1982-1988
($Millions)

Type or Use	1982	1983	1984	1985	1986	1987	1988
All issues, new and refunding, total[a]	$ 79,138	$ 86,421	$ 106,641	$ 214,189	$ 147,011	$ 102,407	$ 108,078
Type of Issue							
General obligation	21,094	21,566	26,485	52,622	46,346	30,589	29,662
Revenue	58,044	64,855	80,156	161,567	100,664	71,818	78,417
Type of Issuer							
State	8,438	7,140	9,129	13,004	14,474	10,102	9,254
Special district and statutory authority[b]	45,060	51,297	63,550	134,363	89,997	65,460	69,447
Municipalities, counties, townships, school districts	25,640	27,984	33,962	78,754	42,541	26,845	29,377
Issues for new capital, total	74,804	72,441	94,050	156,050	83,492	56,789	75,064
Use of Proceeds							
Education	6,482	8,099	7,553	16,658	12,307	9,524	13,722
Transportation	6,256	4,387	7,552	12,070	7,246	3,677	6,974
Utilities and conservation	14,259	13,588	17,844	26,852	14,595	7,912	7,929
Social welfare	26,635	26,910	29,928	63,181	11,353	11,106	17,824
Industrial aid	8,349	7,821	15,415	12,892	6,190	7,474	6,276
Other purposes	12,822	11,637	15,758	24,398	31,802	18,020	22,339

[a] Par amounts of long-term issues based on date of sale.
[b] Includes school districts beginning April 1986.
Source: Public Securities Association and Securities Data Company.

D38. State and Municipal Bond Election Results
Calendar Years 1947-1988

Year	Amount ($Millions)		Percent of Total	
	Approved	Defeated	Approved	Defeated
1947	$ 1,870.0	$ 165.0	92 %	8 %
1948	1,449.7	657.5	69	31
1949	2,217.3	413.3	84	16
1950	1,537.5	498.0	76	24
1951	2,249.6	301.2	88	12
1952	2,284.0	458.3	84	16
1953	1,851.6	388.8	83	17
1954	2,781.9	544.2	84	16
1955	2,885.7	1,524.5	65	35
1956	4,642.5	665.7	87	13
1957	2,733.4	806.8	77	23
1958	3,728.5	1,263.8	75	25
1959	2,752.9	1,087.6	72	28
1960	5,917.0	1,007.9	85	15
1961	2,544.3	1,263.6	67	33
1962	4,263.6	1,850.4	70	30
1963	3,626.9	2,156.8	63	37
1964	5,715.4	1,582.9	78	22
1965	5,611.7	2,095.5	73	27
1966	6,515.8	1,944.8	77	23
1967	7,365.2	2,549.7	74	26
1968	8,686.1	7,549.9	54	46
1969	4,286.5	6,534.0	40	60
1970	5,366.4	3,194.0	63	37
1971	3,142.8	5,862.4	35	65
1972	7,875.5	4,445.9	64	36
1973	6,306.0	5,800.8	52	48
1974	8,021.4	4,865.4	62	38
1975	3,392.3	8,184.2	29	71
1976	5,087.0	3,574.5	59	41
1977	6,092.0	2,929.1	67	33
1978	8,421.3	4,842.3	64	36
1979	6,148.1	2,518.8	71	29
1980	6,279.6	2,560.7	71	29
1981	5,029.2	3,765.9	57	42
1982	8,885.2	1,797.2	83	17
1983	7,162.2	4,557.3	61	39
1984	10,628.4	2,490.2	81	19
1985	9,156.0	1,846.0	83	17
1986	13,371.6	2,804.4	83	17
1987	8,484.9	3,094.4	73	27
1988	21,126.5	5,048.1	81	19

Source: The Bond Buyer.

D39. Income and Expenditure of All Public and Private Institutions of Higher Education[a]

Selected School Years 1953-54 — 1985-86[b]

($Millions)

Item	Public and Private Institutions			Publicly Controlled Institutions		
	1953-54	1975-76	1985-86	1953-54	1975-76	1985-86
Total current income	$ 2,966.3	$ 39,703.2	$ 100,437.6	$ 1,651.4	$ 26,834.9	$ 65,004.6
From public sources	1,259.3	20,355.1	45,160.8	1,033.1	17,463.9	38,398.8
Federal	419.5	6,477.2	12,704.8	217.0	4,001.1	6,852.4
State	751.6	12,260.9	29,911.5	729.7	11,963.3	29,220.6
Local	88.2	1,617.0	2,544.5	86.4	1,499.5	2,325.8
Student fees and tuition	554.2	8,171.9	23,116.6	148.1	3,477.6	9,439.2
Endowment income	127.5	687.5	2,275.9	14.7	97.0	398.6
Private gifts and grants	191.3	1,917.0	5,410.9	38.6	616.4	2,109.8
Sales and services	775.2	7,687.4	21,274.2	390.5	4,686.2	12,990.7
Educational activities	165.5	645.4	2,373.5	93.8	423.3	1,596.9
Auxiliary enterprises	576.8	4,547.6	10,674.1	286.3	2,889.5	6,684.8
Hospitals	c	2,494.3	8,226.6	c	1,373.4	4,708.9
Other	32.9	-	-	10.4	-	-
Miscellaneous	58.8	884.3	3,199.2	26.6	493.8	1,667.6
Total current expenditures	2,902.5	38,903.2	97,535.7	1,597.5	26,184.0	63,193.9
Current general expenses	2,363.1	30,598.7	76,128.0	1,324.9	21,283.0	50,873.0
Instruction	966.8	13,094.9	31,032.1	555.5	9,516.0	21,880.8
Research	374.9	3,287.4	8,437.4	203.2	2,154.4	5,705.1
Administration	290.5	3,615.4	9,350.8	124.2	2,364.8	5,667.1
Libraries	73.4	1,223.7	2,551.3	39.2	824.7	1,685.1
Extension and public service	114.7	1,238.6	3,119.5	108.3	1,035.7	2,515.7
Plant operation and maintenance	280.0	3,083.0	7,605.2	156.8	2,158.4	5,177.3
Scholarships and fellowships	74.8	1,635.9	4,160.2	25.1	798.5	1,575.9
Other	188.0	3,419.8	9,871.5	112.6	2,430.5	6,666.0
Other current expenses	539.3	8,304.4	21,407.8	272.4	4,900.9	12,320.9
Auxiliary enterprises	539.3	4,476.8	10,528.3	227.4	2,828.1	6,830.2
Hospitals	c	2,695.6	8,692.1	c	1,609.7	5,358.7
Other	-	1,132.0	2,187.4	-	463.1	132.0

[a] Includes junior colleges.
[b] Data for 1953-54 include Alaska, Canal Zone, Guam, Hawaii, Puerto Rico, and the Virgin Islands; 1973-74 and 1985-86 data are for 50 states and the District of Columbia.
[c] Included in miscellaneous general income and expenditures.
Source: Department of Education, National Center for Education Statistics.

D40. Higher Education Enrollments and College-Age Population
School Years 1963-64 to 1994-95, Actual and Projected[a]
(Thousands)

School Year	College-age Population[b] (age 18-24)	Fall Enrollment in Institutions of Higher Education		
		Total	Publicly Controlled	Privately Controlled
1963-64	18,268	4,766	3,066	1,700
1964-65	18,783	5,280	3,468	1,812
1965-66	20,293	5,921	3,970	1,951
1966-67	21,376	6,390	4,349	2,041
1967-68	22,327	6,912	4,816	2,096
1968-69	22,883	7,513	5,431	2,082
1969-70	23,723	8,005	5,897	2,108
1970-71	24,712	8,581	6,428	2,153
1971-72	25,874	8,949	6,804	2,144
1972-73	26,076	9,215	7,071	2,144
1973-74	26,635	9,602	7,420	2,183
1974-75	27,233	10,224	7,989	2,235
1975-76	28,005	11,185	8,835	2,350
1976-77	28,645	11,012	8,653	2,359
1977-78	29,174	11,286	8,847	2,437
1978-79	29,622	11,259	8,784	2,475
1979-80	30,048	11,570	9,037	2,533
1980-81	30,350	12,097	9,457	2,640
1981-82	30,428	12,372	9,647	2,725
1982-83	30,283	12,426	9,696	2,730
1983-84	29,943	12,465	9,683	2,782
1984-85	29,390	12,242	9,477	2,765
1985-86	28,749	12,247	9,479	2,768
1986-87	27,968	12,505	9,715	2,790
1987-88	27,336	12,768	9,975	2,793
1988-89	26,904	12,894	10,012	2,882
1989-90	26,590	13,038	10,130	2,908
1990-91	26,141	13,120	10,196	2,924
1991-92	25,700	13,121	10,197	2,924
1992-93	25,271	13,037	10,135	2,902
1993-94	24,991	12,950	10,066	2,884
1994-95	24,602	12,869	10,004	2,865

[a] Beginning 1988-89 data are projected.
[b] As of July 1 preceding the school year; data include armed forces overseas.
Source: Department of Education, National Center for Education Statistics; Department of Commerce, Bureau of the Census.

D41. Capital Outlay of State and Local Governments by Major Function

Selected Fiscal Years 1952-1987

($Millions)

Year	Total[a]	Local Schools	Institutions of Higher Education	Highways	Health and Hospitals	Sewerage	Housing and Urban Development	Parks and Recreation[b]	Utilities[b,c]
1952	$ 7,436	$ 1,421	$ 266	$ 2,700	$ 387	$ 442	$ 629	$ 63	$ 677
1957	12,616	2,715	514	5,211	355	644	283	156	1,330
1960	15,104	2,903	759	6,340	405	767	557	235	1,407
1962	16,791	3,026	949	6,978	407	886	781	269	1,481
1964	19,087	3,042	1,465	7,959	418	1,095	729	332	1,631
1965	20,535	3,287	1,445	8,324	494	1,107	794	360	2,190
1966	22,330	3,879	1,854	8,598	550	1,202	913	378	2,099
1967	24,233	3,966	2,436	9,444	610	1,069	933	418	1,972
1968	25,731	3,967	2,574	9,716	736	1,107	1,024	451	2,246
1969	28,240	4,479	2,646	10,273	761	1,207	1,238	581	2,551
1970	29,650	4,658	2,705	10,762	790	1,385	1,319	684	2,437
1971	33,137	4,845	2,926	11,888	1,046	1,744	1,635	747	2,656
1972	34,627	4,833	2,980	12,340	1,208	2,202	1,665	773	3,017
1973	35,272	4,856	2,731	11,459	1,065	2,428	1,911	863	3,656
1974	38,084	5,108	2,812	12,152	1,374	2,640	2,037	1,060	3,994
1975	44,824	6,532	2,834	13,646	1,781	3,569	1,821	1,261	4,846
1976	46,531	6,547	3,007	14,209	1,843	3,955	1,398	1,314	5,355
1977	45,154	5,681	2,813	12,554	2,150	4,660	1,324	1,612	6,952
1978	44,769	5,709	2,593	12,898	1,878	4,366	1,439	1,552	6,597
1979	53,196	6,370	2,781	15,567	1,984	5,619	1,685	1,791	8,357
1980	62,894	7,362	2,972	19,133	2,443	6,272	2,248	2,023	9,933
1981	67,596	7,441	3,474	19,334	2,559	6,911	2,689	2,072	11,562
1982	66,802	6,864	3,696	18,178	2,503	5,922	3,259	2,029	12,484
1983	67,984	7,200	3,403	18,627	2,710	5,806	2,921	2,100	12,870
1984	70,748	7,258	3,855	20,366	2,380	5,664	3,104	1,962	12,599
1985	79,390	8,848	4,629	23,900	2,745	5,926	3,212	2,196	13,435
1986	90,457	10,274	5,217	26,807	2,817	6,461	3,516	2,554	15,340
1987	98,277	11,633	6,169	28,260	3,056	7,306	3,520	2,835	15,392

[a] Includes functions not shown separately.
[b] Prior to 1977 data apply to local governments only; state governments included beginning 1977.
[c] Electric power, water supply, transit, and gas supply.
Source: Department of Commerce, Bureau of the Census.

D42. Capital Outlay of State and Local Governments by Major Function and State

Fiscal Year 1987

($Millions)

State	Total[a]	Local Schools	Institutions of Higher Learning	Highways	Health and Hospitals	Sewerage and Sanitation	Water Supply Systems	Other Utility Systems[b]
Total	$ 98,276.5	$ 11,632.8	$ 6,168.6	$ 28,260.3	$ 3,055.9	$ 8,365.3	$ 6,019.6	$ 9,372.7
Alabama	1,134.3	106.8	127.1	311.9	102.0	93.7	89.5	36.3
Alaska	1,130.9	203.5	16.7	316.1	20.1	70.3	88.8	93.9
Arizona	2,568.7	472.2	132.9	913.6	9.5	112.0	145.9	326.8
Arkansas	855.4	229.8	33.3	267.6	12.6	44.0	24.4	167.8
California	10,190.5	972.9	802.3	1,658.6	322.1	704.3	1,092.6	1,057.0
Colorado	1,947.6	313.6	80.8	390.6	30.7	120.1	291.5	136.6
Connecticut	1,250.7	94.5	42.3	432.3	13.5	96.0	36.4	67.7
Delaware	217.5	13.0	33.8	95.0	3.4	18.5	3.8	4.3
Florida	6,389.6	765.1	241.0	1,295.4	273.2	561.0	757.0	534.6
Georgia	3,079.3	408.1	124.7	780.7	220.9	122.7	178.6	646.3
Hawaii	610.0	70.9	32.3	72.9	8.3	71.9	39.7	16.2
Idaho	327.2	37.0	38.5	162.5	8.1	16.8	4.1	1.8
Illinois	4,135.5	455.7	299.7	1,447.7	53.8	352.7	165.3	159.2
Indiana	1,412.9	246.8	128.8	496.4	50.8	113.6	23.0	47.2
Iowa	993.1	84.5	128.8	471.0	49.3	73.6	34.9	19.5
Kansas	920.0	96.9	57.8	428.0	18.2	39.4	36.5	40.5
Kentucky	1,155.2	99.9	71.7	508.5	29.1	67.4	40.0	26.3
Louisiana	1,601.8	181.1	83.8	659.0	56.5	184.0	49.2	27.6
Maine	339.0	69.1	31.1	101.3	2.7	56.6	9.8	1.1
Maryland	2,141.9	171.9	134.7	722.2	23.2	205.7	53.8	65.1
Massachusetts	2,188.5	107.1	108.8	458.2	41.7	216.7	80.0	397.1
Michigan	2,327.4	289.9	283.5	592.8	108.5	134.1	115.8	22.6
Minnesota	2,110.4	214.7	132.2	756.6	57.5	196.7	60.9	141.3
Mississippi	641.8	93.9	40.9	272.0	45.5	38.7	11.6	5.2
Missouri	1,613.1	188.5	169.6	544.2	92.3	168.9	55.0	41.3
Montana	384.7	31.1	24.4	199.8	5.2	13.8	4.2	0.4
Nebraska	668.0	58.6	63.8	225.2	42.9	23.4	14.4	136.0
Nevada	542.8	52.9	16.6	180.6	10.9	39.0	26.0	5.2
New Hampshire	330.6	71.7	33.4	111.0	5.1	19.0	25.4	0.0
New Jersey	3,052.9	259.4	135.3	1,157.3	69.9	333.5	97.0	297.3
New Mexico	730.3	128.5	46.2	303.7	10.9	57.8	15.5	24.9
New York	9,137.0	767.9	451.8	1,992.1	331.8	1,083.9	192.1	1,782.5
North Carolina	2,399.5	302.3	239.3	448.9	122.5	50.3	262.3	415.0
North Dakota	273.0	41.6	18.9	118.6	2.3	13.0	15.2	0.3
Ohio	3,134.3	326.6	306.0	919.8	114.5	434.2	158.3	51.1
Oklahoma	1,136.9	231.5	54.1	359.2	24.3	115.9	60.7	58.7
Oregon	948.8	97.3	84.7	375.3	23.8	58.4	32.3	44.4
Pennsylvania	2,984.3	475.2	162.2	1,172.1	53.9	197.3	128.3	173.6
Rhode Island	212.2	13.5	5.4	99.3	8.5	25.9	1.2	2.1
South Carolina	1,117.3	213.6	89.5	271.6	59.7	87.6	77.6	89.4
South Dakota	424.8	22.4	11.3	120.0	1.1	11.9	12.7	2.7
Tennessee	1,686.4	161.1	83.7	543.6	97.1	103.1	113.1	147.6
Texas	9,045.9	1,364.9	442.7	2,587.5	215.1	916.2	940.2	1,036.6
Utah	922.2	93.3	80.3	189.1	5.1	37.7	47.9	215.7
Vermont	155.5	10.3	10.6	73.8	0.8	14.9	1.9	12.8
Virginia	2,122.7	257.9	141.0	841.8	85.8	224.1	114.4	23.9
Washington	2,593.6	338.4	137.3	687.8	50.4	317.1	74.7	432.5
West Virginia	524.0	83.0	17.3	289.6	9.4	26.6	14.1	2.7
Wisconsin	1,488.9	117.0	115.3	560.0	22.7	242.5	48.2	66.2
Wyoming	426.5	72.5	15.7	195.0	26.9	14.0	25.5	8.4
District of Columbia	551.1	53.1	4.9	82.6	1.8	24.8	28.2	210.1

[a] Includes amounts for categories not shown.
[b] Electric, gas supply, and transit systems.
Source: Department of Commerce, Bureau of the Census.

D43. Public Assistance Payments by Type of Program[a]

All Governments
Calendar Years 1936-1987[b]
($Millions)

Year	Total Money and Medical Payments	Money Payments[c] Total Money Payments	Old-Age Assistance[e]	Aid to the Blind[e]	Aid to the Permanently and Totally Disabled[e,f]	Aid to Families with Dependent Children	General Assistance	Medical Vendor Payments[d]
1936	$ 655.1	$ 655.1	$ 155.5	$ 12.8	-	$ 49.7	$ 437.1	-
1937	802.9	802.9	309.6	16.2	-	70.5	406.7	-
1938	987.0	987.0	394.9	19.0	-	97.6	475.6	-
1939	1,050.8	1,050.8	433.5	20.4	-	114.8	482.1	-
1940	1,020.1	1,020.1	475.7	21.8	-	133.8	392.2	-
1941	989.4	989.4	540.1	22.9	-	153.3	273.2	-
1942	956.8	956.8	593.4	24.6	-	158.4	180.4	-
1943	926.3	926.3	650.0	25.0	-	140.4	110.9	-
1944	940.4	940.4	690.7	25.3	-	135.1	89.3	-
1945	987.9	987.9	726.6	26.6	-	149.6	86.3	-
1946	1,179.3	1,179.3	819.8	30.7	-	208.4	120.4	-
1947	1,480.8	1,480.8	986.4	36.2	-	294.0	164.2	-
1948	1,730.7	1,730.7	1,128.2	41.3	-	362.8	198.5	-
1949	2,175.0	2,175.0	1,372.9	48.4	-	472.4	281.3	-
1950	2,354.5	2,354.5	1,461.6	52.7	$ 8.0	551.7	292.8	-
1951	2,382.8	2,279.6	1,427.6	54.5	54.3	548.8	194.5	$ 103.2
1952	2,451.0	2,311.5	1,462.9	59.5	81.5	538.0	169.5	139.5
1953	2,539.9	2,374.2	1,513.3	63.6	102.0	544.0	151.3	165.7
1954	2,642.7	2,451.8	1,497.6	65.2	119.8	573.1	196.0	190.9
1955	2,748.1	2,516.6	1,490.4	68.0	135.2	617.8	214.0	231.5
1956	2,853.1	2,584.2	1,529.0	72.9	150.1	634.9	197.2	268.9
1957	3,090.3	2,788.2	1,609.4	78.7	172.2	716.8	211.1	302.1
1958	3,426.5	3,068.7	1,647.4	81.5	196.6	839.9	303.3	357.8
1959	3,657.7	3,200.8	1,620.7	83.6	217.3	937.2	342.0	456.9
1960	3,798.9	3,276.7	1,629.5	86.2	237.4	1,000.8	322.5	522.2
1961	4,115.2	3,426.9	1,571.3	84.7	256.9	1,156.8	356.0	688.3
1962	4,456.1	3,531.1	1,571.2	84.0	282.7	1,298.8	292.7	925.0
1963	4,731.3	3,666.6	1,615.0	85.3	318.9	1,365.9	279.6	1,064.7
1964	5,097.9	3,842.8	1,613.0	86.6	357.9	1,510.4	272.7	1,255.1
1965	6,134.9	4,022.9	1,600.7	85.1	417.7	1,660.2	259.2	2,112.0
1966	7,066.9	4,334.4	1,633.7	85.6	487.3	1,863.9	263.9	2,732.5
1967	8,591.8	4,956.6	1,702.1	87.7	574.6	2,266.4	325.8	3,635.2
1968	10,311.4	5,694.6	1,676.6	88.9	658.6	2,849.3	421.2	4,616.8
1969	12,168.8	6,668.8	1,752.7	92.2	788.1	3,563.4	472.4	5,500.0
1970	14,752.7	8,431.9	1,862.4	98.3	999.9	4,853.0	618.3	6,320.8
1971	18,198.5	10,143.4	1,888.9	100.8	1,189.6	6,203.5	760.6	8,055.1
1972	20,141.7	11,022.6	1,876.8	105.5	1,390.5	6,909.3	740.5	9,119.1
1973	21,707.0	11,358.0	1,743.5	104.4	1,609.6	7,212.0	688.5	10,349.0
1974	21,367.2	8,749.7	4.7	.1	2.9	7,916.6	825.4	12,619.5
1975	25,454.9	10,356.9	4.6	.1	3.0	9,211.0	1,138.2	15,098.0
1976	28,228.4	11,376.4	4.8	.1	3.1	10,140.5	1,227.9	16,852.0
1977	30,707.8	11,849.8	4.9	.1	3.4	10,603.8	1,237.6	18,858.0
1978	33,062.8	11,944.8	5.1	.1	3.8	10,730.4	1,205.4	21,118.0
1979	36,658.3	12,318.3	9.4	.2	9.1	11,068.9	1,230.7	24,340.0
1980	42,062.2	13,935.2	8.9	.1	8.7	12,475.2	1,442.3	28,127.0
1981	45,256.1	13,001.1	9.4	.2	10.4	12,981.1	n.a.	32,255.0
1982	47,773.9	12,895.9	8.0	.1	9.9	12,877.9	n.a.	34,878.0
1983	51,533.0	13,856.0	7.9	.1	9.8	13,838.2	n.a.	37,677.0
1984	54,958.7	14,522.7	7.8	.1	10.1	14,504.7	n.a.	40,436.0
1985	59,714.7	15,213.9	7.6	.1	10.4	15,195.8	n.a.	44,501.0
1986	64,151.7	16,051.7	7.5	.1	11.0	16,033.1	n.a.	48,100.0
1987	70,585.8	16,390.8	7.4	.1	10.8	16,372.5	n.a.	54,195.0

[a] Does not include insurance programs; also excludes expenditures for administration, services, and training.

[b] Data include Guam beginning July 1959, Puerto Rico and Virgin Islands beginning October 1950, Alaska and Hawaii beginning 1943.

[c] Includes payments under programs not shown separately; emergency assistance payments beginning 1968; and, for 1968 through 1971, payments for institutional services in intermediate-care facilities.

[d] Includes payments under categorical programs and general assistance. Except for general assistance, these programs were initiated in October 1950. Also includes payments under medical assistance for the aged, initiated in October 1960 (terminated in 1969), and medical assistance, initiated in 1966. Beginning 1972, includes institutional services in intermediate-care facilities, previously included under money payments. Data for 1980 and thereafter are not strictly comparable to prior years.

[e] Superseded by supplemental security income program, beginning January 1974. Data for 1974 and thereafter are for Guam, Puerto Rico, and the Virgin Islands.

[f] Program initiated in October 1950.

Source: Department of Health and Human Services; Social Security Administration and Health Care Financing Administration.

D44. Benefit Payments Under Major Public Assistance Programs by Program and State

Selected Calendar Years 1970-1987[a]

($Millions)

State	Aid for Families with Dependent Children (AFDC)					Medical Assistance			
	1970	1975	1980	1985	1987	1975	1980	1985	1987
Total[b]	$ 4,853	$ 9,211	$ 12,475	$ 15,196	$ 16,373	$ 12,292	$ 23,311	$ 37,522	$ 45,098
Alabama	26	59	84	70	64	131	263	375	366
Alaska	6	13	27	42	51	9	28	66	77
Arizona	22	32	40	65	95	-	-	-	-
Arkansas	15	50	51	43	50	93	235	358	410
California	853	1,349	2,328	3,427	3,916	1,491	2,728	4,045	4,816
Colorado	44	75	81	100	119	98	182	316	409
Connecticut	68	130	209	223	220	161	350	595	749
Delaware	9	22	32	26	24	15	45	71	90
Florida	64	118	203	249	300	173	392	943	1,178
Georgia	78	136	138	200	245	256	462	760	901
Hawaii	21	60	91	77	68	37	109	140	139
Idaho	11	18	24	19	20	24	52	76	89
Illinois	275	773	722	881	860	682	1,192	1,653	1,745
Indiana	40	105	139	153	153	172	354	747	924
Iowa	43	95	144	160	164	82	230	360	422
Kansas	38	61	87	86	96	102	197	256	282
Kentucky	49	119	136	138	137	100	296	540	606
Louisiana	55	98	124	156	176	143	415	725	824
Maine	22	48	60	81	82	60	131	232	303
Maryland	74	144	214	244	249	187	322	584	765
Massachusetts	212	415	510	426	526	494	1,009	1,433	1,844
Michigan	206	655	1,063	1,194	1,213	623	1,072	1,517	1,823
Minnesota	74	134	207	309	333	255	590	1,001	1,097
Mississippi	18	32	61	64	82	94	211	274	363
Missouri	57	130	182	198	213	99	295	525	619
Montana	8	13	19	33	41	29	62	96	122
Nebraska	16	27	42	59	59	54	109	167	215
Nevada	5	9	11	13	17	16	45	66	86
New Hampshire	8	24	27	20	19	28	72	118	142
New Jersey	265	437	560	499	479	366	756	1,145	1,565
New Mexico	22	32	42	51	57	29	70	148	183
New York	947	1,448	1,623	2,029	2,088	2,955	4,543	7,588	8,841
North Carolina	50	121	155	167	193	163	401	647	825
North Dakota	8	12	16	19	21	23	47	117	165
Ohio	152	405	561	773	812	366	809	1,767	2,377
Oklahoma	45	67	92	91	114	141	265	460	502
Oregon	50	97	147	111	121	74	179	239	254
Pennsylvania	361	610	771	751	742	709	1,058	1,797	2,077
Rhode Island	29	47	72	75	81	72	160	250	296
South Carolina	15	46	72	95	100	76	258	309	422
South Dakota	11	20	19	18	21	22	55	94	116
Tennessee	53	85	85	92	119	123	380	578	811
Texas	92	146	134	241	328	461	981	1,414	1,767
Utah	20	34	48	52	61	31	80	110	152
Vermont	9	21	32	38	41	31	59	89	103
Virginia	55	135	160	173	172	160	359	547	662
Washington	91	138	251	340	399	176	329	584	759
West Virginia	34	44	60	94	109	29	104	173	244
Wisconsin	61	193	353	568	554	361	687	942	1,004
Wyoming	3	5	9	14	18	5	14	28	45
District of Columbia	32	92	92	76	77	94	168	312	358

[a] Data for 1985 are preliminary.
[b] Includes amounts for Puerto Rico, Guam, and Virgin Islands not shown separately.
Source: Department of Health and Human Services.

D45. Revenue, Expenditures, and Debt on Public Highways and Toll Roads

Selected Calendar Years 1954-1987[a]

(\$Millions)

Item	1954	1959	1965	1987
A. Current Revenue Collections				
Total current revenue	\$ 5,565	\$ 9,168	\$ 13,368	\$ 61,757
Federal government	700	2,428	6,079	14,466
Highway user taxes	-	2,245	3,779	11,980
All other	700	183	300	2,486
State agencies and D.C.	3,518	5,007	7,037	30,861
Highway user taxes	3,244	4,428	6,076	24,335
Tolls	167	396	607	2,261
All other	107	183	354	4,265
Counties and townships	584	743	898	6,480
Property taxes and assessments	420	512	571	2,350
General revenue and all other	150	211	308	4,065
Tolls	14	20	19	65
Municipalities	763	990	354	9,950
Property taxes and assessments	222	389	528	1,600
General revenue and all other	498	547	749	7,750
Tolls	43	54	77	600
B. Expenditures by Road Systems				
Total expenditures	6,580	10,277	13,456	63,579
Capital outlay	4,110	6,657	8,368	31,063
State highways	3,020	5,162	6,293	21,222
Toll facilities only	n.a.	n.a.	214	n.a.
Local roads and streets	1,015	1,392	1,677	9,370
Toll facilities only	n.a.	n.a.	15	n.a.
Not classified by systems[b]	75	103	169	471
Maintenance	1,804	2,481	3,289	18,993
State highways	659	914	1,328	7,179
Local roads and streets	1,138	1,542	1,943	11,663
Not classified by systems[b]	7	25	18	151
Administrative, research, and public safety	437	760	1,275	10,807
Interest on debt	229	379	524	2,716
C. Long-term Obligations Issued, Redeemed, and Outstanding				
Obligations issued[c]	2,684	1,158	1,070	4,427
State	2,317	669	586	1,927
County and other local rural units	94	153	169	900
Municipal	273	336	315	1,600
Obligations redeemed[c]	433	610	855	2,806
State	168	308	459	1,625
County and other local rural units	109	92	123	423
Municipal	156	210	273	758
Obligations outstanding, end of year	8,905	12,576	15,316	37,069
State	6,164	9,004	10,905	22,363
County and other local rural units	911	1,186	1,363	5,629
Municipal	1,830	2,386	3,048	9,077

[a] Data prior to 1985 are not strictly comparable. Federal and state data are for calendar years; local data are for varying fiscal years.
[b] In 1954, includes data for Alaska, Hawaii, and Puerto Rico; thereafter, Puerto Rico only.
[c] Refunding issues and redemptions by refunding are excluded.
Source: Department of Transportation, Federal Highway Administration.

D46. Full-Time Employment of State and Local Governments Per 10,000 Population by Function and State

October 1987

State	All Functions[a]	Higher Education	Elementary and Secondary School Education	Hospitals	Highways	Police Protection	Fire Protection	Correction
Total	496.6	56.1	185.3	42.3	22.1	27.2	10.2	16.5
Alabama	499.2	63.0	178.9	63.5	26.6	22.7	9.9	12.3
Alaska	757.5	70.1	251.2	10.1	66.3	28.7	10.3	20.7
Arizona	481.0	63.4	190.4	12.3	13.4	28.6	8.8	23.7
Arkansas	464.5	49.9	190.3	43.2	30.0	22.4	7.2	10.5
California	463.1	55.1	156.4	35.5	12.9	28.0	12.1	19.9
Colorado	537.3	82.2	195.8	42.7	23.7	27.0	9.4	12.8
Connecticut	478.7	43.0	186.3	40.4	25.1	28.9	13.0	12.6
Delaware	540.5	95.7	176.7	26.4	28.2	26.6	4.2	22.5
Florida	454.3	40.4	165.1	37.0	18.6	31.6	11.9	19.7
Georgia	552.1	46.2	202.3	93.9	21.6	26.1	11.4	17.8
Hawaii	504.7	59.4	166.4	24.8	17.2	27.1	13.7	12.6
Idaho	519.0	87.1	197.4	41.1	31.1	24.9	6.5	9.2
Illinois	446.8	54.9	161.0	27.1	17.2	33.0	11.1	13.3
Indiana	469.7	65.2	187.5	48.3	20.4	21.7	9.4	11.8
Iowa	539.6	94.8	205.7	58.5	30.8	20.1	5.9	8.9
Kansas	555.6	82.5	212.6	45.3	35.1	25.4	9.2	12.3
Kentucky	454.6	50.9	192.8	26.5	25.8	19.6	6.9	12.0
Louisiana	529.8	54.4	198.2	66.1	25.0	26.8	9.2	19.8
Maine	492.2	45.8	218.2	24.2	36.8	22.5	9.3	11.7
Maryland	498.4	60.9	172.5	19.4	23.6	29.3	12.3	21.8
Massachusetts	492.9	38.6	183.0	50.1	19.2	29.7	21.4	13.3
Michigan	485.1	69.2	195.9	40.4	15.9	25.7	7.7	16.8
Minnesota	481.2	76.4	160.2	41.4	28.8	19.7	5.2	9.7
Mississippi	542.0	69.0	209.3	82.9	29.2	21.1	8.2	10.8
Missouri	445.9	39.1	177.3	43.6	22.8	26.8	10.0	13.2
Montana	544.0	77.2	208.1	24.1	39.1	23.6	5.8	12.5
Nebraska	607.2	87.4	206.3	55.9	36.0	23.5	6.9	11.5
Nevada	500.4	53.8	172.3	32.3	21.3	37.9	14.1	20.3
New Hampshire	437.3	50.7	176.0	13.0	32.7	24.8	11.9	10.1
New Jersey	499.6	38.7	197.0	34.6	25.1	39.1	9.5	19.7
New Mexico	591.6	94.3	210.4	44.2	32.0	28.4	8.0	21.6
New York	628.2	35.8	202.6	75.0	27.4	37.5	12.1	26.4
North Carolina	504.0	73.1	195.4	40.9	22.4	23.5	7.2	16.1
North Dakota	548.4	93.6	191.8	35.3	35.0	19.9	4.4	6.4
Ohio	459.5	53.7	177.7	32.3	19.8	23.3	9.8	11.8
Oklahoma	524.8	67.5	195.9	46.0	29.0	25.9	10.9	13.4
Oregon	520.3	84.4	188.6	29.5	26.3	22.4	11.8	14.1
Pennsylvania	395.4	29.7	165.2	22.5	20.6	24.2	5.4	11.4
Rhode Island	450.8	54.7	153.9	27.6	19.7	27.8	19.5	11.6
South Carolina	527.2	67.0	201.2	66.4	20.0	23.2	6.6	20.2
South Dakota	521.3	55.3	214.3	29.2	40.3	21.5	5.2	11.4
Tennessee	479.4	54.0	170.5	52.2	23.8	22.7	11.0	16.2
Texas	499.9	57.0	223.2	40.6	19.9	24.4	9.9	17.1
Utah	480.2	95.3	187.1	26.3	17.9	21.8	7.0	9.2
Vermont	496.0	69.4	206.9	14.5	38.0	21.5	4.9	11.4
Virginia	515.6	61.3	206.6	37.2	24.4	23.8	10.2	21.7
Washington	514.9	78.4	165.4	30.8	24.7	22.3	11.7	16.7
West Virginia	500.9	53.5	230.0	35.6	34.7	17.1	4.6	7.3
Wisconsin	488.1	82.0	172.6	31.3	23.8	26.8	8.6	10.8
Wyoming	714.4	93.9	280.2	72.6	47.2	32.5	7.0	14.6
District of Columbia	896.6	22.9	187.0	85.6	16.9	74.1	28.3	59.6

[a] Includes functions not shown separately.
Source: Department of Commerce, Bureau of the Census.

D47. State and Local Payroll, Employment, and Average Earnings by State

October 1987

State	Monthly Payroll ($millions)	Number (thousands)	Full-time Employment Per 10,000 Population[a]			Average Monthly Earnings[b]		
			Total	State	Local	Total	State	Local
Total	$ 24,457.9	12,086.4	497	143	353	$ 2,023.6	$ 2,090.2	$ 1,996.6
Alabama	334.6	203.7	499	172	327	1,642.6	1,883.8	1,515.8
Alaska	126.3	39.4	750	382	268	3,205.5	3,193.3	3,218.2
Arizona	368.0	162.6	480	114	366	2,263.7	2,764.5	2,107.3
Arkansas	162.5	110.6	463	162	301	1,470.0	1,669.7	1,362.4
California	3,331.5	1,281.1	463	105	358	2,600.6	2,791.1	2,545.0
Colorado	364.3	176.8	536	156	380	2,060.6	2,350.8	1,941.1
Connecticut	342.2	153.7	479	181	297	2,226.9	2,307.7	3,225.3
Delaware	67.4	34.6	537	287	250	1,948.3	1,842.6	2,069.9
Florida	1,052.0	546.1	454	105	349	1,926.5	1,852.1	1,948.8
Georgia	571.4	343.4	552	153	399	1,663.9	1,875.6	1,582.5
Hawaii	103.9	54.5	503	390	114	1,906.0	1,847.6	2,105.9
Idaho	80.7	51.4	515	182	333	1,570.9	1,647.2	1,529.3
Illinois	1,104.9	517.4	447	112	334	2,135.4	2,105.8	2,145.3
Indiana	460.7	259.7	470	138	332	1,773.7	2,006.0	1,677.7
Iowa	276.7	152.7	539	182	357	1,811.9	2,080.3	1,674.9
Kansas	229.4	137.2	554	173	381	1,672.0	1,617.0	1,697.0
Kentucky	270.1	169.1	454	173	281	1,597.3	1,658.5	1,559.6
Louisiana	364.3	236.3	530	191	339	1,541.6	1,674.7	1,466.8
Maine	97.1	58.1	489	178	312	1,672.4	1,801.7	1,598.7
Maryland	503.2	225.8	498	176	322	2,229.0	2,163.4	2,264.8
Massachusetts	610.1	288.3	492	158	334	2,116.1	2,189.2	2,081.5
Michigan	1,012.4	446.3	485	140	345	2,268.5	2,378.0	2,224.0
Minnesota	466.1	204.0	481	150	330	2,284.2	2,278.2	2,286.9
Mississippi	193.7	142.0	541	169	372	1,364.1	1,488.9	1,348.9
Missouri	389.5	227.4	446	130	315	1,712.7	1,621.3	1,750.4
Montana	75.8	43.5	538	198	339	1,742.9	1,915.0	1,642.3
Nebraska	159.5	96.5	606	186	419	1,652.3	1,513.2	1,714.2

Continued

D47. State and Local Payroll, Employment, and Average Earnings by State (continued)

October 1987

State	Monthly Payroll ($millions)	Number (thousands)	Full-time Employment Per 10,000 Population[a]			Average Monthly Earnings[b]		
			Total	State	Local	Total	State	Local
Nevada	105.0	50.0	497	152	345	2,099.0	2,044.1	2,123.1
New Hampshire	80.2	45.9	434	149	286	1,745.8	1,814.3	1,710.0
New Jersey	857.0	383.2	499	129	370	2,236.5	2,405.5	2,177.7
New Mexico	147.5	88.7	592	235	357	1,661.9	1,753.5	1,601.5
New York	2,645.9	1,119.5	628	154	474	2,363.3	2,485.5	2,323.6
North Carolina	580.7	323.1	504	156	348	1,797.2	1,975.0	1,717.8
North Dakota	63.3	36.7	547	227	320	1,724.0	1,756.1	1,701.2
Ohio	976.0	495.3	459	116	343	1,970.5	2,062.7	1,939.2
Oklahoma	274.8	171.6	524	197	328	1,601.2	1,680.6	1,553.6
Oregon	275.1	141.5	520	180	340	1,943.5	1,855.7	1,989.9
Pennsylvania	916.9	471.7	395	105	290	1,943.9	1,942.9	1,944.2
Rhode Island	96.3	44.2	448	201	247	2,180.3	2,116.7	2,232.1
South Carolina	290.6	180.3	526	204	323	1,611.8	1,713.0	1,547.9
South Dakota	57.3	36.5	515	186	329	1,570.8	1,798.9	1,442.1
Tennessee	383.2	232.5	479	146	333	1,647.8	1,768.3	1,595.0
Texas	1,501.5	838.9	500	118	381	1,789.9	1,995.6	1,726.1
Utah	141.9	80.7	480	191	289	1,759.5	1,724.6	1,782.6
Vermont	46.7	26.8	489	215	274	1,743.4	1,921.4	1,603.7
Virginia	569.1	304.2	515	176	339	1,870.5	1,936.5	1,836.3
Washington	491.0	233.2	514	186	328	2,105.0	2,113.1	2,100.4
West Virginia	151.1	94.7	499	177	322	1,595.7	1,609.8	1,587.8
Wisconsin	475.6	234.2	487	132	355	2,029.9	2,188.5	1,970.9
Wyoming	64.7	35.0	714	213	501	1,848.1	1,828.6	1,856.5
District of Columbia	148.3	55.6	888	-	888	2,667.6	-	2,667.6

[a] Population as of July 1, 1987.
[b] Per full-time equivalent employee.
Source: Department of Commerce; Bureau of the Census. Computations by Tax Foundation.

D48. Selected Factors Affecting State and Local Finances

State	Population[a] Total July 1, 1987 (Thousands)	Population[a] Percent Urban in 1980	Retail Sales Calendar 1987[b] ($Millions)	Personal Income Calendar 1988 ($Millions)	Assessed Valuation of Property 1986[c] ($Millions)	Motor Vehicle Registration Calendar 1987[d] (Thousands)
Total	243,400	74%	$ 1,544,897	$ 4,042,110	$ 4,817,779	179,044
Alabama	4,083	60	20,161	52,019	14,367	3,547
Alaska	525	64	4,227	10,014	46,423	357
Arizona	3,386	84	20,435	51,592	17,651	2,417
Arkansas	2,388	52	12,130	29,478	12,251	1,445
California	27,663	91	186,413	531,100	1,059,122	20,294
Colorado	3,296	81	22,021	54,004	19,216	3,033
Connecticut	3,211	79	26,310	73,772	78,302	2,612
Delaware	644	71	4,652	11,682	12,969	491
Florida	12,023	84	85,791	204,792	386,981	10,684
Georgia	6,222	62	39,656	95,887	76,380	5,026
Hawaii	1,083	87	7,393	18,466	50,517	690
Idaho	998	54	5,253	12,644	29,551	947
Illinois	11,582	83	71,233	203,305	90,679	7,662
Indiana	5,531	64	34,272	82,076	28,833	3,708
Iowa	2,834	59	16,425	41,844	74,386	2,699
Kansas	2,476	67	14,357	39,561	11,090	2,188
Kentucky	3,727	51	20,622	47,603	79,337	2,720
Louisiana	4,461	69	25,161	53,891	15,088	2,891
Maine	1,187	48	8,943	18,065	28,642	928
Maryland	4,535	80	32,241	89,692	65,524	3,309
Massachusetts	5,855	84	46,908	121,538	237,511	3,887
Michigan	9,200	71	57,406	152,400	106,244	6,945
Minnesota	4,246	67	28,903	72,285	29,446	3,172
Mississippi	2,625	47	12,445	28,875	8,122	1,761
Missouri	5,103	68	31,999	79,605	31,951	3,712
Montana	809	53	4,654	10,186	2,306	650
Nebraska	1,594	63	9,473	24,305	44,121	1,305
Nevada	1,007	85	8,028	18,479	13,892	812
New Hampshire	1,057	52	9,725	20,860	27,760	874
New Jersey	7,672	89	54,834	168,923	188,260	5,520
New Mexico	1,500	72	8,561	18,842	11,836	1,285
New York	17,825	85	108,682	345,425	163,942	9,593
North Carolina	6,413	48	37,613	92,199	193,999	4,870
North Dakota	672	49	4,337	8,430	986	650
Ohio	10,784	73	65,173	168,344	101,702	8,521
Oklahoma	3,272	67	19,273	43,292	11,051	2,887
Oregon	2,724	68	16,183	41,068	83,199	2,243
Pennsylvania	11,936	69	72,730	194,459	46,993	7,642
Rhode Island	986	87	6,751	16,709	20,989	654
South Carolina	3,425	54	19,006	44,586	5,496	2,366
South Dakota	709	46	4,106	8,917	6,906	674
Tennessee	4,855	60	28,652	67,183	29,293	4,027
Texas	16,789	80	106,553	245,663	678,953	12,298
Utah	1,680	84	8,183	20,315	47,645	1,114
Vermont	548	34	4,344	8,546	169	443
Virginia	5,904	66	40,131	105,774	199,104	4,628
Washington	4,538	74	27,613	76,538	159,789	3,828
West Virginia	1,897	36	10,247	21,960	19,709	1,194
Wisconsin	4,807	64	27,467	75,028	110,648	3,096
Wyoming	490	63	3,809	6,455	7,900	478
District of Columbia	622	100	3,403	13,431	30,548	268

[a] Estimates, Bureau of the Census; excludes armed forces overseas.
[b] Estimated by Sales & Marketing Management, Inc.
[c] Assessed value subject to tax, after deduction of exemptions.
[d] Includes private, commercial, and publicly-owned vehicles.

Continued

D48. Selected Factors Affecting State and Local Finances (continued)

Mileage in State and Local Systems[e] Calendar 1987	Public Elementary and Secondary School Enrollment Fall 1988 (Thousands)	Higher Education Enrollment Fall 1987		Medicaid Recipients[g] Fiscal Year 1987	Percent of Persons Below Poverty Level[h] April 1980	Recipients of Aid to Dependent Children[g] December 1988	State
		Total, Public and Private[f] (Thousands)	Percent Public				
3,874,026	40,196	12,768	78.1%	23,108,760	12.4%	10,881,514	Total
88,166	730	184	88.0	289,285	18.9	132,467	Alabama
12,082	104	27	96.3	27,997	10.7	19,195	Alaska
77,723	578	237	96.6	i	13.2	90,742	Arizona
77,087	456	79	86.1	211,768	19.0	67,199	Arkansas
158,932	4,611	1,788	88.4	3,689,420	11.4	1,708,375	California
76,730	560	184	88.0	189,025	10.1	94,072	Colorado
19,721	463	162	63.6	217,249	8.0	106,689	Connecticut
5,341	96	37	81.1	37,344	11.9	20,177	Delaware
100,423	1,729	490	82.7	639,858	13.5	307,187	Florida
106,767	1,111	224	77.7	505,906	16.6	243,811	Georgia
4,070	167	52	82.7	88,149	9.9	41,184	Hawaii
71,639	215	46	76.1	39,984	12.6	17,501	Idaho
135,310	1,788	687	75.8	1,042,249	11.0	681,000	Illinois
91,535	964	256	78.5	300,625	9.7	150,281	Indiana
112,472	477	158	70.9	232,244	10.1	103,535	Iowa
132,931	426	146	91.1	172,034	10.1	67,358	Kansas
69,629	638	153	79.7	410,680	17.6	154,636	Kentucky
58,272	791	173	86.1	464,185	18.6	271,017	Louisiana
21,964	211	48	72.9	122,875	13.0	51,818	Maine
27,965	689	239	85.4	311,626	9.8	175,832	Maryland
33,807	826	424	44.1	541,470	9.6	233,764	Massachusetts
117,803	1,590	536	85.6	1,125,047	10.4	642,185	Michigan
132,843	724	237	78.5	336,823	9.5	161,297	Minnesota
72,065	503	106	87.7	341,650	23.9	176,246	Mississippi
119,682	807	252	67.9	368,851	12.2	199,986	Missouri
71,811	152	36	88.9	58,143	12.3	28,913	Montana
92,401	269	101	84.2	107,126	10.7	42,720	Nebraska
44,754	177	48	100.0	34,196	8.7	17,067	Nevada
14,611	166	56	55.4	33,341	8.5	10,731	New Hampshire
34,041	1,081	294	79.9	545,876	9.5	320,491	New Jersey
53,749	281	83	97.6	97,391	17.6	59,952	New Mexico
110,321	2,580	993	57.1	2,308,198	13.4	1,018,510	New York
93,234	1,081	321	80.7	386,499	14.8	171,383	North Carolina
86,243	118	37	91.9	42,250	12.6	14,593	North Dakota
112,154	1,782	519	75.5	1,131,736	10.3	648,312	Ohio
111,082	585	173	86.1	270,643	13.4	100,651	Oklahoma
93,915	462	153	87.6	167,757	10.7	81,005	Oregon
115,908	1,655	554	56.1	1,101,734	10.5	538,585	Pennsylvania
5,852	134	72	50.0	98,820	10.3	41,862	Rhode Island
63,420	616	141	80.1	266,956	16.6	121,688	South Carolina
73,469	127	32	75.0	39,674	16.9	18,465	South Dakota
83,691	820	202	76.2	443,392	16.5	181,061	Tennessee
293,530	3,269	802	88.5	985,818	14.7	500,382	Texas
49,901	426	107	69.2	81,673	10.3	44,366	Utah
14,071	96	33	57.6	50,096	12.1	20,331	Vermont
66,125	988	319	86.5	318,364	11.8	144,904	Virginia
79,509	791	246	87.0	391,634	9.8	208,422	Washington
35,173	336	77	88.3	214,706	15.0	110,931	West Virginia
108,925	775	282	85.5	410,637	8.7	270,742	Wisconsin
40,075	98	26	96.2	22,239	7.9	13,100	Wyoming
1,102	89	78	14.1	96,635	18.6	50,244	Dist. of Columbia

[e] Includes mileage in Federal parks, forests, and reservations that are not part of the highway system.

[f] Total includes 60,136 students in U.S. service schools not listed under states.

[g] Medicaid total includes 1,696,882 recipients in Puerto Rico and the Virgin Islands. Total for AFDC includes 184,549 recipients in Guam, Puerto Rico, and the Virgin Islands.

[h] Level based on property index developed by the Social Security Administration in 1964 and subsequently revised by other agencies; nonmoney income is not considered in calculating the poverty threshold.

[i] Arizona has no Medicaid program.

Source: Department of Commerce; Department of Education; Department of Transportation; Department of Health and Human Services; and Sales & Marketing Management, Inc. - Copyright 1988, Sales & Marketing Management's Survey of Buying Power, August 15, 1988, further reproduction is forbidden.

D49. Finances of State-Administered Public Employee Retirement Systems, by Year[a]

Fiscal Years 1950-1987

($Millions)

			Receipts				
		Employee	Government Contributions		Earnings	Benefits	Cash and
	Total	Contribu-	State	Local	on Invest-	and With-	Security
Year	Receipts	tions	Government	Government	ments	drawals	Holdings[b]
1950	$ 609	$ 260	$ 180	$ 98	$ 70	$ 166	$ 2,871
1951	724	311	211	118	84	209	3,441
1952	842	350	263	123	106	256	4,013
1953	917	399	282	116	120	302	4,638
1954	1,109	449	352	166	142	364	5,371
1955	1,172	493	335	177	166	383	6,159
1956	1,316	542	397	185	193	446	7,081
1957	1,504	607	441	231	225	522	8,050
1958	1,755	712	531	253	259	603	9,249
1959	1,883	752	507	300	324	647	10,499
1960	2,217	802	659	358	398	716	12,127
1961	2,480	857	736	406	482	808	13,798
1962	2,697	943	753	443	558	949	15,547
1963	2,998	1,005	862	489	642	1,012	17,465
1964	3,279	1,093	910	541	734	1,125	19,726
1965	3,632	1,208	994	582	849	1,238	22,093
1966	4,026	1,345	1,108	604	969	1,398	24,670
1967	4,656	1,494	1,304	747	1,110	1,606	27,661
1968	5,445	1,672	1,614	878	1,281	1,810	31,102
1969	6,242	1,895	1,733	1,060	1,555	2,088	35,233
1970	7,184	2,149	1,979	1,237	1,820	2,376	39,997
1971	8,196	2,413	2,215	1,381	2,188	2,705	45,288
1972	9,268	2,624	2,442	1,599	2,604	3,175	50,759
1973	11,174	3,338	2,907	1,830	3,099	3,942	58,529
1974	12,199	3,315	3,281	2,193	3,410	4,591	66,155
1975	14,157	3,501	3,974	2,623	4,059	5,160	74,703
1976	16,599	3,915	4,428	3,336	4,920	6,045	85,811
1977	19,287	4,223	4,847	4,051	6,167	6,930	94,913
1978	21,767	4,619	5,741	4,538	6,868	7,811	110,357
1979	24,659	4,968	6,318	5,173	8,200	8,937	125,803
1980	28,545	5,285	7,399	5,611	10,250	10,257	144,682
1981	33,451	6,001	8,328	6,405	12,716	11,419	164,864
1982	37,944	6,674	8,898	6,879	15,492	13,134	193,295
1983	45,127	7,196	9,611	7,585	20,734	14,204	223,262
1984	48,724	7,306	10,458	8,063	22,897	16,492	256,583
1985	56,313	7,913	11,976	8,944	27,480	17,987	296,692
1986	68,982	8,939	12,162	9,531	38,350	19,878	347,361
1987	77,706	9,428	13,199	10,059	45,021	22,189	407,953

[a] Excludes amounts for purchase and liquidation of assets.
[b] End of fiscal years. In 1987, includes other investments such as real property.
Source: Department of Commerce, Bureau of the Census.

D50. Finances of State-Administered Public Employee Retirement Systems, by State[a]

Fiscal Year 1987

($Thousands)

State	Total Receipts	Employee Contri-butions	Receipts — Government Contributions — State Government	Receipts — Government Contributions — Local Government	Earnings on Investments	Benefits and Withdrawals	Cash and Security Holdings
Total	$ 77,706,305	$ 9,427,514	$ 13,198,606	$ 10,058,969	$ 45,021,216	$ 22,188,796	$ 407,953,034
Alabama	1,007,387	156,363	251,341	992	598,691	254,049	5,462,307
Alaska	629,799	86,038	94,584	71,185	377,992	133,289	3,061,367
Arizona	1,137,459	161,921	53,913	111,211	810,414	217,801	5,622,627
Arkansas	603,646	40,896	105,617	19,028	438,105	109,664	2,936,091
California	11,137,385	1,662,309	1,577,607	1,747,593	6,149,876	3,180,498	62,962,618
Colorado	1,490,893	202,798	127,048	229,999	931,048	290,993	6,734,594
Connecticut	991,768	110,346	533,341	17,052	331,029	338,652	4,365,381
Delaware	280,959	15,465	77,442	-	188,052	54,652	1,221,712
Florida	2,765,393	10,736	306,738	882,993	1,564,926	532,209	11,979,640
Georgia	1,713,306	215,888	448,107	113,560	935,751	395,517	8,285,755
Hawaii	578,692	53,834	145,986	47,050	331,822	175,568	2,672,949
Idaho	278,676	43,833	26,150	50,793	157,900	80,943	1,137,599
Illinois	2,862,577	511,336	456,823	156,604	1,737,814	891,220	13,542,920
Indiana	830,973	115,113	219,213	90,640	406,007	290,620	3,799,179
Iowa	576,495	77,985	122,464	2,026	374,020	156,316	3,495,967
Kansas	565,202	89,782	83,120	70,157	322,143	148,911	2,847,188
Kentucky	974,994	178,225	227,228	42,060	527,481	269,810	4,939,130
Louisiana	1,343,451	243,578	360,189	23,703	715,981	625,813	6,633,846
Maine	369,118	51,546	129,936	22,945	164,691	143,592	1,190,518
Maryland	1,422,227	106,023	695,411	37,258	583,535	441,588	6,139,061
Massachusetts	865,414	241,274	437,895	-	186,245	543,523	4,470,172
Michigan	3,009,323	117,137	560,859	223,944	2,107,383	1,004,412	14,966,059
Minnesota	1,542,508	200,804	195,815	98,982	1,046,907	365,748	8,209,810
Mississippi	639,754	111,776	67,997	102,259	357,722	197,696	3,579,241
Missouri	1,132,885	139,105	148,198	150,030	695,552	228,591	7,087,121
Montana	255,726	58,648	21,033	46,430	129,615	103,202	1,188,398
Nebraska	127,503	30,785	6,331	27,475	62,912	20,804	677,477
Nevada	487,314	14,032	37,899	126,875	308,508	92,414	2,165,136
New Hampshire	176,943	33,663	6,383	12,049	124,848	41,355	922,874
New Jersey	2,479,824	397,294	628,380	384,310	1,069,840	875,045	15,271,791
New Mexico	561,590	110,730	67,995	77,179	305,686	151,319	2,742,212
New York	7,346,954	222,259	586,025	1,492,172	5,046,498	2,062,802	48,044,521
North Carolina	2,139,459	342,658	433,595	223,470	1,139,736	532,272	11,503,226
North Dakota	121,576	22,938	10,293	16,106	72,239	25,749	564,330
Ohio	6,397,487	920,490	274,752	1,267,905	3,934,340	1,918,627	30,284,401
Oklahoma	845,999	121,240	281,940	28,583	414,236	334,144	3,756,344
Oregon	855,538	152,357	98,713	174,806	429,662	265,118	6,961,259
Pennsylvania	3,819,792	394,252	877,885	462,439	2,085,216	1,304,410	17,205,254
Rhode Island	290,671	57,070	66,698	40,499	126,404	106,251	1,366,931
South Carolina	928,330	172,207	111,425	128,001	516,697	250,836	7,343,858
South Dakota	189,077	27,861	11,235	15,940	134,041	33,268	972,326
Tennessee	1,176,872	78,700	342,341	29,168	726,663	251,052	5,591,057
Texas	4,030,127	811,638	912,418	86,221	2,219,850	1,140,462	20,406,477
Utah	387,888	80,813	23,108	65,236	218,731	98,619	2,491,786
Vermont	84,770	2,289	33,002	1,122	48,357	24,178	459,293
Virginia	1,700,924	52,758	236,524	376,248	1,035,394	306,298	6,446,739
Washington	1,469,768	276,241	419,631	130,076	643,820	547,281	10,083,574
West Virginia	289,022	81,577	35,241	17,373	154,831	165,101	1,337,899
Wisconsin	2,605,964	12,521	192,799	478,622	1,922,022	424,438	13,428,570
Wyoming	186,903	8,382	29,938	38,600	109,983	42,076	1,104,595

[a] Excluding amounts for purchase and liquidation of investments.
Source: Department of Commerce, Bureau of the Census.

Section E
State Governments

- Summary Data
- Expenditures
- Revenue and Taxation
- Debt

E1. State Expenditures, Revenue, and Debt

Selected Fiscal Years 1902-1987

($Millions)

Year	Expenditures Total	Expenditures Direct	Payments to Other Governments[a]	Revenue Total	From Own Sources	Intergovern-mental[b]	Gross Debt
1902	$ 188	$ 136	$ 52	$ 192	$ 183	$ 9	$230
1913	388	297	91	376	360	16	379
1922	1,397	1,085	312	1,360	1,234	126	1,131
1927	2,047	1,451	596	2,152	1,994	158	1,971
1932	2,829	2,028	801	2,541	2,274	267	2,832
1934	3,461	2,143	1,318	3,421	2,452	969	3,248
1936	3,862	2,445	1,417	4,023	3,265	758	3,413
1938	4,598	3,082	1,516	5,293	4,612	681	3,343
1940	5,209	3,555	1,654	5,737	5,012	725	3,590
1942	5,343	3,563	1,780	6,870	6,012	858	3,257
1944	5,161	3,319	1,842	7,695	6,714	981	2,776
1946	7,066	4,974	2,092	8,576	7,712	865	2,353
1948	11,181	7,897	3,283	11,826	10,086	1,740	3,676
1950	15,082	10,864	4,217	13,903	11,480	2,423	5,285
1952	15,834	10,790	5,044	16,815	14,330	2,485	6,874
1954	18,686	13,008	5,679	18,834	15,951	2,883	9,600
1956	21,686	15,148	6,538	22,199	18,903	3,296	12,890
1957	24,235	16,796	7,440	24,656	20,728	3,927	13,738
1958	28,080	19,991	8,089	26,191	21,427	4,764	15,394
1959	31,125	22,436	8,689	29,164	22,912	6,252	16,930
1960	31,596	22,152	9,443	32,838	26,094	6,745	18,543
1961	34,693	24,578	10,114	34,603	27,821	6,782	19,993
1962	36,402	25,495	10,906	37,595	30,115	7,480	22,023
1963	39,583	27,698	11,885	40,993	32,750	8,243	23,176
1964	42,583	29,616	12,968	45,167	35,703	9,464	25,041
1965	45,639	31,465	14,174	48,827	38,507	10,320	27,034
1966	51,123	34,195	16,928	55,246	43,000	12,246	29,564
1967	58,760	39,704	19,056	61,082	46,793	14,289	32,472
1968	66,254	44,304	21,950	68,460	52,525	15,935	35,666
1969	74,227	49,448	24,779	77,584	59,809	17,775	39,555
1970	85,055	56,163	28,892	88,939	68,691	20,248	42,008
1971	98,840	66,200	32,640	97,233	73,424	23,809	47,793
1972	109,255	72,496	36,759	112,343	84,362	27,981	54,453
1973	118,836	78,014	40,822	129,808	97,108	32,700	59,375
1974	132,134	86,193	45,941	140,815	107,645	33,170	65,296
1975	158,882	106,905	51,978	157,033	119,206	37,827	72,127
1976	180,926	123,069	57,858	183,821	139,104	44,717	84,825
1977	191,225	128,765	62,460	204,426	155,799	48,627	91,640
1978	203,832	136,545	67,287	225,011	171,550	53,461	102,569
1979	224,666	148,691	75,975	247,059	189,972	57,087	111,740
1980	257,812	173,307	84,504	276,962	212,636	64,326	121,958
1981	291,527	198,348	93,180	310,828	240,042	70,786	134,847
1982	310,358	211,615	98,743	330,899	261,733	69,166	147,470
1983	334,019	233,132	100,887	357,661	284,933	72,728	167,290
1984	351,537	243,164	108,373	397,087	315,637	81,450	186,377
1985	390,828	269,257	121,571	438,954	349,032	89,922	211,904
1986	424,205	292,239	131,966	481,279	382,705	98,574	247,715
1987	455,752	314,326	141,426	517,019	414,638	102,381	265,677

[a] Principally shared taxes and fiscal aids. Beginning in 1974, includes state reimbursement to the Federal government, primarily for state share of the supplemental security income program. For state payments to local governments only, see Table E7.

[b] Principally grants-in-aid from the Federal government. Includes minor amounts from localities for shares of programs administered by the states, payments for services performed by the states, and repayment of advances.

Source: Department of Commerce, Bureau of the Census.

E2. State Revenue, Expenditures, and Surpluses or Deficits: Total and General Accounts

Selected Fiscal Years 1942-1987

($Millions)

Year	Total			General[a]		
	Revenue	Expenditures	Surplus or Deficit (-)	Revenue	Expenditures	Surplus or Deficit (-)
1942	$ 6,870	$ 5,343	$ 1,527	$ 5,132	$ 4,549	$ 583
1944	7,695	5,161	2,534	5,465	4,508	957
1946	8,576	7,066	1,510	6,284	5,245	1,039
1948	11,826	11,181	645	9,257	9,469	-212
1950	13,903	15,082	-1,179	11,262	12,250	-988
1952	16,815	15,834	981	13,429	13,697	-268
1954	18,834	18,686	148	15,299	15,788	-489
1956	22,199	21,686	513	18,389	18,857	-468
1957	24,656	24,235	421	20,382	21,086	-704
1958	26,191	28,080	-1,889	21,772	23,537	-1,765
1959	29,164	31,125	-1,961	24,448	26,006	-1,558
1960	32,838	31,596	1,242	27,363	27,228	135
1961	34,603	34,693	-90	28,693	29,118	-425
1962	37,595	36,402	1,193	31,157	31,281	-124
1963	40,993	39,583	1,410	33,882	34,377	-495
1964	45,167	42,583	2,584	37,648	37,292	356
1965	48,827	45,639	3,188	40,930	40,446	484
1966	55,246	51,123	4,123	46,757	46,090	667
1967	61,082	58,760	2,322	52,071	53,305	-1,234
1968	68,460	66,254	2,206	59,132	60,395	-1,263
1969	77,584	74,227	3,357	67,312	68,023	-711
1970	88,939	85,055	3,884	77,755	77,642	113
1971	97,233	98,840	-1,607	85,099	89,118	-4,019
1972	112,343	109,255	3,088	98,632	98,810	-178
1973	129,808	118,836	10,972	113,132	108,086	5,046
1974	140,815	132,134	8,681	122,327	119,891	2,436
1975	157,033	158,882	-1,849	134,611	138,303	-3,692
1976	183,821	180,926	2,895	152,118	153,690	-1,572
1977	204,426	191,225	13,201	169,126	164,351	4,775
1978	225,011	203,832	21,179	189,099	179,802	9,297
1979	247,059	224,666	22,393	208,048	200,534	7,514
1980	276,962	257,812	19,150	233,592	228,223	5,369
1981	310,828	291,527	19,301	258,159	253,654	4,505
1982	330,899	310,358	20,541	275,111	269,490	5,621
1983	357,661	334,019	23,642	290,480	285,042	5,438
1984	397,087	351,537	45,550	330,740	309,775	20,965
1985	438,954	390,828	48,126	365,344	345,133	20,211
1986	481,279	424,205	57,074	393,475	376,429	17,046
1987	517,019	455,752	61,267	419,487	403,937	15,550

[a] Excludes utilities, liquor stores, and insurance trust transactions.
Source: Department of Commerce, Bureau of the Census; and Tax Foundation computations.

E3. State Direct Expenditures for Own Functions

Selected Fiscal Years 1902-1987

($Millions)

| Year | Total[a] | General Expenditures | | | | | | | | Insurance Trust | Liquor Stores |
		Total General	Education	Highways	Public Welfare[b]	Health and Hospitals	Natural Resources	Financial Administration[c]	Other[d]		
1902	$136	$134	$17	$4	$10	$32	$9	$23	$39	-	$2
1913	297	197	55	26	16	53	14	38	95	-	-
1922	1,085	1,031	164	303	38	125	61	69	271	-	-
1927	1,451	1,380	218	514	40	170	94	96	248	$54	-
1932	2,028	1,965	278	843	74	215	119	114	322	71	-
1942	3,563	2,769	391	790	523	299	159	164	443	63	-
1952	10,790	8,653	1,494	2,556	1,410	1,132	539	361	1,161	1,413	288
1954	13,008	10,109	1,715	3,254	1,548	1,276	563	419	1,334	2,096	723
1956	15,148	12,319	2,138	4,367	1,603	1,470	670	477	1,594	1,984	803
1958	19,991	15,449	2,728	5,507	1,944	1,760	753	569	2,188	3,675	845
1960	22,152	17,784	3,396	6,070	2,221	1,896	842	654	2,705	3,461	869
1962	25,495	20,375	4,270	6,635	2,509	2,161	973	763	3,064	4,238	907
1964	29,616	24,275	5,465	7,850	2,796	2,464	1,185	871	3,644	4,364	882
1966	34,195	29,162	7,572	8,624	3,138	2,966	1,532	1,024	4,306	3,952	977
1968	44,304	38,446	10,957	9,819	5,122	3,832	1,954	1,310	5,452	4,626	1,081
1970	56,163	48,749	13,780	11,044	8,203	4,788	2,158	1,720	7,055	6,010	1,233
1972	72,496	62,051	17,153	12,747	12,247	6,008	2,470	2,134	9,293	8,950	1,404
1973	78,014	67,264	18,283	12,072	14,147	6,506	2,623	2,451	11,182	9,167	1,495
1974	86,193	73,950	19,753	12,636	15,169	7,494	2,917	2,799	13,182	10,590	1,583
1975	106,905	86,326	22,902	14,258	17,457	8,968	3,368	3,205	16,168	18,860	1,653
1976	123,069	95,832	25,546	14,860	20,157	9,851	3,641	3,539	18,238	26,455	1,719
1977	128,765	101,891	27,073	13,853	22,646	11,209	3,083	3,983	20,044	23,426	1,781
1978	136,545	112,515	29,577	14,658	25,729	12,319	3,241	4,700	22,291	20,495	1,817
1979	148,691	124,559	31,517	17,079	28,747	13,786	3,594	5,300	24,536	20,107	1,991
1980	173,307	143,718	35,251	20,661	33,242	15,666	4,124	6,114	28,660	24,981	2,068
1981	198,348	160,474	39,664	20,668	38,580	18,028	4,725	6,563	32,246	32,221	2,206
1982	211,615	170,747	42,301	20,103	41,513	19,398	5,165	7,441	34,826	34,730	2,305
1983	233,132	184,154	44,584	21,153	44,876	20,834	5,545	8,266	38,896	42,180	2,408
1984	243,073	201,310	48,573	23,250	49,122	21,567	5,662	8,904	44,232	34,632	2,381
1985	269,257	223,562	53,667	27,167	42,990	23,211	6,395	9,944	60,188	37,940	2,313
1986	292,249	244,553	58,260	30,191	56,256	25,471	6,897	11,262	56,216	39,749	2,391
1987	314,326	262,512	61,647	31,488	61,123	27,202	7,354	12,233	61,465	43,373	2,470

a Includes expenditures for public utilities not shown separately, 1977-1985. Prior to 1977 expenditures for public utilities included in other general expenditures.
b Principally categorical public assistance. See Table E11.
c Includes general control.
d Principally police, correction, interest, and social insurance administration.
Source: Department of Commerce, Bureau of the Census.

E4. Total State Expenditures Including Payments to Other Governments by Function and State

Fiscal Year 1987

($Millions)

State	Total	Education	Highways	Public Welfare	Health and Hospitals	Natural Resources	Financial Administration[a]	Insurance Trust[b]	Liquor Stores	Other[c]
Total	$ 455,751.8	$ 149,900.7	$ 38,272.8	$ 78,453.8	$ 32,130.9	$ 7,815.8	$ 6,839.7	$ 43,372.8	$ 2,470.3	$ 96,495.0
Alabama	6,330.0	2,746.6	555.1	635.8	623.7	120.7	202.6	433.6	130.1	884.8
Alaska	4,416.2	971.1	501.5	280.4	89.1	142.2	201.2	281.8	-	1,949.3
Arizona	5,904.4	2,169.1	1,050.0	586.6	217.4	86.9	186.1	492.0	-	1,116.3
Arkansas	3,473.2	1,346.7	468.4	540.1	230.2	99.0	91.8	253.7	-	443.3
California	62,480.6	22,225.7	2,653.1	12,444.1	3,751.7	1,274.0	1,502.6	7,035.0	-	11,594.4
Colorado	5,456.4	1,970.1	585.4	850.6	363.0	113.9	195.4	742.8	-	635.2
Connecticut	6,665.6	1,539.1	618.0	1,094.5	631.2	59.1	289.8	528.5	-	1,905.4
Delaware	1,553.5	561.4	148.0	139.5	94.6	27.0	77.9	93.1	-	412.0
Florida	15,426.3	5,744.3	1,466.4	1,905.2	1,374.3	516.4	531.0	833.1	-	3,055.6
Georgia	9,060.7	3,645.2	926.8	1,430.8	714.7	232.2	185.7	637.5	-	1,287.8
Hawaii	2,614.2	820.7	93.7	307.5	195.4	53.1	119.9	222.1	-	801.8
Idaho	1,605.2	618.4	208.7	153.8	71.0	65.8	36.4	177.2	28.8	245.1
Illinois	18,820.8	6,027.6	1,830.6	3,724.3	1,054.3	216.4	477.8	1,735.5	-	3,754.3
Indiana	8,341.9	3,529.9	869.0	1,240.9	549.2	124.7	162.9	467.7	-	1,397.6
Iowa	5,074.8	2,012.5	666.7	769.3	376.3	114.4	119.4	302.5	78.8	634.9
Kansas	3,628.9	1,457.5	476.2	515.6	264.1	85.0	141.8	326.7	-	362.0
Kentucky	6,333.8	2,318.4	850.6	985.8	309.8	174.8	251.5	489.4	-	954.5
Louisiana	8,459.8	2,590.5	711.6	1,046.1	725.0	262.0	164.8	1,255.0	-	1,704.8
Maine	2,287.3	673.8	196.4	510.5	112.8	54.3	67.8	194.6	49.2	427.9
Maryland	8,714.3	2,302.3	1,077.6	1,385.5	627.7	170.6	294.2	806.4	-	2,050.0
Massachusetts	14,015.2	3,130.3	668.7	3,063.1	1,200.6	165.5	565.4	978.5	-	4,243.1
Michigan	18,790.8	5,286.7	1,212.9	4,173.6	1,848.8	238.7	411.7	1,873.2	414.1	3,331.1
Minnesota	9,205.0	3,185.4	844.6	1,625.7	580.8	218.4	189.8	780.4	-	1,779.8
Mississippi	3,956.0	1,497.6	386.8	544.8	279.0	102.1	61.4	310.1	90.4	683.8
Missouri	7,094.8	2,841.7	708.3	1,075.5	585.8	150.1	209.6	465.6	-	1,061.2
Montana	1,697.5	466.3	245.4	234.6	83.4	77.6	62.5	235.9	31.9	259.9

Continued

E4. Total State Expenditures Including Payments to Other Governments by Function and State (continued)

Fiscal Year 1987

($Millions)

State	Total	Education	Highways	Public Welfare	Health and Hospitals	Natural Resources	Financial Administration[a]	Insurance Trust[b]	Liquor Stores	Other[c]
Nebraska	2,282.4	755.2	342.2	396.1	206.1	68.0	51.6	72.9	-	390.3
Nevada	2,009.6	614.7	203.0	143.2	63.6	29.8	63.9	334.3	-	557.1
New Hampshire	1,483.6	292.4	182.8	243.7	124.4	24.1	67.3	56.0	132.8	360.1
New Jersey	17,174.9	4,358.5	1,255.9	2,546.6	992.6	159.3	486.2	1,711.5	-	5,664.3
New Mexico	3,306.5	1,298.0	381.9	316.8	234.8	57.8	111.7	232.6	-	672.9
New York	47,504.6	11,376.8	1,922.1	11,548.2	3,855.6	222.8	1,658.5	3,597.2	-	13,323.4
North Carolina	10,133.3	4,473.1	923.1	1,205.3	818.3	197.3	275.6	753.7	-	1,486.9
North Dakota	1,584.3	542.8	170.1	225.9	107.6	51.3	36.8	132.1	-	317.7
Ohio	20,752.6	6,422.4	1,497.1	3,833.9	1,304.5	165.3	407.2	3,650.5	285.2	3,186.5
Oklahoma	5,509.9	1,971.2	543.8	853.4	363.9	89.6	157.1	624.7	-	906.2
Oregon	5,139.9	1,399.4	588.1	562.4	324.3	139.3	231.3	609.7	88.8	1,196.6
Pennsylvania	20,571.4	5,571.4	2,186.1	4,487.5	1,312.4	275.6	530.7	2,376.3	591.6	3,239.8
Rhode Island	2,258.7	556.7	123.7	496.7	192.5	13.0	111.8	225.6	-	538.7
South Carolina	5,958.5	2,355.3	395.3	610.7	588.1	120.2	135.9	380.4	-	1,372.6
South Dakota	1,281.4	318.3	148.6	143.7	67.2	41.0	30.3	45.6	-	486.7
Tennessee	6,641.2	2,353.6	806.3	1,185.3	548.4	96.5	142.4	479.5	-	1,029.2
Texas	21,717.3	9,787.8	2,543.5	2,580.6	1,407.2	289.1	362.0	2,442.6	-	2,304.5
Utah	3,262.5	1,382.5	279.1	390.7	257.0	125.5	85.6	279.5	51.1	411.5
Vermont	1,153.4	355.3	144.6	196.8	51.6	28.6	46.8	49.2	28.0	252.5
Virginia	9,692.9	3,677.6	1,316.4	1,059.1	985.8	142.2	315.4	442.2	210.7	1,543.5
Washington	9,981.6	3,811.3	888.2	1,511.8	530.0	200.4	195.3	1,416.3	183.7	1,244.6
West Virginia	3,884.3	1,286.9	462.6	510.9	161.5	86.4	106.0	594.7	50.8	624.5
Wisconsin	9,427.4	2,767.7	670.3	2,029.4	586.1	168.2	192.9	758.4	-	2,254.4
Wyoming	1,629.7	493.9	278.2	111.3	94.9	79.2	46.8	155.1	24.2	346.1

[a] Includes general control totaling $6,191 million.

[b] Comprises payments to beneficiaries (including withdrawal of retirement contributions) of employee retirement, unemployment compensation, workmen's compensation, and disability benefit social insurance programs.

[c] Principally police protection, correction, interest, employment security administration, utilities, and intergovernmental payments to local governments not elsewhere classified.

Source: Department of Commerce, Bureau of the Census.

E5. State Direct Expenditures by Character and Payments to Other Governments by State

Fiscal Year 1987

($Millions)

State	Total	Total Direct[a]	Current Operation	Direct Capital Outlay	Assistance and Subsidies	Interest	Insurance Trust	Payments to Other Governments
Total	$455,751.8	$314,326.0	$199,659.2	$37,207.0	$14,705.3	$19,381.6	$43,372.8	$141,425.7
Alabama	6,333.0	4,704.1	3,373.5	480.5	160.8	255.7	433.6	1,628.9
Alaska	4,416.2	3,479.1	2,025.4	417.0	83.1	671.9	281.8	937.1
Arizona	5,904.4	3,923.3	2,387.3	838.5	140.9	64.6	492.0	1,981.1
Arkansas	3,473.2	2,482.4	1,725.0	312.9	92.2	98.6	253.7	990.8
California	62,480.6	34,854.9	23,095.9	2,608.7	422.6	1,692.7	7,035.0	27,625.6
Colorado	5,456.4	3,928.9	2,529.2	415.8	34.9	206.1	742.8	1,527.6
Connecticut	6,665.6	5,366.0	3,319.5	644.2	276.9	596.9	528.5	1,299.5
Delaware	1,553.5	1,272.1	817.8	152.9	37.9	170.5	93.1	281.4
Florida	15,426.3	9,536.1	6,219.6	1,445.9	469.2	568.3	833.1	5,890.2
Georgia	9,060.7	9,269.2	4,150.1	1,043.6	274.8	163.1	637.5	2,791.5
Hawaii	2,614.2	2,570.4	1,664.8	382.8	93.3	207.4	222.1	43.8
Idaho	1,605.2	1,171.8	707.3	207.9	30.5	48.9	177.2	433.4
Illinois	18,820.8	13,669.0	7,856.4	1,563.3	1,569.2	944.6	1,735.5	5,151.8
Indiana	8,341.9	5,562.6	4,098.6	691.6	99.8	204.9	467.7	2,779.3
Iowa	5,074.8	3,517.5	2,364.9	506.0	223.9	120.2	302.5	1,557.3
Kansas	3,628.9	2,647.5	1,791.2	401.0	113.1	15.6	326.7	981.3
Kentucky	6,333.8	4,768.4	3,099.3	715.2	183.0	281.5	489.4	1,565.5
Louisiana	8,459.8	6,648.8	3,766.2	817.9	203.2	606.6	1,255.0	1,811.0
Maine	2,287.3	1,822.5	1,229.4	145.9	122.8	129.9	194.6	464.8
Maryland	8,714.3	6,665.5	4,118.5	999.7	367.0	373.8	806.4	2,048.8
Massachusetts	14,015.2	10,123.9	6,647.4	889.6	751.9	856.5	978.5	3,891.3
Michigan	18,790.8	13,646.8	8,737.0	919.8	1,541.9	575.0	1,873.2	5,144.0
Minnesota	9,205.0	5,766.1	3,965.9	644.1	110.6	265.2	780.4	3,438.8
Mississippi	3,956.0	2,609.8	1,785.6	294.2	113.1	106.9	310.1	1,346.2
Missouri	7,094.8	5,003.8	3,196.7	770.1	246.7	324.8	465.6	2,091.0
Montana	1,697.5	1,379.3	762.8	237.7	50.7	92.1	235.9	318.2

Continued

E5. State Direct Expenditures by Character and Payments to Other Governments by State (continued)

Fiscal Year 1987

($Millions)

State	Total	Direct						Payments to Other Governments
		Total Direct[a]	Current Operation	Capital Outlay	Assistance and Subsidies	Interest	Insurance Trust	
Nebraska	2,282.4	1,734.7	1,208.8	250.7	79.3	123.0	72.9	547.7
Nevada	2,009.6	1,359.1	731.3	165.3	24.6	103.5	334.3	650.5
New Hampshire	1,483.6	1,301.6	900.8	142.7	35.6	166.5	56.0	182.0
New Jersey	17,174.9	12,215.7	7,459.5	1,654.6	154.4	1,235.8	1,711.5	4,959.2
New Mexico	3,306.5	2,140.2	1,379.2	336.3	68.7	123.4	232.6	1,166.3
New York	47,504.6	31,255.9	19,936.5	3,966.8	735.0	3,020.5	3,597.2	16,248.7
North Carolina	10,133.3	6,482.0	4,434.2	831.4	286.6	176.0	753.7	3,651.3
North Dakota	1,584.3	1,223.1	879.1	132.1	23.0	56.8	132.1	361.2
Ohio	20,752.6	14,724.8	7,914.3	1,554.5	887.6	717.8	3,650.5	6,027.8
Oklahoma	5,509.9	4,149.0	2,624.8	415.6	181.5	302.5	624.7	1,360.8
Oregon	5,139.9	3,949.3	2,245.0	431.2	155.0	508.4	609.7	1,190.6
Pennsylvania	20,571.4	14,850.9	9,051.2	1,363.4	1,482.0	578.0	2,376.3	5,720.5
Rhode Island	2,258.7	1,891.6	1,193.5	157.1	94.9	220.6	225.6	367.1
South Carolina	5,958.5	4,492.7	3,106.0	567.9	137.9	300.4	380.4	1,465.9
South Dakota	1,281.4	1,076.8	580.8	312.2	26.3	111.9	45.6	204.6
Tennessee	6,641.2	5,055.5	3,549.7	689.8	176.7	159.8	479.5	1,585.7
Texas	21,717.3	15,491.8	9,547.0	2,361.8	673.1	467.3	2,442.6	6,225.4
Utah	3,262.5	2,474.5	1,654.0	347.0	81.0	113.0	279.5	788.0
Vermont	1,153.4	974.0	691.1	89.0	64.0	80.7	49.2	179.5
Virginia	9,692.9	6,931.6	4,879.7	1,016.1	272.3	321.2	442.2	2,761.3
Washington	9,981.6	7,073.4	4,034.2	867.6	477.1	278.1	1,416.3	2,908.2
West Virginia	3,884.3	2,989.8	1,800.1	335.0	121.0	139.1	594.7	894.5
Wisconsin	9,427.4	6,018.4	3,813.9	453.5	624.7	367.9	758.4	3,409.0
Wyoming	1,629.7	1,079.9	609.7	218.7	29.4	67.0	155.1	549.7

[a] Includes expenditures of liquor stores in alcoholic beverage monopoly states, and utility expenditures.
Source: Department of Commerce, Bureau of the Census.

E6. State Direct Expenditures by Character and Payments to Other Governments

Selected Fiscal Years 1902-1987

($Millions)

Year	Total	Direct						Payments to Other Governments
		Total Direct[a]	Current Operation	Capital Outlay	Assistance and Subsidies	Interest	Insurance Trust[b]	
1902	$188	$136	$114	$2	$10	$10	-	$52
1913	388	297	218	48	17	14		91
1922	1,397	1,085	562	302	122	45	$54	312
1927	2,047	1,451	762	492	43	83	71	596
1932	2,829	2,028	982	786	83	114	63	801
1934	3,461	2,143	985	619	356	119	64	1,318
1936	3,862	2,445	1,192	634	416	124	79	1,417
1938	4,598	3,082	1,503	701	448	128	302	1,615
1940	5,209	3,555	1,570	737	517	130	601	1,654
1942	5,343	3,563	1,827	642	466	122	505	1,780
1946	7,066	4,974	2,701	368	663	84	1,158	2,092
1950	15,082	10,864	4,450	2,237	1,891	109	2,177	4,217
1952	15,834	10,790	5,173	2,658	1,402	144	1,413	5,044
1954	18,686	13,008	5,886	3,347	1,486	193	2,096	5,679
1956	21,686	15,148	6,758	4,564	1,531	311	1,984	6,538
1958	28,080	19,991	8,161	5,946	1,813	396	3,675	8,089
1960	31,596	22,152	9,534	6,607	2,015	536	3,461	9,443
1962	36,402	25,495	11,290	7,214	2,118	635	4,238	10,906
1964	42,583	29,616	13,492	8,820	2,175	765	4,364	12,968
1966	51,123	34,195	16,855	10,193	2,301	394	3,952	16,928
1968	66,254	44,304	23,379	12,210	2,960	1,128	4,626	21,950
1970	85,055	56,163	30,971	13,295	4,387	1,499	6,010	28,892
1971	98,840	66,200	35,846	14,736	5,531	1,761	8,327	32,640
1972	109,255	72,496	39,790	15,286	6,337	2,135	8,950	36,759
1973	118,836	78,014	44,838	14,677	6,897	2,434	9,167	40,822
1974	132,134	86,193	50,803	15,417	6,521	2,863	10,590	45,941
1975	158,882	106,905	60,793	17,307	6,673	3,272	18,860	51,978
1976	180,926	123,069	68,175	18,009	7,290	4,140	25,455	57,858
1977	191,225	128,765	75,683	16,964	7,556	5,136	23,426	62,460
1978	203,832	136,545	86,153	16,064	8,341	5,493	20,495	67,287
1979	224,666	148,691	94,533	19,124	8,878	6,048	20,107	75,975
1980	257,812	173,308	108,131	23,325	9,818	7,053	24,981	84,504
1981	291,527	198,348	122,794	24,286	10,889	8,157	32,221	93,180
1982	310,358	211,615	133,152	23,466	10,867	9,400	34,730	98,743
1983	334,019	233,132	144,018	23,351	11,875	11,708	42,180	100,887
1984	351,446	243,073	156,734	25,583	12,386	13,738	34,632	108,373
1985	390,828	269,257	172,210	30,657	12,841	15,606	37,940	121,571
1986	424,216	292,249	186,188	34,550	14,162	17,601	39,749	131,966
1987	455,752	314,326	199,659	37,207	14,705	19,382	43,373	141,426

a Includes expenditures of liquor stores in alcoholic beverage monopoly states, and utility expenditures where applicable.
b Cash payments of contributory employee retirement, unemployment compensation, sickness and other cash benefit social insurance programs. Includes withdrawals of retirement contributions.
Source: Department of Commerce, Bureau of the Census.

E7. State Payments to Local Governments by Function

Selected Fiscal Years 1902-1987

($Millions)

| Year | Total | Specified Function | | | | General Local Government Support |
		Education	Highways	Public Welfare	Other	
1902	$ 52	$ 45	$ 2	-	-	$ 5
1913	91	82	4	-	-	5
1922	312	202	70	$ 4	$ 1	35
1927	596	292	197	6	3	98
1932	801	398	229	28	6	140
1934	1,318	434	247	211	281	145
1936	1,417	573	285	245	151	163
1938	1,516	656	317	346	17	180
1940	1,654	700	332	420	21	181
1942	1,780	790	344	390	32	224
1944	1,842	861	298	368	41	274
1946	2,092	953	339	376	67	357
1948	3,283	1,554	507	648	146	428
1950	4,217	2,054	610	792	279	482
1952	5,044	2,523	728	976	268	549
1954	5,679	2,930	871	1,004	274	600
1956	6,538	3,541	984	1,069	313	631
1958	8,089	4,598	1,167	1,247	390	687
1960	9,443	5,461	1,247	1,483	446	806
1961	10,114	5,963	1,266	1,602	462	821
1962	10,906	6,474	1,327	1,777	489	839
1963	11,885	6,993	1,416	1,919	545	1,012
1964	12,968	7,664	1,524	2,108	619	1,053
1965	14,174	8,351	1,630	2,436	654	1,102
1966	16,928	10,177	1,725	2,882	783	1,361
1967	19,056	11,845	1,861	2,897	868	1,585
1968	21,950	13,321	2,029	3,527	1,079	1,993
1969	24,779	14,858	2,109	4,402	1,275	2,135
1970	28,892	17,085	2,439	5,003	1,408	2,958
1971	32,640	19,292	2,507	5,760	1,823	3,258
1972	36,759	21,195	2,633	6,944	2,235	3,752
1973	40,822	23,316	2,953	7,532	2,741	4,280
1974	45,941	27,107	3,211	7,369	3,450	4,804
1975	51,978	31,110	3,225	8,102	4,412	5,129
1976	57,868	34,084	3,241	9,476	5,393	5,674
1977	61,074	36,964	3,631	8,756	5,350	6,373
1978	65,815	40,125	3,821	8,586	6,464	6,819
1979	74,482	46,206	4,149	8,653	7,250	8,224
1980	82,758	52,688	4,383	9,241	7,802	8,644
1981	91,307	57,257	4,751	11,025	8,704	9,570
1982	96,950	60,684	5,028	11,965	9,229	10,044
1983	99,544	63,118	5,277	11,342	9,443	10,364
1984	106,651	67,485	5,687	11,924	10,810	10,745
1985	119,608	74,937	6,019	12,673	13,659	12,320
1986	129,860	81,929	6,470	14,214	13,863	13,384
1987	138,970	88,253	6,785	14,901	14,786	14,245

Source: Department of Commerce, Bureau of the Census.

E8. State Payments to Other Governments by Function and State[a]

Fiscal Year 1987

($Millions)

State	Total	Specific Function				General Local Government Support
		Education	Highways	Public Welfare	Other[b]	
Total	$141,425.7	$88,253.3	$6,784.7	$17,331.2	$14,811.4	$14,245.1
Alabama	1,628.9	1,240.4	133.5	10.6	159.0	85.4
Alaska	937.1	514.8	61.4	-	164.1	196.8
Arizona	1,981.1	1,159.0	287.0	1.3	81.3	452.5
Arkansas	990.8	729.3	99.4	1.6	112.5	48.0
California	27,625.6	15,304.4[c]	900.5	7,106.2[d]	2,260.8	2,053.8[e]
Colorado	1,527.6	986.6	159.6	274.9	82.2	24.4
Connecticut	1,299.5	876.0	29.9	48.7	172.6	172.3
Delaware	281.4	247.2	5.8	0.7	27.7	-
Florida	5,890.2	4,231.2	202.4	-	556.9	899.8
Georgia	2,791.5	2,303.4	38.9	147.1	286.0	16.1
Hawaii	43.8	-	-	3.7	8.8	31.4
Idaho	433.4	327.1	46.9	-	19.6	39.8
Illinois	5,151.8	3,507.7	355.6	131.3	622.3	535.0
Indiana	2,779.3	1,700.3	262.3	190.9	79.9	545.8
Iowa	1,557.3	1,054.7	202.0	14.7	133.1	152.8
Kansas	981.3	803.9	76.8	-	42.7	57.9
Kentucky	1,565.5	1,289.6	77.1	-	198.8	-
Louisiana	1,811.0	1,449.4	20.1	33.1	147.3	161.1
Maine	464.8	361.2	15.9	15.1	22.1	50.4
Maryland	2,048.8	1,098.2	313.0	f	472.8	164.8
Massachusetts	3,891.3	1,849.3	113.1	124.0	851.1	953.9
Michigan	5,144.0	2,528.0	595.4	183.6	949.3	887.7
Minnesota	3,438.8	1,806.5	238.4	500.3	266.1	627.5
Mississippi	1,346.2	958.2	75.4	2.7	114.4	195.6
Missouri	2,091.0	1,741.8	121.7	6.8	214.6	6.1
Montana	318.2	241.7	14.2	8.4	33.9	20.0
Nebraska	547.7	291.8	94.2	1.8	86.3	73.7
Nevada	650.5	390.9	16.1	4.8	9.6	229.2
New Hampshire	182.0	76.0	13.9	29.0	25.8	37.4
New Jersey	4,959.2	2,824.4	12.7	692.4	394.7	1,035.0
New Mexico	1,166.3	823.8	14.0	-	53.5	274.9
New York	16,248.7	7,291.5[c]	238.9	5,506.9[d]	2,065.8	1,145.5
North Carolina	3,651.3	2,752.2	66.8	200.9	405.3	226.0
North Dakota	361.2	255.3	39.9	12.7	19.4	33.9
Ohio	6,027.8	3,743.1	429.5	656.7	452.7	745.7
Oklahoma	1,360.8	1,099.9	147.4	12.3	90.3	10.9
Oregon	1,190.6	725.3	202.9	2.4	120.8	139.2
Pennsylvania	5,720.5	3,490.7	219.7	732.8	1,186.0	91.3
Rhode Island	367.1	267.2	f	28.7	36.4	34.7
South Carolina	1,465.9	1,233.9	14.8	4.7	58.6	153.8
South Dakota	204.6	129.9	0.5	0.7	27.3	46.2
Tennessee	1,585.7	1,051.0	216.0	26.7	106.5	185.4
Texas	6,225.4	5,920.1[c]	12.9	3.2	245.0	44.2
Utah	788.0	678.7	31.0	3.8	74.4	-
Vermont	179.5	138.9	20.4	7.6	8.4	4.2
Virginia	2,761.3	1,882.3	133.1	273.9	369.7	102.2
Washington	2,908.2	2,297.3	194.9	93.6	258.7	63.7
West Virginia	894.5	849.0	-	-	30.5	15.0
Wisconsin	3,409.0	1,385.6	202.0	229.4	507.5	1,084.5
Wyoming	549.7	344.5	16.3	f	99.5	89.4

[a] Includes payments of $2,455.4 million to Federal government, mostly for state share of supplemental security income program; remainder to local governments.
[b] Primarily health, police and corrections, housing, sewerage, and transportation.
[c] Includes, in millions, $12,666.6 for redistribution of Federal funds to school districts, and $1,894.9 community college grants in California; $6,875.4 general school support, and $291.4 for community college support in New York; $5,501.9 in support to school districts, and $416.2 for junior college support in Texas.
[d] Includes, in millions, $2,506.2 aid to local governments for families with dependent children and $1,354.9 reimbursement to the Federal government for supplemental security income program in California; $1,685.3 aid to local governments for families with dependent children, $888.5 vendor payment to New York City Hospital Corporation, and $451.7 for welfare medical assistance in New York.
[e] Includes $1,132.8 million shared motor vehicle license taxes.
[f] Less than $500,000.
Source: Department of Commerce, Bureau of the Census.

E9. State Direct Expenditures for Education by State
Fiscal Year 1987
($Millions)

State	Total	State Institutions of Higher Education			Other Education[b]			
		Total	Current Operation[a]	Capital Outlay	Total	Current Operation	Capital Outlay	Assistance and Subsidies
Total	$61,647.4	$50,710.3	$45,246.6	$5,463.7	$10,937.1	$6,457.0	$505.8	$3,974.3
Alabama	1,506.2	1,056.1	929.0	127.1	450.0	396.1	11.8	42.2
Alaska	456.3	226.2	209.5	16.7	230.1	213.8	12.9	3.4
Arizona	1,010.1	903.0	797.9	105.1	107.1	69.7	2.0	35.4
Arkansas	617.4	479.5	446.3	33.3	137.9	107.7	8.3	21.9
California	6,921.3	5,947.3	5,245.0	702.3	974.1	548.6	2.9	422.6
Colorado	983.6	918.0	840.4	77.6	65.5	30.0	.6	34.9
Connecticut	663.1	507.8	465.5	42.3	155.3	118.4	9.7	27.2
Delaware	314.2	256.8	223.0	33.8	57.4	43.8	1.9	11.8
Florida	1,513.1	994.6	816.6	178.0	518.5	385.0	5.7	127.8
Georgia	1,341.7	1,171.1	1,047.5	123.5	170.7	131.2	5.1	34.4
Hawaii	820.7	291.9	259.6	32.3	528.8	455.5	70.9	2.4
Idaho	291.4	258.1	220.7	37.4	33.3	25.2	2.2	5.9
Illinois	2,519.9	1,929.4	1,672.6	256.8	590.5	232.8	30.9	326.8
Indiana	1,829.6	1,582.3	1,453.5	128.8	247.3	146.1	9.7	91.4
Iowa	957.7	859.9	747.9	112.0	97.8	43.4	1.1	53.4
Kansas	653.6	586.9	541.1	45.7	66.7	42.9	.2	23.7
Kentucky	1,028.8	829.3	757.6	71.7	199.4	147.3	9.3	42.8
Louisiana	1,141.1	926.5	842.8	83.7	214.6	179.8	1.6	33.2
Maine	312.6	242.4	211.4	31.1	70.2	66.6	.9	26.4
Maryland	1,204.2	934.5	815.8	118.7	269.7	196.2	9.1	64.4
Massachusetts	1,281.0	1,025.4	916.7	108.8	255.6	140.4	.6	114.5
Michigan	2,758.7	2,473.7	2,219.7	254.0	285.0	102.7	2.6	179.8
Minnesota	1,378.9	1,188.2	1,081.3	106.9	190.6	77.2	5.4	108.1
Mississippi	539.4	442.1	411.9	30.2	97.3	61.7	1.7	33.9
Missouri	1,099.9	978.0	827.3	150.8	121.9	80.3	4.4	37.2
Montana	224.6	175.7	151.6	24.1	48.9	35.7	.8	12.3
Nebraska	463.6	413.7	355.7	58.0	49.7	33.0	2.1	14.5
Nevada	223.8	198.8	182.2	16.6	25.1	16.7	-	8.3
New Hampshire	216.4	188.9	155.6	33.4	27.5	14.1	2.3	11.0
New Jersey	1,534.1	1,276.0	1,159.1	116.9	258.1	97.9	5.8	154.4
New Mexico	474.2	411.2	369.9	41.3	63.0	42.9	8.1	12.0
New York	4,085.3	3,010.6	2,593.1	417.5	1,074.6	330.9	8.8	735.0
North Carolina	1,720.9	1,446.8	1,276.0	170.7	274.2	172.7	59.3	42.2
North Dakota	287.5	262.6	243.8	18.9	24.8	15.9	.2	8.8
Ohio	2,679.3	2,472.9	2,183.4	289.5	206.5	83.5	61.9	61.1
Oklahoma	871.3	766.2	712.1	54.1	105.1	74.6	3.2	27.3
Oregon	674.1	595.2	518.8	76.5	78.9	43.8	2.1	33.0
Pennsylvania	2,080.8	1,269.7	1,146.7	123.0	811.1	345.9	33.3	431.9
Rhode Island	289.5	201.7	196.3	5.4	87.7	67.5	2.3	18.0
South Carolina	1,121.4	915.6	826.1	89.5	205.8	154.3	21.6	29.9
South Dakota	188.4	166.7	155.4	11.3	21.7	17.0	.4	4.3
Tennessee	1,302.6	1,013.9	930.3	83.7	288.6	217.1	31.6	39.8
Texas	3,867.6	3,456.8	3,090.7	366.2	410.8	261.7	6.5	142.6
Utah	703.8	636.4	556.2	80.3	67.4	45.1	6.1	16.1
Vermont	216.4	178.4	167.8	10.6	38.0	17.7	.2	20.1
Virginia	1,795.3	1,602.2	1,461.2	141.0	193.1	118.5	5.1	69.6
Washington	1,514.0	1,348.6	1,211.2	137.3	165.4	71.4	28.2	65.9
West Virginia	437.9	357.0	339.7	17.3	80.9	68.6	1.9	10.4
Wisconsin	1,381.1	1,201.7	1,140.9	60.8	179.4	86.8	2.5	90.0
Wyoming	149.4	133.7	122.6	11.2	15.7	5.2	.1	10.4

a Includes $5,921.6 million for auxiliary enterprises such as dormitories and athletic events.
b Includes support of local public schools, state administration and services, tuition grants, aid to private schools, and special programs.
Source: Department of Commerce, Bureau of the Census.

E10. State Direct Expenditures for Highways by State[a]

Fiscal Year 1987

($Millions)

State	Total	Regular Highway Facilities			Toll Highway Facilities		
		Total	Current Operation	Capital Outlay	Total	Current Operation	Capital Outlay
Total	$31,488.1	$29,712.5	$9,569.2	$20,143.3	$1,775.6	$908.1	$867.6
Alabama	421.6	421.6	167.7	253.9	-	-	-
Alaska	440.2	379.2	160.0	219.2	61.0	57.8	3.1
Arizona	763.0	763.0	134.7	628.3	-	-	-
Arkansas	369.0	369.0	132.8	236.1	-	-	-
California	1,752.2	1,699.7	780.6	919.1	52.5	37.7	14.8
Colorado	425.8	425.8	171.6	254.2	-	-	-
Connecticut	588.1	583.5	198.8	384.7	4.6	4.6	-
Delaware	142.2	124.7	51.8	72.9	17.6	5.4	12.1
Florida	1,263.9	1,110.2	297.4	812.8	153.7	41.6	112.2
Georgia	887.8	887.2	200.4	686.8	.6	.6	-
Hawaii	93.7	93.7	32.2	61.5	-	-	-
Idaho	161.7	161.7	24.0	137.7	-	-	-
Illinois	1,475.0	1,372.0	366.3	1,005.7	103.0	50.9	52.1
Indiana	606.7	579.9	155.7	424.1	26.8	15.6	11.2
Iowa	464.5	464.2	127.3	337.0	.3	.3	-
Kansas	399.4	387.1	107.5	279.6	12.3	12.3	-
Kentucky	773.5	752.7	283.1	469.6	20.8	8.9	12.0
Louisiana	691.6	691.6	133.9	557.7	-	-	-
Maine	180.5	158.6	82.5	76.1	21.9	14.9	7.1
Maryland	764.6	699.3	241.9	457.4	65.3	23.7	41.5
Massachusetts	555.6	490.1	153.0	337.1	65.5	37.9	27.7
Michigan	617.6	611.3	198.3	413.1	6.2	5.4	.9
Minnesota	606.2	606.2	178.2	428.0	-	-	-
Mississippi	311.4	311.4	98.3	213.1	-	-	-
Missouri	586.6	586.6	184.0	402.6	-	-	-
Montana	231.1	231.1	45.0	186.1	-	-	-
Nebraska	248.0	248.0	82.7	165.3	-	-	-
Nevada	186.9	186.9	58.7	128.3	-	-	-
New Hampshire	168.9	146.5	76.0	70.5	22.4	8.3	14.0
New Jersey	1,243.2	894.4	114.5	780.0	348.8	196.8	152.0
New Mexico	367.9	367.9	108.6	259.3	-	-	-
New York	1,683.2	1,482.1	316.3	1,165.8	201.1	95.5	105.6
North Carolina	856.3	842.7	459.5	383.2	13.6	11.8	1.9
North Dakota	130.2	130.2	41.4	88.8	-	-	-
Ohio	1,067.5	998.0	348.7	649.3	69.5	33.9	35.6
Oklahoma	396.4	383.8	103.6	280.3	12.6	12.3	.2
Oregon	385.2	384.0	82.0	302.0	1.2	1.2	-
Pennsylvania	1,966.4	1,742.1	882.4	859.7	224.3	90.6	133.6
Rhode Island	123.4	121.5	23.5	98.0	1.9	1.9	-
South Carolina	380.4	380.4	123.4	257.1	-	-	-
South Dakota	148.0	148.0	53.8	94.2	-	-	-
Tennessee	590.3	590.3	143.3	447.0	-	-	-
Texas	2,530.7	2,484.7	738.9	1,745.8	46.0	5.2	40.7
Utah	248.1	248.1	94.3	153.9	-	-	-
Vermont	124.2	124.2	59.7	64.5	-	-	-
Virginia	1,183.3	1,093.7	419.9	673.8	89.6	46.6	43.0
Washington	693.3	572.4	90.7	481.7	120.9	74.6	46.3
West Virginia	462.6	451.1	178.0	273.1	11.5	11.5	-
Wisconsin	468.3	468.3	175.5	292.8	-	-	-
Wyoming	261.9	261.9	87.1	174.8	-	-	-

[a] Includes streets, highways, and structures necessary for their use; snow and ice removal; bridges and levees.
Source: Department of Commerce, Bureau of the Census.

E11. State Direct Expenditures for Public Welfare by State

Fiscal Year 1987

($Millions)

State	Total	Cash Assistance Payments			Vendor Payments	State Welfare Institutions	Other
		Total	Categorical Assistance Programs[a]	Other			
Total	$ 61,122.6	$ 10,729.7	$ 9,589.8	$ 1,139.9	$ 39,380.8	$ 449.8	$ 10,562.3
Alabama	625.2	118.6	118.6	-	375.8	-	130.7
Alaska	280.4	79.7	78.2	1.5	93.4	26.7	80.6
Arizona	585.3	105.4	90.8	14.7	315.6	3.0	161.3
Arkansas	538.4	70.3	49.2	21.1	344.9	-	123.2
California	5,337.8	-	-	-	4,268.4	45.4	1,024.0
Colorado	575.7	-	-	-	403.1	8.9	163.7
Connecticut	1,045.8	249.8	247.8	2.0	632.5	20.0	143.5
Delaware	138.8	26.1	24.4	1.7	30.7	28.5	53.5
Florida	1,905.2	341.3	339.8	1.5	1,196.0	-	367.8
Georgia	1,283.8	240.4	240.4	-	934.4	-	109.0
Hawaii	303.8	90.8	73.6	17.2	161.7	-	51.2
Idaho	153.8	24.6	24.6	-	82.6	2.2	44.3
Illinois	3,593.0	1,242.4	942.2	300.2	1,662.2	19.1	669.3
Indiana	1,050.0	8.4	8.4	b	945.1	21.9	74.6
Iowa	754.6	170.5	168.8	1.8	398.7	20.7	164.7
Kansas	515.6	89.4	89.4	-	246.4	3.0	176.8
Kentucky	985.8	140.2	140.2	-	653.6	-	192.0
Louisiana	1,013.0	170.0	170.0	-	630.0	-	213.0
Maine	495.4	96.3	95.6	.7	319.3	.3	79.4
Maryland	1,385.4	302.6	302.6	-	843.0	1.7	238.1
Massachusetts	2,939.1	637.4	550.4	87.0	1,482.8	25.0	793.9
Michigan	3,989.9	1,362.2	1,116.7	245.4	1,777.7	25.1	825.0
Minnesota	1,125.3	2.5	-	2.5	1,064.7	11.7	46.4
Mississippi	542.1	79.2	79.2	-	377.3	-	85.6
Missouri	1,068.7	209.5	200.3	9.2	619.3	8.1	231.8
Montana	226.2	38.4	38.4	.1	133.2	4.2	50.4
Nebraska	394.3	64.8	64.4	.4	213.7	20.1	95.7
Nevada	138.5	16.3	16.2	.1	77.7	-	44.5
New Hampshire	214.7	24.5	24.5	-	96.4	5.2	88.6
New Jersey	1,854.2	-	-	-	1,473.9	37.7	342.6
New Mexico	316.8	56.6	56.6	-	161.2	5.9	93.1
New York	6,041.3	-	-	-	5,746.1	7.0	288.2
North Carolina	1,004.4	244.4	196.8	47.6	655.3	-	1,415.4
North Dakota	213.2	14.2	14.2	-	178.6	1.0	19.5
Ohio	3,177.1	826.5	826.5	-	2,109.5	17.1	224.0
Oklahoma	841.1	154.2	154.0	.2	494.9	14.1	177.8
Oregon	559.9	122.1	114.4	7.6	220.5	-	217.3
Pennsylvania	3,754.7	1,048.9	769.6	279.2	1,791.1	19.7	895.0
Rhode Island	468.0	76.9	76.9	-	314.8	8.5	67.7
South Carolina	606.0	108.0	103.3	4.7	321.0	-	177.0
South Dakota	143.0	22.0	21.8	.2	87.2	2.3	31.5
Tennessee	1,158.6	136.9	114.1	22.8	831.8	-	189.9
Texas	2,577.3	530.4	530.4	-	1,532.7	-	514.2
Utah	386.8	64.9	57.9	7.0	216.8	-	105.1
Vermont	189.2	44.0	41.7	2.3	94.9	3.8	46.5
Virginia	785.2	202.8	202.8	-	542.7	-	39.7
Washington	1,418.2	411.2	359.8	51.4	714.4	9.4	283.2
West Virginia	510.9	110.6	107.0	3.6	279.2	1.5	119.5
Wisconsin	1,800.0	534.6	530.3	4.4	1,181.9	16.4	67.1
Wyoming	111.0	19.0	16.9	2.1	51.7	4.6	35.7

a Includes Aid to Families with Dependent Children and supplemental security income in those states with state-administered payments.
b Less than $50,000.
Source: Department of Commerce, Bureau of the Census.

E12. State Direct Expenditures for Hospitals by State[a]
Fiscal Year 1987
($Millions)

| State | Total | State Hospitals and Institutions for the Handicapped | | | Other Hospitals[b] |
		Total	Current Operation	Capital Outlay	
Total	$ 17,995.0	$ 17,861.7	$ 16,956.0	$ 905.7	$ 133.2
Alabama	418.1	418.1	382.5	35.7	-
Alaska	27.0	27.7	26.9	.7	-
Arizona	64.1	59.5	58.5	1.0	4.5
Arkansas	133.2	130.4	126.9	3.5	2.8
California	1,604.3	1,604.3	1,526.9	77.4	-
Colorado	232.6	212.2	210.0	2.3	20.4
Connecticut	466.6	466.0	461.6	4.5	.6
Delaware	36.5	36.5	35.0	1.5	-
Florida	392.2	384.5	368.3	16.3	7.6
Georgia	397.0	397.0	384.9	12.2	-
Hawaii	110.9	109.6	103.4	6.3	1.3
Idaho	24.3	24.3	21.5	2.8	-
Illinois	505.2	483.3	468.1	15.3	21.8
Indiana	325.3	325.3	303.7	21.6	-
Iowa	308.5	308.5	277.0	31.4	-
Kansas	215.8	215.8	208.1	7.8	-
Kentucky	156.0	156.0	145.3	10.6	-
Louisiana	554.7	554.7	544.7	10.0	-
Maine	53.4	53.4	52.1	1.3	-
Maryland	272.0	272.0	268.1	3.8	-
Massachusetts	587.0	587.0	563.5	23.5	-
Michigan	729.1	729.1	683.0	46.1	-
Minnesota	427.1	426.2	391.0	35.2	.9
Mississippi	175.2	175.2	168.6	6.6	-
Missouri	370.0	369.4	311.2	58.2	.5
Montana	34.0	34.0	30.4	3.5	-
Nebraska	136.1	135.5	123.5	12.1	.4
Nevada	30.0	30.0	29.9	.1	-
New Hampshire	42.8	42.8	38.9	3.9	-
New Jersey	570.9	562.3	555.3	7.0	8.7
New Mexico	138.1	137.7	131.7	5.9	.5
New York	2,620.2	2,620.2	2,531.7	88.5	-
North Carolina	496.3	496.3	433.4	63.0	-
North Dakota	70.4	70.4	68.6	1.9	-
Ohio	878.5	878.5	815.2	63.3	.2
Oklahoma	234.6	234.5	227.6	6.8	-
Oregon	206.6	206.6	193.7	12.9	7.2
Pennsylvania	826.9	819.7	779.8	39.9	-
Rhode Island	107.4	107.4	104.3	3.1	-
South Carolina	329.8	329.8	300.2	29.6	-
South Dakota	29.6	29.6	29.2	.4	-
Tennessee	296.7	296.7	266.6	30.1	-
Texas	918.8	863.1	842.4	20.7	55.8
Utah	149.4	149.4	148.9	.5	-
Vermont	21.9	21.9	21.7	.3	-
Virginia	672.3	672.3	606.6	65.7	-
Washington	274.6	274.6	265.0	9.6	-
West Virginia	58.9	58.9	58.6	.3	-
Wisconsin	236.8	236.8	235.8	.9	-
Wyoming	27.3	27.3	26.2	1.2	-

[a] Includes general hospitals, sanitariums, and hospitals and institutions for special diseases.
[b] Nongovernmental.
Source: Department of Commerce, Bureau of the Census.

E13. Federal Aid Received by the States by Function[a]

Selected Fiscal Years 1902-1987

($Millions)

Year	Total	Public Welfare	Highways	Education[b]	Employment Security Administration	Health and Hospitals[c]	Natural Resources[c]	General Revenue Sharing	All Other
1902	$3	$1	-	$1	-	-	-	-	$1
1913	6	1	-	3	-	-	-	-	2
1922	99	1	$79	10	-	-	-	-	9
1927	107	1	81	11	-	-	-	-	14
1932	222	1	191	12	-	-	-	-	18
1942	802	369	169	137	$57	-	-	-	69
1950	2,275	1,107	438	345	168	$95	-	-	122
1960	6,382	2,048	2,883	727	319	132	-	-	274
1962	7,108	2,449	2,746	985	423	158	-	-	346
1964	9,046	2,977	3,652	1,152	437	209	$154	-	465
1965	9,874	3,133	3,987	1,393	457	222	172	-	508
1966	11,743	3,573	3,972	2,654	506	270	205	-	562
1967	13,616	4,353	4,033	3,500	553	314	235	-	627
1968	15,228	5,240	4,198	3,891	619	382	262	-	636
1969	16,907	6,477	3,201	4,121	681	427	284	-	716
1970	19,252	7,818	4,431	4,554	769	508	309	-	864
1971	22,754	9,553	4,814	5,468	959	532	350	-	1,078
1972	26,791	12,289	4,871	5,984	1,148	601	393	-	1,505
1973	31,361	13,653	4,648	6,430	1,276	608	437	$2,272	2,037
1974	31,632	13,320	4,503	6,720	1,295	738	472	2,045	2,539
1975	36,148	14,247	5,260	7,879	1,521	1,102	599	2,066	3,473
1976	42,013	16,867	6,262	8,661	1,658	1,235	642	2,102	4,585
1977	45,890	18,723	6,363	9,035	1,833	1,532	637	2,217	5,550
1978	50,200	20,007	6,301	9,819	1,887	1,833	703	2,255	7,394
1979	54,548	22,313	7,015	10,710	1,928	1,988	784	2,261	7,550
1980	61,892	24,681	8,860	12,765	2,050	2,309	851	2,278	8,098
1981	67,868	28,892	9,369	14,100	2,362	2,601	986	1,118	8,440
1982	66,026	31,510	8,304	13,149	2,352	2,510	956	d	7,245
1983	68,985	32,949	8,927	13,208	2,531	2,869	965	d	7,536
1984	76,140	35,423	10,380	13,975	2,606	3,243	998	d	9,515
1985	84,469	38,664	12,702	15,307	2,679	3,416	1,113	d	10,588
1986	92,666	41,802	13,855	16,523	2,790	3,573	1,139	d	12,984
1987	95,463	44,969	12,963	16,883	2,794	3,764	1,960	d	12,130

a Excludes value of any aid in kind rather than cash, such as free transfers of surplus property or of commodities.
b Includes aid for training of defense workers, 1942-1944; from 1954 to 1962, includes Federal reimbursement for atomic research by state universities, previously classified as "All Other"; from 1963, atomic research is again included in "All Other".
c Health and hospitals included in "All Other" for 1902-1948; natural resources included in "All Other" for 1902-1962.
d Federal general revenue sharing program for states ended in fiscal year 1981.
Source: Department of Commerce, Bureau of the Census.

E14. Total State Revenue by Source and State
Fiscal Year 1987
($Millions)

| State | Total | From Own Sources | | | | | | Intergovernmental | |
| | | Total Own Sources[a] | General Revenue | | | Liquor Stores[c] | Insurance Trust | From Federal | From Local |
			Total	Taxes[b]	Charges and Miscellaneous				
Total	$517,019.3	$414,638.6	$317,106.1	$246,933.2	$70,172.8	$5,776.3	$91,756.3	$95,462.9	$6,917.7
Alabama	7,076.6	5,561.3	4,439.3	3,222.2	1,217.1	139.8	982.2	1,481.3	33.4
Alaska	4,892.2	4,403.3	3,756.2	1,062.4	2,693.8	1.8	645.3	485.4	3.6
Arizona	6,673.4	5,673.4	4,213.4	3,469.5	743.9	7.7	1,452.3	912.9	87.2
Arkansas	3,887.6	2,974.6	2,339.5	1,889.1	450.5	—	635.1	908.8	4.2
California	70,335.5	57,641.9	43,190.6	35,790.8	7,399.8	88.0	14,363.3	12,423.0	270.6
Colorado	6,723.3	5,477.7	3,680.0	2,561.5	1,118.5	—	1,797.7	1,219.9	25.7
Connecticut	7,595.2	6,365.9	5,659.0	4,359.2	1,299.8	18.0	688.9	1,208.8	20.5
Delaware	1,980.3	1,699.7	1,420.2	941.9	478.3	3.8	275.7	278.1	2.5
Florida	17,394.3	14,492.2	11,533.6	9,846.2	1,687.4	5.1	2,953.5	2,799.1	103.0
Georgia	10,240.5	7,898.2	6,289.0	5,323.7	965.4	—	1,609.1	2,287.4	54.9
Hawaii	3,164.5	2,734.8	2,208.7	1,697.4	511.2	36.5	526.2	425.6	4.1
Idaho	1,868.0	1,476.0	1,047.5	829.7	217.8	—	392.0	376.4	15.6
Illinois	20,632.0	16,522.6	13,166.8	10,429.5	2,737.3	—	3,355.8	4,027.1	82.3
Indiana	9,037.5	7,115.9	6,280.7	4,774.2	1,506.6	103.5	835.2	1,875.3	46.3
Iowa	5,480.7	4,359.4	3,543.6	2,662.1	881.5	—	712.3	1,044.4	77.0
Kansas	4,111.7	3,295.6	2,615.0	2,085.5	529.5	—	680.6	804.7	11.4
Kentucky	6,926.4	5,501.8	4,435.3	3,520.4	914.9	—	1,066.5	1,411.1	13.5
Louisiana	9,257.4	6,781.3	5,242.6	3,448.6	1,793.9	50.1	1,538.8	2,450.7	25.3
Maine	2,651.4	2,039.9	1,666.6	1,288.5	378.1	58.2	323.2	608.4	3.1
Maryland	9,699.9	7,932.8	6,662.8	5,204.5	1,458.3	32.6	1,211.7	1,721.2	45.9
Massachusetts	14,001.1	11,484.1	10,504.6	8,463.9	2,040.7	425.9	946.9	2,325.6	191.4
Michigan	21,493.3	16,974.8	12,955.8	9,857.1	3,098.6	—	3,593.2	4,019.2	499.2
Minnesota	10,642.7	8,649.3	6,840.2	5,546.4	1,293.7	111.9	1,809.1	1,903.8	89.7
Mississippi	4,413.5	3,247.6	2,451.9	1,943.4	508.5	—	683.9	1,149.6	16.3
Missouri	7,761.2	6,189.8	4,914.4	3,942.3	972.1		1,275.4	1,560.6	10.8
Montana	1,815.7	1,316.4	933.3	591.0	342.3	36.1	346.9	486.3	13.1

Continued

E14. Total State Revenue by Source and State (continued)

Fiscal Year 1987

($Millions)

| State | Total | Total Own Sources[a] | From Own Sources | | | Liquor Stores[c] | Insurance Trust | Intergovernmental | |
| | | | General Revenue | | | | | From Federal | From Local |
			Total	Taxes[b]	Charges and Miscellaneous				
Nebraska	$2,474.9	$1,889.3	$1,699.5	$1,203.3	$496.2	-	$189.8	$561.5	$24.1
Nevada	2,474.5	2,165.9	1,353.6	1,131.3	222.3	$41.7	770.7	299.1	9.5
New Hampshire	1,758.8	1,398.3	1,021.8	562.7	459.1	168.1	208.3	326.9	33.6
New Jersey	19,542.2	16,537.4	12,931.1	9,491.4	3,439.7	315.0	3,291.4	2,876.4	128.3
New Mexico	3,842.2	3,240.8	2,666.5	1,574.7	1,091.8	-	574.2	565.5	35.9
New York	55,571.7	40,901.8	29,930.2	24,676.3	5,253.9	1,735.3	9,236.2	10,758.4	3,911.5
North Carolina	11,874.4	9,680.3	7,570.5	6,235.2	1,335.3	-	2,109.8	2,029.6	164.6
North Dakota	1,545.4	1,163.4	970.0	573.5	396.6	-	193.4	365.7	16.2
Ohio	25,066.9	19,184.3	12,815.1	9,717.1	3,097.9	336.8	6,032.4	3,734.6	148.0
Oklahoma	5,781.3	4,646.8	3,650.2	2,669.2	981.0	170.2	826.4	1,107.1	27.4
Oregon	6,146.4	4,937.8	3,418.0	2,235.1	1,182.9	138.3	1,381.5	1,173.7	34.9
Pennsylvania	23,803.2	19,078.4	14,161.0	11,378.8	2,782.2	613.3	4,304.1	4,645.1	79.7
Rhode Island	2,575.3	2,055.8	1,631.5	1,050.1	581.4	7.0	417.3	490.0	29.5
South Carolina	6,766.0	5,533.5	4,038.7	3,158.5	880.3	480.1	1,014.7	1,197.2	35.4
South Dakota	1,241.3	891.9	695.1	416.4	278.7	-	196.9	342.6	6.7
Tennessee	7,382.6	5,499.2	4,424.9	3,603.3	821.5	-	1,074.4	1,852.3	31.2
Texas	24,038.0	19,512.9	15,082.9	11,227.8	3,855.1	-	4,430.0	4,508.1	17.0
Utah	3,400.5	2,596.2	2,004.6	1,438.3	566.3	68.7	523.0	778.9	25.4
Vermont	1,294.2	956.0	813.0	537.9	275.0	29.3	113.7	333.3	5.0
Virginia	11,173.7	9,088.2	7,138.7	5,526.6	1,612.2	252.5	1,696.9	1,948.9	136.6
Washington	11,575.1	9,486.0	6,682.7	5,639.4	1,043.3	216.0	2,587.3	1,915.4	173.7
West Virginia	3,965.2	3,037.5	2,312.0	1,830.2	481.8	56.7	668.8	914.6	13.1
Wisconsin	12,167.4	9,990.8	7,006.4	5,673.6	1,332.8	-	2,984.4	2,123.7	52.9
Wyoming	1,802.1	1,355.4	1,097.7	631.7	466.0	28.2	229.5	419.6	27.2

[a] Includes utility revenues of $2,964.4 million for 15 states, not shown separately.
[b] Excludes unemployment compensation taxes included in insurance trust revenue, shown separately in Table E47.
[c] Represents sales revenues, not net profits.
Source: Department of Commerce, Bureau of the Census.

E15. Total State Revenue by Source

Selected Fiscal Years 1902-1987

($Millions, Except Per Capita)

Year	Total	Total Own Sources[b]	From Own Sources — General Revenue: Total	Taxes[c]	Charges and Miscellaneous	Insurance Trust[d]	Liquor Stores[e]	Intergovernmental: From Federal	From Local	Per Capita[a]: Total	Taxes
1902	$192	$183	$181	$156	$25	-	$2	$3	$6	$2.46	$2.00
1913	376	360	360	301	59	-	-	6	10	3.92	3.14
1922	1,360	1,234	1,128	947	181	$106	-	99	27	12.49	8.70
1927	2,152	1,994	1,857	1,608	249	137	-	107	51	18.28	13.66
1932	2,541	2,274	2,156	1,890	266	118	-	222	45	20.50	15.25
1942	6,870	6,012	4,274	3,903	370	1,366	373	802	56	51.67	29.36
1952	16,815	14,330	10,944	9,857	1,087	2,462	924	2,329	156	108.87	63.82
1954	18,834	15,951	12,417	11,089	1,328	2,560	974	2,668	215	117.96	69.45
1956	22,199	18,903	15,093	13,375	1,718	2,791	1,019	3,027	269	133.78	80.60
1958	26,191	21,427	17,008	14,919	2,089	3,361	1,058	4,461	302	152.24	86.72
1960	32,838	26,094	20,618	18,036	2,583	4,347	1,128	6,382	363	184.52	101.35
1962	37,595	30,115	23,677	20,561	3,116	5,304	1,134	7,108	373	204.53	111.86
1964	45,167	35,703	28,184	24,243	3,942	6,324	1,195	9,046	417	238.50	128.01
1966	55,246	43,000	34,511	29,380	5,131	7,128	1,361	11,743	503	284.52	151.31
1968	68,460	52,525	43,197	36,400	6,797	7,771	1,557	15,228	707	345.37	183.63
1970	88,939	68,691	57,507	47,962	9,545	9,437	1,748	19,252	995	440.38	237.48
1971	97,233	73,424	61,290	51,541	9,749	10,320	1,814	22,754	1,054	473.05	250.75
1972	112,344	84,362	70,651	59,870	10,780	11,806	1,905	26,791	1,191	539.53	287.53
1973	129,808	97,108	80,432	68,069	12,363	14,690	1,985	31,361	1,339	616.93	323.51
1974	140,815	107,645	89,157	74,207	14,950	16,439	2,049	31,632	1,538	662.91	349.34
1975	157,033	119,206	96,784	80,155	16,629	20,293	2,129	36,148	1,680	732.23	373.76
1976	183,821	139,104	107,401	89,256	18,145	29,508	2,196	42,013	2,704	848.63	412.06
1977	204,426	155,799	120,499	101,085	19,414	32,365	2,244	45,890	2,737	834.71	462.20
1978	225,011	171,550	135,638	113,261	22,377	32,562	2,388	50,200	3,261	1,018.17	512.50
1979	247,059	189,972	150,961	124,963	25,998	35,370	2,504	54,548	2,539	1,105.94	559.39
1980	276,962	212,636	169,265	137,075	32,190	39,301	2,765	61,892	2,434	1,225.83	606.69
1981	310,828	240,042	187,374	149,738	37,636	48,041	2,805	67,868	2,918	1,360.39	655.35
1982	330,899	261,732	205,945	162,607	43,338	50,848	2,854	66,026	3,139	1,433.95	704.66
1983	357,661	284,933	217,752	171,440	46,312	61,971	2,819	68,986	3,742	1,534.97	735.77
1984	397,087	315,637	249,290	196,795	52,495	60,950	2,759	76,140	5,310	1,688.63	836.88
1985	438,954	349,030	275,422	215,320	60,102	67,907	2,753	84,469	5,453	1,829.00	897.19
1986	481,279	382,705	294,901	228,535	66,848	82,090	2,807	92,666	5,908	2,005.30	952.21
1987	517,019	414,638	317,106	246,933	70,173	91,756	2,812	95,463	6,918	2,133.57	1,019.01

a Based on population, excluding armed forces overseas and District of Columbia, January 1, each year.
b Includes utility revenues of $692 million in 1977, $962 million in 1978, $1,137 million in 1979, $1,304 million in 1980, $1,823 million in 1981, $2,085 million in 1982, $2,390 million in 1983, $2,638 million in 1984, $2,948 million in 1985, $2,907 million in 1986, and $2,964 million in 1987, not shown separately. Prior to 1977, utility revenues included in charges and miscellaneous general revenue.
c Excludes unemployment compensation taxes included in insurance trust revenue and shown in Table E17.
d Collections from employers and employees for financing unemployment compensation, accident and sickness, workmen's compensation, retirement, and similar social insurance programs.
e Gross receipts from the sale of liquor and associated products in state alcoholic beverage monopoly systems.
Source: Department of Commerce, Bureau of the Census. Per capita computations by Tax Foundation.

E16. Percentage Distribution of State Tax Collections by Source

Selected Fiscal Years 1902-1988

Year	Total Tax Collections[a]	General Sales, Use, or Gross Receipts	Motor Vehicle Fuel Sales	Tobacco Products Sales	Alcoholic Beverage Sales and Licenses	Motor Vehicle and Operators' Licenses	Income — Total	Income — Individual	Income — Corporation	Property	Death and Gift	Severance	Other
1902	100.0%	-	-	-	b	-	-	-	-	52.6%	b	-	47.4%
1913	100.0	-	-	-	.7%c	1.7%	-	-	-	46.5	b	-	51.2
1922	100.0	-	1.4%	-	-	16.0	10.7%	4.5%	6.1%	36.7	7.0%	-	28.2
1927	100.0	-	16.1	-	-	18.7	10.1	4.4	5.7	23.0	6.6	-	25.5
1932	100.0	.4%	27.9	1.0%	.1	17.7	8.1	3.9	4.2	17.4	7.8	1.0%	18.7
1938	100.0	14.3	24.8	1.8	7.2	11.5	12.2	7.0	5.3	7.8	4.5	1.9	14.0
1940	100.0	15.1	25.3	2.9	7.7	11.7	10.9	6.2	4.7	7.8	3.4	1.6	13.6
1948	100.0	21.9	18.7	5.0	7.4	8.8	16.1	7.4	8.7	4.1	2.7	1.9	13.4
1950	100.0	21.1	19.5	5.2	6.3	9.5	16.5	9.1	7.4	3.9	2.1	2.7	13.3
1952	100.0	22.6	19.0	4.6	5.3	9.4	17.8	9.3	8.5	3.8	2.1	2.8	12.8
1954	100.0	22.9	20.0	4.2	4.9	9.9	16.0	9.1	7.0	3.5	2.2	2.8	13.5
1956	100.0	22.7	20.1	3.8	4.7	9.7	16.9	10.3	6.7	3.5	2.3	2.7	13.6
1958	100.0	23.5	19.6	4.1	4.3	9.5	17.2	10.3	6.8	3.6	2.4	2.5	13.4
1960	100.0	23.8	18.5	5.1	4.1	8.7	18.8	12.2	6.5	3.4	2.3	2.3	12.9
1962	100.0	24.9	17.8	5.2	3.6	8.1	19.6	13.3	6.4	3.1	2.5	2.2	12.9
1964	100.0	25.1	16.7	4.9	4.1	7.9	21.1	14.1	7.0	3.0	2.7	2.0	12.5
1966	100.0	26.8	15.7	5.2	3.8	7.6	21.5	14.6	6.9	2.8	2.8	1.9	11.8
1968	100.0	28.7	14.2	5.2	3.5	6.8	24.0	17.1	6.9	2.5	2.4	1.7	10.9
1970	100.0	29.6	13.1	4.8	3.2	5.7	26.9	19.1	7.8	2.3	2.1	1.4	10.9
1971	100.0	30.0	12.9	4.9	3.2	5.7	26.3	19.7	6.6	2.2	2.1	1.4	11.2
1972	100.0	29.4	12.1	4.7	3.0	5.6	29.1	21.7	7.4	2.1	2.2	1.3	10.6
1973	100.0	29.1	11.8	4.6	2.8	5.3	30.9	22.9	8.0	1.9	2.1	1.2	10.2
1974	100.0	30.5	11.1	4.4	2.6	5.1	31.1	23.0	8.1	1.8	1.9	1.7	9.8
1975	100.0	30.9	10.3	4.1	2.5	4.9	31.8	23.5	8.3	1.8	1.8	2.2	9.6
1976	100.0	30.6	9.7	3.9	2.3	4.9	32.2	24.0	8.2	2.4	1.7	2.3	9.9
1977	100.0	30.6	9.0	3.5	2.2	4.5	34.3	25.2	9.1	2.2	1.8	2.1	9.7
1978	100.0	31.1	8.4	3.2	2.1	4.3	35.2	25.7	9.5	2.1	1.6	2.2	9.7
1979	100.0	31.6	8.0	2.9	1.9	4.1	35.8	26.1	9.7	2.0	1.6	2.3	9.6
1980	100.0	31.5	7.1	2.7	1.9	3.9	36.8	27.1	9.7	2.1	1.5	3.0	9.3
1981	100.0	31.0	6.5	2.6	1.8	3.8	36.8	27.3	9.4	2.0	1.5	4.3	9.7
1982	100.0	31.0	6.4	2.4	1.7	3.7	36.7	28.1	8.6	1.9	1.4	4.8	9.8
1983	100.0	31.3	6.3	2.3	1.6	3.7	36.7	29.0	7.7	1.9	1.5	4.3	10.3
1984	100.0	31.8	6.3	2.0	1.5	3.5	37.8	30.0	7.9	2.0	1.1	3.7	10.2
1985	100.0	32.3	6.2	2.1	1.4	3.6	37.8	29.6	8.2	1.8	1.1	3.3	10.3
1986	100.0	32.8	6.2	2.0	1.4	3.7	37.6	29.6	8.1	1.9	1.1	2.7	10.6
1987	100.0	32.3	6.3	1.9	1.3	3.7	39.2	30.8	8.4	1.9	1.2	1.6	9.9
1988	100.0	33.0	6.5	1.8	1.3	3.7	38.6	30.3	8.2	1.9	1.2	1.6	10.4

a Excluding unemployment taxes.
b Unallocable, included in "Other."
c License taxes included in "Other."

Source: Computed by Tax Foundation from data in Table E17.

E17. State Tax Collections by Source
Selected Fiscal Years 1902-1938 and Fiscal Years 1940-1988[a]
($Millions)

Year	Total Including Unemployment	Total Excluding Unemployment	General Sales, Use, or Gross Receipts	Motor Vehicle Fuel Sales	Tobacco Products Sales	Alcoholic Beverage Sales and Licenses	Motor Vehicle and Operators' Licenses
1902	c	$ 156	-	-	-	$ 2[f] e	$ 5
1913	c	301	-	-	-	-	152
1922	c	947	-	$ 13	-	-	301
1927	c	1,608	-	259	-	-	335
1932	c	1,890	$ 7	527	$ 19	1	305
1934	c	1,979	173	565	25	81	360
1936	$ 2,641	2,618	364	687	44	166	359
1938	3,834	3,132	447	777	55	227	387
1940	4,157	3,313	499	839	97	255	434
1941	4,507	3,606	575	913	106	272	431
1942	4,979	3,903	632	940	130	313	414
1943	5,136	3,964	671	776	141	335	394
1944	5,390	4,071	720	684	159	324	414
1945	5,603	4,349	776	696	145	368	439
1946	5,971	4,937	899	886	198	469	517
1947	6,690	5,721	1,181	1,110	245	480	593
1948	7,802	6,743	1,478	1,259	337	499	665
1949	8,349	7,376	1,609	1,361	388	502	755
1950	8,958	7,930	1,670	1,544	414	497	840
1951	10,270	8,933	2,000	1,710	430	546	924
1952	11,295	9,857	2,229	1,870	449	519	1,012
1953	11,922	10,552	2,433	2,019	469	544	1,098
1954	12,352	11,089	2,540	2,218	464	542	1,184
1955	12,735	11,597	2,637	2,353	459	550	1,295
1956	14,690	13,375	3,036	2,687	515	625	1,368
1957	16,041	14,531	3,373	2,828	556	650	1,415
1958	16,412	14,919	3,507	2,919	616	647	1,492
1959	17,495	15,848	3,697	3,058	675	684	1,573
1960	20,172	18,036	4,302	3,335	923	734	1,641
1961	21,374	19,057	4,510	3,431	1,001	774	1,667
1962	23,210	20,561	5,111	3,665	1,075	740	1,780
1963	25,109	22,117	5,539	3,851	1,124	883	1,917
1964	27,289	24,243	6,084	4,059	1,196	989	2,021
1965	29,120	26,126	6,711	4,300	1,284	1,050	2,236
1966	32,420	29,380	7,873	4,627	1,541	1,120	2,311
1967	34,836	31,926	8,923	4,837	1,615	1,182	2,485
1968	38,947	36,400	10,441	5,178	1,886	1,281	2,685
1969	44,481	41,931	12,443	5,644	2,056	1,379	2,728
1970	50,486	47,962	14,177	6,283	2,308	1,540	2,953
1971	54,031	51,541	15,473	6,628	2,536	1,650	3,340
1972	62,998	59,870	17,619	7,216	2,831	1,820	3,636
1973	72,564	68,069	19,793	8,058	3,112	1,957	3,755
1974	79,336	74,207	22,612	8,207	3,250	2,051	3,941
1975	85,290	80,155	24,780	8,255	3,286	2,110	4,356
1976	95,422	89,256	27,333	8,660	3,462	2,211	4,587
1977	109,608	101,085	30,896	9,088	3,500	2,297	4,835
1978	123,155	113,261	35,280	9,501	3,653	2,454	5,155
1979	136,669	124,908	39,505	9,980	3,640	2,580	5,325
1980	149,746	137,075	43,168	9,722	3,738	2,657	5,695
1981	167,227	149,738	46,412	9,734	3,893	2,826	6,036
1982	178,358	162,607	50,357	10,473	3,958	2,937	6,292
1983	192,091	171,464	53,643	10,793	4,001	2,967	6,933
1984	212,845	196,905	62,564	12,406	3,949	3,161	7,780
1985	232,336	215,893	69,633	13,344	4,534	3,266	8,374
1986	244,686	228,054	74,821	14,087	4,449	3,302	9,037
1987	264,260	247,149	79,819	15,661	4,606	3,343	9,644
1988	n.a.	264,055	87,010	17,196	4,801	3,433	

[a] In 1945, 1943, and prior to 1942, includes all local shares of state-imposed taxes.
[b] In several states, individual and corporation income taxes are not segregable.
[c] Unemployment tax not levied prior to 1936.

Continued

E17. State Tax Collections by Source (continued)

Selected Fiscal Years 1902-1938 and Fiscal Years 1940-1988[a]

($Millions)

Total	Income[b] Individual	Corporation	Property	Death and Gift	Severance	Unemploy- ment[c]	Other[d]	Year
-	-	-	$ 82	e	-	-	$ 74	1902
-	-	-	140	e	-	-	154	1913
$ 101	$ 43	$ 58	348	$ 66	-	-	267	1922
162	70	92	370	106	-	-	410	1927
153	74	79	328	148	$ 19	-	353	1932
129	80	49	273	93	21	-	314	1934
266	153	113	228	117	34	$ 23	354	1936
383	218	165	244	142	58	702	440	1938
361	206	155	260	113	53	844	449	1940
422	225	197	268	118	53	901	445	1941
518	249	269	264	110	62	1,076	502	1942
633	293	340	259	109	75	1,172	547	1943
762	316	446	243	110	71	1,319	605	1944
810	357	453	276	136	83	1,254	643	1945
831	389	442	249	141	90	1,034	737	1946
869	418	451	261	165	94	969	799	1947
1,084	499	585	276	179	131	1,059	905	1948
1,234	593	641	276	176	201	973	963	1949
1,310	724	586	307	168	211	1,028	1,053	1950
1,492	805	687	346	196	222	1,337	1,151	1951
1,751	913	838	370	211	272	1,438	1,262	1952
1,779	969	810	365	222	286	1,370	1,423	1953
1,776	1,004	772	391	247	312	1,263	1,502	1954
1,831	1,094	737	412	249	306	1,138	1,616	1955
2,264	1,374	890	467	310	361	1,315	1,815	1956
2,547	1,563	984	479	338	388	1,510	2,003	1957
2,562	1,544	1,018	533	351	370	1,493	1,998	1958
2,765	1,764	1,001	566	347	394	1,647	2,171	1959
3,389	2,209	1,180	607	420	420	2,136	2,333	1960
3,621	2,355	1,266	631	501	451	2,317	2,496	1961
4,036	2,728	1,308	640	516	451	2,649	2,660	1962
4,461	2,956	1,505	688	595	468	2,992	2,728	1963
5,110	3,415	1,695	722	658	489	3,046	3,019	1964
5,586	3,657	1,929	766	731	503	2,994	3,171	1965
6,326	4,288	2,038	834	808	545	3,040	3,463	1966
7,136	4,909	2,227	862	795	577	2,910	3,688	1967
8,749	6,231	2,518	912	872	618	2,547	3,977	1968
10,707	7,527	3,180	981	996	630	2,550	4,410	1969
12,921	9,183	3,738	1,092	996	686	2,524	5,231	1970
13,577	10,153	3,424	1,126	1,104	733	2,490	5,761	1971
17,412	12,996	4,416	1,257	1,294	758	3,128	6,323	1972
21,012	15,587	5,425	1,312	1,431	850	4,495	6,908	1973
23,093	17,078	6,015	1,301	1,425	1,255	5,129	7,258	1974
25,461	18,819	6,642	1,451	1,418	1,741	5,135	7,712	1975
28,721	21,448	7,273	2,118	1,513	2,029	6,166	8,853	1976
34,667	25,493	9,174	2,260	1,805	2,168	8,523	9,817	1977
39,843	29,105	10,738	2,364	1,837	2,493	9,894	10,988	1978
44,750	32,622	12,128	2,490	1,973	2,893	11,761	11,996	1979
50,410	37,089	13,321	2,892	2,035	4,167	12,671	12,799	1980
55,038	40,895	14,143	2,949	2,229	6,379	17,489	14,584	1981
59,670	45,668	14,002	3,116	2,350	7,830	15,751	15,925	1982
62,942	49,789	13,153	3,281	2,545	7,406	20,627	17,594	1983
74,514	59,002	15,511	3,862	2,226	7,249	15,940	20,041	1984
81,539	63,908	17,631	3,984	2,328	7,211	16,443	22,274	1985
85,832	67,469	18,363	4,355	2,534	6,125	16,632	24,175	1986
96,778	76,038	20,740	4,613	3,023	4,048	17,111	26,222	1987
101,818	80,133	21,685	5,049	3,241	4,326	n.a.	27,537	1988

d Includes taxes on insurance, public utilities, pari-mutuels, corporation licenses, hunting and fishing licenses, documents and stock transfers, other, and unsegregable.
e Unsegregable, included in "Other."
f Licenses included in "Other."
Source: Department of Commerce, Bureau of the Census.

E18. State Tax Collections by Source and State

Excluding Unemployment Tax Collections

Fiscal Year 1988[a]
($Thousands)

State	Total	General Sales, Use or Gross Receipts	Selective Sales, Use, or Gross Receipts[b]	Licenses	Individual Income[c]	Corporation Net Income	Property	Death and Gift	Severance	Other Taxes
Total	$264,055,303	$87,009,688	$43,126,314	$17,019,743	$80,133,133	$21,684,670	$5,049,111	$3,240,929	$4,326,436	$2,465,279
Alabama	3,374,056	927,750	897,490	280,666	929,459	177,657	72,965	15,393	60,603	12,073
Alaska	1,251,021	-	81,710	72,234	449	181,387	96,225	361	818,655	-
Arizona	3,722,112	1,706,342	583,665	257,043	857,710	148,134	138,240	30,978	-	-
Arkansas	2,020,721	777,073	370,648	125,078	596,899	116,202	4,784	5,745	16,302	7,990
California	36,075,033	11,515,266	3,028,719	1,670,571	12,864,291	4,781,873	1,880,708	307,460	26,145	-
Colorado	2,725,767	724,300	490,276	159,078	1,159,923	146,776	6,083	13,175	15,330	10,826
Connecticut	4,376,395	1,983,977	925,011	260,592	352,031	601,212	12	176,852	-	76,708
Delaware	1,018,367	-	144,793	327,530	377,782	119,323	-	11,479	-	37,460
Florida	11,460,299	6,862,627	2,259,870	685,279	-	624,032	222,918	177,168	75,023	553,382
Georgia	5,782,747	1,856,625	772,450	179,259	2,391,771	478,969	20,309	54,204	-	29,160
Hawaii	2,039,375	919,796	374,701	29,709	625,594	78,053	-	7,314	-	4,208
Idaho	893,658	328,453	149,837	70,344	280,991	61,352	80	1,926	675	-
Illinois	11,078,693	3,677,354	2,125,171	814,621	3,161,110	973,704	231,191	82,502	-	13,040
Indiana	5,311,824	2,361,910	656,913	178,452	1,764,498	261,125	23,707	64,544	675	-
Iowa	2,841,657	859,033	442,980	254,887	1,064,816	158,040	-	58,932	-	2,969
Kansas	2,445,284	775,633	356,290	135,926	826,318	195,520	29,280	44,505	81,812	-
Kentucky	3,663,591	951,756	733,034	183,927	1,006,992	255,760	269,912	49,056	210,046	3,108
Louisiana	3,774,225	1,300,885	767,948	368,558	575,693	219,894	26,827	41,550	472,870	-
Maine	1,505,523	491,936	245,176	96,188	555,212	84,704	6,237	11,913	-	14,157
Maryland	5,807,153	1,423,585	1,128,687	204,923	2,432,698	313,070	147,621	58,012	-	98,557
Massachusetts	8,521,404	2,021,093	892,650	248,379	3,984,746	1,068,341	932	254,701	-	50,562
Michigan	10,515,368	2,919,055	1,145,156	579,931	3,587,860	1,856,105	278,656	93,799	43,581	11,225
Minnesota	6,143,956	1,676,632	1,025,896	375,120	2,625,405	411,960	7,536	13,610	7,796	1
Mississippi	2,126,254	1,007,276	395,439	185,431	353,227	96,170	19,774	15,713	53,224	-
Missouri	4,405,501	1,683,481	603,358	337,566	1,515,970	224,228	10,876	28,590	33	1,399

Continued

E18. State Tax Collections by Source and State (continued)

Excluding Unemployment Tax Collections

Fiscal Year 1986[a]

($Thousands)

State	Total	General Sales, Use or Gross Receipts	Selective Sales, Use, or Gross Receipts[b]	Licenses	Individual Income[c]	Corporation Net Income	Property	Death and Gift	Severance	Other Taxes
Montana	$715,083	-	$182,094	$74,058	$243,768	$46,200	$34,958	$8,745	$112,779	$12,481
Nebraska	1,342,868	$447,790	278,803	98,465	432,035	73,783	3,884	3,343	2,571	2,194
Nevada	1,186,445	546,409	435,641	149,346	-	-	39,115	5,279	10,655	-
New Hampshire	583,103	-	256,878	82,680	29,844	145,680	9,894	21,933	-65	36,259
New Jersey	9,762,360	3,136,801	2,015,934	593,844	2,557,694	1,181,849	27,073	163,117	-	86,048
New Mexico	1,793,387	739,904	273,486	127,565	303,733	49,576	3,148	4,095	291,880	-
New York	26,171,524	5,510,790	2,868,213	778,521	13,569,288	2,172,245	-	459,827	-	812,640
North Carolina	6,922,990	1,627,672	1,194,029	456,240	2,784,385	712,975	80,370	65,740	1,579	-
North Dakota	633,339	204,793	121,394	59,495	114,020	39,094	2,148	1,498	90,897	-
Ohio	9,990,514	3,218,959	1,950,318	806,389	3,364,689	582,026	13,562	45,218	9,353	13,223
Oklahoma	3,150,072	756,916	700,151	336,752	832,779	83,725	-	39,846	386,680	1,508
Oregon	2,110,963	-	314,949	298,191	1,283,647	167,047	2	13,647	31,972	
Pennsylvania	11,825,044	3,846,585	2,169,301	1,201,892	2,805,432	1,046,443	140,865	401,404	-	213,122
Rhode Island	1,120,534	383,209	191,421	42,919	388,461	79,194	8,021	21,821	-	5,488
South Carolina	3,438,186	1,249,430	616,552	171,023	1,141,076	203,959	8,029	35,991	-	12,126
South Dakota	475,701	262,348	130,596	37,589	-	26,357	-	10,362	8,449	-
Tennessee	3,855,027	2,142,276	804,454	381,598	79,650	352,120	-	33,484	1,820	59,625
Texas	13,425,516	6,271,018	4,005,775	1,981,504	-	-	-	108,410	1,058,809	-
Utah	1,602,093	589,480	197,340	73,204	637,511	71,663	296	3,443	29,156	-
Vermont	616,553	123,490	179,832	48,338	201,660	44,688	389	6,161	-	11,995
Virginia	6,136,607	1,188,856	1,338,424	342,380	2,757,868	334,382	26,104	43,205	1,668	103,720
Washington	5,994,964	3,553,516	958,117	329,349	-	-	948,787	18,846	45,790	140,559
West Virginia	1,743,871	537,499	386,909	108,372	394,181	176,704	1,651	6,489	128,486	3,580
Wisconsin	6,005,545	1,769,062	905,795	297,811	2,319,967	461,369	128,654	98,086	915	23,886
Wyoming	573,030	151,047	52,040	60,926	-	-	77,288	1,457	230,272	-
District of Columbia	2,060,338	390,646	181,581	38,426	592,828	151,498	609,425	33,559	-	62,375

a Preliminary; unemployment tax collections are shown in Table E47.
b Includes collections of motor fuels, alcoholic beverages, tobacco products, insurance, public utilities, pari-mutuels, amusement, and other selective sales and gross receipts.
c Includes three states (Connecticut, New Hampshire, and Tennessee) where tax applies to limited income base (see Table E23).
Source: Department of Commerce, Bureau of the Census.

E19. Percentage Distribution of State Tax Collections by Source and State

Excluding Unemployment Tax Collections

Fiscal Year 1988

State	Total	General Sales	Selective Sales and Gross Receipts	Licenses	Income	Property	Other
Total	100.0	33.0	16.3	6.4	38.6	1.9	3.8
Alabama	100.0	27.5	26.6	8.3	32.8	2.2	2.6
Alaska	100.0	-	6.5	5.8	14.5	7.7	65.5[b]
Arizona	100.0	45.8	15.7	6.9	27.0	3.7	.8
Arkansas	100.0	38.5	18.3	6.2	35.3	.2	1.5
California	100.0	31.9	8.4	4.6	48.9	5.2	.9
Colorado	100.0	26.6	18.0	5.8	47.9	.2	1.4
Connecticut	100.0	45.3	21.1	6.0	21.8	a	5.8
Delaware	100.0	-	14.2	32.2	48.8	-	4.8
Florida	100.0	59.9	19.7	6.0	5.4	1.9	7.0
Georgia	100.0	32.1	13.4	3.1	49.6	.4	1.4
Hawaii	100.0	45.1	18.4	1.5	34.5	-	.6
Idaho	100.0	36.8	16.8	7.9	38.3	a	.3
Illinois	100.0	33.2	19.2	7.4	37.3	2.1	.9
Indiana	100.0	44.5	12.4	3.4	38.1	.4	1.2
Iowa	100.0	30.2	15.6	9.0	43.0	-	2.2
Kansas	100.0	31.7	14.6	5.6	41.8	1.2	5.2
Kentucky	100.0	26.0	20.0	5.0	34.5	7.4	7.2
Louisiana	100.0	34.5	20.3	9.8	21.1	.7	13.6
Maine	100.0	32.7	16.3	6.4	9.3	.4	1.7
Maryland	100.0	24.5	19.4	3.5	47.3	2.5	2.7
Massachusetts	100.0	23.7	10.5	2.9	59.3	a	3.6
Michigan	100.0	27.8	10.9	5.5	51.8	2.6	1.4
Minnesota	100.0	27.3	16.7	6.1	49.4	.1	.3
Mississippi	100.0	47.4	18.6	8.7	21.1	.9	3.2
Missouri	100.0	38.2	13.7	7.7	39.5	.2	.7
Montana	100.0	-	25.5	10.4	40.6	4.9	18.7
Nebraska	100.0	33.3	20.8	7.3	37.7	.3	.6
Nevada	100.0	46.1	36.7	12.6	-	3.3	1.3
New Hampshire	100.0	-	44.1	14.2	30.1	1.7	10.0
New Jersey	100.0	32.1	20.7	6.1	38.3	.3	2.6
New Mexico	100.0	41.3	15.2	7.1	19.7	.2	16.5
New York	100.0	21.1	11.0	3.0	60.1	-	4.9
North Carolina	100.0	23.5	17.2	6.6	50.5	1.2	1.0
North Dakota	100.0	32.3	19.2	9.4	24.2	.3	14.6
Ohio	100.0	32.2	19.5	8.1	39.5	.1	.5
Oklahoma	100.0	24.0	22.2	10.7	29.1	-	14.0
Oregon	100.0	-	14.9	14.1	68.7	a	2.2
Pennsylvania	100.0	32.5	18.3	10.2	32.6	1.2	5.2
Rhode Island	100.0	34.2	17.1	3.8	41.7	.7	2.4
South Carolina	100.0	36.3	17.9	5.0	39.1	.2	1.4
South Dakota	100.0	55.1	27.5	7.9	5.5	-	4.0
Tennessee	100.0	55.6	20.9	9.9	11.2	-	2.5
Texas	100.0	46.7	29.8	14.8	-	-	8.7
Utah	100.0	36.8	12.3	4.6	44.3	a	2.0
Vermont	100.0	20.0	29.2	7.8	40.0	.1	2.9
Virginia	100.0	19.4	21.8	5.6	50.4	.4	2.4
Washington	100.0	59.3	16.0	5.5	-	15.8	3.4
West Virginia	100.0	30.8	22.2	6.2	32.7	.1	7.9
Wisconsin	100.0	29.5	15.1	5.0	46.3	2.1	2.0
Wyoming	100.0	26.4	9.1	10.6	-	13.5	40.4[b]
District of Columbia	100.0	19.0	8.8	1.9	36.1	29.6	4.7

[a] Less than .05%.
[b] Primarily severance tax collections.
Source: Computed by Tax Foundation from data in Table E18.

E20. State Tax Collections by State

Excluding Unemployment Tax Collections[a]

Selected Fiscal Years 1939-1988[b]

($Thousands)

State	1939	1946	1950	1960	1970	1980	1986	1987	1988
Total	$ 3,076,387	$ 4,937,065	$ 7,929,881	$ 18,035,927	$ 47,961,994	$ 137,056,630	$ 228,053,889	$ 247,148,658	$ 264,055,303
Alabama	47,780	66,607	115,918	273,718	657,361	1,856,789	2,997,093	3,222,201	3,374,056
Alaska	-	-	-	27,110	85,899	1,437,607	1,856,488	1,062,391	1,251,021
Arizona	15,288	31,701	47,836	164,965	474,270	1,716,237	3,195,720	3,469,477	3,722,112
Arkansas	28,030	55,415	85,015	158,118	351,447	1,160,767	1,826,701	1,889,066	2,020,721
California	242,215	480,144	811,206	2,124,369	5,497,548	19,366,696	30,878,427	35,790,750	36,075,033
Colorado	31,360	51,268	89,455	192,542	470,060	1,490,898	2,344,375	2,561,477	2,725,767
Connecticut	40,258	55,783	105,636	238,124	741,789	1,839,678	3,836,804	4,359,175	4,376,395
Delaware	9,776	15,175	25,775	70,776	195,648	515,715	882,666	989,298	1,018,367
Florida	51,191	111,066	170,275	521,682	1,421,109	4,804,298	9,120,166	9,846,189	11,460,299
Georgia	42,128	79,769	124,648	369,080	941,334	2,728,961	4,917,070	5,323,689	5,782,747
Hawaii	-	-	-	124,230	340,450	998,383	1,490,665	1,697,424	2,039,375
Idaho	10,143	18,172	30,052	68,999	155,880	490,346	744,739	829,698	893,658
Illinois	183,247	256,819	380,270	836,372	2,868,694	7,073,077	9,800,757	10,529,524	11,078,693
Indiana	72,617	117,887	202,895	399,379	1,002,418	2,695,759	4,458,168	4,774,190	5,311,824
Iowa	61,071	82,127	146,437	265,787	628,327	1,746,828	2,459,172	2,662,110	2,841,657
Kansas	36,144	59,221	119,349	206,622	430,975	1,269,671	1,911,548	2,085,490	2,445,284
Kentucky	40,787	65,032	107,390	228,507	703,044	2,144,941	3,216,343	3,520,409	3,663,591
Louisiana	70,143	113,157	240,867	452,695	838,792	2,397,215	3,629,513	3,448,641	3,774,225
Maine	19,751	26,049	41,628	86,929	207,617	619,160	1,101,381	1,288,480	1,505,523
Maryland	35,895	57,523	131,464	343,579	1,082,058	2,760,818	4,669,561	5,204,499	5,807,153
Massachusetts	106,826	175,351	234,846	491,123	1,393,653	3,927,303	7,668,440	8,463,874	8,521,404
Michigan	139,610	238,113	393,056	913,920	2,345,090	5,947,650	9,314,194	9,857,122	10,515,368
Minnesota	75,775	99,050	188,610	352,583	1,020,953	3,242,940	4,898,456	5,546,422	6,143,956
Mississippi	27,288	57,943	87,451	194,300	485,755	1,257,932	1,917,330	1,943,388	2,126,254
Missouri	69,071	111,789	162,215	213,895	820,860	2,094,540	3,608,083	3,942,295	4,405,501
Montana	11,007	14,395	30,149	64,868	128,823	435,751	617,108	591,001	715,083
Nebraska	21,474	28,661	54,055	91,052	261,307	816,767	1,119,382	1,203,344	1,342,868
Nevada	3,554	5,375	10,953	44,885	149,128	476,604	1,048,301	1,118,326	1,186,445
New Hampshire	12,445	16,328	19,819	41,757	94,765	267,495	484,478	562,712	583,103
New Jersey	91,730	135,150	147,914	365,232	1,332,251	4,265,830	8,360,193	9,491,417	9,762,360
New Mexico	13,998	27,120	51,070	123,206	273,466	926,048	1,462,123	1,574,692	1,793,387
New York	416,207	668,718	891,783	1,961,008	6,116,519	12,626,027	22,747,419	24,676,346	26,171,524
North Carolina	69,169	137,544	212,728	459,373	1,190,220	3,215,348	5,579,710	6,235,163	6,922,990
North Dakota	11,235	21,196	39,210	60,760	121,646	371,861	616,076	573,465	633,339
Ohio	190,341	242,376	379,403	872,723	1,702,624	4,766,665	9,062,151	9,717,146	9,990,514
Oklahoma	55,721	104,883	158,232	275,379	502,121	1,776,044	2,959,632	2,669,188	3,150,072
Oregon	22,592	52,094	99,829	208,283	430,686	1,455,352	1,931,346	2,235,073	2,110,963
Pennsylvania	238,747	263,406	439,387	1,032,861	2,777,578	7,240,808	10,683,238	11,378,764	11,825,044
Rhode Island	14,162	25,284	38,297	86,095	228,674	550,787	885,557	1,050,144	1,120,534
South Carolina	28,646	61,133	90,019	235,478	543,678	1,678,049	2,887,103	3,339,515	3,438,186
South Dakota	14,879	18,887	37,923	52,993	112,705	270,518	403,741	416,386	475,701
Tennessee	40,553	67,065	149,782	304,590	686,936	1,886,992	3,271,963	3,603,331	3,855,027
Texas	111,375	170,921	315,117	792,800	1,975,087	6,758,706	11,124,708	11,227,796	13,425,516
Utah	15,365	26,181	43,613	100,405	251,596	785,755	1,364,835	1,438,325	1,602,093
Vermont	9,853	13,383	20,425	43,522	135,177	266,317	499,519	537,905	616,553
Virginia	47,365	79,625	147,081	291,664	955,726	2,743,325	4,846,627	5,526,557	6,136,607
Washington	57,474	134,872	201,560	460,770	1,028,028	2,917,445	5,219,292	5,639,369	5,994,964
West Virginia	43,616	62,252	94,029	180,119	384,993	1,219,492	1,848,552	1,830,168	1,743,871
Wisconsin	75,649	126,433	197,546	426,234	1,332,754	3,366,310	5,491,530	5,673,577	6,005,545
Wyoming	6,836	8,622	17,663	41,460	84,475	388,125	795,445	631,669	573,030

[a] Unemployment tax collections by state shown in Table E47.
[b] Data for 1939 not strictly comparable to other years.
Source: Department of Commerce, Bureau of the Census.

E21. Per Capita State Tax Collections by State
Excluding Unemployment Tax Collections
Selected Fiscal Years 1939-1988[a]

State	1939	1946	1950	1960	1970	1980	1986	1987	1988[b]
Total	$ 23.81	$ 37.51	$ 53.63	$ 104.08	$ 239.16	$ 623.91	$ 948.44	$ 1,018.00	$ 1,075.45
Alabama	14.99	24.00	36.84	84.48	191.09	492.65	739.48	789.17	819.94
Alaska	-	-	-	123.23	290.20	3,540.90	3,476.57	2,023.60	2,258.16
Arizona	32.81	53.37	67.00	131.55	273.04	687.51	963.44	1,024.65	1,050.85
Arkansas	14.54	31.45	46.10	88.88	183.72	532.46	770.11	791.07	841.97
California	36.39	51.39	78.48	138.54	278.91	853.38	1,144.45	1,293.81	1,285.00
Colorado	28.20	45.94	69.08	111.32	217.13	537.83	717.59	777.15	813.66
Connecticut	23.91	31.53	51.99	95.44	247.26	590.59	1,203.14	1,357.58	1,352.83
Delaware	38.04	53.06	81.57	161.22	362.31	886.11	1,394.42	1,536.18	1,569.13
Florida	28.91	45.06	63.82	108.91	213.99	542.25	781.17	818.95	935.61
Georgia	13.63	25.58	37.49	94.59	206.84	533.31	805.55	855.62	905.82
Hawaii	-	-	-	200.37	453.93	1,091.13	1,403.64	1,567.34	1,852.29
Idaho	19.77	35.84	52.72	104.86	220.48	541.82	742.51	831.36	885.69
Illinois	23.30	33.79	43.86	83.86	259.87	629.89	848.33	900.49	956.38
Indiana	21.45	34.40	51.26	86.52	194.91	499.21	809.99	863.17	960.37
Iowa	24.49	35.58	56.80	96.83	224.00	601.94	862.56	939.35	1,013.79
Kansas	19.62	34.21	62.00	95.57	192.74	535.95	776.74	842.28	987.20
Kentucky	14.57	25.04	37.69	75.82	219.84	608.15	862.75	944.57	980.09
Louisiana	30.70	46.59	91.45	141.20	231.77	596.53	806.38	773.06	837.41
Maine	23.43	32.56	46.10	90.74	209.29	564.41	938.14	1,085.49	1,261.96
Maryland	20.33	27.44	56.45	112.61	279.75	665.58	1,046.28	1,147.63	1,262.70
Massachusetts	24.47	41.74	49.54	96.62	246.66	680.76	1,314.89	1,445.58	1,456.90
Michigan	27.61	43.49	62.07	117.88	267.06	645.99	1,018.50	1,071.43	1,139.14
Minnesota	27.52	39.04	64.26	104.38	271.67	788.81	1,162.42	1,306.27	1,438.53
Mississippi	12.83	27.72	41.94	89.87	218.81	517.88	730.41	740.34	799.04
Missouri	18.27	31.79	41.79	73.00	176.91	430.37	712.22	772.54	858.44
Montana	19.94	30.18	52.99	97.25	185.62	554.39	753.49	730.53	818.73
Nebraska	16.19	23.67	41.52	64.95	177.28	518.91	700.49	754.92	842.98
Nevada	33.85	36.07	69.76	160.88	310.68	678.92	1,088.58	1,110.55	1,162.04
New Hampshire	25.66	35.57	37.18	69.36	130.89	301.57	471.74	532.37	535.94
New Jersey	22.37	32.90	30.25	61.28	187.77	559.78	1,097.14	1,237.15	1,258.68
New Mexico	27.29	50.50	79.30	132.76	270.49	746.21	988.59	1,049.79	1,151.82
New York	30.80	53.52	59.88	118.00	337.84	720.58	1,279.96	1,384.37	1,474.04
North Carolina	20.11	38.93	54.39	102.04	236.58	573.55	881.33	972.27	1,048.62
North Dakota	17.36	38.82	65.68	96.91	195.89	566.00	907.33	853.37	946.70
Ohio	27.84	35.05	47.59	90.80	161.19	444.20	842.83	901.07	926.85
Oklahoma	23.98	51.72	75.17	119.68	198.08	614.12	895.50	815.77	958.05
Oregon	21.17	41.68	69.76	118.61	208.87	575.92	715.84	820.51	772.40
Pennsylvania	23.99	28.81	42.29	91.93	236.57	617.24	898.58	953.31	997.05
Rhode Island	20.41	32.58	47.81	100.81	245.36	592.88	908.26	1,065.05	1,133.00
South Carolina	15.62	31.61	44.37	99.44	211.55	572.32	854.68	975.04	992.55
South Dakota	22.93	32.62	60.10	78.05	168.72	392.62	570.26	587.29	672.84
Tennessee	14.38	23.30	46.29	85.87	176.27	430.82	681.23	742.19	788.19
Texas	17.99	25.04	41.34	85.08	178.82	505.13	666.87	668.76	780.92
Utah	28.72	44.30	65.00	114.49	240.30	574.80	819.72	856.15	930.37
Vermont	27.68	42.49	55.35	112.75	309.33	540.20	923.33	981.58	1,116.94
Virginia	17.95	24.94	44.68	74.23	207.14	527.87	837.50	936.07	1,026.70
Washington	33.85	61.14	87.86	163.22	307.52	743.11	1,169.46	1,242.70	1,313.53
West Virginia	23.86	36.45	48.72	96.22	220.50	649.36	963.29	964.77	924.64
Wisconsin	24.42	42.70	58.26	108.87	304.42	713.20	1,147.66	1,180.27	1,251.94
Wyoming	27.79	36.08	63.77	127.57	256.76	862.50	1,568.93	1,289.12	1,134.71

[a] Computations based on population as of July 1; data for 1939 not strictly comparable to other years.
[b] Computed by Tax Foundation; population figures are projections.
Source: Department of Commerce, Bureau of the Census.

E22. Dates of Adoption of Major State Taxes by State

State	Individual Income	Corporate Income	General Sales	Gasoline	Cigarettes	Distilled Spirits[a]
Alabama	1933	1933	1936	1923	1935	-
Alaska	1949[b]	1949	-	1946	1949	1945
Arizona	1933	1933	1933	1921	1935	1933
Arkansas	1929	1929	1935	1921	1929	1935
California	1935	1929	1933	1923	1959	1935
Colorado	1937	1937	1935	1919	1964	1933
Connecticut	1969[b]	1915	1947	1921	1935	1937
Delaware	1917	1957	-	1923	1943	1933
Florida	-	1971	1949	1921	1943	1935
Georgia	1929	1929	1951	1921	1937	1937
Hawaii	1901	1901	1935	1932	1939	1939
Idaho	1931	1931	1965	1923	1945	-
Illinois	1969	1969	1933	1927	1941	1934
Indiana	1963	1963	1933	1923	1947	1933
Iowa	1934	1934	1933	1925	1921	-
Kansas	1933	1933	1937	1925	1927	1948
Kentucky	1936	1936	1960	1920	1936	1934
Louisiana	1934	1934	1938	1921	1932	1934
Maine	1969	1969	1951	1923	1941	-
Maryland	1937	1937	1947	1922	1958	1933
Massachusetts	1916	1919	1966	1929	1939	1933
Michigan	1967	1967	1933	1925	1947	-
Minnesota	1933	1933	1967	1925	1947	1934
Mississippi	1912	1921	1932	1922	1932	1966
Missouri	1917	1917	1934	1925	1955	1934
Montana	1933	1917	-	1921	1947	-
Nebraska	1967	1967	1967	1925	1947	1935
Nevada	-	-	1955	1923	1947	1935
New Hampshire	1923[b]	1970	-	1923	1939	-
New Jersey	1976	1958	1966	1927	1948	1933
New Mexico	1933	1933	1933	1919	1943	1934
New York	1919	1917	1965	1929	1939	1933
North Carolina	1921	1921	1933	1921	1969	-
North Dakota	1919	1919	1935	1919	1927	1936
Ohio	1971	1971	1934	1925	1931	-
Oklahoma	1915	1931	1933	1923	1933	1959
Oregon	1930	1929	-	1919	1965	-
Pennsylvania	1971	1935	1953	1921	1937	-
Rhode Island	1971	1947	1947	1925	1939	1933
South Carolina	1922	1922	1951	1922	1923	1935
South Dakota	-	-	1933	1922	1923	1935
Tennessee	1931[b]	1923	1947	1923	1925	1939
Texas	-	-	1961	1923	1931	1935
Utah	1931	1931	1933	1923	1923	-
Vermont	1931	1931	1969	1923	1937	-
Virginia	1916	1915	1966	1923	1960	-
Washington	-	-	1933	1921	1935	-
West Virginia	1961	1967	1933	1923	1947	-
Wisconsin	1911	1911	1961	1925	1939	1934
Wyoming	-	-	1935	1923	1951	-

[a] Excludes excises by the states that own and operate liquor stores, and by North Carolina where county stores operate under state supervision.
[b] Taxes are limited: Connecticut (capital gains and dividends); New Hampshire and Tennessee (interest and dividends). Alaska abolished its individual income tax in 1980.
Source: Advisory Commission on Intergovernmental Relations, and Commerce Clearing House.

E23. State Individual Income Tax Rates and Related Data[a]

As of March 1989

State	Lowest Bracket Rate (Percent)	To Net income of	Highest Bracket Rate (Percent)	Income Above	Maximum Personal Exemption and Credit for Dependents[b] — Married or Head of Family	Single	Each Dependent	Federal Income Tax Deductible
Alabama[c]	2	$1,000	5	$6,000	$3,000	$1,500	$300	Yes
Arizona[c,d,e]	2	1,229	8	7,374	2,250	2,125	1,275	Yes
Arkansas	1	2,999	7	25,000	40[f]	20[f]	20[f]	No
California[c,d,e]	1	7,636	9.3	50,105	104[f]	52[f]	52[f]	No
Colorado	5 percent of Federal taxable income				2,500	1,250	1,250	No
Delaware[c]	3.2	5,000	7.7	40,000	3,000	1,500	1,500	No
Georgia[c]	1	1,000	6	10,000	1,500	1,000	1,000	No
Hawaii[c,g]	2.25	2,400	10	40,400	2,000	1,000	1,000	No
Idaho[d]	2	1,000	8.2	20,000	Federal exemptions			No
Illinois	2.5	All	-	-	2,000	1,000	1,000	No
Indiana	3.4	All	-	-	2,000	1,000	1,000	No
Iowa[j]	.4	1,000	9.98	45,000	40	20	15	Yes[h]
Kansas[j]	4.5	27,500	5.95	27,500	4,000	2,000	2,000	No
Kentucky	2	3,000	6	8,000	40[f]	20[f]	20[f]	No
Louisiana[d]	2	10,000	6	50,000	9,000[i]	4,500[i]	1,000[i]	Yes
Maine[e]	2	6,000	8	16,250	100	60	55	No
Maryland	2	1,000	5	3,000	2,200	1,100	1,100	No
Massachusetts	[j]	All	-	-	4,400[j]	2,200	1,000	No
Michigan	4.6	All	-	-	Federal exemptions		720[m]	No
Minnesota[c,g]	6	19,000	8	19,000	9,500	6,000	1,500	No
Mississippi	3	5,000	5	10,000	2,400	1,200	400	No
Missouri	1.5	1,000	6	9,000	2,280	1,140	1,140	Yes[h]
Montana[e,k]	2	1,400	11	48,100	2,260	1,130	1,130	Yes
Nebraska[c]	2	3,000	5.9	45,000	2,000	1,000	1,000	No
New Jersey[c]	2	20,000	3.5	50,000	Federal exemptions			No
New Mexico[d]	2.4	8,000	8.5	64,000	2,000	1,000	1,000	No
New York	2	1,700	8.75	23,300	2,200	1,100	800	No
North Carolina	3	2,000	7	10,000	Federal exemptions			No
North Dakota[k]	2.67	3,000	12	50,000	Federal exemptions			Yes[h]
Ohio[g]	.751	5,000	6.9	100,000	1,300	650	650	No
Oklahoma[c,j]	.5	2,000	6	15,000	2,000	1,000	1,000	Yes[h]
Oregon[c,e]	5	2,000	9	5,000	178[f]	89[f]	89[f]	Yes[h]

Continued

E23. State Individual Income Tax Rates and Related Data[a] (continued)
As of March 1989

State	Lowest Bracket		Highest Bracket		Maximum Personal Exemption and Credit for Dependents[b]			Federal Income Tax Deductible
	Rate (Percent)	To Net Income of	Rate (Percent)	Income Above	Married or Head of Family	Single	Each Dependent	
Pennsylvania	2.1	All	-	-	Federal exemptions			No
Rhode Island	23.46 percent of taxpayer's Federal tax liability							No
South Carolina[c]	3	4,000	7	10,000		Federal exemptions[n]		Yes[h]
Utah[o]	2.75	1,500	7.75	7,500		Federal exemptions		Yes
Vermont[g]	25.8 percent of taxpayer's Federal tax liability							No
Virginia	2	3,000	5.75	14,000	1,600	800	800	No
West Virginia[c]	3	10,000	6.5	60,000	4,000	2,000	2,000	No
Wisconsin	4.9	10,000	6.93	20,001	50[f]	50[f]	50[f]	No
District of Columbia	6	10,000	9.5	20,000	2,550	1,025	1,025	No

[a] In addition to the states listed, three states tax limited portions of personal income. Connecticut levies a 7% tax on capital gains and a graduated 1% to 12% tax on dividends and interest income for taxpayers with Federal adjusted gross income of $54,000 or more. New Hampshire imposes a 5% tax on dividends and certain interest income. Tennessee taxes income from dividends and interest at 6%.

[b] Does not include exemptions or credits for age or blindness, to offset sales or property taxes paid, or for any other special purpose.

[c] Rates for the following states are for married persons filing jointly: Alabama, California, Georgia, Hawaii, Minnesota, Nebraska, New York, Oklahoma, Utah, and Wisconsin; separate rate schedules apply for single taxpayers and in some cases for heads of households. Rates for Arizona and Oregon are for single taxpayers; in the case of joint returns, the tax is twice the tax that would be due if taxable income of husband and wife were cut in half.

[d] Community property state in which, in general, half of community income is taxed to each spouse.

[e] Subject to annual adjustment for inflation. Brackets shown for Arizona and Montana are indexed for tax year 1988.

[f] Credit allowed in lieu of exemption.

[g] The tax rates are reduced for tax years beginning after 1988 in Hawaii. The rates will be increased after 1987 if there is a revenue shortfall, and for tax years beginning after 1990, the brackets will be adjusted for inflation in Minnesota. The rate in increased to 25% of federal liability for tax years beginning after 1988 in Vermont.

[h] Amount of Federal income tax deduction is limited. After 1987 Delaware's deductibility provision is repealed.

[i] Applies to allowable personal exemption and standard deduction.

[j] No tax is imposed on total income below $12,000 for husband and wife or $8,000 for single individuals. Above these amounts a 5% tax is levied on earned income and a 10% tax on interest, dividends, and net capital gains. Exemptions shown apply to earned income.

[k] A 10% surtax is imposed in Montana (until 1990) and North Dakota.

[l] Different rate schedules apply to taxpayers who choose to deduct Federal income tax in Oklahoma and Kansas.

[m] The credit for each dependent cannot exceed $720 in any tax year, and the total credit for all dependents of a claimant cannot exceed $1,440 in a tax year.

[n] An individual may claim a credit for expenses related to a dependent as provided in Federal Code Sec. 21, except that the term "applicable percentage" means 7% and is not reduced if a taxpayer's adjusted gross income exceeds $10,000 for a tax year.

[o] Personal exemptions for Utah state taxes are equal to 25% of the total amount of federal personal exemptions in the same tax year.

Source: Commerce Clearing House.

E24. State Individual Net Income Tax Collections by State

Selected Fiscal Years 1939-1988[a]

($Thousands)

State	1939	1950	1960	1970	1980	1986	1988
Total	$ 196,044	$ 724,435	$ 2,209,294	$ 9,182,862	$ 37,089,482	$ 67,469,185	$ 80,133,133
Alabama	1,061	14,314[b]	27,360	85,081	396,570	757,289	929,459
Alaska	-	-	8,903	32,455	100,481	556	449
Arizona	372	2,668	10,000	64,974	287,498	701,998	857,710
Arkansas	343	4,343	9,774	42,548	316,644	509,872	596,899
California	20,672	60,500	245,797	1,150,604	6,463,736	11,368,059	12,864,291
Colorado	1,361	11,287	34,542	129,097	461,325	955,931	1,159,923
Connecticut[c]	-	-	-	4,916	100,953	300,687	352,031
Delaware	1,085	7,398	26,393	68,486	235,763	393,705	377,782
Georgia	2,280	10,884	36,442	184,943	872,073	1,945,188	2,391,771
Hawaii	-	-	28,778	105,019	311,404	467,789	625,594
Idaho	520	5,374	20,195	36,662	159,138	255,974	280,991
Illinois	-	-	-	575,601	1,900,676	2,645,364	3,161,110
Indiana	-	-	-	216,384	556,709	1,326,861	1,764,498
Iowa	3,483	15,812	36,671	112,746	602,385	864,475	1,064,816
Kansas	1,325	8,313	24,000	78,423	336,061	582,158	826,318
Kentucky	1,941	11,025	51,686	121,423	505,832	819,893	1,006,992
Louisiana	2,344	18,768[d]	12,500	47,993	247,438	457,636	575,693
Maine	-	-	-	18,885	142,689	337,129	555,212
Maryland	570	18,267	85,010	413,366	1,097,009	1,929,547	2,432,698
Massachusetts	18,875	44,758	151,728	517,952	1,860,033	3,617,300	3,984,746
Michigan	-	-	-	415,345	1,916,626	3,248,238	3,587,860
Minnesota	8,097	37,351	89,328	345,733	1,262,697	1,948,595	2,625,405
Mississippi	861	4,487	7,639	44,162	150,296	272,612	353,227
Missouri	e	25,239[d]	37,659	129,654	603,319	1,116,470	1,515,970
Montana	435	3,687	10,707	38,871	135,012	172,216	243,768
Nebraska	-	-	-	44,444	235,821	351,828	432,035
New Hampshire	745	1,119	1,581	3,462	10,474	24,853	29,844
New Jersey	-	-	-	17,643[f]	1,004,781	2,052,592	2,557,694
New Mexico	268	1,546	7,101[d]	35,730	46,846	102,629	303,733
New York	105,888	262,916	756,364	2,506,435	5,780,045	11,582,305	13,569,288
North Carolina	2,767	24,397	91,814	270,945	1,180,507	2,206,749	2,784,385
North Dakota	275	3,697	4,796	15,379	53,346	73,368	114,020
Ohio	-	-	-	-	1,039,728	2,776,884	3,364,689
Oklahoma	2,469	7,260	16,780	50,516	361,895	687,646	832,779
Oregon	3,338	29,460	94,641	213,053	867,976	1,193,767	1,283,647
Pennsylvania	-	-	-	-	1,671,842	2,655,677	2,805,432
Rhode Island	-	-	-	18,644	153,912	286,649	388,461
South Carolina	1,250	10,292	31,642	95,398	494,789	907,285	1,141,076
South Dakota	e	-	-	-	-	-	-
Tennessee	1,386	3,045	5,218	12,113	30,800	67,432	79,650
Utah	680	4,111	16,234	61,335	265,327	451,543	637,511
Vermont	562	3,057	11,373	43,668	83,182	100,507	201,660
Virginia	2,161	23,993	77,314	282,769	1,103,006	2,174,272	2,757,868
West Virginia	1,311	-	-	40,061	252,362	478,590	394,181
Wisconsin	7,319	45,067	139,324	489,944	1,430,476	2,239,067	2,319,967

[a] Data for 1939 not strictly comparable to other years.
[b] In Alabama, 1950 data include corporate income taxes except on financial institutions; in Alaska, 1986 data reflect residual collections of repealed tax.
[c] In Connecticut, tax applicable to income from capital gains only in 1970, to capital gains and dividends in 1980, and to capital gains, dividends, and interest in 1986; in Tennessee and New Hampshire, the tax is restricted to income from interest and dividends.
[d] Includes corporation income taxes.
[e] Included with corporation income taxes in Table E26.
[f] In New Hampshire, a tax on commuters' income is included. In New Jersey, collections were only from New York and Pennsylvania commuters.
Source: Department of Commerce, Bureau of the Census.

E25. State Property Tax Collections by State

Selected Fiscal Years 1960-1988

($Thousands)

State	1960 Total	1960 General	1970 Total	1970 General	1980 Total	1980 General	1987 Total	1987 General	1988 Total
Total	$ 607,399	$ 231,497	$ 1,091,745	$ 359,262	$ 2,891,744	$ 900,394	$ 4,613,690	$ 1,014,124	$ 5,049,111
Alabama	13,220	13,220	22,853	22,596	44,287	43,356	68,640	67,487	72,965
Alaska	542 [a]	-	-	-	169,016	-	102,491	-	96,225
Arizona	28,470	25,250	67,822	59,983	121,990	86,914	114,852	59,278	138,240
Arkansas	321	68	870	99	3,571	296	5,669	244	4,784
California	125,459	-	233,480	-	677,238	-	1,668,447	-	1,880,708
Colorado	10,646	9,318	1,115	153	3,652	-	7,570	-	6,083
Connecticut	12	-	-	-	12	-	12	-	12
Delaware [b]	1,842	-	303	-	-	-	-	-	-
Florida	18,629	44 [a]	33,623	-	86,091	86,091	221,959	-	222,918
Georgia	1,275	1,275	3,123	-	9,565	8,701	17,801	16,032	20,309
Idaho	2,572	2,546	750	711	175	97	138	34	80
Illinois	918	2 [a]	2,502	25 [a]	103,979	-	222,432	-	231,191
Indiana	9,967	2,784	22,780	743	30,313	1,597	39,957	5,776	23,707
Iowa	3,641	3,448	4,063	3,947	-	-	-	-	-
Kansas	7,949	6,653	10,353	8,961	18,832	14,499	30,426	19,480	29,280
Kentucky	17,080	1,193	26,577	2,256	176,759	88,111	251,246	-	269,912
Louisiana	14,880	14,880	26,935	26,935	32	32	4,552	-	26,827
Maine	1,650	-	3,767	3,135	15,198	15,179	8,156	8,062	6,237
Maryland	12,101	-	34,119	34,014	83,597	82,987	128,523	128,176	147,621
Massachusetts	270	-	349	-	812	-	1,689	-	932
Michigan	51,170	-	83,032	-	133,412	-	205,113	-	278,656
Minnesota	22,518	20,828	5,810	283	4,281	12	6,180	-	7,536
Mississippi	4,448	4,448	3,917	3,917	4,723	4,723	285	285	19,774
Missouri	11,224	5,068	2,815	2,815	5,038	5,038	9,872	-	10,876
Montana	6,247	6,247	8,090	8,090	18,129	18,129	41,957	-	34,958
Nebraska	23,173	25,893	2,006	-	2,502	-	3,574	-	3,884
Nevada	1,841	1,841	4,336	-	21,024	200	38,542	-	39,115
New Hampshire	2,366	-	3,485	8	8,218	82	11,307	-	9,894
New Jersey	2,700	-	49,755	-	73,932	-	29,827	-	27,073
New Mexico	8,234	8,234	14,469	13,172	24,341	23,250	3,260	1,700	3,148
New York	3,474	3,474	12,350	12,350	6,520	6,520	-	-	-
North Carolina	11,155	-	23,680	-	45,908	-	78,316	-	80,370
North Dakota	3,220	3,172	1,406	914	2,174	1,347	2,215	2,215	2,148
Ohio	46,691	12,086	58,563	6	141,980	-	16,136	-	13,562
Oklahoma	-	-	-	-	-	-	-	-	-
Oregon	21	-	2,881	-	77	-	176	-	2
Pennsylvania	1,656	-	32,009	-	181,287	-	137,521	-	140,865
Rhode Island	-	-	-	-	6,280	-	7,156	-	8,021
South Carolina	1,042	1,642	1,655	-	6,042	-	8,456	-	8,029
South Dakota	3	3	-	-	-	-	-	-	-
Tennessee	9 [a]	9 [a]	-	-	-	-	-	-	-
Texas	37,587	37,587	64,063	64,063	47,351	47,351	-	-	-
Utah	8,087	8,087	12,835	12,835	147	147	289	289	296
Vermont	339	-	225	10	327	21	430	35	389
Virginia	13,170	-	12,599	-	23,505	-	23,510	-	26,104
Washington	34,017	9,305	113,061	60,949	471,559	322,906	889,069	580,492	948,787
West Virginia	390	390	250	250	713	713	1,944	1,944	1,651
Wisconsin	30,423	-	72,317	6,287	94,075	19,335	104,469	24,079	128,654
Wyoming	6,750	6,576	10,752	9,755	23,080	22,760	99,517	98,516	77,288

[a] Back taxes only.
[b] For years 1956 and 1960 tax was collected locally for schools operated directly by the State Board of Education.
Source: Department of Commerce, Bureau of the Census.

E26. State Corporation Net Income Tax Collections by State
Selected Fiscal Years 1939-1988[a]
($Thousands)

State	1939	1950	1960	1970	1980	1986	1987	1988
Total	$ 134,895	$ 585,750	$ 1,179,924	$ 3,737,944	$ 13,321,381	$ 18,362,904	$ 20,740,041	$ 21,684,670
Alabama	934	885[b]	9,447	30,797	109,238	156,745	161,832	177,657
Alaska	-	-	1,692	5,301	565,329	177,751	141,068	181,387
Arizona	544	2,897	6,833	20,910	117,764	170,821	198,948	148,134
Arkansas	306	7,809	8,862	26,228	83,714	113,205	115,620	116,202
California	20,230	74,546	240,064	587,577	2,507,183	3,833,261	4,758,950	4,781,873
Colorado	706	6,003	10,723	33,513	110,607	116,937	124,085	146,776
Connecticut	2,834	12,200	30,773	119,538	246,139	616,824	680,242	601,212
Delaware	-	-	7,478	13,446	40,553	88,923	120,993	119,323
Florida	-	-	-	-	371,405	486,925	596,434	624,032
Georgia	2,700	14,589	23,634	84,735	239,713	418,119	449,176	478,969
Hawaii			5,649	14,578	50,259	43,661	76,793	78,053
Idaho	877	3,297	5,778	11,125	42,604	42,652	47,308	61,352
Illinois	-	-	-	140,956	797,927	859,707	862,435	973,704
Indiana	-	-	-	8,597	179,191	183,565	235,709	261,125
Iowa	761	2,652	3,807	24,273	138,564	138,588	149,602	158,040
Kansas	867	3,456	8,434	19,258	149,517	156,344	137,061	195,520
Kentucky	1,518	8,305	20,240	39,459	158,846	233,524	267,378	255,760
Louisiana	2,891	c	18,331	34,770	249,338	263,815	191,189	219,894
Maine	-	-	-	8,257	45,086	51,870	68,336	84,704
Maryland	305	10,463	20,381	60,109	165,857	250,331	270,489	313,070
Massachusetts[d]	1,277	19,450	28,539	218,279	532,383	1,067,987	1,203,940	1,068,341
Michigan	-	-	-	194,602	910,732	1,449,598	1,644,692	1,856,105
Minnesota	6,492	15,568	39,840	79,832	381,217	367,312	422,999	411,960
Mississippi	852	7,637	13,460	19,949	64,369	97,301	102,865	96,170
Missouri	6,173[e]	c	10,000	21,287	135,103	174,199	235,352	224,228
Montana	395	1,678	4,671	9,696	45,623	58,585	34,568	46,200
Nebraska	-	-	-	8,550	57,579	54,559	67,423	73,783
New Hampshire	-	-	-	-[f]	62,786	99,063	151,793	145,680
New Jersey	-	-	27,690	169,178	497,205	954,885	1,088,311	1,181,849
New Mexico	279	1,255	c	8,072	46,272	72,130	99,139	49,576
New York	42,147	180,664	256,309	693,151	1,235,340	1,901,879	2,143,390	2,172,245
North Carolina	6,950	30,015	51,516	112,408	291,752	512,095	566,480	712,975
North Dakota	149	1,306	1,414	2,998	36,348	56,312	33,442	39,094
Ohio	-	-	-	-	517,394	477,794	474,588	582,026
Oklahoma	4,585	7,893	12,166	27,490	89,869	107,077	83,703	83,725
Oregon	1,484	17,017	22,442	39,880	177,425	161,728	136,376	167,047
Pennsylvania	15,141	64,214	142,086	529,770	861,682	963,228	1,015,814	1,046,443
Rhode Island	-	4,382	8,419	23,090	53,620	67,656	87,675	79,194
South Carolina	1,571	14,487	18,797	42,318	153,475	149,465	190,474	203,959
South Dakota[e]	574	143	395	780	3,292	23,617	24,212	26,357
Tennessee	1,784	10,443	21,392	59,633	198,222	268,618	298,644	352,120
Utah	1,024	2,584	5,671	11,790	40,377	66,450	60,891	71,663
Vermont	158	1,172	2,219	5,819	22,425	30,531	38,445	44,688
Virginia	2,077	18,458	31,715	67,369	193,847	280,768	320,598	334,382
West Virginia	-	-	-	3,872	32,889	88,909	89,890	176,704
Wisconsin	6,310	40,315	59,057	104,704	311,321	407,590	470,689	461,369

[a] Data for 1939 not strictly comparable to other years.
[b] Financial institutions only; other corporation income taxes are included with individual income taxes in Table E24.
[c] Unallocable, included with individual income taxes in Table E24.
[d] From 1939 to 1960 excludes corporation taxes measured in part by net income included with license taxes in Table E40; beginning in 1970, includes portion of corporation excise taxes and surtaxes measured by corporate excess. Financial institutions are included only in 1939.
[e] Includes individual income taxes in 1939; in later years shown, tax applies only to financial institutions.
[f] Includes unsegregable amount of business franchise tax.
Source: Department of Commerce, Bureau of the Census.

E27. State Corporation Income Tax Rates[a]

As of May 1989

State	Flat Rate or Lowest Bracket		Highest Bracket		Minimum Tax	Federal Income Tax Deductible[b]
	Rate (Percent)	To Net Income of	Rate (Percent)	Net Income Over		
Alabama	5.0	All	-	-	-	Yes
Alaska	1.0	$9,999	9.4	$90,000	-	No
Arizona	2.5	1,000	10.5	6,000	$50	Yes
Arkansas	1.0	3,000	6.0	25,000	-	No
California[d]	9.3	All	-	-	300[c]	No
Colorado	5.5	50,000	6.0	50,000	-	No
Connecticut	11.5[e]	All	-	-	100	No
Delaware	8.7	All	-	-	-	No
Florida	5.5	All[f]	-	-	-	No
Georgia	6.0	All	-	-	-	No
Hawaii[g]	4.4	25,000	6.4	100,000	-	No
Idaho	8.0[i]	All	-	-	20[h]	No
Illinois	4.0[j]	All[f]	-	-	-	No
Indiana	3.4[j]	All	-	-	-	No
Iowa	6.0[k]	25,000	12.0	250,000	-	Yes
Kansas	4.5[k]	All	-	-	-	No
Kentucky	3.0	25,000	7.25	250,000	-	No
Louisiana	4.0	25,000	8.0	200,000	-	Yes
Maine	3.5	25,000	8.93	250,000	-	No
Maryland	7.0[l]	All	-	-	-	No
Massachusetts	9.5[l]	All	-	-	228	No
Michigan	2.35[m]	All	-	-	-	No
Minnesota	9.5	All	-	-	-	No
Mississippi	3.0	5,000	5.0	10,000	-	No
Missouri	5.0	All	-	-	-	Yes
Montana[n]	6.75	All	-	-	50[o]	No
Nebraska	4.75	50,000	6.65	50,000	-	No
New Hampshire	8.0	All	-	-	-	No
New Jersey	9.0[p]	All	-	-	-	No
New Mexico	4.8	500,000	7.6	1,000,000	-	No
New York	9.0[q]	All	-	-	250	No
North Carolina	7.0	All	-	-	-	No
North Dakota	3.0	3,000	10.5	50,000	-	Yes
Ohio	5.1	25,000[r]	9.2[r]	25,000	50	No
Oklahoma	5.0	All	-	-	-	No
Oregon	6.6	All	-	-	10	No
Pennsylvania	8.5	All	-	-	-	No
Rhode Island	8.0[s]	All	-	-	100	No
South Carolina	5.0	All	-	-	-	No
Tennessee	6.0	All	-	-	-	No
Utah	5.0	All	-	-	100	No
Vermont	5.5	10,000	8.25	250,000	75	No
Virginia	6.0	All	-	-	-	No
West Virginia	9.6[t]	All	-	-	-	No
Wisconsin	7.9	All	-	-	-	No
District of Columbia	10.0[k]	All	-	-	-	No

[a] A special tax on financial institutions is levied in all states, based either on net income or on the value of shares of capital stock.
[b] Some states permitting Federal income tax deduction limit deductions to taxes paid on that part of income subject to own income tax.
[c] $600 for income years beginning in 1989 and $800 for income years beginning after 1989.
[d] For income years beginning on or after July 1, 1988 tax rates are reduced until, for the tax years beginning on or after July 1, 1993, the tax is imposed at a 5% rate.
[e] Additional tax imposed on capital stock and surplus to extent that it exceeds net income tax.
[f] For Florida an exemption of $5,000 and for Illinois $1,000 of net income allowed each corporation.
[g] Capital gains taxed at 4.0%.
[h] Each corporation pays additional $10.
[i] An additional 2.5% personal property replacement tax is levied.
[j] Applies to adjusted gross income. A supplemental 4.5% net income tax is imposed.
[k] Surtaxes: in Kansas, 2-1/4% imposed on taxable income in excess of $25,000; in the District of Columbia a 2.5% surtax is imposed.
[l] Corporations pay excise tax as follows: (a) $2.60 per $1,000 of value of Massachusetts tangible property not taxed locally or net worth allocated to Massachusetts, plus 9.5% of net income; or (b) $400, whichever is greater. Surtax of 14% is imposed.
[m] The first $40,000 of the tax base is exempt from tax ($41,000 for tax years beginning in 1989. This exemption is reduced by $2 for every $1 that business income exceeds the exemption amount.
[n] Corporations electing to use water's edge apportionment are taxed at 7.0%; a 4.0% surtax applies to all corporations after 1987.
[o] Minimum tax on small corporations is $10.
[p] All corporations pay additional tax on net worth. A 7-1/4% corporation income tax is imposed on entire net income of corporations deriving income from New Jersey other than those subject to or exempt from general income tax.
[q] Corporations subject to 9% net income tax on three alternative bases, whichever produces the greatest tax. There is also an additional tax on subsidiary capital.
[r] The 5.1% rate applies to the first $50,000 of income in 1989 and the 9.2% rate is reduced to 8.9% in 1988 and thereafter.
[s] Tax on 8% of net income or 40¢ on each $100 of net worth if tax yield is greater.
[t] Rate will be phased down to 9% by July 1, 1992.
Source: Commerce Clearing House.

E28. State General Sales Tax Collections by State[a]

Selected Fiscal Years 1939-1988[b]

($Thousands)

State	1939	1950	1960	1970	1980	1986	1987	1988
Total	$ 451,213	$ 1,670,028	$ 4,301,997	$ 14,177,082	$ 43,167,534	$ 74,821,130	$ 79,818,707	$ 87,009,688
Alabama	5,921	32,662	89,109	212,383	577,089	838,347	883,762	927,750
Arizona	3,571	16,138	64,164	173,739	814,588	1,459,253	1,547,425	1,706,342
Arkansas	4,937	23,116	54,571	108,719	371,825	696,866	715,636	777,073
California	88,365	321,560	714,991	1,756,935	6,695,242	10,405,892	10,934,653	11,515,266
Colorado	8,455	25,901	50,205	137,768	537,379	736,649	718,646	724,300
Connecticut	-	23,689	77,293	258,659	802,950	1,624,938	1,823,025	1,983,977
Delaware	-	13	-	-	-	-	-	-
Florida	-	23,516	171,335	658,197	2,252,113	5,027,376	5,478,278	6,862,627
Georgia	-	-	146,277	335,807	931,976	1,640,401	1,739,304	1,856,625
Hawaii	-	-	62,067	162,689	498,293	746,697	817,525	919,796
Idaho	-	-	-	41,679	137,114	250,475	297,896	328,453
Illinois	81,696	166,951	374,949	1,008,182	2,379,123	3,366,226	3,405,309	3,677,354
Indiana[c]	19,982	86,550	189,170	380,739	1,331,594	2,161,337	2,252,060	2,361,910
Iowa	15,423	55,741	80,680	223,464	502,055	768,504	826,107	859,033
Kansas	9,744	37,430	73,349	145,371	418,389	560,718	726,833	775,633
Kentucky	-	-	-	267,688	607,604	881,274	892,042	951,756
Louisiana	8,248	45,003	88,489	166,485	739,347	1,135,007	1,189,690	1,300,885
Maine	-	-	27,318	83,240	214,113	383,324	439,399	491,936
Maryland	-	28,378	74,093	236,843	712,815	1,189,603	1,302,463	1,423,585
Massachusetts	-	-	-	168,443	745,996	1,721,345	1,866,748	2,021,093
Michigan	51,838	204,864	363,221	828,491	1,706,728	2,687,022	2,828,516	2,919,055
Minnesota	-	-	-	195,620	650,138	1,359,015	1,468,608	1,676,632
Mississippi	6,296	24,540	71,792	227,930	671,086	1,030,745	1,015,402	1,007,276
Missouri	22,488	72,084	118,934	344,799	792,290	1,530,176	1,624,025	1,683,481
Nebraska	-	-	-	74,883	277,014	349,884	390,546	447,790
Nevada	-	-	12,905	54,710	182,925	519,535	552,995	546,409
New Jersey	-	-	-	355,613	1,180,267	2,614,372	2,911,780	3,136,801
New Mexico	3,440	17,384	40,948	85,709	402,909	625,873	699,564	739,904
New York	-	-	-	1,012,036	2,844,869	4,760,919	5,097,847	5,510,790
North Carolina	10,995	41,848	87,978	264,461	693,564	1,384,069	1,456,024	1,627,672
North Dakota	2,751	11,563	15,876	42,926	124,012	177,042	193,779	204,793
Ohio	47,864	133,016	265,201	658,759	1,445,788	3,165,994	3,382,985	3,218,959
Oklahoma	11,782	34,839	56,184	93,821	317,578	650,048	613,769	756,916
Pennsylvania	-	-	330,419	948,357	1,995,829	3,241,419	3,568,903	3,846,585
Rhode Island	-	5,799	24,666	78,324	169,061	291,377	350,811	383,209
South Carolina	-	-	67,705	192,552	576,489	1,111,500	1,356,473	1,249,430
South Dakota	4,158	17,048	15,748	47,736	147,171	198,929	205,480	262,348
Tennessee	-	42,507	104,923	241,151	982,251	1,865,934	1,994,313	2,142,276
Texas	-	-	-	552,561	2,536,805	4,327,698	4,601,385	6,271,018
Utah	3,725	14,014	28,592	90,976	324,744	558,581	559,208	589,480
Vermont	-	-	-	17,065	40,836	98,576	109,450	123,490
Virginia	-	-	-	210,045	595,060	1,020,192	1,102,670	1,188,856
Washington[c]	20,332	104,771	261,534	546,236	1,625,006	3,113,204	3,284,378	3,553,516
West Virginia[c]	38,125	51,911	85,039	181,710	598,512	811,147	790,406	537,499
Wisconsin	-	-	-	272,614	853,863	1,543,347	1,651,907	1,769,062
Wyoming	1,853	7,192	12,272	30,967	163,134	184,240	150,682	151,047

[a] Includes use tax collections. For information on sales tax rates, see Table E29.
[b] Data for 1939 not strictly comparable to other years.
[c] Includes business occupation taxes for Washington and West Virginia, and gross income tax collections for Indiana. Figures listed for 1960 and earlier years for Indiana refer to gross income tax collections only.
Source: Department of Commerce, Bureau of the Census.

E29. State General Sales Tax Rates[a]

As of March 1989

State	Rate[b] (Percent)	Taxation of Food and Drugs[c]		Local Sales Taxes Levied[d]
		Food[e]	Prescription Drugs	
Alabama	4	T	E	Yes
Arizona	5	E	E	Yes
Arkansas	4	T	E	Yes
California	4.75	E	E	Yes
Colorado	3	E	E	Yes
Connecticut	7.5	E	E	No
Florida	6	E	E	Yes
Georgia	4	T	E	Yes
Hawaii	4	T	E	No
Idaho	5	T	E	No
Illinois	5[f]	E	E	Yes
Indiana	5	E	E	No
Iowa	4	E	E	No
Kansas	4	T	E	Yes
Kentucky	5	E	E	Yes
Louisiana	4	T[h]	T[h]	Yes
Maine	5	E	E	No
Maryland	5	E	E	No
Massachusetts	5	E	E	No
Michigan	4	E	E	No
Minnesota	6	E	E	Yes
Mississippi	6	T	E	No
Missouri	4.225[f]	T	E	Yes
Nebraska	4	E	E	Yes
Nevada	5.75[g]	E	E	Yes[g]
New Jersey	6	E	E	No
New Mexico	4.75	T	T	Yes
New York	4	E	E	Yes
North Carolina	3	T	E	Yes
North Dakota	5.5[f]	E	E	No
Ohio	5	E	E	Yes
Oklahoma	4	T	E	Yes
Pennsylvania	6	E	E	Yes
Rhode Island	6	E	E	No
South Carolina	5	T	E	No
South Dakota	4	T	E	Yes
Tennessee	5.5	T	E	Yes
Texas	6	E	E	Yes
Utah	5.09375[f]	T	E	Yes
Vermont	4	E	E	No
Virginia	3.5	T	E	Yes
Washington	6.5	E	E	Yes
West Virginia	6	E	E	No
Wisconsin	5	E	E	Yes
Wyoming	3	T	E	Yes
District of Columbia	6	E	E	E

[a] In all but two of the states listed, tax is confined to retail or final sales; Hawaii and Mississippi also tax certain preretail sales at special low rates.

[b] Every state with a sales tax levies an accompanying use tax on imports from other states at a rate identical to that of the sales tax. Certain states tax retail sales of automotive vehicles and/or aircraft at lower levels.

[c] E = Exempt; T = Taxable.

[d] See Table F18 for information on local sales taxes.

[e] Exemptions generally apply only to food for consumption away from place of sale; all states tax restaurant meals, although Massachusetts and Vermont do so under separate taxes. Several states that are listed as taxing food, exempt farm products sold directly to consumers by producers.

[f] Missouri's sales tax rate will drop to 4.125% on July 1, 1999; North Dakota's rate will drop to 5% on July 1, 1989; Utah's rate will drop to 5% on January 1, 1990. Illinois' rate will increase to 6.25% on January 1, 1990.

[g] Combined 2% state rate plus a 3.75% state-mandated county rate.

[h] Food is subject to a 3% tax until July 1, 1989 and prescription drugs are subject to a 1% tax until July 1, 1989.

Source: Commerce Clearing House.

E30. State Motor Fuel Sales Tax Collections by State

Selected Fiscal Years 1939-1988[a]

($Thousands)

State	1939	1950	1960	1970	1980	1986	1987	1988
Total	$ 791,161	$ 1,544,436	$ 3,335,356	$ 6,282,916	$ 9,721,569	$ 14,086,947	$ 15,661,127	$ 17,196,209
Alabama	14,360	29,882	71,031	116,760	172,922	254,355	262,744	275,750
Alaska	-	-	3,686	10,372	26,175	22,651	32,117	33,676
Arizona	4,278	10,156	24,974	64,974	118,158	257,445	309,534	314,928
Arkansas	10,316	22,899	38,142	74,897	136,166	197,668	206,457	216,965
California	47,513	137,826	337,530	672,410	854,185	1,193,698	1,248,218	1,292,300
Colorado	7,599	20,559	37,515	71,801	113,442	194,444	291,575	300,032
Connecticut	9,470	18,682	45,786	99,191	153,155	241,861	254,123	292,515
Delaware	2,096	4,201	8,417	18,252	29,319	33,054	33,322	81,402
Florida	23,529	51,205	121,655	225,399	417,133	739,000	716,019	764,040
Georgia	20,530	47,376	84,044	154,699	330,485	392,913	385,698	411,706
Hawaii	-	-	14,577	17,723	34,778	44,070	48,089	49,806
Idaho	4,401	10,168	14,701	25,330	52,793	77,667	82,227	95,204
Illinois	38,099	56,339	141,865	311,313	388,097	618,868	740,786	701,971
Indiana	23,085	40,040	100,872	192,795	256,149	309,405	397,254	401,452
Iowa	13,883	27,325	60,359	100,831	167,463	230,549	252,041	266,094
Kansas	10,097	26,122	39,486	81,402	118,937	151,651	156,753	170,035
Kentucky	12,327	35,152	62,218	104,615	187,446	194,546	294,472	322,736
Louisiana	17,808	42,788	63,926	119,841	188,281	335,619	357,400	366,798
Maine	5,603	12,589	23,116	36,557	51,652	91,445	97,278	105,779
Maryland	10,373	23,117	55,831	111,326	186,658	308,768	328,335	441,618
Massachusetts	20,455	27,900	76,684	135,816	212,035	291,247	310,397	305,517
Michigan	28,421	46,871	146,345	273,735	473,593	593,425	717,796	687,308
Minnesota	17,921	34,193	56,807	122,880	204,955	336,122	356,870	391,657
Mississippi	10,584	23,361	46,540	88,502	127,647	124,542	128,125	229,060
Missouri	12,103	19,800	45,881	115,359	203,177	214,924	215,212	339,738
Montana	4,509	9,847	16,964	28,766	51,089	79,380	85,490	102,404
Nebraska	11,571	23,439	37,762	67,781	104,331	146,596	161,842	165,798
Nevada	1,235	3,618	8,192	24,054	34,625	79,687	97,900	99,238
New Hampshire	3,377	4,983	13,465	23,865	48,046	70,022	83,615	83,016
New Jersey	22,273	32,672	98,374	200,318	288,264	339,001	343,542	330,866
New Mexico	4,108	13,315	24,783	42,516	69,999	104,535	107,684	138,703
New York	67,201	90,095	215,245	374,821	474,798	468,946	495,922	500,180
North Carolina	23,852	52,836	99,134	213,709	295,143	424,208	554,254	596,573
North Dakota	2,542	4,776	11,197	19,819	33,488	50,470	55,441	63,668
Ohio	51,106	76,197	213,587	320,166	397,133	663,692	641,771	811,365
Oklahoma	14,362	36,393	58,533	90,867	129,545	205,681	204,931	311,367
Oregon	10,107	25,454	36,873	64,485	92,880	133,807	150,345	166,072
Pennsylvania	56,192	100,400	155,391	344,966	575,891	635,896	651,124	672,262
Rhode Island	3,910	6,224	15,113	27,699	39,260	47,451	52,666	54,763
South Carolina	11,768	25,248	50,876	87,238	173,412	253,161	262,054	305,989
South Dakota	3,936	6,588	14,531	24,012	41,809	57,477	56,751	61,844
Tennessee	19,170	41,684	76,276	130,625	226,785	369,323	489,224	503,496
Texas	44,217	76,432	185,307	312,349	480,946	1,011,478	1,273,136	1,473,821
Utah	3,622	7,687	20,816	37,805	74,074	117,668	127,378	129,370
Vermont	2,565	4,652	8,801	16,094	21,745	38,499	40,208	42,435
Virginia	17,218	42,728	76,771	146,477	275,141	307,637	438,691	593,677
Washington	15,514	37,333	60,482	140,878	254,637	393,643	448,682	435,456
West Virginia	9,520	16,878	34,470	49,944	101,467	152,120	161,649	167,658
Wisconsin	19,864	31,455	72,241	130,512	194,684	389,523	418,527	491,323
Wyoming	2,571	4,951	8,384	16,370	37,576	37,159	35,458	36,778

[a] Data for 1939 not strictly comparable to other years.
Source: Department of Commerce, Bureau of the Census.

E31. State Motor Fuel Tax Rates[a]

As of April 1989

State	Rate per Gallon (Cents)	State	Rate per Gallon (Cents)
Alabama	11	Nebraska	18.5
Alaska	8	Nevada	16.25
Arizona	17	New Hampshire	14
Arkansas	13.5	New Jersey	10.5
California	9	New Mexico	14.2
Colorado	18 [b]	New York	8
Connecticut	20 [b]	North Carolina	15.7
Delaware	16	North Dakota	17
Florida	4 [b]	Ohio	14.8
Georgia	7.5[c]	Oklahoma	16
Hawaii	16-22.5[d]	Oregon	16 [b]
Idaho	18	Pennsylvania	12
Illinois	13	Rhode Island	15 [e]
Indiana	15	South Carolina	16
Iowa	20	South Dakota	18
Kansas	11 [e]	Tennessee	19
Kentucky	15 [e]	Texas	15
Louisiana	16	Utah	19
Maine	17	Vermont	14
Maryland	18.5	Virginia	17.5
Massachusetts	11 [e]	Washington	18
Michigan	15	West Virginia	15.5
Minnesota	20	Wisconsin	20.8
Mississippi	18 [b]	Wyoming	8
Missouri	11	District of Columbia	15.5[e]
Montana	20		

[a] Exclusive of local taxes, licenses, and inspection fees. Rates shown apply to gasoline and most other motor fuels; however, some states impose different rates on diesel fuel, liquified petroleum or liquid natural gas, and aviation fuels. Also fuels in vehicles not operated on public highways may be taxed at a different rate.

[b] Changes in tax rates are scheduled as follows: Colorado, rate is reduced to 12¢ per gallon July 1, 1989 and special fuel tax rate is reduced to 13¢ per gallon; Connecticut, 22¢, July 1, 1990, and 23¢, July 1, 1991; Mississippi, reduced to 14.4¢, September 1, 2001; Nebraska, the figure includes an additional tax based on the statewide average cost of fuel plus a second additional tax of 1¢ per gallon; Oregon, 18¢, January 1, 1990. Florida lowered its rate from 8¢ to 4¢ April 1, 1983, but now imposes the 5% state sales tax on gasoline.

[c] Additional tax levied at rate of 3% of retail sales price.

[d] Rates are combined state and county levies. Rates vary from 16¢ in Hawaii County to 22.5¢ in Honolulu County.

[e] Rates are adjusted periodically, generally by administrative agencies, to reflect a measure of value in the following states: Kansas (10.5% of average retail price); Kentucky (9% of average wholesale price plus a supplemental highway user motor fuel tax computed to reflect decreases in average wholesale price of gasoline); Massachusetts (10% of weighted average selling price); Nebraska (adjusted quarterly, based on both variable and fixed factors); Rhode Island (11% of wholesale selling price plus an additional excise tax on distributors of 2% of the wholesale price per gallon); and Wisconsin (rate is computed annually based on highway maintenance costs and amount of fuel sold in the state plus an additional 2¢ per gallon).

Source: Commerce Clearing House.

E32. State Alcoholic Beverage Tax Rates[a]
As of July 1, 1988

State	Distilled Spirits (Per Gallon)	Wines (Per Gallon)		Malt Beverages	
		14% or Less Alcohol	14-21% Alcohol	Draught (Per Gallon)	Package[b] (Per Case of 24)
Alabama	56% of retail[c]	$1.70[c]	48% of retail[c]	$ 1.05[d]	$ 2.37[d]
Alaska	$ 5.60	.85	$ .85	.35	.788
Arizona	3.00	.84	.84	.16	.36
Arkansas	2.50	1.00	1.00	.20	.55[e]
California	2.00	.01	.02	.04	.09
Colorado	2.28	.28	.28	.08[e]	.18[e]
Connecticut	3.00	.30	.30	.10	.225
Delaware	2.25	.40	.40	.065	.145
Florida	6.50	2.25	3.00	.481	.44
Georgia	3.78	1.51	2.54	.323[d]	1.08[d]
Hawaii	5.75	1.30	2.00	.50	1.935
Idaho	15% of retail[c,g]	45¢ plus 15% of retail[c,g]	45¢ plus 15% of retail[c,g]	.15	.338
Illinois	2.00	.23	.60	.07[d]	.158[d]
Indiana	2.68	.47	.47	.115	.259
Iowa	f	1.75[c]	1.75[c]	.19	.428
Kansas	2.50	.30	.75	.18[e]	.405[e]
Kentucky	1.92	.50	.50	.081	.181
Louisiana	2.50	.11	.23	.323[d]	.726[d]
Maine	1.25[c]	.30[c]	2.00[c]	.35	.788
Maryland	1.50	.40	.40	.09	.203
Massachusetts	4.05	.55	.55	.106	.240
Michigan	12% of retail[c,g]	.51[c]	.757[c]	.203	.457
Minnesota	5.03	.30	.95	.077	.174[e]
Mississippi	2.50[c]	.35[c]	.35[c]	.43	.960
Missouri	2.00	.34	.34	.06	.135
Montana	26% of retail[c]	1.20[c]	26% of retail[c]	.139[e]	.312[e]
Nebraska	3.00	.75	1.35	.23	.518
Nevada	2.05	.40	.75	.09	.203
New Hampshire	c	.30	.30	.30	.765
New Jersey	2.80	.30	.30	.033	.075
New Mexico	3.94	.95	.95	.18	.405
New York	4.09	.12	.12	.055	.124
North Carolina	28% of retail[c]	.79[c]	.91[c]	.484	1.20
North Dakota	2.50	.50	.60	.08	.36
Ohio	2.25[c]	.26[c]	.62[c]	.081	.36
Oklahoma	5.56	.72	1.44	.403[e]	.907[e]
Oregon	c	.67[c]	.77[c]	.084	.189
Pennsylvania	18% of retail[c]	18% of retail[c]	18% of retail[c]	.08	.24
Rhode Island	2.50	.40	.40	.065	.145
South Carolina	2.72[i]	.90	.90	.768	1.728

Continued

E32. State Alcoholic Beverage Tax Rates[a] (continued)
As of July 1, 1988

State	Distilled Spirits (Per Gallon)	Wines (Per Gallon)		Malt Beverages	
		14% or Less Alcohol	14-21% Alcohol	Draught (Per Gallon)	Package[b] (Per Case of 24)
South Dakota	3.93	.93	1.45	.274[e]	.617[e]
Tennessee	4.00	1.10	1.10	.126 plus 17% of wholesale[d]	.283 plus 17% of wholesale[d]
Texas	2.40	.20	.408	.194[e]	.436[e]
Utah	13% of retail[c]	13% of retail[c]	13% of retail[c]	.355	.798
Vermont	25% of retail[c]	.55[c]	25% of retail[c]	.265	.596
Virginia	20% of retail[c]	1.51[c]	1.51[c]	.256[e]	.636[e]
Washington	17.1	.83 [c,j]	.83[c,j]	.09[j]	.202[j]
West Virginia	c,k	1.00	1.00	.177[e]	.40[e]
Wisconsin	3.25	.25	.45	.065	.145
Wyoming	.946[c]	.284[c]	.284[c]	.02	.045
District of Columbia	1.50	.15	.33	.073	.166

[a] In addition there are special taxes on manufacturers, processors and dealers, and beverage components. Some states tax brandy, vermouth, sparkling wines, or other specified beverages at different rates. Rates on quantities other than those shown may be at proportionate or higher rates; rates are not shown for distilled spirits in excess of 100 proof, on wines with more than 21% alcohol content, and malt beverages of more than 4% alcohol. Rates for beverages manufactured in the state are not shown when they differ from rates on imported beverages.

[b] Per case of twenty-four 12-ounce containers.

[c] Monopoly state, receives most or all revenue through markup. Tax rates shown are in addition to any price markup.

[d] Some or all counties and municipalities in Georgia, Illinois, Louisiana, and Tennessee also levy local taxes on beer.

[e] For beer not over 3.2% in Arkansas, Minnesota, Utah; over 3.2% in Kansas and Oklahoma; under 7% in Montana; 4% and less in Texas and North Dakota.

[f] State sells at wholesale only.

[g] Includes enforcement tax and other levies.

[h] 22.4% for distillers of less than 200,000 proof gallons.

[i] A 9% surtax applies to all taxes on alcoholic beverages.

[j] Additional tax of 7% of basic tax rate imposed on beer and wine.

[k] A 5% tax is imposed on sales of liquor outside municipalities.

Source: Commerce Clearing House, Beer Institute, and Distilled Spirits Council of the U.S.

E33. State Motor Vehicle and Operators' License Collections by State
Selected Fiscal Years 1939-1988[a]
($Thousands)

State	1939	1950	1960	1970	1980	1986	1987	1988
Total	$ 358,325	$ 755,111	$ 1,566,316	$ 2,955,785	$ 5,325,041	$ 8,374,356	$ 9,037,090	$ 9,644,233
Alabama	3,258	6,753	6,356	25,794	44,816	109,170	112,544	117,954
Alaska	-	-	2,032	5,770	11,535	18,276	18,288	18,958
Arizona	1,022	3,046	10,267	21,056	62,020	174,649	186,506	190,519
Arkansas	3,118	7,834	15,046	29,891	78,094	76,019	77,019	73,216
California	13,116	53,820	135,450	271,292	431,066	720,235	1,019,227	1,136,188
Colorado	2,426	6,162	17,205	27,126	54,181	79,472	82,361	88,617
Connecticut	6,510	10,545	17,436	46,885	82,750	154,734	197,002	207,027
Delaware	1,177	1,685	4,385	10,335	24,263	41,691	43,976	46,509
Florida	6,736	22,818	57,263	114,690	268,366	404,936	421,848	449,166
Georgia	2,172	5,630	17,988	37,304	53,408	84,921	87,215	92,738
Hawaii	-	-	-	76	8,398	15,061	17,604	18,411
Idaho	406	844	10,068	14,778	36,560	33,337	53,906	34,763
Illinois	23,507	41,278	104,854	231,197	382,279	598,475	614,380	653,782
Indiana	10,102	22,844	38,211	63,500	98,411	101,788	89,468	129,288
Iowa	11,608	22,680	46,310	80,728	139,399	180,899	188,016	193,869
Kansas	4,040	14,129	22,503	35,430	73,833	79,673	80,079	84,382
Kentucky	3,545	8,041	13,126	30,697	56,045	103,033	146,568	83,039
Louisiana	5,232	6,797	13,153	27,871	49,888	81,441	84,813	86,780
Maine	3,681	6,316	9,715	14,671	36,505	49,211	53,240	61,346
Maryland	4,585	13,134	26,343	57,448	87,727	106,291	93,552	141,367
Massachusetts	7,183	11,184	23,383	50,183	65,424	153,199	179,158	183,000
Michigan	22,034	42,236	75,645	154,482	259,945	344,422	353,714	440,257
Minnesota	9,445	21,687	43,532	66,847	140,739	254,556	274,155	286,566
Mississippi	250	2,992	7,280	14,442	30,901	64,549	63,608	81,334
Missouri	10,214	17,019	38,967	75,144	113,448	190,996	196,918	207,210
Montana	298	1,933	4,262	7,895	22,511	32,448	32,436	31,800
Nebraska	812	4,566	7,261	25,442	44,181	52,068	53,513	53,568
Nevada	277	1,458	4,475	9,477	24,597	49,044	52,994	61,008
New Hampshire	2,883	3,816	6,975	13,580	24,176	43,485	47,522	50,527
New Jersey	19,918	36,215	70,667	133,374	276,804	333,339	349,978	348,187
New Mexico	1,814	5,151	11,700	16,215	37,191	36,780	39,831	102,255
New York	46,666	78,557	141,946	240,943	329,330	483,323	480,000	484,101
North Carolina	7,970	18,088	31,768	67,120	137,047	224,113	237,546	253,167
North Dakota	1,460	5,928	10,549	16,732	26,618	32,467	32,969	35,493
Ohio	26,926	45,049	100,157	159,207	219,949	345,483	351,988	363,889
Oklahoma	5,550	19,406	38,446	65,696	126,948	246,602	227,927	254,250
Oregon	2,817	15,286	30,968	48,541	108,817	168,556	183,072	205,585
Pennsylvania	34,871	53,867	83,224	126,205	327,739	439,862	446,361	463,034
Rhode Island	2,895	4,562	7,279	16,258	18,466	25,815	27,463	31,457
South Carolina	1,717	4,777	9,938	17,790	34,173	71,751	80,385	76,594
South Dakota	845	2,040	6,654	10,741	16,856	26,544	34,960	22,169
Tennessee	4,454	12,372	27,956	62,631	102,651	136,655	144,816	159,566
Texas	8,543	25,515	83,900	165,816	325,195	694,747	745,965	747,530
Utah	1,149	2,583	6,636	10,623	20,380	36,547	44,606	45,689
Vermont	2,469	3,948	7,356	12,208	21,615	32,273	34,260	35,048
Virginia	6,721	12,754	23,639	63,171	111,148	229,666	248,685	255,400
Washington	3,168	12,283	23,658	49,629	89,561	140,783	153,862	172,205
West Virginia	4,904	9,140	19,322	27,379	49,987	65,150	68,401	67,868
Wisconsin	13,183	24,123	43,364	71,443	107,764	168,277	162,883	169,121
Wyoming	648	2,220	7,698	10,031	31,336	38,544	37,106	41,537

[a] Data for 1939 not strictly comparable to other years.
Source: Department of Commerce, Bureau of the Census.

E34. State Alcoholic Beverage Sales Tax Collections by State
Selected Fiscal Years 1939-1988[a]
($Thousands)

State	1939	1950	1960	1970	1980	1986	1987	1988
Total	$ 174,519	$ 419,594	$ 650,467	$ 1,420,216	$ 2,477,568	$ 3,062,102	$ 3,090,589	$ 3,188,693
Alabama	299	1,336	7,292	41,661	87,493	96,245	97,309	97,869
Alaska	-	-	2,188	4,425	7,366	13,337	12,580	12,111
Arizona	662	1,945	3,587	9,240	22,093	40,849	40,819	40,954
Arkansas	1,504	4,895	5,954	11,373	22,041	23,449	24,093	24,229
California	9,854	16,145	50,401	105,792	138,902	133,892	131,319	128,720
Colorado	2,097	3,640	5,828	11,198	23,627	23,830	23,173	21,965
Connecticut	2,931	5,314	7,207	23,730	24,879	31,985	32,934	31,526
Delaware	555	883	1,645	3,587	4,745	5,034	5,129	5,023
Florida	3,772	22,626	45,614	120,533	283,008	435,196	445,817	453,229
Georgia	2,802	17,124	20,333	57,837	96,473	114,786	116,568	119,412
Hawaii	-	-	3,232	7,482	12,948	29,852	34,547	133,824
Idaho	225	842	1,932	3,886	7,749	9,212	10,079	9,160
Illinois	9,472	22,966	31,623	66,989	76,675	69,385	67,287	67,843
Indiana	4,242	12,273	14,075	19,894	34,020	36,438	34,562	35,705
Iowa	1,410	3,310	3,235	9,048	16,403	14,825	13,107	12,645
Kansas	509	5,322	5,286	9,984	29,524	44,788	45,450	47,304
Kentucky	3,346	9,483	17,686	14,293	16,071	48,504	49,109	49,285
Louisiana	2,791	15,943	19,886	31,306	50,944	58,133	52,137	49,848
Maine	1,072	2,056	2,215	4,711	26,357	31,539	33,490	34,008
Maryland	3,625	5,876	8,838	15,663	29,227	27,993	29,063	28,023
Massachusetts	5,345	20,568	25,856	54,821	80,631	70,737	80,693	78,436
Michigan	4,401	6,832	21,940	63,915	90,257	94,353	106,323	120,085
Minnesota	4,910	13,480	15,321	34,111	54,201	51,379	54,370	55,746
Mississippi	623	2,301	4,370	13,097	31,411	35,390	37,139	36,257
Missouri	4,138	5,518	5,935	12,335	24,958	24,813	25,074	23,891
Montana	711	1,512	3,819	6,309	14,207	14,143	13,794	13,208
Nebraska	1,494	2,610	2,680	6,397	12,425	14,602	15,434	15,824
Nevada	180	492	1,152	5,353	10,888	14,121	13,266	11,070
New Hampshire	596	1,024	1,089	2,274	4,544	11,016	11,276	11,383
New Jersey	8,546	14,612	21,411	43,598	55,492	58,563	57,886	55,092
New Mexico	647	1,305	2,098	4,509	7,713	17,759	17,480	17,471
New York	34,246	45,018	57,190	112,623	149,678	160,210	156,384	149,069
North Carolina	1,760	8,398	16,324	57,316	104,753	127,269	131,437	141,794
North Dakota	946	3,104	3,010	4,513	6,352	5,813	5,608	5,630
Ohio	17,660	30,093	37,283	61,192	75,531	69,749	69,395	67,399
Oklahoma	692	4,502	14,439	18,240	37,334	51,989	52,299	55,404
Oregon	599	1,195	1,404	2,403	10,262	10,831	11,214	10,510
Pennsylvania	14,192	40,983	46,120	88,263	120,986	135,083	137,702	138,368
Rhode Island	356	1,633	3,120	5,849	7,420	7,716	7,684	7,755
South Carolina	2,315	12,874	16,109	37,509	85,082	103,491	106,614	107,132
South Dakota	1,219	2,552	2,572	5,169	7,744	8,597	6,918	9,013
Tennessee	807	7,790	8,206	23,238	49,916	61,615	62,335	63,125
Texas	5,682	13,249	35,035	54,643	200,465	348,660	326,192	315,536
Utah	113	743	922	2,269	5,870	16,701	16,653	16,300
Vermont	878	2,553	4,078	9,516	13,106	14,806	14,822	14,700
Virginia	1,449	6,917	8,900	34,212	76,397	97,741	95,257	95,379
Washington	2,054	1,948	13,083	39,481	81,173	97,187	105,493	102,010
West Virginia	950	2,083	3,305	17,303	5,610	7,238	7,401	8,645
Wisconsin	5,513	11,179	15,028	26,261	40,784	29,830	44,588	38,555
Wyoming	329	553	611	865	1,833	1,428	1,286	1,223

[a] Data for 1939 not strictly comparable to other years.
Source: Department of Commerce, Bureau of the Census.

E35. State Tobacco Sales Tax Collections by State

Selected Fiscal Years 1939-1988[a]

($Thousands)

State	1939	1950	1960	1970	1980	1986	1987	1988
Total	$58,998	$414,143	$922,519	$2,308,000	$3,737,798	$4,449,007	$4,605,543	$4,801,425
Alabama	3,156	7,645	18,474	36,876	56,438	72,063	71,351	71,575
Alaska	-	-	1,223	2,711	4,283	7,771	9,875	8,879
Arizona	612	1,793	3,495	19,508	39,883	50,776	51,220	52,407
Arkansas	1,410	4,633	8,823	23,449	49,740	63,111	63,060	64,483
California	-	-	63,860	235,277	269,044	259,494	268,337	252,995
Colorado	-	-	-	12,323	34,856	50,930	80,207	63,835
Connecticut	2,572	7,648	10,992	56,117	76,510	87,920	88,803	87,198
Delaware	-	1,036	2,007	9,022	11,999	12,294	12,249	12,465
Florida	-	8,706	9,252	39,235	255,845	285,991	330,498	340,100
Georgia	2,761	12,684	19,827	40,466	79,946	92,241	91,058	91,020
Hawaii	-	-	1,971	5,803	12,759	19,741	19,060	21,318
Idaho	-	1,644	3,248	4,885	8,027	9,897	11,954	16,253
Illinois	-	28,328	49,320	153,149	176,726	194,787	251,426	249,988
Indiana	-	12,548	16,646[b]	39,890[b]	81,167	75,676	75,761	116,253
Iowa	1,783	4,947	11,489	29,824	46,551	72,260	77,590	83,208
Kansas	1,128	4,929	8,756	20,390	32,671	59,348	61,645	59,659
Kentucky	1,587	4,987	9,693	11,881	21,487	18,289	17,114	14,842
Louisiana	4,522	18,126	26,743	33,178	60,984	82,992	78,786	74,714
Maine	-	5,142	6,551	14,741	24,166	37,718	39,618	40,672
Maryland	-	-	10,940	26,459	52,441	66,951	66,042	65,494
Massachusetts	1,209	25,930	39,168	75,208	144,018	172,414	171,024	168,479
Michigan	-	22,565	53,801	85,893	140,365	218,822	253,828	264,541
Minnesota	-	11,123	21,047	49,437	86,547	101,393	80,189	115,848
Mississippi	2,313	6,774	10,950	19,668	33,231	54,270	53,638	53,342
Missouri	-	-	10,888	47,137	61,182	81,869	82,784	83,214
Montana	-	1,341	5,870	5,846	11,552	13,140	12,616	12,052
Nebraska	-	3,860	5,962	11,966	22,490	30,852	35,892	38,998
Nevada	-	738	1,586	7,696	11,950	25,962	21,052	14,089
New Hampshire	-	2,441	4,100	13,870	25,735	32,731	31,674	31,695
New Jersey	-	17,781	40,817	118,227	170,572	214,203	210,955	221,826
New Mexico	-	2,228	4,630	10,469	14,507	14,765	18,621	18,814
New York	-	56,684	119,188	256,564	332,079	422,832	406,235	400,932
North Carolina	-	-	-	11,738	18,031	16,561	16,141	16,219
North Dakota	499	2,692	3,543	6,278	9,610	11,887	11,276	16,644
Ohio	7,813	18,130	60,147	121,530	207,947	183,149	181,350	229,124
Oklahoma	2,144	10,390	13,839	37,984	80,738	75,304	74,515	84,457
Oregon	-	-	-	12,297	29,816	73,929	77,750	70,306
Pennsylvania	11,159	42,759	63,495	185,672	252,423	233,526	229,927	228,881
Rhode Island	173	3,102	5,943	14,948	24,365	29,385	29,748	33,318
South Carolina	2,369	5,859	11,473	17,402	28,101	29,993	30,303	30,610
South Dakota	576	1,723	3,222	7,033	10,418	14,964	14,878	14,282
Tennessee	2,524	8,511	17,447	50,703	74,432	81,256	82,516	83,142
Texas	6,903	23,532	85,850	186,363	321,765	378,715	370,843	416,997
Utah	325	869	2,295	5,403	10,236	13,166	15,955	21,656
Vermont	348	1,807	3,392	6,532	9,605	12,083	11,891	12,256
Virginia	-	-	-	13,751	17,437	17,310	17,175	17,075
Washington	1,084	6,501	18,132	37,122	63,603	107,064	129,240	129,724
West Virginia	28	2,057	9,511	13,975	37,069	35,344	34,512	34,216
Wisconsin	-	9,950	21,208	58,938	86,951	127,128	129,083	147,284
Wyoming	-	-	1,705	3,166	5,500	4,740	4,278	4,046

[a] Data for 1939 not strictly comparable to other years.
[b] Includes related license taxes.
Source: Department of Commerce, Bureau of the Census.

E36. State Tobacco Tax Rates

As of February 1989

State	Cigarettes (Per Package of 20)[a]	Cigars (Per 1,000)[b]	Smoking Tobacco	Chewing Tobacco and Snuff
Alabama	16.5¢	$1.50 - $20.25[c]	c,d	3/4¢ per ounce[c,e]
Alaska	16	-	-	-
Arizona	15	$2.00 - $20.00	1/2¢ - 2¢ per ounce	2¢ per ounce
Arkansas	21	16% of mfg. price	16% of mfg. price	16% of mfg. price
California	35	-	-	-
Colorado	20	20% of mfg. price.	20% of mfg. price	20% of mfg. price
Connecticut	40	-	-	-
Delaware	14	15% of wholesale	15% of wholesale	15% of wholesale
Florida	24	-	25% of wholesale	25% of wholesale
Georgia	12	13% of wholesale	-	-
Hawaii	40% of wholesale	40% of wholesale	40% of wholesale	40% of wholesale
Idaho	18	35% of wholesale	35% of wholesale	35% of wholesale
Illinois	20 [c]	-	-	-
Indiana	15.5	15% of wholesale	15% of wholesale	15% of wholesale
Iowa	34	19% of wholesale	19% of wholesale	19% of wholesale
Kansas	24	10% of wholesale	10% of wholesale	10% of wholesale
Kentucky	3	-	-	-
Louisiana	16	8 - 20% of mfg. price	33% of mfg. price	-
Maine	28	12% of wholesale	12% of wholesale	45% of wholesale
Maryland	13	-	-	-
Massachusetts	26	-	-	-
Michigan	25	-	-	-
Minnesota	38	35% of wholesale	35% of wholesale	35% of wholesale
Mississippi	18	15% of mfg. price	15% of mfg. price	15% of mfg. price
Missouri	13	-	-	-
Montana	16	12-1/2% of wholesale	12-1/2% of wholesale	12-1/2% of wholesale
Nebraska	27 [c]	15% of wholesale	15% of wholesale	15% of wholesale
Nevada	20 [c]	30% of wholesale	30% of wholesale	30% of wholesale
New Hampshire	17	-	-	-
New Jersey	27	-	-	-
New Mexico	15	25% of value	25% of value	25% of value
New York	21 [c]	-	-	-
North Carolina	2	-	-	-
North Dakota	27	20% of wholesale	20% of wholesale	20% of wholesale
Ohio	18	-	-	-
Oklahoma	23	$10.00 - $20.00	40% of factory list	30% of factory list
Oregon	27	35% of wholesale	35% of wholesale	35% of wholesale
Pennsylvania	18	-	-	-
Rhode Island	27 [c]	-	-	-
South Carolina	7	$11.00 - $20.00	36% of mfg. price	5% of mfg. price
South Dakota	23	-	-	-
Tennessee	13	6% of wholesale	6% of wholesale	6% of wholesale
Texas	26	$7.50 - $15.00	28.125% of factory list	28.125% of factory list
Utah	23	35% of sales price	35% of sales price	35% of sales price
Vermont	17	20% of wholesale	20% of wholesale	20% of wholesale
Virginia	2.5	-	-	-
Washington	31	61.75% of wholesale	61.75% of wholesale	61.75% of wholesale
West Virginia	17	-	-	-
Wisconsin	30 [c]	20% of mfg. list	20% of mfg. list	20% of mfg. list
Wyoming	8	-	-	-
District of Columbia	17	-	-	-

[a] Rate shown is cents per package unless otherwise indicated. In addition to the state tax, local taxes are imposed by some jurisdictions in several states including Alabama, Illinois, Missouri, New Jersey, New York, and Virginia.
[b] A special rate applies to small cigars (less than 3 lbs. per thousand); in many states they are taxed like cigarettes.
[c] State imposes a use tax of equal amount.
[d] Range from 2¢ to 11¢ on packages weighing up to 4 ounces, plus 3¢ per ounce over 4 ounces.
[e] Rate applies to base and any fraction thereof for chewing tobacco; snuff taxed at rates ranging from 1/2¢ to 4¢ on packages weighing up to 6 ounces, plus 1¢ for each additional ounce.
Source: Commerce Clearing House.

E37. State Inheritance Tax Rates and Exemptions
Selected Categories of Heirs
As of February 1989

State[a]	Rate[b] (Percent)			Maximum Rate Applies Above ($Thousands)	Exemptions[c] (Thousands)			
	Spouse, Child, or Parent	Brother or Sister	Other than Relative		Spouse	Child or Parent	Brother or Sister	Other than Relative
Connecticut[d]	3-8	4-10	8-14	$1,000	All	50	6	1
Delaware	1-6	5-10	10-16	200	70	2.5	5	1
Indiana	1-10	7-15	10-20	1,500	All	5[e]	.5	.1
Iowa	1-8	5-10	10-15	150	180	15[e]	None	None
Kansas	1-5	3-12.5	10-15	500	All	30	5	None
Kentucky	2-10	4-16	6-16	500	All	5[e]	1	.5
Louisiana	2-3	5-7	5-10	20	25[f]	25	1	.5
Maryland[g]	1	10	10	[h]	.15[h]	.15[h]	.15[h]	.15[h]
Michigan	2-10[j]	2-10[j]	12-17[j]	750	65[k]	10[e]	10	None
Montana	2-8	4-16	8-32	100	All	7[e]	1	None
Nebraska	1	1	6-18	60	All	10	10	.5
New Hampshire	[i]	15	15	[h]	[i]	None[m]	None[m]	None[m]
New Jersey	6-16[m]	11-16	15-16	3,200	All	20.15[h, n]	None	None[m]
North Carolina	1-12	4-16	8-17	3,000	All	None[o]	None	None
Pennsylvania	6	15	15	[h]	None[o]	None[o]	None	None
South Dakota	3-15	4-20	6-30	100	All	30[p]	.5	.1
Tennessee	5.5-9.5	5.5-9.5	5.5-13	440	600[q]	600[q]	600[q]	850[q]
Wisconsin[r]	2.5-10	5-20	10-20	100	All	50	1	.5

Continued

E37. State Inheritance Tax Rates and Exemptions (continued)

a In addition to an inheritance tax, all states listed also levy an estate tax, generally to assure full absorption of the Federal credit.

b Rates generally apply to excess above graduated absolute amounts.

c Generally, transfers to governments or solely charitable, educational, scientific, religious, literary, public, and other similar organizations in the United States are wholly exempt. Some states grant additional exemptions either for insurance, homestead, joint deposits, support allowance, disinherited minor children, orphaned, incompetent, or blind children, and for previously or later taxed transfers. In many states, exemptions are deducted from the first bracket only. Adopted children generally receive the same consideration as natural children.

d On estates, an additional inheritance tax equal to 30% of the basic tax is imposed. A second additional inheritance tax equal to 10% of the basic tax and the first additional tax is imposed, except on farmland passing to descendants.

e Exemption for child (in thousands): $50 in Iowa; in Montana, all property is exempt. Exemption for minor child (in thousands): $50 in Idaho, $10 in Indiana, $20 in Kentucky. In Michigan, a widow receives $5,000 for every minor child to whom no property is transferred in addition to normal exemption of a spouse.

f Community property state, in which in general, either all community property to the spouse is exempt, or only one-half of the community property is taxable on death of either spouse.

g Where property of a decedent subject to administration in Maryland is $20,000 or less, no inheritance taxes are due. No tax on the share of any beneficiary if the value of the share is less than $150.

h Rates apply to entire share.

i All real property and the first $100,000 of non-real property transferred to a spouse is exempt. For other beneficiaries, no exemption if share exceeds amount stated.

j No tax on the share of any beneficiary if the value of the share is less than $100.

k Spouse entitled to another $10,000 exemption.

l Spouses, children, parents, and adopted children in the decedent's line of succession are entirely exempt.

m Property transferred to a spouse is totally exempt. For transfers made on or after July 1, 1988, there shall be no tax imposed on parents, grandparents, children or grandchildren. No tax on the share of any beneficiary if the value of the share is less than $500.

n Credit. In North Carolina the credit is increased to $26,150 for descendents dying on or after January 1, 1989.

o However, the $2,000 family exemption is specifically allowed as a deduction.

p Rates range fom 3.75-7.5% for a child and from 3-15% for parents. Exemption for parents is $3,000.

q There is a marital deduction equal to 50% of the value of the taxable transfer. Exemptions and rates for other beneficiaries will gradually approach those of close relatives until, by 1990, all beneficiaries will be considered one class for inheritance tax purposes.

r Tax is reduced by 40% for 1989. Additional reductions are scheduled until, by 1992, tax will be repealed entirely.

Source: Commerce Clearing House.

E38. State Death and Gift Tax Collections by State

Selected Fiscal Years 1939-1988[a]

($Thousands)

State	1939	1950	1960	1970	1980	1986	1987	1988
Total	$ 131,060	$ 168,374	$ 420,180	$ 996,396	$ 2,035,269	$ 2,533,696	$ 3,022,580	$ 3,240,929
Alabama	199	914	612	1,380	5,441	11,973	16,351	15,393
Alaska	-	-	54	123	198	672	1,073	361
Arizona	394	118	463	4,245	12,117	13,169	25,693	30,978
Arkansas	167	205	241	743	4,666	7,263	6,010	5,745
California	8,372	19,852	47,180	156,935	463,406	59,679	281,540	307,460
Colorado	919	1,918	6,638	11,934	29,780	13,280	18,254	13,175
Connecticut	3,684	5,869	16,920	42,590	54,764	150,556	176,868	176,852
Delaware	254	2,879	1,088	5,353	7,883	14,936	12,826	11,479
Florida	4,535	3,011	5,488	16,017	69,910	127,783	151,653	177,168
Georgia	236	613	981	5,642	7,517	26,105	30,289	54,204
Hawaii	-	-	587	2,324	4,328	5,971	5,178	7,314
Idaho	108	222	751	785	4,524	3,072	1,522	1,926
Illinois	4,933	7,090	22,027	63,720	122,728	53,721	81,252	82,502
Indiana	945	3,042	7,563	15,013	38,845	49,232	53,943	64,544
Iowa	1,502	3,408	7,294	16,767	47,668	58,261	53,369	58,932
Kansas	500	1,079	3,727	7,234	26,246	32,360	31,645	44,505
Kentucky	1,866	2,618	5,302	12,445	23,295	54,949	49,334	49,056
Louisiana	677	1,510	7,311	6,728	22,691	40,727	40,167	41,550
Maine	578	1,476	3,229	4,944	11,397	14,104	19,482	11,913
Maryland	1,824	2,581	4,987	11,921	20,653	41,770	46,892	58,012
Massachusetts	11,082	9,660	20,535	43,422	78,952	208,068	211,450	254,701
Michigan	4,964	7,929	12,124	26,470	46,281	78,480	89,530	93,799
Minnesota	1,980	2,335	7,335	20,032	41,922	15,617	21,601	13,610
Mississippi	100	231	666	1,980	6,006	12,290	10,421	15,713
Missouri	1,625	2,742	5,259	11,996	26,255	26,661	32,431	28,590
Montana	232	422	1,775	4,235	8,537	8,365	7,212	8,745
Nebraska	87	189	374	816	2,277	3,889	4,480	3,343
Nevada	-	-	-	-	-	-	-	5,279
New Hampshire	743	911	2,093	3,769	8,256	14,264	21,186	21,933
New Jersey	6,354	9,139	20,621	65,574	111,047	188,634	190,368	163,117
New Mexico	51	215	676	1,669	2,327	7,688	3,377	4,095
New York	35,582	22,375	71,611	127,935	124,920	328,465	392,687	459,827
North Carolina	881	2,211	6,644	18,936	42,149	86,702	77,477	65,740
North Dakota	32	113	278	842	2,828	2,318	1,942	1,498
Ohio	2,593	4,194	8,694	17,854	37,208	37,930	45,366	45,218
Oklahoma	565	2,449	6,396	14,459	27,477	39,544	47,381	39,846
Oregon	406	1,467	4,523	14,088	27,359	26,246	33,670	73,647
Pennsylvania	20,893	20,404	51,121	98,850	173,229	322,760	371,860	401,404
Rhode Island	1,318	1,556	3,873	8,618	11,962	15,865	18,462	21,821
South Carolina	191	397	1,596	3,517	9,309	22,710	26,981	35,991
South Dakota	41	375	927	1,952	7,262	11,680	10,104	10,362
Tennessee	1,425	1,947	4,847	18,118	28,798	30,966	31,757	33,484
Texas	610	6,047	12,608	23,123	75,589	119,458	113,742	108,410
Utah	337	363	1,017	3,102	1,695	4,725	2,318	3,443
Vermont	317	371	733	2,307	1,368	4,502	2,554	6,161
Virginia	830	2,028	5,176	12,245	27,281	19,915	32,800	43,205
Washington	2,018	3,559	9,422	25,434	54,598	17,712	22,189	18,846
West Virginia	700	888	2,430	5,009	12,636	19,833	6,761	6,489
Wisconsin	3,367	5,337	14,039	32,569	56,791	75,244	85,604	98,086
Wyoming	43	110	344	632	2,893	3,582	3,528	1,457

[a] Data for 1939 not strictly comparable to other years.
Source: Department of Commerce, Bureau of the Census.

E39. State Estate Tax Rates and Exemptions[a]

As of February 1989

State	Rates (On Net Estate After Exemptions)[b]	Maximum Rate Applies Above	Exemption
Alabama	Maximum Federal credit[c,d]	$ 10,040,000	$ 60,000[c]
Alaska	Maximum Federal credit[c,d]	10,040,000	60,000[c]
Arizona	Maximum Federal credit[c,d]	10,040,000	60,000[c]
Arkansas	Maximum Federal credit[c,d]	10,040,000	60,000[e, c]
California	Maximum Federal credit[c,d]	10,040,000	60,000[c]
Colorado	Maximum Federal credit[c,d]	10,040,000	60,000[c]
Florida	Maximum Federal credit[c,d]	10,040,000	60,000[c]
Georgia	Maximum Federal credit[c,d]	10,040,000	60,000[c]
Hawaii	Maximum Federal credit[c,d]	10,040,000	60,000[c]
Idaho	Maximum Federal credit[c,d]	10,040,000	60,000[c]
Illinois	Maximum Federal credit[c,d]	10,040,000	60,000[c]
Maine	Maximum Federal credit[c,d]	10,040,000	60,000[c]
Massachusetts	5% on first $50,000 to 16%	4,000,000	[e,f,g]
Minnesota	Maximum Federal credit[c,d]	10,040,000	60,000[c]
Mississippi	1.7% on first $100,000 to 18.4%	3,500,000	400,000
Missouri	Maximum Federal credit[c,d]	10,040,000	60,000[c]
Nevada	Maximum Federal credit[c,d]	10,040,000	60,000[c]
New Mexico	Maximum Federal credit[c,d]	10,040,000	60,000[c]
New York	2% on first $50,000 to 21%[g,h]	10,100,000	[e,i]
North Dakota	Maximum Federal credit[c,d]	10,040,000	60,000[e, c]
Ohio	2% on first $40,000 to 7%[g]	500,000	10,000[e,j]
Oklahoma	.5% on first $10,000 to 15%[g]	10,000,000	[e,k,l]
Oregon	Maximum Federal credit[c,d]	10,040,000	60,000[e, c]
Rhode Island	2% on first $25,000 to 9%[g,m]	1,000,000	25,000[n]
South Carolina	6% on first $40,000 to 8%[d,g]	100,000	140,000[e,o]
Texas	Maximum Federal credit[c,d]	10,040,000	60,000[c]
Utah	Maximum Federal credit[c,d]	10,040,000	60,000[c]
Vermont	Maximum Federal credit[c,d]	10,040,000	60,000[e, c]
Virginia	Maximum Federal credit[c,d]	10,040,000	60,000[c]
Washington	Maximum Federal credit[c,d]	10,040,000	60,000[c]
West Virginia	Maximum Federal credit[c,d]	10,040,000	60,000[c]
Wyoming	Maximum Federal credit[c,d]	10,040,000	60,000[c]
District of Columbia	Maximum Federal credit[c,d]	10,040,000	60,000[c]

[a] Excludes states shown in Table E37 which levy an estate tax in addition to their inheritance taxes to assure full absorption of the Federal credit.

[b] The rates generally are in addition to graduated absolute amounts.

[c] Maximum Federal credit allowed under the 1954 Code for state estate taxes paid is expressed as a percentage of the taxable estate (after $60,000 exemption) in excess of $40,000, plus a graduated absolute amount. The $60,000 exemption is allowed under the State Death Tax Credit.

[d] A tax on nonresident estates is imposed on the proportionate share of the estate which the property located in the state bears to the entire estate wherever situated.

[e] Transfers to religious, charitable, educational, and municipal corporations generally are fully exempt. Limited in Mississippi to those located in United States or its possessions and amount increases after October 1, 1989.

[f] A credit equal to the lesser of $1,500 or Massachusetts estate tax liability is allowed on net estates above $200,000. Otherwise, exemption is equal to Massachusetts net estate.

[g] An additional estate tax is imposed to assure full absorption of the Federal credit. In New York, this applies only to residents.

[h] On net estate before exemption.

[i] A credit is allowed, ranging from the full amount of tax if estate tax is $2,750 or less to $500 if estate tax is $5,000 or more. In addition, the unlimited Federal marriage deduction has been adopted.

[j] A credit equal to the lesser of $500 or the amount of tax is allowed. Marital deduction is equal to the lesser of the modified Federal marital deduction; or to half of the difference between the value of the gross estate and deductions or $500,000, whichever is greater.

[k] An estate valued at $100 or less is exempt.

[l] Exemption is a total aggregate of $175,000 for father, mother, child, and named relatives. Property passing to surviving spouse is entirely excluded.

[m] In 1989, tax is 40% of estate tax otherwise payable. This percentage is gradually reduced until, by 1991, estate tax will be equal to maximum Federal death tax credit.

[n] Marital deduction is $175,000.

[o] After June 30, 1989, $170,000; and after July 1, 1990, $320,000.

Source: Commerce Clearing House.

E40. State General Corporation License Tax Collections by State[a]
Selected Fiscal Years 1942-1988
($Thousands)

State	1942	1946	1950	1960	1970	1980	1986	1987	1988
Total	$ 87,736	$ 120,596	$ 175,875	$ 426,217	$ 763,813	$ 1,387,780	$ 3,064,768	$ 3,171,598	$ 3,171,087
Alabama	1,753	1,853	2,343	8,834	15,352	45,087	74,617	88,748	82,311
Alaska	-	-	-	95	402	671	946	896	892
Arizona	45	52	111	875	1,119	2,427	3,677	3,838	3,801
Arkansas	401	304	443	866	1,497	4,045	3,985	4,238	7,722
California	92	381	390	1,355	2,621	4,836	7,873	7,799	8,124
Colorado	104	105	206	998	1,352	2,747	2,424	2,495	3,428
Connecticut	199	339	407	1,208	1,309	3,425	8,242	8,758	9,384
Delaware	3,166	3,354	4,293	9,684	43,924	66,738	132,816	152,152	180,583
Florida	351	499	641	2,027	6,394	8,192	19,431	21,642	22,086
Georgia	442	491	755	2,017	3,800	9,004	17,528	17,873	20,335
Hawaii	-	-	-	158	334	737	987	1,048	881
Idaho	80	68	151	428	715	1,348	184	253	457
Illinois	2,984	3,160	3,756	5,565	27,181	37,013	60,666	74,401	75,261
Indiana	67	218	131	1,321	1,172	2,926	4,941	4,620	5,043
Iowa	111	218	291	286	602	17,238	18,354	13,879	12,090
Kansas	370	370	432	836	1,214	6,240	10,305	10,650	11,505
Kentucky	382	564	886	1,770	4,522	12,394	42,592	65,896	61,618
Louisiana	3,175	3,522	4,479	14,452	25,830	66,570	233,339	241,685	234,616
Maine	224	236	214	417	383	680	862	950	957
Maryland	508	329	432	793	1,459	3,819	4,034	3,907	4,775
Massachusetts	9,790	28,670	44,433	66,245	2873(b)	5,037	11,757	16,160	15,308
Michigan	6,015	7,438	11,005	69,139	124,024	5,349	87,848	89,099	9,979
Minnesota	37	111	90	349	674	1,401	2,116	3,187	2,917
Mississippi	474	666	1,099	3,497	9,392	25,729	51,795	61,041	58,384
Missouri	1,695	1,165	3,042	6,070	20,673	27,326	44,518	49,847	51,722
Montana	18	40	66	136	187	300	801	769	750
Nebraska	151	163	221	510	1,357	2,592	4,499	4,419	4,520
Nevada	48	69	63	480	839	2,223	3,573	4,351	5,058
New Hampshire	31	45	109	256	842	2,773	4,178	4,508	4,748
New Jersey	2,314	7,290	8,643	31,603	49,277	151,817	111,356	127,002	137,789
New Mexico	238	239	355	1,062	1,720	5,384	7,163	5,581	2,112
New York	637	1,956	1,332	3,413	5,475	7,450	18,461	20,031	24,172
North Carolina	2,303	3,023	4,368	8,193	20,340	49,335	95,489	106,048	121,156
North Dakota	23	11	15	34	120	301	644	645	610
Ohio	4,640	6,310	9,327	47,078	114,044	81,471	332,547	329,578	273,225
Oklahoma	964	1,089	1,832	3,439	6,177	17,809	32,919	33,339	30,402
Oregon	348	339	462	687	1,412	2,458	3,631	3,898	3,693
Pennsylvania	31,312	32,993	52,081	55,503	124,920	279,881	473,960	478,111	498,201
Rhode Island	682	3,742	804	190	660	1,774	2,746	2,262	3,048
South Carolina	429	352	509	1,054	1,901	5,601	21,097	19,792	20,491
South Dakota	-	-	21	87	168	385	751	666	800
Tennessee	1,484	2,406	5,057	8,369	17,795	45,640	147,816	155,329	166,504
Texas	2,694	4,385	7,996	60,606	110,276	352,615	924,291	892,607	953,201
Utah	162	62	74	172	-	-	-	-	-
Vermont	90	103	15	27	123	194	573	566	622
Virginia	541	552	715	1,253	2,244	6,143	14,988	18,564	19,263
Washington	331	339	412	1,438	2,260	4,199	6,061	6,425	6,434
West Virginia	727	733	1,098	839	1,649	3,693	4,553	4,565	3,122
Wisconsin	82	214	215	334	948	2,033	4,136	4,996	4,738
Wyoming	22	28	55	169	261	730	2,698	2,484	2,249

[a] Licenses and fees applicable to all corporations. Excludes corporation taxes based on value of property, net income, or gross receipts from sales or taxes imposed on particular types of corporations.
[b] Excludes portion of corporation excise taxes and surtaxes measured by corporate excess included here for prior years.
Source: Department of Commerce, Bureau of the Census.

E41. State Insurance Company Gross Premiums Tax Collections By State

Selected Fiscal Years 1942-1988

($Thousands)

State	1942	1950	1960	1970	1980	1986	1987	1988
Total	$ 113,198	$ 241,185	$ 531,965	$ 1,182,134	$ 3,113,231	$ 5,488,860	$ 6,382,557	$ 6,896,341
Alabama	1,173	2,678	7,964	20,643	68,410	107,212	125,401	138,497
Alaska	-	-	857	2,562	10,436	19,490	23,659	23,661
Arizona	275	823	3,275	9,365	29,457	67,936	79,269	72,433
Arkansas	861	1,916	3,918	9,144	29,969	44,115	52,189	44,416
California	8,558	23,286	62,342	134,954	446,262	839,467	1,008,887	1,152,508
Colorado	870	1,970	4,920	12,021	38,883	52,997	82,331	82,224
Connecticut	4,169	9,276	13,915	40,336	61,977	112,768	140,323	150,968
Delaware	388	729	1,624	4,454	11,381	19,695	23,158	25,188
Florida	1,318	3,832	11,730	34,115	103,524	225,188	254,760	316,325
Georgia	1,110	3,783	10,543	21,905	68,043	99,042	154,462	150,312
Hawaii	-	-	1,883	6,096	23,001	34,806	36,463	38,876
Idaho	371	1,114	2,496	4,471	15,977	23,625	32,519	23,532
Illinois	7,768	15,062	26,604	68,452	82,871	145,722	178,752	187,001
Indiana	2,582	5,514	9,633	24,299	58,291	84,318	96,520	103,489
Iowa	1,828	4,052	7,497	15,704	43,746	72,764	76,490	81,033
Kansas	1,135	2,934	6,315	11,424	34,083	64,157	64,986	72,269
Kentucky	1,541	3,315	6,513	17,556	62,016	122,200	136,642	147,922
Louisiana	1,586	3,974	9,708	22,818	81,724	177,157	182,435	184,822
Maine	705	1,399	2,355	4,348	13,095	24,160	28,167	33,464
Maryland	1,504	3,893	8,557	21,356	56,152	99,208	120,653	128,103
Massachusetts	2,015	5,072	11,813	39,068	111,517	178,728	215,088	248,060
Michigan	4,780	9,789	20,659	44,114	119,678	148,551	160,952	43,882
Minnesota	2,345	4,714	9,421	24,181	63,984	97,645	107,091	126,765
Mississippi	833	1,906	5,124	12,429	36,164	62,689	66,358	76,448
Missouri	3,676	6,448	13,078	23,578	64,064	122,457	145,047	155,402
Montana	361	853	2,207	4,578	11,716	23,758	25,304	39,510
Nebraska	619	1,409	3,712	7,398	20,228	43,128	30,895	34,502
Nevada	81	244	868	2,851	11,924	32,924	40,700	46,446
New Hampshire	471	962	1,888	5,858	13,427	24,690	30,219	35,299
New Jersey	4,992	8,153	18,053	38,740	89,565	124,676	147,891	168,138
New Mexico	233	708	2,050	5,666	20,199	44,129	41,854	43,483
New York	16,428	30,222	64,145	124,297	209,019	371,738	458,965	489,490
North Carolina	2,112	5,141	12,886	29,149	80,496	135,000	139,941	186,833
North Dakota	300	884	1,643	2,951	9,106	12,994	12,203	14,662
Ohio	7,012	13,909	25,792	53,116	131,405	196,393	223,044	240,836
Oklahoma	2,205	4,929	9,921	18,368	54,080	112,543	121,208	137,207
Oregon	1,000	2,458	5,578	7,975	33,039	46,907	55,704	58,730
Pennsylvania	9,470	15,667	29,374	59,541	165,412	259,780	306,497	336,488
Rhode Island	820	1,614	2,601	5,643	13,168	22,850	27,523	30,362
South Carolina	1,148	2,622	5,500	13,314	40,519	61,290	87,537	83,185
South Dakota	316	993	1,942	3,715	10,599	19,214	22,294	23,480
Tennessee	1,928	4,231	9,448	21,607	64,090	109,498	126,575	122,438
Texas	3,973	11,054	32,210	58,565	176,108	424,962	460,963	545,808
Utah	412	993	2,373	4,856	18,043	30,253	28,990	25,286
Vermont	309	619	1,195	2,339	6,380	11,238	14,708	17,175
Virginia	2,133	5,131	11,716	26,685	76,484	131,181	158,495	180,460
Washington	1,831	3,491	7,752	17,111	43,646	78,339	91,876	93,619
West Virginia	1,039	2,485	6,422	10,482	29,035	49,049	43,803	47,155
Wisconsin	2,445	4,478	9,014	26,276	43,828	65,717	73,857	78,414
Wyoming	169	456	1,031	1,660	7,016	10,512	18,909	9,735

Source: Department of Commerce, Bureau of the Census.

E42. State Public Utility Gross Receipts Tax Collections by State
Selected Fiscal Years 1939-1988[a]
($Thousands)

State	1939	1950	1960	1970	1980	1986	1987	1988
Total	$ 93,381	$ 185,175	$ 365,424	$ 918,363	$ 3,197,230	$ 6,003,060	$ 5,982,998	$ 6,179,474
Alabama	1,188	3,153	3,369	30,325	154,392	235,911	246,038	251,884
Alaska	-	-	-	338	1,981	1,946	1,985	2,024
Arizona	194	908	3,300	6,227	23,232	80,345	84,808	91,999
Arkansas	143	14	-	-	-	-	-	-
California	2,400	8,523	12,696	22,998	19,028	34,794	35,146	48,662
Colorado	652	-	-	443	1,148	3,636	7,321	6,317
Connecticut	2,340	5,486	7,895	34,253	142,112	271,605	252,320	254,826
Delaware	7	15	34	64	13,809	19,369	16,614	16,726
Florida	791	2,195	7,640	18,803	91,595	201,936	202,333	217,846
Georgia	2	-	-	-	-	-	-	-
Hawaii	-	-	4,026	14,105	32,458	70,265	61,792	63,587
Idaho	437	649	1,228	404	1,405	2,101	1,819	1,323
Illinois	11,743	22,848	48,570	143,838	464,008	647,935	586,242	757,202
Iowa	158	-	-	-	1,778	-	-	-
Kansas	1,307	245	293	302	588	838	765	704
Kentucky	333	2,546	6,224	-	-	-	-	-
Louisiana	1,335	9,839	7,127	12,406	29,843	39,493	32,472	35,155
Maine	1,211	2,599	4,140	3,772	16,979	30,939	28,960	29,400
Maryland	1,468	4,058	9,874	18,171	59,460	91,029	93,058	95,721
Michigan	1,148	-	-	-	-	-	-	-
Minnesota	6,553	15,102	21,143	33,225	67,697	56,323	114,950	99,953
Mississippi	-	-	200	399	-	-	-	-
Missouri	807	89	111	150	666	1,346	1,202	1,113
Montana	142	494	1,130	2,712	4,520	7,793	9,857	10,494
Nebraska	29	11	4	-	-	1,790	1,811	1,599
Nevada	218	-	-	301	1,251	3,115	2,912	4,419
New Hampshire	-	-	-	1,065	1,812	7,891	6,427	7,074
New Jersey	82	-	37	18,889	226,398	1,002,770	1,018,560	1,002,496
New Mexico	179	527	471	960	2,592	2,238	6,108	6,004
New York	23,190	34,317	68,664	143,614	497,580	966,054	969,056	1,007,926
North Carolina	2,572	10,440	23,943	58,392	199,067	199,209	207,463	225,244
North Dakota	24	4	1	161	3,159	11,303	10,304	10,994
Ohio	10,634	19,466	40,838	87,429	373,937	647,678	620,111	588,233
Oklahoma	1,565	246	630	1,198	6,281	13,573	12,549	13,156
Oregon	1,196	201	184	477	1,478	2,441	2,283	5,145
Pennsylvania	6,800	9,805	16,693	108,195	380,250	518,300	543,624	486,312
Rhode Island	565	2,760	5,023	13,207	36,737	63,126	56,106	54,113
South Carolina	1,311	2,734	4,517	9,612	18,568	26,008	27,504	35,570
South Dakota	25	17	33	42	308	600	600	760
Tennessee	1,172	1,307	1,511	3,928	13,154	20,696	20,336	22,270
Texas	1,907	4,744	18,507	37,477	171,462	234,990	210,474	207,836
Utah	-	62	117	307	997	4,124	4,629	4,728
Vermont	316	681	1,160	2,623	11,198	19,949	19,971	21,066
Virginia	3,754	10,944	18,129	32,943	100,018	133,600	144,132	151,045
Washington	350	5,710	14,682	31,314	101,307	159,246	163,748	170,965
West Virginia	634	-	-	-	-	-	-	18,013
Wisconsin	2,267	2,432	11,279	23,294	84,515	166,755	156,606	149,570
Wyoming	232	4	1	-	-	-	-	-

[a] Data for 1939 not strictly comparable to other years.
Source: Department of Commerce, Bureau of the Census.

E43. State Severance Tax Collections by State
Selected Fiscal Years 1939-1988[a]
($Thousands)

State	1939	1950	1960	1970	1980	1986	1987	1988
Total	$ 47,227	$ 210,695	$ 419,704	$ 685,892	$ 4,167,399	$ 6,125,394	$ 4,047,878	$ 4,326,436
Alabama	355	928	1,598	2,242	32,410	75,072	53,342	60,603
Alaska	-	-	1,449	10,780	506,469	1,432,911	666,870	818,655
Arkansas	521	3,358	5,165	4,334	18,051	22,158	15,130	16,302
California	192	930	1,184	1,632	25,954	19,195	22,847	26,145
Colorado	22	16	2,811	1,058	31,121	22,577	9,694	15,330
Florida	-	30	43	248	121,254	170,902	81,268	75,023
Idaho	242	108	84	264	1,905	522	426	675
Indiana	-	307	353	322	1,582	1,253	556	675
Kansas	-	245	421	605	1,100	102,108	63,601	81,812
Kentucky	42	126	356	191	177,244	229,296	211,203	210,046
Louisiana	9,619	52,281	137,173	251,019	525,297	619,671	449,576	472,870
Michigan	393	932	792	965	43,525	52,821	53,362	43,581
Minnesota	2,198	16,224	14,558	18,976	83,459	9,501	8,266	7,796
Mississippi	-	6,092	10,778	14,262	52,514	72,925	49,190	53,224
Missouri	-	-	29	-	46	31	21	33
Montana	720	1,152	2,951	4,730	94,636	129,934	101,453	112,779
Nebraska	-	-	1,354	766	2,948	4,037	2,396	2,571
Nevada	27	37	49	50	23	26	3	10,655
New Hampshire	-	-	78	71	311	485	85	-65
New Mexico	649	2,404	16,482	35,398	213,643	367,214	235,044	291,880
North Carolina	-	-	-	-	1,292	1,436	1,436	1,579
North Dakota	-	-	2,502	3,198	43,927	146,971	95,808	90,897
Ohio	-	-	-	-	4,596	9,865	9,528	9,353
Oklahoma	9,544	20,599	32,969	50,539	436,098	571,375	370,178	386,680
Oregon	104	524	659	1,937	50,592	32,415	33,309	31,972
South Dakota	1,118	622	466	16	2,423	5,613	5,469	8,449
Tennessee	-	-	-	-	2,204	2,321	1,581	1,820
Texas	17,415	102,692	180,929	273,213	1,525,118	1,552,130	1,181,685	1,058,809
Utah	349	866	3,869	4,272	10,584	43,905	21,548	29,156
Virginia	29	138	272	314	1,012	1,600	1,714	1,668
Washington	144	-	-	-	49,924	36,998	40,483	45,790
West Virginia	3,530	-	-	-	-	-	-	128,486
Wisconsin	14	84	235	222	437	834	1,071	915
Wyoming	-	-	95	4,268	105,700	387,292	259,735	230,272

[a] Data for 1939 not strictly comparable to other years.
Source: Department of Commerce, Bureau of the Census.

E44. State Pari-Mutuel Tax Collections by State

Selected Fiscal Years 1942-1988[a]

(\$Thousands)

State	1942	1950	1960	1970	1980	1986	1987	1988
Total	\$ 23,164	\$ 102,734	\$ 265,068	\$ 515,052	\$ 731,076	\$ 646,623	\$ 642,522	\$ 666,922
Arizona	110	614	2,278	3,904	9,580	12,067	10,882	10,145
Arkansas	335	624	1,529	5,232	15,573	19,769	20,555	20,555
California	1,770	15,341	36,100	59,970	126,306	112,347	113,155	129,544
Colorado	-	738	2,439	3,774	8,366	8,517	8,721	8,517
Connecticut	-	-	-	-	52,934	63,901	65,459	62,505
Delaware	400	1,020	3,700	7,232	1,609	425	63	81
Florida	4,393	12,472	25,973	50,898	102,490	113,127	118,809	119,719
Idaho	-	-	-	66	425	442	483	2,296
Illinois	1,287	7,924	16,863	42,630	79,095	55,836	52,159	49,975
Kentucky	-	683	2,178	5,863	13,951	10,805	7,985	6,525
Louisiana	84	568	3,027	4,933	18,446	23,103	22,048	21,320
Maine	70	320	1,070	1,459	1,313	1,318	1,582	1,853
Maryland	1,175	4,569	8,105	13,112	16,038	2,385	2,450	2,726
Massachusetts	2,471	7,888	12,721	25,603	29,474	37,527	35,679	32,036
Michigan	-	3,389	7,564	19,931	25,959	21,278	24,960	20,173
Montana	-	-	-	-	-	173	166	144
Nebraska	-	-	554	2,083	7,364	7,145	5,405	673
Nevada	-	-	-	-	385	10	9	12
New Hampshire	1,009	1,944	4,220	8,832	12,429	10,695	10,518	11,489
New Jersey	24	11,706	25,063	35,139	15,725	7,632	7,379	8,233
New Mexico	-	253	120	766	3,459	2,928	2,253	2,330
New York	8,266	26,572	86,908	159,231	98,751	90,331	83,836	92,349
Ohio	130	527	9,534	17,193	26,826	10,949	12,354	13,361
Oklahoma	-	-	-	-	-	1,471	1,498	1,624
Oregon	134	697	1,127	2,452	4,711	4,688	4,817	4,186
Pennsylvania	-	-	-	18,099	27,764	9,292	9,454	9,652
Rhode Island	1,242	3,508	6,985	10,795	7,886	5,798	6,605	10,791
South Dakota	2	-	471	1,346	2,337	3,357	3,583	1,000
Vermont	-	-	-	2,922	836	492	239	188
Washington	129	608	1,161	1,474	7,199	8,684	9,244	8,882
West Virginia	142	769	5,378	10,100	13,829	-	-	13,780
Wyoming	-	-	-	13	16	131	172	258

[a] Data for years prior to 1960 not strictly comparable to other years.
Source: Department of Commerce, Bureau of the Census.

E45. State Pari-Mutuel Tax Rates[a]

As of December 1987

State	Tax Rate	Breakage	
		Amount	To State (Percent)
Arizona	3% on first $100,000[b] 5% of excess over $100,000	$.10	-
Arkansas	6.55%	.10	60[c]
California	Annual handle under $250 million; sliding scale beginning at 4.8%.	Annual handle (millions)	
	Annual handle of $250 million or more; 5.7%.	$0-$24 $24-$50 over $50	50 - 100
Colorado	3.5%	.10	-
Delaware	.75%	.10	-
Florida	3.3% of handle in excess of $300,000[d]	.10	-
Idaho	1.25%	n.a.	n.a.
Illinois	Based on sliding scale of 1.75% on first $200,000 to 7.75% over $3,000,000.[j]	.10	100
Kentucky	4.75%	.10	-
Louisiana	3% of excess over $60,000 to $201,000. 4% of excess over $201,000 to $401,000 plus $4,230. 5% over $401,000 plus $12,230.	.10	-
Maine	50% on straight bets, with 16% take out[e]	n.a.	n.a.
Maryland	.5%	.10	-
Massachusetts	3%	n.a.	n.a.
Michigan	4.5% on straight bets[e, j]	.10	50
Minnesota	1.75% on less than $48 million; 6% on over $48 million.	.10	-
Missouri	1% on $0 to $100 million; 2% from $101 to $150 million; and 4% on $151 million and up.		
Nebraska	5% on excess over $100,000,000	.10	-
Nevada	2%	.10	-
New Hampshire	1% on straight bets[e]	.10	50
New Jersey	Based on sliding scale of .30% to 1.30% on less than $1,000,000 and .5% over $1,000,000 at private tracks.	.10	-
New Mexico	2.5% over $250,000 to $350,000, 3.5% over $350,000 to $400,000, 6% over $400,000	.10	-
New York	5% on straight bets[e]	.10[f]	20-55[g]
Ohio	Based on sliding scale at 1% of first $200,000; 2% over $200,000 to $300,000; 3% over $300,000 to $400,000; and 4% on excess over $400,000.	.10	-
Oklahoma	2% on first $100 million; 4% on next $50 million; and 6% over $150 million.[e]	n.a.	n.a.
Oregon	2%	.10	-
Pennsylvania	1.5%	.10	25
South Dakota	3%[i]	.10	-
Tennessee	2% on first $250,000; 2.5% from $250,000 to $500,000; 3% from $500,000 to $750,000; 4% over $750,000[h]	.10	-
Texas	5%	.10	-
Vermont	Based on sliding scale of 3 - 8% on weekdays; 4 - 8% on Sundays	n.a.	n.a.
Washington	1/2% under $200,000; 1% from $200,000 to $400,000; 4% in excess of $400,000	.10	-
West Virginia	2% January-March and October-December 3% April-September	.10	-

[a] Applies to thoroughbred horseracing and may or may not apply to other forms of racing. Excludes racing at fairs when taxed at a lower rate.
[b] Tax starts at 2% at tracks where daily average does not exceed $200,000.
[c] To city where track is located with portion to county.
[d] At Tampa Bay Downs, 3.3% on daily handle over $500,000.
[e] 2.27% on exotic bets in Maine, 6% on "special sweepstakes" in Michigan and 2% on multiple wagering in New Hampshire. In New York, tax is 4% on multiple (2 horses) bets at Aqueduct, Belmont, Saratoga, and 1% at Finger Lakes. State receives 7.5% on exotic (3 horses) bets at Aqueduct, Belmont, Saratoga, and 6.25% at Finger Lakes. In Washington, state receives an additional 1% on exotic bets. In Oklahoma, state receives an additional 2% on Daily Double, Quinella, and Exacta wagers.
[f] Breakage is 10 cents on regular bets and 50 cents on exotic bets.
[g] State receives 20% at Aqueduct, Belmont, and Saratoga; 55% at Finger Lakes.
[h] Additional 3%-7% on multiple wagering interests.
[i] On daily handles under $100,000, state receives 2.25%.
[j] Applies to racetracks in counties over one million in population in Illinois; lower rates apply for counties with less than one million in population. In Michigan, state receives 3.5% from racetracks in counties with less than 200,000 in population.
Source: Association of Racing Commissioners International, Inc. *Pari-mutuel Racing 1987*, pp. 14-18.

E46. State Unemployment Compensation Tax Rates and Related Data by State

Regular State Programs Only[a]
Calendar Year 1987

State	Employer Contributions[b] Total ($Millions)	As a Percent of Taxable Wages	As a Percent of Total Wages	Taxable Wage Base As of Dec. 31, 1987	Average Weekly Wages In Covered Employment Taxable Wages	Total Wages	Average Weekly Benefit[c] Amount	As Percent of Total Wages	Average Duration (Weeks)
Total[d]	$17,567.9	2.60%	1.05%	$7,000	$157.52	$396.77	$139.74	35.3%	14.6
Alabama	162.4	1.72	.78	8,000	152.61	344.90	100.87	29.3	11.4
Alaska	84.3	3.46	2.26	21,500	339.96	502.72	159.12	29.6	17.0
Arizona	115.8	1.34	.54	7,000	146.69	367.43	120.07	32.1	14.4
Arkansas	119.1	2.38	1.10	7,500	144.00	310.92	122.98	39.2	12.8
California	1,916.9	2.64	.85	7,000	147.22	439.05	121.29	27.4	15.8
Colorado	207.2	2.02	.86	9,000	153.64	393.79	159.05	40.3	14.0
Connecticut	211.4	1.98	.64	7,100	149.63	473.07	165.28	35.4	10.9
Delaware	61.5	2.94	1.15	8,500	158.58	405.45	138.37	34.8	11.1
Florida	297.7	1.00	.41	7,000	144.35	350.60	128.39	36.1	13.3
Georgia	265.1	1.50	.60	7,500	150.86	376.99	120.06	32.0	10.3
Hawaii	76.0	1.74	1.19	16,500	236.63	345.17	154.79	43.7	13.4
Idaho	85.4	2.96	2.01	16,200	223.60	323.81	136.01	42.2	12.9
Illinois	1,211.0	3.60	1.37	8,500	160.92	429.35	147.15	34.6	17.7
Indiana	185.7	1.44	.51	7,000	137.62	381.32	104.26	27.7	12.3
Iowa	240.0	2.96	1.69	12,300	188.95	330.41	142.73	43.3	14.3
Kansas	158.4	1.99	.99	8,000	166.76	351.19	159.40	45.4	14.6
Kentucky	220.1	2.82	1.22	8,000	148.05	343.70	107.56	31.4	13.6
Louisiana	306.5	3.80	1.47	7,000	140.35	364.97	142.38	40.0	18.6
Maine	75.4	2.67	1.15	7,000	141.85	329.14	131.02	39.8	11.2
Maryland	169.6	1.47	.54	7,000	142.37	394.25	150.72	37.9	13.7
Massachusetts	424.9	2.05	.76	7,000	160.08	434.05	173.85	40.3	13.9
Michigan	1,132.0	4.59	1.67	9,500	176.81	452.22	158.33	35.8	15.5
Minnesota	383.9	2.68	1.25	11,200	182.24	390.11	176.75	45.2	14.9
Mississippi	62.4	1.27	.60	7,000	137.35	303.95	99.98	33.2	13.7
Missouri	226.5	1.70	.67	7,500	142.24	376.47	113.62	30.5	13.5
Montana	51.8	1.89	1.37	12,400	217.95	308.60	131.01	42.5	14.3
Nebraska	48.0	1.38	.60	7,000	128.64	312.02	111.87	35.6	12.5

Continued

E46. State Unemployment Compensation Tax Rates and Related Data by State (continued)

Regular State Programs Only[a]
Calendar Year 1987

State	Employer Contributions[b]			Taxable Wage Base As of Dec. 31, 1987	Average Weekly Wages In Covered Employment		Average Weekly Benefit[c]		
	Total ($Millions)	As a Percent of							
		Taxable Wages	Total Wages		Taxable Wages	Total Wages	Amount	As Percent of Total Wages	Average Duration (Weeks)
Nevada	$ 76.7	1.65%	.95%	$ 11,700	$ 211.58	$ 362.47	$ 140.69	37.8%	13.5
New Hampshire	24.4	.77	.30	7,000	145.86	375.50	121.86	32.8	5.6
New Jersey	979.4	2.41	1.42	11,300	207.34	458.84	167.79	36.8	15.1
New Mexico	66.3	1.91	1.03	10,700	177.54	327.10	121.65	36.5	17.8
New York	1,351.3	2.95	.90	7,000	147.66	479.98	139.54	29.5	17.3
North Carolina	206.5	1.06	.50	9,600	173.91	338.46	124.09	36.4	9.5
North Dakota	56.5	4.17	2.19	10,800	169.09	305.89	144.33	47.2	14.7
Ohio	1,089.9	3.47	1.48	8,000	151.02	397.17	149.33	38.0	14.7
Oklahoma	168.2	2.34	1.05	9,100	163.48	354.35	140.91	40.1	15.7
Oregon	294.7	3.11	1.90	14,000	217.20	354.23	143.49	40.0	14.3
Pennsylvania	1,394.8	4.51	1.84	8,000	150.74	388.75	158.22	40.7	15.1
Rhode Island	127.4	3.61	1.97	11,400	190.83	349.60	140.32	39.1	12.3
South Carolina	153.5	1.99	.83	7,000	137.57	324.52	103.92	31.7	10.7
South Dakota	12.5	.96	.48	7,000	126.94	276.39	112.10	40.0	10.3
Tennessee	196.3	1.70	.67	7,000	139.76	349.02	98.11	28.1	11.7
Texas	911.7	2.42	.85	7,000	144.49	393.68	161.67	41.4	16.5
Utah	77.8	1.66	.96	12,900	196.77	340.95	157.74	45.9	14.0
Vermont	60.3	3.91	1.84	8,000	153.55	337.09	128.72	38.2	12.5
Virginia	159.4	1.04	.40	7,000	140.61	371.81	132.90	35.7	8.7
Washington	610.8	4.03	2.22	13,200	214.31	376.63	150.21	39.3	15.1
West Virginia	152.1	4.29	1.86	8,000	151.30	362.75	144.62	40.3	15.2
Wisconsin	628.8	4.23	2.08	10,500	175.18	359.69	144.11	39.9	13.4
Wyoming	33.3	2.84	1.41	10,300	178.15	352.64	164.18	46.0	19.5
District of Columbia	63.4	2.09	.76	8,000	166.44	497.46	177.35	35.2	19.1

[a] Excludes Federal-state extended benefits and reimbursable employer programs.

[b] Includes contributions from employees in states which tax workers - Alaska, New Jersey, and Pennsylvania.

[c] Includes dependents' allowances in Alaska, Connecticut, District of Columbia, Illinois, Indiana, Iowa, Maine, Maryland, Massachusetts, Michigan, New Jersey, Ohio, Pennsylvania, and Rhode Island.

[d] Total includes Puerto Rico and Virgin Islands.

Source: Department of Labor, Employment and Training Administration.

E47. State Unemployment Compensation Tax Collections by State

Selected Fiscal Years 1939-1987[a]

($Thousands)

State	1939	1950	1960	1970	1980	1985	1986	1987
Total	$ 801,113	$ 1,028,033	$ 2,135,933	$ 2,524,066	$ 11,615,657	$ 18,276,207	$ 18,632,383	$ 17,521,362
Alabama	8,134	11,913	17,739	24,219	154,185	307,971	266,864	179,496
Alaska	-	-	5,322	15,474	61,168	92,183	84,286	79,852
Arizona	2,140	3,824	9,149	21,727	96,473	136,160	134,992	121,859
Arkansas	3,303	4,332	8,842	15,388	73,544	148,458	125,261	118,743
California	75,351	128,456	268,217	531,108	1,597,909	2,188,157	1,925,324	1,807,862
Colorado	4,875	3,490	5,501	13,986	78,697	263,199	230,219	204,249
Connecticut	15,670	13,285	42,766	67,117	180,922	250,185	244,135	223,228
Delaware	2,205	1,458	9,677	6,287	34,163	57,408	57,512	59,408
Florida	6,109	7,542	35,967	34,939	279,045	374,377	335,020	303,729
Georgia	8,869	13,013	27,084	37,764	187,347	247,417	262,627	270,929
Hawaii	-	-	4,464	14,203	64,382	63,594	62,587	71,815
Idaho	2,016	4,263	5,103	8,789	44,204	88,990	83,947	84,116
Illinois	65,909	56,031	121,051	53,425	830,067	1,329,437	1,315,647	1,247,512
Indiana	19,623	18,156	42,998	49,786	163,656	305,309	235,766	179,017
Iowa	8,091	10,848	9,811	14,114	153,509	238,384	243,526	242,313
Kansas	5,703	5,966	10,605	16,384	85,810	170,152	162,228	157,198
Kentucky	10,939	14,833	29,297	27,990	140,533	263,911	246,841	227,331
Louisiana	9,810	15,350	20,217	31,882	222,098	370,043	332,292	307,563
Maine	4,032	6,173	8,560	10,134	58,820	82,166	74,453	73,985
Maryland	11,844	12,294	44,372	22,235	279,444	318,029	329,667	213,129
Massachusetts	37,803	49,018	78,435	121,586	444,874	490,473	430,318	420,629
Michigan	36,563	68,839	154,185	125,788	635,369	515,526	1,367,822	1,233,863
Minnesota	14,100	9,184	22,123	46,554	209,129	334,684	352,331	372,733
Mississippi	2,143	4,118	13,319	7,531	78,348	133,564	119,054	74,088
Missouri	19,567	23,327	30,003	37,369	159,966	289,812	314,217	253,355
Montana	2,682	4,178	4,106	6,608	44,577	52,138	70,161	57,679
Nebraska	3,986	2,724	6,754	7,102	36,861	52,242	56,089	54,749
Nevada	937	1,515	6,013	12,232	76,572	99,312	87,582	77,722
New Hampshire	2,734	4,538	6,785	6,127	28,187	37,880	31,810	24,295
New Jersey	43,978	43,601	109,894	181,058	661,230	963,703	1,017,137	991,162
New Mexico	1,481	4,058	5,996	7,060	41,573	65,956	69,219	66,575
New York	119,215	208,227	293,185	323,597	1,272,486	1,371,325	1,421,183	1,394,252
North Carolina	10,691	17,987	37,627	49,124	234,923	427,482	405,520	292,251
North Dakota	1,112	1,869	3,122	5,342	28,795	49,067	43,204	46,618
Ohio	56,889	44,029	107,558	87,788	495,430	1,050,916	1,000,638	964,348
Oklahoma	5,621	7,310	11,171	11,216	77,927	169,198	173,098	165,614
Oregon	6,439	12,788	34,338	29,631	216,329	258,038	270,996	288,955
Pennsylvania	75,745	57,937	239,053	163,477	720,798	1,467,008	1,551,608	1,448,682
Rhode Island	7,594	10,927	19,071	19,040	64,275	120,293	127,335	132,304
South Carolina	4,438	7,377	11,765	25,563	117,288	150,433	151,596	152,564
South Dakota	1,144	1,368	1,970	2,021	11,432	17,722	16,605	14,896
Tennessee	8,486	12,396	29,737	45,766	157,304	278,588	205,257	193,139
Texas	22,740	26,927	42,698	24,667	124,181	890,802	942,975	884,745
Utah	2,627	3,096	6,793	12,147	54,326	132,472	101,349	79,874
Vermont	1,506	1,569	2,585	6,396	29,218	51,890	57,584	60,087
Virginia	9,913	8,644	23,365	13,320	107,761	281,295	215,623	177,402
Washington	10,061	34,756	50,512	47,962	340,653	471,878	495,478	561,687
West Virginia	9,453	9,604	22,701	18,489	81,799	147,844	154,995	144,416
Wisconsin	15,415	13,222	31,759	59,815	265,031	562,540	576,457	682,890
Wyoming	1,427	1,673	2,568	2,739	14,039	46,596	51,948	36,454

[a] Data for 1939 are not strictly comparable to other years.
Source: Department of Commerce, Bureau of the Census.

E48. Unemployment Compensation Benefits and Reserves by State

Calendar Year 1987

(Dollar Figures in Millions)

State	Current Income[a]	Funds Available for Benefits as of Dec. 31, 1986[b]	Reserves as of Dec. 31, 1987	Benefits Amount[c]	As Percent of Current Income	As Percent of Funds Available[d]
Total[e]	$ 19,442.2	$ 19,932.4	$ 25,228.7	$ 13,648.0[f]	70.2%	68.5%
Alabama	205.0	459	503.8	157.7	76.9	34.4
Alaska	90.4	90	65.4	117.2	129.6	129.8
Arizona	152.6	392	425.9	120.5	79.0	30.7
Arkansas	127.5	95	100.7	122.4	96.0	129.3
California	2,253.1	3,477	4,017.1	1,755.9	77.9	50.5
Colorado	214.4	78	96.1	207.3	96.7	265.7
Connecticut	231.8	190	267.5	156.5	67.5	82.4
Delaware	71.8	94	140.6	24.9	34.6	26.6
District of Columbia	70.3	70	77.9	58.6	83.3	83.7
Florida	445.5	154	1,745.4	260.3	58.4	169.4
Georgia	332.3	706	803.1	230.6	69.4	32.7
Hawaii	96.3	202	253.9	43.5	45.1	21.5
Idaho	92.8	97	126.2	66.0	71.1	68.2
Illinois	1,225.3	461	313.6	784.6	64.0	170.3
Indiana	227.2	437	508.5	154.0	67.8	35.2
Iowa	258.2	146	282.8	121.4	47.0	83.2
Kansas	189.3	331	362.6	155.1	82.0	46.9
Kentucky	237.9	151	251.5	136.1	57.2	90.1
Louisiana	306.7	-16	0.7	336.3	109.6	g
Maine	85.8	100	138.3	48.6	56.7	48.4
Maryland	217.8	527	555.8	186.3	85.5	35.3
Massachusetts	517.4	987	1,097.0	404.4	78.2	41.0
Michigan	1,138.0	884	978.2	932.5	81.9	105.4
Minnesota	391.3	47	155.1	305.9	78.2	649.4
Mississippi	95.0	371	369.9	95.2	100.2	25.7
Missouri	257.7	329	366.0	224.1	87.0	68.1
Montana	54.9	29	45.3	43.0	78.3	149.8
Nebraska	55.1	79	87.0	47.6	86.4	60.4
Nevada	96.3	207	235.9	67.2	69.8	32.5
New Hampshire	38.0	142	164.6	15.4	40.5	10.8
New Jersey	1,115.4	236	1,824.2	543.0	48.7	230.3
New Mexico	76.4	110	120.2	67.6	88.4	61.6
New York	1,569.6	2,165	2,705.5	1,040.0	66.3	48.0
North Carolina	311.3	1,124	1,248.1	186.7	60.0	16.6
North Dakota	56.9	-1	15.0	36.0	63.3	g
Ohio	1,094.6	-11	213.6	624.4	57.0	g
Oklahoma	176.0	69	112.4	138.0	78.4	200.2
Oregon	326.3	307	427.3	206.2	63.2	67.3
Pennsylvania	1,398.5	143	705.3	860.9	61.6	600.7
Rhode Island	142.7	137	216.3	60.0	42.0	44.0
South Carolina	168.7	134	215.2	86.4	51.2	64.5
South Dakota	16.1	39	43.5	11.9	73.6	30.6
Tennessee	237.9	427	506.5	161.6	67.9	37.8
Texas	911.7	1	-	1,059.8	116.3	-
Utah	91.4	155	161.3	86.6	94.8	56.0
Vermont	68.7	72	116.9	23.7	34.4	32.8
Virginia	209.8	526	606.9	131.4	62.6	25.0
Washington	653.7	346.7	654.5	348.5	53.3	100.5
West Virginia	153.5	-2.7	65.3	120.0	78.2	g
Wisconsin	647.6	3.4	404.4	302.8	46.8	-
Wyoming	35.3	35.4	18.4	53.1	150.5	149.9

[a] Includes interest credits to trust fund, employer contributions, and contributions from employees in states which tax workers. Includes interest and penalties for those states in which state law requires these items to be used to pay benefits.
[b] Sum of balances in state clearing accounts, benefit-payment accounts, and state accounts in Federal unemployment trust fund.
[c] Includes states' share of extended benefits of $45.3 million.
[d] Funds available for benefits as of December 31, 1986.
[e] Total includes Puerto Rico and Virgin Islands.
[f] Includes advances from the Federal Unemployment Account in the Federal Unemployment Trust Fund.
[g] Funds available are in deficit position.
Source: Department of Labor, Employment and Training Administration.

E49. Insured Unemployment and Related Data for State Programs[a]

Selected Calendar Years 1940-1987

Year	Insured Unemployment		Initial Claims[c] (Thousands)	Weeks Compensated (Millions)	Number of Exhaustions[d] (Thousands)	Benefits Paid[e]		Funds Available for Benefits[f] ($Millions)
	Number[b] (Thousands)	Percent of Covered Employment				Total ($Millions)	Average Weekly Check	
1940	1,282	5.6%	214	51.1	2,596	$ 518.7	$ 10.56	$ 1,817
1945	589	2.1	116	24.2	254	445.9	18.77	6,914
1950	1,503	4.6	236	67.9	1,853	1,373.1	20.76	6,972
1955	1,254	3.5	226	56.1	1,272	1,350.4	25.04	8,264
1960	1,906	4.8	331	85.6	1,603	2,726.7	32.87	6,643
1961	2,290	5.6	350	104.2	2,371	3,422.7	33.80	5,802
1962	1,783	4.4	302	79.3	1,638	2,675.4	34.56	6,273
1963	1,806	4.3	298	80.1	1,569	2,774.7	35.28	6,648
1964	1,605	3.8	268	71.4	1,371	2,522.1	35.96	7,296
1965	1,328	3.0	232	58.8	1,086	2,166.0	37.19	8,357
1966	1,061	2.3	203	46.5	781	1,771.3	39.76	9,828
1967	1,205	2.5	226	52.9	867	2,092.3	41.25	10,778
1968	1,111	2.2	201	48.7	848	2,031.6	43.43	11,717
1969	1,101	2.1	200	47.9	812	2,127.9	46.17	12,638
1970	1,805	3.4	296	78.9	1,295	3,848.5	50.34	11,896
1971	2,150	4.1	295	94.3	2,007	4,957.0	54.02	9,703
1972	1,848	3.5	261	81.3	1,809	4,471.0	56.75	9,423
1973	1,632	2.7	247	71.2	1,495	4,007.6	59.00	10,934
1974	2,262	3.5	363	97.8	1,926	5,974.9	64.25	10,599
1975	3,986	6.0	478	175.3	4,195	11,754.7	70.23	4,523
1976	2,991	4.6	386	127.4	3,270	8,974.5	75.16	3,343
1977	2,655	3.9	375	113.2	2,850	8,357.2	78.79	4,387
1978	2,359	3.3	364	101.0	2,039	7,717.2	83.67	9,307
1979	2,434	2.9	388	106.1	2,037	8,612.9	89.67	12,470
1980	3,350	3.9	488	149.0	3,076	13,761.1	98.92	11,446
1981	3,047	3.5	460	135.9	2,989	13,262.1	106.70	11,588
1982	4,061	4.6	583	185.3	4,175	20,649.6	119.37	7,482
1983	3,396	3.9	438	155.5	4,180	17,762.8	123.59	7,264
1984	2,476	2.8	377	112.1	2,613	12,594.7	123.28	11,557
1985	2,611	2.9	396	119.3	2,575	13,977.8	128.23	15,999
1986	2,650	2.8	378	121.5	2,703	15,402.8	135.72	19,932
1987	2,332	2.4	328	105.6	2,421	14,276.2	139.90	25,229

[a] Excludes programs for Federal employees and for ex-servicemen; includes programs for state and local government employees where covered by state law.
[b] Weekly average, workers reporting completion of at least one week of unemployment.
[c] Notices filed by workers to indicate they are starting periods of unemployment.
[d] Individuals receiving final payment in benefit year.
[e] Beginning 1971, excludes Federal and state payments under extended benefits provisions; through 1970, includes state share of such benefits.
[f] Sum of balances in state clearing accounts, benefit payment accounts, and state accounts in Federal unemployment trust fund.
Source: Department of Labor.

E50. State Debt by Length of Maturity
End of Selected Fiscal Years 1902-1987
($Millions)

Year	Gross Debt Outstanding			Offsets to Long-term Debt	Net Long-term Debt
	Total	Short-term	Long-term		
1902	$ 230	$ 9	$ 221	n.a.	n.a.
1922	1,131	30	1,101	n.a.	n.a.
1932	2,832	235	2,597	n.a.	n.a.
1942	3,257	161	3,096	$ 533	$ 2,563
1952	6,874	235	6,640	1,020	5,620
1960	18,543	415	18,128	2,533	15,595
1962	22,023	411	21,612	2,967	18,645
1964	25,041	641	24,401	3,479	20,922
1966	29,564	1,060	28,504	4,016	24,488
1968	35,666	2,045	33,622	4,256	29,366
1970	42,008	3,104	38,903	4,425	34,478
1972	54,453	3,912	50,542	5,309	45,233
1973	59,375	3,674	55,701	6,377	49,324
1974	65,296	3,599	61,697	7,850	53,847
1975	72,127	4,580	67,548	9,160	58,388
1976	84,825	6,011	78,814	15,880	62,934
1977	91,640	3,016	88,624	19,600	69,023
1978	102,569	2,897	99,671	27,582	72,089
1979	111,740	2,291	109,449	28,111	81,338
1980	121,958	2,137	119,821	40,011	79,810
1981	134,487	2,325	132,521	50,983	81,538
1982	147,470	3,768	143,702	56,655	87,047
1983	167,290	2,595	164,695	69,915	94,779
1984	186,377	3,169	183,208	81,527	101,681
1985	211,904	2,792	209,112	98,764	110,348
1986	247,715	1,606	246,109	116,990	129,119
1987	265,677	1,606	264,071	122,256	141,815

Source: Department of Commerce, Bureau of the Census.

E51. State Gross Long-Term Debt by Character
End of Selected Fiscal Years 1942-1987
($Millions)

Year	Total	Full Faith and Credit		Nonguaranteed	
		Amount	Percent of Total	Amount	Percent of Total
1942	$ 3,096	$ 2,641	85.3	$ 455	14.7
1952	6,640	4,926	74.2	1,714	25.8
1960	18,128	8,912	49.2	9,216	50.8
1962	21,612	10,313	47.7	11,300	52.3
1964	24,401	11,147	45.7	13,254	54.3
1966	28,504	12,709	44.6	15,795	55.4
1968	33,622	14,698	43.7	18,923	56.3
1970	38,903	17,736	45.6	21,167	54.4
1972	50,542	25,228	49.9	25,314	50.1
1973	55,701	28,443	51.1	27,258	48.9
1974	61,697	30,855	50.0	30,842	50.0
1975	67,548	33,736	49.9	33,812	50.1
1976	78,814	38,842	49.3	39,972	50.7
1977	88,624	43,010	48.5	45,613	51.5
1978	99,671	46,316	46.5	53,356	53.5
1979	109,449	48,286	44.1	61,163	55.9
1980	119,821	49,364	41.2	70,457	58.8
1981	132,521	52,582	39.7	79,940	60.3
1982	143,702	51,507	35.8	92,195	64.2
1983	164,695	55,079	33.4	109,617	66.6
1984	183,208	57,349	31.3	125,859	68.7
1985	209,112	60,432	28.9	148,680	71.1
1986	246,109	64,640	26.3	181,469	73.7
1987	264,071	66,758	25.3	197,314	74.7

Source: Department of Commerce, Bureau of the Census.

E52. State Gross Long-Term Debt by Function and State

End of Fiscal Year 1987

($Millions)

State	Total	Highways		Education			Veterans' Bonuses	Hospitals	Other and Unallocable[a]
		Toll Facilities	Other Highways	State Institutions of Higher Learning	Local Schools	Other Education			
Total	$264,071.2	$8,746.2	$10,170.3	$32,664.3	$3,798.8	$4,381.1	$153.1	$29,090.8	$175,066.5
Alabama	3,728.6	-	393.9	375.2	-	842.0	-	5.5	2,112.0
Alaska	6,182.4	-	3.4	21.0	-	-	-	11.4	6,146.6
Arizona	1,936.7	-	650.5	383.4	-	-	-	686.7	216.2
Arkansas	1,441.0	-	-	257.5	-	6.2	-	39.0	1,138.3
California	22,405.1	90.9	-	2,193.1	1,126.1	-	-	3,621.6	15,373.4[b]
Colorado	2,308.4	-	-	505.1	-	-	-	671.0	1,132.3
Connecticut	8,003.5	0.4	348.0	302.7	179.7	-	-	312.5	6,860.3[b]
Delaware	2,778.2	197.6	164.9	112.1	55.6	-	0.7	338.1	1,909.2
Florida	7,805.8	1,393.1	230.6	447.4	-	2,544.3	-	-	3,190.5
Georgia	2,600.8	-	-	416.5	84.4	-	-	14.0	2,085.8
Hawaii	2,796.5	-	-	7.5	-	-	-	-	2,789.0
Idaho	613.7	-	-	48.1	-	-	-	157.1	408.5
Illinois	12,655.5	568.0	-	1,224.9	-	197.4	-	3,178.5	7,486.6[b]
Indiana	2,691.5	297.5	-	863.5	-	21.7	-	127.8	1,381.0
Iowa	1,290.2	2.9	-	662.2	-	-	-	-	625.1
Kansas	369.9	113.3	151.5	65.3	-	-	-	-	39.8
Kentucky	4,669.0	351.9	1,013.5	1,120.8	175.8	6.9	22.2	67.2	1,910.8
Louisiana	11,075.0	-	139.9	1,162.9	133.9	-	4.8	1,038.5	8,595.1[b]
Maine	1,621.0	4.4	91.5	50.1	4.0	-	-	238.0	1,233.0
Maryland	5,330.4	201.9	-	152.4	760.7	394.3	-	595.5	3,225.6
Massachusetts	12,606.7	232.3	887.6	2,073.5	-	-	-	2,217.8	7,195.6[b]
Michigan	7,669.1	7.9	403.6	1,096.5	-	-	15.0	2,684.0	3,441.5
Minnesota	3,586.9	-	91.0	912.9	38.5	20.7	21.0	-	2,516.4
Mississippi	1,322.5	-	199.1	36.1	59.4	7.2	-	-	888.9
Missouri	4,306.7	-	-	513.7	75.6	138.9	-	906.2	2,811.2

Continued

E52. State Gross Long-Term Debt by Function and State (continued)

End of Fiscal Year 1987

($Millions)

State	Total	Highways		Education			Veterans' Bonuses	Hospitals	Other and Unallocable[a]
		Toll Facilities	Other Highways	State Institutions of Higher Learning	Local Schools	Other Education			
Montana	1,118.6	-	154.3	168.2	-	-	-	84.3	711.7
Nebraska	1,463.6	-	3.0	101.7	-	98.5	-	108.4	1,152.0
Nevada	1,226.2	-	28.0	29.9	-	-	-	-	1,168.3
New Hampshire	2,362.1	79.3	41.3	272.3	-	-	-	157.9	1,811.4
New Jersey	17,480.6	2,966.9	953.1	785.0	-	-	-	2,402.3	10,373.4[b]
New Mexico	1,777.3	-	20.3	317.0	-	4.8	-	17.9	1,417.3
New York	40,403.5	540.9	520.0	6,494.6	-	-	-	5,504.0	27,344.0[b]
North Carolina	2,713.3	-	250.0	295.5	60.0	-	-	871.4	1,236.3
North Dakota	791.7	-	-	322.9	-	-	-	-	468.9
Ohio	9,329.6	4.8	373.2	2,039.7	-	-	-	923.3	5,988.6[b]
Oklahoma	4,105.1	170.9	-	202.0	271.3	-	45.0	23.6	3,392.3
Oregon	6,958.4	6.4	24.0	174.8	-	-	-	-	6,753.2[b]
Pennsylvania	8,817.0	807.6	1,514.4	1,309.0	259.5	-	-	-	4,926.4[b]
Rhode Island	2,732.4	48.8	5.8	296.2	3.7	-	40.0	142.0	2,196.0
South Carolina	3,722.3	-	16.5	274.7	12.0	-	4.4	-	3,414.7
South Dakota	1,544.1	-	-	17.5	55.1	-	-	213.5	1,258.0
Tennessee	2,183.7	-	62.1	351.9	-	70.8	-	3.7	1,695.3
Texas	5,325.9	346.0	-	1,785.0	-	-	-	145.3	3,049.6
Utah	1,412.1	-	-	262.9	-	-	-	-	1,149.2
Vermont	952.3	-	51.1	55.6	-	27.7	-	123.5	694.4
Virginia	4,199.0	152.7	-	1,088.7	256.1	-	-	-	2,701.5
Washington	3,841.0	66.0	755.1	508.2	73.4	-	-	573.8	1,864.5
West Virginia	2,240.8	93.9	629.4	176.4	114.0	-	-	401.5	825.7
Wisconsin	4,795.2	-	-	289.9	-	-	-	483.7	4,021.5
Wyoming	780.4	-	-	40.5	-	-	-	-	739.9

[a] Includes utility debt of $11,894.7 million, housing and community development debt of $6,069.7 million, sewerage debt of $3,183.7 million, parks and recreation debt of $2,067.2 million, water transport and terminals debt of $1,288.3 million, and air transportation debt of $676.7 million.

[b] Includes debt of Veterans' Farm and Home Building and Housing Finance Agency in California; Housing Finance Agency and Development Authority in Connecticut; miscellaneous capital development, transportation bonds in Illinois; Housing Finance Agency and Public Facilities Authority in Louisiana; Housing Finance Agency and miscellaneous capital development in Massachusetts; Economic Development Authority and Housing Finance Authority in New Jersey; Municipal Assistance Corporation, State Mortgage Agency and Urban Development Corporation in New York; Air Quality Development Authority and Department of Development Authority in Ohio; Veterans' Welfare Bonds in Oregon; miscellaneous development and Housing Finance Agency in Pennsylvania.

Source: Department of Commerce, Bureau of the Census.

E53. State Long-Term Debt by Character and State

End of Fiscal Year 1987

(Dollar Figures in Millions)

State	Gross Long-term Debt	Full Faith and Credit		Nonguaranteed	
		Total[a]	General Obligation	Amount	Percent of Total
Total	$264,071.2	$66,757.6	$54,743.2	$197,313.6	74.7%
Alabama	3,728.6	1,868.2	1,868.2	1,860.4	49.9
Alaska	6,188.8	1,448.5	1,448.5	4,733.9	76.5
Arizona	1,936.7	-	-	1,936.7	100.0
Arkansas	1,441.0	-	-	1,441.0	100.0
California	22,405.1	5,109.9	3,732.2	17,295.2	77.2
Colorado	2,308.4	-	-	2,308.4	100.0
Connecticut	8,003.5	2,252.8	1,599.0	5,750.7	71.9
Delaware	2,778.2	524.1	524.1	2,254.0	81.1
Florida	7,805.8	1,780.4	1,615.6	6,025.4	77.2
Georgia	2,600.8	1,608.3	1,608.3	992.5	38.2
Hawaii	2,796.5	1,823.7	1,823.7	972.8	34.8
Idaho	613.7	-	-	613.7	100.0
Illinois	12,655.5	3,806.2	3,806.2	8,849.2	69.9
Indiana	2,691.5	-	-	2,691.5	100.0
Iowa	1,290.2	-	-	1,290.2	100.0
Kansas	369.9	-	-	369.9	100.0
Kentucky	4,669.0	142.5	142.5	4,526.5	96.9
Louisiana	11,075.0	3,463.2	3,463.2	7,611.8	68.7
Maine	1,621.0	296.6	296.6	1,324.5	81.7
Maryland	5,330.4	2,040.9	2,040.9	3,289.5	61.7
Massachusetts	12,606.7	4,406.7	3,944.1	8,200.0	65.0
Michigan	7,669.1	561.3	561.3	7,107.8	92.7
Minnesota	3,586.9	1,142.4	1,142.4	2,444.5	68.2
Mississippi	1,322.5	421.0	352.1	901.5	68.2
Missouri	4,306.7	686.5	686.5	3,620.2	84.1
Montana	1,118.6	99.4	99.4	1,019.2	91.1
Nebraska	1,463.6	-	-	1,463.6	100.0
Nevada	1,226.2	367.2	367.2	859.0	70.1
New Hampshire	2,362.1	454.5	299.9	1,907.6	80.8
New Jersey	17,480.6	2,774.4	2,774.4	14,706.1	84.1
New Mexico	1,777.3	115.3	97.4	1,662.0	93.5
New York	40,403.5	4,717.9	3,654.3	35,685.6	88.3
North Carolina	2,713.3	780.7	780.7	1,932.6	71.2
North Dakota	791.7	-	-	791.7	100.0
Ohio	9,329.6	2,731.5	717.8	6,598.2	70.7
Oklahoma	4,105.1	88.6	88.6	4,016.5	97.8
Oregon	6,958.4	6,231.4	576.3	727.0	10.4
Pennsylvania	8,817.0	4,371.9	4,371.9	4,445.1	50.4
Rhode Island	2,732.4	301.5	265.0	2,430.9	89.0
South Carolina	3,722.3	693.5	665.4	3,028.8	81.4
South Dakota	1,544.1	-	-	1,544.1	100.0
Tennessee	2,183.7	802.1	802.1	1,381.6	63.3
Texas	5,325.9	2,080.6	2,080.6	3,245.3	60.9
Utah	1,412.1	255.2	255.2	1,157.0	81.9
Vermont	952.3	266.7	266.7	685.6	72.0
Virginia	4,199.0	389.7	72.3	3,809.2	90.7
Washington	3,841.0	3,073.2	3,073.2	767.8	20.0
West Virginia	2,240.8	619.9	619.9	1,620.9	72.3
Wisconsin	4,795.2	2,159.4	2,159.4	2,635.8	55.0
Wyoming	780.4	-	-	780.4	100.0

[a] Total includes general obligation debt plus $12,014.4 million payable initially from specified nontax revenue.

Source: Department of Commerce, Bureau of the Census. Percentage computations by Tax Foundation.

E54. Total and Per Capita Gross Debt and Net Long-Term Debt by State[a]

End of Selected Fiscal Years 1960-1987

State	Gross Debt Total in Millions 1960	Gross Debt Total in Millions 1970	Gross Debt Total in Millions 1987	Per Capita 1987	Net Long-Term Debt 1987 Total in Millions	Net Long-Term Debt 1987 Per Capita
Total	$18,543.1	$42,007.7	$265,676.8	$1,094.32	$141,815.1	$584.13
Alabama	241.0	742.9	3,728.6	913.21	1,797.9	440.33
Alaska	2.9	222.3	6,182.4	11,788.18	1,967.0	3,746.67
Arizona	12.4	90.9	1,936.7	571.98	1,159.5	342.45
Arkansas	105.9	100.8	1,441.0	603.41	431.7	180.76
California	2,087.9	5,334.5	22,405.1	809.93	12,919.2	467.02
Colorado	70.5	124.4	2,308.4	703.77	630.3	191.22
Connecticut	902.5	1,919.5	8,003.5	2,495.74	4,730.6	1,473.25
Delaware	219.6	420.9	2,778.2	4,327.64	2,355.9	3,658.28
Florida	282.8	891.0	7,805.8	649.24	3,282.2	272.99
Georgia	295.3	970.2	2,600.8	418.00	2,026.0	325.62
Hawaii	195.7	528.2	2,796.5	2,648.15	2,270.6	2,092.75
Idaho	7.0	33.1	613.7	614.92	144.4	144.71
Illinois	675.6	1,305.9	12,655.5	1,093.52	6,863.6	592.61
Indiana	408.5	583.8	2,691.5	493.83	1,004.1	181.54
Iowa	53.9	98.0	1,290.2	626.58	579.0	204.29
Kansas	202.3	223.6	369.9	149.41	339.6	137.15
Kentucky	147.0	1,224.1	4,669.0	1,252.74	2,942.9	789.61
Louisiana	354.7	865.0	11,075.0	2,482.66	7,303.3	1,637.13
Maine	136.2	232.3	1,621.0	1,365.65	309.4	260.69
Maryland	584.1	1,145.9	5,330.4	1,176.65	2,658.7	586.27
Massachusetts	1,289.9	1,861.8	12,606.7	2,186.21	5,774.0	986.51
Michigan	775.7	958.5	7,669.1	836.99	3,097.8	336.71
Minnesota	228.6	462.5	3,586.9	844.76	1,438.7	338.85
Mississippi	180.6	455.2	1,322.5	503.79	558.6	212.81
Missouri	85.4	141.9	4,306.7	843.95	1,809.5	354.60
Montana	49.0	81.8	1,118.6	1,416.74	360.8	445.96
Nebraska	13.1	73.5	1,463.6	927.48	572.7	359.29
Nevada	4.0	34.1	1,226.2	1,217.66	577.1	573.09
New Hampshire	92.1	157.9	2,362.1	2,234.75	1,526.5	1,444.15
New Jersey	914.9	1,762.8	17,480.6	2,279.54	11,829.4	1,541.89
New Mexico	50.7	120.7	1,777.3	1,186.68	390.2	260.13
New York	2,902.1	7,387.8	40,403.5	2,279.43	22,286.1	1,250.27
North Carolina	276.3	541.6	2,713.3	425.03	1,707.9	266.31
North Dakota	14.6	37.3	791.7	1,178.13	41.4	61.60
Ohio	910.8	1,631.9	9,329.6	875.34	7,071.0	655.81
Oklahoma	193.4	739.6	4,105.1	1,254.63	2,150.3	657.17
Oregon	281.2	689.7	6,958.4	2,622.40	1,743.8	640.17
Pennsylvania	1,446.7	3,220.4	8,817.0	738.90	6,878.1	576.24
Rhode Island	96.4	373.2	2,732.4	2,824.72	1,286.4	1,304.69
South Carolina	271.6	350.5	3,722.3	1,086.86	2,386.4	696.76
South Dakota	6.3	29.9	1,544.1	2,177.88	227.6	321.02
Tennessee	123.6	416.2	2,183.7	465.66	996.8	205.32
Texas	324.8	1,013.1	5,325.9	317.40	2,740.1	163.21
Utah	14.5	103.1	1,412.1	843.76	334.4	199.07
Vermont	42.1	220.6	952.3	1,742.82	336.0	613.21
Virginia	188.2	323.2	4,199.0	711.21	670.4	113.56
Washington	420.3	719.7	3,841.0	846.41	3,210.0	707.36
West Virginia	296.7	554.6	2,240.8	1,167.70	1,303.9	687.36
Wisconsin	55.0	536.2	4,795.2	997.54	2,761.7	574.52
Wyoming	8.7	51.1	780.4	1,592.61	31.6	64.42

[a] Gross debt includes short- and long-term debt (see amounts in Table E50).
Source: Department of Commerce, Bureau of the Census.

Section F
Local Governments

- Summary Data
- Expenditures
- Revenue and Taxation
- Debt
- Education

F1. Local Expenditures, Revenue, and Debt

Selected Fiscal Years 1902-1987

($Millions)

Year	Expenditures			Revenue			Gross Debt
	Total	Direct	Payments to State Governments[a]	Total	From Own Sources	Intergovern-mental[b]	
1902	$ 959	$ 959	-	$ 914	$ 858	$ 56	$ 1,877
1913	1,960	1,960	-	1,755	1,658	97	4,035
1922	4,567	4,567	-	4,148	3,827	321	8,978
1927	6,359	6,359	-	6,333	5,728	605	12,910
1932	6,375	6,375	-	6,192	5,381	811	16,373
1934	5,699	5,699	-	6,363	4,962	1,401	15,681
1936	6,056	6,756	-	6,793	5,147	1,646	16,061
1938	6,906	6,906	-	7,329	5,646	1,683	16,093
1940	7,685	7,685	-	7,724	5,792	1,932	16,693
1942	7,351	7,351	-	8,114	6,278	1,836	16,080
1944	7,180	7,180	-	8,535	6,665	1,870	14,703
1946	9,093	9,093	-	9,561	7,416	2,145	13,564
1948	13,363	13,363	-	13,167	9,666	3,501	14,980
1950	17,041	17,041	-	16,101	11,673	4,428	18,830
1952	20,229	20,073	$ 156	19,398	14,117	5,281	23,226
1954	23,814	23,599	215	22,402	16,468	5,933	29,331
1956	28,273	28,004	269	26,352	19,453	6,899	35,978
1958	34,023	33,721	302	31,348	22,970	8,378	42,793
1960	39,056	38,847	209	37,324	27,209	10,114	51,412
1961	42,641	42,445	196	40,483	29,579	10,904	55,030
1962	45,279	45,053	226	43,147	31,506	11,642	59,255
1963	47,237	47,002	235	45,586	32,995	12,591	61,881
1964	51,199	50,964	235	49,578	35,749	13,829	67,181
1965	55,482	55,221	262	53,408	38,242	15,165	72,478
1966	60,994	60,711	283	59,268	41,499	17,769	77,487
1967	66,648	66,274	374	64,608	44,419	20,188	81,185
1968	72,357	71,930	427	70,171	47,875	22,295	85,492
1969	82,698	82,152	546	79,274	53,192	26,082	93,995
1970	92,522	91,889	633	89,082	59,557	29,525	101,563
1971	105,167	104,566	601	100,993	66,521	34,473	111,034
1972	118,568	118,001	567	114,791	75,097	39,694	120,705
1973	128,254	127,452	802	129,119	81,253	47,866	129,110
1974	140,387	139,498	889	143,132	88,391	54,741	141,320
1975	162,614	161,336	1,278	159,726	97,772	61,954	147,798
1976	181,802	179,980	1,822	178,338	108,592	69,746	155,707
1977	196,307	194,403	1,904	196,458	119,626	76,831	169,458
1978	211,081	208,768	2,313	214,518	130,464	84,053	177,864
1979	233,323	231,684	1,639	234,630	139,853	94,777	192,363
1980	260,777	259,019	1,757	258,298	155,873	102,425	213,645
1981	288,571	286,827	1,744	287,834	176,391	111,443	229,045
1982	313,365	311,409	1,957	315,322	198,703	116,619	257,109
1983	335,098	332,093	3,005	337,921	218,522	119,399	287,211
1984	359,378	355,781	3,597	366,156	239,425	126,732	318,653
1985	390,961	386,931	4,030	402,544	264,461	138,083	356,539
1986	427,980	421,961	4,019	434,751	287,459	147,256	411,160
1987	463,826	458,592	5,234	469,317	313,032	156,285	452,980

[a] Amounts prior to 1952 are minor and not segregable from direct expenditures.
[b] Largely shared taxes and fiscal aids from state governments.
Source: Department of Commerce, Bureau of the Census.

F2. Per Capita Amounts of Selected City Finance Items by Population-Size Groups

Fiscal Year 1987[a]

Item	All Municipalities	Population Size[b]						
		1,000,000 or More	500,000 to 999,999	300,000 to 499,999	200,000 to 299,999	100,000 to 199,999	75,000 to 99,999	Less Than 75,000
Revenue, total	$ 1,133	$ 2,423	$ 1,835	$ 1,292	$ 1,227	$ 1,074	$ 918	$ 724
General Revenue, total	869	1,892	1,419	1,022	985	812	747	536
Intergovernmental revenue	252	630	481	244	273	234	192	136
From Federal government	56	96	182	71	55	49	37	31
From state government	176	512	271	139	194	161	144	89
From local government	20	22	28	35	24	23	11	16
Own-source general revenue	617	1,262	938	778	712	578	555	400
Taxes	369	923	577	401	363	335	332	211
Property	181	350	278	178	175	203	207	121
General Sales	64	147	85	84	73	56	65	38
Selective Sales	40	100	58	57	52	38	28	21
Income	54	252	106	43	34	13	7	12
Other	30	73	49	38	30	25	26	18
Current Charges	129	193	186	176	171	127	111	99
Miscellaneous general revenue	119	146	176	202	178	116	112	91
Utility and liquor strore revenue	194	226	266	188	182	223	144	178
Employee-retirement revenue	69	305	142	82	60	39	27	10
Expenditures, total	1,095	2,272	1,771	1,219	1,236	1,068	901	711
General expenditures, total	831	1,783	1,331	949	987	806	731	517
Education	90	260	155	70	160	119	103	29
Highways	67	67	80	70	80	69	74	64
Public-welfare	43	244	85	6	16	13	4	3
Hospitals	36	107	64	19	25	21	16	23
Health	13	37	41	20	12	10	5	4
Police protection	99	171	139	115	106	100	98	73
Fire protection	53	74	73	71	68	67	61	38
Sewerage	61	73	97	76	60	59	53	52
Sanitation other than sewerage	30	56	37	35	36	28	24	22
Parks and recreation	40	50	61	66	64	44	42	28
Housing and urban development	37	107	72	50	42	36	32	14
Libraries	11	19	14	15	13	13	11	7
Financial administration	22	23	30	27	24	22	25	20
General control	21	42	47	25	23	21	12	13
General public buildings	11	19	16	12	13	14	7	8
Interest on general debt	62	90	103	111	97	54	62	42
All other	137	345	218	163	146	115	101	78
Utility and liquor store expenditure	225	310	362	227	227	243	153	187
Employee-retirement expenditure	38	180	71	44	22	19	17	5
Exhibit: Expenditure for salaries and								
wages	370	851	596	394	442	371	326	217
Gross debt outstanding, total	1,200	1,839	2,010	1,942	1,911	1,097	1,110	813
Long-term	1,171	1,754	1,976	1,924	1,884	1,071	1,096	795
Full faith and credit	381	662	780	504	560	350	334	240
Nonguaranteed	790	1,092	1,196	1,420	1,324	722	761	556
Short-term	29	85	34	18	26	26	15	18
Utility debt only	272	372	569	355	410	243	165	202
Cash and security holdings	1,183	3,273	2,069	1,732	1,136	935	937	546
Exhibit: City contribution to own retirement systems	36	162	81	37	19	18	15	5

[a] For coverage of fiscal years, see Introductory Notes to Tables.
[b] Population as of 1982.
Source: Department of Commerce, Bureau of the Census.

F3. Local Direct Expenditures by Character and Payments to State Governments

Selected Fiscal Years 1902-1987[a]

($Millions)

Year	Total	Direct Expenditures Total[b]	Current Operation	Capital Outlay[c]	Assistance and Subsidies	Interest[d]	Insurance Trust[e]	Payments to State Governments[f]
1902	$ 959	$ 959	$ 682	$ 203	$ 5	$ 69	-	-
1913	1,960	1,960	1,287	500	7	159	-	-
1922	4,567	4,567	2,915	1,216	30	385	$ 8	-
1927	6,359	6,359	3,828	1,864	50	579	21	-
1932	6,375	6,375	4,197	1,090	305	726	38	-
1942	7,351	7,351	5,230	835	590	584	57	-
1950	17,041	17,041	11,498	3,810	1,027	504	122	-
1952	20,229	20,073	13,360	4,778	1,070	580	202	$156
1954	23,814	23,599	15,622	5,778	1,148	723	258	215
1956	28,273	28,004	18,771	6,843	1,089	910	327	269
1958	34,023	33,721	22,701	8,040	1,346	1,141	392	302
1960	39,056	38,847	26,785	8,497	1,503	1,492	490	209
1962	45,279	45,053	31,446	9,577	1,590	1,789	575	226
1964	51,199	50,964	36,197	10,267	1,709	2,061	651	235
1966	60,994	60,711	43,357	12,137	2,014	2,374	730	283
1968	72,357	71,930	51,932	13,521	2,689	2,761	830	427
1970	92,522	91,889	66,943	16,355	3,703	3,624	1,027	633
1971	105,167	104,566	75,983	18,402	4,573	4,142	1,263	601
1972	118,568	118,001	87,033	19,344	5,212	4,811	1,466	567
1973	128,254	127,452	94,266	20,595	5,290	5,394	1,599	802
1974	140,387	139,498	104,007	22,667	4,769	5,977	1,907	889
1975	162,614	161,336	120,183	27,517	4,473	6,815	2,077	1,278
1976	181,802	179,980	136,212	28,522	5,205	7,542	2,350	1,822
1977	196,307	194,403	149,967	28,190	5,522	8,001	2,499	1,904
1978	211,081	208,768	163,070	28,705	5,413	8,551	2,723	2,313
1979	233,323	231,684	179,633	34,072	5,170	9,415	3,031	1,639
1980	260,777	259,019	199,690	39,568	5,404	10,552	3,394	1,757
1981	288,571	286,827	220,829	43,311	5,971	12,354	3,815	1,744
1982	313,365	311,409	241,905	43,336	6,468	14,920	4,361	1,957
1983	335,098	332,093	258,026	44,633	6,809	17,470	4,779	3,005
1984	359,378	355,781	276,730	45,166	7,308	20,701	5,154	3,597
1985	390,961	386,931	300,333	49,273	7,865	23,209	5,876	4,030
1986	427,980	423,961	326,149	55,907	8,426	26,769	6,251	4,019
1987	463,826	458,592	350,402	61,068	8,904	30,719	6,710	5,234
							7,499	

[a] Data by state for 1987 appear in Table F6.
[b] Includes utility and liquor store expenditures. Utility covers water supply, electric power, gas supply, and transit systems owned and operated by local governments.
[c] Capital outlay data are gross; i.e., no allowance has been made for depreciation or repair.
[d] Includes payments on general and utility debt.
[e] Benefit payments and refunds of contributions received in connection with contributory retirement, life insurance, and social insurance programs comprise this category of expenditure.
[f] Amounts prior to 1952 are minor and not segregable from direct expenditures.
Source: Department of Commerce, Bureau of the Census.

F4. Local Direct Expenditures for Own Functions

Selected Fiscal Years 1902-1987[a]

($Millions)

Year	Total	General								Utility	Liquor Stores	Insurance Trust
		Total	Education[b]	Highways	Public Welfare	Health and Hospitals	Police and Fire	General Control[c]	Other[d]			
1902	$959	$879	$238	$171	$27	$28	$90	$118	$207	$80	-	-
1913	1,960	1,767	522	393	36	55	164	173	424	186	-	$7
1922	4,567	4,187	1,541	991	81	133	344	244	853	359	-	21
1927	6,359	5,830	2,017	1,295	111	185	466	316	1,440	491	-	38
1932	6,375	5,800	2,033	898	370	241	513	356	1,389	457	$1	57
1934	5,699	5,172	1,603	771	526	295	465	324	1,268	553	5	69
1936	6,056	5,421	1,880	671	405	246	500	370	1,349	636	8	77
1938	6,906	6,181	2,144	835	616	283	560	396	1,347	1,090	10	81
1940	7,685	6,499	2,263	780	629	309	566	410	1,542	804	14	86
1942	7,351	6,421	2,195	700	702	292	590	414	1,528	822	33	112
1944	7,180	6,197	2,304	660	556	325	624	437	1,291	1,014	56	128
1946	9,093	7,875	2,838	1,059	729	394	728	511	1,616	1,612	76	148
1948	13,363	11,498	4,298	1,526	1,137	566	985	614	2,372	2,005	80	177
1950	17,041	14,754	5,819	1,745	1,374	801	1,179	724	3,112	2,246	98	202
1952	20,073	17,444	6,824	2,094	1,378	1,053	1,419	832	3,844	2,577	102	285
1954	23,599	20,593	8,842	2,272	1,512	1,133	1,653	956	4,225	3,119	101	327
1956	28,004	24,392	11,082	2,586	1,536	1,302	1,909	1,083	4,894	3,720	104	392
1958	33,721	29,403	13,192	3,060	1,874	1,704	2,269	1,274	6,030	4,066	115	492
1960	38,847	34,092	15,323	3,358	2,183	1,898	2,607	1,459	7,264	4,445	126	570
1962	45,053	39,831	17,946	3,722	2,575	2,181	2,978	1,574	8,855	5,067	140	651
1964	50,964	45,027	20,822	3,814	2,970	2,446	3,273	1,697	10,004	6,042	159	730
1966	60,711	53,680	25,715	4,146	3,620	2,944	3,767	1,950	11,540	6,721	216	830
1968	71,930	63,966	30,200	4,663	4,735	3,715	4,517	2,337	13,799	7,820	223	1,027
1970	91,889	82,582	38,938	5,383	6,477	4,880	5,830	2,961	18,113	8,675	230	1,263
1971	104,566	94,196	43,613	5,792	7,708	5,806	6,733	3,349	21,195	9,715	188	1,466
1972	118,001	106,499	48,661	6,274	8,869	7,014	7,685	3,786	24,210	11,204	248	1,599
1973	127,452	114,093	51,431	6,543	9,435	7,338	8,567	4,202	25,577	12,487	265	1,907
1974	139,498	124,668	56,085	7,310	9,576	8,451	9,181	4,737	29,328			2,077
1975	161,336	143,421	64,956	8,270	9,733	9,877	10,734	5,435	34,416	15,276	290	2,350
1976	179,990	159,720	71,670	9,047	11,278	10,836	12,017	6,133	38,739	17,451	310	2,499
1977	194,403	170,938	75,707	9,205	11,883	11,830	13,288	6,764	42,261	20,463	279	2,723
1978	208,768	182,995	81,181	9,951	11,950	12,632	14,425	7,595	45,261	22,416	326	3,031
1979	231,684	201,470	87,931	11,361	11,676	14,432	15,530	8,512	52,028	26,473	348	3,394
1980	259,019	223,621	97,960	12,650	12,310	16,507	17,151	9,303	57,740	31,198	385	3,815
1981	286,827	245,102	106,121	13,915	13,667	18,073	19,013	10,208	64,105	36,943	421	4,361
1982	311,408	264,355	111,982	14,417	14,704	21,483	21,141	11,400	69,208	41,840	434	4,779
1983	332,093	280,924	119,281	15,502	14,281	23,284	22,894	12,617	73,055	45,579	436	5,154
1984	355,781	301,974	127,535	16,266	15,588	24,852	24,671	13,591	79,471	47,504	427	5,876
1985	390,961	332,665	139,228	17,912	18,194	26,967	26,785	14,860	88,719	51,613	432	6,251
1986	423,961	359,902	152,559	19,177	18,390	28,142	28,944	16,435	96,255	56,900	449	6,710
1987	458,592	391,095	165,010	20,711	18,967	29,769	31,959	17,810	106,869	59,537	461	7,499

a Data by state for 1987 appear in Table F7.
b Principally elementary and secondary schools.
c Includes financial administration.
d Includes natural resources, sanitation, recreation, interest on general debt, housing and urban renewal, nonhighway transportation, correction, local libraries, general public buildings, and other general government.

Source: Department of Government, Bureau of the Census.

F5. Detail of Local Expenditures by Function and Unit of Government

Fiscal Years 1982 and 1987

($Millions)

Type and Function	1987 Total	1982 — Unit of Government					
		Total	County	Municipality	Township	School District	Special District
Total[a]	$463,826	$313,365	$67,107	$112,833	$10,137	$93,398	$34,821
Intergovernmental[a]	5,234	1,957	3,070	2,123	527	413	756
Direct	458,592	311,408	64,037	110,710	9,610	92,986	34,066
General	391,095	264,355	61,505	83,132	8,919	92,836	17,963
Education	165,010	111,982	8,703	9,760	2,450	91,009	60
Highways	20,711	14,417	5,709	6,874	1,591	-	243
Public welfare	18,967	14,704	10,106	4,488	110	-	-
Health	7,656	5,112	3,658	1,228	68	-	158
Hospitals	22,113	16,371	7,245	3,955	59	-	5,113
Police	21,049	14,115	3,481	9,859	775	-	-
Fire	10,910	7,026	637	5,422	448	-	519
Local parks and recreation	9,102	6,140	1,224	4,009	282	-	625
Natural resources	2,384	1,403	649	54	6	-	693
Sanitation and sewerage	20,918	14,581	1,965	9,248	780	-	2,589
Housing and urban renewal	10,458	8,096	444	4,641	50	-	2,961
Air transportation	4,400	2,518	490	1,426	10	-	593
Water transport and terminals	1,209	860	57	333	-	-	469
General control[b]	17,810	11,400	6,087	4,639	674	-	-
Interest on general debt	23,233	11,145	2,456	4,306	288	1,827	2,268
Other and unallocable[c]	20,127	24,485	8,594	12,890	1,328	-	1,672
Utility	59,537	41,840	1,577	23,637	628	-	15,998
Water supply system	18,244	11,334	944	7,521	346	-	2,523
Electric power system	26,317	18,634	49	11,185	276	-	7,123
Transit system	12,097	9,306	571	2,952	3	-	5,781
Gas supply system	2,879	2,566	13	1,979	4	-	571
Liquor stores[d]	461	434	184	250	-	-	-
Insurance trust	7,499	4,779	770	3,691	63	150	104
Employee retirement	7,425	4,679	770	99	63	150	104
Unemployment compensation	74	99	-	3,592	-	-	-

[a] To avoid duplication, intergovernmental transactions between units of government are eliminated in the total for all units.
[b] Includes financial administration.
[c] Includes libraries, social insurance administration, parking facilities, correction, protective inspection and regulation, and other and unallocable expenditures.
[d] Includes purchase of goods for resale.
Source: Department of Commerce, Bureau of the Census.

F6. Local Expenditures by Character and State
Fiscal Year 1987
($Millions)

State	Total	Direct								Local Payments to State Governments
		Total[a]	Current Operation			Assistance and Subsidies	Capital Outlay	Interest on General Debt	Insurance Trust	
			Total	Salaries and Wages	Other					
Total	$463,826.1	$458,592.2	$350,401.6	$193,062.2	$157,339.4	$8,904.2	$61,067.8	$30,719.4	$7,499.3	$5,233.7
Alabama	5,403.7	5,399.6	4,376.9	2,350.2	2,026.7	.5	653.8	343.6	24.8	4.1
Alaska	2,434.1	2,434.0	1,376.5	773.4	603.1	-	713.9	339.4	4.1	.8
Arizona	7,632.1	7,535.8	4,927.7	2,711.8	2,215.9	-	1,730.1	857.0	21.0	96.3
Arkansas	2,735.7	2,735.2	2,006.7	1,169.4	837.3	b	542.5	178.6	7.4	.5
California	67,157.5	67,081.6	50,394.2	27,776.8	22,617.4	4,370.2	7,581.8	3,219.8	1,515.8	75.9
Colorado	7,442.7	7,440.0	5,019.7	2,888.7	2,131.0	192.1	1,531.8	635.9	60.6	2.6
Connecticut	5,028.2	5,027.8	4,133.5	2,184.0	1,949.5	33.1	606.6	177.2	77.4	.4
Delaware	844.3	844.3	704.5	385.7	318.8	-	64.6	67.5	7.7	b
Florida	23,528.3	23,510.1	16,397.9	8,918.2	7,479.7	4.9	4,943.7	2,029.5	134.1	18.3
Georgia	11,743.3	11,721.9	8,773.2	4,514.7	4,258.5	-	2,035.7	840.0	72.9	21.4
Hawaii	822.2	822.2	597.4	289.3	308.1	-	227.3	57.6	-	-
Idaho	1,190.0	1,183.5	1,026.4	593.6	432.8	.1	119.3	37.0	.7	6.6
Illinois	19,763.0	19,745.0	15,634.4	8,812.7	6,821.7	.3	2,572.2	992.4	545.7	18.0
Indiana	7,844.4	7,835.2	6,535.8	3,664.8	2,871.0	172.6	721.4	345.2	60.2	9.2
Iowa	4,500.5	4,448.2	3,692.8	1,920.8	1,772.0	.7	487.2	244.4	23.1	52.3
Kansas	4,320.8	4,320.5	3,388.2	1,767.3	1,620.9	-	519.0	479.7	13.7	.2
Kentucky	4,113.0	4,111.3	3,185.9	1,717.3	1,468.6	2.4	440.0	457.7	25.3	1.7
Louisiana	6,361.7	6,341.4	4,933.7	2,801.7	2,132.0	3.8	783.9	565.0	54.9	20.3
Maine	1,418.6	1,417.8	1,161.1	641.7	519.4	.1	193.1	63.3	b	.8
Maryland	7,366.7	7,317.9	5,507.3	3,492.4	2,014.9	-	1,142.0	561.4	107.2	48.8
Massachusetts	11,099.1	10,854.6	8,536.2	4,887.9	3,648.3	1.9	1,298.8	475.8	541.9	244.4
Michigan	17,034.4	16,948.6	14,415.2	7,660.1	6,755.1	5.9	1,407.6	693.5	426.4	85.8
Minnesota	10,258.3	10,189.7	7,211.1	3,849.4	3,361.7	428.3	1,466.3	962.3	121.6	68.7
Mississippi	3,442.7	3,442.1	2,907.0	1,512.4	1,394.6	.2	347.6	179.5	7.7	.6
Missouri	6,871.7	6,870.2	5,627.5	3,238.5	2,389.0	.2	843.0	315.5	83.9	1.5
Montana	1,258.7	1,249.5	1,016.8	578.5	438.3	b	147.0	85.6	.1	9.2

Continued

F6. Local Expenditures by Character and State (continued)

Fiscal Year 1987

($Millions)

State	Total	Total[a]	Direct							Local Payments to State Governments
			Current Operation			Assistance and Subsidies	Capital Outlay	Interest on General Debt	Insurance Trust	
			Total	Salaries and Wages	Other					
Nebraska	3,740.0	3,732.4	3,000.2	1,335.3	1,664.9	.1	417.3	289.5	25.2	7.6
Nevada	1,950.1	1,949.6	1,408.0	804.1	603.9	-	377.4	164.1	-	.5
New Hampshire	1,334.7	1,315.5	1,078.2	551.8	526.4	2.0	187.8	47.2	.3	19.2
New Jersey	14,254.9	14,076.2	11,387.9	6,451.4	4,936.5	531.3	1,398.3	739.4	19.4	178.6
New Mexico	2,352.0	2,342.2	1,701.6	967.5	734.1	-	394.0	246.6	-	9.6
New York	55,565.1	51,909.8	39,431.1	21,990.4	17,440.7	2,611.4	5,170.2	2,353.0	2,344.1	3,655.3
North Carolina	10,454.3	10,346.4	7,906.0	4,151.2	3,754.8	73.7	1,568.0	794.3	4.4	107.8
North Dakota	916.9	906.3	879.1	339.8	539.3	23.0	139.9	57.3	2.8	10.6
Ohio	16,850.7	16,781.5	14,245.9	7,788.8	6,457.1	228.2	1,579.8	693.7	34.0	69.1
Oklahoma	4,451.3	4,448.7	3,405.8	2,054.4	1,351.4	b	721.3	311.8	9.7	2.5
Oregon	4,995.4	4,988.6	4,191.3	2,159.1	2,032.2	-	517.6	254.4	25.3	6.8
Pennsylvania	18,547.0	18,396.0	14,667.7	8,029.6	6,638.1	b	1,620.9	1,786.6	320.8	151.1
Rhode Island	1,168.1	1,168.0	1,021.0	613.9	407.1	19.2	55.0	44.4	28.3	b
South Carolina	4,273.9	4,260.4	3,347.4	1,925.5	1,421.9	-	549.4	361.8	1.8	13.5
South Dakota	871.8	868.3	727.7	385.8	341.9	b	112.4	26.3	1.9	3.6
Tennessee	8,902.3	8,882.5	7,282.2	2,851.1	4,431.1	.5	996.6	498.8	104.5	19.8
Texas	31,796.4	31,787.9	21,285.9	13,048.4	8,237.5	1.3	6,684.1	3,666.3	150.4	8.5
Utah	3,171.0	3,165.2	2,019.8	1,041.3	978.5	-	575.1	570.2	-	5.9
Vermont	698.2	698.1	604.5	301.0	303.5	-	66.5	25.9	1.2	.1
Virginia	8,685.8	8,663.3	6,983.9	4,220.8	2,763.1	65.1	1,106.1	426.9	80.9	22.4
Washington	10,274.7	10,157.5	7,116.7	3,676.8	3,439.9	.2	1,726.0	1,249.0	65.6	117.2
West Virginia	2,067.7	2,067.0	1,660.9	1,115.6	545.3	-	189.0	208.6	8.6	.6
Wisconsin	9,074.6	9,059.7	7,584.3	3,960.5	3,623.8	50.8	1,035.4	316.6	72.7	14.9
Wyoming	1,366.2	1,345.7	1,031.5	578.1	453.4	-	207.8	105.4	.9	20.5
District of Columbia	4,387.3	4,387.3	3,198.9	1,566.9	1,632.0	102.5	551.1	276.8	258.0	-

[a] Includes utility and liquor store expenditures, including payments on local utility debt.
[b] Less than $50 thousand.
Source: Department of Commerce, Bureau of the Census.

F7. Local Direct General Expenditures for Own Functions by State

Fiscal Year 1987
($Millions)

State	Total	Education	Highways	Public Welfare	Health and Hospitals	Police and Fire	Financial Administration[a]	Other[b]
Total	$ 391,095.1	$ 165,010.5	$ 20,711.1	$ 18,967.1	$ 29,769.1	$ 31,958.8	$ 17,810.2	$ 106,868.3
Alabama	4,332.4	1,684.5	289.5	16.6	711.8	155.1	187.1	1,287.8
Alaska	2,127.0	789.4	143.4	10.8	60.2	133.5	118.2	871.5
Arizona	6,069.2	2,614.6	467.9	140.8	231.7	499.9	339.9	1,774.4
Arkansas	2,324.3	1,275.2	141.6	4.8	208.3	140.2	82.2	472.0
California	56,767.3	20,092.2	2,152.3	5,954.4	5,130.8	5,591.1	3,264.5	14,582.0
Colorado	6,159.2	2,435.0	394.0	347.5	336.8	485.2	325.4	1,835.3
Connecticut	4,630.7	2,186.6	226.4	140.8	60.2	466.4	166.1	1,384.2
Delaware	757.4	425.7	33.3	.2	.3	60.2	31.5	206.2
Florida	19,590.4	7,520.4	839.8	153.6	1,795.7	1,836.8	998.9	6,445.2
Georgia	9,280.6	3,884.5	347.7	19.1	2,149.1	600.6	444.3	1,835.3
Hawaii	718.1	.1	54.2	5.0	5.2	156.0	67.3	430.3
Idaho	1,112.3	524.0	89.0	16.1	127.8	85.9	59.3	210.2
Illinois	17,236.4	7,479.4	1,073.8	311.5	812.6	1,729.1	832.2	4,997.8
Indiana	6,861.6	3,178.2	368.4	360.4	656.3	412.4	349.2	1,536.7
Iowa	3,990.0	1,850.8	427.0	102.4	363.4	240.9	167.4	838.1
Kansas	3,848.7	1,721.6	376.7	14.0	244.5	245.2	172.7	1,074.0
Kentucky	3,496.6	1,650.3	153.0	20.4	236.0	243.4	139.1	1,054.4
Louisiana	5,619.6	2,274.2	324.3	40.4	583.4	475.4	305.5	1,616.4
Maine	1,358.9	733.7	105.7	11.8	31.8	94.8	52.8	328.3
Maryland	6,844.7	3,038.7	405.0	19.9	128.1	638.9	250.6	2,363.5
Massachusetts	8,416.7	3,724.4	417.4	107.8	441.7	972.1	271.8	2,481.5
Michigan	15,302.5	7,242.1	1,010.6	257.0	1,415.0	1,173.0	755.2	3,449.6
Minnesota	8,944.4	3,423.3	731.7	910.4	558.5	441.2	403.7	2,475.6
Mississippi	3,109.9	1,391.8	240.5	14.2	606.9	168.2	132.2	556.1
Missouri	6,014.6	2,938.0	378.1	39.5	544.2	514.9	244.1	1,355.8
Montana	1,219.4	645.7	75.9	21.1	39.5	62.3	55.2	319.7
Nebraska	2,288.0	1,110.0	204.8	20.5	261.3	131.2	106.6	453.6

Continued

F7. Local Direct General Expenditures for Own Functions by State (continued)

Fiscal Year 1987
($Millions)

State	Total	Education	Highways	Public Welfare	Health and Hospitals	Police and Fire	Financial Administration[a]	Other[b]
Nevada	1,849.9	582.4	93.8	24.9	136.4	202.1	128.1	682.2
New Hampshire	1,252.5	638.0	107.1	55.8	7.7	111.3	47.3	285.3
New Jersey	13,654.1	6,113.2	582.8	834.3	405.6	1,112.3	573.9	4,032.0
New Mexico	2,133.6	1,034.4	109.6	12.3	69.0	168.6	83.9	655.8
New York	45,716.3	16,176.7	2,128.4	5,381.2	3,599.6	3,659.6	1,195.1	13,575.7
North Carolina	7,596.7	4,048.0	179.3	258.8	673.0	523.5	282.9	1,631.2
North Dakota	854.3	439.1	95.7	22.9	6.3	47.3	34.8	208.2
Ohio	15,466.4	6,940.4	832.6	1,042.4	1,130.8	1,305.5	680.9	3,533.8
Oklahoma	3,990.6	1,878.1	263.3	6.1	353.6	286.6	163.1	1,039.8
Oregon	4,402.6	2,226.1	240.3	19.3	219.7	375.0	203.4	1,118.8
Pennsylvania	16,166.9	7,827.4	614.3	670.0	562.0	949.7	763.1	4,780.4
Rhode Island	1,104.8	587.4	40.1	23.9	1.5	152.9	65.2	233.8
South Carolina	3,622.1	1,907.2	77.4	14.8	432.8	230.8	138.5	820.6
South Dakota	772.1	401.3	98.1	11.5	19.2	47.7	41.1	153.2
Tennessee	5,510.9	2,098.3	340.1	57.0	741.0	418.7	226.3	1,629.5
Texas	25,967.6	11,886.5	1,508.9	1,533.1	1,766.1	1,861.6	1,180.5	6,230.9
Utah	2,132.2	1,083.1	112.4	5.7	61.2	161.2	112.0	596.6
Vermont	609.8	389.2	61.7	.7	.7	31.5	23.5	102.5
Virginia	7,888.2	3,740.7	311.1	325.8	326.3	673.3	443.7	2,067.3
Washington	7,128.7	3,065.7	437.4	8.4	420.7	559.0	444.0	2,193.5
West Virginia	1,969.0	1,173.3	44.1	.3	120.8	87.2	84.1	459.2
Wisconsin	8,406.5	3,730.7	783.5	541.4	512.2	688.0	337.9	1,812.8
Wyoming	1,267.0	641.8	60.4	2.7	166.4	69.2	48.9	277.6
District of Columbia	3,211.3	566.9	116.4	558.1	301.9	319.3	173.9	1,174.8

[a] Includes general control.
[b] Includes sewerage and other sanitation, local parks and recreation, interest on general debt, and all other direct general expenditures.
Source: Department of Commerce, Bureau of the Census.

F8. Local Expenditures by Function and Unit of Government
Selected Fiscal Years 1942-1987
($Millions)

Function and Unit of Government	1942	1952	1962	1972	1982	1987
Total expenditures[a]	$ 7,351	$ 20,229	$ 45,279	$ 118,568	$ 313,365	$ 463,826
County	n.a.	4,095	8,879	24,410	67,107	102,977
City	n.a.	8,383	17,328	43,669	112,833	164,146
Township	n.a.	924	1,723	4,207	10,137	14,747
School district	n.a.	5,357	14,913	39,241	93,398	138,288
Special district	n.a.	1,665	3,154	8,602	34,821	50,865
Intergovernmental[a]	b	156	226	567	1,957	5,234
County	n.a.	216	586	1,173	3,070	5,054
City	n.a.	68	193	500	2,123	4,903
Township	n.a.	18	44	130	527	632
School district	n.a.	n.a.	89	255	413	378
Special district	n.a.	47	34	73	756	1,463
Direct	7,351	20,073	45,053	118,001	311,408	458,592
County	n.a.	3,877	8,294	23,237	64,037	97,922
City	n.a.	8,314	17,136	43,170	110,710	159,243
Township	n.a.	906	1,679	4,078	9,610	14,115
School district	n.a.	5,357	14,824	38,986	92,985	137,909
Special district	n.a.	1,619	3,120	8,529	34,066	49,403
General	6,421	17,444	39,831	106,499	264,355	391,095
County	1,438	3,802	8,105	22,757	61,505	94,303
City	2,926	6,235	13,282	35,400	83,132	119,711
Township	303	874	1,588	3,853	8,919	13,168
School district	1,642	5,342	14,778	38,893	92,836	137,678
Special district	112	1,190	2,078	5,595	17,963	26,235
Education	2,195	6,824	17,946	48,661	111,982	165,010
County	182	413	1,063	3,528	8,703	13,110
City	491	933	1,925	5,767	9,760	13,180
Township	55	230	526	1,329	2,450	3,500
School district	1,467	5,248	14,338	37,836	91,009	135,166
Special district	-	-	94	200	60	55
Highways	700	2,094	3,722	6,274	14,417	20,711
County	396	912	1,508	2,614	5,709	8,049
City	219	853	1,690	2,787	6,874	10,043
Township	81	248	394	707	1,591	2,157
School district	-	-	-	-	-	-
Special district	4	81	131	167	243	462

Continued

F8. Local Expenditures by Function and Unit of Government (continued)
Selected Fiscal Years 1942-1987
($Millions)

Function and Unit of Government	1942	1952	1962	1972	1982	1987
Public welfare	702	1,378	2,575	8,869	14,704	18,967
County	388	882	1,811	5,813	10,106	13,573
City	272	432	686	2,992	4,488	5,168
Township	42	64	79	64	110	226
School district	-	-	-	-	-	-
Special district	-	-	-	-	-	-
Health and hospitals	292	1,053	2,181	7,014	21,483	29,769
County	119	541	1,029	3,026	10,903	14,915
City	153	471	874	2,718	5,183	7,300
Township	6	5	15	44	127	173
School district	-	-	-	-	-	-
Special district	14	33	264	1,224	5,271	7,382
Other general[c]	2,532	6,095	13,407	35,681	101,769	156,638
County	353	1,054	2,694	7,776	26,084	44,656
City	1,791	3,546	8,107	21,136	56,827	84,020
Township	119	327	574	1,709	4,641	7,112
School district	175	94	440	1,057	1,827	2,512
Special district	94	1,076	1,589	4,004	12,389	18,336
Utility and liquor stores	818	2,344	4,571	9,903	42,274	59,998
County	n.a.	61	130	319	1,761	2,448
City	n.a.	1,845	3,329	6,472	23,887	33,710
Township	n.a.	30	86	208	628	839
School district	n.a.	-	-	-	-	-
Special district	n.a.	407	1,026	2,905	15,998	23,001
Insurance trust	112	285	651	1,599	4,779	7,499
County	n.a.	13	60	162	770	1,171
City	n.a.	234	524	1,299	3,691	5,822
Township	n.a.	2	6	16	63	109
School district	n.a.	15	46	93	150	231
Special district	n.a.	21	16	29	104	167

[a] To avoid duplication, intergovernmental transactions between units of government are eliminated in the total for all units; consequently, this figure is less than the sum of the components.
[b] Minor amount, not segregable from "direct expenditure."
[c] Includes natural resources, sanitation, recreation, police and fire, housing and community development, general control, interest on general debt, and other unallocable expenditures.
Source: Department of Commerce, Bureau of the Census.

F9. Per Capita Direct General Expenditures of Local Governments in Selected Metropolitan Areas by Major Function

Fiscal Year 1983

Area	Total	Education	Highways	Public Welfare	Health and Hospitals	Police Protection	Fire Protection	Interest on General Debt	All Other
Total, 75 major SMSAs	$ 1,374	$ 538	$ 63	$ 87	$ 105	$ 85	$ 42	$ 64	$ 390
Anaheim-Santa Ana-Garden Grove, California	1,316	583	67	95	27	86	48	53	357
Atlanta, Georgia	1,236	489	37	5	229	63	35	57	322
Baltimore, Maryland	1,269	515	153	1	60	82	44	62	352
Boston-Lowell-Brockton-Lawrence-Haverhill, Massachusetts	1,127	493	49	8	79	74	66	34	325
Buffalo, New York	1,699	618	105	217	96	62	37	81	482
Chicago, Illinois	1,253	532	65	12	49	102	46	70	378
Cincinnati, Ohio-Kentucky-Indiana	1,029	437	44	42	67	65	36	43	295
Cleveland, Ohio	1,416	527	59	98	159	95	53	59	365
Columbus, Ohio	1,130	459	46	78	61	72	43	75	295
Dallas-Ft. Worth, Texas	1,255	549	66	3	91	69	40	95	343
Denver-Boulder, Colorado	1,397	619	72	84	63	87	39	73	361
Detroit, Michigan	1,438	601	72	12	122	100	40	59	431
Ft. Lauderdale-Hollywood, Florida	1,335	431	76	2	255	123	39	37	372
Hartford-New Britain-Bristol, Connecticut	1,077	534	57	33	9	63	39	35	308
Houston, Texas	1,527	708	86	4	100	80	47	113	388
Indianapolis, Indiana	1,048	442	43	53	149	50	30	34	246
Kansas City, Missouri-Kansas	1,164	473	84	4	78	80	36	78	333
Los Angeles-Long Beach, California	1,587	558	47	196	142	109	49	37	448
Miami, Florida	1,504	532	40	14	145	119	51	77	525
Milwaukee, Wisconsin	1,604	610	88	83	153	105	43	57	466
Minneapolis-St. Paul, Minnesota-Wisconsin	1,560	510	115	154	118	68	37	110	449
Nassau-Suffolk, New York	1,885	926	84	93	80	158	29	105	410
Newark, New Jersey	1,470	611	54	134	45	88	46	47	447
New Orleans, Louisiana	1,157	389	60	8	126	79	37	75	382
New York, New York-New Jersey	2,114	559	77	361	214	122	60	92	629
Philadelphia, Pennsylvania-New Jersey	1,224	477	44	57	71	82	24	73	395
Phoenix, Arizona	1,389	582	96	22	69	94	39	77	409
Pittsburgh, Pennsylvania	1,188	484	58	38	66	51	18	108	365
Portland, Oregon-Washington	1,363	637	67	9	28	71	65	61	424
Riverside-San Bernardino-Ontario, California	1,556	592	56	203	167	84	35	46	372
Rochester, New York	1,594	730	98	146	54	62	29	75	400
Sacramento, California	1,537	561	43	249	54	77	60	30	464
St. Louis, Missouri-Illinois	949	467	59	7	62	73	24	27	231
San Antonio, Texas	1,091	543	36	3	84	49	26	57	293
San Diego, California	1,391	553	47	146	161	70	33	31	350
San Francisco-Oakland, California	1,719	490	63	155	250	97	58	63	544
San Jose, California	1,577	657	72	139	170	79	51	33	378
Seattle-Everett, Washington	1,293	490	87	1	89	72	41	66	448
Tampa-St. Petersburg, Florida	1,126	444	50	15	82	82	31	48	374
Washington, D.C.-Maryland-Virginia	1,790	653	51	139	129	105	52	106	554

Source: Department of Commerce, Bureau of the Census.

F10. City Expenditures by Character and Function
Selected Fiscal Years 1952-1987
($Millions)

Character or Function	1952	1960	1970	1980	1986	1987
Total expenditures	$ 8,383	$ 15,251	$ 34,173	$ 93,699	$ 152,181	$ 164,146
Expenditure by character and object						
Direct expenditures	8,315	15,093	33,792	91,692	147,961	159,243
Current operation	5,519	9,874	22,895	66,687	106,330	113,396
Capital outlay	1,850	3,691	7,103	16,285	23,878	25,862
Construction	1,511	2,884	5,649	13,341	17,693	19,188
Land and existing structures	156	436	733	2,944	6,185	6,674
Equipment	183	372	722	-	-	-
Interest on debt[a]	341	684	1,547	4,182	10,485	12,056
Assistance payments	370	386	1,245	1,546	2,093	2,108
Insurance benefits and repayments	234	458	1,002	2,992	5,175	5,822
Intergovernmental expenditure	68	158	381	2,007	4,220	4,903
Expenditure by function						
General	6,303	11,818	27,682	72,433	114,864	124,614
Police	685	1,275	2,994	8,200	13,637	14,835
Fire	504	885	1,762	4,535	7,303	7,893
Public welfare	438	608	2,215	3,801	6,254	6,395
Education	954	1,801	4,548	9,284	12,361	13,417
Libraries	100	185	407	883	1,446	1,607
Highways	860	1,573	2,499	5,976	9,336	10,086
Health and hospitals	481	799	1,944	4,457	7,055	7,383
Sanitation	728	1,332	2,553	7,907	12,359	13,515
Parks and recreation	277	551	1,306	3,433	5,430	5,975
General control[b]	367	598	1,233	3,858	6,816	7,343
Interest on general debt	202	431	1,098	3,054	8,097	9,300
All other	707	1,781	5,123	17,044	24,770	26,865
Utility[c]	1,845	2,915	5,382	18,052	31,899	33,464
Water supply	855	1,424	2,337	5,933	10,641	11,815
Electric power and gas	543	1,002	2,071	9,930	17,560	17,714
Transit	407	489	974	2,189	3,698	3,935
Liquor stores	40	60	107	222	243	246
Insurance trust	234	458	1,002	2,993	5,175	5,822
Employee retirement	233	453	992	2,928	5,109	5,748
Unemployment compensation[d]	2	5	10	65	66	74

[a] Includes interest on general debt and on utility debt. See "Expenditure by function."
[b] Includes financial administration beginning 1960.
[c] Includes interest on utility debt (in millions): 1952, $114; 1960, $253; 1970, $449; 1980, $1,128; 1986, $2,388; 1987, $2,756.
[d] Washington, D.C.
Source: Department of Commerce, Bureau of the Census.

F11. Per Capita General Expenditures in the 49 Largest Cities By Function and City

Fiscal Year 1987

City	Total	Police and Fire	Health and Hospitals	Highways	Education	Public Welfare	Financial Administration[a]	Other[b]
Total	$ 1,460	$ 222	$ 111	$ 71	$ 283	$ 233	$ 64	$ 670
Albuqerque	946	160	12	78	-	-	50	646
Atlanta	1,171	169	c	53	44	9	54	842
Austin	1,181	172	198	133	2	2	53	621
Baltimore	1,715	267	55	164	525	1	78	625
Baton Rouge	707	118	56	47	-	2	85	399
Boston	2,002	301	230	73	593	4	63	736
Buffalo	1,648	182	3	73	778	-	42	570
Charlotte	859	140	4	97	-	1	45	571
Chicago	888	240	22	92	11	29	28	467
Cincinnati	1,041	242	70	75	-	-	40	614
Cleveland	879	284	26	63	-	1	61	444
Columbus	712	208	29	49	-	-	48	378
Dallas	774	186	10	75	-	-	35	467
Denver	1,711	265	207	64	-	171	95	909
Detroit	1,228	285	68	95	6	-	85	690
El Paso	368	93	20	22	-	1	25	208
Fort Worth	733	160	16	107	-	-	39	411
Honolulu	642	134	6	45	-	-	53	402
Houston	813	195	17	55	-	-	29	517
Indianapolis	879	124	160	56	1	73	57	409
Jacksonville	791	148	45	53	c	12	87	447
Kansas City, KS	1,037	210	5	157	-	-	41	624
Long Beach	1,136	290	21	72	2	-	78	674
Los Angeles	755	228	2	39	2	-	52	433
Memphis	1,020	159	20	24	481	-	29	307
Miami	718	257	56	41	c	5	61	298
Milwaukee	784	225	20	79	-	-	48	412
Minneapolis	1,359	183	21	107	-	-	50	998
Nashville-Davidson	1,426	140	119	64	488	15	61	538
Newark	930	242	19	8	-	112	61	487
New Orleans	953	149	12	77	-	27	95	593
New York City	3,343	282.8	347	78	707	642	75	1,212
Oakland	1,125	224	2	47	5	-	51	797
Oklahoma City	606	121	118	43	-	-	24	301
Omaha	521	137	1	80	1	-	21	280
Philadelphia	1,260	229	110	38	9	84	116	673
Phoenix	852	185	1	149	6	1	50	460
Pittsburgh	786	197	18	49	-	c	44	478
Portland	1,420	158	83	109	526	33	37	474
St. Louis	1,112	235	110	86	6	7	73	596
San Antonio	750	112	32	73	5	3	33	492
San Diego	660	151	1	33	-	c	33	442
San Francisco	2,039	263	419	20	56	254	154	874
San Jose	793	162	-	89	-	-	36	506
Seattle	1,044	221	14	26	-	-	184	598
Toledo	547	205	12	54	-	-	43	234
Tucson	882	177	-	120	-	6	73	507
Tulsa	1,023	166	12	87	c	-	24	735
Washington, D.C.	5,331	510	482	186	906	891	278	2,079

[a] Includes general control.
[b] Includes sewerage and sanitation, housing and urban renewal, parks and recreation, libraries, interest on general debt, general public buildings, and miscellaneous expenditures.
[c] Less than one-half of unit shown.
Source: Department of Commerce, Bureau of the Census.

F12. Total Local Revenue by Source
Selected Fiscal Years 1902-1987
($Millions)

Year	Total[a]	Total Own Sources	From Own Sources — General Revenue — Total General	General Revenue — Total	Taxes — Property	Taxes — Sales and Gross Receipts	Taxes — Income[b]	License and Other	Charges and Miscellaneous	Utility	Liquor Stores	Insurance Trust[c]	Intergovernmental — From States	Intergovernmental — From Federal[d]
1902	$ 914	$ 858	$ 798	$ 704	$ 624	-	-	$ 80	$ 94	$ 60	-	-	$ 52	$ 4
1913	1,755	1,658	1,540	1,308	1,192	$ 3	-	113	232	116	-	$ 2	91	6
1922	4,148	3,827	3,545	3,069	2,973	20	-	76	476	266	-	16	312	9
1932	6,192	5,381	4,879	4,274	4,159	26	-	89	605	463	-	39	801	10
1940	7,724	5,792	5,007	4,497	4,170	130	$ 18	179	510	704	$ 13	68	1,654	278
1950	16,101	11,673	9,586	7,984	7,042	484	64	394	1,602	1,808	94	185	4,217	211
1960	37,324	27,209	22,912	18,081	15,798	1,339	254	692	4,831	3,613	136	549	9,522	592
1965	53,408	38,242	32,362	25,116	21,817	2,059	433	807	7,245	4,908	177	795	14,010	1,155
1969	79,274	53,192	45,861	34,781	29,692	2,470	1,381	1,239	11,080	5,931	245	1,155	23,837	2,245
1970	89,082	59,557	51,392	38,833	32,963	3,068	1,630	1,173	12,558	6,608	258	1,299	26,920	2,605
1971	100,993	66,521	57,491	43,434	36,726	3,662	1,747	1,298	14,058	7,276	269	1,484	31,081	3,391
1972	114,791	75,097	65,549	49,739	41,620	4,268	2,230	1,621	15,810	7,701	223	1,622	35,143	4,551
1973	129,119	81,253	70,526	53,032	43,970	4,924	2,406	1,731	17,493	8,622	291	1,814	39,963	7,903
1974	143,132	88,391	76,693	56,466	46,404	5,542	2,413	2,108	20,227	9,392	306	2,000	44,553	10,188
1975	159,726	97,772	84,353	61,310	50,040	6,468	2,635	2,166	23,043	10,867	338	2,214	51,068	10,886
1976	178,338	108,592	93,186	67,557	54,884	7,156	3,127	2,390	25,628	12,573	357	2,477	56,169	13,576
1977	196,458	119,626	102,214	74,852	60,267	8,278	3,754	2,552	27,362	14,299	306	2,808	60,277	16,554
1978	214,518	130,464	110,730	80,381	64,058	9,326	4,071	2,926	30,349	16,290	371	3,073	64,661	19,393
1979	234,630	139,853	117,209	80,606	62,454	10,579	4,309	3,264	36,603	18,594	394	3,657	74,162	20,616
1980	258,298	155,873	130,027	86,387	65,607	12,072	4,990	3,718	43,640	21,055	435	4,355	81,289	21,136
1981	287,834	176,391	145,736	94,776	72,020	13,220	5,531	4,005	50,960	24,794	474	5,388	89,017	22,427
1982	315,322	198,703	164,426	103,783	78,952	14,824	6,097	3,910	60,643	28,612	489	5,176	95,363	21,256
1983	337,921	218,522	178,994	112,996	85,824	16,352	6,445	4,375	65,998	31,643	492	7,393	98,378	21,021
1984	366,156	239,425	196,504	123,399	92,595	18,296	7,215	5,293	73,105	34,736	481	7,704	105,820	20,912
1985	402,544	264,461	216,013	134,473	99,772	20,956	7,974	5,770	81,630	38,630	482	9,246	116,359	21,724
1986	434,751	287,497	233,406	144,406	107,356	22,628	8,536	5,886	88,409	56,900	449	12,639	126,824	20,433
1987	469,317	313,032	254,062	158,216	116,618	24,455	9,663	7,480	95,846	59,537	461	14,936	136,752	19,533

[a] Duplicative transactions between levels of government are excluded in arriving at aggregates.

[b] Principally individual income.

[c] Includes collections for unemployment compensation and employee retirement funds.

[d] Amounts received directly from Federal government, not transfers of Federal funds received initially by states.

Source: Department of Commerce, Bureau of the Census.

F13. Local Revenue, Expenditures, and Surpluses or Deficits: Total and General Accounts

Selected Fiscal Years 1942-1987

($Millions)

Year	Total			General[a]		
	Revenue	Expenditures	Surplus or Deficit (-)	Revenue	Expenditures	Surplus or Deficit (-)
1942	$ 8,114	$ 7,351	$ 763	$ 7,122	$ 6,421	$ 701
1944	8,535	7,180	1,355	7,340	6,197	1,143
1946	9,561	9,093	468	8,227	7,875	352
1948	13,167	13,363	-196	11,373	11,498	-125
1950	16,101	17,041	-940	14,014	14,754	-740
1952	19,398	20,229	-831	16,952	17,600	-648
1954	22,402	23,814	-1,412	19,562	20,808	-1,246
1956	26,352	28,273	-1,921	23,137	24,661	-1,524
1958	31,348	34,023	-2,675	27,723	29,705	-1,982
1960	37,324	39,056	-1,732	33,027	34,301	-1,274
1961	40,483	42,641	-2,158	35,899	37,393	-1,494
1962	43,147	45,279	-2,132	38,346	40,057	-1,711
1963	45,586	47,237	-1,651	40,558	41,721	-1,163
1964	49,578	51,199	-1,621	44,084	45,262	-1,178
1965	53,408	55,482	-2,074	47,528	48,667	-1,139
1966	59,268	60,994	-1,726	53,172	53,963	-791
1967	64,608	66,648	-2,040	58,235	59,475	-1,240
1968	70,171	72,357	-2,186	63,181	64,393	-1,212
1969	79,274	82,698	-3,424	71,943	74,029	-2,086
1970	89,082	92,522	-3,440	80,916	83,215	-2,299
1971	100,993	105,167	-4,174	91,964	94,797	-2,833
1972	114,791	118,568	-3,777	105,243	107,066	-1,823
1973	129,119	128,254	865	118,392	114,895	3,497
1974	143,132	140,387	2,745	131,434	125,557	5,877
1975	159,726	162,614	-2,888	146,307	144,699	1,608
1976	178,338	181,802	-3,464	162,931	161,542	1,389
1977	196,458	196,307	151	179,045	172,842	6,203
1978	214,518	211,081	3,437	194,783	185,308	9,475
1979	234,630	233,323	1,307	211,986	203,109	8,877
1980	258,298	260,777	-2,479	232,453	225,379	7,074
1981	287,834	288,571	-737	257,179	246,846	10,333
1982	315,322	313,365	1,957	281,045	266,312	14,733
1983	337,921	335,098	2,823	298,394	283,929	14,465
1984	366,156	359,378	6,778	323,236	305,570	17,666
1985	402,455	390,910	11,545	354,098	328,586	25,512
1986	434,751	427,980	6,771	380,663	359,902	20,761
1987	469,317	463,826	5,491	410,347	391,095	19,252

[a] Excludes utilities, liquor stores, and insurance trust transactions.

Source: Department of Commerce, Bureau of the Census; and Tax Foundation computations.

F14. Percentage Distribution of Local General Revenue by Source

Selected Fiscal Years 1902-1987

Year	Amount ($Millions)	From Own Sources				Intergovernmental	
		Total	Taxes		Charges and Miscellaneous	From State	From Federal
			Property	Other			
			Percent of Total				
1902	$ 854	93.4%	82.4%	73.1%	9.3%	11.0%	6.1%	.5%
1913	1,637	94.1	79.9	72.8	7.1	14.2	5.6	.4
1922	3,866	91.7	79.4	76.9	2.5	12.3	8.1	.2
1932	5,690	85.7	75.1	73.1	2.0	10.6	14.1	.2
1940	6,939	72.2	64.8	60.1	4.7	7.3	23.8	4.0
1950	14,014	68.4	57.0	50.2	6.8	11.4	30.1	1.5
1960	33,027	69.4	54.7	47.8	6.9	14.6	28.8	1.8
1965	47,528	68.1	52.8	45.9	6.9	15.2	29.5	2.4
1970	80,916	63.5	48.0	40.7	7.3	15.5	33.3	3.2
1971	91,964	62.5	47.2	39.9	7.3	15.3	33.8	3.7
1972	105,243	62.3	47.3	39.5	7.8	15.0	33.4	4.3
1973	118,392	59.6	44.8	37.1	7.7	14.8	33.8	6.7
1974	131,434	58.4	43.0	35.3	7.7	15.4	33.9	7.8
1975	146,307	57.7	41.9	34.2	7.7	15.7	34.9	7.4
1976	162,931	57.2	41.5	33.7	7.8	15.7	34.5	8.3
1977	179,045	57.1	41.8	33.7	8.1	15.3	33.7	9.2
1978	194,783	56.8	41.3	32.9	8.4	15.6	33.2	10.0
1979	211,986	55.3	38.0	29.5	8.5	17.3	35.0	9.7
1980	232,453	55.9	37.2	28.2	9.0	18.8	35.0	9.1
1981	257,179	56.7	36.9	28.0	8.9	19.8	34.6	8.7
1982	281,045	58.5	36.9	28.1	8.8	21.6	33.9	7.6
1983	298,394	60.0	37.9	28.8	9.1	22.1	33.0	7.0
1984	323,236	60.8	38.2	28.6	9.5	22.6	32.7	6.5
1985	354,098	61.1	38.0	28.2	9.8	23.1	32.8	6.1
1986	380,663	61.3	38.1	28.2	9.9	23.2	33.3	5.4
1987	410,347	61.9	38.5	28.4	10.1	23.4	33.3	4.8

Source: Department of Commerce, Bureau of the Census; percentage computations by Tax Foundation.

F15. Local General Revenue by Source and State

Fiscal Year 1987
($Millions)

State	Total	From Own Sources					Intergovernmental	
		Total	Taxes			Charges and Miscellaneous	From State	From Federal
			Total	Property	Other			
Total	$ 410,347.3	$ 254,062.4	$ 158,216.0	$ 116,617.6	$ 41,598.4	$ 95,846.4	$ 136,752.4	$ 19,532.6
Alabama	4,485.4	2,732.6	1,218.7	436.5	782.2	1,513.9	1,491.8	261.0
Alaska	2,026.4	1,185.9	597.5	520.9	76.6	588.4	765.7	74.8
Arizona	5,936.9	3,549.4	1,930.0	1,469.5	460.5	1,619.4	2,124.4	263.1
Arkansas	2,233.2	1,239.7	586.2	464.0	122.2	653.5	885.4	108.1
California	59,624.1	31,429.9	17,481.7	12,034.2	5,447.5	13,948.2	26,227.1	1,967.1
Colorado	6,185.8	4,464.6	2,718.8	1,877.7	841.1	1,745.8	1,512.0	209.3
Connecticut	4,597.2	3,290.6	2,756.6	2,704.5	52.1	534.0	1,142.3	164.2
Delaware	743.4	381.1	186.3	155.2	31.1	194.8	322.9	39.5
Florida	19,969.6	13,376.6	6,566.0	5,222.7	1,343.3	6,810.6	5,723.9	869.1
Georgia	10,237.2	6,641.4	3,211.1	2,143.3	1,067.8	3,430.3	3,127.2	468.6
Hawaii	706.5	537.6	419.8	346.2	73.6	117.8	66.0	102.9
Idaho	1,131.4	650.9	346.4	333.7	12.7	304.5	433.8	46.7
Illinois	17,893.4	11,960.0	8,683.2	6,375.4	2,307.8	3,276.8	4,813.9	1,119.9
Indiana	7,307.7	4,132.5	2,439.4	2,264.3	175.1	1,693.1	2,840.4	334.8
Iowa	4,449.9	2,769.9	1,674.2	1,638.8	35.4	1,095.7	1,497.4	182.7
Kansas	4,242.8	3,257.3	1,647.4	1,363.9	283.5	1,609.9	890.5	95.0
Kentucky	3,610.1	1,949.0	990.7	511.5	479.2	958.3	1,484.7	176.4
Louisiana	5,747.4	3,749.2	2,024.7	877.2	1,147.5	1,724.5	1,714.1	284.1
Maine	1,311.3	816.1	627.6	621.6	6.0	188.5	420.4	74.8
Maryland	7,278.7	4,810.5	3,428.7	1,974.2	1,454.5	1,381.8	1,979.7	488.5
Massachusetts	9,629.7	5,161.1	3,863.2	3,745.1	118.1	1,297.9	3,676.5	792.0
Michigan	15,525.2	9,874.3	6,478.4	5,951.4	527.0	3,395.9	4,949.1	701.8
Minnesota	9,555.2	5,502.1	2,539.9	2,424.6	115.3	2,962.2	3,682.5	370.6
Mississippi	3,326.9	1,876.3	655.4	615.4	40.0	1,220.9	1,286.4	164.2
Missouri	5,778.8	3,898.3	2,419.3	1,375.3	1,044.0	1,479.0	1,586.9	293.6
Montana	1,184.6	814.9	514.4	491.6	22.8	300.5	291.3	78.5

Continued

F15. Local General Revenue by Source and State (continued)

Fiscal Year 1987

($Millions)

State	Total	From Own Sources				Intergovernmental	
		Total	Taxes		Charges and Miscellaneous	From State	From Federal
			Property	Other			
Nebraska	2,420.1	1,838.4	1,010.6	114.0	713.8	466.2	115.5
Nevada	1,836.5	1,060.1	324.0	177.6	558.5	679.0	97.4
New Hampshire	1,271.2	1,055.5	899.4	6.2	149.9	154.2	61.5
New Jersey	13,657.6	8,571.8	6,456.5	157.5	1,957.8	4,539.0	546.7
New Mexico	2,228.2	1,006.3	225.8	161.5	619.0	1,090.7	131.2
New York	51,649.7	33,211.7	14,249.3	10,495.9	8,466.5	16,724.6	1,713.4
North Carolina	8,176.3	4,355.2	1,788.3	716.5	1,850.4	3,468.2	352.9
North Dakota	905.3	515.8	269.5	14.2	232.1	332.2	57.3
Ohio	15,980.8	9,791.5	4,444.4	2,116.2	3,230.9	5,383.2	806.1
Oklahoma	3,925.7	2,481.0	802.2	515.2	1,163.6	1,275.0	169.7
Oregon	4,554.7	3,147.5	1,948.3	208.2	991.0	1,098.4	308.7
Pennsylvania	17,557.4	11,118.2	4,785.5	2,382.9	3,949.8	5,435.9	1,003.3
Rhode Island	1,102.3	738.9	636.5	9.5	92.9	302.1	61.2
South Carolina	3,613.5	2,196.4	976.5	87.6	1,132.3	1,262.1	155.0
South Dakota	823.9	581.6	351.1	78.9	151.6	179.9	62.4
Tennessee	5,622.6	3,752.3	1,206.5	802.0	1,743.8	1,591.1	279.2
Texas	26,491.8	18,902.1	9,215.2	1,869.6	7,817.3	6,497.5	1,092.1
Utah	2,344.2	1,467.0	660.3	185.4	621.3	761.7	115.5
Vermont	609.4	420.6	352.1	3.6	64.9	160.1	28.7
Virginia	7,982.5	5,049.8	2,512.6	1,101.6	1,435.6	2,617.7	315.0
Washington	7,514.2	4,005.2	1,302.7	759.7	1,942.8	2,980.5	528.6
West Virginia	1,985.8	1,027.6	407.3	97.2	523.1	885.2	73.0
Wisconsin	8,275.0	4,519.9	2,864.8	53.4	1,601.7	3,461.0	294.1
Wyoming	1,405.2	895.3	443.5	48.6	403.2	470.4	39.5
District of Columbia	3,694.6	2,301.3	546.2	1,368.5	386.6	-	1,393.3

Source: Department of Commerce, Bureau of the Census.

F16. Total Local Revenue by Source and Unit of Government
Selected Fiscal Years 1942-1987
($Millions)

Source and Unit of Government	1942	1952	1962	1972	1982	1987
Total revenue[a]	$ 8,114	$ 19,398	$ 43,147	$ 114,791	$ 315,322	$ 469,317
County	n.a.	4,013	8,694	24,174	68,621	105,803
City	n.a.	8,278	16,794	42,114	115,493	169,814
Township	n.a.	862	1,716	4,149	10,226	15,084
School district	n.a.	5,097	14,199	39,364	96,326	139,291
Special district	n.a.	1,054	2,565	6,861	30,961	49,194
Intergovernmental[a]	1,836	5,281	11,642	39,694	116,619	156,285
County	655	1,541	3,276	9,956	28,002	37,240
City	491	1,212	2,674	11,528	31,621	37,740
Township	73	290	368	878	2,898	3,980
School district	616	2,158	5,769	17,653	52,131	76,584
Special district	2	80	376	1,550	8,271	10,610
Revenue from own sources	6,278	14,117	31,506	75,097	198,702	313,502
County	n.a.	2,472	5,418	14,218	40,619	68,563
City	n.a.	7,067	14,121	30,586	83,871	132,074
Township	n.a.	622	1,348	3,271	7,328	11,105
School district	n.a.	2,938	8,431	21,711	44,195	62,707
Special district	n.a.	1,017	2,189	5,311	22,690	38,584
General revenue, from own sources	5,286	11,671	26,705	65,549	164,426	254,062
County	1,070	2,385	5,209	13,695	38,653	63,989
City	2,620	5,139	10,453	23,471	59,643	92,476
Township	267	594	1,267	3,105	6,718	10,202
School district	1,138	2,920	8,370	21,603	43,879	61,979
Special district	192	632	1,405	3,679	15,533	25,417
Taxes	4,625	9,466	20,993	49,739	103,783	158,216
County	920	1,918	4,149	10,076	22,970	37,240
City	2,314	4,183	7,934	17,009	37,077	55,366
Township	250	540	1,145	2,765	5,350	8,114
School district	1,052	2,655	7,320	18,939	35,539	51,809
Special district	90	170	445	952	2,846	5,687

Continued

F16. Total Local Revenue by Source and Unit of Government (continued)
Selected Fiscal Years 1942-1987
($Millions)

Source and Unit of Government	1942	1952	1962	1972	1982	1987
Property taxes	4,273	8,282	18,414	41,620	78,952	116,618
County	893	1,835	3,879	8,625	17,744	27,362
City	1,999	3,144	5,807	10,937	19,519	27,163
Township	241	515	1,068	2,584	5,014	7,489
School district	1,051	2,618	7,216	18,572	34,408	50,488
Special district	90	170	445	903	2,266	4,116
Other taxes	352	1,184	2,579	8,119	24,831	41,598
County	27	83	270	1,451	5,226	9,878
City	315	1,039	2,127	6,072	17,558	28,203
Township	9	25	77	181	336	625
School district	1	37	104	367	1,131	1,321
Special district	-	-	-	49	580	1,571
Charges and miscellaneous	661	2,205	5,711	15,810	60,643	95,846
County	150	468	1,060	3,619	15,682	26,748
City	306	956	2,519	6,461	22,566	37,110
Township	17	54	122	339	1,367	2,088
School district	86	265	1,051	2,664	8,340	10,170
Special district	102	462	960	2,727	12,687	19,730
Utility and liquor stores	904	2,184	4,174	7,924	29,100	43,034
County	n.a.	65	117	240	874	1,413
City	n.a.	1,718	3,213	5,940	20,740	29,103
Township	n.a.	26	74	150	546	766
School district	n.a.	-	-	-	-	-
Special district	n.a.	375	770	1,592	6,940	12,752
Insurance trust	88	262	627	1,622	5,176	14,936
County	n.a.	22	92	283	1,092	3,162
City	n.a.	209	454	1,175	3,488	10,494
Township	n.a.	2	6	16	64	137
School district	n.a.	18	60	108	316	728
Special district	n.a.	10	14	40	217	416

[a] To avoid duplication, intergovernmental transactions between units of government are eliminated in the total for all units.
Source: Department of Commerce, Bureau of the Census.

F17. Per Capita General Revenue of Local Governments in Selected Standard Metropolitan Areas By Source

Fiscal Year 1982-1983

Area	Total	From Own Sources					Intergovernmental Revenue		
		Total	Taxes			Charges and Miscellaneous	Total	From State	From Federal
			Total	Property	Other				
Total, 75 major SMSAs	$1,493	$913	$609	$440	$169	$304	$580	$464	$116
Anaheim-Santa Ana-Garden Grove, California	1,362	795	516	395	121	279	567	526	42
Atlanta, Georgia	1,447	1,009	536	411	124	473	438	313	125
Baltimore, Maryland	1,327	729	520	303	217	208	598	485	113
Boston-Lowell-Brockton-Lawrence-Haverhill, Massachusetts	1,390	782	611	602	9	171	609	420	189
Buffalo, New York	1,680	894	656	468	189	238	785	668	118
Chicago, Illinois	1,428	953	729	531	197	225	475	310	165
Cincinnati, Ohio-Kentucky-Indiana	1,123	674	457	317	140	217	449	352	97
Cleveland, Ohio	1,563	972	645	405	239	327	592	468	124
Columbus, Ohio	1,188	695	438	302	129	263	493	411	82
Dallas-Fort Worth, Texas	1,252	894	524	419	105	370	358	297	61
Denver-Boulder, Colorado	1,543	1,093	717	443	274	376	450	379	72
Detroit, Michigan	1,483	980	672	604	68	308	503	350	153
Ft. Lauderdale-Hollywood, Florida	1,397	1,062	547	442	105	515	335	281	54
Hartford-New Britain-Bristol, Connecticut	1,068	724	602	595	7	122	344	270	75
Houston, Texas	1,500	1,088	728	616	112	360	412	343	69
Indianapolis, Indiana	1,089	636	364	343	21	272	452	388	64
Kansas City, Missouri-Kansas	1,210	835	528	310	218	308	375	252	123
Los Angeles-Long Beach, California	1,686	799	483	314	169	316	888	797	91
Miami, Florida	1,629	1,021	556	438	118	464	608	374	235
Milwaukee, Wisconsin	1,653	904	574	566	8	330	749	665	84
Minneapolis-St. Paul, Minnesota-Wisconsin	1,667	993	517	491	28	474	674	571	103
Nassau-Suffolk, New York	1,915	1,334	1,124	944	180	210	581	520	61
Newark, New Jersey	1,510	843	683	668	15	160	668	564	103
New Orleans, Louisiana	1,278	846	488	164	324	358	432	302	130
New York, New York-New Jersey	2,576	1,600	1,171	625	547	429	976	821	155
Philadelphia, Pennsylvania-New Jersey	1,350	823	595	392	203	227	527	392	136
Phoenix, Arizona	1,575	940	389	276	113	551	636	540	96
Pittsburgh, Pennsylvania	1,263	780	536	397	139	245	483	341	142
Portland, Oregon-Washington	1,431	932	624	537	87	307	499	369	130
Riverside-San Bernardino-Ontario, California	1,634	766	422	316	106	344	868	794	74
Rochester, New York	1,611	965	721	525	196	244	646	547	99
Sacramento, California	1,620	745	399	298	102	346	874	797	77
St. Louis, Missouri-Illinois	1,008	653	474	300	175	178	355	273	82
San Antonio, Texas	1,054	561	316	238	78	245	493	373	120
San Diego, California	1,534	838	425	320	105	413	696	616	80
San Francisco-Oakland, California	1,934	1,103	576	389	187	528	830	693	138
San Jose, California	1,744	988	578	392	187	410	756	669	87
Seattle-Everett, Washington	1,451	844	443	266	177	401	607	516	91
Tampa-St. Petersburg, Florida	1,167	737	370	294	76	367	429	342	87
Washington, D.C.-Maryland-Virginia	1,998	1,350	1,039	541	498	311	648	226	422

Source: Department of Commerce, Bureau of the Census.

F18. Local General Sales Taxes and Rates by State and Level of Government[a]

As of March 1, 1989

State	Municipalities		Counties	
	Number	Rate (Percent)	Number	Rate (Percent)
Alabama[b]	338	.5 – 4.0	56	.25-3.0
Alaska	95	1.0 – 6.0	-	-
Arizona	81	1.0 – 4.0	-	-
Arkansas	117	1.0 – 2.0	44	1.0
California[c]	380	1.0	58	1.25
Colorado[c]	200	.5 – 4.0	34	.25 – 4.0
Georgia	-	-	235[d]	1.0-2.0
Illinois[c]	1,276	.5 – 1.5	102	.5 – 1.25
Iowa	75	1.0	9	1.0
Kansas	116	.5 – 1.0	62	.5 – 1.0
Louisiana	201	.3 – 3.0	62[e]	1.0 – 5.0
Minnesota	3	.5 – 1.0	-	-
Missouri	510	.5 – 1.5	125	.125 – 1.5
Nebraska	30	.5 – 1.5	-	-
Nevada[c]	-	-	7	3.75
New Mexico	101	1.25 – 1.5	33	.125 – .625
New York	25	1.0 – 4.25[f]	60	1.0 – 4.0
North Carolina	-	-	100	2.0
North Dakota	5	.5-1.0	-	-
Ohio	-	-	84[g]	.5 – 1.5
Oklahoma	467	1.0 – 4.0	25	.5 – 2.0
South Dakota	134	1.0 – 4.0	-	-
Tennessee	13	.25 – .75	95	1.0 – 2.75
Texas[h]	1,023	1.0 – 1.5	82	.5
Utah[i]	14	.25 – 1.0	29	.906 – 2.156
Virginia	All	1.0	All	1.0
Washington	256	.5-1.6 [j]	39	.5 – 1.0
Wisconsin	-	-	24	.5
Wyoming	-	-	16	1.0 – 2.0
District of Columbia	1	6.0	-	-

[a] Applies to retail sales of tangible personal property; may or may not apply to services and other categories. Number includes only those local taxes on which authoritative information is available. Local taxes are in addition to state rates shown in Table E29.

[b] In 4 Alabama counties, county sales taxes do not apply in certain municipalities. Rates shown are general rates; rates on sales of automobiles and machinery are different.

[c] City taxes may be credited against county taxes in California. Nine counties impose a tax of .5% to 1% for transportation purposes. In addition, Alameda County imposes a second additional .5% tax, and the cities of Los Angeles and San Francisco levy special gross receipts taxes. In Colorado, one transit district levies a sales tax of .6%; in Illinois, two transit districts impose the tax at rates from .25-1.0%, and the city of Chicago levies an additional 1% sales and use tax; and in Nevada the 3.75% county tax is state mandated, and counties levy an additional, optional, .25% sales tax.

[d] Eleven counties have a 2% tax effective for one year; the last 2% tax will be phased out 3/31/90. Jurisdictions in the Metropolitan Atlanta Rapid Transit Authority (City of Atlanta and five other counties) impose a 1% transit tax.

[e] In some parishes (counties) in Louisiana, tax is imposed by school boards and/or police juries.

[f] City pre-empts portion of county tax in some jurisdictions. Highest combined rate is 8.25% in New York City and three other municipalities.

[g] Three counties also levy a transit tax at rates ranging from .5% to 1.0%.

[h] Rapid transit taxes are also levied by six municipal transit authorities ranging from 25% to 1.0%.

[i] In Utah, rates include resort and transportation taxes levied in several localities. Two cities impose special gross receipts taxes.

[j] In Washington, if the county in which the city is located imposes a sales tax, the rate of the city tax may not exceed .425% and city taxes are credited against the county tax. Qualified localities may also levy an additional transit sales tax of up to .6%.

Source: Commerce Clearing House.

F19. Local Income Taxes and Rates by State[a]

As of January 1989

State and Locality	Rate (Percent)	State and Locality	Rate (Percent)
Alabama		**Ohio-continued**	
Birmingham	1.0	Cleveland Heights	2.0
Delaware		Columbus	2.0
Wilmington	1.25	Dayton	2.25
Indiana		Elyria	1.5
75 counties	.2 – 1.5	Euclid	2.0
Iowa	(% of state tax)	Hamilton	1.75
52 school districts	2.5 – 19.25[c]	Kettering	1.75
Kentucky		Lakewood	1.5
Covington	2.5	Lima	1.5
Lexington-Fayette	2.0	Lorain	1.5
Louisville	2.2[b]	Mansfield	1.25
Owensboro	1.0	Parma Heights	1.0
76 cities under 50,000	.25 – 2.5	Springfield	2.5
25 counties	.15 – 1.45	Toledo	2.25
Maryland	(% of state tax)	Warren	1.5
Baltimore	50.0	Youngstown	2.0
24 counties	20.0 – 50.0	Over 490 cities and	
Michigan		villages[e] under 50,000	.25 – 2.5
Detroit	3.0	**Pennsylvania[f]**	
Flint	1.0	Abington Township	1.0
Grand Rapids	1.0	Allentown	1.0
Highland Park	2.0	Altoona	1.0
Lansing	1.0	Bethlehem	1.0
Pontiac	1.0	Erie	1.0
Saginaw	1.0	Harrisburg	1.0
17 cities	1.0	Lancaster	.5
Missouri		Penn Hills Township	1.6
Kansas City	1.0	Philadelphia	4.96
St. Louis	1.0	Pittsburgh	4.0[g]
New York		Reading	1.0
New York City	1.5 – 3.5[d]	Scranton	2.2
	(% of state tax)	Wilkes-Barre	2.5
Yonkers	19.25	York	1.0
	2		
Ohio		Approx. 3,000 other	
Akron	2.0	local jurisdictions	.036 – 2.0
Canton	2.0	**District of Columbia**	6.0 – 9.5[d]
Cincinnati	2.0		
Cleveland	2.0		

[a] Rates shown separately for cities with 1980 population of 50,000 or more. Where rates differ for resident and nonresident income, only rates on residents are given. In Ohio and Pennsylvania cities, rates are the same; the nonresident rate is markedly lower in New York City and is half the resident rate in most Michigan cities. In addition to the areas shown, certain local jurisdictions in Arkansas and Georgia may impose an income tax with voter approval, although none have done so to date. Also, payroll taxes are imposed on employers in several localities in California, New Jersey, and Oregon.

[b] Includes rates levied for Jefferson County and for school boards.

[c] The school district surtax rates were reported for fiscal year 1988.

[d] In New York City rates for 1989, range between 2.2% and 3.4%; for 1990, 2.4% and 3.4% and after 1990 2.7% and 3.4% unless the Legislature continues higher rates. Resident income tax rates are graduated in New York City and Washington, D.C.

[e] School districts may also levy a tax at rates ranging from .25% to 1% if approved by voters.

[f] Except for Philadelphia, Pittsburgh, Scranton, Wilkes-Barre and several other jurisdictions, the total rate payable by any taxpayer is limited to 1%. If overlapping jurisdictions impose the tax, the rate in each is limited to one-half the maximum potential rate.

[g] Includes school district tax of 1.875.

Source: Commerce Clearing House.

F20. City Revenue by Source
Selected Fiscal Years 1952-1987
($Millions)

Source	1952	1960	1970	1975	1980	1985	1986	1987
Total revenue	$ 8,278	$ 14,915	$ 32,704	$ 59,744	$ 94,862	$ 147,648	$ 158,886	$ 169,814
General revenue	6,351	11,647	26,621	49,853	76,055	114,627	122,100	130,217
Taxes	4,183	7,109	13,647	21,135	31,256	47,647	50,859	55,366
Property	3,144	5,197	9,127	13,046	16,859	23,459	25,061	27,163
Sales and gross receipts	598	1,217	2,422	4,555	8,208	13,877	14,644	15,598
General	360	797	1,479	2,769	5,096	8,569	9,021	9,567
Selective	239	420	943	1,786	3,112	5,307	5,623	6,031
Other	440	695	2,098	3,534	6,189	10,312	11,154	12,606
Intergovernmental	1,212	2,321	7,906	19,648	28,270	35,838	37,131	37,740
From state governments	1,073	1,868	6,173	13,053	15,939	23,082	24,626	26,384
From other governments	139	453	1,733	6,595	12,331	12,756	12,505	11,357
Charges and miscellaneous	956	2,217	5,068	9,071	16,530	31,142	34,110	37,110
Utility	1,669	2,790	5,047	8,217	15,472	26,225	27,555	28,833
Water supply	758	1,253	2,201	3,266	4,989	8,504	9,203	9,883
Electric power	542	1,006	1,883	3,682	8,007	13,377	14,204	14,929
Gas supply	49	162	292	448	1,444	2,796	2,570	2,278
Transit	320	370	671	821	1,032	1,548	1,578	1,743
Liquor stores	50	71	121	192	247	260	267	270
Insurance trust	209	407	915	1,482	3,088	6,536	8,965	10,494
Employee retirement	203	400	904	1,460	3,028	6,492	8,871	10,408
Unemployment compensation[a]	5	7	11	22	60	44	94	86

[a] Washington, D.C.

Source: Department of Commerce, Bureau of the Census.

F21. Per Capita General Revenue in the 49 Largest Cities by Source And City

Fiscal Year 1987

| City | Total | Total Own Sources[a] | From Own Sources | | | | Intergov- ernmental |
| | | | Taxes | | | | |
			Total[b]	Property	General Sales	Income	
Total	$ 1,556	$ 1,060	$ 703	$ 288	$ 163	$ 452	$ 496
Albuquerque	1,083	734	224	103	77	-	349
Atlanta	1,283	1,035	392	217	-	-	248
Austin	1,294	1,197	337	191	94	-	98
Baltimore	2,043	1,018	702	469	-	136	1,025
Baton Rouge	826	710	390	152	184	-	117
Boston	2,264	1,195	835	754	-	-	1,069
Buffalo	1,640	554	340	300	-	-	1,087
Charlotte	796	600	316	286	-	-	196
Chicago	780	557	401	127	82	-	223
Cincinnati	1,375	803	451	83	-	335	573
Cleveland	810	590	418	79	-	4	220
Columbus	701	583	369	33	-	314	117
Dallas	814	691	419	228	107	-	124
Denver	1,580	1,255	600	177	315	-	325
Detroit	1,331	678	461	162	-	243	653
El Paso	445	381	162	90	45	-	65
Fort Worth	772	679	350	211	82	-	94
Honolulu	632	489	376	311	-	-	143
Houston	722	638	352	212	78	-	84
Indianapolis	898	557	324	269	-	24	341
Jacksonville	1,155	953	285	211	-	-	202
Kansas City, KS	1,406	1,250	288	199	69	-	156
Long Beach	1,121	911	310	130	62	-	210
Los Angeles	821	694	411	146	76	-	127
Memphis	1,053	393	224	165	-	-	659
Miami	706	546	395	295	-	-	160
Milwaukee	856	444	215	200	-	-	412
Minneapolis	1,802	1,370	391	331	-	-	432
Nashville-Davidson	1,568	1,224	743	386	252	-	344
Newark	980	401	248	163	-	-	580
New Orleans	1,002	799	410	158	151	-	204
New York City	3,624	2,264	1,761	692	291	544	1,360
Oakland	325	159	98	10	60	-	167
Oklahoma City	671	598	271	49	177	-	72
Omaha	593	451	331	153	136	-	143
Philadelphia	1,342	1,041	816	157	-	508	301
Phoenix	928	623	280	94	120	-	305
Pittsburgh	901	618	527	240	-	147	282
Portland	785	647	404	285	-	-	138
St. Louis	1,175	975	610	79	121	212	200
San Antonio	629	513	183	97	64	-	115
San Diego	779	610	255	94	89	-	169
San Francisco	2,566	1,764	917	479	98	-	802
San Jose	728	603	341	129	81	-	125
Seattle	1,007	846	507	174	92	-	161
Toledo	686	583	332	32	-	281	103
Tucson	896	584	305	53	210	-	312
Tulsa	1,035	974	375	49	286	-	61
Washington, D.C.	5,383	3,618	3,058	872	606	1,081	1,765

[a] Includes amounts for charges and miscellaneous general revenue not shown separately.
[b] Includes amount for miscellaneous tax revenue not shown separately.
Source: Department of Commerce, Bureau of the Census; and Tax Foundation computations.

F22. Local Debt by Character and Unit of Government
Selected Fiscal Years 1902-1987[a]
($Millions)

A. All Units

			Character		
				Long-term	
Year	Gross Debt	Short-term	Total	Full Faith and Credit	Nonguaranteed
1902	$ 1,877	$ 91	$ 1,786	n.a.	n.a.
1922	8,978	624	8,354	n.a.	n.a.
1932	16,373	1,096	15,277	n.a.	n.a.
1942	16,082	772	15,310	n.a.	n.a.
1944	14,703	617	14,086	n.a.	n.a.
1946	13,564	230	13,334	n.a.	n.a.
1948	14,980	623	14,357	n.a.	n.a.
1950	18,830	942	17,888	$ 15,570	$ 2,317
1952	23,226	1,146	22,080	17,510	4,571
1954	29,331	1,750	27,581	21,222	6,359
1956	35,978	1,846	34,132	25,603	8,529
1958	42,793	2,122	40,672	28,495	12,177
1960	51,412	2,739	48,673	32,738	15,938
1962	59,255	3,324	55,931	38,008	17,923
1964	67,181	4,055	63,126	42,119	21,007
1966	77,487	4,991	72,497	47,091	25,405
1968	85,492	6,382	79,109	50,380	28,730
1970	101,563	9,051	92,512	57,601	34,911
1971	111,034	11,738	99,296	62,523	36,773
1972	120,705	12,149	108,556	71,099	37,457
1973	129,110	12,205	116,905	74,502	42,403
1974	141,320	13,064	128,256	80,095	48,161
1975	149,096	15,206	133,890	81,836	52,054
1976	155,707	12,766	142,941	92,222	50,718
1977	169,458	9,826	159,632	93,496	66,136
1978	177,864	8,532	169,332	96,207	73,125
1979	192,363	9,510	182,853	97,100	85,753
1980	213,645	11,010	202,635	100,439	102,196
1981	229,045	13,237	215,808	99,168	116,639
1982	257,109	15,025	242,084	102,439	139,645
1983	287,211	15,959	271,252	108,043	163,208
1984	318,653	16,792	301,861	109,546	192,316
1985	356,539	16,614	339,925	115,728	224,197
1986	411,160	15,210	395,950	121,517	274,433
1987	452,980	14,170	438,810	134,708	304,102

B. By Unit

Unit	1952	1962	1972	1982	1984	1985	1987
Gross debt	$ 23,226	$ 59,255	$ 120,705	$ 257,109	$ 318,653	$ 356,539	$ 452,980
Short-term	1,146	3,324	12,149	15,025	16,792	16,614	14,170
Long-term	22,080	55,931	108,556	242,084	301,861	339,925	438,810
Full faith and credit	17,510	38,008	71,099	102,439	109,546	115,728	134,708
Nonguaranteed	4,571	17,923	37,457	139,645	192,316	224,197	304,102
County	2,018	5,381	13,985	44,671	63,081	72,260	99,154
Short-term	80	173	934	2,581	2,638	3,068	2,277
Long-term	1,938	5,208	13,051	42,090	60,442	69,192	96,877
City	12,659	26,857	52,583	98,421	124,970	140,961	179,860
Short-term	546	1,758	6,678	4,822	5,296	5,049	4,323
Long-term	12,113	25,099	45,905	93,598	119,673	135,912	175,537
Township	619	1,391	3,866	5,568	6,166	6,556	7,933
Short-term	15	88	1,223	1,472	1,218	1,274	1,161
Long-term	604	1,303	2,643	4,096	4,948	5,282	6,772
School district	3,806	13,931	25,272	29,770	30,477	31,104	35,136
Short-term	91	275	1,168	1,519	1,678	1,781	1,723
Long-term	3,715	13,656	24,104	28,251	28,799	29,323	33,413
Special district	4,125	11,695	25,000	78,680	93,959	105,657	130,897
Short-term	415	1,030	2,146	4,631	5,961	5,440	4,685
Long-term	3,710	10,665	22,854	74,049	87,998	100,217	126,212

[a] Data for 1902-1950 are as of June 30; beginning in 1952 data are as of the end of the fiscal year.
Source: Department of Commerce, Bureau of the Census.

F23. Local Debt Outstanding by Unit of Government and State[a]
End of Fiscal Year 1987
($Millions)

State	All Units	Counties	Municipalities	Townships	School Districts	Special Districts
Total	$ 452,980	$ 99,154	$ 179,860	$ 7,933	$ 35,136	$ 130,897
Alabama	5,655	389	4,090	-	195	981
Alaska	4,986	1,592	3,274	-	-	120
Arizona	12,166	3,342	3,443	-	1,548	3,833
Arkansas	2,880	896	1,300	-	479	205
California	49,556	9,114	26,426	-	733	13,283
Colorado	8,881	2,491	3,500	-	938	1,952
Connecticut	2,739	-	1,136	862	33	707
Delaware	1,029	623	268	-	12	127
Florida	32,821	14,346	11,389	-	1,135	5,952
Georgia	11,652	2,769	2,111	-	746	6,026
Hawaii	636	162	473	-	-	-
Idaho	532	124	183	-	151	75
Illinois	14,811	921	6,922	18	1,877	5,073
Indiana	4,958	444	2,455	12	317	1,729
Iowa	3,116	455	2,373	-	262	26
Kansas	6,288	1,404	4,071	-	426	386
Kentucky	7,750	3,381	3,516	-	624	229
Louisiana	8,715	3,950	3,349	-	1,138	277
Maine	985	15	207	228	205	329
Maryland	8,573	4,244	1,689	-	-	2,640
Massachusetts	6,436	40	1,833	1,253	69	3,240
Michigan	10,974	3,293	3,280	335	2,491	1,574
Minnesota	13,642	509	8,537	24	1,063	3,508
Mississippi	4,016	2,602	919	-	269	226
Missouri	4,351	874	2,346	-	668	463
Montana	1,076	169	653	-	167	87
Nebraska	4,842	135	1,009	1	259	3,438
Nevada	2,115	1,364	330	-	177	244
New Hampshire	701	51	249	155	155	90
New Jersey	11,463	1,708	1,848	1,351	981	5,575
New Mexico	3,517	212	3,024	-	229	51
New York	36,616	8,333	20,112	2,923	2,204	3,044
North Carolina	11,010	3,371	1,449	-	-	6,190
North Dakota	887	140	521	-	67	158
Ohio	9,924	2,976	4,487	17	1,060	1,384
Oklahoma	4,439	1,133	2,536	-	387	382
Oregon	3,801	274	2,030	-	489	1,009
Pennsylvania	27,689	1,670	5,340	267	2,805	17,606
Rhode Island	615	-	272	210	-	133
South Carolina	5,197	1,636	696	-	903	1,963
South Dakota	424	39	183	1	42	158
Tennessee	8,780	2,648	4,684	-	19	1,429
Texas	47,945	7,586	18,561	-	6,764	15,034
Utah	7,702	746	805	-	532	5,619
Vermont	361	-	189	47	50	74
Virginia	6,882	2,962	3,090	-	-	830
Washington	15,880	676	2,121	-	1,288	11,796
West Virginia	2,936	2,006	639	-	121	170
Wisconsin	4,952	590	2,935	229	826	372
Wyoming	1,371	750	297	-	230	94
District of Columbia	3,711	-	2,709	-	-	1,002

[a] Includes long- and short-term debt.
Source: Department of Commerce, Bureau of the Census.

F24. Public and Private Elementary and Secondary School Enrollments[a]
Selected School Years 1899-1900 to 1993, Actual and Projected[b]
(Thousands)

School Year[c]	Total Public and Nonpublic All Grades	Total All Grades		Kindergarten Through Grade 8		Grades 9-12 and Post Graduate	
		Public	Nonpublic	Public	Nonpublic	Public	Nonpublic
1899-1900	16,855	15,503	1,352	14,984	1,241	519	111
1909-1910	19,372	17,814	1,558	16,899	1,441	915	117
1919-1920	23,278	21,578	1,700	19,378	1,486	2,200	214
1929-1930	28,329	25,678	2,651	21,279	2,310	4,399	341
1939-1940	28,045	25,434	2,611	18,832	2,153	6,601	458
1949-1950	28,492	25,112	3,380	19,387	2,708	5,725	672
1959	40,857	35,182	5,675	26,911	4,640	8,271	1,035
1960	42,181	36,281	5,900	27,692	4,800	8,589	1,100
1961	43,364	37,464	5,900	28,095	4,800	9,369	1,100
1962	44,849	38,749	6,100	28,637	4,900	10,112	1,200
1963	46,487	40,187	6,300	29,304	5,000	10,883	1,300
1964	47,716	41,416	6,300	30,025	5,000	11,391	1,300
1965	48,473	42,173	6,300	30,563	4,900	11,610	1,400
1966	49,239	43,039	6,200	31,145	4,800	11,894	1,400
1967	49,891	43,891	6,000	31,641	4,600	12,250	1,400
1968	50,744	44,944	5,800	32,226	4,400	12,718	1,400
1969	51,119	45,619	5,500	32,597	4,200	13,022	1,300
1970	51,272	45,909	5,363	32,577	4,052	13,332	1,311
1971	51,281	46,081	5,200	32,265	3,900	13,816	1,300
1972	50,744	45,744	5,000	31,831	3,700	13,913	1,300
1973	50,429	45,429	5,000	31,353	3,700	14,077	1,300
1974	50,053	45,053	5,000	30,921	3,700	14,132	1,300
1975	49,791	44,791	5,000	30,487	3,700	14,304	1,300
1976	49,484	44,317	5,167	30,006	3,825	14,311	1,342
1977	48,717	43,577	5,140	29,336	3,797	14,240	1,343
1978	47,635	42,550	5,085	28,328	3,732	14,223	1,353
1979	46,645	41,645	5,000	27,931	3,700	13,714	1,300
1980	46,318	40,987	5,331	27,674	3,992	13,313	1,339
1981	45,599	40,099	5,500	27,245	4,100	12,855	1,400
1982	45,252	39,652	5,600	27,156	4,200	12,496	1,400
1983	45,067	39,352	5,715	26,997	4,315	12,355	1,400
1984	44,993	39,293	5,700	26,918	4,300	12,375	1,400
1985	45,066	39,509	5,557	27,049	4,195	12,460	1,362
1986	45,437	39,837	5,600	27,404	4,300	12,434	1,300
1987	45,371	40,024	5,347	27,886	4,118	12,138	1,229
1988	45,438	40,196	5,241	28,390	4,036	11,806	1,206
1989	45,595	40,323	5,272	28,818	4,097	11,505	1,175
1990	46,112	40,772	5,340	29,373	4,176	11,399	1,164
1991	46,718	41,306	5,412	29,803	4,237	11,503	1,175
1992	47,369	41,883	5,486	30,189	4,292	11,694	1,195
1993	48,011	42,455	5,556	30,473	4,332	11,982	1,224

[a] Beginning in 1959, data include Alaska and Hawaii. Nonpublic school enrollment estimated.
[b] Beginning in 1989, enrollments are projected. Data for 1988 are preliminary.
[c] Fall enrollment reported beginning 1959. Fall enrollment prior to 1962 was not reported by grades; grade breakdowns for years 1959 through 1961 are estimates.
Source: Department of Education, National Center for Education Statistics.

F25. Public Elementary and Secondary School Expenditures by Character

Selected School Years 1939-40 — 1979-80[a]

Character and Function	Amount ($Millions)					Percentage Distribution				
	1939-40	1949-50	1959-60	1969-70	1979-80	1939-40	1949-50	1959-60	1969-70	1979-80
Total	$ 2,344	$ 5,838	$ 15,613	$ 40,683	$ 95,962	100.0%	100.0%	100.0%	100.0%	100.0%
Current expenditures	1,955	4,723	12,462	34,854	87,582	83.4	80.9	79.8	85.7	91.3
Public elementary and secondary schools	1,942	4,687	12,329	34,218	86,984	82.8	80.3	79.0	84.1	90.6
Administration	92	220	528	1,607	4,264	3.9	3.8	3.4	3.9	4.4
Instruction	1,403	3,112	8,351	23,270	53,258	59.9	53.3	53.5	57.2	55.5
Plant operation	194	428	1,085	2,537	9,745[f]	8.3	7.3	6.9	6.2	10.2[f]
Plant maintenance	73	214	423	975		3.1	3.7	2.7	2.4	
Fixed charges[b]	50	261	909	3,267	11,794	2.1	4.5	5.8	8.0	12.3
Other school services[c]	129	452	1,033	2,562	7,924	5.5	7.7	6.6	6.3	8.3
Other programs[d]	13	36	133	636	598	.6	.6	.9	1.5	.6
Capital outlay[e]	258	1,014	2,662	4,659	6,506	11.0	17.4	17.0	11.5	6.8
Interest on school debt	131	101	490	1,171	1,874	5.6	1.7	3.1	2.9	2.0

a Beginning in 1959-60, data include Alaska and Hawaii.
b Includes expenditures relative to attendance, transportation, health, and food services.
c Payments to teacher retirement funds, social security, insurance premiums, and rent.
d Includes summer and adult programs, community services, community colleges and technical institutes under the jurisdiction of local school district. In 1949-50 and prior years, community services included in "Current expenditures" for full-time day schools.
e Prior to 1965-66, data exclude capital outlay by nonschool agencies.
f Includes plant maintenance.

Source: Department of Education, National Center for Education Statistics.

F26. Public Elementary and Secondary School Revenue by Government Source of Funds

Selected School Years 1929-30 — 1986-87[a]

School Year	Amount[b] ($Millions)				Percentage Distribution			
	Total	Federal	State	Local[c]	Total	Federal	State	Local[c]
1929-30	$ 2,088.6	$ 7.3	$ 353.7	$ 1,727.6	100.0%	.4%	16.9%	82.7%
1933-34	1,810.7	21.5	423.2	1,365.9	100.0	1.2	23.4	75.4
1937-38	2,222.9	26.5	656.0	1,540.4	100.0	1.2	29.5	69.3
1941-42	2,416.6	34.3	760.0	1,622.3	100.0	1.4	31.4	67.1
1945-46	3,059.8	41.4	1,062.1	1,956.4	100.0	1.4	34.7	63.9
1949-50	5,437.0	155.8	2,165.7	3,115.5	100.0	2.9	39.8	57.3
1953-54	7,866.9	355.2	2,944.1	4,567.5	100.0	4.5	37.4	58.1
1957-58	12,181.5	486.5	4,800.4	6,894.7	100.0	4.0	39.4	56.6
1959-60	14,746.6	651.6	5,768.0	8,326.9	100.0	4.4	39.1	56.5
1961-62	17,527.7	761.0	6,789.2	9,977.5	100.0	4.3	38.7	56.9
1963-64	20,544.2	897.0	8,078.0	11,569.2	100.0	4.4	39.3	56.3
1965-66	25,356.9	1,997.0	9,920.2	13,439.7	100.0	7.9	39.1	53.0
1967-68	31,903.1	2,806.5	12,275.5	16,821.1	100.0	8.8	38.5	52.7
1969-70	40,266.9	3,219.6	16,062.8	20,984.6	100.0	8.0	39.9	52.1
1971-72	50,003.6	4,468.0	19,133.3	26,402.4	100.0	8.9	38.3	52.8
1973-74	58,230.9	4,930.4	24,113.4	29,187.1	100.0	8.5	41.4	50.1
1975-76	71,206.1	6,318.3	31,776.1	33,111.6	100.0	8.9	44.6	46.5
1977-78	81,443.2	7,694.2	35,013.3	38,735.7	100.0	9.4	43.0	47.6
1979-80	96,881.2	9,503.5	45,348.8	42,028.8	100.0	9.8	46.8	43.4
1980-81	105,949.1	9,768.3	50,182.7	45,998.2	100.0	9.2	47.4	43.4
1981-82	110,191.3	8,186.5	52,436.4	49,568.4	100.0	7.4	47.6	45.0
1982-83	117,497.5	8,340.0	56,282.2	52,875.4	100.0	7.1	47.9	45.0
1983-84	126,055.4	8,576.5	60,233.0	57,245.9	100.0	6.8	47.8	45.4
1984-85	135,294.7	9,105.6	67,168.7	61,020.4	100.0	6.6	48.9	44.4
1985-86	149,004.9	9,956.0	73,673.2	65,375.7	100.0	6.7	49.4	43.9
1986-87	158,827.5	10,145.9	79,022.6	69,659.0	100.0	6.4	49.8	43.9

[a] Beginning in 1959-60, data include Alaska and Hawaii. Data for 1986-87 are preliminary.
[b] Excludes nonrevenue receipts principally from bond sales, loans, and sale of property; includes in-kind payments.
[c] Includes a small amount from nongovernmental sources and private contributions.
Source: Department of Education, National Center for Education Statistics.

F27. Public Elementary and Secondary School Expenditures by State[a]
Selected School Years 1949-50 — 1988-89[b]
($Thousands)

State	1949-50	1959-60	1969-70	1979-80	1988-89
Total	$ 5,837,643	$ 15,613,255	$ 40,683,429	$ 95,961,561	$ 185,953,328
Alabama	79,374	191,165	467,665	1,239,247	2,221,000
Alaska	4,101	24,195	103,436	411,378	872,007
Arizona	41,535	139,697	337,814	1,172,300	2,895,792
Arkansas	54,354	100,548	259,691	780,115	1,235,931
California	623,359	2,021,625	4,343,580	9,665,006	20,646,773
Colorado	59,458	189,508	433,801	1,450,888	2,598,039
Connecticut	83,748	231,407	659,331	1,289,667	3,315,900
Delaware	13,118	55,667	161,260	286,276	515,900
Florida	97,319	367,207	1,152,451	3,077,765	8,479,538
Georgia	95,225	236,764	749,583	1,813,222	4,680,545
Hawaii	19,412	48,766	175,002	383,135	685,730
Idaho	26,267	52,527	121,644	362,417	658,525
Illinois	358,198	846,734	2,233,552	4,958,981	7,757,832
Indiana	158,180	393,626	1,093,271	2,125,255	3,814,547
Iowa	114,174	235,678	643,820	1,297,080	2,045,541
Kansas	72,391	216,003	402,975	917,270	1,899,789
Kentucky	68,092	148,236	389,028	1,145,428	2,288,530
Louisiana	112,753	298,618	583,918	1,468,959	2,667,730
Maine	25,143	59,674	179,119	417,914	1,024,430
Maryland	94,545	286,550	912,117	1,961,052	3,712,824
Massachusetts	145,559	368,907	1,051,256	2,775,469	4,415,193
Michigan	274,534	811,973	2,205,337	5,087,137	7,315,203
Minnesota	118,163	352,448	977,943	2,013,849	3,557,320
Mississippi	40,786	148,791	318,478	815,894	1,535,200
Missouri	112,463	300,749	778,690	1,632,389	3,140,741
Montana	31,607	64,021	143,512	416,812	665,677
Nebraska	47,193	112,836	279,605	650,111	1,006,217
Nevada	8,757	32,641	104,921	344,630	752,413
New Hampshire	16,939	41,114	125,663	318,927	742,649
New Jersey	199,986	599,007	1,600,815	3,866,103	7,765,200
New Mexico	33,509	88,902	209,466	609,717	1,218,602
New York	617,811	1,742,717	4,656,111	9,347,402	17,741,608
North Carolina	151,323	294,744	762,982	2,011,922	4,143,800
North Dakota	24,905	59,694	110,445	245,955	427,100
Ohio	291,920	799,953	1,963,251	4,137,251	7,506,466
Oklahoma	87,611	185,751	386,799	1,194,278	1,964,000
Oregon	93,325	185,229	462,980	1,303,410	2,197,400
Pennsylvania	348,118	797,498	2,534,175	5,008,640	9,260,030
Rhode Island	21,538	53,035	164,571	373,504	742,519
South Carolina	63,465	136,686	433,895	1,143,666	2,266,311
South Dakota	27,071	53,855	125,609	240,939	440,584
Tennessee	104,576	214,459	563,338	1,480,292	2,696,693
Texas	303,013	757,092	1,827,857	6,047,189	13,568,398
Utah	33,800	97,490	208,181	702,166	1,188,000
Vermont	11,548	28,144	109,993	207,602	485,750
Virginia	100,902	266,942	848,073	2,123,297	4,807,601
Washington	113,845	319,393	856,033	2,188,119	4,170,622
West Virginia	69,666	122,434	282,483	768,395	1,303,605
Wisconsin	123,868	332,960	930,978	2,085,592	3,842,600
Wyoming	14,737	46,844	73,614	298,056	551,500
District of Columbia	27,871	52,752	173,317	299,495	517,423

[a] Includes current expenditures, capital outlay, and interest for public day schools, expenditures for operation of summer and adult programs, community services, and community colleges.

[b] Beginning in 1959-60, totals include Alaska and Hawaii.

Source: Department of Education, National Center for Education Statistics; National Education Association-Copyright 1989, *Estimates of School Statistics 1988-89.*

F28. Public Elementary and Secondary School Expenditures By Character and State

School Year 1988-89

($Millions)

State	Total Expenditures	Current Expenditures			Capital Outlay	Interest on Debt
		Total	Full-time Day Schools	Other Programs		
Total	$ 185,953.3	$ 170,795.5	$ 167,931.4	$ 2,864.1	$ 12,026.6	$ 3,131.2
Alabama	2,221.0	2,020.0	2,000.5	19.5	180.0	21.0
Alaska	872.0	736.0	711.2	24.8	72.5	63.4
Arizona	2,895.8	2,156.1	2,146.8	9.3	619.1	120.6
Arkansas	1,235.9	1,115.5	1,110.3	5.2	88.5	31.9
California	20,646.8	19,465.0	18,598.4	866.6	1,152.0	29.7
Colorado	2,598.0	2,388.9	2,384.8	4.1	121.0	88.2
Connecticut	3,315.9	3,160.6	3,127.8	32.8	119.1	124.0
Delaware	515.9	498.0	488.0	10.0	13.7	4.2
Florida	8,479.5	7,380.5	7,380.5	-	999.6	99.4
Georgia	4,680.5	4,310.4	4,287.6	22.8	329.7	40.4
Hawaii	685.7	652.6	631.1	21.5	32.9	.1
Idaho	658.5	594.2	593.7	.5	53.1	11.2
Illinois	7,757.8	7,247.8	7,059.5	188.3	340.1	170.0
Indiana	3,814.5	3,384.7	3,381.6	3.1	363.0	66.8
Iowa	2,045.5	1,926.5	1,926.5	-	102.6	16.5
Kansas	1,899.8	1,748.5	1,689.7	58.8	121.9	29.4
Kentucky	2,288.5	2,110.1	2,098.1	12.0	134.9	43.5
Louisiana	2,667.7	2,388.7	2,371.2	17.5	185.6	93.5
Maine	1,024.4	967.0	957.0	10.0	42.0	36.2
Maryland	3,712.8	3,448.9	3,398.6	50.3	238.2	25.7
Massachusetts	4,415.2	4,163.9	4,148.8	15.1	196.8	54.5
Michigan	7,315.2	6,901.2	6,692.3	208.9	287.1	126.9
Minnesota	3,557.3	3,245.7	3,144.6	101.1	251.6	60.0
Mississippi	1,535.2	1,394.6	1,394.6	-	79.3	61.3
Missouri	3,140.7	2,840.7	2,792.7	48.0	250.0	50.0
Montana	665.7	600.1	592.5	7.6	55.0	10.5
Nebraska	1,006.2	949.5	947.2	2.3	38.7	18.1
Nevada	752.4	640.6	635.8	4.8	86.1	25.7
New Hampshire	742.6	663.3	661.5	1.8	71.8	7.6
New Jersey	7,765.2	7,591.1	7,537.8	53.3	74.1	100.0
New Mexico	1,218.6	1,000.8	996.2	4.6	166.8	51.1
New York	17,741.6	16,861.0	16,701.0	160.0	675.0	205.6
North Carolina	4,143.8	3,928.8	3,908.8	20.0	215.0	-
North Dakota	427.1	392.6	390.0	2.6	30.0	4.5
Ohio	7,506.5	6,915.7	6,800.0	115.7	489.8	101.0
Oklahoma	1,964.0	1,771.0	1,745.0	26.0	165.0	28.0
Oregon	2,197.4	2,055.8	2,049.5	6.3	104.2	37.4
Pennsylvania	9,260.0	8,731.7	8,404.4	327.3	307.3	221.1
Rhode Island	742.5	733.5	727.5	6.0	7.5	1.5
South Carolina	2,266.3	2,014.7	1,992.5	22.2	181.0	70.6
South Dakota	440.6	412.7	398.4	14.3	23.9	3.9
Tennessee	2,696.7	2,561.7	2,536.3	25.4	70.0	65.0
Texas	13,568.4	11,656.2	11,632.9	23.3	1,420.0	492.1
Utah	1,188.0	1,067.0	1,041.9	25.1	82.3	38.7
Vermont	485.8	459.5	445.0	14.5	17.5	8.8
Virginia	4,807.6	4,406.5	4,350.5	56.0	328.5	72.6
Washington	4,170.6	3,265.8	3,199.1	66.7	788.0	116.8
West Virginia	1,303.6	1,227.8	1,208.8	19.0	52.6	23.2
Wisconsin	3,842.6	3,630.7	3,560.3	70.4	159.2	52.7
Wyoming	551.5	501.5	500.0	1.5	35.0	15.0
District of Columbia	517.4	509.5	452.4	57.1	7.9	-

[a] Includes summer school, adult programs, community services, and community colleges (under jurisdiction of local boards of education).
Source: National Education Association - Copyright 1989, *Estimates of School Statistics 1988-89.*

F29. Current Expenditures Per Pupil by State[a]

Selected School Years 1949-1950 — 1986-1987[b]

State	1949-50	1959-60	1969-70	1979-80	1986-87
U.S. average[b]	$ 209	$ 375	$ 816	$ 2,272	$ 3,977
Alabama	117	241	544	1,612	2,573
Alaska[c]	-	546	1,123	4,728	8,010
Arizona	241	404	720	1,971	3,544
Arkansas	112	225	568	1,574	2,733
California	n.a.	424[d]	867	2,268	3,728
Colorado	220	396	738	2,421	4,147
Connecticut	255	436	951	2,420	5,435
Delaware	259	456	900	2,861	4,825
Florida	181	318	732	1,889	3,794
Georgia	123	253	588	1,625	3,374
Hawaii	-	325	841	2,322	3,787
Idaho	186	290	603	1,659	2,585
Illinois	258	438	910	2,587	4,106
Indiana	235	369	728	1,882	3,556
Iowa	231	368	844	2,326	3,808
Kansas	219	348	771	2,173	3,933
Kentucky	121	233	545	1,701	2,733
Louisiana	214	372	648	1,792	3,069
Maine	157	283	693	1,824	3,850
Maryland	213	393	918	2,598	4,777
Massachusetts	236	409	859	2,819	5,145
Michigan	220	415	904	2,640	4,353
Minnesota	242	425	904	2,387	4,180
Mississippi	80	206	501	1,664	2,350
Missouri	174	344	709	1,936	3,472
Montana	268	411	782	2,476	4,194
Nebraska	217	337	736	2,150	3,756
Nevada	246	430	770	2,088	3,573
New Hampshire	211	347	723	1,916	3,933
New Jersey	280	488	1,016	3,191	5,953
New Mexico	222	363	707	2,034	3,558
New York	295	562	1,327	3,462	6,497
North Carolina	141	237	612	1,754	3,129
North Dakota	226	367	690	1,920	3,437
Ohio	202	365	730	2,075	3,671
Oklahoma	207	311	604	1,926	3,099
Oregon	272	448	925	2,692	4,337
Pennsylvania	216	409	882	2,535	4,616
Rhode Island	240	413	891	2,601	4,985
South Carolina	122	220	613	1,752	3,237
South Dakota	230	347	690	1,908	3,097
Tennessee	132	238	566	1,635	2,827
Texas	209	332	624	1,916	3,409
Utah	179	322	626	1,657	2,415
Vermont	193	344	807	1,997	4,399
Virginia	146	274	708	1,970	3,780
Washington	248	420	915	2,568	3,964
West Virginia	150	258	670	1,920	3,784
Wisconsin	230	413[e]	883	2,477	4,523
Wyoming	263	450	856	2,527	5,201
District of Columbia	256	431	1,018	3,259	5,742

[a] Data are for pupils in average daily attendance in full-time public elementary and secondary day schools.
[b] Beginning in 1959-1960, totals include Alaska and Hawaii.
[c] Because of the high cost of living in Alaska, per pupil expenditure data for this state cannot be readily compared to those for other states.
[d] Estimated by Office of Education.
[e] Excludes vocational schools not operated as part of the regular public school system.
Source: Department of Education, National Center for Education Statistics.

F30. Average Annual Salaries of Classroom Teachers in Public Elementary and Secondary Day Schools by State

Selected School Years 1965-1966 to 1987-1988

State	1965-1966	1969-1970	1975-1976	1979-1980	1985-1986	1987-1988
U.S. average	$ 6,500	$ 8,520	$ 12,448	$ 15,970	$ 25,313	$ 28,044
Alabama	5,150	6,817	10,597	13,060	22,934	23,320
Alaska[a]	8,240	10,560	19,312	27,210	41,480	40,424
Arizona	7,025	8,715	12,394	15,054	24,680	27,388
Arkansas	4,740	6,273	9,648[b]	12,299	19,538	20,340
California	8,150	9,750	15,200	18,020	29,132	33,159
Colorado	6,391	7,600	12,000	16,205	25,892	28,651
Connecticut	7,200	9,080	11,874	16,229	26,610	33,487
Delaware	7,150	8,900	12,545	16,148	24,624	29,575
Florida	6,435	8,300	10,496	14,149	22,250	25,198
Georgia	5,350	7,170	10,622	13,853	22,080	26,177
Hawaii	6,929	9,572	15,209	19,920	25,845	28,785
Idaho	5,685	7,103	10,212	13,611	20,969	22,242
Illinois	7,123	9,250	n.a.	17,601	27,190	29,663
Indiana	7,050	9,139	11,165[c]	15,599	24,274	27,386
Iowa	6,050	8,050	11,570	15,203	21,690	24,867
Kansas	5,785	7,620	10,710	13,690	22,644	24,647
Kentucky	4,930	7,041	9,770	14,520	20,940	24,274
Louisiana	6,039	6,990	10,092[b]	13,760	20,460	21,209
Maine	5,550	7,575	10,620	13,071	19,583	23,425
Maryland	6,878	9,383	13,709	17,558	27,186	30,933
Massachusetts	7,100[d]	8,980	11,900	17,253	26,800	30,019
Michigan	6,850	9,823	15,540	19,663	30,168	32,926
Minnesota	6,641	9,592	12,261	15,912	27,360	29,900
Mississippi	4,190	5,870	9,314	11,850	18,443	20,669
Missouri	5,857	7,825	10,490	13,682	21,974	24,703
Montana	5,800	7,650	11,000	14,537	22,482	23,798
Nebraska	5,225	7,526	10,017	13,516	20,939	23,246
Nevada	7,025	9,248	12,716	16,295	25,610	27,600
New Hampshire	5,650	7,715	10,500	13,017	20,263	24,091
New Jersey	6,968	9,125	13,375	17,161	27,170	30,720
New Mexico	6,356	7,840	11,005	14,887	22,644	24,351
New York	7,700	9,700	15,950[d]	19,812	30,678	34,500
North Carolina	5,337	7,444	11,165	14,117	22,795	24,900
North Dakota	5,120	6,760	9,888	13,263	20,816	21,660
Ohio	6,350	8,242	11,400	15,269	24,500	27,606
Oklahoma	5,650	6,987	9,600	13,107	21,419	22,006
Oregon	6,650	8,975	12,400	16,266	25,788	28,060
Pennsylvania	6,410	8,700	12,350	16,515	25,853	29,174
Rhode Island	6,325	8,808	13,381	18,002	29,470	32,858
South Carolina	4,675	6,750	9,904	13,063	21,570	24,241
South Dakota	4,650	6,300	9,314	12,348	18,095	19,750
Tennessee	5,100	7,200	10,299	13,972	21,800	23,785
Texas	5,950[e]	7,275	11,373	14,132	25,160	25,655
Utah	6,260	7,644	11,360	14,909	22,341	22,621
Vermont	5,640	7,960	9,975	12,484	20,325	23,397
Virginia	5,650	8,000	11,300	14,060	23,382	27,436
Washington	6,825	9,025	13,615	18,820	26,015	28,116
West Virginia	4,990	7,610	10,480	13,710	20,627	21,736
Wisconsin	6,425[b]	9,000	12,816	16,006	26,525	28,998
Wyoming	6,119	8,282	11,100	16,012	27,224	27,260
District of Columbia	7,500	10,660	15,297[c]	22,190	33,990	34,705

[a] Because of the high cost of living in Alaska, data for this state cannot readily be compared with those for other states.
[b] Includes some personnel in addition to instructional staff.
[c] Data are for school year 1974-1975 in Indiana. In District of Columbia, data are for 1966-1967.
[d] Salary data reported as median salary.
[e] Excludes nursery and kindergarten schools.
Source: Department of Education, National Center for Education Statistics.

F31. Revenue Receipts for Public Schools by Source of Funds and State

School Year 1986-1987

State	Amount ($Millions)				Percent of Total		
	Total	Federal	State	Local and Other[a]	Federal	State	Local and Other[a]
Total	$ 158,827.5	$ 10,145.9	$ 79,022.6	$ 69,659.0	6.4%	49.8%	43.9%
Alabama	2,070.6	241.4	1,373.0	456.3	11.7	66.3	22.0
Alaska	731.2	85.3	465.6	180.3	11.7	63.7	24.7
Arizona	2,106.6	189.0	1,017.4	900.1	9.0	48.3	42.7
Arkansas	1,111.6	128.2	608.8	374.7	11.5	54.8	33.7
California	17,219.5	1,218.0	11,961.8	4,039.6	7.1	69.5	23.5
Colorado	2,395.7	117.6	935.2	1,343.0	4.9	39.0	56.1
Connecticut	2,606.4	114.9	1,043.4	1,448.1	4.4	40.0	55.6
Delaware	429.4	33.0	297.3	99.1	7.7	69.2	23.1
District of Columbia	439.8	45.5	2.7	391.6	10.3	.6	89.0
Florida	6,610.6	475.2	3,581.7	2,553.7	7.2	54.2	38.6
Georgia	3,708.4	263.1	2,213.2	1,232.1	7.1	59.7	33.2
Hawaii	592.8	70.2	522.1	.5	11.8	88.1	.1
Idaho	544.5	48.2	342.3	154.0	8.9	62.9	28.3
Illinois	6,025.4	261.5	2,358.2	3,405.8	4.3	39.1	56.5
Indiana	3,563.5	176.3	2,070.5	1,316.8	4.9	58.1	37.0
Iowa	1,846.3	94.6	821.1	930.7	5.1	44.5	50.4
Kansas	1,681.7	81.0	712.4	888.2	4.8	42.4	52.8
Kentucky	1,656.3	192.3	1,069.0	395.0	11.6	64.5	23.8
Louisiana	2,416.4	277.6	1,331.2	807.6	11.5	55.1	33.4
Maine	779.8	49.7	391.5	338.6	6.4	50.2	43.4
Maryland	3,223.0	164.3	1,241.1	1,817.7	5.1	38.5	56.4
Massachusetts	4,103.3	201.8	1,850.7	2,050.8	4.9	45.1	50.0
Michigan	7,242.9	425.5	2,525.8	4,291.6	5.9	34.9	59.3
Minnesota	3,101.7	131.7	1,765.8	1,204.2	4.2	56.9	38.8
Mississippi	1,076.3	112.6	701.8	261.8	10.5	65.2	24.3
Missouri	2,749.6	173.0	1,132.2	1,444.4	6.3	41.2	52.5
Montana	633.0	53.8	302.8	276.3	8.5	47.8	43.7
Nebraska	1,005.6	61.7	226.7	717.2	6.1	22.5	71.3
Nevada	595.8	26.4	235.6	333.8	4.4	39.5	56.0
New Hampshire	647.1	21.8	38.1	587.2	3.4	5.9	90.7
New Jersey	6,593.0	290.8	2,837.6	3,464.6	4.4	43.0	52.5
New Mexico	1,008.3	123.2	757.3	127.8	12.2	75.1	12.7
New York	15,757.0	762.1	6,688.7	8,306.2	4.8	42.4	52.7
North Carolina	3,474.0	274.7	2,294.4	904.9	7.9	66.0	26.0
North Dakota	421.8	39.7	214.1	168.0	9.4	50.8	39.8
Ohio	6,293.6	348.8	3,122.7	2,822.1	5.5	49.6	44.8
Oklahoma	1,727.8	96.0	1,097.7	534.2	5.6	63.5	30.9
Oregon	1,863.5	123.0	522.2	1,218.3	6.6	28.0	65.4
Pennsylvania	8,259.3	418.5	3,825.2	4,015.6	5.1	46.3	48.6
Rhode Island	630.2	28.2	268.3	333.7	4.5	42.6	52.9
South Carolina	1,987.7	175.9	1,113.7	698.0	8.9	56.0	35.1
South Dakota	417.6	49.3	113.4	254.8	11.8	27.2	61.0
Tennessee	2,064.0	228.5	918.7	916.8	11.1	44.5	44.4
Texas	11,900.9	846.5	5,603.1	5,451.3	7.1	47.1	45.8
Utah	1,153.4	70.0	627.1	456.3	6.1	54.4	39.6
Vermont	388.0	19.7	133.3	235.0	5.1	34.4	60.6
Virginia	b	b	b	b	b	b	b
Washington	3,118.2	196.0	2,258.4	563.8	6.3	72.4	21.3
West Virginia	1,237.9	93.3	864.1	280.4	7.5	69.8	22.7
Wisconsin	3,303.2	154.3	1,141.3	2,007.7	4.7	34.5	60.8
Wyoming	609.2	22.6	261.9	324.8	3.7	43.0	53.3

[a] Includes revenue from local and intermediate sources, gifts, and tuition and fees from patrons.
[b] Data not reported.
Source: Department of Education, National Center for Education Statistics.

Glossary

Terms generally associated with a particular Federal agency or level of government are identified by the following abbreviations:

BC	Bureau of the Census	**BEA**	Bureau of Economic Analysis
BLS	Bureau of Labor Statistics	**DA**	Department of Agriculture
DC	Department of Commerce	**IRS**	Internal Revenue Service
OMB	Office of Management and Budget	**TD**	Treasury Department
TF	Tax Foundation	**S-L**	State-local governments as reported by the Bureau of the Census

Adjusted gross income (IRS): For Federal individual income tax purposes, gross income from all sources not specifically excluded minus certain deductions, primarily business expenses.

Appropriations (OMB): Legal authorization to make specified amounts of expenditures or to enter into obligations to make expenditures from the general fund or from special funds for specified purposes.

Assistance and subsidies (BC): Cash contributions and subsidies to persons and foreign governments, not in payment for goods or services or for claims against the government; includes direct cash assistance to public welfare recipients; veterans' bonuses; direct cash grants for tuition, scholarships, and aid to nonpublic educational institutions; and payments for agricultural support programs and foreign aid.

Budget surplus or deficit (OMB): The difference between budget receipts and budget outlays (i.e., expenditures and net lending) in a given year. (See "Federal budget receipts" and "Federal budget expenditures.") Cash balances, appropriation balances, and surpluses or deficits of previous years are not part of the calculation of the budget surplus or deficit. Excludes deficits incurred on off-budget transactions.

Business saving (BEA): Undistributed corporate profits with inventory valuation and corporate capital consumption adjustments, and corporate and noncorporate capital consumption allowances (with adjustment).

Capital consumption adjustment (BEA): The tax-return based capital consumption allowances less capital consumption allowances that are based on estimates of economic service lives, straight-line depreciation, and replacement cost.

Capital consumption allowances (BEA): A measure of the plant and equipment depreciated, worn out, damaged, or rendered obsolete during a given period of time.

Capital outlay (BC): Expenditures for the acquisition of or addition to fixed assets. Included are amounts for replacements and major alterations, but not for repair.

Character and object classification of expenditures (BC): A classification which focuses on the nature of spending apart from the functions served; distinguishes among purchases of goods and services for current operation and capital outlay; assistance and subsidies; interest on debt; and insurance benefits and repayments.

Charges and miscellaneous revenue (BC): Nontax revenue derived chiefly from fees, assessments, and other reimbursements for current services, interest earnings, and from rents and sales of commodities or services furnished incident to the performance of particular general government functions.

Consumer price index (BLS): A measure of the average level of prices in a fixed market basket of goods and services bought by urban wage earners and clerical workers and by all urban consumers, compared to the average level in a base period.

Corporate profits tax liability (BEA): Federal, state, and local taxes levied on corporate income of a given period, measured on an accrual basis.

Corporation income taxes (BC): Taxes on net income of corporations, including distinctively imposed net income taxes on special kinds of corporations (e.g., financial institutions) and on unincorporated businesses.

Current operation expenditures (BC): Expenditures for compensation of own employees, and for supplies, materials, and contractual services, except amounts for capital outlay.

Depreciation charges (BEA, IRS): Charges made by private business and nonprofit institutions against receipts to account for the decrease in value of capital assets as a result of wear, accidental damage, and obsolescence, plus an estimate of corresponding depreciation in owner-occupied dwellings. Accepted accounting and tax practice permits various methods of deducting estimated depreciation to account for the gradual exhaustion of durable capital assets.

Direct expenditures (BC): Payments to employees, suppliers, contractors, beneficiaries, and other final recipients of government payments, i.e., all expenditures other than intergovernmental expenditures.

Disposable personal income (BEA): Personal income less personal tax and nontax payments to government.

Employment (BLS): Employed persons are those who did any work for pay during a specified week, or who worked without pay for 15 hours or more in a family enterprise (farm or business); also included are persons who did not work or look for work but who had a job or business from which they were temporarily absent during the week. Unemployed persons comprise those who did not work at all during the week and who were looking for work, or were on layoff from a job.

Expenditures: (See Government expenditures, Federal expenditures, etc.)

Farm output, index of (DA): A measure of the variation in the volume of farm output compared to the average in a base period. Farm output consists of farm production available for human use through sales from farms or consumption in farm households.

Federal budget expenditures (OMB, TD): In the unified budget concept, covers expenditures of all Federal agencies and trust funds. Expenditures are distinguished from net lending, and total budget outlays are the sum of expenditures and net lending. Expenditures of public enterprise funds and trust revolving funds are shown net of the receipts of such funds. Certain other receipts are also offset against expenditures in the new budget concept.

Federal budget outlays (OMB): (See Federal budget expenditures.)

Federal budget receipts (OMB, TD): In the unified budget concept, covers receipts, net of refunds, of all Federal agencies and trust funds. Interfund and intragovernmental transactions are excluded. Does not include proceeds of borrowing or receipts of public enterprise and revolving funds.

Federal debt limit (OMB, TD): A limit imposed by law (Second Liberty Bond Act as amended) on the aggregate face amount of outstanding obligations issued, or guaranteed as to principal and interest, by the United States except such guaranteed obligations as may be held by the Secretary of the Treasury.

Federal expenditures (BEA): Federal purchases of goods and services, transfer payments, grants-in-aid to state and local governments, net interest paid, and subsidies less current surplus of government enterprises. The basic differences between this and the unified budget basis for expenditures, apart from the fact that these data are converted to a calendar year basis, are that they are on an accrual basis, and exclude capital transactions that do not represent current production.

Federal funds (OMB, TD): Accounts designed for general support functions of the Federal government and not earmarked by law for a specified purpose.

Federal internal revenue collections (IRS): Total Federal taxes collected through the Internal Revenue Service. They make up 99 percent of all Federal taxes (customs and a few miscellaneous taxes are excluded).

Federal tax burden (TF): Estimates of the geographic origin of Federal taxes in terms of their ultimate incidence rather than the point of collection, based on a framework of assumptions and methods developed by the Tax Foundation.

Federal tax collections (TD): All internal revenue collections plus customs collections plus railroad unemployment insurance taxes collected by the Railroad Retirement Board, before refunds.

Federal tax receipts (BEA): Differ from tax receipts above chiefly in that business taxes are included on an accrual basis.

Federal tax receipts (OMB, TD): Internal revenue collections plus customs and railroad unemployment insurance taxes, net of refunds.

Financial administration expenditures (BC): Expenditures for tax assessment and collection, accounting, auditing, budgeting, purchasing, custody of funds, and other central finance activities.

Full faith and credit debt (BC, S-L): State and local debt for which the credit of the government, implying the power of taxation, is unconditionally pledged.

Function classification of expenditures (OMB, BC): Focuses on the purposes that particular kinds of expenditures are designed to serve or facilitate. The classification used by the Office of Management and Budget distinguishes more than a dozen major groups of programs (each with subgroups), including national defense, veterans' benefits and services, health, education and related services, agriculture, commerce and housing credit, income security, interest, and general government. The function classification used by the Bureau of the Census is more appropriate to the analysis of state and local government programs. The categories include education, public welfare, highways, police and fire protection, health and hospitals, sewerage, interest, and general control. The Census Bureau classifies most veterans' services and benefits according to the type of service provided (e.g., education, health and hospitals, etc.) rather than under a single category as does the Office of Management and Budget.

General control expenditures (BC): Expenditures of the legislative and judicial branches, the office of the chief executive, and central staff services and agencies concerned with personnel administration, law, recording, planning and zoning, and the like.

General expenditures (BC): Total expenditures (see Government expenditures) less utility, liquor store, and insurance trust expenditures when used in reference to state or local governments separately.

General revenue (BC): Total revenue (see Government revenue) less utility, liquor store, and insurance trust revenue when used in reference to state or local governments separately. When combined for state-local totals, it refers only to taxes and charges and miscellaneous revenue to avoid duplicating intergovernmental revenue (see Revenue from own sources).

General revenue sharing (OMB, TD): Funds distributed to states and local general purpose governments by the Federal government under the State and Local Fiscal Assistance Act of 1972 and subsequent laws.

Government expenditures, total (BC): All money paid out by a government – net of recoveries and other correcting transactions – other than for retirement of debt, investment in securities, extension of credit, or as agency transactions. Expenditures include only external transactions of a government and exclude noncash transactions such as the provision of perquisites or other payments in kind. Aggregates for groups of governments exclude intergovernmental transactions among the governments involved. (See also Direct expenditures, General expenditures, and Direct general expenditures.)

Government revenue, total (BC): All money received by a government from external sources – net of funds and other correcting transactions – other than from issue of debt, liquidation of investments, and as agency and private trust transactions. Excludes noncash transactions such as receipts of services, commodities, or other "receipts in kind."

Grants-in-aid (BC, OMB): Payments made by one government unit to another government unit for specified or general purposes. They represent Federal support for a state or locally administered program, or state support for a local program.

Gross debt (BC): All long-term credit obligations incurred and outstanding whether backed by a government's full faith and credit or nonguaranteed, and all interest-bearing short-term credit obligations.

Gross national product or expenditure (BEA): The market value of the output of all goods and services produced by the nation's economy, before deduction of depreciation charges and other allowances for capital consumption.

Gross private domestic investment (BEA): Purchases of newly produced capital goods plus the value of the change in the volume of inventories held by business. Purchases include all new private dwellings, whether leased to tenants or owner-occupied.

Guaranteed debt (TD): Obligations of certain semi-public and public corporations which are guaranteed by the Federal government as contingent liabilities.

Guarantees (OMB): A Federal credit aid in which the Federal government pledges its financial liability for loans made by private, state, or local government institutions.

Highway trust fund (OMB, TD): A Federal trust fund (created under the Highway Revenue Act of 1956) to finance the expanded program of Federal highway aid. Appropriations based on certain highway user tax collections (on motor fuels, vehicles, and parts) are made to the fund, and from it Federal payments to states for highway construction are made.

Implicit price deflator for gross national product (BEA): A measure of the average level of market prices of goods and services represented in the national income and product accounts, compared to the average level in a base period.

Income: (See National income, Adjusted gross income, Personal income, Disposable personal income.)

Indirect business tax and nontax liability (BEA): All tax liabilities incurred by business, except for corporate income and social insurance taxes, plus general government nontax revenues from business. Nontax liabilities consist mainly of certain charges for government products and services, of fines and penalties, of donations, and of special assessments by state and local governments. Tax and nontax liabilities are measured on an accrual basis.

Individual income taxes (BC): Taxes on individuals measured by net income, including distinctive taxes on income from interest, dividends, and the like.

Insurance trust expenditures (BC): Cash payments to beneficiaries of contributory social insurance programs, such as Old-Age, Survivors, Disability, and Health Insurance; government employee retirement; unemployment compensation; sickness insurance; etc. Excludes cost of administration, intergovernmental expenditures for social insurance, and noncontributory payments to former employees.

Insurance trust revenue (BC): Revenue from contributions required of employers (excluding government as an employer) and employees for financing social insurance programs, and earnings on assets of such systems.

Intergovernmental expenditures (BC): Payments to other governments as grants-in-aid, shared revenues, payments in lieu of taxes, or as reimbursements for the performance of services for the paying government.

Intergovernmental revenue (BC): Revenue received from other governments as grants-in-aid, shared revenues, receipts in lieu of taxes, or as reimbursements for services performed.

Inventory valuation adjustment (BEA): Corporate profits and income of unincorporated enterprises include inventory profit or loss in customary business accounting. Current output in the national income accounts, however, includes only the value of the change in volume in inventories. The adjustment is that necessary to take account of this departure from business accounting. No valuation adjustment is necessary for farm inventories because farm income is measured exclusive of inventory profits.

Labor force (BLS): All persons 16 years or age or over who are employed or unemployed, according to established criteria. Total labor force includes members of the armed forces stationed either in the United States or abroad. These are excluded from civilian labor force. (See Employment.)

License taxes (BC, S-L): Taxes exacted (either for revenue raising or for regulation) as a condition to the exercise of a business or nonbusiness privilege, at a flat rate or measured by such bases as capital stock, number of business units, or capacity. Excludes taxes measured directly by transactions, income, or property value, except those to which only nominal rates apply.

Liquor store expenditures (BC, S-L): Expenditures by government-owned facilities for purchase of liquor for resale and provision and operation of stores. Excludes expenditures for law enforcement and licensing activities carried out in conjunction with liquor store operations.

Liquor store revenue (BC, S-L): Revenue from sale of liquor and from related operations of publicly operated stores. Excludes collections from sales taxes and license taxes on alcoholic beverages, classified as tax revenue.

National income (BEA): The aggregate earnings of labor and property which arise from the current production of goods and services by the nation's economy. It consists of compensation of employees, profits of corporate and unincorporated enterprises, net interest, rents paid to individuals, plus taxes on earnings.

National income and product accounts (BEA): Accounts prepared and published by the Department of Commerce showing various aspects of the total output of the economy and of the total income received in the economy.

National resources expenditures (BC): Payments for conservation and development of agriculture, fish and game, forestry, and other soil and water resources, including irrigation, drainage, flood control, and the like. Includes agricultural experiment stations and extension services, and Federal programs relating to farm price stabilization programs, farm insurance, and credit activities. Excludes hydroelectric power activities classified under utility expenditures.

Net exports of goods and services (BEA): The excess of exports of goods and services (domestic output sold abroad, and the production abroad credited to U.S.-owned resources) over imports (U.S. purchases of foreign output, production in the United States credited to foreign-owned resources, and net private cash remittances to abroad).

Net interest (BEA): The net interest component of national income is total interest (monetary and imputed) received by or accruing to individuals and governments less total interest paid by governments. Government interest paid is excluded because it is not considered income arising out of current production.

Net long-term debt (BC, S-L): Total long-term debt less cash and investment assets of sinking funds and other reserve funds specifically held for redemption of long-term debt.

Net national product (BEA): The market value of the net output of goods and services produced by the nation's economy. It equals gross national product less capital consumption allowances.

Nonguaranteed debt (BC, S-L): Long-term debt payable solely from earnings of revenue-producing activities, from special assessments, or from specific nonproperty taxes. It does not constitute an obligation on any other resources of the government if the pledged sources are insufficient.

Offsets to long-term debt (BC, S-L): Cash and investment assets of sinking funds, bond reserve and other reserve funds that are specifically held for redemption of long-term debt, and assets of credit funds that are pledged to redeem debt incurred to finance loan activities of such funds.

Parity ratio (DA): A measure of the change in the relationship between prices farmers receive for farm products and prices they pay for goods and services, compared to this relationship in the base period, 1910-1914.

Personal consumption expenditures (BEA): The sum of money and imputed expenditures made by consumers (individuals, nonprofit institutions such as hospitals, etc.) for goods and services. It excludes purchases of dwellings (included in gross private domestic investment), but includes rental value of owner-occupied houses.

Personal income (BEA): National income less various kinds of income not actually received by individuals, nonprofit institutions, etc. (i.e., undistributed corporate profits, corporate taxes, employer contributions for social insurance) plus certain receipts which do not arise from current production (i.e., transfer payments and government interest).

Personal saving (BEA): The difference between disposable personal income and personal consumption expenditures. It includes the changes in cash and deposits, security holdings, indebtedness, reserves of life insurance companies and mutual savings institutions, the net investment of unincorporated enterprises, and the acquisition of real property net of depreciation. Personal saving includes saving by individuals, nonprofit institutions, and private pension, health, welfare, and trust funds.

Producer price index (BLS): A measure of the average level of prices received by producers of commodities in all stages of processing, compared to the average level in a base period. Includes items produced, as well as those imported for sale; generally applies to the first significant commercial transaction in primary markets in the United States. Formerly known as the wholesale price index.

Production workers (BLS): Working foremen and all nonsupervisory workers, including trainees, engaged in any type of production operation or closely associated services. Excludes supervisory employees (above the working foremen level) and their clerical staffs.

Property taxes (BC, S-L): Taxes conditioned on ownership of property and measured by its value. Includes general property taxes relating to property as a whole, real and personal, tangible or intangible, whether taxed at a single rate or at classified rates, and taxes on selected types of property, such as motor vehicles or certain intangibles.

Public enterprise funds, Federal (OMB): Revolving funds (see definition below) with receipts primarily from outside the government. They include nearly all of the government corporations, the postal fund, and various unincorporated business-type enterprises.

Public welfare (BC): Support of and assistance to needy persons contingent upon their need. Expenditures for public welfare include cash assistance payments directly to needy persons, vendor payments to private purveyors for medical care and other services, welfare institutions, and others.

Purchasing power of the dollar (BLS): A measure of the quantity (not quality) of goods and services that a dollar will buy in a specified market (e.g., consumer or producer) compared with the amount that it could buy in some base period. It is obtained by taking the reciprocal of an appropriate price index.

Revenue from own sources (BC): Total revenue from own sources consists of taxes, charges, and miscellaneous revenue, and revenue from utility, liquor stores, and insurance trust. General revenue from own sources is limited to taxes (as defined by the Bureau of the Census to exclude insurance trust fund taxes), charges, and miscellaneous revenue.

Revolving and management funds, Federal (OMB): Revolving funds are those which finance a cycle of operations in which the expenditures generate receipts that are available for continuing use. They include public enterprise funds and intragovernmental funds (funds with receipts primarily from inside the government). Management funds facilitate accounting for and administration of activities financed by two or more appropriations. The receipts of revolving and management funds are not included in budget receipts. They are deducted from expenditures of these funds in deriving budget expenditures.

Sales and gross receipts taxes (BC): Taxes, including "licenses" at more than nominal rates, based on volume or value of transfers of goods or services, upon gross receipts therefrom, or upon gross income, and related taxes based on use, storage, production, importation, or consumption of such goods. *General sales or gross receipts taxes* apply to all types of goods, services, or gross income except to items that are specifically exempted. *Selective sales and gross receipts taxes* are imposed distinctively on selected commodities, services, or businesses. Selective sales taxes are also known as "excise" taxes.

Severance taxes (BC): Taxes imposed on removal from land or water of natural products, such as oil, gas, other minerals, timber, and fish.

Shared revenue (OMB, TD): Payments to the states and localities of a portion of the proceeds from the sale of certain Federal property, products and services, and payments to the Territories of certain Federal tax collections derived within their boundaries or from transactions affecting them.

Short-term debt (BC, S-L): Interest-bearing debt payable within one year from date of issue, such as bond anticipation notes, bank loans, and tax anticipation notes and warrants. It includes obligations having no fixed maturity date if payable from a tax levied for collection in the year of their issuance.

Special districts (L): Independent governmental units created to provide a single function or limited functions and having the power to tax, impose service charges, or incur debt therefor.

Special Issues (TD): Securities issued by the Treasury for investment of reserves of government trust funds and for certain payments to veterans.

Standard Metropolitan Statistical Area (BC): Also known as Metropolitan Statistical Areas, these are integrated economic and social units having at least one city with 50,000 or more inhabitants; or Census Bureau-defined urbanized areas of at least 50,000 inhabitants and a total area population of at least 100,000 (75,000 in New England).

Surplus or deficit (BC, BEA): Government revenues less expenditures in a given period. Cash balance carry-overs and surpluses or deficits of prior years are not part of the calculation of surplus or deficit.

Tax Index (TF): A measure of the average level of taxes compared to the average level in a base period. A separate Tax Index is available for all governments, for the Federal government, and for state-local governments combined, as well as for each major type of tax at different levels of government.

Taxable Income (IRS): For Federal individual income tax purposes, adjusted gross income less personal deductions and exemptions.

Taxes: Compulsory contributions exacted by a government for public purposes. The Bureau of the Census's definition of "taxes" is limited to general taxes only; it excludes taxes or contributions paid by employers and employees that go into insurance trust funds – e.g., social security, railroad retirement, and unemployment compensation taxes. Amounts received by a government from a tax it imposes are counted as tax revenue of that government, even though initially collected by another government.

Total debt (BC): All long-term obligations of the government and its agencies (whether backed by the unit of government's full faith and credit or nonguaranteed) and all interest-bearing short-term credit obligations. Long-term obligations are those repayable more than one year after issue.

Transfer payments (BEA): Payments to individuals by government and business for which no goods or services are currently rendered. Examples are benefits from social insurance funds, welfare payments, military pensions, mustering-out pay, and corporate gifts to nonprofit institutions.

Treasury obligations (TD): Treasury certificates and bills are short-term Federal securities; certificates mature in 1 year, bills in 90 or 91 days. Treasury notes are Federal securities with maturities ranging from 2 to 5 years. Treasury bonds are Federal securities with maturity dates ranging from 6 to 50 years.

Trust funds, Federal (OMB, TD): Funds that are established to account for receipts which are held in trust by the government for use in carrying out specific purposes and programs in accordance with a trust agreement or a statute.

Unemployment: (See Employment.)

Utility (BC, S-L): A water supply, electric light and power, gas supply, or transit system owned and operated by a government.

Utility expenditures (BC, S-L): Expenditures for construction or acquisition of publicly owned utility facilities or equipment, for production and distribution of utility commodities and services, and for interest on debt. Expenditures for administering utility debt and investments and for providing services to the local government are not included. Such costs are general expenditures of the local government.

Utility revenue (BC, S-L): Receipts from the sale of utility services or commodities to the public or to other governments.

Index

A

Adjusted gross income, see *Individual income tax, Federal*

Administration
Public expenditures, 9
  Financial, 8, 9
    Percentage of all expenditures, 10
  Social insurance, 8

Africa, Grants and credits to, 111

African Development Fund, 111

Agricultural Trade Development and Assistance Act
Credits, 110

Agriculture, see also *Commodity Credit Corporation*
Department
  Employment, 156
  Federal outlays, 99
  Public enterprise funds, 114
Employment, 44
Farm income, 73
  Part of national income, 50
Farm output index, 74
  Defined, *Glossary*
Farms, number, 73
Federal outlays, 91, 98, 101
  Aid to state and local governments, 101, 103
Government payments to farmers, 73
Loans, direct and guaranteed, 113
Net direct loan outlays, 112
Price index
  Paid by farmers, 74
  Parity ratio, 74
    Defined, *Glossary*
  Received by farmers, 74
Price support program
  Costs and losses, by commodity, 109
  Federal outlays, 105
Production expenses, 73

Agriculture, forestry, and fisheries
Corporate profits, taxes, and dividends, 60-61

Aid, see also *Expenditures, Public-Intergovernmental; General revenue sharing; Grants-in-aid; Revenue-Intergovernmental; Expenditures, Public and Revenue,* subdivided by level of government
Federal expenditures

To state and local governments, 100
  By form of aid, 103
  By function, 101, 103
  By state, 104, 150
    Tax burden per dollar, 150, 151
To state governments by function, 237
Percent change by level of government, 3
State expenditures, 231

Aid, Foreign, see *Foreign assistance*

Aid to families with dependent children, 31, 210
By state, 211
Recipients by state, 216-217

Air transportation, 8, 9
Expenditures
  By level of government, 8
  Local, by unit of government, 293
  Percentage of all government expenditures, 10
Federal excise collections, 139
Federal excise rates, 140-141
Revenue from charges, state and local, 195

Airport and airway trust fund
Federal aid to state and local governments, 103
Receipts and expenditures, 115

Airports
Federal aid to states, 237

Alcoholic beverage tax
Federal excise collections, 139
Federal excise rates, 140-141
Revenue, 14
  By level of government, 13
  Percent of all government revenue, 15
State, dates of adoption, 249
State collections, 242-243
  By state, 263
  Percent of total state taxes, 241
State rates, by state, 260-261

Appropriations, defined, *Glossary*

Armed forces, 44, 160

Asian Development Bank, Investment in, 111

Assessed valuation of property, by state, 216-217

Assessments, Special
State and local revenue, 195

Assistance and subsidies
Defined, *Glossary*
Expenditures
  Federal, 107
  Local, 291